BAPTIST THEOLOGIANS

Edited by TIMOTHY GEORGE
and DAVID S. DOCKERY

BROADMAN PRESS
NASHVILLE, TENNESSEE

© Copyright 1990 • Broadman Press
All Rights Reserved
4265-88
ISBN: 0-8054-6588-X
Dewey Decimal Classification: 286
Subject Headings: BAPTISTS—BIOGRAPHY // BAPTISTS—DOCTRINES // THEOLOGIANS
Library of Congress Catalog Number: 89-29532
Printed in the United States of America

Library of Congress Cataloging-in-Publication Data

Baptist theologians / edited by Timothy George and David Dockery.
    p.   cm.
    Includes biographical references.
    ISBN 0-8054-6588-X
    1. Baptists—Doctrines—History.   2. Theologians   I. George,
Timothy.   II. Dockery, David S.
BX6331.2.B29   1990
230′.6′0922—dc20
    [B]   89-29532
                                                                      CIP
                                                                      r89

For
J. Ralph McIntyre and Darold H. Morgan
beloved pastors who ordained us to the gospel ministry
and taught us to cherish our
Baptist heritage

Contributors

Paul A. Basden, Pastor
Valley Ranch Baptist Church
Dallas, Texas

Stephen Brachlow, Professor of Church History
North American Baptist Seminary

L. Russ Bush III, Dean and Academic Vice President
Southeastern Baptist Theological Seminary

Mark Coppenger, Executive Director-Treasurer
State Convention of Baptists in Indiana

R. Alan Culpepper, Professor of New Testament Interpretation
The Southern Baptist Theological Seminary

Alan Day, Pastor
First Baptist Church
Edmond, Oklahoma

Mark E. Dever, Ph.D. Candidate, J. B. Lightfoot Fellow
Cambridge University

David S. Dockery, Editor
Broadman Press

Lewis A. Drummond, President
Southeastern Baptist Theological Seminary

Keith E. Eitel, Professor of Missions
Criswell College

Duane A. Garrett, Associate Professor of Old Testament
Canadian Baptist Seminary

James Leo Garrett, Jr., Professor of Theology
Southwestern Baptist Theological Seminary

Timothy George, Dean
Beeson Divinity School, Samford University

Stanley J. Grenz, Professor of Theology and Ethics
Carey Hall, Regent College

Fisher Humphreys, Professor of Divinity
Beeson Divinity School, Samford University

John N. Jonsson, W. O. Carver Professor
The Southern Baptist Theological Seminary

Molly Marshall-Green, Associate Professor of Theology
The Southern Baptist Theological Seminary

R. Albert Mohler, Jr., Editor
The Christian Index

Thomas J. Nettles, Associate Professor of Church History
Trinity Evangelical Divinity School

Bob E. Patterson, Professor of Theology
Baylor University

Harry L. Poe, Assistant Professor of Evangelism
The Southern Baptist Theological Seminary

Robert V. Rakestraw, Associate Professor of Theology
Bethel Theological Seminary

Kurt A. Richardson, Assistant Professor of Historical Theology
Southeastern Baptist Theological Seminary

Phil Roberts, Associate Professor of Evangelism and Church Growth
Southeastern Baptist Theological Seminary

L. Joseph Rosas III, Assistant Professor of Religion
Union University

Robert Sloan, Associate Professor of New Testament
Baylor University

Harold S. Smith, Manager
General Trade Books, Broadman Press

James Spivey, Assistant Professor of Church History
Southwestern Baptist Theological Seminary

Danny R. Stiver, Assistant Professor of Christian Philosophy
The Southern Baptist Theological Seminary

Gerald Thomas, Ph.D. candidate, Martin Luther King, Jr., Fellow
The Southern Baptist Theological Seminary

J. Barry Vaughn, Assistant Professor of Religion
Samford University

Timothy P. Weber, Professor of Church History
Denver Seminary

Contents

Preface

"Whoever writes a Book seems by custom obliged to write a preface to it; wherein it is expected, he should show the motive which induced him to write the same." So declared Thomas Crosby in 1738 in the opening lines of his four-volume study of *The History of the English Baptists*.

We can trace the origin and motive of this book to a cemetery. One summer afternoon in 1987 the two of us walked together through Cave Hill Cemetery in Louisville, Kentucky where several of the theologians featured in this volume lie buried. We discussed the debt each of us felt to the rich theological legacy of these and other great men of God. We lamented the fact that so many Baptist giants of days gone by are either no longer remembered at all or, at best, relegated to the realm of affectionate obscurity. We determined to collect a volume of essays which we hoped would serve as a resource for pastors, students and teachers, an introduction to the life and thought of the most notable shapers of Baptist theology.

There was also, however, another motive behind our desire to assemble these essays on Baptist theologians. When the idea of editing this book first occurred to us, we were then professors at two institutions deeply implicated in the current controversy in the Southern Baptist Convention, namely, The Criswell College in Dallas, Texas and The Southern Baptist Theological Seminary in Louisville, Kentucky. Our personal friendship had emerged through our tentative efforts to reach out to one another across the boundaries of divergence which had placed us (without asking us) on opposite sides of the polemical divide in our denominational quarrel. In the process a marvelous thing happened: we experienced a mutual conversion as we discovered a surprising confluence of ideas and commitments, not only between the two of us but also among a wider circle of colleagues and friends. Through correspondence and conversation, through times of prayer and fellowship, we came to see that we had far more in common than our stereotypes of one another had encouraged us to suppose.

Thus, what began as a scholarly effort to recover a neglected part of our Baptist heritage became a project we hoped would serve the mission and unity of the denomination we love and belong to. We desired to foster a forum where scholars from diverse perspectives within the Baptist family could share the results of their research and in the process experience, perhaps, the miracle of dialogue—not a raucous shouting at one another, nor a snide whispering behind each other's backs, but a genuine listening and learning in the context of humane inquiry and disciplined thought. Since that walk through the cemetery several years ago, we have both received new job descriptions and new addresses, but we still sense, even more urgently, the need for considered reflection on the theme of this volume.

In our search for common ground, we do not declare theological neutrality. We rejoice in the renewed commitment to biblical faith within our own denomination, as well as in reports of evangelical awakening among Baptists throughout the world. However, such movings of the Spirit, if they are not to degenerate into shallow piosity, must also be accompanied by theological revival. The Christian faith is deeper and wider than the spiritual experience of any one believer: it is the confession of Jesus Christ as Lord, and the living out of that confession by the power of the Holy Spirit in the midst of the people of God. Theology is not an ivory-tower exercise for stuffy academics: it is the serious responsibility of every Christian and every church that seeks to be faithful to its Lord. By seeing how others before us have articulated the faith, we will be better able to formulate a proper theology for our own turbulent times. Thus, in one sense, the essays in this volume are a preparatory, albeit necessary, study for other books yet to be written.

In the nineteenth century Leopold von Ranke, the father of modern historiography, declared that the business of historians was to describe the past "as it really happened." However worthy such an ideal may seem as a corrective to polemical distortions of past events, history is never merely the simple recounting of the past "as it really happened." It is always and inevitably an interpretation of the past, a retrospective vision of the past, a vision conditioned both by the historical sources themselves and by the historian who selects and evaluates them. We have deliberately chosen the contributors to this volume from a wide spectrum of Baptist life, and we have encouraged them not only to analyze but also to evaluate their assigned theologians. With only minor editorial changes, we have allowed the essays to stand as submitted, in hopes that the diversity of theologians considered and interpretations given might stimulate further research and dialogue. At the same time, in the opening and closing chapters of the volume we have not hesitated to state plainly our own perspective on the course and future of Baptist theology.

One of our most difficult tasks was deciding which theologians should be examined in this anthology. Early Baptists were legally excluded from the English universities and were slow in developing their own theological academies, the first developing from a fund for ministerial education established at Bristol in 1679. Theology in that age tended to be written by pastors and evangelists who, if lacking in formal training, were far from unlearned. Bunyan, Keach, Gill, and Fuller are only four of the better known representatives of this tradition which lives on today in pastor-theologians such as W. A. Criswell and Herschel H. Hobbs, arguably the two most influential figures in Southern Baptist theology in the post-war period. Another group represented in this volume are professional academic theologians who produced systematic theologies while training ministers for service in the church. James P. Boyce, Augustus H. Strong, E. Y. Mullins, and W. T. Conner were leaders in this effort. However, considering the crucial role the Bible has played in Baptist history, we have not limited our selection to "systematic" theologians proper but have also included several leading biblical scholars as well, each with considerable theological influence within his own denomination and beyond. H. Wheeler Robinson, George E. Ladd, and George R. Beasley-Murray fall into this category. There are still others whose theological labors and legacy are best interpreted in a context wider than their own Baptist constituency: Walter Rauschenbusch's vision of the social gospel was widely heralded as a linchpin of modern Protestant liberalism, Deotis Roberts' agenda for black theology is not restricted to the Baptist branch of the black church, and Carl F. H. Henry and E. J. Carnell are major shapers of contemporary transdenominational evangelicalism. Each chapter includes: (1) biography; (2) exposition; (3) evaluation; and (4) selected bibliography of important works. Endnotes are found at the conclusion of each chapter.

The majority of theologians selected represent our own contexts and horizons: Baptists from North America—primarily Southern Baptists at that. Certainly in the growing ranks of Baptists around the world, new theological giants will step forward as well. Within the limits of our task, we have selected representatives from some other sectors of Baptist life. The concluding overview points us to dozens of other shapers of the Baptist world. Obviously there remains the possibility for a second volume. Doubtless, some of our contributors will themselves be objects of scrutiny for similar studies in the future. It is our prayer that this volume is the first of many others that will enhance the renewal of Baptist theology.

A volume of this magnitude cannot be put together without the enablement of many people. We wish to thank the contributors who share our vision for the renewal of Baptist theology, though, by the variety of the contributions, it will become plain to the readers that the vision may be described differently. Words of gratitude are also due to those who have read the manuscript or portions of it and offered valuable suggestions. To those at the Historical Commission in Nashville, Tennessee, who provided resources and photographs, we say thanks. We have dedicated this volume to the two men who ordained us and have greatly shaped our understanding of what it means to be Baptist ministers. Our families have gone the extra mile on more than one occasion in order for us to bring this project to completion. We are appreciative to them for their ongoing love and support. Expecially are we appreciative for the careful index prepared by Larese H. Dockery and David P. Smith. Finally, and ultimately, to our Lord who has graced us with His call to salvation and ministry, we offer our praise and thanksgiving.

Soli Deo Gloria,

David S. Dockery
Timothy George

1

The Renewal of Baptist Theology
Timothy George

There is a crisis in Baptist life today which cannot be resolved by bigger budgets, better programs, or more sophisticated systems of data processing and mass communication. It is a crisis of identity rooted in a fundamental theological failure of nerve. The two major diseases of the contemporary church are spiritual amnesia (we have forgotten who we are) and ecclesiastical myopia (whoever we are, we are glad we are not like "them"). While these maladies are not unique to the people of God called Baptists, they are perhaps most glaringly present among us.

Baptists began as a small, persecuted sect in pre-Revolutionary England, but by the late-twentieth century, in America at least, we could boast one of the largest religious "empires" in the world. There are over thirty million members in some twenty-odd Baptist groupings in this country. Not even Texas is large enough to contain all of the Baptists! We educate more students in our colleges and seminaries, sponsor more missionaries through our boards and agencies, and produce more religious literature through our publishing houses than any other comparable body of Christians in the history of the world. Yet despite such notable success all is not well in Zion. As Baptists have gained influence and status, we have also tended to approximate the values of our environing culture, including its secularity. We have lost touch with the great historic traditions which have given us our vitality and identity. Seduced by the lure of modernity ("whatever is latest is best"), we find ourselves awash on the sea of pragmatism ("whatever works is right"), indifference, and theological vacuity. The results are all about us: Church rolls stuffed with so-called "inactive members" no one has seen or heard from in years, trendy sermons which lack both biblical depth and spiritual power, a generation of young people uninstructed in the rudiments of the faith, fractious controversies which sap our strength and strain our fellowship, shallow worship services geared more to the applause of man than the praise of God, a slackening interest in evangelism and missions, all amidst a hurried activism steeped in this-worldly priorities.

This volume examines the contribution of thirty-three Baptist theologians, many of whom raised their voices against doctrinal apathy and spiritual decline in their own day. It is a measure of the dire straights we are in that so many of these giants of faith remain virtually unknown to their spiritual descendants today. It is hoped that a study of their lives and labors, not excluding their shortcomings and blind spots, will encourage others, especially pastors and ministerial students, to think theologically about the Baptist tradition. How can the theology of these great teachers challenge and correct and inform our own efforts to theologize faithfully on the basis of the Word of God? We must ask not only *what it meant* then and there, but also *what it means* here and now. Theology is about more than getting our doctrine correct; in its most basic and comprehensive sense, it is about being rightly related to God. In the first theology textbook used at Harvard College, the Puritan divine William Ames gave the following definition: *Theologia est scientia vivendo deo;* "Theology is the knowledge of living in the presence of God." Baptists today face a theological challenge. Will we listen reverently and obediently to what God has once and for all said in Holy Scripture and once and for all done in Jesus Christ? Will we forsake our flirtation with the false gods of this age and reclaim the godly heritage of those who did not flinch in the hour of temptation? How we respond to this challenge is not a matter of academic speculation or ecclesiastical gamesmanship. It is a question of life or death. It is the decision of whether the church will serve the true and living God of Jesus Christ, the God of the Old and New Testaments, or else succumb to the worship of Baal.

Theology that Matters

In 1919 George W. McDaniels, a leading pastor and later president of the Southern Baptist Convention, lamented the growing apathy about theology which he could discern in his day.

> In other decades Baptists were better indoctrinated than they are today. The environment in which they lived, sometimes inimicable to them, was conducive to the mastery of their principles. Of later years, a tendency to depreciate doctrinal discussion is easily discernible, and young converts particularly are not rooted and grounded in the faith. Modern nonchalance acts as if it made little difference what one believes.[1]

What McDaniels identified as a trend has more recently accelerated into a full-blown ideology of indifference. A new mythology of Baptist identity has emerged which runs something like this: "Baptists are not essentially a doctrinal people. We have no creed but the Bible, which everyone should be left to interpret according to his or her personal predilection. The basic criterion of theology is individual experience. The right of private judgment in matters religious supremely overrules fixed norms of doctrine. Baptist means freedom, freedom to think, believe, and teach without constraints." The practical upshot of such radical subjectivism is seen in the way that Baptist ordinands are frequently admitted to the ministry: A sweet smile and a pious declaration of "Jesus in my heart" will often satisfy the well-wishing examination committee.

It is sometimes claimed that doctrinal laxity is the necessary corollary to the Baptist principles of religious liberty, soul competency, and the priesthood of all believers. Clearly, each of these principles is a cherished distinctive of the Baptist tradition. However, as they are not equivalent terms, it is necessary to define each one carefully. The doctrine of religious liberty declares that, since God alone is Lord of the conscience, the temporal realm has no authority to coerce religious commitments. As Thomas Helwys put it in his famous appeal to King James in 1612: "Let them be heretics, Turks, Jews, or whatsoever, it appertains not to the earthly power to punish them."[2] However, religious liberty guarantees not only the right of each individual to believe as he or she chooses without fear of penal reprisal, but also the ability of every congregation, indeed every voluntary society, to order its own internal life and its doctrine and discipline, in accordance with its own perception of divine truth. Thus the Standard Confession of the General Baptists, published in 1660, juxtaposed a clear call for liberty of conscience with the right, indeed the responsibility, of each congregation to maintain its own doctrinal integrity. Article 24 of this document asserts that "all men should have the free liberty of their own consciences in matters of Religion, or Worship, without the least oppression, or persecution." This follows the admonition of article 17 that the true church should "reject all Hereticks" along with any others who teach "contrary to the Doctrine (of Christ) which they have learned."[3] For these and other Baptists, including Roger Williams, liberty of conscience did not imply a fluid notion of religious authority. It presupposed instead "a free church in a free state," that is, a church not only freed *from* improper civil constraints, but also freed *for* unswerving obedience to its Lord.

Soul competency is closely related to religious liberty in that it affirms for all persons the inalienable right of direct access to God. Put otherwise, all persons created in the image of God stand in a unique and inviolable relation to their Creator and, when quickened by divine grace, are fully "competent" or capable of responding to God directly. Soul competency pertains universally to all persons, not merely to Christians. It means that *every* individual is responsible to God. Thus, it is the basis of our indiscriminate evangelistic appeals for repentance and faith.

Baptists, however, do not teach the "*priesthood* of all human beings." Priesthood applies only to those who, through repentance and faith, have been admitted into the covenant of grace and, consequently, have been made participants in the priestly ministry of their Mediator, Jesus Christ (i.e., to believers only). The Reformation principle of the priesthood of all believers, with which Baptists have gladly identified themselves, does not merely, nor even primarily, refer to the Christian's freedom to come before God without a human mediator. It speaks instead of the Christian's evangelical responsibility to (as Luther put it) "be a little Christ" to his fellow believers in the church and to his lost neighbors in the world. It has more to do with service than status and more to do with the community of faith, its purpose and mission, than with individual rights. The Reformers did not speak of the priesthood of "the" believer, a lonely, isolated seeker of truth, but rather of a band of faithful believers (plural) united in a common confession as a local, visible *congregatio sanctorum*.[4]

Regrettably, for some, the doctrine of the priesthood of all believers, removed from its original Reformation and historic Baptist setting, has degenerated into the theology of "every tub sitting on its own bottom." In this context, the concepts of priesthood of believers and soul competency are frequently conflated, the one becoming virtually interchangeable with the other. Winthrop S. Hudson, one of the most perceptive interpreters of Baptist history, has pointed to the devastating impact of this development on Baptist ecclesiology.

> To the extent that Baptists were to develop an apologetic for their church life during the early decades of the twentieth century, it was to be on the basis of this highly individualistic principle. It has become increasingly apparent that this principle was derived from the general cultural and religious climate of the nineteenth century rather than from any serious study of the Bible. . . . The practical effect of the stress upon "soul competency" as the cardinal doctrine of Baptists was to make every man's hat his own church.[5]

The appeal to individual experience and private judgment corresponded to the shift away from biblical authority and the dogmatic consensus of historic Christianity. With Friedrich Schleiermacher and "the turn to the subject" in theology, "thus saith the Lord" was replaced by "it seems to me." Historically, for Baptists, the subject of theology has been the revelation of God in Jesus Christ, and its method, the exposition of Holy Scripture. Moreover, the revelation of God in His Word has been understood as something unquestionably given, objective, rational, and self-authenticating. In much of contemporary theology, however, the objectivity of divine revelation has been displaced by the religious self-consciousness as the starting point for theological reflection. In some quarters this has led to the virtual trashing of the classical documents of the Christian tradition, as in Don Cupitt's claim that "all theology written before 1800 is only of relative value."[6] In other circles the result has been a deliberate discarding of the great themes of biblical revelation in favor of "the trendy ideas of minor modern heresies."[7] In such a schema the very possibility of theology, understood as the coherent unity of biblical teaching, is denied outright while the assumptions and prejudices of the contemporary culture are accepted without being brought under Christian judgment or subjected to Christian critique. What passes as theology in many seminaries and divinity schools is little more than a thinly veiled apology for the latest item on the current social and political agenda, a better rationale for which can usually be found among secular theorists who do not sugarcoat their ideas with religious terminology. The net result is a kind of theological faddism which signals what Thomas J. J. Altizer, not known for his traditionalism, has called "a moment of profound theological breakdown . . . the ultimate moment of breakdown of theological tradition in the West."[8] The strictures of Jeremiah against the false prophets of ancient Israel apply to the present-day purveyors of religion without revelation: "Do not listen to what the prophets are prophesying to you. . . . They speak visions from their own minds, not from the mouth of the Lord. . . . But which of them has stood in the council of the Lord to see or hear his word? Who has listened and heard his word?" (Jer. 23:16,18, NIV)

Objectivity and Commitment

Theology, *theo-logia,* God-speech, is an office in the liturgy of the church. It arises out of the wonder and terror of having been confronted with the living God. It issues in confession, thanksgiving, and praise; its special function is fulfilled in that province between baptism and communion, in the realm between the Scriptures and their exposition and proclamation. Thus, the renewal of Baptist theology hinges significantly upon the recovery of an unbroken doctrine of Holy Scripture. The Scriptures are interpreted in the context of the living community of faith, the communion of saints which extends from the prophets and apostles through the Fathers and Reformers to the evangelists, missionaries, pastors, and teachers who have come before us and on whose shoulders we stand. Such an ideal presupposes a vital relationship between theology and the theologian in which the true and total person is claimed. Theology as a Christian vocation is not merely the academic study of religion, not even Christian religion. It is rather the elucidation of the confession of the church from the standpoint of one who recognizes that confession as his or her own context of commitment.

Edward Farley has traced the evolution of two distinct senses of the word *theology* in the history of Christianity. In its basic, primal meaning, theology refers to "a cognitive disposition and orientation of the soul, a knowledge of God and what God reveals."[9] In this sense theology was a vital, if not the only, component in true spirituality. It had to do with the daily strengthening of believers in their inner being, the process of growth and sanctification "which shows itself in the just and devout life called for by the truth" (Eph. 4:24, NEB). In the course of time, however, the word *theology* assumed a more precise, technical meaning: It came to refer to a discipline of study, a self-conscious, scholarly enterprise carried out in a specific pedagogical setting. So long as these two definitions functioned within a common field of Christian meaning, they were mutually enriching and reinforcing. Theology, like ministry, belonged to the whole body of Christ. Just as certain individuals were set aside as pastors, so others were assigned to be teachers. The purpose, if not the function, of both were the same—the building up of the people of God through the faithful proclamation and exposition of His Holy Word.

With the rise of the Enlightenment, however, the ideal of theology as *primarily* a discipline of critical rationality deliberately divorced (at least methodologically) from the commitment of faith became the normative paradigm for doing theology "in a world come of age." The resultant split between intellect and piety, between critical inquiry and religious experience, between head and heart, has become a standard feature in contemporary theological education. An able practitioner of the academic study of religion has expressed the dilemma posed by such a dichotomy. While acknowledging that scholars of religion should take seriously the specific faith commitments of the groups they study, he concludes that they "must ultimately regard their own modes of understanding as the arbiter of truth."[10] It is difficult to see how one who approaches the study of theology from a posture of neutrality, or on the basis of independently secured epistemological premises, could arrive at any other assessment. However, the luxury of such imperious independence is precisely what is denied to the Christian theologian, whose special vocation it is to listen for and expect to find the Word of God in the documents of the church.

Schleiermacher tried to hold together the two traditional meanings of theology—spiritual discipline and critical inquiry—by replacing the objectivity of divine revelation with the Christian self-consciousness as the starting point for theological reflection. In the end, however, Schleiermacher's dictum that "certain doctrines may be 'entrusted to history for safe keeping' became an axiom by means of which other thinkers could consign much of the orthodox tradition to irrelevance."[11] The effort of liberal theology to identify the "essence" of Christianity, which paralleled the elusive "quest for the historical Jesus," yielded a concept of God which was little more than the sum total of human dreams, fantasies, and self-projections. To the extent that Baptist theology has been seduced by this pattern of thought, it has lost touch with the historical roots which have sustained and nurtured it as a vital expression of classical Protestant Christianity.

John L. Dagg, whose *Manual of Theology* was the first textbook in systematic theology used at The Southern Baptist Theological Seminary, opened his great study with these words:

> The study of religious truth ought to be undertaken and prosecuted from a sense of duty, and with a view to the improvement of the heart. When learned, it ought not to be laid on the shelf, as an object of speculation; but it should be deposited deep in the heart, where its sanctifying power ought to be felt. To study theology, for the purpose of gratifying curiosity, or preparing for a profession, is an abuse and profanation of what ought to be regarded as most holy. To learn things pertaining to God, merely for the sake of amusement, or secular advantage, or to gratify the mere love of knowledge, is to treat the Most High with contempt.[12]

Here we see the two strands in our definition of theology brought together in a beautiful balance—theology as a discipline of faith pursued arduously but not dispassionately in the service of the church to the glory of God, its gracious and sovereign Object. From this perspective every act of theological work is at one and the same time an act of prayer. Theology must take place in a realm which has both open windows and a skylight—open windows through which the life of the church and the world can be glimpsed, and a skylight so that communion with God can constantly inform and correct and illumine the theologian at work.[13] It is significant that Anselm of Canterbury's famous ontological argument for the existence of God assumed the literary form of a direct address to God. The opening lines of this treatise present a model of supplication, reverent submission, and humble entreaty, which is the only proper posture for anyone who approaches those matters which "ought to be regarded as most holy."

> And do thou, O Lord my God, teach my heart where and how to seek thee, where and how to find thee. . . . When wilt thou enlighten our eyes and "show us thy face"? When wilt thou give us back thyself. Look upon us, O Lord, hear us, enlighten us, show us thy own self. . . . I am not trying, O Lord, to penetrate thy loftiness, for I cannot begin to match my understanding with it, but I desire in some measure to understand thy truth, which my heart believes and loves. For I do not seek to understand in order to believe, but I believe in order to understand.[14]

The Faith Once Delivered

The burden of this essay can be summarized in one sentence: The crisis of Baptist identity is closely related to the loss of a defining theological vision epitomized by the coinherence of intellect and piety.[15] As a leader in the American Baptist churches put it recently in a blunt statement: Mere pluralism and diversity "is a lousy identity."[16] It is not doubted that Baptists have disagreed among themselves on a host of minor matters throughout their history. Foot washing, hymn singing, tongue speaking, the laying on of hands, the appointment of missionaries, the ordination of pastors, and the proper limits of cooperation and fellowship have all produced countless splits and hurtful disharmony among Baptist peoples. There have also been several major doctrinal defections such as the Unitarian invasion of General Baptist ranks in eighteenth-century England. However, despite such incidents, for much of their history Baptists have enjoyed a remarkable unity of purpose and vision which has been a source of wonder both to themselves and others. Thus Francis Wayland, not known for his doctrinaire spirit, could write in 1861:

> I do not believe that any denomination of Christians exists, which, for so long a period as the Baptist, have maintained so invariably the truth of their early confessions. . . .
> The theological tenets of the Baptists, both in England and America, may be briefly stated as follows: they are emphatically the doctrines of the Reformation, and they have been held with singular unanimity and consistency.[17]

Shortly after the turn of the century, however, Augustus H. Strong, perhaps the leading Baptist theologian of his day, was lamenting "some common theological trends of our time." If left unchecked, he believed, such trends would undermine historic Baptist adherence to the essential truths of the gospel.

> Under the influence of Ritschl and his Kantian relativism, many of our teachers and preachers have swung off into a practical denial of Christ's deity and of his atonement. We seem upon the verge of a second Unitarian defection, that will break up churches and compel secessions, in a worse manner than did that of Channing and Ware a century ago. American Christianity recovered from

that disaster only by vigorously asserting the authority of Christ and the inspiration of the Scriptures. We need a new vision of the Savior like that which Paul saw on the way to Damascus and John saw on the isle of Patmos, to convince us that Jesus is lifted above space and time, that his existence antedated creation, that he conducted the march of Hebrew history, that he was born of a virgin, suffered on the cross, rose from the dead, and now lives forevermore, the Lord of the universe, the only God with whom we have to do, our Savior here and our Judge hereafter. Without a revival of this faith our churches will become secularized, mission enterprise will die out, and the candlestick will be removed out of its place as it was with the seven churches of Asia, and as it has been with the apostate churches of New England.[18]

From the perspective of the late-twentieth century we are tempted to read Strong's warning through the lenses of the Fundamentalist-Modernist controversies which have left deep scars on most Baptist bodies. Baptist theologians would do well to transcend the obscurantism, sectarianism, and legalism which marked vast areas of church life in the period of retrenchment and reaction which followed the storms of the early-twentieth century. We dare not minimize, however, the urgency of Strong's warning against the unbelieving theology of his day, nor his constructive mission of presenting a contemporary account of "the faith that was once for all delivered to the saints," which he hoped would be a corrective to the "fast advancing tide" of revision and denial. (The word *demythologizing* had yet to be coined!) Nor should we forget that Strong's counterpart in the South, E. Y. Mullins, also identified himself with the early fundamentalists and supported their legitimate concerns by writing one of the famous tracts included in *The Fundamentals*.

As Baptists approach the twenty-first century, what are the great theological themes which press for clarification and restatement? Among many topics which could be mentioned, the following five concerns constitute an urgent agenda for Baptist theology.

The Authority of Scripture

Historically, Baptists have used a variety of words to describe the Bible: *inspired, infallible, certain, true, without error,* and so forth. All of these terms underscore a fundamental commitment to the authority of Holy Scripture. Roger Williams spoke for many early Baptists when he declared that "every word, syllable and tittle in that Scripture or writing is the word, or immediate revealed will of God."[19] Baptists cannot avoid the issues raised by the current debate over biblical inerrancy. The question is not whether the word *inerrancy* should be used to describe the Bible, but rather to what extent one can appropriate the "advances" of modern biblical scholarship while still remaining faithful to the historic Baptist confidence in the Bible as the totally true and authoritative Word of God. It is precisely this tension which underlies the *Chicago Statement on Biblical Inerrancy* (1978), a document which seems to be gaining wider acceptance among Baptists and other evangelicals. In practice, of course, the affirmation of *sola Scriptura* cannot be separated from the difficult hermeneutical task of actually listening to the Bible and applying its message to our lives. There is no shortcut past serious engagement with the text of Scripture itself. The purpose of such an exercise, however, is not to make the Bible "relevant" to our modern world, but rather, in the light of the Bible through which God has once and for all spoken, to see how *irrelevant* the modern world—and we ourselves—have become in our rebellion against God. Let us affirm clearly: what the Bible says, God says; what the Bible says happened, happened—every miracle, every event in every book of the Old and New Testaments is altogether true and trustworthy. But let us not think that such an affirmation excuses us from accountability. Most assuredly, it places us in the arena of judgment, that judgment which begins with the family of God (1 Pet. 4:17).

The Doctrine of God

Throughout our history, Baptists have been explicitly orthodox in our continuity with the Trinitarian and Christological consensus of the early church. Our confessions usually begin with an affirmation of the being and attributes of God, who is portrayed as utterly transcendent, graciously beneficent, and immutably just in all His dealings with humankind. While thus asserting the *absoluteness* of God ("immutable, immense, eternal, incomprehensible, Almighty, every way infinite"),[20] Baptists strongly resisted the deist notion of an "absentee-landlord" God who seldom if ever interfered with His creation. In their doctrine of providence, Baptists echoed Calvin's idea that in every one of life's events human beings have direct "business with God" *(negotium cum Deo):* The God who, without violating human responsibility or making Himself the author of sin, "from eternity, decrees or permits all things that come to pass, and perpetually upholds, directs and governs all creatures and all events."[21]

Baptists should resist efforts to replace this robust, biblical view of God with the transcendence-starved deity of process theology. Little comfort can be offered by a limited God who struggles with us against the chaos but who finally is too impotent to prevent it or even possibly to overcome it. We need a fresh emphasis on the priority and absolute authority of the living God, the real God with whom we have to do in life and death, in judgment and grace. In former days Baptist associational sermons frequently focused on the attributes of God, His holiness and power, His love and omniscience, His eternity and truth. Why are these grand themes so neglected in our preaching and teaching today? Who can deny that a broken doctrine of Scripture has produced an attenuated view of God? We cannot truly reclaim the one without embracing the other. Isaiah's prophetic ministry began when he saw the Lord high and lifted up. His response was confession, adoration, and commitment. True theology is born in the tremors of such a vision.

The Person and Work of Jesus Christ

Baptists have never understood the sovereignty of God in an abstract or metaphysical sense. As preachers of the gospel, we know that the only saving revelation of God is embodied in the historical existence of Jesus Christ, the incarnate Son of God. We have emphasized both the complete deity and full humanity of Jesus Christ, just as we have stressed both the objectivity of the atonement ("Christ . . . hath fully satisfied the justice of God [and] procured reconciliation"—Second London Confession) and the experiential appropriation of the same in regeneration.

It is a sign of proper humility to confess the mystery of the incarnation, for who, this side of heaven, can fully plumb the depths of its meaning? However, it is a mark of outrageous blasphemy to deny its reality, as a prominent Baptist leader recently did when he compared belief in the incarnation to a child's belief in the tooth fairy.[22] We must beware of revisionist Christologies which dismiss such verities as the virginal conception of Jesus on the grounds that "it won't do in an age that knows what genes are and has, with regrettable exceptions, a more enlightened view of the equality of men and women."[23] The centrality and finality of Jesus Christ is at the heart of the Baptist commitment to evangelism and missions. Yet, confronted with the fact of religious pluralism, some have begun to question the most basic presupposition of Christian witness, namely that "Salvation is found in no one else, for there is no other name under heaven given to men by which we must be saved" (Acts 4:12, NIV). A potent expression of this perspective appeared in 1932 in a report published by a committee representing seven American Protestant denominations. It declared that the task of the evangelist and missionary

> is to see the best in other religions, to help the adherents of those religions to discover, or to rediscover, all that is best in their own traditions. . . . The aim should not be conversion. The ultimate aim . . . is the emergence of the various religions out of their isolation into a world fellowship in which each will find its appropriate place.[24]

Is it any surprise that the sending of missionaries from these denominations has dwindled to a trickle, while *evangelism* has become for many a dirty word not to be spoken about in polite company? The doctrine of hell, the necessity of conversion, and the preaching of the cross have all given way to the implicit universalism of many contemporary theologies. The vision of "sinners in the hands of an angry God" has been displaced by a more palatable view—"a God without wrath who brings men without sin into a kingdom without judgment through the ministrations of a Christ without a cross." Certainly, the truth about Jesus must be conveyed in the spirit of Jesus, not with blustering arrogance or cultural chauvinism. Christians should be good listeners as well as bold proclaimers. It is good to remember, however, that Paul did not establish an interfaith dialogue with the Stoics and Epicureans of Athens. He called on them to repent and believe in Jesus and the resurrection.

The Ministry of the Holy Spirit

Once the early church had struggled through the debates over the essential oneness of the Son and Father, it became necessary to defend the full deity of the Holy Spirit against the "spirit fighters" who conceived of His ministry as that of a mere creature. Thus the Nicene Creed (as it was received by the Western churches) calls the Spirit "the Holy One, the Lord and Giver of Life who proceeds from the Father and the Son, who together with the Father and the Son is adored and glorified." The Holy Spirit is not an It but a Thou, not a force or power, but a Person, the divine Person who regenerates, indwells, and baptizes every true believer, because "Anyone who does not have the Spirit of Christ does not belong to him" (Rom. 8:9, RSV).

A renewed focus on the work of the Holy Spirit in salvation will bring to Baptist churches a deeper appreciation for the long-neglected doctrines of grace. It is the Holy Spirit who convicts of sin, draws the lost person to Christ, and effects the miracle of the new birth. This truth stands as an indictment against much of the "quick-fix" evangelism of our times which ignores the great biblical themes of human depravity, repentance, justification by faith, and the role of the Holy Spirit in the process of salvation. The Holy Spirit also superintends the study of Scripture through His ministry of illumination. We must never forget that the same Spirit who inspired the prophets and apostles to commit to writing the divine revelation is also present to open our minds and hearts as we approach the received text with reverence and prayer. Baptists have experienced great movings of the Spirit throughout our history and are doing so now, particularly in Great Britain and some Third World countries. Charismatic renewal must be matched with doctrinal insight lest it degenerate into mere enthusiasm. But, conversely, dead orthodoxy without the invigorating power of the Spirit will produce stale congregations and stultified Christians. Baptists have an opportunity to make a significant theological contribution to the entire body of Christ because our tradition has taught us to hold in tension the two ideals of a balanced piety—sound doctrine and Spirit-filled living. Together they issue in a life of faith which is active in love.

The Church

More than any other doctrine, early English Baptists' understanding of the church led them to separate from the established religious structures of their country and also set them apart from other dissenting groups such as the Presbyterians, Congregationalists, and Methodists. Baptist ecclesiology most closely approximates the Anabaptist ideal in its emphasis on the church as an intentional community of regenerated and baptized believers who are bound to one another and to the Lord by a solemn covenant. Historically, the ritual of covenant taking was both the means of gathering a newly formed congregation at its inception and also a rite of passage into the fellowship for new members. Church discipline, in accordance with the procedures of admonition, censure, and excommunication as outlined in Matthew 18:15-18, was regarded as an essential mark of a true, visible church. The practice of discipline served a twofold function in Baptist life: it aimed at restoring the lapsed brother or sister to full fellowship if possible, and it marked off clearly the boundaries between the church and its environing culture. In both of these ways, discipline helped preserve the purity of the church's witness in the world.

As Baptists have evolved from small sectarian beginnings into what one historian has called "the catholic phase of their history," both the covenantal and disciplinary features of our church life have become marginal to our identity. The loss of these historic distinctives has resulted in the crisis of Baptist spirituality which pervades so much of our church life today. Theological renewal cannot evade the issues raised by this devolution. What are the standards of personal holiness which ought to distinguish a man or woman of God? What are the ethical implications of our corporate decisions? Without engaging in partisan politics, can the church speak prophetically to the great moral concerns of our day such as the proliferation of violence and war, the persistence of racial injustice, and the genocidal slaughter of the innocent unborn? Can we recover a structure of accountability in our congregational life without relapsing into narrow judgmentalism? Such issues of "practical" theology along with other pressing concerns such as worship, pastoral care, and church governance, cannot be resolved merely by better administrative procedures or more "how-to" manuals. They go to the very heart of the doctrine of the church itself.

At the turn of the century, J. B. Gambrell observed that "heresies have their habitation in cold hearts and cold churches." The awakening that must come will have its start in local congregations where there is an atmosphere of hospitality to the truth. It will be reflected in a renewal of doctrinal preaching and systematic expository study of the Scriptures. It will issue in a greater burden for the lost, a wider missionary vision, and the equipping of God's people in the discipling of *panta ta ethne* in fulfillment of the Great Commission. Like all true spiritual phenomena, theological revival cannot be brought about by mere human means. We cannot work it up; only God can send it down. However, we can pray for it and prepare ourselves for it through the study and reclamation of the theological legacy we have received and are charged as a sacred duty to pass on.

Notes

1. George W. McDaniels, *The People Called Baptists* (Nashville: The Sunday School Board of the SBC, 1919), 8.

2. Thomas Helwys, *A Short Declaration of the Mystery of Iniquity* (London: n.p., 1612), 46. For a fuller treatment of Helwys in the context of the early Baptist literature of toleration, see Timothy George, "Between Pacifism and Coercion: The English Baptist Doctrine of Religious Toleration," *Mennonite Quarterly Review* 58 (1984): 30-49.

3. W. L. Lumpkin, ed., *Baptist Confessions of Faith* (Valley Forge, Pa.: Judson Press, 1959), 230-32.

4. For a fuller elucidation of these themes, see Timothy George, "The Priesthood of All Believers and the Quest for Theological Integrity," *Criswell Theological Review* 3 (1989): 283-94.

5. Winthrop S. Hudson, ed., *Baptist Concepts of the Church* (Valley Forge, Pa.: Judson Press, 1959), 215-16. Cf. also the lament of Carlyle Marney, *Priests to Each Other* (Valley Forge, Pa.: Judson Press, 1974), 12.

6. Don Cupitt, *The Debate About Christ* (London: SCM Press, 1979), 110.

7. Thomas C. Oden, *Agenda for Theology* (San Francisco: Harper and Row, 1979), 11.

8. Mark C. Taylor, *Deconstructing Theology* (New York: Crossroad, 1982), xi.

9. Edward Farley, *Theologia: The Fragmentation and Unity of Theological Education* (Philadelphia: Fortress Press, 1983), 35.

10. Herbert Burhenn, "The Study of Religion and Liberal Education," *Bulletin, The Council of Societies for the Study of Religion*, 18 (April 1989): 28.

11. Jaroslav Pelikan, *Historical Theology: Continuity and Change in Christian Doctrine* (Philadelphia: Westminster Press, 1971), 160.

12. John L. Dagg, *Manual of Theology and Church Order* (Harrisonburg, Va.: Gano Books, 1982), 13.

13. The metaphor of the skylight is that of Karl Barth, *Evangelical Theology* (Grand Rapids, Mich.: Eerdmans, 1963), 161.

14. E. R. Fairweather, ed., *A Scholastic Miscellany: Anselm to Ockham* (New York: Macmillan, 1970), 70-73.

15. The crisis is felt in varying measures among most of the more than twenty-five distinct Baptist groups in North America. The continuing controversy in the Southern Baptist Convention is but one symptom of this wider phenomenon. As recently as 1984 the American Baptist Churches in the U.S.A. authorized a "blue ribbon commission on Denominational Identity" to address this theme.

16. Quoted, William H. Brackney, " 'Commonly, (Though Falsely) Called . . .': Reflections on the Search for Baptist Identity," in *Perspectives in Churchmanship: Essays in Honor of Robert G. Torbet,* ed. David M. Scholer (Macon, Ga.: Mercer University Press, 1986), 81.

17. Francis Wayland, *The Principles and Practices of Baptist Churches* (London: J. Heaton and Son, 1861), 15-16.

18. Augustus H. Strong, *Systematic Theology* (Valley Forge, Pa.: Judson Press, 1907), ix.

19. Roger Williams, *The Complete Writings of Roger Williams* (New York: Russell and Russell, 1963), 5:387. Cf. David S. Dockery, "Toward a Balanced Hermeneutic in Baptist Life," *Search* 19 (1989): 47-51.

20. This from the article "Of God and of the Holy Trinity" in the Second London Confession of 1677. The complete text is in Lumpkin, *Confessions,* 244-95.

21. From the article on providence in the *Abstract of Principles,* the guiding confessional document of The Southern Baptist Theological Seminary. Printed in Robert A. Baker, ed., *A Baptist Source Book* (Nashville: Broadman Press, 1966), 138.

22. Cf. H. Leon McBeth, *The Baptist Heritage* (Nashville: Broadman Press, 1987), 517-18.

23. Eric James, ed., *God's Truth: Essays to Celebrate the Twenty-fifth Anniversary of Honest to God* (London: SCM Press, 1988), 197.

24. Quoted, Jaroslav Pelikan, *Jesus Through the Centuries* (New York: Harper and Row, 1985), 299.

2

John Bunyan

Harry L. Poe

Biography

John Bunyan stands in contrast to many of the Nonconformists who fell heir to the Puritan tradition after the Puritan movement had disintegrated in controversy. The debates that rocked the Civil War period continued into the Restoration period, solidifying in the form of various sectarian groups struggling for identity and survival during the fierce persecution of the last two Stuart kings. John Bunyan, though a committed Nonconformist and a decided Baptist, took a different tack from his Nonconformist brethren. Instead of accenting the differences that separated the different groups, he emphasized the fundamentals of the faith which all true believers shared. He defended the gospel as the basis of Christian unity and communion and devoted his ministry to the proclamation of that gospel. When he involved himself in controversy, he did so because he saw a challenge to the gospel itself.

Born in Elstow, Bedfordshire, in 1628, John Bunyan grew up in a poor home. He described his family as "a low and inconsiderable generation; my father's house being of that rank that is meanest and most despised of all the families in the land."[1]

Despite the family's limited means, his parents sent Bunyan to school where he learned to read and write, ". . . according to the rate of other poor men's children."[2] Bunyan recalled his childhood as one in which he had ". . . but few equals . . . both for cursing, swearing, lying, and blaspheming the holy name of God."[3] Bunyan also recalled dreams and thoughts of the day of judgment which terrified him as a child, but his newfound pleasures, lusts, and vices put these thoughts behind him as he grew older.

In 1644 Bunyan's mother and sister died, and his father remarried. Before the end of the year, young Bunyan enlisted in the Newport Pagnell garrison of the Parliamentary Army.[4] He remained in the army until the middle of 1647.[5] Some time after his military career ended, Bunyan took a wife whose total dowry consisted of two books left to her by her father: *The Plain Man's Pathway to Heaven* by Arthur Dent and *The Practice of Piety* by Lewis Bayly.[6] These products of contemporary piety inspired some interest in religion for Bunyan, but he later lamented that his interest had been superstitious adoration and devotion of the "high place, priest, clerk, vestment, service, and what else belonging to the church."[7] Among his other religious fancies, Bunyan wanted to be a member of the tribes of Israel, but when informed by his father that he was not, he became depressed.[8]

John Bunyan (1628-88)

Bunyan began attending the Separatist church at Bedford which had John Gifford for its pastor. During this period, Bunyan went through the crisis of his conversion experience described in *Grace Abounding*. In 1653 he joined Gifford's church. Gifford became rector of St. John's parish church in Bedford that same year as an appointee of the state church under Cromwell. Two years later Gifford died and John Burton took his place. Bunyan began preaching at the invitation of the church soon after Burton began his tenure.

Bunyan found that he had a gift for evangelistic preaching. His concern for the gospel, however, led him into his first controversy in 1656 when he published his first book. *Some Gospel-Truths Opened* attacked the Quaker doctrine of the inner light and presented Bunyan's understanding of the simplicity of the gospel as it related to the person and work of Christ. He stressed the objective significance of the incarnation and the atonement in salvation. Edward Burrough responded to Bunyan in *The True Faith of the Gospel of Peace Contended for in the Spirit of Meekness* (1656). Bunyan replied to Burrough in *A Vindication of Gospel Truths Opened* (1657), and Burrough responded in turn with *Truth (the Strongest of All)* (1657). Bunyan remained critical of the Quakers throughout his life, but he devoted no more tracts exclusively to them.

Bunyan's wife died in 1658, and he remarried the following year. Also in 1659 he published perhaps his most important theological treatise, *The Doctrine of the Law and Grace Unfolded*, in which he elaborated a covenantal understanding of the atonement and justification. In this work he built on the foundation of Calvinist tradition that salvation lay totally within the gracious promise of God.[9]

At the Restoration of Charles II in 1660, Bunyan found himself in prison for six years. He put his time to good use, writing *Grace Abounding* (1666) and eight other books.[10] Freed for a brief time in 1666, Bunyan soon found himself imprisoned again for another six-year term. During this confinement he wrote *A Defence of the Doctrine of Justification* (1672) to refute *The Design of Christianity* (1671) by the latitudinarian Edward Fowler. This debate constituted his second literary controversy. His second imprisonment came to an end in 1672 under the terms of the Declaration of Indulgence, ironically intended to benefit Quakers. The Church at Bedford chose Bunyan to serve as pastor on January 21, 1672.[11]

Bunyan's third controversy engaged the Baptists in a debate over the necessity of believer's baptism by immersion for communion. In light of his strong position on the gospel as the way to salvation, Bunyan regarded the gospel, rather than baptism, as the door to the church and defended this position in *Confession of My Faith, and a Reason of My Practice* (1672). Several prominent London Particular Baptists responded to Bunyan. William Kiffin and Henry D'Anvers collaborated with Thomas Paul in *Some Serious Reflections* (1673). John Denne, a General Baptist, also replied to Bunyan in *Truth Out-Weighing Error*. Bunyan responded in 1673 with *Differences in Judgment about Water-Baptism, No Bar to Communion*. Kiffin replied to

Bunyan in *A Sober Discourse of Right to Church Communion*. Bunyan's final answer in the matter came in *Peaceable Principles and True*.[12]

Bunyan spent another six-month period in Bedford jail in the mid-1670s. Tradition holds that he wrote *The Pilgrim's Progress* during this imprisonment.[13] The success of that effort led to a series of works in that literary style, including *The Life and Death of Mr. Badman* (1680), *The Holy War* (1682), and the second part of *The Pilgrim's Progress* (1684).

Bunyan devoted the remaining years of his life to his writing, to his congregation, and to the evangelization of the Bedford area. His church cooperated with other Nonconformist churches of the area in a systematic plan of evangelization.[14] Bunyan died August 31, 1688, as a result of a fever he developed from riding through a heavy rain on his way to preach in London.[15]

Exposition

Bunyan cried to God to know the gospel of Jesus Christ and when he discovered it, he found "the wonderful work of God, in giving Jesus Christ to save us."[16] The elements of Bunyan's gospel included the conception and birth of Jesus, His life ". . . from the cradle to the cross," His death to pay the penalty of sin, His resurrection and ascension to the right hand of God, and His second coming to judge the world.[17] The objective testimony of the Bible and the historical work of Christ in salvation became the principle dynamics in Bunyan's theology. When Bunyan first began preaching, he still labored under a guilty conscience and preached what he "smartingly did feel."[18] He preached condemnation. As his understanding of God's grace through Christ increased, his message began to change: "Wherefore now I altered in my preaching, for still I preached what I saw and felt; now therefore I did much labour to hold forth Jesus Christ in all his offices, relations, and benefits unto the world. . . ."[19] Bunyan settled the gospel on Christ and never left that settlement.

Bunyan preached evangelistically. Indeed, he saw evangelism as the primary purpose of preaching:

> In my preaching I have really been in pain, and have, as it were, travailed to bring forth children to God; neither could I be satisfied unless some fruits did appear in my work. If I were fruitless it mattered not who commended me; but if I were fruitful, I cared not who did condemn.[20]

Bunyan continued to preach in the framework of a Calvinistic theological system, but he was not interested "to see people drink in opinions if they seemed ignorant of Jesus Christ."[21] Instead, he concentrated on the greatness of sin and the need of Christ.

Bunyan's stress on Christ protected him from becoming involved in the ecclesiological controversies of his age. He said,

> I never cared to meddle with things that were controverted, and in dispute amongst the saints, especially things of the lowest nature; yet it pleased me much to contend with great earnestness for the word of faith and the remission

of sins by the death and sufferings of Jesus; but I say, as to other things, I should let them alone, because I saw they engendered strife, and because that they neither, in doing nor in leaving undone, did commend us to God to be his. Besides, I saw my work before me did run in another channel, even to carry an awakening word; to that therefore did I stick and adhere.[22]

Bunyan avoided controversy except in what he considered the fundamentals of the gospel.[23] Rather than waste his energy on controversies that divided the church and brought salvation to none, he devoted himself to evangelism.

The Gospel

Despite his professed desire to avoid controversy, Bunyan's concern for the content of the gospel precipitated the first controversy in which he engaged. Throughout his career, Bunyan preached the gospel in terms of Jesus Christ, but in the Quaker doctrine of the inner light, Bunyan saw a teaching that discarded the incarnation and the atonement. Bunyan wrote his first book, *Some Gospel-Truths Opened* (1656), to correct errors he perceived in the contemporary preaching of the gospel by radical sectaries. In this treatise he explained his understanding of the simplicity of the gospel as it related to the person and work of Christ.[24]

Though election and predestination formed the backdrop of Bunyan's presentation of the gospel, he did not make these doctrines the content of his gospel. Bunyan stressed the work of Christ. Knowing that humans would sin, God foreordained a Savior before the foundation of the world and ". . . did before *choose* some of those that would fall, and give them to him that should afterward purchase them actually, though in the account of God, his blood was shed before the world was."[25] God made a bargain with the Savior to give Him some of the "poor souls" upon the satisfaction of "such and such terms."[26] By the terms of the bargain, the Savior agreed to "take upon him flesh and blood . . ." and to spill "his most precious blood" in order to accomplish the eternal righteousness and justification of the chosen.[27]

After the fall, God began to make known to the world, through the prophets, His design of love to send a Savior. Christ, born of a virgin, fulfilled the expectations for a Savior foretold in the prophecies.[28] Having affirmed the basis upon which Christ is Savior, Bunyan added to that affirmation His "godhead, birth, death, resurrection, ascension, *and* intercession; *together with* his most glorious and personal appearing the second time, *which will be* to raise the dead, and bring every work to judgment."[29] In the final admonition of *Some Gospel-Truths Opened,* Bunyan made an earnest plea to his readers who had "not yet laid hold on the Lord Jesus Christ, for eternal life, [to] lay hold upon him; upon his righteousness, blood, resurrection, ascension, intercession, and wait for his second coming to 'judge the world in righteousness.' "[30] Bunyan believed that these essential points about Christ formed the "fundamentals of religion" and the message of the gospel.[31]

Throughout his ministry, Bunyan stressed the content of the gospel which he found implicit in Romans 1:16 rather than the preaching act itself which

Puritans had stressed since the time of Archbishop Grindal. Though he lacked the theological training of the great Puritan preachers who preceded him, Bunyan realized that the preaching which God used to save people had a specific content. The gospel had a basic simplicity, and Bunyan warned against the "comixture" of other doctrine with it.[32]

The incarnation.—The Quakers had spiritualized Christ out of the gospel in Bunyan's opinion; therefore, he made the historical activity of Christ the primary focus of his preaching. Bunyan followed *Some Gospel-Truths Opened* with *A Vindication of . . . Some Gospel-Truths Opened* wherein he accused the Quakers of denying the blood atonement, ascension, bodily resurrection, second coming, and intercession of Christ because of their method of spiritualizing the historical Christ, or to use Bunyan's expression, "the Son of the Virgin Mary."[33]

Bunyan considered the incarnation a necessity for salvation. Christ had to come in the flesh to do what human beings could not do. By coming in the flesh, Christ came into the human condition of living under the law and took both sin and guilt upon himself. Bunyan would not allow justification and salvation to be separated from the incarnation and atonement. This early battle for the gospel crystallized a theme that Bunyan continued to sound throughout his writing ministry.

Bunyan stressed the messiahship of Christ. His coming fulfilled the promises made by God to the prophets, because God raised Him up to be the Savior of the elect, called "Israel" in the Scriptures.[34] Belief in the prophecies of a Savior constituted the grounds for the salvation of the patriarchs.[35] Bunyan found the promise of the Messiah throughout the Old Testament: "Indeed, the Scriptures of the Old Testament are filled with promises of the Messias to come, prophetical promises, typical promises; for all the types and shadows of the Saviour are virtually so many promises."[36] The birth of Christ fulfilled the promises of a Messiah. Born of the virgin Mary, of the seed of David, in flesh as a man, Christ came to die for sinners.[37] Bunyan believed that the miracles played a part in the gospel as a testimony of the messiahship of Christ,[38] while His frailty testified to His humanity.[39] Bunyan insisted on maintaining the two natures of Christ.

The atonement.—Bunyan based salvation on justification obtained by the incarnate Christ. If Christ had not actually taken both sin and guilt upon Himself, then those two could not be forgiven:

> Sever not sin and guilt asunder, lest thou be an hypocrite like these wicked men, and rob Christ of his true sufferings. Besides, to see sin upon Christ, but not its guilt; to see sin upon Christ, but not the legal punishment, what is this but to conclude that either there is no guilt and punishment in sin, or that Christ bore our sin, but we the punishment.[40]

Bunyan repudiated those who taught that Christ did not take on sin in any "real" sense.[41]

Substitutionary atonement lay at the center of Bunyan's soteriology. By shedding His blood, Christ paid ". . . the full price to Divine justice for sinners."[42] Bunyan's view of the atonement also included the dramatic view of Divine victory over the forces of darkness. Christ not only had to satisfy Divine justice; He also had to gain a victory over "death, devil, hell, and the grave."[43] In his passion, Christ engaged "sin, the devil, death, and hell, as a Saviour."[44] Bunyan declared that the priestly work of Christ "is the first and great thing presented to us in the gospel—namely, how that he died for our sins, and gave himself to the cross, that the blessings of Abraham might come upon us through him."[45]

Bunyan pointed to several demonstrations that Christ has obtained the "eternal redemption" of the "souls of sinners" by paying "the full price to God."[46] The first of these demonstrations was the resurrection. The second was the ascension into heaven to sit on the right hand of God. The third was the giving of the Holy Spirit.[47] Bunyan condemned those that thought

> . . . that it is not material to salvation to venture upon a crucified Christ, neither do they trouble their heads or hearts with inquiring whether Christ Jesus be risen and ascended into heaven, or whether they see him again or no, but rather are for concluding that there will be no such thing . . .[48]

Those who did not accept and hold to these essentials of the gospel, Bunyan called "anathematized of God."[49]

Conversion

In his spiritual autobiography, *Grace Abounding to the Chief of Sinners,* Bunyan marked the beginning of his conversion from the time he first felt guilt for sin. Bunyan concluded that he, who had never before been sensible of sin, was such a great sinner that Christ would not forgive him:

> Then I fell to musing upon this also; and while I was thinking on it, and fearing lest it should be so, I felt my heart sink in despair, concluding it was too late; and therefore I resolved in my mind I would go on in sin: for, thought I, if this case be thus, my state is surely miserable; miserable if I leave my sins, and but miserable if I follow them; I can but be damned, and if I must be so, I had as good be damned for many sins, as to be damned for few.[50]

He made sin the object of his study and experience for a month after this episode.

In later years, Bunyan would write that "conversion begins at conviction, though all conviction doth not end in conversion."[51] He observed that, like himself, most people under the guilt of conviction will "look any ways, and that on purpose to divert their minds, and to call them off from thinking on what they have done. . . ."[52] In bringing conviction, however, God intends for the sinner to experience self-judgment for the things one has done. Bunyan lamented the poor sinner whose "dull head could look no further than to the conceit of the pitiful beauty and splendour of his own stinking righteousness."[53]

In the account of his conversion, which he described as taking a number of years, Bunyan repeatedly encountered Christian people, the Spirit, and the Bible. He recalled a number of people who played a part in his conversion, including John Gifford.[54] The Spirit played a part in Bunyan's conversion by bringing conviction, over and over again.[55] Most importantly in his conversion, Bunyan found that the Bible spoke the word that could bring him through his trial and make his salvation sure.[56] In each situation of temptation, trial, or despair, Bunyan found that a word of Scripture would finally come to his mind which stilled his spirit or gave him peace. Bunyan further understood these words as having been brought to him by the Spirit. The periods of distress lasted for moments, weeks, and even years before Bunyan found peace for what troubled him.[57] Because of the power of the Word to give him comfort and hope in his lengthy conversion experience, the objective word of Scripture continued to play a primary role in the form Bunyan's theology would take.

Calvinism and conversion.—Though a confirmed Calvinist, Bunyan found no peace in the doctrines of Dort as he struggled for his own salvation. The questions of election and predestination drove him to despair. Rather than leading him to faith, Bunyan found the dark points of Calvinism a hindrance: .

> Neither as yet could I attain to any comfortable persuasion that I had faith in Christ; but instead of having satisfaction, here I began to find my soul to be assaulted with fresh doubts about my future happiness; especially with such as these, Whether I was elected? But how, if the day of grace should now be past and gone.[58]

Though temporarily calmed for more than a year by a passage from Ecclesiasticus 2:10, "Look at the generations of old, and see; did ever any trust in the Lord, and was confounded?", Bunyan continued to fear that the day of grace had passed.[59] Though comforted by the passage from Luke 14:22, ". . . and yet there is room," Bunyan later had a renewed fear that God had not called him.[60] This fear lasted many months until a new word came to him from Joel 3:21, "I will cleanse their blood that I have not cleansed: for the Lord dwelleth in Zion," which he took as a special encouragement from God.[61] Some time later, he suffered yet another fear that he might be reprobate.[62] Bunyan's preoccupation with the dark points of Calvinism continued to stifle his faith.

Scripture and conversion.—The vacillation between peace and doubt continued, but each time Bunyan found that Scripture alone could bring him out of his doubt and give him comfort. He believed that God spoke to him through the Bible. Theology only aggravated his sense of lostness, and the ordinances of the church gave affliction rather than assurance.[63] When he finally believed that he had faith, his assurance came from Scripture:

> I remember that one day, as I was travelling into the country and musing on the wickedness and blasphemy of my heart, and considering of the enmity that was in me to God, that scripture came in my mind, He hath "made peace through the blood of his cross." Col. i. 26. By which I was made to see, both again, and again, that day, that God and my soul were friends by his blood;

yea, I saw that the justice of God and my sinful soul could embrace and kiss each other through this blood. This was a good day to me; I hope I shall not forget it.[64]

As his conversion process continued, Bunyan stood convinced that only those truths borne out by the Bible and confirmed by the experience of the Holy Spirit had validity.

Casuistry and conversion.—The casuistry of the Puritans, with its reliance on rational arguments, proofs, objections, answers to objections, and cases studied did nothing to bring Bunyan the peace and assurance that Martin Luther's commentary on Galatians brought.[65] Bunyan cherished Luther's book above all others, except the Bible, because of the deep, personal, experiential quality he felt in reading it.[66] In reading the cases of conscience of the Puritans, Bunyan thought ". . . that they had writ only that which others felt, or else had, through the strength of their wits and parts, studied to answer such objections as they perceived others were perplexed with, without going down themselves into the deep."[67] But in Luther's commentary Bunyan found his own condition reflected in Luther's experience. This encounter with Luther probably influenced Bunyan's methodology more than his theology. In his writing and preaching, Bunyan made his essential appeal to the experience of people more than to their intellect. Rather than elaborating the Calvinist system of salvation, Bunyan presented Christ in a way to draw out an experiential identification with what he preached: "the worth of their own salvation, sound conviction for sin, especially for unbelief, and an heart set on fire to be saved by Christ, with strong breathing after a truly sanctified soul. . . ."[68]

Faith.—When a sinner appears before God justified by the imputed righteousness of Christ, God blesses this soul with the forgiveness of sin and the Holy Spirit. After God has given these blessings, the justified Christian can believe the gospel and be brought by this belief to repentance and "to hungering and thirsting vehemently after this righteousness."[69] Bunyan believed that God accomplished this work on a passive soul: "And in his own time he shall show me, that I am a justified person, a pardoned person, a person in whom the Spirit of God had dwelt for some time, though I knew it not."[70] Imputed righteousness must come before the forgiveness of sins because forgiveness is granted on the basis of righteousness. Imputed righteousness must come before justification, otherwise God would have no basis for declaring the condemned justified.[71] Those that God justifies and gives the Holy Spirit believe by the power of the Spirit who reveals God through the preaching of the gospel:[72]

He then that believeth shall be saved; for his believing is a sign, not a cause, of his being made righteous before God by imputation: And he that believeth not shall be damned, because his non-belief is a sign that he is not righteous, and a cause that sins abide upon him.[73]

Though Bunyan held to the strong doctrines of election and predestination of the Puritan tradition, he did not make these doctrines the object of faith.

The object of faith in salvation is Christ and His blood. To believe in Christ and His blood is "to believe that while we were yet sinners Christ died for us, that even then, when we were enemies, we were reconciled to God by the death of his Son: To believe that there is a righteousness already for us completed."[74] Bunyan's Calvinism touched his teaching on faith primarily to protect it from being viewed as a human work that might earn justification. Even in his teaching on faith, he made a distinction between how faith operates and the message of the gospel which faith appropriates. He called faith

> . . . a gift, Ep. ii. 8. first, Ga. v. 22. or work, of the Spirit of God, whereby a soul is enabled, under a sight of its sins, and wretched estate, to lay hold on the birth, righteousness, blood, death, resurrection, ascension and intercession of the Lord Jesus Christ, I Th. ii. 7. and by the assistance of the Spirit, whereby it is wrought, to apply all the virtue, life and merit of what hath been done and suffered, or is doing by the same Lord Jesus Christ, to its own self in particular, Ga. ii. 20., Ro. vii. 24, 25. as if itself had really done all that the Lord Jesus Christ hath done . . . .[75]

Faith comes as a gift of God, but it grasps the truths of the gospel.

In the preaching of the gospel, Christ calls and produces ". . . a sound sense of the absolute need that a man hath . . ." of Him.[76] Bunyan viewed conviction as the first step to faith and repentance. By the doctrine of Christ having died for sinners, sinners that are awake and see themselves as sinners are encouraged to come to God for mercy.[77] In drawing forth the absolute need for Christ, the gospel empowered by the Spirit produces faith:

> Thus I speak of the sinner, the salvation of whose soul is graciously intended and contrived of God; for he shall by gospel light be wearied out of all; he shall be made to see the vanity of all, and that the personal righteousness of Jesus Christ, and that only, is it which of God is ordained to save the sinner from the due reward of his sins.[78]

Thus, Bunyan called the gospel "the word of faith preached."[79]

Repentance.—Bunyan insisted that the preaching of the gospel demanded repentance as well as faith. Faith leads to repentance, but Bunyan made the point that repentance, like faith, comes as a gift from God and could not be viewed as the basis upon which God grants forgiveness of sin.[80] Bunyan repudiated Edward Fowler's suggestion in *The Design of Christianity* that God could make repentance the basis for pardoning sin ". . . without any other satisfaction."[81] Repentance does not cause remission of sins but serves as "a sign of our hearty reception thereof."[82] Bunyan believed that the response of repentance was a necessary element of salvation, but that it came by grace, just as faith came by grace, as a gift of God.[83] Without faith one cannot receive the gospel, but without repentance, one cannot receive it "unfeignedly."[84]

Repentance manifests itself first in confession. A person's self-judgment and self-condemnation draw out confession when he sees himself in the light of the gospel. Bunyan called confession a "mighty act" like venturing forth ". . . upon hot burning coals," but it is brought about by the "supernatural power" of God who "secretly" prompts the sinner.[85] Before confession, the Spirit convinces the soul of sin. Before confession, the sinner must have a ". . . sound knowledge of God, especially as to his justice, holiness, righteousness, and purity."[86] Without a true knowledge of God, one cannot make a true confession. Bunyan also believed that to have a proper ". . . dread, terror, or frightful apprehension . . ." of sin, one must have a grasp of the certainty of a day of judgment.[87] This conviction accounts for the importance of the second coming and final judgment in Bunyan's preaching. Deep confession would be impossible, however, without a belief in the probability of mercy. Without belief in mercy, no one would ever turn to God when he fell under conviction. Confession cannot be mingled with any false apprehension of the worthiness of past good deeds because this reliance on past deeds would mitigate the crime and shame of sin as well as God's mercy in pardoning the sinner.[88]

Bunyan identified repentance as sorrow for sins.[89] Saving repentance, however, involves much more than simple sorrow which even the vilest of reprobates could manifest. Bunyan described repentance that does not lead to salvation as involving: (a) awakening, (b) acknowledgement of sin, (c) a cry under the burden of sin, (d) humiliation, (e) loathing of sin, (f) prayers and tears against sin, (g) delight in doing the things of God, and (h) fear of sinning against God. Someone could manifest all of these elements of repentance and still perish for lack of saving repentance.[90]

True repentance involves a contrition and brokenness of heart that has knowledge of sin, hell deserved, and heaven lost, but which also knows "that Christ, and grace, and pardon may be had."[91] Christ is the overriding dynamic in true repentance, ". . . for saving conversion lieth more in the turning of the mind and will to Christ, and to the love of his heavenly things, than in all knowledge and judgment."[92]

Salvation

In his most famous work, *The Pilgrim's Progress,* Bunyan presented an allegorical description of his understanding of salvation. In the journey from the City of Destruction to the Celestial City, Bunyan describes salvation as more than a static experience. He elaborates the elements of justification, sanctification, and glorification, as well as the place of perseverance and assurance. While he describes salvation in the context of the experience of a believer, he interprets the experience by Scripture and applies the significance of the gospel to each dimension of salvation.

Throughout his writing, Bunyan stressed that salvation has many parts. It involves both a work in process and a work completed so that Bunyan could argue "to save is a work that hath its beginning before the world began, and shall not be completed before it is ended."[93] Because people consist of "body and soul" and Christ gave Himself for bodies as well as spirits, none can "be completely saved until the time of the resurrection of the dead."[94] Thus, Bunyan counted the second coming of Christ to be as important as His death on the cross in the total work of salvation. Christ accomplished the justification of sinners on the cross: "To be saved is to be delivered from guilt of sin that is by the law, as it is the ministration of death and condemnation, or, to be set free therefrom before God."[95] While Christ accomplished the finished work of salvation, the Holy Spirit carries out the sanctification of those whom Christ has justified:

> . . . the Spirit makes us meet for heaven; not by electing, that is the work of the Father; not by dying, that is the work of the Son; but by his revealing Christ, and applying Christ to our souls, by shedding the love of God abroad in our hearts, by sanctifying of our souls, and taking possession of us as an earnest of our possession of heaven.[96]

Thus, the giving of the Holy Spirit to believers played as crucial a role in Bunyan's gospel as the death on the cross. Bunyan explained that "the Holy Spirit coming into us, and dwelling in us, worketh out many salvations for us now, and each of them in order also to our being saved forever."[97]

Bunyan based the perseverance of the saints largely on his understanding of the priestly work of the ascended Christ in making constant intercession on behalf of the elect.[98] Perseverance is not "an accident in Christianity," rather it is a necessity for the "complete saving of the soul" accomplished by the power of God.[99] Bunyan insisted that full salvation meant "to be preserved in the faith to the end."[100] While Christ accomplishes perseverance by His intercession, the Holy Spirit serves as the agent of perseverance by setting up "his kingdom in the heart, and by that means keepeth out the devil after he is cast out."[101]

While Bunyan made Christ the content of his preaching, his theological frame of presentation remained Calvinistic. Bunyan's brand of Calvinism came through clearly in his concept of the order of salvation. The beginning of good for a person is the forgiveness of sins,

> and if they have missed of the first, of the beginning good, they shall never, as so standing, receive the second, or the third: Justification, sanctification, glorification, they are the three things, but the order of God must not be perverted. Justification must be first, because that comes to man while he is ungodly and a sinner.[102]

Bunyan believed that pardon must be given before the sinner can stand justified. Effectual believing comes after forgiveness has been granted by God, otherwise faith would be the cause of God's forgiveness of sin instead of the death of Christ.[103] Instead of being the grounds for forgiveness, Bunyan made faith the grounds for assurance: "The peace and comfort of it cometh not to the soul, but by believing. Yet the work is finished, pardon procured, justice being satisfied already, or before, by the precious blood of Christ."[104] Though Bunyan believed the Calvinistic doctrines concerning salvation, he preached pragmatically, knowing that those whom God had forgiven would trust Christ when they heard Him preached.

The Church

In *The Pilgrim's Progress,* shortly after coming to the cross and gaining release from his burden of sin, Christian came to a stately palace called Beautiful. The palace represented the church in the allegory, and guarding its entrance stood a porter. The porter either granted or denied admission "according to the rules of the house."[105] In order to determine Christian's qualifications to enjoy the "relief and security" of the place, the porter entrusted the pilgrim to his daughters who made inquiry of Christian's experience.[106] On the basis of his suitable account of how he had come to the place, Christian gained the hospitality of the place.

The questioning of Discretion, Piety, Prudence, and Charity continued in open-ended fashion to give Christian ample opportunity to describe his experience in his own words. In the conversation that followed, Bunyan depicted his characters as reviewing the elements of the gospel he counted so precious in his own conversion. Once satisfied that Christian had come to the palace by way of the cross, the daughters instructed him more completely in the things the "Lord of the hill" had done. Finally, the daughters equipped Christian with the best armor in the armory, "lest, perhaps, he should meet with assaults in the way."[107] Thus confirmed, refreshed, and equipped for what lay ahead, the pilgrim renewed his journey.

In this brief vignette, Bunyan presented his basic understanding of the function of the church. Built as a place of "relief and security" by the "Lord of the hill," the church supplied familial love, fellowship, teaching, and equipping to live a life of holiness in spite of grave spiritual threats. Bunyan also presented his understanding of how one gained entry to the church. He based it solely on discovery of one as a "visible saint" by virtue of faith in Christ as revealed in the gospel. This understanding of the basis for fellowship in the church and the conspicuous absence of baptism as a rite of entry in his theology set Bunyan at odds with many Baptists who held strict communion views.

According to tradition, John Gifford baptized Bunyan in the Ouse River sometime between 1651 and 1655.[108] In *The Heavenly Foot-man,* published posthumously in 1698, Bunyan declared that he called himself an "Anabaptist."[109] The Bedford church practiced believer's baptism, but it did not make believer's baptism a condition of church membership. The church and Bunyan reflected the teaching of their founding pastor John Gifford who exalted faith in Christ and holiness of life as the only conditions for entry into the church. No doubt as a result of the often violent ruptures in church life that had attended the disintegration of Puritanism with dozens of factious opinions, Gifford counseled his congregation not to cause divisions over "Baptisms, Laying on of hands, Anoynting with Oyls, Psalmes, or any externalls."[110]

The lax administration of baptism in the Bedford church occasioned a great deal of talk among the careful Baptists of London. In 1672 Bunyan issued *A Confession of My Faith, and A Reason of My Practice* in which he distinguished between the practice of baptism and the doctrine of baptism. The doctrine of baptism refers to the belief in the saving death and resurrection of Christ, and the believer's death and resurrection with Christ. While the practice of baptism symbolizes the salvation experience of the believer with Christ, its absence does not invalidate the experience. Bunyan insisted that baptism served as neither the door to the church nor as an initiation rite into the new covenant. He argued "that by the word of faith, and of good works, moral duties gospelized, we ought to judge of the fitness of members by, by which we ought also to receive them to fellowship. . . ."[111] Rather than as a basis for church membership, Bunyan believed that baptism provided a "sign to the person baptized, and a help to his own faith."[112]

The London Baptists attacked Bunyan's position in *Some Serious Reflections* (1673) which he quickly answered in *Differences in Judgment About Water-Baptism, No Bar to Communion*. Bunyan criticized his "Brethren of the Baptized-way" for making baptism "an essential of the gospel."[113] Bunyan stressed "that Christ, not baptism, is the way to the sheep fold."[114] While his opponents considered baptism as a law of Christ and an ordinance of worship for the church, Bunyan considered baptism a personal ordinance that contributed to the edification and assurance of the believer. Bunyan insisted that his adversaries failed to appreciate the difference between ceremonial laws such as baptism which did not comprise an essential element of holiness, and moral laws such as faith which did comprise an essential element of holiness.[115]

William Kiffin responded to Bunyan in *A Sober Discourse of Right to Church-Communion* and charged him with failing to follow the command of God expressed in Scripture. Bunyan gave his final response in *Peaceable Principles and True* in which he declared, "I do not deny, but acknowledge, that baptism is God's ordinance; yet I have denied, that baptism was ever ordained of God to be a wall of division between the holy and the holy. . . ."[116]

While he held that the primitive church baptized those that it received, he could not find scriptural basis for excluding those of faith who were not baptized.[117] In an age of theological and ecclesiological chaos, Bunyan feared making anything but the gospel the basis for church membership. His opinion, however, did not prevail within the Baptist community.

Though Bunyan described the church without reference to baptism in *The Pilgrim's Progress,* in The Second Part (1684) of *The Pilgrim's Progress,* Christina washes in the bath of Sanctification because "her master" would have her do it. Water baptism by immersion seems intended here rather than the baptism of the Spirit, since the latter would lie outside Christina's power.[118] The episode reflects Bunyan's continuing conviction about baptism by immersion for professing adults despite his willingness to forbear.

Evaluation

The Pilgrim's Progress secured John Bunyan's place as a most influential Baptist theologian. The book has had an unprecedented publication history for over three hundred years. Remarkably, it still is an effective evangelistic tool in the conversion of souls.[119] For the most part, Bunyan's theological tracts do not rise above the ordinary, but perhaps this very emphasis on the simple and the ordinary fostered the masterpiece that is *The Pilgrim's Progress*.

Bunyan's works boldly express his preoccupation with the simple gospel message, the experience of conversion, and the work of salvation. Bunyan had and proclaimed a practical, evangelistic theology. He had neither the training nor the inclination to pursue the depth of theological inquiry pursued by his contemporaries Thomas Goodwin, John Owen, and Richard Baxter. Yet, those giants of theology lie largely forgotten except to the specialists in Puritan studies. Bunyan's theology centered around his own salvation experience and his evangelistic calling. Whatever he preached or wrote had some practical relationship to the gospel as the basis for conversion and salvation.

While Bunyan clung to the gospel to avoid disputes over theology or ecclesiology which might hinder the advance of the kingdom, his commitment to the gospel led to his involvement in controversy on several occasions. All of his major controversies involved a defense of his understanding of the gospel. He did not seem to pursue controversy as William York Tindell has suggested, but he never avoided it when the gospel stood in issue. In his writings Bunyan either defended the gospel, explained the gospel, or presented the gospel with an evangelistic purpose in mind.

Even in Bunyan's choice of genre for presenting the gospel, he encountered controversy. *The Pilgrim's Progress* constituted a radical departure from what had been the norm for evangelism in England. From the time of Archbishop Grindal, the Calvinistic clergy of England had insisted that the "public and continual preaching of God's word is the ordinary mean and instrument of the salvation of mankind."[120] While the Puritans had enlarged this view in practice by the dissemination of books of sermons, they still relied on the sermon as the form evangelism should take. The printed sermon bore fruit. William Kiffin was influenced in his conversion by reading Thomas Goodwin's *A Childe of Light* and Thomas Hooker's *The Souls Preparation for Christ*. Richard Baxter was influenced in his conversion though reading the sermons of Richard Sibbes. Bunyan himself began his pilgrimage by reading *The Plain Man's Pathway to Heaven* by Arthur Dent and *The Practice of Piety* by Lewis Bayly, but Bunyan was especially helped by Luther's *Commentary on Galatians*. While several people had written on the theme of the pilgrimage of life, none had succeeded like Bunyan. To some Calvinists his approach amounted to innovation![121]

His willingness to depart from the overwhelming body of popular opinion has made Bunyan difficult to categorize, but without that trait his genius might never have flourished in *The Pilgrim's Progress*. One might easily tag him as a Calvinistic Baptist, if one were prepared to qualify all specificity from the designation by adding the phrase "in many respects." While these terms do not apply without qualifications, neither would any other except "Nonconformist" which he personified even in respect to the body of other dissenters.[122]

While Bunyan fit nicely into Calvinistic orthodoxy, the extent of Luther's influence on him was significant. Richard Greaves has elaborated much of this influence in his study of Bunyan's theology.[123] While many have come to recognize Bunyan's debt to Luther in terms of his emphasis on experience, more work needs to be done on the extent to which Luther may have influenced his expression of the atonement. Because Bunyan so clearly expresses Calvin's view of substitutionary atonement, as one would expect of an orthodox Calvinist, one might not notice that Bunyan expresses more than one view of the atonement. Though he holds strongly to substitutionary atonement in the satisfaction of Divine justice, Bunyan also consistently presents the Classic view of the atonement whereby Christ defeats sin, death, the devil, and hell. Gustaf Aulen has argued convincingly that Luther expressed the Classic view in, among other writings, his *Commentary on Galatians*.[124]

Bunyan mentions the *Christus Victor* motif in *Light for Them That Sit in Darkness*.[125] In *The Pilgrim's Progress*, while visiting the stately palace Christian remarks, "I perceived that he had been a great warrior, and had fought with and slain 'him that had the power of death. . . .' "[126] The most obvious example, of course, appears in *The Holy War*, in which the drama of salvation appears as a divine struggle against the tyrant who dominates Mansoul. Mansoul is freed from the reign of Diabolus by Emmanuel's victory. Bunyan believed that atonement involved more than the legal satisfaction of sin as usually expressed in the Calvinist framework.

In another significant area Bunyan departed from the English Puritan tradition. William Perkins popularized Calvin's thought and made it more accessible in his widely circulated *A Golden Chaine* (1591). In the order of salvation, Perkins placed faith before remission of sins and imputation of righteousness.[127] In *A Defence of the Doctrine of Justification* (1672) and *The Pharisee and the Publican* (1685) Bunyan completely reversed the order: imputation of righteousness, remission of sins, and faith.[128] Furthermore, while Perkins placed faith prior to justification as an element of effectual calling, Bunyan suggested that it comes after justification as an element of sanctification.[129] Bunyan insisted it must be this way, otherwise faith would be the basis of salvation rather than the grace of God.

One other significant point from this brief survey distinguishes Bunyan from the common view of English Calvinists. While he espoused a covenant theology in the tradition of Perkins, Preston, and Sibbes, Bunyan rejected the commonly held view that baptism corresponded to circumcision as a basis for entry into and participation in the covenant of grace.[130] This divergence from the Puritan tradition placed Bunyan not only at odds with the strict communion Baptists over the place of baptism in the church, but also with the vast majority of "orthodox" churchmen in England.

If one classifies Bunyan a Baptist, one should not think in terms of a fully developed denominational orientation. Though he practiced believer's baptism, he distanced himself from the developing organization of Calvinistic Independent churches practicing believer's baptism that came to be called the Particular Baptists. Richard Baxter distinguished between two sorts of Anabaptists in 1675 when he described one group as "sober Godly Christians, who when they are rebaptized to satisfy their consciences, live among us in Christian love and peace," while the other group held it "unlawful to hold communion with such as are not of their mind and way, and are schismatically troublesome and unquiet, in labouring to increase their Party."[131] William Orme, the biographer of William Kiffin, distinguished between strict and free communion Baptists.[132] Tindall divided the Baptists of the day into four groups: the Seventh Day Baptists, strict-communion Particular Baptists, open-communion Particular Baptists, and General Baptists.[133]

As one who practiced believer's baptism, Bunyan took part in the debate that helped draw the parameters of institutional Particular Baptist life. At the end of the debate, Bunyan stood outside the camp of how Baptists came to be defined. In his own time, however, when "baptist" and "congregational" were still adjectives more than proper nouns, Bunyan could easily call himself an "Anabaptist."[134] When he registered to obtain a license to preach under the terms of the king's Indulgence, Bunyan identified himself as a "congregational person."[135] In his final rejoinder to the Strict-communion Baptists, however, Bunyan would only say, "I tell you, I would be, and hope I am, a CHRISTIAN. . . ."[136]

Bibliography

Works by Bunyan

The Acceptable Sacrifice. London: n.p., 1689.

The Barren Fig-Tree. London: n.p., 1688.

A Book for Boys and Girls. London: n.p., 1686.

A Case of Conscience Resolved. London: n.p., 1683.

A Caution to Stir up to Watch against Sin. London: n.p., [1684].

Christian Behaviour. London: n.p., 1663.

Come, & Welcome, to Jesus Christ. London: n.p., 1678.

A Defence of the Doctrine of Iustification, by Faith. London: n.p., 1672.

Differences in Judgment about Water-Baptism, No Bar to Communion. London: n.p., 1673.

A Discourse of . . . the House of God. London: n.p., 1688.

A Discourse upon the Pharisee and the Publican. London: n.p., 1685.

The Doctrine of the Law and Grace Unfolded. London: n.p., 1659.

Ebal and Gerizzim, ad cal. One Thing is Needful. 3d ed. London: n.p., 1688.

A Few Sighs from Hell. London: n.p., 1658.

Good News for the Vilest of Men. London: n.p., 1688.

Grace Abounding to the Chief of Sinners. London: n.p., 1666.

Idem. 2d ed. London: n.p., 1687.

Idem. 6th (enlarged) ed. London: n.p., 1688.

The Greatness of the Soul. London: n.p., 1683.

The Heavenly Foot-Man. London: n.p., 1698.

The Holy City. London: n.p., 1665.

A Holy Life. London: n.p., 1684.

The Holy War. London: n.p., 1682.

Instruction for the Ignorant. London: n.p., 1675.

I will Pray with the Spirit. London: n.p., 2d ed. 1663.

The Life and Death of Mr. Badman. London: n.p., 1680.

Light for Them That Sit in Darkness. London: n.p., 1674.

One Thing Is Needful. 3d ed. London: n.p., 1688.

The Pilgrim's Progress. London: n.p., 1678.

Idem. The Second Part. London: n.p., 1684.

Prison-Meditations, ad cal. One Thing Is Needful. 3d ed. London: n.p., 1688.

Profitable Meditations. London: n.p., [1661].

Questions about . . . the Seventh-Day-Sabbath. London: n.p., 1685.

The Resurrection of the Dead. London: n.p., [c. 1665].

Seasonable Counsel. London: n.p., 1684.

Solomon's Temple Spiritualiz'd. London: n.p., 1688.

Some Gospel-Truths Opened according to the Scriptures. London: n.p., 1656.

The Strait Gate. London: n.p., 1676.

A Treatise of the Fear of God. London: n.p., 1679.

A Vindication of . . . Some Gospel-Truths Opened. London: n.p., 1657.

The Water of Life. London: n.p., 1688.

The Work of Jesus Christ as an Advocate. London: n.p., 1688.

Doe, Charles. *The Works of That Eminent Servant of Christ, Mr. John Bunyan.* n.p., 1692.

Offor, George, ed. *The Whole Works of John Bunyan,* 3 vols. London: Blackie and Sons, 1875.

Sharrock, Roger, ed. *Grace Abounding to the Chief of Sinners, and, The Pilgrim's Progress.* New York: Oxford University Press, 1966.

Sharrock, Roger, and Forrest, James F., eds. *The Holy War.* Oxford: Clarendon Press, 1980.

_____. *The Life and Death of Mr. Badman.* Oxford: Clarendon Press, 1988.

Sharrock, Roger, ed. *The Miscellaneous Works of John Bunyan,* 12 vols. Oxford: Clarendon Press, 1976- . (in progress).

_____. *The Pilgrim's Progress.* 2d ed. Oxford: Clarendon Press, 1967.

Works about Bunyan

Brittain, Vera. *Valiant Pilgrim: The Story of John Bunyan and Puritan England*. New York: Macmillan, 1950.

Brown, John. *John Bunyan (1628-1688): His Life, Times, and Work*. Tercentenary ed., rev. Frank Mott Harrison. London: The Hulbert Publishing Co., 1928.

Greaves, Richard L. *John Bunyan*. Courtenay Studies in Reformation Theology, No. 2. Grand Rapids, Mich.: Eerdmans, 1969.

Hill, Christopher. *A Tinker and a Poor Man: John Bunyan and His Church, 1628-1688*. New York: Knopf, 1989.

Kaufmann, U. Milo. *The Pilgrim's Progress and Traditions in Puritan Meditation*. Yale Studies in English, vol. 163. New Haven: Yale University Press, 1966.

Keeble, N. H. *John Bunyan Conventicle and Parnassus: Tercentenary Essays*. Oxford: Clarendon Press, 1988.

Sharrock, Roger. *John Bunyan*. London: Hutchinson's University Library, 1954.

Talon, Henri. *John Bunyan: The Man and His Works*. Cambridge, Mass.: Harvard University Press, 1951.

Tindall, William York. *John Bunyan Mechanick Preacher*. New York: Columbia University Press, 1934.

Winslow, Ola Elizabeth. *John Bunyan*. New York: Macmillan, 1961.

Notes

1. John Bunyan, *Grace Abounding* in *The Whole Works of John Bunyan*, ed. George Offor (London: Blackie & Sons, 1875; reprinted by Baker Book House, 1977), 1:6. This old edition continues to be the only recent complete edition of Bunyan's works; therefore, all citations will reference the edition by citing the particular book by Bunyan and the Offor volume and page. For a critical text of some of Bunyan's works, see the critical edition in progress produced by the Clarendon Press.

2. Ibid.

3. Ibid.

4. John Brown, *John Bunyan (1628-1688) His Life, Times, and Work*, rev. Frank Mott Harrison (London: The Hulbert Publishing Co., 1928), 47.

5. Ibid., 48. His irreligious bent testifies to the diversity that made up the Parliamentary Army.

6. Ibid., 53.

7. Bunyan, *Grace-Abounding* (1666), 1:7.

8. Ibid., 8.

9. Richard L. Greaves, ed., *The Doctrine of the Law and Grace Unfolded and I Will Pray with the Spirit, The Miscellaneous Works of John Bunyan* (Oxford: The Clarendon Press, 1976), 2:xxiv-xxv.

10. Richard L. Greaves, *John Bunyan*, Courtenay Studies in Reformation Theology, No. 2 (Grand Rapids, Mich.: Wm. B. Eerdmans Publishing Company, 1969), 21.

11. Ibid., 22.

12. For a discussion of this controversy, see my article "John Bunyan's Controversy with the Baptists," *Baptist History and Heritage* 23:2 (April 1988): 25-35.

13. Roger Sharrock, *John Bunyan* (London: Hutchinson's University Library, 1954), 49.

14. Richard L. Greaves, "The Organizational Response of Nonconformity to Repression and Indulgence: The Case of Bedfordshire," *Church History* 44 (December 1975): 472-84.

15. Sharrock, 50.

16. Bunyan, *Grace Abounding* (1666), 1:20.

17. Ibid., 20-21.

18. Ibid., 42.

19. Ibid.

20. Ibid., 43-44.

21. Ibid., 44.

22. Ibid., 43.

23. For a contrary opinion, see William York Tindall, *John Bunyan Mechanick Preacher* (New York: Columbia University Press, 1934), 42-67. Tindall says, "As an evangelist, solicitous for his threatened flock he constantly lent his passions to oral and pamphlet controversies; and as a mechanick he was often compelled by disagreeable contact with the learned to defend not only the freedom of grace but his ignorance and his authority to preach. In his capacity of evangelist and mechanick, and delegated by his conventicle to defend the truth, Bunyan was prodigal of his talent for controversy; for in addition to the eight or nine tracts which are exclusively contentious, most of his works reveal disputative passages, and his oral debates appear to have been innumerable," 43. Among the controversial tracts, Tindall includes *The Pilgrim's Progress* and *Grace Abounding*.

24. Bunyan, *Some Gospel Truths Opened* (1656), 2:141.

25. Ibid.

26. Ibid., 141-42.

27. Ibid., 142.

28. Ibid., 143-46.

29. Ibid., 148.

30. Ibid., 169.

31. Bunyan, *A Vindication of Gospel Truths Opened* (1657), 2:176.

32. Bunyan, *Light for Them That Sit in Darkness* (1674), 1:391.

33. Bunyan, *A Vindication of Gospel Truths Opened* (1657), 2:176-77. This second book appeared specifically to answer the disputation of Edward Burrough, a Quaker whom Bunyan charged with heresy. See, Edward Burrough's *The True Faith of the Gospel of Peace Contended For* (London: n.p., 1656).

34. Bunyan, *Light for Them That Sit in Darkness* (1674), 1:394.

35. Ibid., 397.

36. Ibid., 396.

37. Ibid., 393, 397, 402.

38. Ibid., 400.

39. Ibid., 398.

40. Ibid., 409.

41. Ibid., 411.

42. Ibid., 402.

43. Ibid.

44. Ibid., 395.

45. Bunyan, *Christ a Complete Saviour* (1692), 1:238.

46. Bunyan, *Light for Them that Sit in Darkness* (1674), 1:416.

47. Ibid., 416 *ff*.

48. Ibid., 436.

49. Ibid.

50. Bunyan, *Grace Abounding* (1666), 1:8.

51. Bunyan, *The Strait Gate* (1676), 1:387.

52. Bunyan, *The Pharisee and the Publican* (1685), 2:274.

53. Ibid., 268.

54. Bunyan, *Grace Abounding* (1666), 1:9-10, 15-16.

55. Ibid., 12, 15.

56. Ibid., 10-20.

57. Ibid., 13.

58. Ibid.

59. Ibid., 13-14.

60. Ibid., 14.

61. Ibid., 15.

62. Ibid., 16.

63. Ibid., 18.

64. Ibid., 20.

65. For discussions of Bunyan's dependence on Luther, see Richard L. Greaves, *John Bunyan,* Courtenay Studies in Reformation Theology, vol. 2 (Grand Rapids, Mich.: William B. Eerdmans Publishing Company, 1969), passim; John R. Knott, Jr., *The Sword of the Spirit: Puritan Responses to the Bible* (Chicago: The University of Chicago Press, 1980), 132 *ff*.

66. Bunyan, *Grace Abounding* (1666), 1:22.

67. Ibid.

68. Ibid, 44.

69. Bunyan, *The Pharisee and the Publican* (1685), 2:251.

70. Ibid.

71. Ibid., 255.

72. Bunyan, *Light for Them That Sit in Darkness* (1674), 1:431.

73. Bunyan, *The Pharisee and the Publican* (1685), 2:258.

74. Bunyan, *A Defence of the Doctrine of Justification* (1672), 2:295.

75. Bunyan, *Some Gospel Truths Opened* (1656), 2:170.

76. Bunyan, *Come and Welcome to Jesus Christ* (1678), 1:248.

77. Bunyan, *Light for Them That Sit in Darkness* (1674), 1:433-34.

78. Bunyan, *Saved by Grace* (1692), 1:351.

79. Bunyan, *Some Gospel Truths Opened* (1656), 2:152.

80. Bunyan, *A Defence of the Doctrine of Justification* (1672), 2:298.

81. Ibid., 294.

82. Bunyan, *The Jerusalem Sinner Saved* (1688), 1:70.

83. Bunyan, *Saved by Grace* (1692), 1:349.

84. Bunyan, *The Jerusalem Sinner Saved* (1688), 1:70.

85. Bunyan, *The Pharisee and the Publican* (1685), 2:260.

86. Ibid., 262.

87. Ibid.

88. Ibid., 264.

89. Bunyan, *The Jerusalem Sinner Saved* (1688), 1:70.

90. Bunyan, *The Strait Gate* (1676), 1:384.

91. Bunyan, *The Acceptable Sacrifice* (1689), 1:719.

92. Bunyan, *The Strait Gate* (1676), 1:368.

93. Bunyan, *Saved by Grace* (1692), 1:338.

94. Ibid., 341.

95. Bunyan, *Christ a Complete Saviour* (1692), 1:207.

96. Bunyan, *Saved by Grace* (1692), 1:347.

97. Ibid., 346.

98. Bunyan, *Some Gospel Truths Opened* (1656), 2:160.

99. Bunyan, *Saved by Grace* (1692), 1:339.

100. Ibid.

101. Ibid., 346.

102. Ibid., 266.

103. Bunyan, *A Defence of the Doctrine of Justification* (1672), 2:295.

104. Ibid.

105. Bunyan, *The Pilgrim's Progress* (1678), 3:106.

106. Ibid., 106-7.

107. Ibid., 111.

108. Joseph D. Ban, "Was John Bunyan a Baptist? A Case Study in Historiography," *The Baptist Quarterly* 30 (October 1984): 369-70.

109. Bunyan, *The Heavenly Footmen* (1698), 3:383.

110. *The Church Book of Bunyan Meeting, 1650-1821* (New York: E. P. Dutton & Co., 1928), 3.

111. Bunyan, *A Confession of My Faith* (1672), 2:607.

112. Ibid., 610.

113. Bunyan, *Differences in Judgment* (1673), 2:633.

114. Ibid., 634.

115. Ibid., 620.

116. Bunyan, *Peaceable Principles and True* (1692), 2:648.

117. Ibid.

118. Sharrock, 144.

119. This semester one of my students came to faith in Christ through reading *The Pilgrim's Progress,* which I used as a text.

120. Edmund Grindal, *The Remains of Edmund Grindal, D. D.* (Cambridge: The University Press, 1843), 379.

121. Harry L. Poe, "Bunyan's Departure from Preaching," *The Evangelical Quarterly* 58 (April 1986): 145-55.

122. Barrie White, perhaps the most careful historian of early Baptists, prefers to speak of Bunyan as belonging to "Independency." See B. R. White, "The Fellowship of Believers: Bunyan and Puritanism," in *John Bunyan Conventicle and Parnassus: Tercentenary Essays,* ed. N. H. Keeble (Oxford: Clarendon Press, 1988), 8-9, 12-13, 19.

123. Greaves, *John Bunyan*. Greaves credits the influence of Luther for giving Bunyan's writings and preaching "a more personal appeal than would have been the case had he relied solely on the more logic-bound orthodox Calvinism," 25.

124. Gustaf Aulen, *Christus Victor* (New York: Macmillan, 1969).

125. Bunyan, *Light for Them That Sit in Darkness* (1674), 1:395, 402.

126. Bunyan, *The Pilgrim's Progress* (1678), 3:109.

127. See William Perkins, "A survey, or Table declaring the order of the causes of Salvation and Damnation, according to God's word" in *The Works of William*

Perkins, ed. Ian Breward (Berkshire, England: The Sutton Courtenay Press, 1970).

128. Bunyan, *A Defence of the Doctrine of Justification* (1672), 2:295; Idem, *The Pharisee and the Publican* (1685), 248-58.

129. Bunyan, *The Pharisee and the Publican* (1685), 2:258; Bunyan, *A Holy Life* (1684), 2:518-19.

130. Greaves, *The Doctrine of Law and Grace,* xxviii.

131. Richard Baxter, *More proofs of Infants Church-membership* (London: n.p., 1675), A4.

132. William Orme, ed., *Remarkable Passages in the Life of William Kiffin* by William Kiffin (London: n.p., 1823), 128.

133. Tindell, 3.

134. For an examination of the debate over Bunyan's "denominational affiliation" see Greaves, *John Bunyan,* 22; Ban, 367-76; Brown, 219-25, 234-38; W. T. Whitley, "The Bunyan Christening, 1672," *Transactions of the Baptist Historical Society* 2 (1910-11): 255-63.

135. Brown, 235.

136. Bunyan, *Peaceable Principles and True* (1692), 2:648.

Benjamin Keach

J. Barry Vaughn

Biography

Born as England prepared to fight the Civil War, Benjamin Keach lived through a tumultuous half century. He witnessed events that shaped English politics and religion for the next three hundred years—the outbreak of fighting between Crown and Parliament (1642), the execution of Charles I (1649), the restoration of Charles II (1660), the restoration of the episcopacy (1662), the "Glorious Revolution" (1688), the toleration of religious dissenters (1689), and the accession of Queen Anne (1702). More important for the purposes of this essay, however, Keach's life coincided almost exactly with the rise and decline of the Calvinistic (or Particular) Baptists. In 1644 the Particular Baptists emerged as a distinct group with the publication of the First London Confession and in 1692 the Particular Baptists of London split over the singing issue.

Keach was no mere bystander during these events. William Kiffin (1616-1701),[1] Hanserd Knollys (1599?-1691),[2] and Benjamin Keach formed a "trinity" of extraordinary Baptist leaders in late-seventeenth-century England. Keach was at the center of Baptist life in London between his arrival there in 1668 and his death in 1704. He was pastor of a large Baptist church in the Southwark area of London, the Horsleydown church; he signed the Second London Confession; and his colleagues enlisted his aid in putting forward the case for congregations to provide adequate financial support for their ministers, which he did in *The Gospel Minister's Maintenance Vindicated* (1689). Above all, Keach was influential in advocating the corporate singing of hymns, an issue which deeply divided the Particular Baptists of London.

Keach was born in the village of Stoke Hammond in Buckinghamshire. The parish records show that Benjamin Keach, son of John and Fodora Keach was christened in 1640.[3] There is no evidence that Benjamin had any formal education. His son-in-law, Thomas Crosby,[4] does not tell us what Keach's trade was, but the record of one of his arrests for unlicensed preaching informs us that he was a tailor and "a teacher in their new-fangled way."[5] Crosby also notes that Keach "applied himself very early to the study of Scripture, and the attainments of divine knowledge."[6]

Keach presented himself for believer's baptism at the age of fifteen. Again, Crosby records:

. . . observing the Scripture to be entirely silent concerning the *baptism of infants,* he began to suspect the validity of the *Baptism* he had received in his infancy, and after he had deliberated upon this matter, was in the *fifteenth* year of his age *baptized* upon the profession of his faith, by Mr. *John Russel,* and then joined himself to a congregation of that persuasion in that country.[7]

The fact that John Russel baptized Keach tells us that the congregation which he joined was not a Particular Baptist church, but a General Baptist church, for Russel was a signer of the General Baptists' "Orthodox Confession."[8] Because Keach's first wife, Jane Grove, was from Winslow, it is extremely probable that the congregation which Keach joined was in that Buckinghamshire village. Present-day Winslow contains a seventeenth-century Baptist chapel which residents know as "Keach's Meeting-House," but this structure was not built until 1695, long after Keach had moved to London.[9]

Keach married Jane Grove in 1660. She died in 1670, but in those ten years she bore her husband five children, of whom three survived, Mary, Elias, and Hannah. Crosby tells us that Hannah became a Quaker and that when her father was in his last illness, she visited him: ". . . when he saw her, he endeavoured to talk with [her] and shewed a great eagerness and desire so to do, but his speech failing, prevented him . . ."[10] Keach's only surviving son, Elias, was instrumental in founding several Baptist churches in the area of Philadelphia. These churches adopted his father's Articles of Faith (1697), and through this document two of Keach's distinctive doctrines (corporate singing and the laying on of hands) found their way into the Philadelphia Confession (1742).[11]

Keach first emerges from obscurity with the publication of a primer for children, *The Child's Instructor,* in 1664. This book has disappeared, and it is possible that Keach would have remained unknown had it not been for the stir caused by its publication. In addition to being a primer, *The Child's Instructor* also advocated Baptist views on baptism. Publishing such a book in 1664 was a dangerous act. The restoration of the monarchy in 1660 and the Established Church in 1662 brought an end to the relatively tolerant regime of the Commonwealth. The intolerance of 1664 was demonstrated by the trial that year of twelve General Baptists in Aylesbury, the seat of Buckinghamshire, who were convicted and sentenced to death for their views. Significantly, they were the last religious dissenters who were sentenced to death in England. They were saved by a wealthy Baptist merchant, William Kiffin, who personally interceded with King Charles II.[12]

The authorities noted Keach's book, seized it because of the religious views it expressed, and bound Keach over to the assizes. Keach was challenged for his views on infant baptism and for his eschatology. The court clerk asked Keach to plead guilty or not guilty after the indictment had been read to him, but Keach declined to plead until he had had a chance to read the indictment himself. The judge viewed this as a delaying tactic and insisted that Keach enter a plea. Keach pleaded not guilty, was given a summary trial, found guilty, and sentenced to stand in the pillory for two hours on each of two successive Saturdays at Aylesbury and Winslow. At Aylesbury, Keach

Benjamin Keach (1640-1704)

Photo courtesy of Southern Baptist Historical Library and Archives

was verbally abused by a clergyman of the Church of England but was defended by the crowd. They silenced the clergyman by reminding him that he had been found drunk twice—once in a ditch and once under a haystack. In spite of the jailer's interruptions, Keach managed to preach to the crowd from the pillory. At Winslow he suffered the additional indignity of having his book burned before him as he stood in the pillory.[13]

Crosby was of the opinion that Keach's encounters with the state's rough treatment of Dissenters made him look toward London:

> His publick trial and suffering rendering him more acceptable to *informers* than others, so that it was unlikely he could enjoy any quiet settlement in those parts for the service of the church of Christ; and he, having not then taken upon him the charge of any people, thought of removing to *London,* where he might have an opportunity of doing more good.[14]

Perhaps he also sensed that there were greater opportunities in London. So in 1668 Keach, his wife, and their children set out for the capital.

At this time, Keach was still a General Baptist. Crosby relates that Keach succeeded General Baptist William Rider as pastor of London's Tooly Street church. Crosby notes that Keach was "solemnly ordained, with prayer, and *laying on of hands,* in the year 1688 [sic]; being the 28th year of his age . . ."[15]

The date and circumstances of Benjamin Keach's acceptance of Calvinism is the greatest puzzle of his life. We know that he had worshiped with the General Baptists in Buckinghamshire. However, we have no literature from Keach's pen which expresses General Baptist sentiments. Sometime between 1655 (the date of his baptism) and 1672 (the year that Keach's church moved to Horsleydown in Southwark), Keach made the transition from General Baptist to Particular Baptist.

Crosby does not go into detail about Keach's change. The Baptists who nurtured his faith "were generally, tho' not all, such as held the *Remonstrants* scheme . . . and went under the name of *Arminians.*"[16] Crosby tells us that

> when he came to London, where he had a greater opportunity of consulting both men and books, and found that the different opinions in this article gave a denomination to two parties of the *Baptists,* he examined the point more closely, and in a few years came to such a determination as fixed his judgment in this point for his whole life-time afterwards.[17]

One source of Calvinist influence was Keach's acquaintance with Hanserd Knollys. He and Keach must have become acquainted before 1672, because in that year Knollys officiated at Keach's wedding to Susannah Partridge of Rickmansworth, Hertfordshire.[18] Beyond that, nothing can be known with certainty about Keach's "conversion" to Calvinism.

Keach did not escape persecution by his move to London. Crosby relates that the authorities harassed him and his congregation and eventually arrested him for his new edition of *The Child's Instructor.* On another occasion, Keach was arrested and fined twenty pounds, a large sum of money in late-seventeenth-century England. A member of Keach's congregation, John Roberts, a physician, stood bail for him.[19]

The 1680s were a productive decade in Keach's life. The first clear sign that he had become accepted by the Particular Baptist community is their endorsement of his *The Gospel Minister's Maintenance Vindicated* in 1689. Keach was also useful to the Particular Baptists as an evangelist. In 1689 the General Assembly sent "Brother Benjamin Keach and one more . . . to visit our friends at Colchester, Suffolk, Norfolk, etc."[20] As a result of this journey a Baptist church was established at Lavenham.

The most significant and best-known controversy in which Keach took part was corporate hymn singing.[21] He introduced the singing of a hymn (as opposed to a psalm or a canticle) into the worship of the Horsleydown church between 1673 and 1675.[22] Furthermore, Keach went on to introduce singing "in *mixt Assemblies, on Days of Thanksgiving . . .*"

The hymn-singing controversy consisted of three components. Keach struggled with a group in his congregation who opposed corporate singing and also battled with the leaders of the Particular Baptist community in London (and elsewhere). Keach also engaged in a vitriolic printed debate.

The printed debate began and ended with books by Isaac Marlow (1649-1719):[23] *A Brief Discourse* appeared in 1690 and *An Answer to a Deceitful Book* in 1698. Marlow represented the Mile End Green Church at the 1689 assembly and was appointed by that assembly to be one of the treasurers of the Particular Baptist Fund.[24] His wife and children are listed as members of the Horsleydown church.[25] Following the singing controversy, Marlow became a member of the Leominster church.[26]

Keach published two books related to the singing controversy: *The Breach Repaired in Gods Worship* (1691) and *A Sober Reply to Mr. Steed's Epistle concerning Singing* (1691).[27] The printed debate tells us much about the struggle among the leaders of the Particular Baptists. About the battle between Keach and the antisinging members of his church, we know little.

It is possible that the conflict was born long before Marlow published *A Brief Discourse*. Marlow was sensitive to the charge that he had started the singing controversy. At the end of *Truth Soberly Defended,* Marlow added, "Some short observations made on . . . *The Breach Repaired . . .*" and pointed out that not only had Hercules Collins defended corporate singing in 1680, but Keach had defended it in two books prior to *The Breach Repaired—Tropologia* and *Gold Refin'd.*[28]

Keach claimed to have introduced the singing of a hymn following the administration of the Lord's Supper in 1673, eighteen years before the publication of *The Breach Repaired*. Next, Keach introduced hymn singing into services of thanksgiving or fasting.[29] His hymn books, *Spiritual Melody* and *Spiritual Songs,* include several funeral hymns. These three categories of services at which hymns were sung indicate a high degree of acceptance of hymn singing prior to the congregational meeting on March 1, 1691, at which a majority of members present voted to allow singing following the sermon each Lord's Day. However, the bitterness with which not only

Marlow and the antisingers, but Keach as well, conducted the debate makes it seem likely that the issue had been simmering for some time.

The motion in favor of singing did not go uncontested. A small but significant group opposed corporate singing, and after the motion passed, they petitioned for withdrawal from the church. The antisingers also objected that the motion had not been discussed thoroughly, although by their own record, Keach had announced the meeting and its subject one week before it took place.[30] The next episode in the singing controversy took place at the General Assembly of Particular Baptists in June. It seems Thomas Whinnel of Taunton asked the assembly to censure persons who wished to withdraw from their churches because of corporate singing, although the assembly had renounced this kind of authority.[31] The Maze Pond records include the testimony of three persons, Nathaniel Crabb, Robert Steed, and Isaac Marlow, who assert that Whinnel was also out of order because he proposed it on the last day of the assembly when many members had gone home, and no new business was to be discussed. Crabb insisted that the meeting on June 8 was "only to ratify what had gone before and not to discuss new business."[32] Marlow concurred:

> As to what was proposed to advise such persons that were not for the common way of Singing in Gods Worship to keep their Communion with those Churches that were in the practise of it there arose a long debate among the Brethren, and it being put to the voate it was strongly oposed and protested against as new matter . . . and after a long dispute it was as I and others desired put aside but I accedentally understanding that some who were for Singing did think otherwise I moved for Sattisfaction whether it was pas't or not upon which severall that were for Singing said that it was pas't others immeadiately protested against it as not being fairly past, and as fresh matter which was not then to be brought before us, and in this confution the matter was left . . .[33]

Keach issued "A Sober Appeal for Right and Justice" on May 30, 1691, in which he suggested that a committee, half the members to be chosen by Keach and half by Marlow, be formed to mediate the conflict. Marlow reported that the assembly endorsed Keach's suggestion.[34]

The members of the committee chosen by Keach were Joseph Maisters, William Collins, Leonard Harrison, and Samuel Bagwell. Marlow's choices were Edward Man, George Barret, Robert Steed, and Richard Halliwell. However, this group never fulfilled their mandate. Marlow withdrew from the project sometime after November 9, 1691, because of a disagreement with Keach over the ground rules of the committee. Marlow wanted the rules to be agreed upon in advance; Keach wanted the committee to work out the rules as they proceeded.[35]

In the context of this tension, the Particular Baptist churches assembled in London in June 1692 and, among other business, took up the singing issue. Murdina MacDonald emphasizes the seriousness of the situation:

> The singing issue ultimately involved, on one level or another, virtually the entire leadership of the London Calvinistic Baptist community. Those who

wrote in favour of singing 1690-1692 included Benjamin Keach, William Collins and Hanserd Knollys. Others who demonstrated approval of the singing position were Joseph Maisters, Richard Adams, James Jones, Hercules Collins, Leonard Harrison, Benjamin Dennis and Richard Allen. Those who opposed singing in print 1690-1691 included Isaac Marlow, Robert Steed, William Kiffin, Richard Halliwell, George Barret and Edward Man. Others who became involved in the controversy due to their sympathetic assistance of the anti-singers in their settlement were John Scot, Richard Baxter, David Towler and John Ward, while Nathaniel Crabb had added his protest to the events of 8 June 1691 by writing a testimony for the Horsleydown dissidents.[36]

The result of the 1692 assembly's investigation was a ruling that both prosingers and antisingers had engaged in "unbrotherly Censures," "unsavoury Expressions," and a "great wrong to the first Baptized Churches."[37] The parties in the dispute were asked to "call in and bring all their books hereafter mentioned into the *assembly,* or to whom they shall appoint, and leave them to their dispose. . . . Moreover, we entreat and determine . . . that none of the members of the churches do buy, give, or disperse any of these books aforesaid underwrit . . . ." The books "underwrit" are *A Sober Reply, Truth Soberly Defended, A Serious Answer,* and *Truth Cleared.*[38] Keach was singled out for having endorsed (if not written) the anonymous pamphlet *A Sober Reply* which implied that Baptist churches in the past had been reluctant to provide their ministers with an adequate salary. Evidently, the Particular Baptist leaders were eager not to convey the impression that Calvinistic Baptists were reluctant to provide their ministers with an adequate stipend.[39] Keach agreed to abide by the Assembly's ruling; Marlow did not and neither did the prosinger, Thomas Whinnel. Marlow immediately issued the book *Some Brief Remarks* (1692).

The hymn-singing conflict left the Particular Baptists of London divided and disorganized. There were no more assemblies after 1693. Particular Baptist organization withered, but hymn singing prospered. Although the printed debate ended in 1698, it is not too extravagant to suggest 1736 as the year in which the drama finally came to an end. In that year the Maze Pond church, established by the antisingers of Horsleydown, called Abraham West to be their pastor. West made it a condition of his accepting their call that the church should sing hymns. The church agreed.[40]

Throughout his years in London, Keach was first and foremost pastor of a church. Crosby tells us that his father-in-law's church had to be enlarged more than once, and eventually held "near a *thousand* people."[41] Also, Keach established "mission" or "satellite" churches. In 1682 it was reported that "Mr. Ceah" (probably Keach) had two houses, three ministers, and about 350 members.[42] These two buildings were the Goat Street and Rotherhithe churches. Crosby writes that Keach was successful in "getting several meeting houses erected for the public worship of God; as, one at *Limehouse,* another at *Rotherhithe;* one in *White-street, Southwark,* and another at *Barkin* in Essex."[43]

Benjamin Keach died on July 18, 1704. He had requested Seventh Day

Baptist leader Joseph Stennet to preach his funeral sermon, but Stennet was too ill. Crosby tells us that Stennet subsequently published it, but there is no record of such a sermon by Stennet.

Exposition

Keach pioneered in one significant area: corporate hymnody. His other contributions can best be understood as clarifications and consolidations of ideas which Baptists already held. Keach's output was enormous; he published fifty-four books, and his sermons run to more than a thousand pages. This essay will focus on four of Keach's most significant contributions: soteriology, baptism, hymn singing, and religious education.

Soteriology

Justification was a hotly debated theological topic in seventeenth-century England. For Keach, justification was "that great Truth, in which mainly the Reformation consisted . . ."[44] Theological enemies castigated each other as "Arminian" and "Antinomian," although the reality very seldom corresponded to the name.[45] Most persons found themselves somewhere in between the two extremes, and persons branded with both labels claimed that their point of view was an authentic expression of Calvinism.

A form of Calvinism (perhaps influenced by Zwingli's successor, Heinrich Bullinger[46]) dominated the Church of England until the 1620s. Thereafter, the Church of England came under the sway of Arminians, and the Puritans, previously distinguished from other Anglicans chiefly by their objection to certain ceremonies, became known as distinctly Calvinistic. During Keach's lifetime, most of the old Puritan party had been excluded from the Established Church by the restoration of the episcopacy in 1662, thus the Nonconformists (formerly Puritans), that is, the Presbyterians, Independents, and Baptists, were dominated by Calvinists. The chief statement of English Calvinism was the Westminster Confession, the doctrinal standard of English Presbyterians. In a somewhat modified form known as the Savoy Declaration, it became the confessional document of the Independents (later known as the Congregationalists). Following suit, the Particular Baptists modified the Savoy confession and issued it as their Second London Confession in 1689.

Although Calvinism dominated Nonconformist thought, there was a very influential party within Nonconformity which held a soteriology significantly at variance from Calvin. These were the "Middle Way Men;" their leader was Richard Baxter;[47] and Keach opposed them unrelentingly. There was legitimate reason for Keach's concern, because Baxter believed in a kind of justification by works:

> . . . as the Blood and Merits of Christ . . . must be the matter of our justification from the guilt of all other sins . . . so must our own personal Faith, Repentance, and sincere Obedience be the matter of our Justification from the particular false Accusation . . . of final non-performance of these conditions of

the Gospel . . . this is the Justification by works . . . which I do assert and defend . . .[48]

Further, Baxter denied that in justification Christ's righteousness is imputed to believers; he maintained instead that the believer's righteousness is imputed to be righteous for Christ's sake:

> . . . as God reputeth Christ's righteousness to be the *prime meritorious Cause* for which we are justified by the Law of Grace . . . so he truly reputeth our *own Faith* and *Repentance* (or *Covenant-consent*) to be our *moral Qualification* for the *gift,* and our *Holiness* and *Perseverance* to be our *moral Qualification* for final Justification and Glory . . .
>
> Therefore God may in this Sence be truly said, both to *impute Righteousness* to us, and to *impute our Faith for righteousness* . . .[49]

Keach wrote five books which defend unconditional justification and attack "Baxterianism"—*The Marrow of True Justification* (1692); *The Everlasting Covenant* (1693); *Christ Alone the Way to Heaven* (1698); *The Display of Glorious Grace* (1698); and *A Medium Betwixt Two Extremes*[50] (1698). In addition to these, there are extensive references to unconditional justification in his collections of sermons: *A Golden Mine Opened* (1694) and *Gospel Mysteries Unveil'd* (1701).

Keach defined justification in *Medium,* his rebuttal of Samuel Clark.

> Justification [is] by the imputation of Christ's active and passive Obedience, through the free Grace of God, apprehended and received by Faith alone, without any thing wrought in us, or done by us; not by imputing Faith or any other act of Evangelical Obedience, but the imputing of Christ's Obedience and Satisfaction exclusively of all things else whatsoever. And that Faith is only said to justify us objectively, or in respect had to the Object Jesus Christ, which it taketh hold of.[51]

A significant aspect of this definition is that Keach held that justification is an effect of having both Christ's active and passive obedience imputed to the believer. (Christ's active obedience meant His complete fulfillment of the precepts of the law; His passive obedience was His suffering the penalty due to the sins of the elect.) Baxterians held that only Christ's passive obedience played a part in justification.

Central to Keach's soteriology is a high view of the Person of Christ and His offices. He implied that Baxterianism encouraged a low view of Christ which tended toward Socinianism.[52] For Keach, union with Christ is the effective cause of justification because Christ, as a priest, represents believers before the Father. The heart of the error of the Baxterian party, according to Keach, was that they regarded justification as the act of Christ the King, not Christ the Priest: "Christ doth not reconcile God to us as a King, but as a Priest, and it is not done by what he works in us, but by what he hath done for us."[53] Keach did not deny that Christ does, in fact, work "in us," as well as "for us." However, he denied that justification is a human act, even a human act assisted by divine grace.

Another central concept in Keach's soteriology was the covenant. Keach argued that the Baxterians were wrong in believing that salvation under the covenant of grace can be had at an "easier rate"; he believed that human credibility before God was utterly lost in the fall. Now, God needs someone to act as a "surety" for the human race. The Baxterians were wrong about the covenant of grace, because God does not enter into a new covenant with the elect in themselves but with the elect as they are in Christ:

> I would know whether in the Covenant of Grace God is said to enter into Covenant with Man, simply considered as in himself; or whether 'tis not with Christ, and so in him with us . . . certainly, our credit was so lost and gone with God, that he would not trust us, with any Covenant-Transaction any more without a Surety . . .[54]

In spite of the high Calvinist nature of Keach's soteriology, he was no quietist; the individual did have a role to play in justification. Although justification is unconditional, Keach held out hope to those who make diligent use of the "means" of grace:

> If any Soul *believes* in Christ, *thirsteth* for Christ, *looketh* to Christ, or *cometh* to Christ, and yet Christ rejecteth him, then charge him with injustice: But where lives that Man, tho he was never so Vile and Ungodly that did thus, but he found Mercy? O see how Free and Universal the Proclamation is![55]

Similarly, those who do not "thirst after Christ" should not presume upon God's mercy by hoping that they may be saved in spite of their unreformed lives: ". . . He that leads an ungodly Life, and pursues his filthy Lusts, may assure himself . . . he shall be damned for ever . . . Men ought to endeavour to believe and repent, and close with Christ upon a Peradventure."[56]

What, then, is the individual's responsibility in justification? It is "to labour after true Faith"[57] because faith is the preeminent "vehicle" of grace. God has also provided a "means" of awakening faith—preaching: "[The preaching of the] Gospel is the instrumental means, through the Spirits Operations of the Sinner's Reconciliation to God . . ."[58] Keach allowed that there were other "ordinances" of the gospel, especially baptism, the Lord's Supper, the laying on of hands, prayer, and praise. He believed that these ordinances were "as *golden Pipes* to convey Heavenly Riches, or Sacred Treasure to our Souls."[59]

But did a person in any sense "cause" his or her own justification? The answer is a qualified "yes." Keach allowed that, in a sense, faith was a cause of justification, but only in an instrumental and very limited sense. He quoted Bishop George Downham's *A Treatise of Justification* (1633) to underscore his point: "*Manus accipientis,* saith Dr. *Downham,* the hand of the Receiver is the Grace of justifying Faith: 'Tis not Faith, but the Object and Righteousness Faith apprehends or takes hold of, that *justifies the ungodly.*"[60]

But faith is not a *material* cause of the believer's justification:

> . . . Faith . . . is said to justify us only in respect of the Object Jesus Christ, whom it apprehended; and it is no part of the matter which doth justify us (the

Righteousness of Christ being alone the material cause of our justification) . . .[61]

Keach expressed the paradox of justification in the following quotation:

> Tho' Faith be required of them that are saved, yea, and Repentance, Regenera-
> tion, Holiness and a new Heart also; yet these Blessings are all promised in the
> Covenant, as part thereof: But Faith it self is no foederal Condition, but only
> serves to shew what God will do for, and work in such that he as an Act of free
> Grace will save.[62]

Faith is "required of them that are saved," but it is "promised in the Covenant, as part thereof." Here Keach is reminiscent of Augustine's prayer,
"Demand what Thou wilt, and give what Thou demandest." The "condition" of justification (faith) is given by God and becomes a source of assurance to the believer.

Keach's doctrine of assurance had two parts. With the Baxterians, he believed that sanctification was evidence of justification. However, he also believed that the "Spirit witnesses with our spirits that we are children of God."
Keach seems to have been more aware than the Baxterians that basing assurance on sanctification is dangerous and can lead to despair for "weak
Saints":

> . . . divers weak Saints are ready to judge of their Justification according to the
> degree and measure of their Sanctification; and can hardly be brought to be-
> lieve, such vile Creatures as they are, who find such evil and deceitful
> Hearts . . . can be Justified in the sight of God . . .[63]

He believed that the Baxterian soteriology led to a doctrine of assurance
which stranded believers in a morass of self-doubt:

> . . . for all your Faith and constant trusting in God, you have much Unbelief,
> and many Fears and Doubtings arising in your Spirits: tho' you have prayed
> often, and have not fainted; yet with what Deadness, with what Coolness, with
> what Wanderings of Heart and Vanity of Thoughts; and tho' you have done
> much good, will not your Consciences tell you, you might have done much
> more? you gave a *Shilling* may be to this poor, and that poor and distressed
> Object, when may be you ought to have given a *Pound*. O Sirs! your Relief lies
> in Christ, and in the Covenant of Grace . . . or you have none, nor ever will.[64]

The preceding quotation implies that Keach believed in the Reformed doctrine *simul justus et peccator,* a realistic, pastoral doctrine which should
caution against making assurance entirely a matter of seeking evidence of
sanctification. The Baxterians were not as cautious.

However, Keach did allow that signs of sanctification may be evidence of
justification:

> No Mans Faith is known to be true, but by its fruits or good Works, tho'
> Holiness and good Works cannot justifie our Persons, yet they justifie our
> Faith, and render us justified Persons before men, and to our own Consciences
> also.[65]

The danger of Keach's doctrine of assurance is that assurance could come to be nothing but a feeling:

> The Holy Spirit witnesses by it self, by an inward and secretd [sic] Persuasion or Suggestion, that God is our Father, and we his Children, and also by the Testimony of his Graces and powerful Operations, tho' not in the like Degree and Clearness to all Believers . . .[66]

But he did stress that assurance comes from being directed toward Christ:

> Quest. How may I know that I have Christ, or an Interest in him?
> Answ. 1. If thou hast Christ, thou hast Life, thou art spiritually quickned . . .
> 2. Thou canst remember the time when thou hadst no God, no Christ, or wast without Christ.
> 3. If Christ be thine, he is very *precious* to thee.
> 4. Doth Jesus Christ rule and reign in thee by his Spirit? He that hath Christ in him, may feel his ruling Power . . .
> 5. . . . if Christ is in thee, and thou by Faith art in him, then thou art a new Creature.[67]

The danger of Keach's high Calvinism was that it could slip over into hyper-Calvinism. The distance between the doctrine of *unconditional* justification (which Keach held) and the doctrine of *eternal* justification (which Keach rejected) is not great.[68] Keach was clearly not a hyper-Calvinist. The main point of his book, *A Medium betwixt Two Extremes* (1698) is to deny eternal justification:

> . . . do we not all preach to all out of Christ as unto ungodly ones, to such that are under Wrath and Condemnation in their own Persons, and so remain until they believe or have Union with Christ. Our Lord *came not to call the Righteous,* as such . . . *but Sinners to Repentance;* to such that were really lost in the first *Adam* . . .[69]

Yet, it is likely that Keach's high Calvinist soteriology did contribute to the development of hyper-Calvinism in the succeeding generation. Keach was close to the hyper-Calvinists in his attitude toward foreign missions:

> [God] might have sent the whole Lump of fallen Mankind to Hell . . . Why we, and not those in *India,* and few or none in *England?* why should we have the Gospel here in this Isle, and almost all the Word [sic] lie in the Darkness of Popery, Mahometanism, or Paganism? If Christ died for all, why is not the Gospel preached to all? . . . the Gospel he doth not give to all, nor his Spirit, Faith, and other Gifts that are necessary to Salvation, to many thousands in the world; therefore he did not give his Son to die to save them all.[70]

Keach's attitude was much like that which Baptist missionary William Carey (1761-1834) encountered. At a meeting of the Ministers' Fraternal of the Northampton Baptist Association in 1787 Carey proposed the following topic for discussion: "Whether the command given the apostles to teach all nations was not binding on all succeeding ministers to the end of the world."

Distinguished Baptist leader John Ryland, Sr., reportedly replied: "Sit down young man. You are an enthusiast! When God pleases to convert the heathen, He will do it without consulting you or me."[71]

Baptism

Between 1689 (the year of Keach's first book challenging pedobaptist views) and 1696 (the year of his last book on the subject) Keach was the most vigorous champion of antipedobaptist views. Keach published six books and one broadsheet attacking pedobaptism: The broadsheet, *Mr. Baxter's Arguments for Believers Baptism* (1674), was Keach's first foray into the baptism debate and is no longer extant. It was based on Richard Baxter's arguments for confirmation in *Confirmation and Restauration.*[72] The six books are *Gold Refin'd* (1689), *Paedobaptism Disproved* (1691), *The Rector Rectified* (1692), *The Ax Laid to the Root* (1693), *A Counter-Antidote* (1694), and *Light Broke forth in Wales* (1696). *Believers Baptism* (1705) is identical to *Light Broke forth in Wales*.

Keach's critique of infant baptism was closely related to his critique of Baxterian soteriology. To Keach, infant baptism implied a conditional soteriology. He believed that infant baptism was the source of this conditionalist soteriology: the "Spring or Rise of this grand *Baxterian* Error [i.e., the conditional covenant] is from Infants-Baptismal Covenant."[73]

This was certainly Baxter's opinion; he explicitly stated that the covenant into which believers' children were baptized was a conditional covenant:

> . . . Remission and Justification are given by a Morall Act of God, even by the promise or grant of the New Covenant, which Covenant is conditionall and universall: when any performeth the condition (as Infants do by their parents faith) the Covenant presently pardoneth and Justifieth them without any new Act of God . . . and if this person do by unbelief deprive himself afterward of the benefit, the Covenant which still remaineth Conditionall, will condemn him, as before it did justifie him . . .[74]

The standard case for pedobaptism made by Anglicans, Presbyterians, and Independents was that under the New Covenant, baptism performed the same function that circumcision had under the Old Covenant. Therefore, if circumcision was administered to infants, then so should baptism. According to Keach this put baptized infants in a worse condition, not a better one. If circumcision was the antitype of baptism, Keach reasoned, then baptism would oblige all those who received it to keep the law as circumcision had:

> The Covenant or Precept that profited none, unless they kept the Law, could not belong to the Covenant of Grace . . . 'Tis strange to me that Circumcision should be a Gospel Covenant, and yet not profit any, unless they perfectly kept the Law, and also obliged them so to do . . . O see how the Law and Circumcision agree, and comport together in their nature, end, use and design, and never plead for it as a Gospel Precept any more, unless you have a mind to bring your Selves and Children under the Old Covenant, and the Curse thereof . . .[75]

Many pedobaptists charged that the Baptists believed that all dying infants were damned. Although not regarding all dying infants as inheritors of eternal life, Keach *did* believe that God would save *elect* infants.

> . . . we have ground to hope our children that Die are as happy as yours, tho' never baptized; and that from Gods word. Hath not Christ said, *Of such are the Kingdom of Heaven,* no doubt God hath comprehended Infants in his eternal electing Love that Die, for whom he also gave his Son, and in some secret way doth Sanctifie them, or makes them meet for glory above; and we have as much ground to hope, that God will give Grace to those Children of ours that live, as you have to hope he will give Grace to yours.[76]

Although Keach acknowledged not only the possibility but the likelihood that at least some dying infants received justifying grace, he denied that such infants should be baptized, even if the minister were capable of distinguishing between elect and nonelect infants: "But if we did know which Infants would dye, who do belong to the Election of Grace, or are in Covenant with God, yet we ought not to Baptize them, because we have no Command from Jesus Christ, so to do . . ."[77]

If Keach believed that infants were capable of receiving justifying grace, then why did he believe that baptism should be withheld from infants? The sole condition of baptism in the New Testament, as Keach read it, was the possession of personal and actual faith.

> . . . Baptism doth not by God's appointment, belong all to them who are capable of the Benefits or Blessings signified thereby, as Remission of Sin and Regeneration, &c. but only to such who are capable to repent and profess Faith in Christ.[78]

Keach accused the pedobaptists of twisting Scripture to make their case for infant baptism. Scripture teaches plainly, not obscurely, Keach insisted. If pedobaptism were the will of God, then surely Scripture would teach it explicitly, not implicitly:

> . . . Consequences that are genuine, or are naturally deduced from the Scripture, to prove and demonstrate Matter of Faith . . . and Consequences brought to prove a Positive Law or Institutions are another thing. Pray, did God by *Moses* give forth any Law, or positive Rite or Precept so darkly, that it could not be proved but by Consequences? . . . *Moses* delivered every Law, Statute and Ordinance so plainly to the People of *Israel,* that *he that ran might read it.* . . .[79]

If we may do whatever is not forbidden by Scripture, then rites and ceremonies may proliferate *ad infinitum*. The final result would be a return to Roman Catholic practices: "If therefore any thing may be done in God's Worship, which you suppose is not forbid, and bears also some proportion in Signification with Jewish Rites; all Popish Rites and Ceremonies may be let in at the same Door . . ."[80]

It might be concluded that baptism for Keach was a "mere" sign or an empty ritual. It did not convey justifying grace, nor would it serve, in the absence of personal and actual faith, to incorporate a person into the new covenant. However, Keach's writings on baptism do show that he regarded baptism to some extent as a real vehicle of divine grace. Its significance is fourfold. First, God's promises are associated with it: "God hath also promised to assist, stand by, help and enable all Believers Baptized, with farther supplies of Grace, nay, they being actually United to Christ, have his blessed influences flowing to them . . ."[81] Secondly, Christ's baptism shows that each person of the Trinity is involved in baptism:

> . . . No Ordinance in all the New-Testament was ever so grac'd, nor honoured with such a Presence as this was at the Baptism of Christ; the three Persons manifest their Presence at this Solemnity . . . 1. The Father seals it and honours it. 2. The Son is there, and subjects to it, shewing what an honourable respect he has to it; nay and came many Miles upon no other Business but to be baptized . . . 3. The Spirit also *descended like a Dove, and rested upon him;* the Holy Ghost puts his Seal upon it, and in a glorious manner owns it.[82]

Thirdly, it affects the religious emotions:

> . . . we cannot but be much affected with the great Love and Goodness of our Blessed Saviour in the Institution of these two great Ordinances, it being his gracious Design and Condescention, [sic] hereby to hold forth, or preach, as I may say, to the very light of our visible Eyes, by these fit and proper Mediums, the glorious Doctrine of his Death, Burial, and Resurrection, which in the Ministration of the Word, is preached or held forth to the hearing of our Ears, that so we might the better and more effectually be established and grounded in the sure and steadfast belief thereof . . .[83]

And fourthly, baptism is a form of communion with Christ: "We have Fellowship with Christ in his Death in Baptism, or the Efficacy of his Death evidenced to us, as the outward Symbol of it is held forth in the external Administration of it."[84]

Corporate Hymn Singing

Benjamin Keach has been chiefly celebrated as a pioneer of corporate hymn singing among English Protestants. Undoubtedly, he deserves his fame in this matter. However, both the quality and extent of his contribution has consistently been either over or underestimated. The fairest statement about Keach, the hymn writer, was made by Hugh Martin: ". . . he was the first to introduce the regular singing of hymns into the normal worship of an English congregation."[85] If the emphasis is placed firmly on "regular" and "normal," Martin's statement is almost certainly true. Hymns (and psalms, too, it goes without saying) were sung by English Protestants before Keach, but Keach was the first, (of whom we know) in spite of vehement opposition, to lead his congregation to sing a hymn every Sunday as a part of the normal course of worship.

Although Keach's hymns were soon forgotten, his precedent had an impact. Isaac Watts was aware of Keach, and Enoch Watts urged his brother to clear the Dissenters from the "scandal" that lay upon them because of "their imagined aversion to poetry":

. . . you cannot be ignorant what a load of scandal lies on the Dissenters, only for their imagined aversion to poetry. You remember what Dr. Steed says:

> So far hath schism prevailed they hate to see.
> Our lines and words in couplings to agree,
> It looks too like abhorred conformity:
> A hymn so soft, so smooth, so neatly drest,
> Savours of human learning and the beast.

And, perhaps, it has been thought there were some grounds for his aspersion from the admired poems of Ben. Keach, John Bunyan, etc., all flat and dull as they are; nay, I am much out if the latter has not formerly made more ravishing music with his hammer and brass kettle.[86]

Keach's defense of hymn singing consists of two parts: he argued both for the usefulness of hymn singing and for its permissibility (i.e., that it is enjoined by Scripture as a perpetual gospel ordinance).

Hymns were not only vehicles of praise, they were also instruments of religious education. Quoting Augustine, in the preface to his first collection of hymns, Keach observed,

> the Holy Ghost seeing the souls of mankind struggling in the way of godliness, and being inclined to the delights of this life, hath mixed the power of his doctrine with sweet singing, that whilst the soul was melted with the sweetness of the verse, the divine word might the better be grafted with profit.[87]

He also saw godly "hymns, psalms, and spiritual songs" as useful replacements for secular songs and ballads:

> . . . this book [*Spiritual Melody*] may prove of great advantage to their children, who generally are taken with verse, and are much addicted to learn such songs and ballads which generally tend to corrupt youth; and 'tis a shame to godly Christians they should suffer their children to learn many of them . . .[88]

Keach also endeavored to show that singing is both a moral duty (i.e., taught by natural law), and that it is a positive duty (i.e., commanded by God in Scripture).

> And what is more clear . . . than that Passage of the Children of *Israel's* Singing after their great Deliverance at the Red Sea . . . Plain it is, this was before the Law was given forth; which clearly shews . . . it was no *Levitical Ceremony* (as some are ready to assent) but a Duty it was, and it has been practiced by Multitudes that never had any knowledge of the Scripture or positive Precepts.[89]

Thus, Keach showed that singing is part of God's law written on the human heart and did not require divine revelation. However, he believed that singing was also commanded by God: ". . . 'tis evident there are more Precepts than injoin all Men to sing the Praises of God in the Old Testament, than there are for them to pray unto him . . ."[90]

However, Keach was hard-pressed to find corporate hymn singing explicitly commanded in the New Testament. That was the main point on which

Isaac Marlow challenged him. Marlow acknowledged that the New Testament commands or at least allows singing, but not that it allows *corporate* hymn singing:

> This we have plainly and clearly delivered to us in I Cor. 14.26 to 34. . . . Here is the Rule for our Practice, *one by one,* or one after another, by course or turns, they may speak with Tongues, and prophesy. And though only these two Gifts are particularized in the Rule, yet the Order stands for all the rest . . .[91]

Another area of disagreement between Keach and Marlow was over the nature of "spiritual worship." Christian worship, Marlow argued, should be "spiritual." Therefore, the singing practiced in Christian worship must be "spiritual": ". . . the *Essence* or *Being of Singing* consists of an inward spiritual Exercise of the Soul or Mind of Man. . . ." Prayer, he goes on to argue, "may be made in our Hearts to God without the use of our Voice . . ."[92]

Marlow seems to have regarded "nature" and "spirit" as irreconcilable opposites: "Have you not been for many years a Preacher up of spiritual Worship? how is it then that you are now so zealous for that which is asserted to be Natural?"[93] Thus, if forms were "natural," they could not be instruments of the Spirit:

> . . . if there be a spiritual Power, it refuses and denies the invented Form; for then there is no need of a prescribed nor pre-composed humane Form: and if we use such a Form we deny the Power, and reject the sufficient successive Gifts of the Holy Spirit, by relying on that Form.[94]

A stock weapon in Marlow's armory was that if forms of singing were permissible then so were forms of prayer. He referred to Keach's hymnbook (*Spiritual Melody*) as a "common Praise-Book"[95] and argued that forms of praise open "a wide door for Forms of Prayer . . ."[96]

Keach did not make such an absolute distinction between "nature" and "spirit." He believed that the Spirit can work in and through nature. To say otherwise is to open the door to silent worship such as that of the Quakers. Keach reduced Marlow's argument that the essence of singing is spiritual (i.e., nonphysical) to absurdity:

> . . . Is not the Essence of Preaching in our Spirits, as much as the Essence of Singing is there? And are we not as capable in our Spirits to worship God, in all other Ordinances, without the Verbal or Vocal Instruments of the Body, as well as in Singing without Voice, by your Argument?[97]

Religious Education

It could be argued that the touchstone by which to understand Keach's entire published output is religious education. His first book, *The Child's Instructor* (1664), was a primer. Nearly every other book which he published can be read as an instrument of catechesis. The various editions of the primer and the catechism were the only formal instruments of religious education which Keach issued, but the hymns and allegories were clearly intended for use as means of religious nurture.

The book attributed to Keach which was most clearly intended for use in religious education was the catechism. However, its authorship is disputed. Crosby does not attribute any catechism to Keach's pen, and it is not clear when the so-called "Baptist catechism" began to be associated with Keach.[98] Thomas Nettles remarks, "William Collins had at least as much to do with the catechism as Keach did."[99] However, Nettles' comment appears to be based on the assumption that the catechism is a précis of the Second London Confession, but it is not. Two facts suggest that the "Baptist Catechism" was largely, if not wholly, the work of Keach. First, the catechism is not a précis of the Second London Confession; it is a summary of the Westminster divines' Shorter Catechism. Keach adapted the Shorter Catechism for use in *The Child's Delight* and *Instructions for Children*.[100] Much of the material of the two catechisms is found in his primers. Second, the order of the subjects in the catechism is the order Keach used in his Articles of Faith. Unlike the Westminster Confession and the Second London Confession, Keach's articles begin with the doctrine of God and move to the doctrine of Scripture. Keach followed the same order in the catechisms he included in *Instructions for Children*. William Collins was undoubtedly responsible for the Second London Confession, so if he had also been responsible for the *Baptist Catechism,* it seems unlikely that he would have changed the order he found acceptable in the confession.

The catechism appears to have been part of the Particular Baptist attempt to rehabilitate their image in the popular mind. The choice of the Westminster Confession as the basis for the Second London Confession and the Shorter Catechism as the basis for Keach's catechism suggest a desire on the part of the Calvinistic Baptists to display their doctrinal solidarity with other English Protestants.

The apologetic purpose of Keach's catechism distinguishes it from the catechisms produced by Jessey, Bunyan, and Hercules Collins. Jessey directed his catechism to children, and Bunyan directed his to new converts. Collins, in choosing the Heidelberg Catechism as a model, came closest to Keach's intention. However, the relative unfamiliarity of the Heidelberg Catechism made it a poorer choice than the better-known Shorter Catechism. Choosing familiar words which were routinely taught to children was an ideal way to demonstrate that the Particular Baptists were in conformity with other English Protestants.

Keach's first book, *The Child's Instructor* (1664), was a primer. Its precise nature will never be known, because it was burned before Keach as he hung in the stocks in Aylesbury, but Crosby tells us that he later rewrote it from memory. Two similar primers by Keach are extant—the third edition of *The Child's Delight: Or Instructions for Children and Youth,* and the ninth edition of *Instructions for Children*—and can be consulted without much difficulty.[101] Unfortunately, neither book gives a date of publication.[102] The two books show us that Keach, in a manner typical of his age, did not make a rigid distinction between religious and "secular" education. Both include catechisms and as well as instruments for teaching reading and simple arithmetic. Keach believed it was impossible to draw a distinct line between the secular and religious purpose of education. One of the first precepts in both primers is:

> To learn to Read, good Child, give heed,
> For 'tis a precious Thing:
> What may compare with Learning rare!
> From hence doth Virtue spring.[103]

Keach's motivation in encouraging children to learn to read may not have been entirely altruistic; he was also the author of several popular religious allegories and the larger the reading public, the greater potential for sales! These allegories were his most innovative instruments of religious education.

The Nonconformist imagination flowered in the late-seventeenth century. Not only did Bunyan publish *The Pilgrim's Progress,* parts 1 and 2; *The Life and Death of Mr. Badman;* and *The Holy War,* but General Baptist Thomas Sherman "improved" on part 1 of *The Pilgrim's Progress* and published his own imaginative accounts of salvation and damnation, *Youth's Comedy* (1680) and *Youth's Tragedy* (1671). Keach's colleague, London pastor Hercules Collins, published *The Marrow of Gospel History,* a metrical account of the life of Christ, in 1696.

Benjamin Keach was one of the most popular writers in this school of Nonconformist literature. Certainly, Keach was vastly inferior to Bunyan in his ability to create dramatic situations, draw characters, and write dialogue. However, the two Baptists were both engaged in conveying heavenly truths through earthly symbols, and Keach carried out this program far more thoroughly than did Bunyan.

Keach published four books which portray the Christian life imaginatively—*War with the Devil* (1674), *The Glorious Lover* (1679) (an epic poem modeled on Milton's *Paradise Lost* and *Paradise Regained*), *The Travels of True Godliness* (1683), and *The Progress of Sin* (1684). Keach produced other poetry, especially *Zion in Distress* (1666) and *Distressed Zion Relieved* (1689), as well as the anti-Quaker pamphlet "The Grand Impostor Discovered" (1675). However, *War with the Devil, The Glorious Lover, Travels of True Godliness,* and *The Progress of Sin* belong together as books in which the Christian experience is portrayed in dramatic terms.

The thought of creating "art for art's sake" never occurred to Benjamin Keach. His imaginative writings were created for a purpose, and that purpose, just as with a great amount of Keach's writing, was to be an instrument of religious instruction. *The Glorious Lover* states this explicitly; it is intended to convey "heavenly manna, though but homely drest."[104]

Evaluation

No Baptist of Keach's generation defended the Baptist understanding of baptism at greater length or with more passion. This passion was also evident (along with bitterness) in the singing controversy of the 1690s. On this latter issue Keach showed himself to be a leader and innovator for English Protestantism in general, and not for the Baptists alone. It is not too much to claim that on March 1, 1691, when Keach's church voted to sing a hymn each Sunday following the sermon, the great tradition of English Protestant hymnody began. Although this essay has not dealt with Keach's sermons, they form an invaluable, though largely unexplored, treasure for Baptists. The nearly one thousand pages of *A Golden Mine Opened* (1694) and *Gospel Mysteries Unveiled* (1701) exceed any two volumes of sermons published by Keach's fellow seventeenth-century Baptists.

The point of this exercise is not merely recovery of the hidden past; much as in Keach's day, Baptists today are seeking a way forward in the midst of uncertainty and conflict. Baptists would do well to note that Keach's Articles of Faith differ significantly from the Second London Confession in confessing God first and the Bible second. We should also take heed of Keach's conciliatory spirit toward those with whom he differed. With regard to those who disagreed with them about the laying on of hands and corporate singing, Keach urged his congregation to show "Tenderness, Charity and Moderation to such as differ from you in those Cases . . . [do] not refuse Communion with them . . ."[105]

Bibliography

Works by Keach

The Articles of Faith of the Church of Christ or Congregation Meeting at Horsley-down. London: n.p., 1697.

The Ax Laid to the Root, or One Blow More at the Foundation of Infant Baptism and Church Membership. London: n.p., 1693.

The Banquetting-house. London: n.p., 1692.

The Baptist Catechism, or a Brief Instruction in the Principles of the Christian Religion. London: n.p., 1793. (This book was not published under Keach's name until 1793.)

The Breach Repaired in God's Worship; or Singing of Psalms, Hymns, and Spiritual Songs proved to be an Ordinance of Jesus Christ. London: n.p., 1691.

The Child's Instructor; or, a new and easy primmer. London: n.p., 1664.

Christ Alone the Way to Heaven, or Jacob's Ladder Improved. London: n.p., 1698.

A Counter Antidote to purge out the Malignant Effects of a Late Counterfeit prepared by Mr. Gyles Shute to prevent the prevalency of Anabaptism. London: n.p., 1694.

The Counterfeit Christian: or the Danger of Hypocrisy. London: n.p., 1691.

The Display of Glorious Grace of the Covenant of Peace Opened. London: n.p., 1698.

Distressed Zion Relieved, or the Garment of Praise for the Spirit of Heaviness. London: n.p., 1689.

The Everlasting Covenant or a Sweet Cordial for a Drooping Soul. London: n.p., 1693.

A Feast of Fat Things. London: n.p., 1696.

The Glorious Lover, A Divine Poem Upon the Adorable Mystery of Man's Redemption. London: n.p., 1679.

The Glory of a True Church and Its Discipline Displayed. London: n.p., 1697.

God Acknowledged, or The True Interest of the Nation and All that Fear God. London: n.p., 1696.

Gold refin'd, or Baptism in its Primitive Purity. London: n.p., 1689.

A Golden Mine Opened; or the Glory of God's Rich Grace displayed in the Mediator to all Believers; and His direful wrath against impenitent sinners. London: n.p., 1694.

The Gospel Minister's Maintenance Vindicated. London: n.p., 1689.

Gospel Mysteries Unveil'd; or an Exposition of all the Parables and Many Express Similitudes contained in the Four Evangelists Spoken by Our Lord and Saviour Jesus Christ. London: n.p., 1701.

Laying-on-of-Hands upon Baptized Believers, as such, Proved an Ordinance of Christ. London: n.p., 1698.

Light Broke forth in Wales Expelling Darkness; or the Englishman's Love to the Antient Britains. London: n.p., 1696.

The Marrow of True Justification or Justification without Works. London: n.p., 1692.

A Medium betwixt two Extremes. London: n.p., 1698.

Pedo-baptism disproved. Being an Answer to two printed Papers by the Athenian Society called the Athenian Mercury. London: n.p., 1691.

The Progress of Sin; or, The Travels of Ungodliness. London: n.p., 1684.

The Rector Rectified and Corrected or Infant Baptism Unlawful. London: n.p., 1692.

Spiritual Melody containing near three hundred sacred hymns. London: n.p., 1691.

Spiritual Songs, Being the Marrow of the Scripture in Songs of Praise to Almighty God; from the Old and New Covenant. London: n.p., 1700.

The Travels of True Godliness from the Beginning of the World to the present day, in an Apt and Pleasant Allegory. London: n.p., 1683.

Keach, Benjamin and Thomas Delaune. *Tropologia* [in Greek characters], *or a Key to Open Scripture Metaphors*. London: n.p., 1681. [Only Book I of *Tropologia* was Delaune's work; it was a translation of Solomon Glassius's *Philologia Sacra*. Books II and III were Keach's catalog of biblical metaphors.]

Troposchematologia [in Greek characters]. London: n.p., 1682.

War with the Devil. London: n.p., 1673.

Works Related to Keach

Allison, C. F. *The Rise of Moralism*. London: SPCK, 1966.

Benson, Louis. *The English Hymn: Its Development and Use in Worship*. New York: Hodder and Stoughton, 1915.

Brown, Raymond. *The English Baptists of the Eighteenth Century*. London: Baptist Historical Society, 1986.

Carnes, James P. "The Famous Mr. Keach: Benjamin Keach and his Influence on Congregational Singing in Seventeenth Century England." M.A. thesis, North Texas State University, 1984.

Clifford, Alan. "Benjamin Keach and Non-Conformist Hymnody." In *Spiritual Worship*. London: Westminster Conference, 1985.

Crosby, Thomas. *The History of the English Baptists*, 4 vols. London: n.p., 1738-40.

Greaves, Richard. *John Bunyan*. Abingdon, Berkshire: Sutton Courtenay Press, 1969.

Greaves, Richard and Zaller, R. *Biographical Dictionary of British Radicals in the Seventeenth Century*, 3 vols. 1982-84.

Hill, Christopher. "Antinomianism in Seventeenth Century England." In *The Collected Essays of Christopher Hill*, vol. 2, *Religion and Politics in Seventeenth Century England*. Brighton: The Harvester Press, 1986.

Holifield, E. Brooks. *The Covenant Sealed: The Development of Puritan Sacramental Theology in Old and New England, 1570-1720*. New Haven, Conn.: Yale University Press, 1974.

Keeble, N. H. *The Literary Culture of Nonconformity*. Athens: University of Georgia Press, 1987.

Kendall, R. T. *Calvin and English Calvinism to 1649*. Oxford: Oxford University Press, 1979.

Lumpkin, William L. *Baptist Confessions of Faith*. Philadelphia: Judson Press, 1959.

Music, David W. "The Hymns of Benjamin Keach: An Introductory Study." *The Hymn* 34 (July 1983): 147-54.

Nettles, Thomas J. *Baptist Catechisms: "To Make Thee Wise Unto Salvation."* Thomas J. Nettles, 1983.

_____. *By His Grace and for His Glory: A Historical, Theological, and Practical Study of the Doctrines of Grace in Baptist Life*. Grand Rapids, Mich.: Baker Book House, 1986.

Royal Commission on the Historical Monuments of England. *An Inventory of Nonconformist Chapels and Meeting-Houses in Central England*. London: Her Majesty's Stationery Office, 1986.

Spears, W. E. "The Baptist Movement in England in the late Seventeenth Century as Reflected in the Work and Thought of Benjamin Keach, 1640-1704." Ph.D. thesis, University of Edinburgh, 1953.

Toon, Peter. *The Emergence of Hyper-Calvinism in English Nonconformity. 1689-1765*. London: The Olive Tree, 1967.

Vaughn, J. Barry. "Public Worship and Practical Theology in the Work of Benjamin Keach (1640-1704)." Ph.D. thesis, University of St. Andrews, 1989.

Wallace, Dewey D., Jr. *Puritans and Predestination: Grace in English Protestant*

Theology, 1525-1695. Chapel Hill: The University of North Carolina Press, 1982.

Watts, Michael. *The Dissenters: From the Reformation to the French Revolution.* Oxford: Oxford University Press, 1982.

White, B. R. *The English Baptists of the Seventeenth Century.* London: The Baptist Historical Society, 1983.

_____. "John Gill in London, 1719-1729: A Biographical Fragment." *Baptist Quarterly* 22 (April 1967): 72-91.

_____. "Thomas Crosby, Baptist Historian: (I) The First Forty Years, 1683-1723." *Baptist Quarterly* 21 (1965-66).

_____. "Thomas Crosby, Baptist Historian: (II) Later Years." *Baptist Quarterly* 21 (1965-66).

Whitley, W. T. *A History of British Baptists.* London: The Kingsgate Press, 1932.

_____. "An Index to Notable Baptists." *Transactions of the Baptist Historical Society* 7, 1920-21.

_____. *Baptist Bibliography,* 2 vols. London: The Kingsgate Press, 1916 and 1922.

Notes

1. For William Kiffin, see Richard Greaves and R. Zaller, *Biographical Dictionary of British Radicals in the Seventeenth Century* (1982-84), 155-56 and Dictionary of National Biography (DNB), 11:98-100.

2. For Hanserd Knollys, see Richard Greaves and R. Zaller, *Biographical Dictionary of British Radicals in the Seventeenth Century* (1982-84), 160-62; B. R. White's *Hanserd Knollys and Radical Dissent in the 17th Century* (London: Dr. Williams's Trust, 1977); Thomas Crosby, *The History of the English Baptists from the Reformation to the Beginning of the Reign of King George I.* 4 vols (1738-1740), 1:334-44; and DNB, 11:279-81.

3. The parish records show that Keach was born on Feb. 29, 1639, but because March 1 was regarded as the beginning of the year, Keach's birth fell in 1640 by modern reckoning.

4. Thomas Crosby (1685?-1752), mathematician and schoolmaster, is the principal source of information about his father-in-law. His *The History of the English Baptists* was based on the work of another Keach son-in-law, Benjamin Stinton (1676-1719), who succeeded Keach as pastor of the Horsleydown church. Stinton's work was never published because of his untimely death. Crosby's work was based on manuscripts, as well as personal access to some of the persons about whom he wrote, and is generally considered an accurate and reliable source. See also B. R. White, "Thomas Crosby, Baptist Historian: (I) The First Forty Years, 1683-1723," *Baptist Quarterly* (BQ) 21 (1965-66): 154-68 and "Thomas Crosby, Baptist Historian: (II) Later Years," BQ 21, (1965-66), 219-34.

5. *Calendar of State Papers, Domestic* (1663-64), 595.

6. Crosby, 4:269.

7. Ibid.

8. Arnold H. J. Baines, "The Signatories of the Orthodox Confession of 1679," BQ 17 (1957-58): 171.

9. See *An Inventory of Nonconformist Chapels and Meeting-Houses in Central England* (London: Her Majesty's Stationery Office, 1986), 27-29.

10. Crosby, 4:308-09.

11. For an account of Elias Keach's work in the colonies, see Morgan Edwards, *Materials toward a History of Baptists in Pennsylvania* (1770), 9-10. See also Whitley, "Baptists in the Colonies till 1750," Transactions of the Baptist Historical Society (TBHS) 7 (1920-21): 31-48.

12. For an account of this incident, see Michael Watts, *The Dissenters: From the Reformation to the French Revolution* (Oxford: Oxford University Press, 1982), 224. Also, Whitley, *History of British Baptists,* 114, and Crosby, 2:184.

13. See Crosby, 2:185-209 for a full account of Keach's trial which Crosby ascribes to an eyewitness.

14. Crosby, 3:143-44.

15. Crosby, 4:272.

16. Ibid., 270.

17. Ibid., 271.

18. Keach's first wife died in childbirth in 1670. The record of Keach's second marriage is in "A perfect and Compleat Register of all Marriages, Nativites, and Burials belonging to the Congregation that meeteth on Horsly-downe, over whom Benjamin Keach is Overseer," MS, Public Records Office, London. An entry for 1672 reads, "Benjamin Keach and Susannah Partridge his wife were maried [sic] the two and twentyth [sic] of April by Mr. han: knowles."

19. Crosby, 3:146-47.

20. *A Narrative of the Proceedings of the General Assembly* (1690), 5. See also A. J. Klaiber, "Early Baptist Movements in Suffolk," BQ 4 (1928-29): 116-20.

21. The best account of the hymn-singing controversy is given in Murdina Mac-Donald's "London Calvinistic Baptists, 1689-1727: Tensions within a Dissenting Community under Toleration" (D.Phil. diss., Regent's Park College, 1983). Throughout the following section I have drawn heavily on her account.

22. Benjamin Keach, *The Breach Repaired in Gods Worship* (1691), "Epistle Dedicatory," viii.

23. Marlow, who represented the Mile End Green church at the 1689 assembly, may never have been a member of Keach's church and is not mentioned in the Maze Pond records as a member of the group who withdrew over the singing issue. However, his wife and children are mentioned in "A Perfect and Compleat Regester of all Marrages, Nativites, and Burials, belonging to the Congregation that meeteth on Horsly-downe, over whom Benjamen Keach is Overseer" (on deposit in the Public Records Office) as members. Furthermore, Marlow and the Horsleydown dissidents shared virtually identical beliefs about singing.

24. *Narrative of the Proceedings* (1689).

25. "A perfect and Compleat Register of all Marriages, Nativites, and Burials belonging to the Congregation that meeteth on Horsly-downe, over whom Benjamin Keach is Overseer," MS, Public Records Office, London.

26. W. T. Whitley, "An Index to Notable Baptists," TBHS 7 (1920-1921): 218.

27. *A Sober Reply to Mr. Steed's Epistle concerning Singing* (1691) was printed anonymously. However, the general assembly censured Keach as though he were the writer (*A Narrative of the Proceedings* (1692, 9-10), and the discussion of ministerial maintenance is characteristic of Keach. I conclude that Keach wrote it.

28. Isaac Marlow, *Truth Soberly Defended* (1692), "Some Short Observation . . . ," 3. *Tropologia* also contains some hymnic verses: "An Epithalamy on the Soul's Marriage with Christ. By E. D." (Bk. II, 107); "On the Rose of

Sharon" (Bk. II, 202); "You gentle Youths whose chaster Breasts do beat" (Bk. III, 16-17); and "Mr. John Flavel's Poem upon the Plough" (Bk. III, 66).

29. Benjamin Keach, *The Breach Repaired in Gods Worship* (1691), viii.

30. Maze Pond Church Book (MPCB), 1:31: ". . . the 22 day of the 12 Month 1690 [February 22, 1691] Mr. Benjamen Keach on the Lords day imeadatly after the Church had broke Bread moved for publick singing in the Church . . .

"Agreed to discours the point of Singing next first Day afternoon, after the publick Worship is over."

31. *Narrative of Proceedings* (1689), 10: ". . . we disclaim all manner of *Superiority, Superintendency,* over the Churches; and that we have no *Authority* or *Power,* to prescribe or impose any thing upon the Faith or Practice of any of the Churches of Christ."

32. Maze Pond Church Book (MPCB), 1:35.

33. Ibid., 37.

34. Marlow, *Truth Cleared* (n.d.), 5-6. Marlow included Keach's "Sober Appeal" in his work.

35. Ibid., 15-21.

36. MacDonald, "London Calvinistic Baptists," 62-63.

37. *Narrative of Proceedings* (1692), 9-10.

38. Crosby, 3:269-70.

39. MacDonald, 65.

40. Crosby, 4:301: ". . . after the death of the reverend Mr. *Edward Wallin,* they chose Mr. West to be their pastor, who made it one condition of his acceptance, that they should *sing the praises of God in the assembly for public worship;* with which they complied, and do now practise accordingly."

41. Ibid., 273.

42. Whitley, "London Churches in 1682," BQ 1 (1922-23): 82.

43. Crosby, 4:306.

44. Benjamin Keach, *A Medium Betwixt Two Extremes* (1698), 36.

45. Jacob Arminius (1560-1609), a Dutch theologian, has given his name to a school of theology which emphasizes human freedom and is perceived as the opposite of Calvinism (although Arminius regarded himself as a faithful interpreter of Calvin). Arminius's theology was condemned at the Synod of Dort (1618-1619). In the seventeenth century, Arminianism was the name given to many groups and movements, usually by their opponents (e.g., the Anabaptists, although they held general atonement and freedom of the will before Arminius). The groups and individuals accused of holding Arminian principles almost invariably denied it (e.g., Richard Baxter).

46. In *Anti-Calvinism: The Rise of English Arminianism, c. 1590-1640* (Oxford: Clarendon Press, 1987) Nicholas Tyacke argues that the standard theology of the Church of England until the 1620s was Calvinism and only thereafter was there a distinctive "Puritan" (i.e., Calvinist) theology as opposed to an Arminian theology (7-8). For the influence of Bullinger and other modifiers of Calvinism, see Dewey D. Wallace, Jr., *Puritans and Predestination: Grace in English Protestant Theology, 1525-1695* (Chapel Hill: The University of North Carolina Press, 1982), x-xi.

47. Richard Baxter (1615-1691) was probably the most influential divine among the first generation of Nonconformists. For a life of Baxter, see Geoffrey Nuttall's *Richard Baxter* (London: Thomas Nelson and Sons, 1965). C. F. Allison extensively critiqued Baxter's soteriology in *The Rise of Moralism* (London: SPCK, 1966).

48. Richard Baxter, *Richard Baxter's Confession of his Faith, Especially con-*

cerning the Interest of Repentance and sincere Obedience to Christ, in our Justification & Salvation (1655), ix-x. Baxter uses "works" ambiguously. In his preface to Allen's *A Discourse of the Nature, Ends, and Difference of the Two Covenants* (1673), he writes: ". . . we shall be all *judged according to our Works*, by the Rule of the Covenant of Grace, though not *for our Works* by way of . . . *Legal proper Merit,*" (9), and on the next page writes: ". . . no Works of Mans are to be *trusted* in, or *pleaded* . . ."

49. Baxter, *An End of Doctrinal Controversies* (1691), 257-58.

50. Keach may have had in mind Baxter's claim "I stand between two extreams, and therefore must speak against both." Baxter, *Treatise of Justifying Righteousness* (1676).

51. Keach, *Medium,* 36.

52. "Socinianism" is named after Italian writer Paolo Sozzini (1539-1604) who denied the divinity of Christ.

53. Keach, *The Display of Glorious Grace or The Covenant of Peace Opened* (1698), 68-69. Also Keach, *Medium,* 17-18.

54. Keach, *The Everlasting Covenant or a Sweet Cordial for a Drooping Soul* (1693), 10.

55. Keach, *Gospel Mysteries Unveil'd; or an Exposition of all the Parables and Many Express Similitudes contained in the Four Evangelists Spoken by Our Lord and Saviour Jesus Christ* (1701), Bk I, 192-94.

56. Ibid.

57. Ibid.

58. Ibid.

59. Keach, *A Golden Mine Opened; or the Glory of God's Rich Grace displayed in the Mediator to all Believers; and His direful wrath against impenitent sinners* (1694), 412. Also note the following passage: "Sirs, Men will not be condemned for not doing that which they had not Power to do, but for neglecting that which they might have done; their Destruction is of themselves, though their Salvation is wholly of God, and of the free Grace of God in Jesus Christ . . . They who say we put the Creature to do nothing, falsely charge us; we press Men to leave their wicked Practices upon a right foot of Account, and to wait upon God in his blessed Ordinances, which he has appointed for the begetting of Faith." (448.)

60. Keach, *Medium,* 6.

61. Keach, *Medium,* 23-24.

62. Keach, *Gospel Mysteries,* Bk I, 192-94.

63. Keach, *Marrow,* 3.

64. Keach, *Everlasting Covenant,* 37.

65. Keach, *Gospel Mysteries,* Bk I, 156-57.

66. Keach, *Everlasting Covenant,* 34.

67. Keach, *Golden Mine,* 499.

68. For hyper-Calvinism, see Peter Toon, *The Emergence of Hyper-Calvinism in English Nonconformity. 1689-1765* (London: The Olive Tree, 1967), 144-45.

69. Keach, *Medium,* 31. John Gill, successor to Keach and Stinton as pastor of the Horsleydown church, is generally identified as a leading hyper-Calvinist of the next generation. He undoubtedly believed in eternal justification. Note the following quotations from his *A Body of Doctrinal Divinity,* 1 (1769): 335: "It is objected, that men, cannot be justified before they exist; they must *be,* before they can be justified . . . whatever is in this objection, lies as strongly against eternal election, as against eternal justification; for it may as well be said, how can a man be elected before he exists?"

Also: "It is asserted, that justification cannot be from eternity, but only in time, when a man actually believes and repents; otherwise it would follow, that he who is justified, and consequently has passed from death to life, and is become a child of God, and an heir of eternal life, abides still in sin, abides in death . . . and in a state of damnation . . . but this latter especially cannot be admitted of, with respect to God's elect, even while unconverted." 339.

70. Keach, *Gospel Mysteries,* Bk II, 75-76.

71. Leon McBeth, *The Baptist Heritage: Four Centuries of Baptist Witness* (Nashville: Broadman Press, 1987), 185.

72. For an account of Baxter's views on baptism, see E. Brooks Holifield, *The Covenant Sealed: The Development of Puritan Sacramental Theology in Old and New England, 1570-1720* (New Haven, Connecticut: Yale University Press, 1974), 87-88.

73. Benjamin Keach, *Believers Baptism: or, Love to the Antient Britains Displayed* (1705), xvii.

74. Baxter, *Plain Proof of Infants Church-membership* (1649), 315.

75. *The Ax Laid to the Root, or One Blow More at the Foundation of Infant Baptism and Church Membership* (1693), 23. See also *The Rector Rectified and Corrected or Infant Baptism Unlawful* (1692), 6: "Circumcision bound those who came under that Rite, to keep the whole Law of *Moses:* Baptism signifies we are delivered from that Yoke of Bondage."

76. Keach, *Believers Baptism,* 243.

77. Keach, *The Ax,* 25.

78. Keach, *Rector,* 77-78.

79. Ibid., 33.

80. Keach, *Rector Rectified,* 7.

81. Keach, *Believers Baptism,* 270. Cf. 173: ". . . Consider the great Promises made to those who are obedient to it, amongst other things, *Lo, I am with you always, even to the end of the World.* And again, *He that believeth, and is baptized, shall be saved.*"

82. Ibid., 172.

83. Ibid., 43.

84. Keach, *Golden Mine,* 133.

85. Hugh Martin, "The Baptist Contribution to Early English Hymnody," BQ 19 (1962): 199.

86. Letter from Enoch Watts to Isaac, March 1700, quoted in E. Paxton Hood, *Isaac Watts: His Life and Writings, His Homes and Friends* (London: The Religious Tract Society, 1875), 86.

87. Keach, *Spiritual Melody containing near three hundred sacred hymns,* "Epistle to the Reader," i.

88. Ibid. Cf. *Breach,* 184: " 'tis so natural for all, especially in Youth, to learn to sing, and so easily attained, ought not Parents to instruct their Children about what they should sing, and what not . . ."

89. Keach, *Breach,* 30.

90. Ibid., 34.

91. Marlow, *Brief Discourse concerning Singing in the Publick Worship of God in the Gospel Church* (1690), 22.

92. Ibid., 4-5.

93. Marlow, *Prelimited Forms of Praising God, vocally sung by all the Church together, Proved to be no Gospel-ordinance* (1691), "The Author's Epistle to Mr. Benjamin Keach," 14.

94. Marlow, *A Brief Discourse*, 18. Also, *Purity of Gospel Communion* (1694), 53: ". . . Mr. *Keach* has pleaded so much for Art in Divine Worship that if the Spirit of the Lord does not lift up a spirituall standard against it, we may fear the increase of Artificial Worship in our Churches . . ."

95. Marlow, *Truth Soberly Defended* (1692), xiv. Also, Marlow, *Purity of Gospel Communion*, 46.

96. Marlow, *Prelimited Forms*, 19. Cf. Marlow, *A Brief Discourse*, 20.

97. Keach, *Breach*, 13-14. Richard Allen concurred in *An Essay to prove Singing of Psalms with Conjoin'd Voices, a Christian Duty* 8: 'Tis a moral Duty for Men to praise God with all the Faculties wherewith he has endowed them. To glorify him, not only with the Faculties of their Souls, but also with all the members of their *Bodies*. . . ."

98. In his *Baptist Bibliography* W. T. Whitley erroneously attributes the *Covenant and Catechism of the church of Christ meeting at Horsley Down in Southwark* to Keach, but this was actually by Independent divine Joseph Jacob.

99. Thomas J. Nettles, *Baptist Catechisms: "To Make Thee Wise unto Salvation"* (1983), 76.

100. The third edition of *The Child's Delight* was probably published in 1703 and the ninth edition of *Instructions for Children* was published in 1710.

101. Benjamin Keach, *The Child's Delight*, 3d ed. (1703) (hereafter referred to as *Delight*) and *Instructions for Children* 9th ed. (1710). All references are to these two editions.

102. The British Library holds a third edition of *The Child's Delight* [1702?]. There are four copies of *Instructions for Children*: the ninth edition [1710]; fifteenth edition (1723); an edition believed to have been issued in 1745; and the thirtieth edition (1763).

103. Keach, *Instructions*, 6 and *Delight*, 8. Keach's verse was borrowed by Manasseh King on v-vi of his *A New and Useful Catechism; Very necessary and Teachable, both for Young Children and Young Christians*, 4th ed. (1699).

104. Keach, *The Glorious Lover, A Divine Poem Upon the Adorable Mystery of Man's Redemption* (1679), 26, 1. 27.

105. Keach, "Epistle Dedicatory," *The Articles of Faith of the Church of Christ or Congregation Meeting at Horsley-down* (1697).

John Gill
Timothy George

Biography

Shortly after the death of John Gill in 1771, Augustus Toplady, famed as the author of the hymn *Rock of Ages* gave the following estimate of the legacy of his deceased friend: "While true religion and sound learning have a single friend remaining in the British Empire, the works and name of GILL will be precious and revered."[1] Toplady's sentiment was echoed by Christian leaders on both sides of the Atlantic who mourned the loss of the greatest Baptist theologian of the eighteenth century. One admirer expressed his grief in verse:

> What doleful tidings strike my list'ning ear,
> or wound the tender feelings of my heart?
> Must the bright star forever disappear?
> Must the great Man, the learned Gill depart?
> Zion may mourn, for grief becomes her well.
> To lose the man whose Heav'n instructed pen
> Taught knowledge clearly, while before him fell
> Gigantic errors of deluded men.[2]

John Gill was the first Baptist to develop a complete systematic theology and also the first Baptist to write a verse-by-verse commentary on the entire Bible. An indefatigable scholar and writer, "Dr. Voluminous," as he was affectionately called, published more than ten thousand pages during his lifetime, more than many ordinary mortals are able to read over a similar span. Undoubtedly the leading light among the Calvinistic Baptists of his day, Gill influenced an entire generation of younger ministers through his remarkable preaching and pastoral labors, which he discharged faithfully in the same congregation for nearly fifty-two years![3]

Despite these accomplishments, it has not fallen the lot of Gill to be remembered by future generations "as one of the Fathers of the Church," as an early-nineteenth-century historian thought he might.[4] When he is mentioned in standard denominational histories, he is invariable caricatured as the bogeyman of hyper-Calvinism, a dour pedant whose "high and dry" theology single-handedly doused the flames of revival among English Baptists, spawning instead "a spiritual dry-rot" among churches within that fellowship.[5]

We can discern at least three reasons for the prevailing negative assessment of Gill and his legacy. First, like most polemical theologians, Gill was more interested in defending "the cause of God and truth," to quote the title of one of his best-known writings, than in winning friends or influencing people. He attracted ardent adversaries as well as admiring disciples. On one occasion the famous Welsh evangelist Christmas Evans remarked to the English preacher Robert Hall, "How I wish, Mr. Hall, that Dr. Gill's works had been written in Welsh."

"I wish they had, sir," replied Hall. "I wish they had, with all my heart, for then I should never have read them. They are a continent of mud, sir."[6]

Second, just as the disciples of John Calvin transmuted as well as transmitted the legacy of the great Genevan reformer, so the "Gillites" carried certain positions of their mentor to extremes he would not, or at least did not, himself embrace. Later historians tended to interpret Gill, and his significance for Baptist history, exclusively through the lenses of the Gillite-Fullerite dispute rather than in terms of the issues of his own day. Inevitably, such faulty methodology resulted in a distorted image.

Third, whether or not one *should* interpret Gill as a hyper-Calvinist, he was such an effective proponent of the doctrines of grace that this dimension of his theological work has tended to overshadow the many other important doctrinal concerns which occupied his prodigious mind and pen. A more balanced presentation of his life and work is long overdue.

John Gill was born at Kettering, Northamptonshire, on November 23, 1697. He was the son of Edward and Elizabeth Gill.[7] His father, who made his living in the woolen trade, was known as a man of "grace, piety, and holy conversation." He later became a deacon in the Particular Baptist congregation at Kettering. Young Gill was an ardent student, mastering the rudiments of Latin and Greek before he was forced to withdraw from the local grammar school at the age of eleven due to the schoolmaster's insistence that all his pupils, including those from dissenting families, attend daily prayer services in the neighboring parish church. Thereafter, Gill continued his studies on his own, becoming almost a fixture among the shelves of the local bookstore. John Rippon reports that when the residents of Kettering wanted to speak of anything as certain they would say, "It is as sure as that John Gill is in the bookseller's shop."[8] By the age of ten Gill had read through the entire Greek New Testament. Thereafter, he taught himself Hebrew with the aid of a secondhand grammar and lexicon he had acquired.

When he was about twelve years old, Gill heard a sermon by William Wallis, the founding pastor of the Baptist church his family attended, on the text, "And the Lord God called unto Adam, and said unto him, Where art thou?" (Gen. 3:9). Through this message he was made aware of his need for Christ and, being under conviction, was drawn to the Lord finding "a comfortable hope and faith of interest in Him, from several exceeding great and precious promises, powerfully applied to his soul."[9] Gill postponed baptism until he was nearly nineteen years old, partly because of the propriety of making such a profession at a more tender age, but also because he sensed that his church was overeager to thrust him into the ministry before he was ready for this step. On November 1, 1716, he was immersed in a river near

John Gill (1679-1771)

Photo courtesy of Southern Baptist Historical Library and Archives

Kettering and, on the following Sunday, was received into the fellowship of his home church, partaking for the first time of the Lord's Supper.

Almost immediately Gill began to exercise his gifts as a preacher and expositor of the Scriptures. With the blessing of his fellow church members, he moved to the village of Higham Ferrers where he boarded with the local minister, John Davis, and assisted as a pastoral intern in the congregation. Here he met Elizabeth Megus, whom he married in 1718 and who shared the labors of his ministry for more than forty-six years. They had three children who survived infancy, one of whom, Elizabeth, died at age thirteen.

Following a brief stint back in Kettering as assistant minister in his home church, Gill was invited to London to preach in view of a call as pastor of the church meeting at Goat Yard, Horsleydown, in Southwark. This congregation, located about a mile from London Bridge, was one of the leading Particular Baptist churches of the metropolis, having been founded by the venerable Benjamin Keach in 1672 and served by his son-in-law, Benjamin Stinton. Gill was perhaps brought to the attention of this church through John Noble, a London pastor who had been impressed with his young friend's pulpit work in Northamptonshire. Noble had nominated him for a grant from the Particular Baptist Fund, a scholarship for young ministers jointly sponsored by several Calvinistic Baptist churches in the city.

Gill's call to the Horsleydown church has all the drama of an ecclesiastical soap opera. On September 13, 1719, a majority of the congregation voted to invite Gill to become their pastor. This decision was strongly contested by the minority who protested that, contrary to the custom of the church, women members had been allowed to vote and that this irregularity had tilted the decision in favor of Gill. For a while the anti-Gill faction secured control of the meeting house and excluded their opponents, who were forced to conduct their worship services in a neighboring schoolhouse. When the lease on the Goat Yard property expired, the pro-Gill group negotiated its renewal and thus reclaimed the original building for their use, the others removing themselves to a new meeting house at Unicorn Yard. Meanwhile, Gill united with the church which had called him as pastor. His former congregation in Kettering granted a letter of dismissal commending John Gill as a "Dear Brother" and one who "hath walked in all good conscience and holy conversation amongst us."[10]

B. R. White has summarized well the dilemma which Gill faced at this critical juncture of his ministry:

> Gill's own stand was the key to the situation: if he remained firm long enough he could hope to live down the initial opposition; if he faltered, his own future as a minister in London was in grave doubt. Whilst there can be no doubt that his firmness stemmed from his own certainty that this was God's will for him the prospect was one before which most men of his age would have quailed.[11]

In fact, Gill appeared undaunted as he set his face towards London to assume his first "full-time" pastoral charge. Perhaps we have a clue to Gill's overwhelming personality in the remark of Robert Morgan, one of the members who had voted against calling a pastor so young and untested: "Mr. Gill might become a useful man, if it should please God to keep him humble."[12]

On March 22, 1720, Gill was formally installed as pastor of the Horsleydown church in a public service of ordination. Following a time of psalm-singing and prayer, the presiding minister, John Skepp of Cripplegate, posed the standard questions concerning Gill's call by the church and his acceptance of this work. Gill's friend, John Noble, then led the congregation to reaffirm its choice of Gill as pastor by solemnly lifting up their hands. Then turning to Gill, he said: "If you as in the presence of God do heartily accept this solemn call of this church to the pastoral office, signify the same to this church now by a free and solemn declaration."[13] Thomas Crosby, one of the deacons, reported that Gill did so, committing himself to take God's Word for his rule, God's Spirit for his guide, God's promises for his support, and Christ's fullness for the supply of all his wants. Gill then received the laying on of hands, and following the ordination of several deacons, the service concluded with the singing of Psalm 133 and an apostolic benediction by the newly inducted pastor.

Having survived a church split and the boycott of his ordination by certain key pastors (only ten ministers participated in the event), Gill had surmounted the first major challenge to his full acceptance by the London Baptist community. Other tests would follow, including a second splintering off of other leading church members and a bout with the fever which left the young pastor physically depleted.[14] Gradually, however, Gill was emerging as a force to be reckoned with among the religious leaders of the day. In 1724 he became a manager of the Particular Baptist Fund. The same year he began his phenomenal writing career, breaking into print with a funeral sermon he preached for one of his deacons. Other books and pamphlets followed, including a sermon entitled "The Urim and Thummin found with Christ" (based on Deut. 33:8); his *Exposition of the Song of Solomon* (1728); and a defense of baptism by immersion, written at the request of Northamptonshire Baptists to refute the arguments of an Independent pastor, Matthias Maurice, who had attacked the Baptist practice of this ordinance. Gill's treatise on baptism circulated widely among Baptists in America as well as in England and helped gain his reputation as a spokesman for the Baptist interest on both sides of the Atlantic. Charles Haddon Spurgeon, who was an ardent admirer of Gill and yet critical of him at points, looked back on Gill's early labors in London and remarked: "Little did the friends dream what sort of man they had chosen to be their teacher, but had they known it, they would have rejoiced that a man of such vast erudition, such indefatigable industry, such sound judgment and such sterling honesty had come among them."[15]

By 1729 Gill's popularity had reached beyond the Baptist community to the other dissenting denominations as well. In that year a circle of his friends from various London churches formed a society to sponsor a weekly lecture by Gill to be delivered each Wednesday evening at Great Eastcheap. For some twenty-seven years Gill spoke from this forum to eager audiences who regarded their speaker as not only one of the great living preachers of the day but also as the seminal theologian for Calvinistic dissent. Many of Gill's major writings, including his treatises on the Trinity and justification, his classic defense of Calvinistic soteriology, *The Cause of God and Truth,* and several of his commentaries on both the Old and New Testaments, were originally presented at the Great Eastcheap lectures.

Gill took a special delight in the study of Hebrew and amassed a considerable library in rabbinics and Oriental languages. He applied this expertise to the study of the New Testament, recognizing that it was written by men, all of whom had been Jews. Gill's biblical studies are interlaced with references to the Mishnah, the Talmud, and ancient Jewish commentaries. In 1748 Marichal College of the University of Aberdeen conferred on Gill the degree Doctor of Divinity in recognition of his outstanding work in this field, which was truly a remarkable accolade for a self-taught Baptist preacher! When the deacons of his church congratulated him on receiving this prestigious award, he thanked them and then added, "I neither thought it, nor bought it, nor sought it."[16]

A hundred years after his death, William Cathcart made the following evaluation of Gill's scholarly reputation: "It is within bounds to say that no man in the eighteenth century was so well versed in the literature and customs of the ancient Jews as John Gill. He has sometimes been called the Doctor John Lightfoot of the Baptists. This compliment, in the estimation of some persons, flatters Doctor Lightfoot more than Doctor Gill."[17]

Although Gill is frequently portrayed as a stern logician who artificially conformed the truth of theology to the rigors of a preconceived system, it is important to recognize that he was a careful exegete of Holy Scripture who wrote a massive commentary on every book, chapter, and verse in the Bible. His *Exposition of the New Testament,* completed in 1748, filled three hefty volumes, while his *Exposition of the Old Testament,* which kept him busy until 1766, was a six-volume project. Only after he had worked his way through the valleys and peaks of scriptural revelation did he attempt a systematic gleaning of doctrinal truth. In 1769 he published in two volumes *A Body of Doctrinal Divinity.* Rippon wrote of this, Gill's *magnum opus:* "Here is the Doctor's whole creed. Here his very heart appears, while he states, maintains, and defends the Truth as it is in Jesus." Divided into seven books, this compendium of Christian theology took up, in order, the being and attributes of God; the internal acts of God (i.e. the eternal decrees); the external acts of God (creation, providence, permission of the Fall); the acts of God's grace in time; the person, work, and offices of Christ; the blessings of grace in the elect; and the final state of man. Gill was well aware that "systematical divinity," as he called it, had fallen onto hard times in his day. "Formulas and articles of faith, creeds, confessions, catechisms, and summaries of divine truths, are greatly decried in our age." Gill asked, "Why should divinity, the most noble science, be without a system?" He defined the task of theology as gathering out of Scripture the principles of evangelical truth and arranging them in an orderly method to show their connection, harmony, and agreement. In pursuing this task, Gill saw himself in continuity with the great tradition of historic Christianity beginning with the Apostles' Creed and including the major Fathers, schoolmen, and reformers, many of whom had produced "bodies or systems of divinity," which proved "very serviceable to lead men into the knowledge of evangelical doctrine, and confirm them in it."[18]

Throughout his long career, Gill sought to apply the doctrines he believed and proclaimed to the practical issues of the Christian life. "Doctrine and practice should go together," he said. "In order both to know and do the will of God, instruction in doctrine and practice is necessary; and the one being first taught will lead on to the other."[19] In this spirit Gill published *A Body of Practical Divinity* in 1770 to complement his earlier summary of Christian theology. A volume of over five hundred pages, this book reflected a series of sermons Gill had preached to his congregation dealing with such themes as public worship, church membership, baptism and the Lord's Supper, family responsibilities, and so forth. A visitor was asked what he thought of the message that day. "Why," said he, "if I had not been told it was the great Dr. Gill who preached, I should have said that I had heard an Arminian!"[20] Although Gill was justly revered as a "distinguished patron of the doctrines of grace," as his biographer aptly put it, he was nonetheless a champion of "practical experimental godliness." In the best tradition of Reformed theology, he emphasized the cementing bond between what Calvin called the twofold grace *(duplicem gratiam)* of justification and sanctification, that is, the connection between the free imputation of Christ's righteousness and actual holiness of life.[21]

In 1757 Gill's congregation moved from their location at Horsleydown to a new meetinghouse in Carter Lane. Gill used this occasion to review his ministry and reaffirm his commitment as a preacher of God's Word.

> What doctrines may be taught in this place, after I am gone, is not for me to know; but, as for my own part, I am at a point; I am determined, and have been long ago, what to make the subject of my ministry. It is now upwards of forty years since I entered into the arduous work; and the first sermon I have preached was from these words of the apostle, "For I am determined not to know any thing among you, save Jesus Christ, and him crucified"; and, through the grace of God, I have been enabled, in some good measure, to abide by the same resolution hitherto, as many of you here are my witnesses; and I hope, through divine assistance, I ever shall, as long as I am in this tabernacle and engaged in such a work.[22]

Gill was an energetic preacher who sometimes went through three or four handkerchiefs in a single sermon. A contemporary witness declared that he was "blessed with ready utterance and with great volubility of speech. . . . With what gravity and majesty had he used to stand and feed the Church of God! How did his listening audiences hang as it were upon his lips, while evangelical truths did sweetly drop from his mellifluous tongue."[23] If this reads like the assessment of an uncritical admirer, it is well to remember that Gill every Sunday was not everyone's cup of tea. One old man in his congregation frequently responded to his pastor's exertions by asking in a cynical tone, "It that preaching?"

Gill suffered such abuse with good humor for a while, but one day exploded in anger against his detractor. With the full strength of his voice, he pointed toward the pulpit and said, "Go up and do better—Go up and do better!"[24]

This last anecdote, taken from Rippon's biography, shows us a very human Gill who was not above losing his temper or venting his anger. Samuel Stennett, who delivered the eulogy at Gill's funeral, recalled this aspect of his friend's personality, along with his capacity for self-judgment and forgiveness.

> And though he knew how with a spirit to resent an injury, he knew how also with becoming meekness to endure and forgive it. His warmth might indeed on some occasions exceed, yet he had prudence and resolution to check it; and failed not afterwards like a good man as he was, to feel great pain on account of it.[25]

John Wesley, who crossed polemical swords with Gill, referred to him as "a positive man" who "fights for his opinions through thick and thin." Doubtless, Gill was the kind of man who engendered feelings of love and loyalty, as well as dislike and contempt, from those who encountered the force of his strong personality. When, as an old man, he thought he had outlived his usefulness to his congregation and offered to resign, his church members sent him the following letter:

> Another grievous circumstance is, that if the Church is willing, you seem inclined to resign your office as Pastor. This expression is extremely alarming to us, and is what can by no means find a place in our thoughts, it being our fixed desire and continual prayer, that you may live and die in that endeared relation. We say with united voice, "How can a father give up his children, or affectionate children their father?" Dear sir, we beseech you not to cast us off, but bear us upon your heart and spiritual affections all your days and let us be remembered to God through your prayers, and who knows but the Lord may visit us again and make us break forth on the right hand and on the left?[26]

Following a prolonged illness, Gill died on October 14, 1771. Shortly before his demise, Gill had penned some "Dying Thoughts" on the importance of a godly preparation for death which he defined as "the time of the Lord's in-gathering of his people to himself; then it is he who comes into his garden, and gathers his lilies, and this and the other flower, to put into his bosom."[27] To his nephew and namesake, John Gill of Saint Albans, he declared that his hope was not based on any services he had been permitted to perform for the good of the church, but rather upon "my interest in the Persons of the Trinity, the free grace of God, and the blessings of grace streaming to me through the blood and righteousness of Christ." Thus, as Samuel Stennett put it, "sinking under the gradual decay of nature, he gently fell asleep in Jesus, in the 74th year of his age."[28] There was great mourning throughout the land, especially among Baptists who had lost one of their brightest lights, and a general recognition by all Christians that "a great man is fallen in Israel."

Exposition

John Gill belonged to that period of English Nonconformity which has been characterized as the "Old Dissent."[29] This term is used in contrast to the "New Dissent" which was the result of the evangelical revival led by John and Charles Wesley, George Whitefield, and, among Baptists, Dan Taylor and Andrew Fuller. Following the English Civil War in the seventeenth century, those Christians who refused to attend the Church of England, or conform to its legally imposed pattern of worship, were severely persecuted by the established authorities. Both John Bunyan and Benjamin Keach, already considered in this volume, were imprisoned on account of their religious convictions.

The "Glorious Revolution" of 1688, which brought William III and his wife Mary to the throne, restored statutory freedom of worship to the dissenters and ushered in a long period of toleration and decline. Although many Anglicans still showed "an implacable hatred to the Nonconformists," they were permitted to convene national assemblies, erect stately meetinghouses, publish confessions of faith, establish their own theological academies, and sustain a public presence in the community.[30] As a recent historian has put it, for the most, dissenters "were now able to go about their daily business without fear of the informer, the constable, and the magistrate."[31]

Unfortunately, however, material prosperity and spiritual vitality did not go hand in hand. If the blood of the martyrs was the seed of the church, then toleration bred moral apathy, doctrinal laxity, and general unconcern. At the height of his career in 1750, Gill reviewed the religious torpor which had beset all of the dissenting denominations, but especially his own Baptist fellowship.

> Of late years, there has been a very visible decline; and a night is coming on, which we are entered into; the shadows of evening are stretching out apace upon us, and the signs of eventide are very manifest. A sleepy form of spirit has seized us; both ministers and churches are asleep; and being so, the enemy is busy in sowing the tares of error and heresies, and which will grow up and spread more and more.[32]

Historian Carl L. Becker has described the Augustan Age in which Gill flourished in the following way: "What we have to realize is that in those years God was on trial."[33] In 1696 the publication of John Toland's *Christianity Not Mysterious* marked the rise of Deism with its belief that natural religion alone, apart from the special revelation of the Christian faith, was quite sufficient. Various strands of "rational theology" had led many thinkers to question the most basic presuppositions of historic Christian orthodoxy such as the doctrines of God and Christ inherent in the Nicene and Athanasian

Creeds. By the mid-eighteenth century the General Baptists and the Presbyterians had succumbed almost entirely to Unitarianism while many others, both inside the established church and among the dissenters, found the supernatural dimension of Christianity increasingly an embarrassment. John Gill believed that there was an intrinsic connection between the doctrinal erosion he observed and the spiritual decay he lamented in the life of the church. Like Athanasius in the fourth century, and Luther and Calvin during the Reformation, Gill dared to say "no" to those forms of teaching which, if carried out consistently, would have threatened the truth of divine revelation itself. In so doing, he helped to preserve the theological integrity of the Particular Baptists and thus, indirectly, prepared them to receive the awakening which came once he was gone.

Holy Scripture

In 1729 Gill led his congregation to renew its church covenant and to include a confession of faith to which each person would give assent before being admitted to church membership. The first article of this confession presented a succinct statement of the common Baptist understanding of the Bible. "We believe that the Scriptures of the Old and New Testament are the word of God, and the only rule of faith and practice."[34] While this brief affirmation suffers by comparison with the extensive article on Scripture which is found in the 1689 Second London Confession, one should not take this as a weakened view of the Bible on Gill's part. Although Gill does allow for a measure of divine revelation imparted through nature and reason, these channels are utterly insufficient, for "The light of nature leaves man entirely without the knowledge of the way of salvation by the Son of God."[35] This predicament has occurred because the rupture of the fall left humankind groping helplessly in the dark apart from God's gracious revelation of Himself in the history of salvation and the inscripturation of revelation.

The first two chapters in book 1 of Gill's *Body of Doctrinal Divinity* deal with the being of God and Holy Scripture. After defining the scope of Scripture to coincide with those books which have been received by the church as canonical (excluding the Apocrypha and other "spurious writings"), Gill expounds in turn the authority, perfection, and perspicuity of the Bible.

Gill asserts without equivocation the divine inspiration and total truthfulness of God's written Word. To be sure, he does not spend much time trying to explain precisely *how* the Scriptures were inspired. However, he clearly affirms the divine origin of the Bible; the biblical authors were "under the impulse and direction of God in all they wrote." Nor did this divine impulsion obliterate their role as instruments in the process of inspiration. Gill, ever a careful student of the Bible, recognized the various genres of literature and differences of style among the different strata of Scripture. Like Calvin, Gill appealed to the principle of accommodation to account for such phenomena. God simply adapted Himself "to the style such persons were wont to use, and which was natural to them, and agreeable to their genius and circumstances."[36] In this way, Gill affirms the humanity of the biblical writers without sacrificing the divine character of the biblical text. Indeed, far from proposing a so-called "mechanical dictation" theory of inspiration, Gill allows for a kind of source theory of composition claiming that Moses and other writers of Scripture may well have made use of "diaries, annals and journals of their own and former times."[37] However, the final product included precisely what God intended for it to contain, even to the very words which God was pleased to employ in disclosing His holy oracles.

Although Gill lived prior to the frontal assault against the integrity of Scripture by rationalistic critics of the last two centuries, he anticipated many of the arguments used by later theologians in their defense of the doctrine of biblical inerrancy. Since the Scriptures are given by God, a perfect Being, they can contain nothing of "ignorance, error, or imperfection." As God's work in creation, providence, and redemption is perfect, so is His work in providing the Scriptures to His people. Of course, Gill fully supported the discipline of textual criticism and made important contributions to it himself. Only the "original exemplars" in the original languages could be regarded as free from every error of transmission, translation, and so forth. Gill also saw the perfection of the Bible displayed in the way it contained a refutation for every heresy and false doctrine which had arisen in the history of the church, as well as a corrective word for every sin which could be committed.

In contending for the perspicuity of the Bible, Gill harked back to a cardinal tenet—the Reformation principle of *sola Scriptura*, the "clarity and certainty of the Word of God," as Zwingli's famous treatise of 1523 put it. Gill admitted that not all Scriptures were equally plain: He quoted Gregory the Great as saying that the Bible is like a great river in which a lamb may walk, and an elephant swim, at different places. Moreover, he also discerned the principle of progressive revelation—"the light of the Scriptures has been a growing one; it was but dim under the dispensation of the law of Moses; it became more clear through the writings of the prophets; but most clear under the gospel dispensation."[38] Still, not everyone who read or studied the Bible could necessarily understand it. It is "a sealed book, which neither learned nor unlearned men can understand and interpret without the Spirit of God."[39] Gill's emphasis on the internal witness of the Holy Spirit saved him from the error of biblical rationalism and from an overreliance on the kind of evidentialist arguments which characterized Protestant apologetics during the age of reason.

Gill believed that Scripture was its own best interpreter, and he appealed to the infallibility of the Bible against two opposing errors. On the one hand, he rejected the Roman Catholic attempt to subordinate the Scriptures to the church. Neither the church nor its pastors, neither councils, nor popes, may sit in judgment on the Word of God. On the other hand, Gill dismissed at once the claims of those "enthusiastic persons" (perhaps Quakers?) who were so enamoured of the Spirit that they saw little need for the written Word. He did acknowledge a legitimate private interpretation of the Bible ("which every Christian may make, according to his ability and light") as well as a duly ordered public one (the preaching of the Word). In both cases, however, both are subject to, and to be determined by, the Scripture itself, which is the only certain and infallible rule of faith and practice.

Trinity

When the General Baptist churches of the Midlands published their "Orthodox Creed" in 1678, they included the Apostles', Nicene, and Athanasian creeds which, they declared, "ought thoroughly to be received, and believed: and used both to edify believers and to prevent heresy in doctrine and practice."[40] In the preface to this document they went so far as to assert that "the denying of baptism is a less evil than to deny the Divinity or Humanity of Christ."[41] Such concerns were well placed for in the decades which followed serious divisions arose among General Baptists concerning both the person of Christ and the doctrine of the Trinity. The sources of such deviant Christology and anti-Trinitarianism were complex, and soon spread to other Dissenting denominations. In the year of John Gill's disputed call to the pastorate of the Horsleydown congregation, a major dispute arose among the Presbyterian, Congregationalist, and General and Particular Baptist ministers of London concerning their subscription to a Trinitarian affirmation. Significantly, all but two of the Particular Baptists present at this conference, held at Salters' Hall, willingly signed this confessional statement, while only one of the General Baptists did so. Raymond Brown has aptly described the sequence of events which ensued: "Resistance to subscription became the prelude to heterodoxy. People who refused to sign the articles came eventually to deny them and those General Baptists who were theologically uncertain ultimately became committed Unitarians."[42]

While few Particular Baptist churches became Unitarian, Gill was well aware of the dangers which confronted all orthodox Christians on these cardinal tenets of the faith. It was this concern which prompted him to publish his *Treatise on the Defense of the Trinity* in 1731, issue a second edition virtually unchanged in 1752, and incorporate much of the same material in his *Body of Doctrinal Divinity* in 1769. Gill vigorously defended the attention he paid to this doctrine by showing how vital it was to every aspect of the Christian life.

> The doctrine of the Trinity is often represented as a speculative point, of no great moment whether it is believed or no, too mysterious and curious to be pried into, and that it had better be left alone than meddled with; but, alas! it enters into the whole of our salvation, and all the parts of it; into all the doctrines of the gospel, and into the experience of the saints.[43]

Gill proceeds to show how all three Persons of the one Triune God are involved in all the works of creation, providence, and redemption. He points out that in the economy of salvation election is usually ascribed in Scripture to the Father, redemption to the Son, and sanctification to the Holy Spirit. Yet the plurality in the Godhead must never be set over against the primal unity which is implied in the very existence of God as a necessary Being, all-sufficient, omnipotent, and supreme in all perfections. In discussing the particularizing characteristics of the divine Persons, Gill follows the distinctions set forth by the Cappadocian Fathers of the fourth century: The Father is *begetting,* the Son *begotten,* and the Holy Spirit *breathed.* Gill echoes Augustine and the Western Church generally in affirming the dual procession of the Holy Spirit: He proceeds from the Father and the Son. Gill also returns to the patristic notion that the personal relations within God is a necessary reflection of the nature of God.

> As he is the best, the greatest and most perfect of Beings, his happiness in himself must be the most perfect and complete; now happiness lies not in solitude, but in society; hence the three personal distinctions in Deity, seem necessary to perfect happiness, which lies in that glorious, inconceivable, and inexpressible communion the three Persons have with one another; and which arises from the incomprehensible in-being and unspeakable nearness they have to each other.[44]

Gill interpreted modern anti-Trinitarianism as a revival of the "old stale error" of Sabellianism and Arianism. He was alarmed that "some who profess evangelical doctrines have embraced it, or are nibbling at it."[45] In defending classical Trinitarian orthodoxy, he was required, as Calvin before him had done, to move beyond the strict use of biblical language for the sake of biblical truth. An earlier meeting of the General Assembly of the General Baptists had decided that the controversy "respecting the Trinity and the Christ of God" should be voiced "in Scripture words and terms and in no other terms."[46] Gill saw this principle as unduly restrictive and intentionally deceptive. Rather than reflecting a true reverence for the biblical text, it frequently camouflaged doctrinal deviance. He contended that "words and phrases though not literally expressed in scripture, yet if what is meant by them is to be found there, they may be lawfully made use of."[47] While Gill, in good Baptist fashion, could acclaim the Bible only, and not confessions, catechisms, or articles of faith, as the proper standard of orthodoxy, he nonetheless showed remarkable respect for the doctrinal consensus of the early Fathers and was most reluctant "to oppose a doctrine the church of God has always held, and especially being what the Scriptures abundantly bear testimony unto."[48] In this sense he was a true catholic theologian.

Sovereign Grace

John Gill was a leading exponent of the Calvinistic doctrines of grace which had characterized Particular Baptist churches since their emergence in the late 1630s. The substance of these doctrines was summarized at the Dutch Reformed Synod of Dort (1618-19) in five major assertions: (1) the decrees of election and reprobation are absolute and unconditional; (2) the scope of the atonement is restricted to the elect although the death of Christ is sufficient to expiate the sins of the whole world; (3) because of the fall human beings are totally incapable of any saving good apart from the regenerating work of the Holy Spirit; (4) God's call is effectual and hence His grace cannot be ultimately thwarted by human resistance; (5) those whom God calls and regenerates He also keeps so that they do not totally nor finally fall from faith and grace.[49] These teachings were repeated in the Westminster Confession (1647), the official creed of English Presbyterianism; the Savoy Declaration (1658) of the English Congregationalists, and in the First (1644) and Second (1677/1689) London Confessions of the Particular Baptists. Gill was heir to this theological tradition, which in his day had come increasingly under attack from Deists and Unitarians on the left and from evangelical Arminians such as the General Baptist leader Thomas Grantham who blasted the "cruel and soul-devouring doctrines of Calvinism" and the great Puritan divine Richard Baxter who proposed a mediating compromise between the two camps.

Gill, like Augustine and Calvin, was drawn into predestinarian polemics when challenged by opposing views which seemed to disparage the grace of God and His sovereignty in salvation. It was Toplady's judgment that no one since Augustine himself had written so extensively or so persuasively in defense of the doctrines of grace as Gill. After reading Gill's reply to Wesley's attack on the doctrine of perseverance, his Anglican friend wrote:

> Between morning and afternoon service, read through Dr. Gill's excellent and nervous tract on Predestination, against Wesley. How sweet is that blessed and glorious doctrine to the soul, when it is received through the channel of inward experience! I believe it may be said of my learned friend, as it was of the Duke of Marlborough, that he never fought a battle which he did not win.[50]

Gill's major defense of the Calvinistic doctrines, *The Cause of God and Truth,* was published in four parts between 1735 and 1738. This work, originally delivered as lectures in Gill's Great Eastcheap series, was intended as a definitive reply to Daniel Whitby's *Discourses on the Five Points* which many considered an unanswerable attack on "the Calvinistical System." The Gill-Whitby exchange surely deserves a place among the classic debates on the doctrine of election. The first two parts of *The Cause* consist of detailed considerations of the scriptural passages, pro and con, which are alleged against the doctrines of grace. Part 3 examines the philosophical arguments for these views and refutes the charge of Stoic fatalism against them. Gill was greatly concerned to vindicate the basic tenets of Calvinism on rational grounds, believing that "they are no more disagreeable to right reason than to divine revelation."[51] Here, perhaps, we see most clearly Gill's indebtedness to the broader intellectual environment of Protestant Scholasticism in its desire to correlate philosophy and dogmatics, that is, to express and formulate the faith in terms compatible with the leading systems of rational inquiry. Gill followed the Protestant dogmatician Herman Witsius (1636-1708) whose writings he often quoted and helped to edit. Part 4 of *The Cause* is a masterful excursus into patristic literature intended to show that, far from being a novel teaching, the doctrines related to predestination were supported by "the whole stream of antiquity."[52]

The kernel of Gill's predestinarian theology was present in the articles of faith which he led his congregation to incorporate into their church covenant in 1729.

> We believe, that before the world began, God did elect a certain number of men unto everlasting Salvation whom he did predestinate to the adoption of children by Jesus of his own free grace and according to the good pleasure of his will, and that in pursuance of this gratious design, he did contrive and make a covenant of grace and peace with his Son Jesus Christ, on ye behalf of those persons, wherein a Saviour was appointed, and all spritual blessings provided for them; as also that their persons with all their grace and glory, were put into ye hands of Christ, and made his care and charge . . . . We believe, yt that Eternal Redemption which Christ has obtained by the shedding of his blood, is special and particular . . . that the Justification of God's Elect, is onely by the righteousness of Christ imputed to them, without ye consideration of any works of righteousness done by them . . . yt the work of regeneration, conversion, sanctification, and faith is not an act of man's free will and power, but of the mighty, efficacious and irresistible grace of God . . . that all those who are chosen by the father, redeemed by the son and sanctified by the spirit shall certainly and finally persevere, so yt none of 'em shall ever perish, but shall have everlasting life.[53]

While this is certainly a *strict* Calvinist statement, it hardly merits the pejorative label, hyper-Calvinist. Bunyan and Keach before him, and Fuller and Spurgeon after him, could have embraced without reservation Gill's congregational confession which, in reality, was merely an abstract of the 1689 Second London Confession. Why, then, has Gill been portrayed as the paradigm of hyper-Calvinism?

Richard Condon has written that "a nuance in an ideological difference is a wide chasm."[54] On three distinct issues Gill's writings were taken to lend support to extreme views which appeared to undermine the necessity of conversion, the moral requirements of the Christian life, and the evangelistic mission of the church. It can be shown that Gill never intended for his ideas to have such questionable consequences. Nor was he himself guilty of pressing the logic (or illogic?) of his position to such nonevangelical conclusions. It is another question, however, of whether he sufficiently anticipated or guarded against such misinterpretations.

Gill's doctrine of *eternal justification* was a stumbling block to many who could not square it with the necessity of conversion as a personal experience of grace. In his *Body of Doctrinal Divinity,* Gill considers justification under two distinct rubrics. In book 2, chapter 5, he treats justification as one of the "eternal and immanent acts in God"; in book 6, chapter 8, he deals with the same topic "as it terminates in the conscience of a believer."[55] This distinction was not original with Gill but followed the pattern of covenant theology expounded by earlier Reformed theologians such as Witsius, Macovius, and Ames who had distinguished active justification, God's eternal act based on His sovereign goodwill, and passive justification, the personal application of the former to the elect believer within space and time. Gill defended this teaching, stressing the priority of justification over faith. Faith, he said, is the effect, not the cause of our justification: "The reason why we are justified is not because we have faith, but the reason why we have faith is because we are justified."[56] To those who objected that no one could be justified before he or she existed, Gill replied that while no one *actually* existed before conception and birth, the elect did enjoy a *representative* existence in their Mediator, Jesus Christ, who, as the eternal Son of God, participated in the decree of election which He would fulfill on their behalf in the course of the history of salvation.

Clearly, Gill did not intend to exalt so highly the initiative of God in salvation that he preempted the requirements of repentance, faith, and conversion. Yet, the doctrine of eternal justification was a perilous teaching, insofar as it encouraged sinners to think of themselves as actually justified regardless of their personal response to Christ and the gospel. Doubtless, for this reason the framers of the Second London Confession (echoing the Westminster divines) had declared that although "God did from all eternity decree to justify all the Elect . . . nevertheless they are not justified personally, until the Holy Spirit, doth in due time actually apply Christ unto them."[57] Happily, on this controverted issue most Particular Baptists followed the fathers of the Second London Confession rather than John Gill.

Closely related to the fear that Gill's theology of grace might disrupt the morphology of conversion was the frequently articulated concern that it would also lead to antinomianism. *Antinomianism* is the view that, since Christ both bore the penalty of sin and fulfilled the law, those under grace are not required to obey the moral law. Although Gill did republish the works of Tobias Crisp and John Skepp, two earlier theologians whose writings were considered a haven for antinomian interpretations, he strenuously resisted the temptation to make light of the importance of good works in the life of a Christian. "I *abhor* the thought of setting the law of God aside as the rule of walk and conversation; and constantly affirm . . . that all who believe in Christ for righteousness should be careful to maintain good works, for necessary uses."[58] Anyone who has examined Gill's *Body of Practical Divinity* or looked at his sermons on "The Law Established by the Gospel" (1756) and "The Law in the Hand of Christ" (1761) will know how spurious is the charge of antinomianism against him. As John Rippon expressed it, "His preaching was as pointed on the *agenda* as on the *credenda* of the Christian system." Just as Christ was crucified between two thieves, continued Rippon, so Gill was pilloried between two robbers—Arminianism, which robs God of His grace, and antinomianism, which robs Him of His glory.[59] Gill could not be an Arminian for he maintained the five distinguishing doctrines which they denied, nor could he be an antinomian, because he denied the axiom which they affirmed, namely, that the moral law did not apply to believers as their rule of conduct.

The third issue on which Gill's hyper-Calvinist reputation is based was his presumed refusal to preach the gospel promiscuously to the lost. This controversy went back to a book published by the Congregationalist minister

Joseph Hussey entitled *God's Operations of Grace but No Offers of His Grace* (1707). Hussey declared that anyone who claimed to believe in God's election and yet offered Christ to all was only a "half-hearted Calvinist." Peter Toon has traced the birth of hyper-Calvinism to Hussey and his writings.[60] It is true that Gill regarded Hussey, along with Tobias Crisp, as "men of great piety and learning, of long standing and much usefulness in the Church of Christ."[61] And Gill, like Hussey, believed that the word *offer* could be misleading when applied to the presentation of the gospel to the lost. Just as we might object to an evangelist who loosely talks about his (as opposed to God's) saving of souls, Gill maintained that, in a proper sense, only the Holy Spirit could truly "offer" Christ and salvation to sinners. Hussey's writings formed the backdrop for the controversy over the "Modern Question," so called from the title of a pamphlet published in 1737 by Matthias Maurice, against whom Gill had earlier written on the topic of infant baptism. In *A Modern Question Modestly Answer'd,* Maurice raised the question of whether it was "the duty of poor unconverted sinners, who hear the gospel preached or published, to believe in Jesus Christ."[62] Those who answered this question in the negative (i.e. the true hyper-Calvinists), saw little need for the promiscuous preaching of the gospel, since it was obviously useless to exhort unconverted sinners to do what they neither *could* do, nor indeed had any obligation to do! There is no doubt that such views gained currency among Particular Baptists in the late eighteenth century and consequently, as Spurgeon put it, "chilled many churches to their very soul," leading them "to omit the free invitations of the gospel, and to deny that it is the duty of sinners to believe in Jesus."[63] It was precisely against such theology that Andrew Fuller reacted in his epochal *The Gospel Worthy of All Acceptation* (1785).

In light of the later Gillite-Fullerite debate and in view of the fact that many exponents of what Joseph Ivimey called the "non-invitation, non-application scheme" appealed to his writings, many historians have traced the source of such "false Calvinism" (Fuller's phrase) to Gill himself. However, a close reading of his sermons and doctrinal treatises will show this to be a hasty judgment which may need to be reconsidered. For example, Thomas Nettles has shown that Gill's interpretation of the words of Jesus, "Come unto me" (Matt. 11:28), differ markedly from that of Hussey. The latter understood these words to refer to the literal "coming on their feet to Christ" of the Jews in ancient Palestine. Gill's exposition extends their meaning greatly.

> Those who come to Christ aright, come as sinners, to a full, suitable, able, and willing Saviour; venture their souls upon him, and trust in him for righteousness, life, and salvation, which they are encouraged to do, by this kind of invitation, which shows his willingness to save, and his readiness to give relief to distressed minds.[64]

Gill persistently encouraged young ministers to "preach the gospel of salvation to all men, and declare, that whosoever believes shall be saved: for this they are commissioned to do."[65] At the ordination service of a certain John Davis, Gill delivered the following charge:

> Souls sensible to sin and danger, and who are crying out, What shall we do to be saved? you are to observe, and point out Christ the tree of live to them; and say, as some of the cherubs did to one in such circumstances, Believe on the Lord Jesus Christ and thou shalt be saved, Acts XVI: 31. Your work is to lead men, under a sense of sin and guilt, to the blood of Christ, shed for many for the remission of sin, and in this name you are to preach the forgiveness to them.[66]

On another occasion, he declared that if a minister fails to exhort sinners to repent and believe in Christ, "their blood will be required at his hands . . . . What can, or does, more strongly engage ministers to take heed to themselves than this? That they may be useful in the conversion and so in the salvation of precious and immortal souls, which are of more worth than the world."[67] We may justly conclude that while Gill believed in harmony with the wider Augustinian tradition, that God, to the praise of His glory, had chosen from eternity to save a certain number of persons from the lost race of humanity, he disparaged neither the means God had ordained to effect the conversion of the elect nor the evangelical mandate to proclaim the good news of God's gracious provision to all the lost.

Recent research has shown that it is inaccurate to lump together indiscriminately Crisp, Hussey, Skepp, Brine, and Gill.[68] Each of these theologians presented a nuanced discussion of the doctrines of grace with distinctive corollaries and diverging consequences. On the "Modern Question," Fuller himself acknowledged that

> Dr. Gill took no active part in the controversy . . . . It cannot be denied that, when engaged in other controversies, he frequently argues in a manner favorable to our side; and his writings contain various concessions on this subject which, if any one else had made them, would not be much to the satisfaction of our opposing brethren.[69]

Still, we cannot quite exonerate Gill of all responsibility in the fostering of an atmosphere in which the forthright promulgation of the missionary mandate of the church was seen to be a threat to, rather than an extension of, the gospel of grace. What Fuller said of Hussey could also be applied to Gill; he was of "that warm turn of mind which frequently misleads even the greatest of men, especially in defending a favorite sentiment."[70] True, Gill did not go so far as the real hyper-Calvinists; but he was so preoccupied in defending the gospel from dangers on the left that he did little to stay the erosion on his right.

Evaluation

The visitor to modern London can find the stately tomb of John Gill in the famous Nonconformist cemetery at Bunhill Fields, which is across from the house on City Road where John Wesley, who died twenty years later, spent the last years of his life. It is ironic that these two great leaders, paradigms of the Old and the New Dissent, should thus find themselves in such close proximity at the end of their earthly walks. Gill lies buried amongst other notables of the dissenting tradition including John Bunyan; John Owen; George Foxe; Isaac Watts; and his successor and biographer, John Rippon. On his tomb is a Latin inscription describing Gill, among other things, as "a sincere disciple of Jesus, an excellent preacher of the gospel, a courageous defender of the Christian faith." At his death the church he had served for so long voted to raise a mortgage and go into debt in order to pay for a portrait of their beloved pastor, from which small prints were provided for every member of the congregation.[71] John Fellows summed up Gill's life in the following couplet from an elegy he published shortly after the death of his friend:

> Zion was his delight; his whole design
> Was to adorn the church, and make her shine.[72]

Gill's influence within the Baptist tradition remained strong for many years after his death. His books were required reading for many young ministerial students whose mentors preferred Gill's hefty tones to "the frothy and flimsy productions of the present day," as one of them put it.[73] Gill's courage in resisting laxity and error inspired Spurgeon during the Downgrade Controversy as he sought to stave off "the boiling mudshowers of modern heresy" which were beginning to descend on Baptist life in his day.

> My eminent predecessor, Dr. Gill, was told by a certain member of his congregation who ought to have known better, that, if he published his book, *The Cause of God and Truth,* he would lose some of his best friends, and that his income would fall off. The doctor said, "I can afford to be poor, but I cannot afford to injure my conscience," and he has left his mantle as well as his chair in our vestry.[74]

At the same time, Spurgeon could be critical of Gill's lack of zeal in pursuing an aggressive evangelistic strategy. His own ministry embodies the best of both Gill and Fuller: a concern for doctrinal integrity on the essentials of the faith and an unswerving commitment to the evangelistic and missionary purpose of the church.

The theology of grace in Christian history oscillates between the poles of divine sovereignty and human responsibility. Both are biblical and evangelical truths which must be held in tension if the gospel is to be proclaimed in its purity and urgency. If Gill erred in overstressing God's initiative in salvation, it was because he believed this foundational fact was being undermined by the inroads of Deism, rationalism, and the misdirected message of Arminianism. His theology was a corrective to these trends which, if left unchecked, might well have so eviscerated the Particular Baptists (as they did in fact the Generals) that there would have been little, if anything, to awaken when revival did come.

The vital springs of piety which nourished Gill's life and thought are sometimes obscured by the abstract form his theology assumed. Yet Luther's dictum that it is "not speculating but rather living, dying and being damned" which make one a theologian applies to Gill as well. As his twelve-year-old daughter Elizabeth lay dying, he hovered over her bed and tried to calm her fears about not being yet baptized. He listened as she confessed great affection for the Savior. "She would sometimes say within herself, *I love him, me thinks, I could hug him in my arms*."

"My dear," he asked, "can you say, Christ died for you?"

"Yes," she replied, "Christ died for me."

"Nay," he later recalled, "one time she said she thought she even saw Christ."

At her funeral service Gill related the testimony of his daughter's assurance in Christ and preached a powerful sermon on the hope of the resurrection. He spoke to himself as well as to the gathered mourners when he observed: "So hard a thing is it for us to keep the doctrines of the gospel always in view; and harder still to make sure of them, and live up to them, when we most want them."[75] Precisely in the midst of such trials Gill found himself sustained by the God of grace, the grace he had proclaimed to others, the grace he had defended at length against its detractors, the grace which overcomes every obstacle in life and in death.

Along with Gill's piety it is also easy to miss his humility. He sometimes sounds, as Castellio said of Calvin, that he has just returned from conversing with the angels! Yet in the end Gill knew, as all true theologians must, that all of our efforts to describe God's glory and power, His majesty and mercy, fall far short of their ineffable object. Unlike Augustine, Gill never wrote a volume of retractions. But the proviso which governed his massive theological output is the confession which should be in the heart of every person who dares to speak, with reverence and fidelity, for the living God.

> If I have written anything contrary to the divine perfections, or what may reflect any dishonor on the dear name of Jesus, or be any way injurious to the truth as it is in him, or be detrimental to the intent of pure and undefiled religion, I do most humbly intreat forgiveness at the hands of God.[76]

Bibliography

Works by Gill

The Cause of God and Truth. Grand Rapids: Baker, 1980 [reprint of the 1855 London edition].

A Collection of Sermons and Tracts. Streamwood, Ill.: Primitive Baptist Library, 1981 [reprint of the 1814 London edition].

A Complete Body of Doctrinal and Practical Divinity. Paris, Ark.: The Baptist Standard Bearer, 1984 [reprint of the 1839 London edition].

The Dissenter's Reasons for Separating from the Church of England. London: n.p., 1753.

A Dissertation Concerning the Antiquity of the Hebrew Language. London: n.p., 1767.

The Doctrine of Grace Cleared from the Charge of Licentiousness. London: n.p., 1751.

The Doctrine of Predestination Stated. London: n.p., 1752.

The Faithful Minister of Christ Crowned. London: n.p., 1767.

The Form of Sound Words Held Fast. London: n.p., 1766.

Gill's Commentaries (6 vols.) Grand Rapids, Mich.: Baker Book House, 1980 [reprint of the 1852-1854 London edition].

The Law Established by the Gospel. London: n.p., 1756.

The Quiet and Easy Passage of Christ's Purchased People. London: n.p., 1763.

A Sermon on the Death of Elizabeth Gill. London: n.p., 1738.

Treatise on the Doctrine of the Trinity. London: n.p., 1752.

The Work of a Gospel Minister Recommended to Consideration. London: n.p., 1763.

Works About Gill

Brantley, W. T. "Gill and Fuller." *Columbian Star and Christian Index* 2 (Jan. 16, 1830): 39-40.

Brown, Raymond. *The English Baptists of the Eighteenth Century.* London: Baptist Historical Society, 1986.

Bush, L. Rush and Thomas J. Nettles. *Baptists and the Bible.* Chicago: Moody Press, 1980.

Cathcart, William. "John Gill." *The Baptist Encyclopedia* I (1881): 452-54.

Clipsham, E. P. "Andrew Fuller and Fullerism: A Study in Evangelical Calvinism." *Baptist Quarterly* 20 (1965): 99-114.

Daniel, Curt. "Hyper-Calvinism and John Gill." Ph.D. dissertation, Edinburgh University, 1983.

Nettles, Thomas J. *By His Grace and for His Glory.* Grand Rapids, Mich.: Baker, 1986.

Nuttall, G. F. "Northamptonshire and *The Modern Question*." *Journal of Theological Studies* 16 (1965).

Price, Seymour. "Dr. Gill's Confession of 1729." *Baptist Quarterly* 4 (1928-29).

Rippon, John. *A Brief Memoir . . . of the late Rev. John Gill.* London: n.p., 1838.

Robison, O. C. "The Legacy of John Gill." *Baptist Quarterly* 24 (1971): 111-25.

Sell, Alan P. F. *The Great Debate: Calvinism, Arminianism and Salvation.* Grand Rapids, Mich.: Baker Book House, 1983.

Seymour, R. E. "John Gill—Baptist Theologian." Ph.D. dissertation, Edinburgh University, 1954.

Stennett, Samuel. *The Victorious Christian Receiving the Crown.* London: n.p., 1771.

Toon, Peter. *The Emergence of Hyper-Calvinism in English Nonconformity, 1689-1765.* London: The Olive Tree, 1967.

Watts, Michael. *The Dissenters.* Oxford: The Clarendon Press, 1978.

Wallin, Benjamin. *The Address at the Interment of Gill. Sacred Remains*. London: n.p., 1852.

White, B. R. "John Gill in London, 1719-1729: A Biographical Fragment." *Baptist Quarterly* 22 (1967): 72-91.

Notes

1. Augustus M. Toplady in the "Memoir of the Life, Labours, and Character of the Reverend and Learned John Gill, D.D." printed in the 1830 London edition of Gill's *A Body of Doctrinal and Practical Divinity*, xxxiv. This memoir, including Toplady's eulogy, first appeared as an introductory preface to a two-volume *Collection of Sermons and Tracts* of Gill published in 1773. John Rippon drew on this source in gathering his more definitive account of Gill's life: *A Brief Memoir . . . of the late Rev. John Gill* (London, 1838). The Rippon memoir was originally drafted in 1800.

2. Quoted, Thomas J. Nettles, *By His Grace and for His Glory* (Grand Rapids, Mich.: Baker, 1986), 75.

3. In 1719 Gill became the third pastor of the Baptist congregation meeting at Goat Yard, Horsleydown in Southwark, succeeding Benjamin Stinton, who had served this church for fifteen years, and the venerable Benjamin Keach, who had founded it in 1672. In turn, Gill was succeeded by his biographer, John Rippon, who served the church for a period of sixty-three years, from 1773 to 1836. In 1854 Charles Haddon Spurgeon became pastor of this congregation, which under Gill's ministry (1757) had relocated to Carter Lane, Tooley Street, near London Bridge.

4. Walter Wilson, *The History and Antiquities of Dissenting Church and Meeting Houses in London, Westminster, and Southwark* (London: n.p., 1810), 4:221.

5. Henry C. Vedder, *A Short History of the Baptists* (Valley Forge, Pa.: Judson Press, 1907), 241. H. Leon McBeth, *The Baptist Heritage* (Nashville: Broadman Press, 1987), gives a somewhat more objective account of Gill, recognizing him as "the most eminent Particular Baptist of his age." He too, however, alleges that Gill's theology "brought the kiss of death to Particular Baptists," 176-78. Nettles, *By His Grace*, 73-107, has reviewed the historiography on Gill and challenged many of the misrepresentations of him.

6. Olinthus Gregory and Joseph Belcher, eds., *The Works of the Rev. Robert Hall* (New York: Harper and Bros., 1854), 3:82.

7. This sketch draws on the two memoirs cited in note 1, as well as the following studies: William Cathcart, "John Gill," *The Baptist Encyclopedia*, 1 (1881): 452-54; B. R. White, "John Gill in London, 1719-1729: A Biographical Fragment," *Baptist Quarterly* 22 (1967): 72-91; O. C. Robison, "The Legacy of John Gill," *Baptist Quarterly* 24 (1971): 111-25. There are also two unpublished Ph.D. dissertations on Gill, both submitted to the University of Edinburgh: R. E. Seymour, "John Gill— Baptist Theologian" (1954); and Curt Daniel, "Hyper-Calvinism and John Gill" (1983).

8. Rippon, *Memoir*, 4. This saying was later paraphrased by his parishioners who frequently remarked, "as surely as Dr. Gill is in his study."

9. Gill, *Sermons and Tracts*, 1:ix. Gill later commented on this text recalling the effect the words must have had on him as a young man, as well as on Adam in the Garden of Eden. They were, he says, a summons to appear before "the Judge of all,

and answer for his conduct; it was in vain for him to secrete himself, he must and should appear, the force of which words he felt, and therefore was obliged to surrender himself." *Gill's Commentary* (Grand Rapids, Mich.: Baker Book House, 1980; London: William Hill, 1852-54), 1:20-21.

10. White, "Gill in London," 76.

11. Ibid., 75.

12. Ibid.

13. Ibid., 79.

14. Ibid., 81-88. The second division centered on Thomas Crosby, Gill's erstwhile supporter and a strong-willed deacon in the church. Apparently, Crosby's mother-in-law, Susannah Keach, who was also the widow of the church's founding pastor, had spoken critically of Elizabeth Gill who had taken a longer than expected time to recover from a miscarriage in 1720. White has suggested that Gill may have been pleased to be rid of Crosby and his meddlesome relatives who left with him since their exit freed the church of "the foremost living exponents of the Keach-Stinton tradition."

15. Charles H. Spurgeon, *The Metropolitan Tabernacle, Its History and Work* (London: n.p., 1876), 40.

16. Rippon, "Memoir," in *Commentary*, 1:xx. The diploma refers to Gill as "praeclaros in Sacrio Literis, Linguis Orientalibus et Antiquitatibus Judaicis progressus fecisse." Gill's most technical work in this field was his *Dissertation concerning the Antiquity of the Hebrew Language, Letters, Vowel Points and Accents*, published in 1767.

17. Cathcart, "Gill," 1:453.

18. Gill, *Body*, xxxvi.

19. Ibid., xxxv.

20. Gill, *Commentary*, 1:xxix.

21. *Calvini Opera*, 4:55: "Neque tamen a gratuita iustitiae imputatione separetur realis (ut loquar) vitae sanctitas." Seymour's claim that Gill so emphasized the doctrine of salvation by sovereign grace that he failed to exhort his people to good works is not borne out by a close examination of his sermons. See his "Gill—Baptist Theologian," 297-98. Gill frequently applied the moral law to Christians and in 1756 published a sermon on *The Law Established by the Gospel*.

22. John Gill. *Attendance in Places of Religious Worship* (London: n.p., 1757), 43-44.

23. Thomas Craner, *A Grain of Gratitude* (London: n.p., 1771), 31-32.

24. Rippon, "Memoir," in *Commentary*, xxxiii.

25. Samuel Stennett, *The Victorious Christian Receiving the Crown* (London, 1771), 32-33.

26. Gill's letter tendering his resignation, along with the church's reply, are found in the Church Record Book, which is housed at the Metropolitan Tabernacle in London. Portions of both letters are reproduced in Seymour, "Gill—Baptist Theologian," 305-06.

27. Gill, *Sermons and Tracts*, 3:569.

28. Stennett, *Victorious Christian*, 48.

29. David M. Thompson, ed., *Nonconformity in the Nineteenth Century* (London: Routledge and Kegan Paul, 1972), 1.

30. Gilbert Burnet, *The History of My Own Times* (Oxford, 1833), IV, Bk. VI, 550.

31. Michael R. Watts, *The Dissenters* (Oxford: Clarendon Press, 1978), 1:264.

32. John Gill, *The Watchman's Answer* (Oxford: Clarendon Press, 1978), 1:264.

33. Quoted, Roland N. Stromberg, *Religious Liberalism in Eighteenth Century England* (London: n.p., 1965), 1.

34. "A Declaration of the Faith and Practice of the Church of Christ at Horsleydown under the Pastoral Care of Mr. John Gill," in *Commentary,* 1:xi. This confession, which displaced the earlier articles of faith adopted under Benjamin Keach in 1697, became a model for other Particular Baptist church covenants and confessions. See Robison, "Legacy," 113-15.

35. Gill, *Body,* 25.

36. Ibid., 13.

37. Ibid., 12.

38. Ibid., 20.

39. Ibid., 21. A helpful analysis of Gill's doctrine of Scripture is found in L. Russ Bush and Tom J. Nettles, *Baptists and the Bible* (Chicago: Moody Press, 1980), 101-09.

40. W. L. Lumpkin, ed., *Baptist Confessions of Faith* (Valley Forge, Pa.: Judson Press, 1959), 326.

41. Ibid., 295.

42. Raymond Brown, *The English Baptists of the Eighteenth Century* (London: The Baptist Historical Society, 1986), 23.

43. Gill, *Body,* 138.

44. Ibid., 140.

45. Ibid., 128.

46. W. T. Whitley, ed., *Minutes of the General Assembly of General Baptists* (London: n.p., 1909-10), 1:43.

47. Gill, *Body,* xli.

48. Gill, *Sermons and Tracts,* 3:555. This quotation is from Gill's *Dissertation Concerning the Eternal Sonship of Christ,* published in 1773. This treatise is a veritable catena of citations from theologians throughout the history of doctrine which Gill adduces in support of this "fundamental doctrine of the Christian religion." Gill felt so strongly about the eternal generation of the Son that in 1768 he led his church to withdraw fellowship from one of its members, a certain James Harmon, who had long opposed it. See Seymour, "Gill—Baptist Theologian," 89.

49. The Canons of Dort are printed in Philip Schaff, *Creeds of Christendom* (New York: Harper and Bros., 1877), 3:550-97.

50. Quoted, Alan P. F. Sell, *The Great Debate: Calvinism, Arminianism and Salvation* (Grand Rapids, Mich.: Baker Book House, 1983), 82.

51. John Gill, *The Cause of God and Truth* (Grand Rapids, Mich.: Baker Book House, 1980), iii.

52. Ibid., 220.

53. Gill, *The Declaration of Faith and Practice,* is given in full in Seymour J. Price, "Dr. John Gill's Confession of 1729," *Baptist Quarterly* 4 (1928): 366-71. This excerpt is quoted in Sell, *Debate,* 80.

54. Quoted, J. Sears McGee, *The Godly Man in Stuart England* (New Haven: Yale University Press, 1976), 1.

55. Gill, *Body,* 201, 503.

56. John Gill, *The Doctrine of God's Everlasting Love to His Elect, and Their Eternal Union with Christ* (London: n.p., 1752), 40.

57. Lumpkin, *Confessions,* 266. There is a striking parallel between Gill's doctrine of eternal justification and Karl Barth's understanding of "the covenant as the

presupposition of reconciliation." Barth writes, "Jesus Christ alone is the content of the eternal will of God, the eternal covenant between God and man. He is this as the Word of God to us and the work of God for us, and therefore in a way quite different from and not to be compared with anything we may become as hearers of this Word and those for whose sake this work is done." *Church Dogmatics* 4:1 (Edinburgh: T. & T. Clark, 1956), 54.

58. Quoted, Sell, *Debate,* 79.

59. Gill, *Commentary,* 1:xxviii-xxix.

60. Peter Toon, *The Emergence of Hyper-Calvinism in English Nonconformity, 1689-1765* (London: The Oliver Tree, 1967), 70-89.

61. Gill, *Sermons and Tracts,* 2:81.

62. G. F. Nuttall, "Northamptonshire and *The Modern Question,*" *Journal of Theological Studies* 16 (1965): 110.

63. Quoted, Brown, *Baptists,* 76.

64. Nettles, *By His Grace,* 101-02. Cf. *Commentary,* 5:101.

65. Gill, *Cause,* 164.

66. John Gill, *The Doctrine of the Cherubim Opened and Explained. A Sermon at the Ordination of the Reverend Mr. John Davis at Waltham-Abbey* (London: n.p., 1754), 36. Quoted, Robison, "Legacy," 118.

67. Ibid., 117.

68. See Nettles, *By His Grace,* 73-130. See also the very helpful study of E. P. Clipsham, "Andrew Fuller and Fullerism: A Study in Evangelical Calvinism," *Baptist Quarterly* 20 (1963): 99-114.

69. *The Complete Works of the Rev. Andrew Fuller,* ed. Joseph Belcher (Philadelphia: American Baptist Publication Society, 1845), 2:422.

70. Ibid. In 1830 W. T. Brantley wrote an article entitled "Gill and Fuller" in which he acknowledged the importance of both for Baptist theology, while also recognizing the nuanced differences between them." Both were ardent and honest in their attachment to the doctrines of grace, firmly persuaded of the humbling facts of human impotence and guilt, animated with the most blessed affections towards the blessed Jesus, as an all-sufficient Saviour in whom believers are complete in righteousness and salvation. To both we are greatly indebted." *Columbian Star and Christian Index* 2 (Jan. 16, 1830):39-40.

71. This fact, along with other details of Gill's funeral, are given in Horton Davies, *Worship and Theology in England, 1690-1850* (Princeton, N.J.: Princeton University Press, 1961), 136.

72. John Fellows, *An Elegy on the Death of the Rev. John Gill* (London: n.p., 1771), 16.

73. Gill, *Body,* xxxii.

74. Charles Haddon Spurgeon, *Autobiography* (London: Passmore and Alabaster, 1900), 4:261-62.

75. John Gill, *A Sermon Occasioned by the Death of Elizabeth Gill* (London: n.p., 1738), 37-41, also 4.

76. Quoted, E. J. Carnell, *The Case for Orthodox Theology* (London: Marshall, Morgan and Scott, 1961), 14.

5

Isaac Backus

Stanley J. Grenz

By the turn of the eighteenth century the energies that had given rise to the founding of the first Baptist churches in New England had largely dissipated, leaving the Baptists a small and divided sect tolerated by the Puritan commonwealth. The ecclesiastical status quo did not continue indefinitely, however, but was soon radically altered by a new wave of dissent which arose within the Congregational establishment itself and from which the Baptists greatly profited.

The event that changed the ecclesiastical face of New England was "the Great Awakening," a revival of such significance that it has been called the American "national conversion." The revival was not enthusiastically greeted everywhere. It produced a deep cleavage within the established Congregational churches of New England.

At first the "New Lights"—those who had been touched by revival or who supported the revivalists—were content to remain within the established churches, seeking to be catalysts for the new life the revival had produced in them and for the ecclesiastical reform the revival demanded. Inevitably, however, conflict arose, as their efforts were met with antagonism and opposition, especially among the clergy, and as the revival party in turn began questioning the spiritual integrity of an ecclesiastical system that opposed itinerant preaching and failed to emphasize what had become a hallmark of the revival, the necessity of personal conversion. These fundamental disagreements led finally to schism, as many New Lights began holding worship services apart from the established churches, earning for themselves the name "Separates."

The Separates' program included a renewed emphasis on the authority of the New Testament in all ecclesiastical matters. However, this "back to the Bible" movement introduced a new and explosive controversy among the schismatic congregations, the issue of baptism. The ensuing debate eventually resulted in the demise of the Separate movement, as many adherents came to adopt an immersionist position and to form closed-communion churches. These "Separate-Baptist" congregations gradually joined fellowship with the older Baptists of New England. In so doing, they brought life to the immersionist cause, but also redefined what it meant to be a Baptist in America.

A man whose ecclesiastical pilgrimage was typical of many Separate Baptists, a man who became the leading figure in raising again the Baptist banner

Isaac Backus (1724-1806)

Photo courtesy of E. C. Dargan Research Library
Sunday School Board of the Southern Baptist Convention

and in redefining the nature of the Baptist movement in eighteenth-century New England, was Isaac Backus. His importance for Baptists in America lies in at least four dimensions. First, he was instrumental in bringing together the older Baptist churches and the newly forming antipedobaptistic Separate churches into one denomination. Second, he became the bearer of the theological thought which came to characterize the denomination at this crucial stage in its establishment, as the evangelical Calvinism which he inherited from the Separates replaced the Arminianism prevalent in the older Baptist churches. Third, Backus played an instrumental role in winning for the denomination a place in the reformation tradition. He placed this outcast group within the Protestant myth of reformation and then helped to win for them a place of equality among the leading denominations of America. Finally, Backus articulated anew the traditional Baptist call for some sort of broad religious liberty and struggled with the ramifications of that call for New England society.

The role which Backus played during the formative years of his denomination was so crucial that he has been termed "the father of American Baptists."[1] Similarly, his efforts on behalf of separation of church and state caused one observer to say concerning him, "no individual in America since Roger Williams stands out so preeminently as the champion of religious liberty."[2]

Biography

Isaac Backus was born on a Connecticut farm in 1724. Prior to the Awakening, his parents were nominal Congregationalists, but the fervent preaching of the itinerants which was sweeping the area in 1731 resulted in revival in the life of young Isaac's recently widowed and severely depressed mother. Isaac was deeply impressed with what he saw happening in Norwich and desired the conversion so many others were experiencing. Not knowing how one received such an experience, he went to his minister, who, in keeping with the outlook of New England rationalist theology (if the sinner leads an upright life, God will in due time grant him salvation), advised his inquirer, "Be not discouraged, but see if God does not appear for your help."[3] Backus found this advice totally unacceptable and continued his search for salvation until he finally concluded that personal striving was totally useless. It was only then that his quest was rewarded, and on August 24, 1741, while alone in a field, he experienced conversion.[4] Soon after his experience of "divine light," Backus received the "inner witness" which assured him that he was indeed a true saint predestined for salvation.

Five years later (September 1746) he was the recipient of a second divine encounter, "an internal call to preach the gospel." In the meantime the Backus family had become part of the Separate congregation that had formed in the neighboring community of Norwich, Connecticut. Immediately after receiving his call, Isaac "tested his gift" by preaching the Sunday sermon at the New Light church. He spent the next year on the itinerant circuit, and then at the age of twenty-four and lacking any formal theological education, he was called to the pastorate of a group in Titicut parish, Massachusetts.

The years as a Separate were filled with strife. Because theirs was an illegal congregation, his church members faced conflicts with the Massachusetts government concerning religious taxation. Backus's involvement in the struggle for separation of church and state, which was triggered by this incident and would occupy him throughout his life, was interrupted in the summer of 1749, when the grave theological controversy which was already threatening to split the entire Separate movement came to Titicut—the explosive issue of believer's baptism. A two-year personal struggle followed. To abandon pedobaptism was to secede from the Separate movement just when success appeared on the horizon. On the other hand, Backus was beginning to see that the New England form of covenant theology was not taught by the Bible and that it was used to justify the ecclesiastical evils of the day—the Halfway Covenant,[5] the parish system, religious taxes, and the aristocratic structure of the church.[6] Backus accepted the antipedobaptist position on July 25, 1751, and was baptized by immersion on August 22.

During the ensuing five years he struggled to maintain an open-communion congregation, but the presence of theological controversy within the church proved too divisive. Finally, in 1756 the pastor dissolved the congregation and formed an immersionist church in adjacent Middleboro. Soon thereafter the new closed-communion group joined fellowship with the Baptists.

The story of the Middleboro congregation was repeated in many other Separate churches. Their attempts to gain dissenting status posed a new problem for the Puritan establishment. Although they were now clearly baptistic, these churches had previously been part of the old order, hence their members should not be dismissed from their duty to support financially the Standing Churches. To prevent any loophole by which these Separate Baptists might obtain dissenting status, the Massachusetts legislature in 1753 added a new requirement to the law, stipulating that the exemption certificates issued by individual churches must be validated by three other "Anabaptist" churches in the region.

This change, however, failed miserably. First, it alarmed the old Baptists, who drafted a remonstrance to the Massachusetts general court and raised funds to send a representative to England with their grievances. Second, because it did not define "Anabaptist," the act made an even bigger loophole, for the Separate Baptist churches merely validated certificates for each other. Third, the law accelerated the movement of open-communion churches to closed-communion status and caused the closed-communion churches to realize their fundamental ties first to each other and then with the old Baptists, whom they had themselves previously ostracized. In short, the Massachusetts law was the first step in the rejuvenation of the New England Baptists.

This process received added impetus from the efforts of Isaac Backus, who saw almost immediately the importance of close ties among all churches holding Baptist beliefs. Between 1756 and 1767, he traveled nearly 15,000 miles within the region,[7] visiting old Baptist churches, open-communion congregations, and new groups which sought his help in the task of organizing as churches. The Philadelphia Baptist Association sent key leaders to encourage their New England coreligionists. Their assistance led to the establishment of Rhode Island College (now Brown University) and in 1767 the Warren Baptist Association.

The Warren Association was originally established for the purpose of aiding local churches. But it soon became the political arm of the New England Baptists in a renewed struggle against the Standing Order, a struggle triggered by the difficulties faced by many of the newer churches in their efforts to obtain exemption from religious taxation. In 1769 the association appointed a grievance committee to collect the complaints of churches and under Backus's leadership to formulate a petition to the Massachusetts legislature. Drawing from the slogans of the independence-minded colonists, the petition condemned the certificate system as "taxation without representation" and claimed that liberty of conscience was a natural right. Despite the pleas of the Baptists, the certificate system and the injustices in its administration continued. These injustices led to a turning point in Backus's thinking.

Between 1772 and 1773, Backus developed his theory of the two governments. God had appointed two kinds of government, the civil and the ecclesiastical, which ought never to be confounded. Based on this theory, Backus concluded that the union of the two governments in the New England colonies must be broken if America were to become a truly Christian land.[8] In September 1772, the grievance committee was reactivated under the leadership of Backus himself. Utilizing his theory as well as its corollary, the right of the Christian to disobey when the governments had indeed been confounded, the committee suggested to the association meeting of September 1773 a new course of action—the mass refusal by the Baptists to turn in exemption certificates. In typical Baptist fashion the association voted to leave this decision with each church but to aid financially those who suffered as a result of their noncompliance with the certificate law.

During this time the struggle between the colonies and England intensified. The Baptists viewed the first meeting of the Continental Congress in Philadelphia on September 5, 1774, as their opportunity to appeal to a body higher than the Massachusetts legislature without appearing to be disloyal. Backus was among those sent by their constituents to join with a group being formed by the Baptists and Quakers of Philadelphia. At the suggestion of the Quakers, a meeting was sought with the Massachusetts congressional delegation together with several sympathetic delegates from other colonies. At this meeting, held on October 14, the Baptists presented a statement which included Backus's two-government theory and the Baptist arguments on behalf of their concept of liberty of worship.[9]

The meeting turned out to be a mistake. Not only did the Baptists fail to accomplish their goal of focusing national attention on their plight, their association with Tory Quakers and neutral, if not Tory Philadelphia Baptists added to the suspicion in New England that they too were unpatriotic. Having failed in Philadelphia, the Baptists were forced again to appeal to the Massachusetts assembly, doing so in July 1775. Soon after, the Revolutionary War began.

The next opportunity to bring about change in Massachusetts came in 1779, when a convention was called for the purpose of writing a new state constitution. Backus lobbied intensively for the inclusion of a bill of rights, but the new constitution did not totally separate church and state and leave the "rational soul" free to find "true religion," as Backus had desired. Despite voting irregularities, the legislature declared the constitution law in 1780. In the wave of renewed persecution against the Baptists who refused once again to pay the religious tax, the legislature ignored completely any petitions and protests. As a result the struggle shifted to the courts.

The Baptists won an important victory in 1782, only to see the decision reversed two years later. The second court decision made the situation worse, for it stated that only legally incorporated religious societies were entitled to legal recognition. For the Baptists this meant that whereas local churches had previously been able to receive a proportionate share of all taxes collected, they would no longer be reimbursed unless they sought incorporation. Against the advice of Backus, many churches began complying with the law—seeking incorporation, paying the tax, and then suing to have their taxes go to their own minister.

The Baptist efforts to eliminate religious taxation had not been successful. Yet, a climate of broad acceptance and toleration had been attained by 1785, and the group now began to turn their attention away from the political struggle to the task of evangelism. Even Backus found himself forced to devote much of his effort to other needs, for new sects and non-Calvinistic theologies were making inroads among the Baptists. He sought to counter these trends through sermons and tracts which attacked the heresies and defended the outlook he had experientially found to be true. Then, Middleboro honored their Baptist minister by electing him as a delegate to the Massachusetts convention which debated the newly proposed United States Constitution, a trust to which Backus gave much attention before finally voting against the consensus of his constituents and in favor of ratification.

Finally, the new evangelism thrust of the denomination drew Backus's attention as well. This occurred in a somewhat unusual way at the Warren Association meeting on September 6, 1788. After Backus had suggested a renewal of the struggle against the Establishment, the association appointed a committee to write a petition and present it to the legislature at its own discretion, but then presented Backus with a new challenge—a southern journey to aid in a revival currently taking place there. In 1790 he returned from his journey full of enthusiasm, but he was unable to produce a similar renewal in his home state.

Backus continued his ministry in Middleboro, where he had served since organizing the Titicut Separate church. When Backus's health began to fail in 1798 and his wife died in 1800, the church began to see the need of obtaining an assistant for their aging pastor. In 1804 they called to this post Ezra Kendal, who, as a member of the new generation of Baptist pastors, held certain Arminian outlooks. Backus suffered a stroke in March 1806 and preached his last sermon on April 3. He suffered a second stroke on April 23, but lingered until November 24. Although he did not live to see the disestablishment of the Congregational churches, his lifetime goal nevertheless became a reality on November 11, 1833.

Exposition

In keeping with the Puritan heritage, the pen became a strategic weapon in the wars Isaac Backus waged as a dissenter from the reigning ecclesiastical system and as a defender of orthodox theology. Backus's literary career began in 1754, soon after his acceptance of the immersionist position. Over the course of fifty-two years, he published thirty-seven tracts and pamphlets, a three-volume ecclesiastical history of New England (written at the request of the Warren Association), a subsequent abridgement, and numerous petitions and newspaper articles. His unpublished output included sermon manuscripts, a lengthy diary and other personal accounts, parts of several autobiographical works, and an assortment of short pieces on various topics.

Backus wrote with the goal of providing direction for his friends and enemies in matters of personal and corporate living in a turbulent era. He spoke out concerning the Calvinism/Arminianism conflict, covenant theology, nature of the church—its officers and its ordinance of baptism, and the relationship between the ecclesiastical and civil spheres. In his attempt to advance his own developing positions, he marshaled arguments from any available source—common opinions of the day, the books and tracts of the New England fathers and his contemporaries, personal experience, and, of course, the Bible. His writings reveal a man of conviction, who, in spite of lack of formal education, was so motivated by what he saw as God's truth and so keenly aware of the mood of his times, that he was able to interpret his convictions to his contemporaries and by so doing be a catalyst for change.

Backus's writings reveal a conservative-radical, a man who fought for a deep reordering of the entire social structure of New England, but for basically conservative reasons. He believed that his program stood squarely on the tradition, ideals, and designs of the original planters of New England and that the social reordering he advocated was merely a further unfolding of the Reformation begun by Luther and Calvin and advanced by the English Puritans and the Separatist fathers of New England.

In this endeavor Backus gained a degree of success, for the New England that emerged from the eighteenth century was molded to a great extent by ideas for which he fought. Subsequent history has shown this "young upstart" and "honest gumphead," as Backus was labeled by his opponents, to have been more than merely a spokesman for his own denomination in his own age. Rather, he stands at a crucial stage in the development of the theological and political thought of the Baptist denomination whose concepts came to be accepted to some degree by the nation as a whole.

Theological Foundation

Backus lived in an age in which religion played a determinative role in society. Social structures were seen as the result of, and as based on, theology. As a result, Backus saw his first task as that of calling New England back to right theology, believing that doctrinal and ecclesiastical purity would result in the proper ordering of society. At the same time, Backus was not a great innovative theological thinker. He accepted the Calvinist theology of Jonathan Edwards, mediated to him by the Awakening, with which he then blended the philosophy of John Locke so important to the colonists. Three theological themes loom as central to his thinking and as foundational to his theory of church and state.

First, Backus stressed the Calvinist emphasis on the sovereignty of God. For him God is the absolutely sovereign governor of the universe to whom all earthly governments must appeal for legitimization:

> That there is one supreme BEING whose kingdom ruleth over all is the first and capital article of truth which no nation upon earth were ever able to erase entirely out of their minds. For no government could ever be established among themselves without appeals to HIM for the truth of what was asserted, and to avenge injustices and the violation of contracts and engagements.[10]

A second area of theological interest was anthropology. Influenced by Edwards and Locke, Backus saw the intellect as the controlling faculty in the human person, dominating even the will: "the will of man is always determined in its choice by motive or by what they at present prefer and think the best."[11] Freedom, then, rather than being the ability to act without any motive (which is impossible), is actually acting consistently with reason, albeit reason informed by revelation.[12]

This in turn affected Backus's understanding of the nature of knowledge and truth. Although he exhibited early in life an indebtedness to the Great Awakening and the pietistic tradition by speaking of "the distinction between doctrinal and experimental knowledge; between right notions of truth in the head, and knowing them in the heart,"[13] he came to see the inconsistency of this with his Lockean anthropology. In 1771 he repudiated his earlier view, declaring that "right ideas will always produce right effects upon our hearts and lives."[14]

Backus viewed truth as an objective force which "certainly would do well enough if she were left to shift for herself."[15] His optimism was based in part on his high regard for the power of reason and the innately human striving after truth. In keeping with this, he could speak of sin as occurring whenever

> evil imaginations have usurped the place of reason and a well informed judgment and hold them in such bondage that instead of being governed by those noble faculties, they are put to the horrid drudgery of seeking out inventions for the gratification of fleshly lusts which war against the soul.[16]

Building on Locke, Backus maintained that humans as created by God were to be governed by "reason and a well informed judgment" which would be influenced by the externally applied "motive" of the divine command to love God. But then another external motive, "the conceit that man could advance either his honor or happiness by disobedience instead of obedience," was injected by "the father of lies." This evil imagination "usurped" the place of a properly informed reason, a usurpation which continues in the history of every person and brings with it the state of rebellion in which each one exists. The result is the depraved state of humanity, in which reason is no longer given the position of leadership over the actions of the individual.

At one major point, however, Backus parted company with Locke. He agreed with the philosopher that liberty consists in the ability to hinder one's desires from determining one's will to any action until the good and evil of that action has been examined. But for the Calvinist Baptist, this was impossible by unaided human ability, in that "evil imaginations and desires have already got the start of reason, so that it can never bring them back to a fair examination without divine influence.[17]

And for Backus the necessary divine influence is mediated to the individual by the Scriptures, which are designed to act against the "evil imaginations" and to combat ignorance, thereby bringing freedom.[18] This divine assistance results in entrance into the state of faith—the acceptance of the truth about God and oneself, which occurs whenever the gospel proclamation (i.e. the demands of God in the law plus the saving work of Christ) is so impressed by the Holy Spirit on an individual that the conscience is pricked, and the mind, impressed with the reasonableness of the message, embraces its truth.

In all of this Backus emphasized the individual. It is the individual in whom reason was originally designed to rule, in whom reason's role has been usurped by evil imaginations, and therefore in whom God's solution is to be operative. Likewise, it is the individual whom the Holy Spirit teaches the truths of God's Word. For this reason "religion is ever a matter between God and individuals,"[19] "a voluntary obedience unto God,"[20] a relationship mediated only by the Word as it is illuminated to the believer by the Holy Spirit.

The third doctrine foundational to Backus's thinking is ecclesiology. He was in agreement with the widely accepted differentiation between the invisible church of all the elect and the visible church, the earthly institution. But in contrast to the Congregationalists, he demanded a radical application of the pure church ideal. Individual religion plus the pure church ideal meant that the visible church is a voluntary society of believers,[21] an outlook for which he found precedence in Locke's definition of the church.[22] For Backus, the local church, is united by a voluntary covenant. From this idea he drew radical conclusions:

> This is the exact nature of a church covenant; which shows that no person can be brought into it without his own consent, that the covenant cannot bind any person or community to act any thing contrary to the revealed will of God, nor ever exempt any from their obligation to act agreeably thereto with their hearts.[23]

Church and State

Out of this theological-philosophical foundation emerged Backus's theory of church and state. First, Backus held that government is intrinsic to the existence of humanity. As creatures of God, humans are placed within the framework of government, in that they fall under the providence of the God who governs creation. Further, humans are designed to be governed internally by reason (not merely carried along by impulse).

In contrast, then, to the teaching of many of his contemporaries including Locke, Backus emphasized with Roger Williams that government and liberty are not incompatible. Rather, because humanity was created under divine providence,

> it is so far from being necessary for any man to give up any part of his real liberty in order to submit to government that all nations have found it necessary to submit to some government in order to enjoy any liberty and security at all.[24]

Human government becomes for Backus the agent of God, divinely instituted and necessitated because of human rebellion against the government of God.[25]

Second, Backus held that there were two different governments instituted by God, the civil and ecclesiastical, each one with differing tasks and spheres of responsibility: "Men have three things to be concerned for, namely, soul, body, and estate. The two latter belong to the magistrate's jurisdiction, the other does not."[26] In order to fulfill its task of governing the bodies and estates of humans, the civil government has two basic duties. It is "to punish such as work ill to their neighbor," and to carry out this duty, and this one alone, the magistrate "bears the sword."[27] Likewise, "all who are in authority" are to "protect and encourage such a quiet and peaceable life in all Godliness and honesty."[28]

Although there are certain structural similarities between the two governments, there is a major difference, for unlike the situation in the church, "dominion" in the civil sphere is not "founded in grace." Backus opposed the widely held viewpoint that "religion endows its subjects with a right to act as lawgivers and judges over others."[29] Rather, he envisioned the civil government defending its citizens against the hostilities of others and promoting upright living by means of respectable magistrates who are elected by the entire population regardless of religious persuasion.

Distinct from civil government is the ecclesiastical with jurisdiction over the souls of humans.[30] Backus found the distinction between the two governments, which is based on the inward nature of religion as opposed to the outward nature of civil jurisdiction, not only in Locke,[31] but more importantly in Christ's teaching. The Lord commanded the church, "Put away from among yourselves that wicked person," but said to the state, "Let both grow together until the harvest."[32]

The distinction between the civil and ecclesiastical governments suggested to Backus that there be a twofold separation of the two. On the one hand, the church must not interfere in the civil sphere. This is demanded by the Lord's exclusion of the sword from His kingdom[33] and by the nature of religion itself. On this basis Backus wrote, "as the Baptists hold all religion to be personal, between God and individuals, and that all church power is in each particular church, it is impossible for them ever to form any great body, that can be dangerous to any civil government."[34]

Worse than the threat of ecclesiastical interference in the civil sphere is the use of secular force in religious affairs. According to Backus the civil government must not legislate in the ecclesiastical sphere, because Jesus declared that His kingdom "does not receive its support from earthly power, but from TRUTH."[35] For support Backus appealed to Locke's concept of the nature of truth:

> The business of laws is not to provide for the truth of opinions, but for the safety and security of the commonwealth, and of every man's goods and person; and so it ought to be; for truth certainly would do well enough if she were once left to shift for herself. She seldom has received, and I fear never will receive, much assistance from the power of great men; to whom she is but rarely known, and more rarely welcome. She is not taught by laws, nor has she any need of force to procure her entrance into the minds of men. Errors indeed prevail by the assistance of foreign and borrowed succours.[36]

In spite of this radical separation, Backus did not see the two spheres as being competitive. Rather, because both are God's institution, a harmonious relationship ought to exist between them:

> as civil rulers ought to be men fearing God, and hating covetousness, and to be terrors to evil doers, and a praise to them who do well; and as ministers ought to pray for rulers, and to teach the people to be subject to them; so there may and ought to be a sweet harmony between them.[37]

Nor did the Baptist leader dispute the long-held view that religion is important to society.[38] The point of fundamental disagreement with his opponents lay with the popular suggestion that the importance of religion to society granted to the civil government the right to seek to secure the benefits of religion through legislative action.[39] Backus questioned whether that worthy goal could ever be attained by such means and advocated a different approach to securing the piety necessary to society. Civil government must limit its role to creating a climate in which truth is free to act. Piety in turn would be guaranteed to society by the sovereign God through the convincing power of truth by means of the missionary enterprise of the church as individuals are converted and become good citizens. "If the church of Christ were governed wholly by his laws, enforced in his name, she would be an infinite blessing to human society."[40] For "if all were protected impartially, they who act from heavenly motives would strengthen the hands of civil rulers, and hold up light to draw others out of evil ways, and to guard against all iniquity."[41]

Herein, then, is the "sweet harmony" Backus envisioned between church and state. Christ is to be sovereign in His church. Through His people He draws the individual members of society to acknowledge the truth of Christianity. This in turn benefits the state, because "real Christians are the best subjects of civil government in the world."[42]

Third, while denying the civil sphere a role in matters of the church, Backus did advocate governmental activity in the realm of morality. Following Locke and the Enlightenment, Backus held to the twofold source of truth. Certain truths of morality and religion were present to all humans regardless of confessional persuasion, being mediated to them by reason. These truths or duties taught by natural religion, including justice, peace, sobriety, and even petition and thanksgiving to God,[43] fall under the sphere of the civil government. Legislation in these areas does not entail a denial of religious liberty. The citizen is merely forced thereby to act according to reason, which is freedom in the true sense. On the other hand, other truths are available only by special revelation. These lie outside the civil sphere.[44]

This, then, was the program outlined by Backus and adopted to a large extent by the new nation. Government is a legitimate institution derived from God. The civil and religious spheres are distinct entities, separated in function and in fact. Morality falls under the domain of both, being divided into each sphere according to the twofold source of truth (i.e., natural truth of reason and supernatural truth of revelation).

The Role of the Baptists

Backus's importance goes beyond his work in defending "evangelical Calvinism" and struggling to enshrine separation of church and state into the civil life of the new American republic. For Baptist history, his most significant contribution lies in his ability to transform an outcast, sectarian group on the fringe of the Puritan commonwealth into an accepted and respected member of the American religious community. The Middleboro minister became an antipedobaptist at a time in which New England society cast scorn on all "Anabaptists." But by the closing decades of the eighteenth century a broad climate of toleration had developed, even in Puritan Massachusetts. Although there were many factors which contributed to this amazing transformation of public sentiment, Backus's activities in formulating, articulating, defending, and gaining sympathy for the Baptist position was of crucial importance.

Backus's success in winning a place for the Baptist movement within the broader Puritan reformation was due to a large degree to his keen ability to utilize history as an ally in the fight to advance his denomination's cause. He was completely convinced that the stands he and the Baptists were formulating were not only logical and biblical, but actually formed the natural outgrowth of the entire Puritan heritage of both Old and New England. In keeping with this conviction, he sprinkled his writings with references to and quotations from many leading figures in the Puritan movement.

Beyond this, Backus became convinced that his adopted denomination, rather than being a sectarian group, actually stood at the forefront of the entire Reformation. These despised "Anabaptists," he maintained, constituted the vanguard of Christ's work of reformation in His church.

To this end Backus's apologetic developed further the Protestant myth articulated by Lutherans, such as Moses Mosheim, and Calvinists, including Jonathan Edwards. In contrast to the contention of his contemporaries that Puritan New England formed the climax of the Reformation, he claimed that the final battle between Christ and Antichrist was still raging, and the scene of this battle was his own land. Many still clung to the national church concept, thereby refusing to allow Christ to be sole ruler and supporter of His church. Likewise, many still maintained that corollary principle of a national church, infant baptism. But when true separation of church and state was inaugurated, truth would be set free to do its work of convincing all God's people of all the principles of Reformation theology and polity. This would constitute the church's victory over Antichrist and the dawning of the era of truth and righteousness marked by Christ's complete rule in His church.[45]

In other words, having accepted the Protestant, Reformed dream and with it the interpretation of the Antichrist which stood behind it, Backus altered this interpretation to fit his own times. The traditional English understanding viewed the bishop of Rome as the Antichrist, an interpretation accepted even by the New England Separates.[46] But Backus never equated the Antichrist with the pope himself. Rather, he saw this apocalyptic figure as constituted by the mingling of church and state. He believed that the union of church and state had been responsible for thwarting the reformation process and preventing a return to the primitive purity of Christ's church. It was, therefore, this church-state intermingling which must be rooted out. When this should occur, truth—the gospel truth of God—would finally be freed from human restrictions to do its work of converting individuals. Truth, being free, would in turn bring the one truly reformed church into being, a church which would follow the ancient baptism practice as well. Then the utopia would dawn.

This alteration of the Protestant interpretation of the Antichrist freed Backus to level his sharp criticism of the governmental system of both Old and New England. The Book of Revelation foresaw the rise of two beasts, which traditional Protestant thought equated with the Roman emperor and the pope respectively. But for Backus, the pope was the first beast (not the second), and the second beast did not arise until the Protestants, following the church against which they were protesting, joined church and state and became persecutors, utilizing the power of the state against their dissenting sisters and brothers. In this manner Antichrist, wounded in the Reformation, had raised its ugly head first in England and subsequently in the colonies. The very Massachusetts fathers who had built a Christian commonwealth to combat the anti-Christian pope were responsible for giving place to the real Antichrist, the church-state union, within the city upon a hill.

By means of his acceptance of the Puritan dream and because of his subtle alteration of the Puritan myth, Backus was able to accomplish for the Baptists something of immeasurable importance. In his interpretation of history he brought this small, despised, dissenting sect into the mainstream of the Puritan myth and, in fact, placed them on its pinnacle. The Baptist minister claimed that none other than this group stood as the end product of the reformation process. They were the most reformed of the Reformation churches. The Massachusetts fathers had thought that the Reformation culminated with them, giving their experiment the significance of constituting a city on a hill for the rest of the world. Backus declared that subsequent history disproved this claim. The Middleboro pastor sought to show that the despised Baptists actually constituted a stage of God's reformation beyond that of colonial Congregationalism. His vision, therefore, was that of a not-too-distant day when *all* Christians would see the light God had allowed the Baptists to see already. He anticipated a day when the principles of believer's baptism and the sole lordship of Christ over His church apart from the meddling of human legislators, now adhered to by the "advance company" of the final reformation, would one day be acknowledged by all true Christians everywhere.

Evaluation

Isaac Backus left a far-reaching legacy to Baptists in America and to the nation as a whole. His legacy included his theology, church-state theory, and understanding of the role of the Baptist movement in the on-going reformation. These three contributions, however, have enjoyed differing degrees of influence in the subsequent two centuries.

Even before Backus's death, his theological bequest was called into question. By the turn of the century, the Arminianism over which he had momentarily been victorious gained adherents among the Baptists, even within the leadership of the Middleboro congregation. During the nineteenth century, under the influence of revivalism, the Arminian tide swept the land. Even the residue of Calvinism found among contemporary Baptists reflects the impact of the intervening two centuries.

Although Backus saw himself as a staunch Calvinist, the Middleboro minister helped pave the way for the revivalism of the nineteenth century. He held unwaveringly to the Calvinist distinctive of the sovereignty of God in election. Yet, Backus's understanding of this principle was shaped by the Great Awakening and the Enlightenment. His attention had been shifted by Edwards and Locke to the human person—especially the human faculty of reason—as the location in which God's eternal decisions find their outworking. It was a short step from his emphasis on individual reason to the revivalist emphasis on individual will, generally expressed in terms of "decisions for Christ."

Although Backus's Lockean anthropology may appear naive in the modern post-Kantian era, as may his understanding of the relationship between Scripture and reason, nevertheless his understandings of God's sovereignty and of conversion have lasting implications. Backus was surely correct in finding the basis of evangelism in the sovereignty of God and the importance of human obedience, rather than in God as the source of human happiness, so prevalent in revivalism. Similarly, Backus's emphasis on covenant (conversion as a covenant with God and the church as a covenant community) offers a needed corrective for much Baptist thinking that builds largely on the individualism of the Baptist heritage while ignoring the corporate dimension, which for earlier Baptists formed the context for an emphasis on the individual.

Of more lasting influence for the nation as a whole has been Backus's view of church and state, for the program he outlined was adopted to a large extent by new republic and has remained the dominant position into the present. By means of an emphasis on the freedom of truth, the Middleboro minister sought a balance between a transcendent grounding of government and individual religious liberty, and he championed liberty of the individual conscience while acknowledging the importance of religion to the well-being of society. Two hundred years of American history have confirmed the basic correctness of his position. Personal religious conviction does contribute to the well-being of society. And such conviction ultimately cannot be forced or legislated but must arise from the hearts of its citizens.

At the same time his theory is not without problems. It appears that Backus and the framers of our government may have purchased too much from the Enlightenment. The twofold source of truth and the division of morality into two spheres on which the theory is based is workable in a democratic society when a consensus of morality and religious belief exist. But what happens when the consensus dissipates? Theoretically, any reduction in the number of commonly held moral beliefs results in a corresponding reduction in governmental enforcement of public morality, and this in the name of religious liberty. Once set in motion the continuation of such a process could result in the systematic exclusion of government not only from the strictly religious, but also from the moral life of its citizens. The frightening possibility exists that given sufficient time a society could grow so pluralistic so as to eliminate any type of religious consensus. Should this situation arise government would no longer play any role in the area of morality.

Recent developments in American society suggest that such a situation is a possibility. Since the days of Backus, many generally held religious and moral beliefs have been called into question, to the extent that some observers wonder if any natural basis can be formulated for civil enforcement of any tenets of public morality. The public school system has been especially vulnerable. An open question today is whether schools are endowed with either the power or the task of instilling any ethical and moral standards beyond "values clarification." The current situation serves to emphasize the problem of basing governmental theory on the optimistic concepts of the Enlightenment in a situation in which the consensus concerning what constitute the natural truths of reason has been lost.

The intervening two centuries have also raised the question as to whether Backus's vision concerning the role of the Baptists in Reformation history is adequate. Although Backus may have correctly pinpointed the significance of the growth of the Baptist movement in eighteenth-century New England, the ecumenical goal he anticipated simply was not attained. The churches in America did in time come to embrace disestablishment, as Backus had hoped, but this victory brought neither the universal acceptance of believer's baptism nor the one truly reformed, baptistic church. As the next century unfolded, other Christian bodies arose, claiming to constitute yet additional stages beyond the Baptists in God's work in reforming the church.

In the ensuing years many of Backus's spiritual children lost his vision. Rather than continuing his struggle for the reformation of the one church, they settled for the enjoyment of the place in the American religious community his efforts in part won for them. As respected members of the community of churches, the Baptists by and large embraced the denominationalism that gained widespread adherence in the nineteenth century as the best solution to the presence of a plurality of Christian bodies in the republic. By the means of this outlook the various competing groups could affirm each other as comprising together the one body of Christ, despite their lack of theological and organizational unity.

The reformation which Backus envisioned, the goal which he inherited from the Puritans and which marked him as a Puritan, has never been completed. Reformation remains the task of the church in every age. Backus's declaration that the Baptists have an important role to play in that reformation is one aspect of his thought that has lasting value. The Baptists have made crucial contributions to church renewal. As a "left wing" Protestant group, they have called other Protestants to apply consistently the principles of their protest against traditionalism, sacramentarianism, sacerdotalism, and authoritarianism. To this end they have sought to measure all creeds and ecclesiological systems against the Scriptures and have continually emphasized the importance not only of the individual congregation, but also of the individual believer, the personal nature of the Christian faith and religious liberty. The Baptist witness has not been unsuccessful. However, the gains of the past are never sufficient. Therefore, today's Baptists must reaffirm the goal of Isaac Backus and his vision of their role in that vision, so they may join with all Christians in fulfilling the mission of the one body of Christ.

Bibliography

Works by Backus

Most of the various tracts Backus published during his lifetime are unavailable in book form. All, however, are found in the Evans Microcard Series. Likewise, his papers and manuscripts are part of Publication 424 of the Historical Commission of the Southern Baptist Convention, Nashville, TN. The following is a list of books and compilations more readily available:

A History of New England with Particular Reference to the Denomination of Christians Called Baptists 2d ed., 2 vols. Edited by David Weston. Newton, Mass.: Backus Historical Society, 1871.

An Abridgment of the Church History of New England from 1602-1804 containing a View of Their Principles and Practices, Declensions and Revivals, Oppression and Liberty, with a Concise Account of the Baptists in the Southern Parts of American and a Chronological Table of the Whole. Boston, 1804. (Second edition with a memoir of the author. Philadelphia Baptist Tract Depository, 1839).

Isaac Backus on Church, State, and Calvinism. Pamphlets, 1754-1789. Edited by William G. McLoughlin. Cambridge, Mass.: Harvard University, 1968.

Works About Backus

Backman, Milton Vaughn, Jr. "Isaac Backus: A Pioneer Champion of Religious Liberty." Ph.D. diss., University of Pennsylvania, 1959.

Grenz, Stanley J. "Isaac Backus and the English Baptist Tradition." *Baptist Quarterly* 30/5 (1984).

_____. "The Ultimate Significance of Isaac Backus for the American Baptist Movement." *Quarterly Review* 44/2 (1984).

_____. "Church and State: The Legacy of Isaac Backus and the Contemporary Situation." *Center Journal* 2/2 (1983).

_____. "Isaac Backus and Religious Liberty." *Foundations* 22/4 (1979).

_____. *Isaac Backus—Puritan and Baptist.* NABPR Dissertation Series, No. 4. Macon, GA.: Mercer University, 1983.

Hovey, Alvah. *A Memoir of the Life and Times of the Rev. Isaac Backus, A. M.* Boston: (n.p.), 1859.

Jones, Dewey H. "Isaac Backus: Champion of Religious Freedom, 1724-1806." Thesis, Claremont Graduate School, 1958.

Lyon, Edward N. "A Discussion of the Contribution of Isaac Backus to the Problem of the Relationship of Church and State." Thesis, Gordon Divinity School, 1955.

Maston, Thomas Bufford. "The Ethical and Social Attitudes of Isaac Backus." Ph.D. diss., Yale University, 1939. Published abridgment, *Isaac Backus: Pioneer of Religious Liberty.* Rochester, N.Y.: American Baptist Historical Society, 1962.

McLoughlin, William G. *Isaac Backus and the American Pietistic Tradition.* In Oscar Hardlin, ed. *The Library of American Biography.* Boston: Little, Brown and Co., 1967.

_____. "Isaac Backus and the Separation of Church and State in America." *The American Historical Review* 73/5 (1968).

_____. *Isaac Backus on Church, State, and Calvinism: Pamphlets, 1754-1789.* Cambridge, Mass.: Harvard University, 1968.

Tull, James E. "Isaac Backus: Leader of the Separate Baptists." In *Shapers of Baptist Thought.* Valley Forge, Penn.: Judson, 1972.

Notes

1. Mary Hewitt Mitchell, *The Great Awakening and Other Revivals* (New Haven: Yale University, 1934).

2. William Henry Allison, "Isaac Backus," in *Dictionary of American Biography,* ed. Allen Johnson (New York: Charles Scribner's Sons, 1928), 1:471.

3. Isaac Backus, *Isaac Backus' Life: An Account of the Life of Isaac Backus,* unpublished manuscript, 11. Also found in Isaac Backus, *Isaac Backus, His Writing Containing Some Particular Account of My Conversion,* unpublished manuscript, 5.

4. Backus describes this event in *Account of Life,* 16-18; and in *Account of Conversion,* 5-6.

5. The Halfway Covenant was so named because it allowed children of unregenerate church members to join the church but not to take communion. They became "halfway" members.

6. William McLoughlin, *Isaac Backus and the American Pietistic Tradition* (Boston: Little, Brown and Co., 1967), 62.

7. Robert G. Torbet, *A History of the Baptists* (Philadelphia: Judson, 1950), 235.

8. See McLoughlin, *Backus,* 123-27.

9. Ibid., 131.

10. Backus, "Truth Is Great and Will Prevail," in *Isaac Backus on Church, State, and Calvinism: Pamphlets, 1754-1789,* ed. William McLoughlin (Cambridge, Mass.: Harvard University, 1968), 402.

11. Isaac Backus, *The Sovereign Decree of God* (Boston: n.p., 1773) in McLoughlin, *Isaac Backus on Church, State, and Calvinism,* 297.

12. Isaac Backus, *The Doctrine of Sovereign Grace Opened and Vindicated* (Providence: n.p., 1771), 60-62.

13. Isaac Backus, *True Faith Will Produce Good Works* (Boston: n.p., 1767), 15. See also *All True Ministers of the Gospel . . . The Nature and Necessity of an Internal Call* (Boston: n.p., 1754) in McLoughlin, *Isaac Backus on Church, State, and Calvinism,* 73.

14. Backus, *Sovereign Grace,* 44-45.

15. Isaac Backus, *A Seasonable Plea for Liberty of Conscience* (Boston: n.p., 1770), 12.

16. Isaac Backus, *An Appeal to the Public for Religious Liberty* in McLoughlin, *Isaac Backus on Church, State, and Calvinism,* 311.

17. Backus, *Sovereign Grace,* 62.

18. See, for example, Isaac Backus, *The Doctrine of Particular Election and Final Perseverance* (Boston: n.p., 1789) in McLoughlin, 451.

19. Isaac Backus, *A Door Opened for Religious Liberty* (Boston: n.p., 1783) in McLoughlin, *Isaac Backus on Church, State, and Calvinism,* 432.

20. Isaac Backus, *Government and Liberty Described* (Boston: n.p., 1778) in McLoughlin, *Isaac Backus on Church, State, and Calvinism,* 351.

21. Backus, *A Door Opened,* 432.

22. Isaac Backus, *Policy as Well as Honesty Forbids the Use of Secular Force in Religious Affairs* (Boston: n.p., 1779) in McLoughlin, *Isaac Backus on Church, State, and Calvinism,* 376. Here Backus quotes John Locke, *A Letter Concerning Toleration,* 3d ed. (Boston: n.p., 1743), 17.

23. Isaac Backus, *A History of New England,* 2d ed. (Newton, Mass.: Backus Historical Society, 1871), 2:304.

24. Isaac Backus, *An Appeal to the Public for Religious Liberty* (Boston: n.p., 1773) in McLoughlin, *Isaac Backus on Church, State, and Calvinism,* 312.

25. Backus, *History,* 2:321.

26. Backus, *Policy as Well as Honesty,* 381.

27. Backus, *History,* 2:265.

28. Isaac Backus, *An Address to the Inhabitants of New England* (Boston: n.p., 1787) in McLoughlin, *Isaac Backus on Church, State, and Calvinism,* 446.

29. Backus, *History,* 1:373.

30. Ibid., 2:561.

31. Backus, *Seasonable Plea*, 12.

32. Backus, *Policy as Well as Honesty*, 375. Also see Backus, *Doctrine of Particular Election*, 468.

33. Backus, *Policy as Well as Honesty*, 375.

34. Backus, *History*, preface to vol. 3, 2:viii.

35. Isaac Backus, *A Letter to a Gentleman* (n.p., 1771), 5.

36. Ibid., 5-6, quoting from Locke, *A Letter on Toleration*.

37. Isaac Backus, *A Fish Caught in His Own Net* (Boston: n.p., 1768) in McLoughlin, *Isaac Backus on Church, State, and Calvinism*, 190-91.

38. Backus, *Policy as Well as Honesty*, 371.

39. Ibid., 374-75.

40. Isaac Backus, *The Kingdom of God Described by His Word* (Boston: n.p., 1792), 14.

41. Backus, *History*, 2:378.

42. Isaac Backus, *An Abridgment of the Church History of New England* (Boston: n.p., 1804), 245.

43. Backus, *History*, 1:361.

44. For a fuller discussion see Stanley J. Grenz, "Isaac Backus and Religious Liberty," *Foundations* 22:4 (1979): 352-60.

45. Isaac Backus, *The Testimony of the Two Witnesses* (Providence: n.p., 1786), 31.

46. This is documented in a quotation from the Separate leader, Elisha Paine. Backus, *History*, 2:100.

6

Andrew Fuller
Phil Roberts

Biography

Lowly his birth,
And though his manners rough—his aspect stern—
Th' observing eye must soon a DIAMOND discern![1]

Thus the ode *Carmen Flebile* described the roots and character of Andrew Fuller, the man who exercised the single greatest theological influence on English Particular Baptists in their pilgrimage to becoming a missionary people.

Fuller was born on February 5, 1754, in Wicken, Cambridgeshire, England. His father was a yeoman farmer, and both parents, from dissenting stock, were Baptists. Fuller was born when England was on the verge of becoming a vast world empire. He would live through the American conflict, and the French would be the constant enemy of England throughout his life. The rise of Napoleon, whose final defeat at Waterloo came the month after Fuller's death, caused evangelicals to believe he might be the beast of Revelation. A greater measure of prosperity and a slightly increasing life span were concomitants of the burgeoning agricultural revolution. Increasing world trade had introduced tea drinking, among other customs, into the average Englishman's life.

Philosophically and religiously, matters were fluid. Orthodoxy was being challenged by rationalism and empiricism. Many churchmen had tired of the religious wars and controversies of the 1600s. Arianism, Socinianism, and Unitarianism became respectively and increasingly popular and forceful as the century progressed. On the other hand, much of Anglicanism initially, and then after 1750 orthodox dissent itself, had been revived by the Methodist Revival under the influence of its leaders, the Calvinist George Whitefield (1714-70) and the Arminian John Wesley (1703-91).

In 1754 the Particular Baptists were as yet mostly untouched by the Revival. They were generally strict Dissenters, closed communionists and many of them were hyper or "high Calvinists." The appellation hyper or "high" meant that they were not merely Calvinists of the "five-point" variety, but that for them evangelism in an open and indiscriminate manner did a disservice to God's sovereignty. Baptists generally viewed themselves as the final outgrowth of the Reformation, the *ecclesia semper reformanda,* the manifestation of congregations ordered and governed only by the New Testament. They had yet to embrace the missionary mandate that would be such an essential element of their character in the nineteenth century.

Andrew Fuller was reared in a high Calvinistic context. He wrote that as a youth the preaching of his pastor "was not adapted to awaken my conscience" and seldom did he say anything to unbelievers.[2] Consequently his conversion was a protracted, troubled affair and mirrored the questions he would later forcefully address: May one apply directly to Christ for salvation without any certainty that he or she is elect? Should everyone be exhorted to believe in Christ?

A "warrant" or evidence of election was necessary, Fuller had been led to believe, before one could have confidence that God would accept any person for salvation. On one occasion, preservation from a dangerous situation ignited his hope that he might be a "favourite of heaven."[3] The habit of "lying, cursing and swearing," however, often left him in despair.[4]

Fuller's reading encouraged him to continue to seek Christ. John Bunyan's *The Pilgrim's Progress,* among other works, spoke to him about Christ's sufficiency to save,[5] but he was still not convinced "that any poor sinner had a warrant to believe in Christ."[6] Concern came and went, but he found no encouragement to trust Christ from his parents, church, or pastor. He was "like a man drowning, looking every way for help."[7]

Finally, the Bible was to provide the answer he needed. He read Job's resolution, "Though he slay me, yet will I trust in him." He read of Esther who entered the king's presence *"contrary to the law."* "Like her," he wrote, "I seemed reduced to extremities, impelled . . . to run all hazards, even though I should perish in the attempt."[8] Biblical proof texts and a fear of damnation drove Fuller to believe. He came to the point of complete trust—"I must—I will trust . . . my sinful . . . soul in his hands. In this way I continued above an hour, weeping and supplicating mercy for the Saviour's sake; . . . my guilt and fears were gradually . . . removed."[9]

In 1770 he was baptized and became a member of the Baptist church in Soham. He was made its pastor in May 1775 but still continued for several years in high Calvinism, not daring to "address an invitation to the unconverted to come to Jesus."[10] By 1781, however, having studied his Bible carefully, reread Bunyan, and made acquaintance with pastors John Sutcliff of Olney and Robert Hall of Arnesby, who in turn introduced him to the writings of Jonathan Edwards and other New England divines, Fuller changed his position. In that year he wrote a work advocating indiscriminate gospel preaching. Four years later he published it as *The Gospel of Christ Worthy of All Acceptation: or The Obligations of Men Fully to Credit, and Cordially to Approve, Whatever God Makes Known. Wherein is Considered the Nature of Faith in Christ, and the Duty of Those Where the Gospel Comes in That Matter.* In eighteenth-century style, its title described the contents and almost rivaled them in length. Although Fuller would write other pieces (the Sprinkle edition of his *Works* covers 2,419 pages), some dealing with the same issue, none would be so important as *The Gospel Worthy.*

Both high Calvinists and Arminians attacked this first piece. Other trea-

Andrew Fuller (1724-1806)

Photo courtesy of Southern Baptist Historical Library and Archives

tises, however, followed. They included *The Calvinistic and Socinian Systems Compared* (1793), *Socinianism Indefensible* (1797), *The Gospel Its Own Witness* (1799), *Letters to Mr. Vidler on the Doctrine of Universal Salvation* (1802), *Strictures on Sandemanianism* (1810), as well as a second edition of *The Gospel Worthy* (1801). In addition to these major pieces, he wrote and published numerous sermons, tracts, letters and book reviews appearing in, among others, both the *Baptist* and *Evangelical Magazines.*

His concern for evangelism and world missions went beyond theory because the work of his life was the organization, management, and support of the Baptist Missionary Society (hereafter the BMS).[11] Much of his missiological/soteriological thought and theology was worked out in the matrix of sending and supporting missionaries. Fuller attended the organizational meeting of the missionary society on October 2, 1792, and was elected its first secretary. He retained that position until his death and worked tirelessly on its behalf in fund-raising, promotion, and defense in the face of occasional political opposition.

Throughout his life, Fuller remained a pastor, serving two congregations—the church at Soham from 1775 to 1782 and one in Kettering from 1782 to his death.

The Kettering church never exceeded 150 members, although up to a thousand people attended worship in the last decade of Fuller's life.[12] While not a particularly eloquent or exciting preacher, (one friend said his "voice was heavy" and his speech was "deformed by colloquialisms") seemingly no one in his preaching had "greater warmth" or more "holy zeal" than Fuller.[13] As an evangelist he was, forgiving the pun, always desirous to practice what he preached, being often "occupied in village preaching" (i.e. evangelistic itinerations).[14] His gospel preaching was punctuated and concluded with forceful evangelistic appeals, if not in a twentieth-century altar-call style at least with a personal exhortation to belief and trust in Christ.[15]

In recognition of his theological contribution, even though he mastered no biblical languages, Princeton University, then the College of New Jersey, awarded him the D.D. in 1798, and Yale University followed with the same honor in 1805. He refused the Princeton degree, feeling himself intellectually inadequate for it, but accepted Yale's, sensing the same inadequacy, while never using the title.[16] Having earlier contracted an "affection [sic] of the lungs" Andrew Fuller died of tuberculosis on May 7, 1815. The assurance of salvation remained with him to the end. "I can go into eternity with composure," he wrote shortly before his death—"Come, Lord Jesus."[17]

Exposition

Unmov'd by clamor, unseduc'd to wrong
  Fuller the truth maintain'd;
Resolv'd, in consciousness of right, to stand—
  By fear and lure ungain'd!

(Carmen Flebile)

As was the case with every Baptist theologian of his day and earlier, Fuller developed his theology as an active pastor. His published work was the result of his preaching and counseling and was often shaped by the questions of his own as well as his congregation's experience. Additionally, due to his unusual intellectual curiosity, his commitment to Scripture and particularly its application to evangelism, and given the unknowns of his character, Fuller's theology work was primarily polemical. He was not a systematizer like John Gill but more a "Valiant-for-Truth." Controversy seemed to fuel his theological production even though he often tired of it and was quite interested in systematic theology.[18] This was true of his first major work *The Gospel of Christ Worthy of All Acceptation* (hereafter the *GWAA*) and much of that which was to follow.

Although having mainly sprung from English Congregationalism and with a debated measure of influence among Baptists, eighteenth-century high Calvinism had a pervasive influence on Fuller's life. Through the work of John Gill (1703-71), a London Baptist pastor, and perhaps more especially that of his neighbor John Brine (1703-65) the particularly important high-Calvinistic doctrine of eternal justification (the view that the elect were justified from eternity even before their conversion) was often utilized to justify excluding open invitations to believe the gospel. The high Calvinists believed that only people who evidenced signs of election, or a "warrant to believe," should be exhorted to put their faith and trust in Christ.

On the other hand, many English Particular Baptists were by the last quarter of the 1700s greatly under the theological influence of the evangelical Calvinism of the Methodist Revival. English Baptist Calvinism then was not a monolithic system with all of its emphases originating from John Calvin. Fuller's conversion to active and open evangelism was aided by the influence of his contemporaries—Robert Hall; John Ryland, Jr.; William Carey; and John Sutcliff—who had read the works of Jonathan Edwards and who admired the zeal of George Whitefield. Hall's father, in fact, Robert Hall, Sr., published *Help to Zion's Travellers,* a sermon advocating general evangelism, in 1781. He had also advised Fuller to read Edwards. Fuller's first full treatise, the *GWAA,* brought together the best of the ideas of evangelical Calvinism and served as its definitive apologetic in its conflict with its hyper-counterpart. The work served to justify identifying evangelical Calvinism in Baptist and Congregational ranks as "Fullerism."

The *GWAA* was issued in Northampton in 1785 and was comprised of 196 pages. It included an introductory first part with "the subject stated, defined and explained" with an "introduction on the importance of the subject."[19] For our purposes, part two is more important, because there Fuller lists six arguments, backed and supported primarily by biblical proof texts, to encourage open evangelism. They are: (1) Faith in Christ is commanded in the Bible of unconverted sinners; (2) Every person is bound to approve of what God reveals; (3) The gospel even as a message of grace, requires obedience; (4) Lack of faith in Christ is sin; (5) God will punish unbelief; and (6) As other spiritual disposition and exercises such as forgiveness, charity, and the like are required by biblical demands, so is faith a duty. He then answers objections, makes certain inferences from his propositions, and clarifies that he is not intending "to vindicate all the language that has been addressed" to the unconverted nor "all the principles" of those who do. Finally, he spends eleven pages clarifying the moral inability argument he adopted from Jonathan Edwards' *Treatise on the Freedom of the Will*. Simply put, it states that human unwillingness to believe stems from a perverted moral nature and not from any physical or natural incapacity, as high Calvinists often argued.

The *GWAA* touched off significant debate within Baptist ranks on both sides of the question. While his arguments may appear to be obvious to a twentieth-century observer, they, in fact, were directed straight at the logic of high Calvinism. William Button, pastor of Dean Street London, was the first who sought to refute it with *Remarks on a Treatise Entitled, The Gospel Worthy*. Button relied on a classically eighteenth-century high-Calvinistic line of argument: (1) Saving faith is of a unique and supernatural character and is distinct from general faith in God. It is that "which none ever had, or was . . . possible to have" except the elect; (2) Man does not have the natural or moral capacity for such faith (making exception with Fuller and Edward's inability argument); (3) God never requires what man cannot do in and of himself. The conclusion, in Button's opinion, is that faith should not be demanded of any person except the elect.[20]

Fuller was well aware of these arguments, having grown up with them and having addressed them in the *GWAA*. However, he replied to Button in 1787 with *A Defense of a Treatise Entitled, the GWAA*. Therein he reasserted that the theories of high Calvinism have been "assumed instead of being proved."[21] He sought then to demonstrate not only the rationale of a free offer of the gospel but its biblical nature as opposed to its opponents conjectures. Then he questioned Button's failure, as well as that of other high Calvinists, to exegete clearly biblical passages encouraging universal faith and obedience. "I ask . . . in what manner do Mr. B.'s sentiments lead him to EXPOUND SCRIPTURE? How has he expounded the second psalm and the sixth of Jeremiah? What has he made these passages to require more than eternal obedience?"[22]

This feature of the warfare between the two views carried over to the next year (1788) when another London Baptist pastor John Martin published *Thoughts on the Duty of Man Relative to Faith in Jesus Christ*. As a high Calvinist, he also attacked Fuller's arguments that in Scripture faith is commanded of unregenerated sinners and that every person is bound to receive what God reveals. He reworded but used Button's same arguments and logic with little appeal to Scripture.

Fuller responded to Martin with *Remarks on Mr. Martin's Publications*. He answered him tersely in only forty pages, perhaps revealing his impatience with the reiteration of old arguments. Fuller asserted that his views were reflective of contemporary Baptist leaders. He also restated his main position that Scripture calls all persons indiscriminately to faith in Christ, and therefore, they are obliged to respond. Martin answered in 1789 with part two of *Thoughts on the Duty of Man*. In it he repeated previous arguments, but by this time Fuller had lost interest in the debate and did not reply. His reticence did not deter Martin who produced a third part to which, once again, Fuller did not respond.

The Button and Martin writings revealed that among English Particular Baptists high Calvinism was not dead but had stagnated by the late 1780s, seemingly due to its inability to convince people that it was biblically justifiable. Fuller, confessedly a former high Calvinist, as well as other Baptists, had become disenchanted with the lack of adequate scriptural exegesis on the part of their stricter Calvinistic brethren.

Additionally, Fuller was challenged by Daniel Taylor (1738-1816) and Archibald McLean of Scotland (1753-1812). Taylor released his piece pseudonymously—"Philanthropos," or "lover of all men" under the title *Observations on the Rev. Andrew Fuller's Late Pamphlet Entitled the GWAA*. As the founder of the evangelical Arminian Baptist group the "New Connexion" of General Baptists, he had no argument with Fuller's general thesis that faith is the duty of all. He did disagree with Fuller's Calvinism. Taylor maintained that if God has "determined not to save" everyone "why should they seek after salvation?"[23] And he, ironically in agreement with the high Calvinists, argued that it is not morally justifiable that God should punish people for what the evangelical Calvinists themselves admit they are not able to do without the renewing power of the Holy Spirit (i.e., to believe in Christ).[24] Taylor continued that God, in universally offering salvation to all people, removed their inability to believe, implying that their inability was due only to their ignorance of the truth.

Fuller responded with his *A Defense of a Treatise Entitled the Gospel of Christ . . . With a Reply to Mr. Buttons Remarks and the Observations of Philanthropos* (1787). He argued that Taylor had failed to recognize the thorough perversity of sin in corrupting the will to believe. Grace alone can overcome that, Fuller maintained. According to Taylor, as Fuller saw it, God offers not grace to sinners but a natural ability to believe. Fuller wrote that natural ability already belongs to sinners in their rational faculties, in the fact that there are not natural impediments in the way of their belief, and because God has clearly manifested His love to them in the giving of His Son.[25] Also Fuller argued that Taylor ignored biblical texts which proved, in his view, that God assures the salvation of the elect in the giving of Jesus Christ. Given the moral inability of sinners, which could only be overcome by grace, it seemed absurd to him that people would be exhorted to believe unless the salvation of those who believed were guaranteed.[25] Fuller's concern then was with the maintenance of what he believed to be a clear scriptural principle— the election of God's people, one which also supported his Calvinism.

Taylor responded twice to Fuller although the latter seemingly ignored Taylor's further argumentation perhaps due to what he considered more pressing concerns.

Archibald McLean of the Sandemanians, a Scottish Baptist element which argued that saving faith is the simple intellectual acceptance of the revelation of the gospel, challenged Fuller that making faith anything more (i.e., trust and continuation in obedience—according to Fuller) hampered free invitations to belief. It seemed to him that it was asking people to seek a "warrant" for faith; something Fuller had struggled with in his own conversion, rather than to view faith as the simple intellectual acceptance of Christ's saving work. Fuller, however, chose to stick with his definition of faith that went beyond the intellectual and included at its root trust and reliance on Christ. Given the nature of faith and the depravity of man, Fuller maintained that conviction and regeneration must precede and accompany faith. McLean agreed with the primacy of regeneration but continued to reject Fuller's view of faith. Notably, neither Taylor nor McLean argued with Fuller on the principle of calling all, indiscriminately, to faith in Christ.

The issue of regeneration surfaced again in the course of Fuller's writings before 1800. In 1796, Abraham Booth (1734-1806), a London Baptist pastor at Prescott Street, former General Baptist, and now Particular Baptist, published *Glad Tidings to Perishing Sinners or, The Genuine Gospel a Complete Warrant for the Ungodly to Believe in Jesus*. His purpose was to argue in support of the free invitation of the gospel and to defend the doctrine of justification by faith alone, which he felt was threatened by an emphasis on regeneration as anterior to saving faith, a view synonymous with classic Calvinism. Regeneration was being made a prerequisite for indiscriminate evangelism, he felt, and possibly limited its universality. "The genuine gospel" he argued "is a complete warrant . . . to believe in Jesus; and that no degree of holiness, (i.e., regeneration), is necessary for that purpose."[27] Specifically, he was remonstrating against Fuller's the *GWAA* wherein Fuller had argued for the primacy of regeneration, or efficacious conviction, before repentance and public faith.

Booth was answered directly by Thomas Scott (1747-1821), evangelical vicar of Olney, in his *Warrant and Nature of Faith Considered* (1718), in which he supported the necessity of regeneration for belief. Consequently Booth, in 1800, revised and reissued *Glad Tidings* in which he lengthened his argument by thirty-four pages. Therein he accused Fuller's position of promulgating preparationism and hindering the gospel's free call. Ironically, Fuller as the champion of evangelical Calvinism was now being charged with hindering the gospel. Fuller reviewed Booth's new edition but saved the weight of his argument for a second edition of the *GWAA* in 1801.

In the 1801 edition, Fuller added an appendix "on the question whether the existence of a holy disposition of heart be necessary to believing." Its arguments were aimed straight at Archibald McLean as well as Abraham Booth. Cogently, Fuller presented the case that true belief foregoes "all claim and expectation of favour on the ground of our own deservings" and that "the only hope which remains for us is in the free mercy of God through Jesus Christ." He expressed surprise that anyone would believe that a faith "which implies contrition" should be supposed to oppose the true gospel.[28] While Fuller could hold the tension of his beliefs between the mandate to evangelize everyone and the primacy of regeneration in the *ordo salutis,*

McLean and Booth felt they could not. They also sensed that Fuller's views might hamper evangelism. Interestingly, the Fuller-Booth, McLean, and Taylor controversies demonstrated the triumph of evangelical Calvinism because the issue was no longer a question of whether or not to offer the gospel but was an attempt to remove all hindrances to such ministry.

In a later shorter work "The Nature of Regeneration," Fuller was reticent on the *modus* of the Holy Spirit's operation in regeneration but not its nature.[29] Sin is so terrible in the extent and nature of its influence—exercised primarily on the heart and character—and is total in its ability to destroy proper spiritual judgment. Therefore, regeneration (i.e., conviction and the renewal of the heart) is and must remain absolutely primary in God's order of salvation.

It must be emphasized then that not only was Fuller concerned with high Calvinism and its deadening influence on missions but also with intellectual believism, easy believism, or, in eighteenth-century nomenclature, Sandemanianism. The flowering of his work in this area was his 1810 publication of *Strictures on Sandemanianism, In Twelve Letters To A Friend*. He dealt in greater detail with the necessity of "regeneration" for belief, of the deceptive nature of unbelief, of the shallowness of "mere acceptance of Gospel facts" as being the "faith of devils," of the nature of justification resting in our union and identity with Christ—the fruit of faith—and not the reward of it, and of the danger of allowing the primacy of regeneration, as he saw it, to deter or restrict evangelism.[30]

For the twentieth-century evangelical, the regeneration debate falls into seemingly two parts with a "split decision" going to Andrew Fuller. Abraham Booth's argument raises the important question of nomenclature. Part of Booth's concern, it seems, focuses on whether it is proper to employ the term "regenerate" except for persons who have already put their faith in Jesus Christ. Does it not create confusion to do otherwise? In addition, Fuller's clear stance for the necessity of genuine conviction and the efficacious work of the Holy Spirit in conversion, reminds us of the spiritual nature of salvation. True belief is the fruit of not mere persuasion but genuine regeneration. He held this belief in tension with the indelible command of Scripture for believers to evangelize in a positive and forceful manner—"calling all men everywhere to repent."

The important note regarding Fuller's Calvinistic soteriology was its intensely practical and evangelical nature based upon biblical exegesis. For instance, when discussing the issue of election, he was desirous to have it understood practically. It was to be applied "to declare the source of salvation to be mere grace . . . to cut off all hopes of acceptance with God by works of any kind"; to account for the unbelief of the greater part of the Jewish nation, "without excusing them in it"—in regards to Romans 9; and "to show the certain success of Christ's undertaking as it were in defiance of unbelievers."[31]

His soteriology was intensely evangelical and evangelistic—desiring always to support the *Missio Dei*. He summarized it in seven points:

(1) "There is no way of obtaining eternal life but by Jesus Christ"; (2) "They that enjoy eternal life must come to Christ for it"; (3) "It is the revealed will of Christ that everyone who hears the gospel should come to him for life"; (4) "The depravity of human nature is such that no man, of his own accord, will come to Christ for life"; (5) "The degree of this depravity is such that, . . . men cannot come to Christ for life"; (6) "A conviction of the righteous of God's government, of the . . . goodness of his law . . . our lost condition by nature . . . is necessary in order to our coming to Christ"; and (7) "There is absolute necessity of a special Divine agency in order to our coming to Christ."[32] The first three points establish Fuller clearly as evangelical, and they also motivated him to be evangelistic. The next four place him firmly in the Calvinistic camp. His avoidance of excessive Calvinistic jargon and high-Calvinistic convictions, however, makes him less than extreme. Point 6 sets him in opposition to antinomianism.

His uncompromising advocacy of the exclusiveness of salvation through Christ alone led him into controversy with the universalist William Vidler (1758-1816). Vidler was a former Particular Baptist who had been attracted to universalism by what he felt to be the harshness of the evangelical doctrine of eternal punishment. He joined a small, but growing, number of universalist congregations in the last quarter of the eighteenth century.[33]

Vidler published *God's Love to His Creatures asserted and vindicated* in 1799. It was released partly in response to a series of published letters by Fuller to Vidler which appeared in the *Evangelical Magazine* and the *Universalist's Miscellany,* beginning in 1795. The twelve letters were collected and published in 1802 under the title *Letters to Mr. Vidler, on the Doctrine of Universal Salvation*. They represent clear evangelical argument on the issue.

In response to Vidler's view that damnation calls into question both God's mercy and justice, Fuller maintained that universalism obscures and distorts the meaning of the cross. In Vidler's view, cleansing came through temporary punishment for sin in perdition. This concept of cleansing undermined Christ's atoning death.[34] Universalism also encouraged unbelievers to continue in their sin, believing that punishment is not eternal. More importantly, perhaps, Fuller spent most of his time exposing Vidler's exegetical and philological weaknesses. In much the caustic style of the period, he surmised, "I never recollect to have seen so much violence done to the word of God in so small a compass. According to your scheme, all things work together for good to them that love not God, as well as to them that love him."[35] Fuller's own exegesis reveals expert and insightful handling of Scripture.

Vidler counterattacked in his *Letters to Mr. Fuller on the Universal Restoration* (1803). Fuller did not respond.

These pieces, as well as his well-known polemics against Deism and Socinianism, clearly established Fuller as an important apologist not just for Calvinism, which later in his life bore proportionately much less of his attention, but for the gospel in broader and more evangelical terms.[36]

Abraham Booth, however, felt that by 1801 Fuller had slipped his Calvinistic moorings. With the release that year of a new edition of the *GWAA*

Fuller had seemingly adopted a less strict view of particular redemption than evidenced in the first edition. In the period between the two editions, Fuller had read extensively many of the New England divines and had corresponded with several of them—Jonathan Edwards the younger, Joseph Bellamy, Samuel Hopkins, and Timothy Dwight. Their view of the atonement tended to reflect the thought of Hugo Grotius, a sixteenth-century Dutch divine who had postulated the moral-government view of the cross. This theory stressed God's position as "moral governor of the universe" and not so much as offended Deity, and emphasized His love for order, peace, and forgiveness rather than on His wrath against individual sin. This view tended toward a more general and a less-personalized soteriology.[37]

The New England position militated against that propounded by Tobias Crisp, John Gill, and other high Calvinists, which asserted that Christ had the actual sin of the elect imputed to Him on the cross and that He was punished proportionately to the amount of their sin.[38] In the 1801 version of the *GWAA*, Fuller strongly suggested that interpretation might support a restricted offer of the gospel:

> If the atonement of Christ were considered as the literal payment of a debt . . . it might be inconsistent with indefinite invitations . . . if the atonement of Christ proceed on the principle . . . of moral justice . . . no such inconsistency can justly be ascribed to it.[39]

Fuller was apparently wrong if he thought that Booth's soteriology would significantly hamper Booth's evangelism; while Booth charged Fuller with denying "that Christ died as a substitute," a serious accusation against a self-confessed strict Calvinist.[40] Subsequent publication demonstrates that Fuller rejected any merely symbolic view of the atonement; he countered that Christ suffered indeed as a substitute for sinners while not being made a "sinner" or being made culpable of their sins, a direction in which high Calvinism and antinomianism tended. Additionally, he adopted, if not wholly at least partially, some New England thought in arguing that the atonement was the "great end of moral government" and was in itself "not a pecuniary, but a moral ransom."[41] In so doing, however, it is clear that his goal was to protect the free offer of the gospel while upholding the uniqueness and substitutionary nature of Christ's death on the cross.

Although Fuller was principally concerned with soteriological issues, as has been noted, other issues occupied his thinking as well. He believed firmly in congregational church order and strict discipline and oversight of members in both morals and doctrine; he argued vehemently for believer's baptism as well as for closed communion. Momentum for a relaxation of communion practice to admit nonbaptized members increased by the close of the eighteenth century, but Fuller maintained that to do so was an inversion of the New Testament order of baptism first and then the Lord's Supper. His publication of *The Discipline of the Primitive Churches Illustrated and Enforced* in 1799 made his position clear.[42] Through his influence, as well, missionaries with the BMS were required to practice strict or closed communion.

In his final work before his death, he delved into a new area of theological discourse—eschatology. As late as 1799 he wrote to William Carey—"I have never been deeply versed in prophecies."[43] But he gave himself more completely to its study over the next fifteen years and published *Expository Discourses on the Apocalypse* in 1815. Therein he revealed his adherence to "Latter-Day-Glory" postmillennialism. He had accepted the popular contemporary view first widely promulgated by Jonathan Edwards, and held by Carey as well, that the eighteenth-century revivals and awakenings, the subsequent reformation of society, the rise of missionary activity, and the general revitalization of the church were the prolegomena to Christ's reign upon the earth to be expressed through the conquest of the church. He accepted a historicist view of the Apocalypse, believing along with Edwards that history was then in the period of the sixth vial (cf. Rev. 16:12-16), the period of the overthrow of the temporal power of Antichrist and the introduction to the final vial when God's truth and morality will exercise "its spiritual dominion, or the hold which it has on the minds of men."[44] His eschatology, however unpopular it might be at present, was nonetheless his because he believed it was the accurate biblical position which in turn went the furthest to encourage the evangelization of the world.

Evaluation

Finally what conclusions may be drawn from the theology of Andrew Fuller? First, it is clear that his main work and contribution was soteriological, with emphases on its practical application for evangelism and missions. While some thinkers would tend to lead us to think that Fuller combated Calvinism generally, it must be noted that his concern was to oppose high Calvinism and to promote a thoroughly evangelistic and evangelical form of that theology.

In so doing, Fuller manifested a willingness to deal with the intricate issues of conversion and salvation that today are so often treated glibly and superficially. The two enemies in the camp, so to speak, of evangelical Calvinism were in his view an antimissionary, imbalanced hyper-Calvinism and a mechanical, rationalistic Sandemanianism. In taking the stand that he did, he demonstrated the value of a thoughtful, biblical theology of conversion as an incentive for evangelism and as a check to mental assent alone as being synonymous with genuine repentance and faith.

For most of the nineteenth-century, evangelical Calvinism would typify the theological position of the vast majority of English and American Baptists, including those who would constitute the Southern Baptist Convention (1845). Andrew Fuller's work, particularly the *Gospel Worthy of All Acceptation,* made perhaps the most notable contribution towards providing a missionary theology and incentive for world evangelism in the midst of a people both Calvinistic and church oriented. He helped to link the earlier Baptists, whose chief concern was the establishment of ideal New Testament congregations, with those in the nineteenth century driven to make the gospel known worldwide. His contribution helped to guarantee that many of the leading Baptists of the 1800s would typify fervent evangelism and world missions. Charles Spurgeon and J. P. Boyce would be fervent evangelical Calvinists rather than stricter and more scholastic Calvinists typical of Fuller's predecessors at Kettering and London pastors like John Gill and John Brine.

Notably as well, Fuller built his theology on scriptural grounds. It was the Bible and mainly the Bible that proved decisive in his conversion. While friends and other theologians, especially Jonathan Edwards, encouraged him toward an evangelical/evangelistic Calvinism, their influence, it seems, was measured only insofar as Fuller felt them to be faithful to Scripture itself. He wrote several short apologies on the necessity of revelation for divine truth and on the Bible as being the written revelation of God passed on to men, the only source of complete and reliable theology. While eschewing mechanical dictation, he affirmed that at the least biblical inspiration meant for him "a Divine superintendence, preserving him [the biblical writer] from error, and from other defects and faults, to which ordinary historians are subject."[45] His faithfulness to Scripture kept him firmly in the Baptist tradition and contributed to the continuum of Baptist concern with biblical theology.

Additionally, his concern for truth and his view that the preservation of theological and biblical veracity was vital to evangelical missions led him to the conviction that controversy should not be eschewed but initiated if the truth was in danger of dilution or perversion. He wrote, "If you love Christ, you will root up those principles which degrade his dignity and set aside his atonement."[46] Without his courage and doctrinal integrity in the face of what he considered to be theological aberrations, the Baptist mission movement might have been stillborn. Theological truth is often preserved and balance achieved only in the crucible of conflict and controversy, a lesson Fuller believed and which many timid twentieth-century Christians should well learn. He believed, additionally, that confessions and creeds were useful to protect doctrinal integrity. While all truth was in Scripture, he argued that it was not wrong "for a number of individuals, who agree in their judgments [on biblical doctrines], to express that agreement in explicit terms, and consider themselves as bound to walk by the same rule."[47]

For him the truth was the fuel and one's personal relationship to God through Christ the flame of the fire of vital biblical Christianity.

For Fuller correct doctrine and theology were not the niceties of the faith but indispensable building blocks of the kingdom of God. In his understanding that meant a Chalcedonian Christology, evangelical Calvinism, and a Baptist church order. Each of these was to be expressed with Christian love and applied practically to world evangelization and mission.

Bibliography

Works by Fuller

An Account of the Particular Baptist Society (used for propagating the gospel among the heathen). 1792.

An Address to the Baptist Churches of the Northamptonshire Association. Northampton: n.p., 1818.

The Admission of Unbaptized Persons to the Lord's Supper, inconsistent with the New Testament, A Letter, published by Dr. W. Newman. London: n.p., 1815.

Antinomianism Contrasted with the Religion Taught and Exemplified in the Holy Scriptures. 2d ed. Bristol: n.p., 1817.

An Apology for the Late Christian Mission to India. New York: American Tract Society, 1854.

The Backslider; or, an Enquiry into the Nature, Symptoms, and Effects of Religious Declension, with the Means of Recovery. Philadelphia: American Baptist Publication Society, 1856.

"The Blessedness of the Dead Who Die in the Lord" (funeral sermon for Beeby Wallis). London: n.p., 1792.

Calvinistic and Socinian Systems compared. Philadelphia: 1796.

Christian Patriotism. A Discourse. Demstable: n.p., 1803.

A Collection of Sermons and Tractates, 2 vols. 1784-1817, London, n.d.

A Collection of Tracts and Sermons, 2 vols. Clipstone: n.p., 1801.

The Complete Works of Andrew Fuller. London: n.p., 1841.

The Complete Works of Andrew Fuller, 3 vols. Sprinkle edition with preface by Dr. Tom Nettles, Harrisonburg, Virginia, 1988.

The Complete Works of Andrew Fuller, 8 vols. London: n.p., 1824.

The Complete Works of the Rev. Andrew Fuller, 5 vols. With a memoir of his life by Andrew G. Fuller. 3 vols. Philadelphia: n.p., 1852.

A Defence of a Treatise entitled the Gospel of Christ worthy of all Acceptation. With a reply to Mr. Button's Remarks and the observations of Philanthropos. Philadelphia: n.p., 1810.

"Dialogues, Letters and Essays on Various Subjects." Harford: n.p., 1820.

The Discipline of the Primitive Churches Illustrated and Enforced. New York: n.p., 1825.

The Christian Doctrine of Rewards. Boston: n.p., 1802.

An Essay on Truth. Boston: n.p., 1806.

"The Excellence and Utility of the Grace of Hope" (circular letter of the Northamptonshire Association). Northampton: n.p., 1782.

Expository Discourses on the Apocalypse. Kettering: n.p., 1815.

Expository Discourses on the Book of Genesis. London: n.p., 1836.

Expository Remarks on the Discipline of the Primitive Church. Providence: n.p., 1820.

God's Approbation of Our Labours Necessary to the Hope of Success. Boston: n.p., 1802.

The Gospel of Christ Worthy of All Acceptation. Boston: n.p., 1846.

The Gospel its own Witness. Philadelphia: n.p., 1803.

The Great Question Answered. London: n.p., 1803.

The Harmony of Scripture. London: n.p., 1817.

Hints to Ministers and Churches. London: n.p., 1826.

The Importance of a Deep and Intimate Knowledge of Divine Truth. London: n.p., 1796.

An Inquiry into the Nature, Symptoms, and Effects of Religions Declension, with the Means of Recovery (circular letter). Philadelphia: n.p., 1832.

Jesus the True Messiah. London: n.p., 1811.

"Joy in God" (circular letter). Northampton: n.p., 1793.

Letters to Mr. Vidler on the Doctrine of Universal Salvation. Ohio: n.p., 1832.

Memoirs of Pearce. 4th ed. London: n.p., 1816.

Miscellaneous Pieces on various religious Subjects. London: n.p., 1826.

Missionary Correspondence: Extracts of Letters from Samuel Pearce and John Thomas. London: n.p., 1814.

"Moral and Positive Obedience" (circular letter). Spalding: n.p., 1807.

A Narrative of Facts relative to a late occurrence in the Country of Cambridge, in Answer to a Statement contained in a Unitarian Publication called 'The Monthly Repository.' London: n.p., 1810.

The Nature and Importance of Walking by Faith. Boston: n.p., 1802.

"Open Communion Unscriptural: A Letter to the Rev. William Ward." London: n.p., 1824.

"Oration Delivered at the Funeral of the Rev. Robert Hall, Sr." London: n.p., 1791.

"The Pastor's Address to His Christian Hearers, Entreating Their Assistance in Promoting the Interest of Christ." Leicester: n.p., 1806.

The Pernicious Influence of Delay in religious Concerns (a sermon at Clipstone). Clipstone: n.p., 1791.

The Practical Uses of Christian Baptism. Montpelier, Vt.: n.p., 1814.

The Principal Works and Remains of the Rev. Andrew Fuller (with a New Memoir by His Son the Rev. Andrew G. Fuller). London: n.p., 1864.

The Principles and Prospects of a Servant of Christ (a sermon preached at the funeral of the Rev. John Sutcliff). Kettering: n.p., 1814.

The Reality and Efficacy of Divine Grace; by Agnostos. London: n.p., n.d.

"On Religious Declension: as an Inquiry into Its Nature, Symptoms, and Effects, With the Means of Recovery." London: n.p., n.d.

Remarks on Mr. Martin's Publication entitled "Thoughts on the Duty of Man relative to Faith in Jesus Christ." London: n.p., 1789.

Remarks on the state of Baptist churches in Ireland after his trip in 1804. London: n.p., 1804.

Salvation Through a Mediator Consistent with Sober Reason. London: n.p., n.d.

"A Sermon Delivered at the Ordination of Thomas Morgan." Birmingham, n.p., 1802.

"The Situation of the Widows and Orphans of Christian Ministers" (circular letter). Northampton: n.p., 1815.

Socinianism Indefensible on the Ground of its Moral Tendency. London: n.p., 1797.

A Statement of the Committee of Shacklewell. 1807.

Strictures on Sandemanianism. New York: n.p., 1812.

"The Substance of Two Discourses Delivered at the Settlement of the Rev. Robert Fawkner at Thorn in Bedfordshire." London: n.p., 1787.

"Substance of the Charge Delivered to the Missionaries at the Parting Meeting at Leicester." Clipstone: n.p., 1793.

Summary of the Principal Evidences for the Truth, and Divine Origin of the Christian Revelation. New York: n.p., 1801.

"Thoughts on Open Communion in a Letter from the late Rev. Andrew Fuller to the Rev. William Ward." London: n.p., 1817.

"A Vindication of Protestant Dissent" (from the charges of the Rev. Thomas Robinson) Vicar of St. Mary's. Leicester: n.p., 1804.

Fuller, Andrew, and Sutcliff, John. *"Two Discourses delivered at a Meeting of Ministers at Clipstone"* (April 27, 1791). London: n.p., 1791.

Works About Fuller

Anonymous. *Carmen Flebile: Or, An Ode, to the Memory of the late Andrew Fuller.* London: n.p., 1815.

Clipsham, E. P. "Andrew Fuller and Fullerism: a Study in Evangelical Calvinism," *The Baptist Quarterly,* vol. 20, 1963-64.

_____. "Andrew Fuller's Doctrine of Salvation," B.D. thesis, Oxford University, 1971.

Duncan, Pope A., Sr. "The influence of Andrew Fuller on Calvinism," Th.D. thesis, The Southern Baptist Theological Seminary, 1917.

Eddins, John W., Jr. "Andrew Fuller's theology of grace," Th.D. thesis, The Southern Baptist Theological Seminary, 1957.

Fuller, Andrew G. *Andrew Fuller,* London: n.p., 1882.

_____. *The Complete Works of the Rev. Andrew Fuller in one volume: with a Memoir of His Life.* London: n.p., 1841. This memoir also appears in the third and fifth volume edition of Fuller's *Works.*

Fuller, T. E. *A Memoir of the Life and Writings of Andrew Fuller.* London: n.p., 1863.

Ivimey, Joseph. *The Perpetual Intercession of Christ for His Church; A Source of Consolation Under The Loss of Useful Ministers. A Sermon To The Memory of the late Rev. Andrew Fuller*. London: n.p., 1815.

Keown, Harlice E. "The Preaching of Andrew Fuller," Th.M. thesis, The Southern Baptist Theological Seminary, 1957.

Kirkby, A. H. "Andrew Fuller—Evangelical Calvinist," *Baptist Quarterly* 15 (1953-54).

_____. "The Theology of Andrew Fuller and Its Relation to Calvinism," Ph.D. thesis, University of Edinburgh, 1956.

Laws, Gilbert. *Andrew Fuller, Pastor, Theologian, Ropeholder*. London: n.p., 1942.

Morris, J. W. *Memoirs of the Life and Writings of the Rev. Andrew Fuller*. London: n.p., 1826.

Nelson, Thomas. *The Gospel Its Own Witness, with a Life of the Author*. Edinburgh: n.p., 1830.

Newman, William. *Reflections on the Fall of a Great Man. A Sermon Occasioned by the Death of the Rev. Andrew Fuller*. London: n.p., 1815.

Ryland, John. *The Work of Faith, the Labour of Love, and the Patience of Hope, illustrated; in the Life and Death of the Rev. Andrew Fuller*. London: n.p., 1818.

Notes

1. Quoted from the anonymous work *Carmen Flebile: or an Ode to the Memory of the late Reverend Andrew Fuller of Kettering, Who Departed this Life, Much and Justly Lamented May 7, 1815* (London: n.p., 1815).

2. Andrew Fuller, *Andrew Fuller* (London: n.p., 1882), 11.

3. Andrew Fuller, *The Gospel Its Own Witness, with a Life of the Author by Thomas Nelson* (Edinburgh: n.p., 1830), xlv-xlvi.

4. Andrew Fuller, *The Complete Works of the Rev. Andrew Fuller: with a Memoir of His Life by Andrew Gunton Fuller*, ed. Joseph Belcher, 3d ed. in three vols., (reprinted by Sprinkle Publications, Harrisonburg, Va., 1988), 1:2. Hereafter Fuller, *Complete Works*.

5. Ibid., 3.

6. John Ryland, *The Work of Faith, the Labour of Love, and the Patience of Hope, illustrated; in the Life and Death of the Rev. Andrew Fuller*, 2d ed. (London: n.p., 1818), 18.

7. Fuller, *Complete Works*, 1:5.

8. Ibid.

9. Ibid., 1:6.

10. Andrew Fuller, personal correspondence to Dr. Stuart, Liverpool, February 1815. Fuller Correspondence—Angus Library, Regent's Park College, Oxford, England.

11. William Newman in *Reflections on the Fall of a Great Man. A Sermon Occasioned by the Death of the Rev. Andrew Fuller* (London: n.p., 1815), wrote that the work of the mission was "always in his head, always in his heart, always in his hands," 13.

12. J. W. Morris, *Memoirs of the Life and Writings of the Rev. Andrew Fuller* (London: n.p., 1826), 90.

13. Ibid.

14. Ibid., 49.

15. For examples of his evangelistic preaching see his *Works* in 3 vols., Sprinkle edition—1:236-37, 265-66, 298-300, 421, 444, 453, and 471-72.

16. See Gilbert Laws, *Andrew Fuller, Pastor, Theologian, Ropeholder* (London: n.p., 1942), 96. Fuller felt that there should be no distinctive titles among Christian brethren.

17. Newman, *Reflections,* 21.

18. See, for instance, his "Letters on Systematic Divinity," *Works*—Sprinkle edition 1:684-711.

19. The *GWAA* (Northampton: n.p., 1785), III.

20. See Button's *Remarks on a Treatise,* 1785, 15-19, 76 *ff,* 87 *ff.,* 94 *ff.*

21. Fuller, *A Defense of a Treatise Entitled The GWAA,* 15.

22. Ibid., 87.

23. Dan Taylor, *Observations on the Rev. Andrew Fuller's late Pamphlet, entitled The Gospel of Christ Worthy of All Acceptation, In Nine letters to a Friend* (London: n.p., 1786), 49.

24. Ibid., 57.

25. Fuller, *Complete Works,* 1:459-83.

26. Ibid., 1:483-511.

27. Booth, *Glad Tidings* (London: n.p., 1796), 2.

28. Fuller, *Works,* Sprinkle edition 2:407.

29. Ibid., 3:776-79.

30. Ibid., 3:561-646.

31. Ibid., 3:808-09.

32. Ibid., 1:667-69.

33. See Geoffrey Rowell, "The Origins and History of Universalist Societies in Britain, 1750-1850," *Journal of Ecclesiastical History* (1971): 39-55.

34. Fuller, *Works,* Sprinkle edition, 2:301-04.

35. Ibid., 304.

36. His anti-Deistic and Socinian polemics included *The Calvinistic and Socinian Systems Compared* (1793), *Socinianism Indefensible* (1797), *The Gospel its own Witness* (1799). They will not be considered here as they were not primarily theological treatises but attempts to demonstrate the ethical superiority of Calvinism versus Socinianism and Deism.

37. F. H. Foster, *A Genetic History of the New England Theology* (Chicago: n.p., 1907), 114 *ff,* 199 *ff.* See also Joseph A. Conforti, *Samuel Hopkins and the New Divinity Movement* (Grand Rapids, Mich.: Wm. B. Eerdmans, 1981), 159-74.

38. This was the view expounded in Crisp's *Christ Alone Exalted,* first published in 1643 and republished in 1691, under the aegis of Hanserd Knollys. It was reissued in 1755 by John Gill. Fuller identified this view as "Crispianism," *Works* (1818), 2:449-51.

39. Fuller, *The Gospel Worthy* (1801) in *Works* (1841), 1:170-71.

40. Ibid., 317.

41. Fuller, *Works,* Sprinkle edition, 2:81.

42. See as well the collection of his "Essays, Letters, etc., on Ecclesiastical Policy" in volume 3 of the Sprinkle edition of his works. He expressed opinion there of

everything from the state of dissenting discipline to his thoughts on singing and the use of instrumental music in Christian worship.

43. Personal correspondence housed at the Angus Library, Regent's Park College, Oxford University. See the letter to Carey dated April 18, 1799.

44. Ibid., and Fuller, *Works* (1841), 470.

45. Fuller, *Works,* Sprinkle edition, 1:699.

46. See his article on "Creeds and Subscriptions," Ibid., 3:449-51.

47. Ibid., 487. For additional perspective see 3:335, 487, 490. Fuller always advocated that theological disagreement, however, must be handled only in an attitude of Christian love.

7

Richard Furman

Thomas J. Nettles

Richard Furman was known for "exemplary piety and holy living." In his preaching, "He intermingled doctrine and practice, experimental religion and pathetic appeal."[1] Furman was a Southern embodiment of the best of Puritanism. Piety and intellect formed a unit; doctrine, by its nature, demanded application; and application had no focus or relevance unless it was doctrinal.

Biography

Richard Furman was born to Wood and Rachel Furman on October 9, 1755, in Esopus, New York. On his father's side, he was five generations removed from the Puritan stock which originally settled Massachusetts Bay under Governor John Winthrop. John Firmin, a passenger on the *Arbella,* was one of the original settlers of Watertown. Richard Furman's paternal grandmother, Sarah Wood, descended from Jonathan Wright, who fought in the Puritan revolution in Cromwell's army.[2] This staunch Puritan background did not prevent Wood Furman from returning to the Anglican fold.

While Richard was still an infant, the family moved to South Carolina to the High Hills, an untamed frontier settlement in Central South Carolina in Saint Mark's Parish. One Baptist preacher, Jeremiah Dargan, called this country "a wild, wild place, a wicked, wicked, neighborhood." Wood Furman soon moved his family to the more civilized Saint Thomas Parish, where he served as a schoolmaster in a school sponsored by the parish vestry and financed from the will of Richard Beresford. After five years he moved to Daniel's Island, and then in 1770, after approximately nine more years, he moved back to the High Hills, by this time much more civilized, populated, governed, and even churched.[3]

Revival of the Separate Baptist variety had just begun in the High Hills under the preaching of Joseph Reese. The Furmans attended his services late in 1771. After having heard Reese preach the Edwardsian conversionism of the Separate Baptists and the believer's baptism of the Baptists, Richard Furman set out to study these issues for himself. Other theological matters also gained his attention as he studied sin, justification, atonement, and grace. He became convinced that the system taught by Reese was the system taught in the Bible. His heart, however, still resisted. Furman came under deep conviction, became overwhelmed by a "sense of guilt and unworthiness"[4] and eventually came as "a sinner willing to accept the free grace of the Gospel."[5]

Richard Furman (1755-1825)

Photo courtesy of Southern Baptist Historical Library and Archives

Before his baptism he was questioned thoroughly by Joseph Reese. His answers, clear and thorough, became the means for the conversion of his mother. They were baptized together by Reese.[6]

After a period of isolation for study of the Scriptures, Furman began witnessing to family, friends, and servants. Also, he became an exhorter. Robert Baker states, "Visiting ministers knew that after they had preached at this infant church, they could call upon young Furman to exhort the congregation to faithfulness in the Christian walk."[7] His peers mocked and ridiculed him. Cathcart's *Encyclopedia* records, "Crowds flocked to hear the boy preacher, and his precocious intellect and profound piety produced a deep impression on those who heard him." In May 1774, after preaching for two years at the High Hills church and engaging in extensive itinerant evangelistic work, he was ordained to the gospel ministry.

Reverends Evan Pugh and Joseph Reese came from their respective churches to participate in the ceremony. Six months later, the church in which he had already preached for two years called him as pastor. During 1774 Furman met Oliver Hart, pastor of the Charleston church, and John Gano, from the Philadelphia Association. He eventually developed close relationships with these men, respecting them highly and gaining much from their ministries. The possible nature of their influence on Furman will be mentioned later.

Furman showed himself a capable minister though only nineteen years old. His zeal for preaching gave him an effective popularity at High Hills and sent him on various preaching missions throughout South Carolina and even into Virginia.

His activities for the cause of independence in the Revolutionary War created great sympathy for the revolutionary government and converted many Tories to the effort for freedom. With the fall of Charleston in 1780, he was forced to move into territory still controlled by the United States. He returned in 1782, having spent the intervening time in North Carolina. He was recognized as a great patriot for the remainder of his life. On February 22, 1800, he preached before the American Revolution Society and the State Society of Cincinnati, a sermon occasioned by the death of George Washington, entitled "Humble Submission to Divine Sovereignty the Duty of a Bereaved Nation." On July 4, 1802, he preached "America's Deliverance and Duty" again before the State Society of Cincinnati. In this he affirmed that the American Revolution was effected, not merely by the permission, but by the special agency of God and contended that, at that time, "the body of our people were Christians." In general, he argued, the people were committed to the righteous providence, clear revelation, gracious redemption, and just judgment of God.[8] Furman could easily have been describing himself when he characterized the clergy's contribution to the demands of the Revolution.

> [T]he clergy, though acting in an humbler, did not render a less essential service to the national interests; by inculcating those sentiments, setting those examples, and taking that lead in religion, which inspired our citizens with zeal in the cause of liberty; formed their minds into a suitable temper for

receiving the Divine blessing, and rendered them, in the expectation of it, courageous to meet the dangers they had to encounter.[9]

In 1787, after going through a three-year struggle with the decision, Furman accepted a call to First Baptist Church in Charleston, South Carolina. He found the church greatly weakened by the war and distracted by internal problems. Thirty-seven years later, he left it strong and united.

Furman's influence in virtually every area of life expanded greatly from this time. Furman was a well-known name and a revered influence in Baptist life in America and England. David Benedict records, "I do not know of any one in the Baptist ranks, at that time, who had a higher reputation among the American Baptists for wisdom in counsel, and a skill in management, in all the affairs of the denomination."[10] Cathcart's *Encyclopedia* says, "Probably no minister of any denomination has ever exerted a wider, more varied, or more beneficient influence."[11]

Furman served as moderator of the Charleston Association for more than twenty-five years. His constant insistence on ministerial education led the association to form a General Committee of which Furman was president for thirty-four years. This committee collected and administered funds to give educational aid to young men preparing for the ministry. Furman's arguments for ministerial education, built on the principle of *sola scriptura* and its implications, undergirded the foundation of Columbian College, Furman University, Mercer University, and The Southern Baptist Theological Seminary.

When the Baptist Convention of South Carolina was formed in 1821, the first state convention in Baptist life, Furman was its chief advocate. He served as its president four years. It bore the marks of his concerns as it set as objects the "increase of Evangelical and useful knowledge, and of vital, practical religion." In addition organizers urged the "promotion of religious Education, and particularly that of indigent, pious young men, designed for the Gospel Ministry." Missions, Sunday School, and family education gained attention also.[12]

In 1814 he was unanimously elected first president of the Triennial Convention and was reelected in 1817. Through his influence the Convention almost became a denominational structure. In 1817 it added ministerial education and home missions to foreign missions as its objectives. Furman eventually opposed the venture into education pursued by the General Missionary Convention because he felt that the project arose too rapidly and without enough general information and support.

Furman's death came August 25, 1825. Baker remarks, "Eulogies were delivered in Baptist Zion when this great man fell, but his life exceeded all of them in eloquence."[13]

Exposition

Doctrinal Influences

That Furman observed Hart and Gano closely in their theological commitments is seen from addresses he gave upon the death of each. About Hart he noted the following:

> In his religious principles he was a fixed Calvinist, and a consistent, liberal Baptist. The doctrines of *free efficacious grace* were precious to him. Christ Jesus, and Him crucified, in the perfection of his righteousness, the merit of his death, the prevalence of his intercession, and efficacy of his grace, was the foundation of his hope, the source of his joy, and the delightful theme of his preaching.[14]

In his friendship with Gano, he had admired him as "one who shone like a star of the first magnitude in the American churches" and enjoyed his "unaffected humility, candour and good-will to men" as well as his "pungent, forcible addresses to the heart and conscience." He also knew that "the doctrines he embraced were those which are contained in the Baptist Confession of Faith, and are commonly styled Calvinistic." These doctrines he maintained "with consistent firmness" while he was careful to avoid giving offense or "grieving any good man who differed with him in sentiment."[15]

The variety of influences in Furman's life has prompted several writers to consider Furman something of a fusion between the back country religion of the Separate Baptists and the more stable rational religion of the Regular Baptists. Baker speaks of Pugh and Reese, who ordained Furman as "the vanguard of a new Breed in South Carolina, uniting the strengths of both the Regulars and the Separates." He then remarks, "Richard Furman was the finest example of this union."[16] James A. Rogers gives some specific ideas concerning the ingredients and benefits of this union.

> The Separates needed the stabilizing influence of Lowcountry Regulars, their emphasis upon an educated ministry, and their more rational approach to worship. The Regulars needed the evangelistic enthusiasm of the Separates to inspire a more urgent mission concern. When the two eventually merged, the resulting Baptists bore the better marks of both.[17]

None can doubt that the combination between Regulars and Separates produced a unique and felicitous expression of Baptist life in the South. Exactly what aspects were contributed by what group may be more difficult to determine. Evangelistic zeal is normally stated as a Separate contribution. While their aggressive evangelism can not be denied, one should be careful not to minimize the evangelistic concerns of the Regulars. The Regulars of the Philadelphia and Charleston Associations consistently engaged in church planting. Sending preachers into unchurched areas on evangelistic tours was common and seen as one of the strengths of associational life. The "Summary of Church Discipline" adopted by the Charleston Association in 1773 listed several advantages of such a connection. Two of these were: "[4] The churches will be more closely united in promoting the cause and interest of Christ. . . . [8] Ministers may alternately be sent out to preach the gospel to those who are destitute, Gal. ii. 9." Sixteen years before the adoption of this "Summary" the Charleston Association had sent John Gano in the area of North Carolina known as the Yadkin and afterwards to "bestow his labors wherever Providence should seem to direct." In 1757 the Association commended Gano for his labor and rejoiced that "Many embraced and professed the Gospel."[18]

George Whitefield found a warm reception among the Regular Baptists in the South. The small group of General Baptists opposed the preaching of Whitefield, and Thomas Simmons, the pastor of the Charleston church who had (to the dismay of his congregation) Arminian leanings, opposed him. His opposition, however, led to an "unhappy difference" between him and his people. The other Baptists received Whitefield's theology and his evangelism so well that he often preached in Baptist meetinghouses. He called the minister at Ashley River "a gracious Baptist minister" and recognized that "there are some faithful ministers among the Baptists."[19] Seeing that it was the influence of Whitefield that gave rise to the Separate Baptist movement and that Whitefield found such enthusiastic approval and fellowship among the Regular Baptists, the historian must be careful in drawing hard and fast distinctions between Regulars and Separates on their evangelistic commitment.

Whatever the various possible blendings of practical matters, the theological wedding posed few difficulties. Though more exuberant in worship and less disposed to be governed by formal confessions of faith, most of the Separates were Calvinistic in doctrine.[20] Thus, Calvinistic theology, with its heavy emphasis on the necessity of an efficacious work of God for salvation, became by heritage and conviction the guiding force in Furman's ministry.

The doctrinal statements of the Charleston Association also influenced Furman. In 1767 the Charleston Association adopted the Second London Confession as its official theological statement and also adopted the "Baptist Catechism" as the mean of training children doctrinally in the home. The Second London Confession and the Baptist Catechism, with their noble and powerful heritage, served as more than figurehead documents. These were taken seriously in the churches and gave theological form to the content of the teaching and preaching. A charming reminiscence of one of the children he catechised gives a clear picture of the importance Furman attached to these formulas. A 1926 edition of *In Royal Service* quotes the remembrance a grandchild had of her grandmother's experience under Furman.

> We had no Sabbath school then, but we had the Baptist Catechism, with which we were as familiar as with the Lord's Prayer. At our quarterly seasons, we children of the congregation repeated the Baptist Catechism standing, in a circle round the font. We numbered from sixty to a hundred. The girls standing at the south of the pulpit, the boys meeting them in the center from the north, Dr. Furman would, in his majestic, winning manner, walk down the pulpit steps and with book in hand, commence asking questions, beginning with the little ones (very small indeed some were, but well taught and drilled at home). We had to memorize the whole book, for none knew which question would fall to them. I think I hear at this very moment the dear voice of our pastor saying, "A little louder, my child," and then the trembling, sweet voice would be raised a little too loud. It was a marvel to visitors on these occasions, the

wonderful self-possession and accuracy manifested by the whole class. This practice was of incalculable benefit, for when it pleased God to change our hearts, and when offering ourselves to the church for membership, we knew what the church doctrines meant and were quite familiar with answering questions before the whole congregation, and did not quake when pastor or deacon or anyone else asked what we understood by Baptism, the Lord's Supper, Justification, Adoption, Sanctification. Oh, no; we had been well taught. . . . What a pity that such a course of instruction has been abandoned.[21]

The two major influences, therefore, on Furman's doctrinal stance were the Charleston Association's theological documents, decidedly Calvinistic in content, and the Whitefieldian conversionism of the First Great Awakening. His own experience and that of his mentors, especially Hart and Gano, enforced these two factors in the most positive and healthy way. The marriage of experimental Christianity with a doctrinally precise Calvinism gave Furman a dowry from which he shared riches for all his ministry.

Furman's Theology

The use of confessions.—Furman had a strong commitment to confessional theology and promoted an open adherence to the essentials of the faith by the use of confessions. As already indicated, an important part of his ministry consisted of catechising young people.

In a sermon entitled "Unity and Peace," based on Ephesians 4:3, Furman emphasized the importance of singling out and stating clearly the doctrines which are "particularly taught and declared to be of highest moment in the Scriptures," while not making a test of faith those which are "less clear or doubtful in their meaning." Since the church is the pillar and foundation of the truth, such commitment is essential for "the satisfaction of those who know and love the truth" as well as for the instruction of those who are "ignorant of religion." Because of this, "objections against the use of confessions of faith in churches, must appear ill-founded, and the consequences of such objections be pernicious."[22]

Faithfulness to God demands a clear statement of essential truths and contending for these in the face of error. "The cause of God, involving the consideration of his being, perfections, and government, is the cause of eternal truth and righteousness." In fact, "whatever he has revealed, concerning his person, office, redemption, law, and grace . . . the purity of his doctrines, ordinances, and worship" must be maintained "in opposition to schemes of imposture and error . . . [and] false doctrines."[23]

A comprehensive, balanced, and experimental acquaintance with doctrine is an essential qualification of one who is to serve as pastor of a church. The bishop must be "well instructed in the sacred doctrines of the gospel." Pivotal doctrines include the "nature and perfections of the Deity; the person and offices of Christ, and salvation through him; the influence and operation of the divine spirit; and the nature of grace and holiness." He must not only know these doctrines but "be truly acquainted with experimental religion, and deeply affected with its reality and importance."[24]

Preaching partakes of this strong doctrinal character. A preacher must take heed to his doctrine. How intimately biblical doctrine relates to the cognitive element of faith can be seen clearly in this notable passage.

> To his *doctrine* he must take heed, that it be the truth of God; not the fancies of his own mind. . . . Here again he must distinguish between law and gospel; and between the characters of men, as saints or sinners: Must point out the ruined and guilty state of all, by nature, under the curse of a broken law; sound, as it were, Mount Sinai's thunder in the sinners ear; present the flaming mountain to his eye; and thus produce the awful evidence, to that momentous truth, "that by the deeds of the law, shall no flesh living be justified." To the humbled sinner, and believing soul, he must describe Jesus, as "the Lamb of God, who taketh away the sins of the world:" As the only, the almighty, and the willing savior. He must describe him, in his person, his offices, his works of love and grace, his bleeding passion, and triumphant state. He must open, as it were, Immanuel's heart, in the description of divine compassion, . . . must shew the abundant grace contained in the promises, and the foundation on which faith may rest, in the faithfulness, infinite goodness, sovereign mercy, and unchangeable purpose of the promiser. To him, belongs the important work of drawing aside the veil of time, and opening the awful scenes of eternity, on his hearers minds: Of describing the joys of paradise; and the terrors of the infernal world.[25]

Furman's concerns did not focus on the fine contours and coherent organization of theology as an intellectually delightful system. He knew that belief and experience of the truth far exceeded in importance its formal expression. For Furman, however, belief and form did not contradict each other but were complementary. If one possessed true faith, one would believe the truth.

Theology of the Bible.—With such a clear commitment to a unified and coherent system of thought built on biblical teachings, Furman's commitment to the Bible as an unerring special revelation from God should come as no surprise. While "the divine bounty shines gloriously in the heavens and in the earth, . . . written in fair characters on the works of creation and providence"[26] and "the mind of man, roused by the dictates of reason and conscience" perceives something of future scenes, only special revelation and the facts of the gospel bring life and immortality to light in "the most striking colours, and with the strongest evidence."[27]

In harmony with the Second London Confession, Furman considered the apostles "immediately inspired by the Holy Ghost."[28] This inspiration, as well as special revelation, came only in the apostolic age and vanished after it. Any claim for a continuance of it Furman considered "folly and presumption in the extreme."[29]

Furman's belief in the uniqueness of the revelatory era bolstered his arguments for the necessity of ministerial education. While some in his day neglected education, assuming they would be "supernaturally assisted," Furman insisted they "ought to remember, miraculous assistance is not to be expected in these days." Instead, "the aids of grace are to be obtained in the use of suitable and rational means."[30] Those convictions, pronounced in 1791, diminished none in the years to follow. In 1824, before the State Convention of the Baptist Denomination in South Carolina, he argued for the uniqueness of the inspiration given to the apostles and applied it to the advantage of ministerial education.

> Will the opponents to a regular course of instruction, for the work of the gospel ministry, say that men are inspired by the Holy Ghost *now,* as the Apostles were?—Or that they *still* have the power of working miracles? Surely they cannot. If men are not divinely inspired *now,* and *the age of miracles* has past away, then, surely, it is necessary that attention should be paid to the education of those whom God has been pleased to call to this work without it.[31]

In reflecting on apostolic admonitions to pastors for the earnest toil at improving gifts of ministry, Furman remarks, "If this rule applied with propriety and force to apostolic times, when inspiration and extraordinary influences of the Spirit were afforded, how much more is it now applicable, when these extraordinary influences have ceased." There is, thus, a qualitative difference in the Spirit's work of revelation and inspiration in apostolic times as compared with the illumination of today. Knowledge today "except by gracious illumination is only obtained in use of rational means, or connected with human effort."[32]

Education, therefore, fosters understanding of, demonstrates a commitment to, and prepares for the defense of the Bible as special revelation. Furman's concern for pursuing learning as a tool to honor God's self-disclosure in Scriptures permeates the following passage from his address "To the Different Baptist Associations in the State of South Carolina." He contemplates the dangers involved in the confrontation of educated Unitarianism with uneducated Baptists. After mentioning how Unitarianism alters the doctrines of the deity of Christ, the atonement, regeneration, and the personality of the Holy Spirit, Furman writes:

> To support all which sentiments, and others connected with them, we are told that the scriptures have been wrongly translated or corrupted and that some parts of them are not of divine authority. A copy is made out professing strict conformity to the original, in favor of these sentiments; and notes are added to give confirmation to this meaning. Tracts controversial and didactic, are written with ingenuity and address, and with a great show of learning and reason, and industriously circulated, especially among the higher circles of society, in order to win over to the scheme as many as possible. Now how can it be expected that successful opposition can be made to such a scheme and to such measures, without the instrumentality of learned men, on the spot, where the attack on truth and righteousness is made, and that in so formidable a manner. Had not God furnished us with the means of obtaining such advocates for truth, we might expect his extraordinary, even his miraculous interpostion; but when our deficiency is owing to our supineness, neglect, and want of zeal, or public spiritedness in his cause, what can we expect but to be scourged with the overflowing of error?[33]

Casual phrases Furman uses to describe Scripture show his commitment to its divine authority: "oracles of heavenly truth and wisdom";[34] "whose word stands firmer than the foundations of the heavens and earth."[35] "Scriptures of truth";[36] "a revelation from heaven";[37] "unerring counsels";[38] In setting forth the biblical view of the ordinances he called them the "institutions of heaven" leaving little doubt as to his view of the Scripture which describes and enforces these ordinances.[39] Furman believed the minister must hold Scripture as "a revelation containing the sovereign will of Almighty God, and his unerring guide through the labyrinths of life."[40] Furman's clear commitment to the divine origin of Scripture combined with his view of God's sovereignty renders anomalous any hint of real discrepancy, moral confusion, or error of any kind in Scripture.

Furman also functioned with the assumption of the perspicuity of Scripture. In his sermon *Unity and Peace* he stated, "Similar attention to and acquaintance with the sacred scriptures will produce unity of sentiments in the great truths of religion."[41] Though the Christian must do all possible to avoid controversy, he must also be careful "not to give up sacred and clearly revealed truths" or even be indifferent toward them.

Perspicuity and mystery are both corollaries of divine revelation. Revelation denotes the disclosure of what was formerly hidden. If the disclosure is itself unclear in its leading principles and overall effect, then its purpose of revealing has not been accomplished. On the other hand, one must expect some difficulties and mysteries to remain even in the revelatory material. Some truths can be grasped only after a mature absorption of a great body of leading principles in Scripture (2 Pet. 3:15-16; Heb. 5:12-14; Eph. 4:13; Phil. 3:15-16). Other elements in the revelatory material seem designed to humble us by reminding us of the ultimate infinitude of the person with whom we have to do. It is *divine* revelation. Like Job, we must be pushed beyond the edges of our understanding so that revelation, rather than puffing us up, humbles us. Like Paul, we must confess, "His ways [are] past finding out!" (Rom. 11:33). On this point, Furman's view of Scripture corresponds perfectly with his view of confessions.

God.—Furman never spoke or wrote of God without a sense of reverence, awe, wonder, and holy dread. His exalted view of God is quite evident in his characterization of American society at the time of the Revolution. Furman believed that the vast majority of people during that period "had felt the ameliorating influence of the christian doctrines" and believed in the "eternal existence, transcendent perfection, and righteous universal providence of an infinite God."[42] This harmonized beautifully with the Baptist Catechism, which Furman taught so faithfully. It defined God as a "spirit, infinite, eternal, and unchangeable in his being, wisdom, power, holiness, justice, goodness, and truth." Each of these elements had its place in Furman's discussion of God; each element also has striking applicatory and experiential power in Furman's treatment.

He clearly believed in God as a Trinitarian being, each Person of the Godhead existing eternally as a separate personal subsistence. In baptism, a person dedicates oneself to the service of "the adoreable [*sic*] Trinity."[43]

He is infinite in His holiness, so that "in an exalted and peculiar sense of the word" the term *good* is to be applied to God alone. Those born of God must, and will, share a degree of that same goodness.

God is omnipotent, or infinite in power. These attributes manifest themselves specifically in creation and providence. His is the "almighty arm which rolls thunder through the vault of heaven, which shakes the earth with strong convulsions, stills the raging waves, guides the furious tempest, supports the universe."[44] In His omnipotence, He is "the righteous, dread creator" and thus the "great sovereign of heaven and earth." This thought overwhelmed Furman. He is confident of the "eternal existence, transcendent perfection and righteous, universal Providence of an infinite God."[45] Anyone who would seek to dispose of God's providence must be a "madman."[46] God's absolute providence is inscrutably, as well as indivisibly, connected with His infinite and unchangeable wisdom. In fact, Furman considered the "evident and miraculous interposition of Divine Providence" as one strand in a rope of evidence for the truth and supernatural origin of the Christian faith.

The Charleston Confession of Faith states:

> God hath decreed in himself from all eternity, by the most wise and holy counsel of his own will, freely and unchangeablely all things whatsoever comes to pass; yet so as thereby is God neither the author of sin nor hath any fellowship with any therein, nor is violence offered to the will of the creature, nor yet is the liberty, or contingency of second causes taken away, but rather established, in which appears his wisdom in disposing all things, and power, and faithfulness in accomplishing his decree.[47]

This conceptional balance informed Furman's discussion of Providence in all historical events. He states his presupposition clearly before a discussion of the peculiar providence of God in the events during and after the Revolutionary War.

> A belief of God's infinite wisdom, and universal dominion will exclude the idea, that any event can take place without his permission; and therefore, it must be admitted, that his counsel and providence are, in some sense, concerned in whatever exists or transpires, throughout the creation. But there is an infinite difference between his permitting an event (for in this manner all evil comes into existence) and his producing it, as his proper work, and the object of his approbation. An important distinction, also is to be made between his immediate act, and his effecting a purpose by the intervention of second causes. This use of second causes and his approbation of the event are principally intended in the proposition before us.[48]

God, as "righteous and dread sovereign" whose "throne is established eternally," has a "sovereign right to demand our services." He is the "great sovereign of heaven and earth."[49] He is omniscient, or infinite in knowledge; and, to Him, the "real and apparent are the same." God discerns the "first springs of action in the human soul" and knows fully those "genuine and secret actions which flow in the most free and unguarded manner from the heart."[50] His omniscience is a holy omniscience. This makes Him not only invested with absolute providence and an ability to execute perfectly His decrees but also establishes Him as the absolute, just judge, the "unerring eternal Judge"[51] of all rational beings, who owe Him perfect obedience. So He is both "dread sovereign and righteous judge," even "the judge of all the earth, whose eyes are as pure flames, piercing into the recesses of the soul, discerning every thought and every action and who will decide on the everlasting state of men." His court is the "bar of eternal rectitude."[52]

This perfect knowledge and holiness is displayed not only in judgment but in a settled, immutable, infinite antagonism and enmity toward all that is unholy. This is one reason the word *dread* so often drips from the pen of Furman and why he can speak of the "frown of an angry God"[53] and the "great day of final retribution," yea, even, "that awful, glorious day of perfect retribution."[54] One can see clearly that retributive justice is a major factor in Furman's view of God and man. This permeates every other area of theology and experience.

Only against such a background can one understand Furman's sober style and exalted worship of Jehovah. But, according to Furman, it was possible to "make the judge your friend"[55] and know him as a "God of great mercy." More than that, he is a "God of infinite mercy." But this is most clearly seen in the Person and Work of the Savior.

Christology.—One doctrinal concern often expressed by Furman as necessary for a gospel minister was the proper representation of "the person and offices of Christ."[56] In fact, the eternal interests of convicted sinners focus on the minister's true representation of Jesus and his ability to describe Him "in his person, his offices, his works of love and grace, his bleeding passion, and triumphant state."[57]

Furman expressed his Christology in crystal clear language in an address "To the Different Baptist Associations in the State of South Carolina." Arguing that ministerial ignorance not only violated clear implications of Scripture and was a "positive embarassment," Furman also expressed alarm that Baptist ignorance was yielding the day to Unitarianism and its denial of the deity of Christ. By that scheme, "the proper divinity of our Divine Lord is denied, together with the merit of his atoning blood, the necessity of his renewing grace, and the reality of regeneration."[58] This note still rang clear when Furman called on the faithful minister of Jesus Christ "who believes in his proper Deity" to demonstrate concern "for the advancement of the kingdom of God's co-equal Son" and help "put to silence the proud philosopher, the artful sophist, who would oppose Christ's divine character."[59]

Christ represented Himself to His disciples as their "Great Lord and Master."[60] When quoting the words of Christ, Furman speaks of Him as "Our Divine Lord."[61] In an imaginary address to the National Convention of France, Furman lauded Christ as "mediator . . . possessed of infinite excellence."[62]

Not only is Christ God, "proper divinity," but He shares human nature. As Furman hypothetically told the French, Jesus "partakes also of the nature and sympathizes in the frailties of man."[63] One element of the church's union with Christ is a natural union "by his assuming human nature."[64]

Furman's Christology is concordant with the simple statement in the Baptist Catechism where Christ, the redeemer of God's elect, "being the eternal Son of God, became man, and so was and continueth to be God and man, in two distinct natures and one person, forever"; and, in consideration of the Father, "the same in essence, equal in power and glory."[65]

Christ's work is bound up in what Furman called His "bleeding passion." The substitionary and propitiatory aspects of the atonement dominated Furman's images and expressions. In discussing James 5:20 ("will cover a multitude of sins"), he relates the meaning in part to the psalmist's affirmation of blessedness to the one whose "sin is covered." This is expressive of "justification and peace with God, through Christ's obedience and propitiatory sacrifice." Later he says, "Their guilt, through his atonement, is completely removed; and, by the act of grace, cast, as it were, into the depths of the sea, to be seen or remembered no more."[66]

Furman conceived of Christ as bearing, in His passive obedience, the actual punishment due to sinners, by which action they are forgiven; and as gaining, by His active obedience, the righteousness of the law, the imputation of which constitutes their justification. Christ left the "mansions of glory" and lived a "life of pain, labor and sorrow" and finally died "the bitter, ignominious death of the cross" to effect redemption.[67]

These ideas find reinforcement in Furman's picture of the saint's entrance into rest. "Their reconciled God, who has accepted them through the righteousness and intercession of his son, looks on them with propitious eye."[68] Again the themes of active and passive obedience, removal of enmity between God and man, imputed righteousness, and propitiatory death undergird Furman's picture of the sinner's acceptance before God.

These same themes recur in Furman's summary of Christ's work in his recommendation of the Christian faith to the consideration of his fellow Americans. Preaching on July 4, 1802, Furman spoke of "America's Deliverance and Duty." Having displayed several elements demonstrating to Furman's satisfaction the sure providence of God in the success of the Revolution, he then called on all Americans to consider the great necessity of religion, for "can we suppose he will be faithful to his country, who is not faithful to his God." The religion of Jesus Christ surely is a revelation from heaven bringing with it all the evidence "sufficiently clear to satisfy the mind of every candid, humble enquirer." Part of this compelling evidence is the clarity with which it points out "the way to reconciliation and bliss, through the meritorious obedience, complete atonement, and prevalent intercession of a Divine Mediator and Redeemer."[69]

Anthropology.—Furman appears to conceive of the "soul" as constituting the image of God in man. The soul, though now fallen, still retains all the natural faculties with which it was endowed at creation. "According to the constitution of human nature," the powers of the soul consist of understanding, will, and affection, with the attendant powers of thought and memory.[70]

These constituent parts, in the fall, were not destroyed but were perverted to uses alien to God. This has brought man into a state of condemnation, corruption, and moral inability. Furman mourned the "guilty, corrupt, condemned state of human nature."[71] Furman paints the sinner's condemnation in striking images. A man "must be converted or perish,"[72] for all men are "ruined and guilty in the first Adam."[73] A preacher is to point out "the ruined and guilty state of all by nature, under the curse of a broken law."[74] Should a man die in such a condition "how certain and awful must [his] ruin be," for he speeds to stand in the presence of him "whose eyes are like pure flames, while his lightnings fearfully flash around, his thunders roll, the elements melt with fervent heat, and convulsed nature utters her last expiring groan."[75] The minister, then, in true sincerity, must cry, "Flee, O! flee from the wrath to come."[76] The sinner who neglects gospel privileges will be brought into "the heaviest condemnation" when "he sinks under the burden of his sins and horrors seize his guilty soul." Everyone should therefore make it his earnest business "to escape from hell and fly to heaven."[77] If we find no relief from guilt, then we must labor eternally "under the frowns and vengeance of the Almighty in a state of fixed, unutterable woe."[78]

With no less urgency does Furman describe man's corruption. All man's faculties, because "alienated from God by sin," are "rebellious" and "employed in seeking their chief happiness in the creatures." Our "natural state" is one not only of guilt, but of "pollution and misery."[79] Furman contends that before sin is brought into action "it exists in a state of embryo, in the heart, in manifold evil propensities, or corrupt affections." One of the obstacles overcome by God's design of grace toward "careless, insensible sinners" is "man's own perverse heart."[80]

It comes as no surprise, then, that Furman views man as bound in a moral inability because of this corrupt perverseness. Sinners are "held under the power of sin" in a "state of thraldom." So strong are the ties that bind the sinner, that Furman says, "A man cannot change his own heart."[81]

Man's sinfulness is also subtle and extremely deceitful. True repentance from sin is extremely difficult because love for sin is so strong. But there are many who feign repentance and may even deceive themselves. Furman gives a penetrating analysis of a self-deceived hypocrite who has stopped short of true conversion.

> But there are self-deceived hypocrites, who have never suspected themselves to be guilty of hypocrisy; but who, notwithstanding, possess not that simplicity and godly sincerity which the gospel calls for. They will, perhaps, be zealous for the most orthodox doctrines of christianity; for its spirituality and experimental nature, as far as these are considered in theory; while in spirit, and conduct, they are quite the reverse of what the christian should be, and really is: they being, in truth, influenced by carnal, worldly motives, and, at heart, more concerned to obtain the approbation and praise of men, or to provide for their present ease and indulgence, than to be interested in the favour of God, or

to serve and glorify him. So blinded are they by self-love, and a good opinion of themselves, that the glaring inconsistency of their conduct, though perhaps evident to everyone else, is not discovered by themselves. . . . Much is set down by them to the account of human imperfections, the corruption of nature, and the force of temptation—while in fact, imperfection is not sincerely lamented by them, corruption not mortified, and temptation not truly resisted.[82]

Salvation, under this view of sin and its dominance over man, is impossible for man. But what is impossible for man is possible for God. Salvation is of grace.

The experience of salvation.—The burden of Furman's soteriology lay on the experiential aspect of it. Regeneration, conversion, sanctification, preservation, perseverance, and assurance all received clear treatment in his published material.

Regeneration.—The initial experience of salvation, culminating the experience of calling, is regeneration or conversion. Both its priority and necessity arise from prior theological truths. As Furman says, "For predicated on the correspondent doctrines of human depravity, and God's holiness the necessity of conversion is maintained and powerfully enforced by the divine oracles."[83] Furman knew and accepted the technical theological distinction between regeneration and conversion. Regeneration is a "change wrought in the Soul, by the implantation there of a Principle of Divine Life, with all its essential Qualities and Dispositions" in which the soul of man is passive. In conversion, however, the faculties of man in their renewed state come into action and cause a man actually to forsake sin and devote himself to the love and service of God. For practical consideration, Furman preferred to combine both concepts under the definition, "a renovation of the soul by the Spirit of God."[84]

This change neither diminishes nor augments the natural faculties, for the natural faculties and powers remain intact "according to the constitution of human nature."[85] The moral and spiritual disposition of the faculties changes: the mind, will, and affection jointly desire the knowledge of God above all things and treasure that knowledge as the individual's chief joy.

Furman shows clearly his Edwardsian Calvinistic orientation both in the distinction between natural and moral abilities and in the *ordo salutis*. Repentance, faith, and all attendant graces proceed from and depend upon the prior work of regeneration.

> It is therefore, beyond all contradiction a supernatural change produced by the spirit of God: And there is something in its nature which is mysterious and wonderful; . . . but however inscrutable . . . . its effects are certain. . . . [I]ts effects will be, repentance toward God, and faith toward our Lord Jesus Christ; a hatred to sin, and a love to holiness; supreme love to God, and unfeigned benevolence to men.[86]

Sanctification and perseverance.—Sanctification follows inevitably and progressively from conversion. This is as surely connected with the determination of God to honor His law as is atonement and justification. "Holiness is necessary for the enjoyment of compleat happiness," says Furman, and without it "No man shall see the Lord." The "wise scheme of redemption" has been so ordered that "the righteousness of the law, should be fulfilled in those, who walk, not after the flesh, but after the spirit."[87] The service of Christ is such a high calling that "no unsanctified mind *will,* or *can,* be faithful in the performance of it." The character of true service is such that "without sanctified affections no acceptable service can be rendered to God," even the acts done professedly for His glory; and, by contrast, the common actions of life under the "exercise of pure affections" are consecrated to God's glory.[88] "No lukewarm, double-minded wavering man can have a part in the Kingdom of Christ and of God." One gains heaven only by "labours and conflicts" and perhaps even a violent death for Christ's sake. Some may fall under the pressures and "final apostasy is the result in the case (I will not say of souls truly regenerate, but) of many professors."[89]

The crown of life is given only to those who are faithful unto death; but the apostate can look only for the dire reward of eternal death. Furman urges, "Beware of apostasy, beware of declension in religion, beware of sin, beware of every temptation."[90] Because conversion produces such a change of affections, the true Christian will certainly persevere, and Furman issued strong challenges to faithfulness.

> O! Christian, see to it that thy heart be right with God; that it feel for his honour, and for the interests of his kingdom; that it be regulated by the principles of Divine love and holy zeal, of eternal truth, justice and benevolence; and that loyalty to thy God, be fully evinced by thy faithfulness to men. The Christian's motto should ever be, "It is better to suffer than to sin."[91]

And because more afraid to sin than to suffer, true Christians will suffer all the way to death. False professors find that "Dungeons, chains, racks, flames, and gibbets appal them" and they cannot sacrifice life for the Redeemer.[92]

Warnings and admonitions to "professors" could be multiplied. These must be seen in the light of Furman's understanding of grace and means. God's grace does, in fact, so radically alter a sinner's moral disposition that perseverance in holiness is inevitable. Great and heroic human effort is both required and certain: Required, for "without holiness no man will see the Lord," and if, by the Spirit, we mortify the deeds of the flesh, we shall live; Certain, for the Spirit lusts against the flesh and He who began the work in you will continue perfecting it until the day of Christ Jesus. The means by which this occurs, other than the immediate work of God's Spirit, is the faithful proclamation of the gospel together with all its warnings, exhortations, admonitions, promises, and comforts.

The gospel minister is vitally involved in the use of means, since one purpose of his ministry is the perfecting of the saints. Furman holds this process to be "an advancement in love, knowledge, holiness and virtue, by the means of grace, until their translation to heavenly blessedness." This process then has no static or finally achieved results, since advancement always may occur in this life, a perpetual state of imperfection. There is a

Christian maturity, however, that can be called "perfection." He describes this as "an eminent degree of virtue and holiness; in which the Christian is not found wanting, in any of the essential parts of the Christian character, or in the acts of religion, suitable to his state and abilities."[93]

The process of perfection, therefore, must in this life never be confused with sinless perfection. Furman was fully aware of such teaching and recoiled against the notion. He argued that *sinless perfection* was not attained in the present life for the following reasons.

> The Scriptures assert, "there is no man which sinneth not;" "if we say we have no sin, we deceive ourselves, and the truth is not in us:" And in the Lord's prayer, we are taught to pray for the forgiveness of our sins, as well as our daily bread. All which passages, expressing the present time, and applying to any supposeable state of excellency, or improvement; plainly prove, the imperfection of all on earth. To which may be added: Men of the greatest attainments in religion, who have even laid down their lives in the cause of God, and have been most sensible of their imperfections; while others, who have made pretensions to this excellent state, have discovered, to almost every observer, ample proof that they were yet wanting; and in some instances, have fallen into most scandalous crimes. And, lastly, reason bears testimony against it, while she observes, that all on earth, are subjects of pain and death: Her dictate is that the perfectly holy, should be perfectly happy. We cannot therefore subscribe to this principle; or consider it as a matter of indifference [sic]; especially when it is asserted such an attainment is necessary to salvation: Since the belief of it, must distress the humble, pious soul, who feels his imperfections; and elevate the blind, conceited professor, to a height of pride and delusion.[94]

Preservation.—The flip side of perseverance is preservation. We certainly persevere but only because God preserves. Those truly regenerate seeking true faithfulness to God will find themselves "the objects of his preserving care, and enjoy his peace which passeth all human understanding." God honors them with "special interpositions of his providence and grace" and supports and comforts them in "sufferings, persecutions and death."[95] God's faithfulness to Himself and His Word prompts His sustenance of weak and faltering Christians; and when they arrive in heaven, having remained faithful unto death, "they have proved the faithfulness of their Redeemer's promise, the riches of his grace, the unchangeable, freeness and fulness of his everlasting love."[96] In this state only will they enjoy that absolute creaturely perfection to be described later.

Assurance and self-examination.—The nature of regeneration and its relation to perseverance, preservation, and the possibility of apostasy obligates every person to a practice of self-examination in the quest for assurance. Furman never allowed the sovereignty of God in regenerating grace to create a careless spirit in the professing Christian. Hatred of and flight from sin is, according to Furman, the major distinction of the truly regenerate person. "Beware of apostasy, . . . declension in religion, . . . sin, . . . every temptation . . . which leads from one sin to another by a fatal gradation."[97] The nature of grace and the glory of a faithful covenant God should never produce presumption.

> The proof that we are of that number is best furnished to our own souls, as well as to the souls of others, not by our confidence that if we sin we shall be recovered; but by our resisting and hating every sin; by our taking heed lest we fall; by our mortifying the deeds of the body through the spirit; and by our cleaving to the Lord with full purpose of heart, in faith, love and holy obedience. He, and only he, that endures to the end shall be saved. "If any man draw back," says the blessed God, "my soul shall have no pleasure in him."[98]

Furman brings a comprehensive sweep of perspicuous doctrinal affirmations to bear upon the process of self-examination. The professing Christian ("Profession may exist where there is no real religion!") must review the whole truth of God in an applicatory way seeking to determine if he not only knows these truths mentally, but affirms them and loves them for their holiness and grace. Does a person "possess the spirit and character which properly belong" to union with Christ? Notice how vividly and passionately Furman imposes this examination on his readers.

> Have we awoke to the serious consideration of eternal things; to a discovery of our guilt and depravity, and of divine wrath as ready to overwhelm a guilty, impenitent world? Has divine mercy also, appeared to us in the gospel, and Christ been endeared in all the amiableness of his character and sufficiency of grace? Have we, in the exercise of a divine faith, fled for refuge to his mediation; do we trust in his immaculate righteousness for justification before God, and to his atoning blood for pardon? Has our faith a sanctifying efficacy on the whole temper of our hearts? Can we say that we truly love God and our Redeemer? Is sin hateful and holiness delightful; have we sincerely renounced our former sinful deeds, and devoted ourselves to God by an entire surrender of our hearts, our souls, our all: and do we look forward to future scenes, big with the hope of eternal life; panting for perfection, immortality, and God? Is the cause of God endeared to us; are his saints, in our view, the excellent of the earth; do we possess, in truly loving them, the strong evidence of a share in spiritual life and happiness; and does a tender regard to their happiness, as well as to the honor of our Redeemer, manifest itself in our endeavouring to keep the unity of the spirit in a peaceful state?[99]

Furman's sensitivity to human experience, knowledge of the full biblical teaching about false faith, awareness of the deceitfulness of the human heart, and identification with the saints' growing sense of the corruption of nature made him especially full in his grasp of the issue of assurance. True Christians may indeed be reduced at times to despair about the state of their soul. The Charleston Confession taught clearly the possibility of the temporary loss of assurance. Furman's representation of this speaks of "their dark hours" when "they have many distressing doubts."

> Even when fully assured that the blessings of salvation are secure to all those who are true believers, or subjects of grace; yet from their knowledge of the deceitfulness of the human heart, of the presumptuous hope indulged by many,

and of their own manifold imperfections, they feel the impressions of fear, lest, at last, they themselves should be found wanting.[100]

Joyful assurance, in spite of all the factors which militate against it, can come in this life. Faithfulness to the service of God and the pursuit of "unaffected piety, benevolence, humbleness and purity" constitute the accompanying conditions of assurance. Where these grow in unceasing measure "the children of God gain a pleasing persuasion, that they are interested in the divine favor; and, while walking in the light of Jehovah's countenance, that persuasion grows up to a good degree of assurance."[101]

In a funeral sermon for Edmund Botsford, Furman gives a description of Botsford's loss of and struggle for assurance during a particularly distressing time of life. Furman's perception of the way emotional, theological, and even physical factors impact assurance shows an admirable sensitivity to the intricacies of the God/man relation.

> He had also severe spiritual conflicts. . . . In one of these conflicts, he was so violently assailed by temptation to doubt of his interest in the favour of God, that he was almost driven to despair; and at the very time too, when bodily affliction lay heavily upon him. The evidences of his gracious state were quite obscured; the errors and imperfections of his life, since he had become a Christian professor, and minister of the Gospel, distressed him; he was filled with self-loathing and reproach; and could not exercise faith in the Redeemer as one interested in him. But finally he obtained complete deliverance, and triumphant joy; by going, deeply humbled, as a sinner, to the all gracious Saviour; making the humbling confession of his sins and errors and casting his immortal soul, with all its important concerns for time and eternity, and with its deep sense of guilt, pollution and unworthiness on the infinite merit, and free grace of the Redeemer, as they afford hope of salvation to the most vile and wretched who apply to him for salvation.[102]

Church.—Furman's ecclesiology was set forth most cogently in his sermon "The Constitution and Order of the Christian Church." Furman accepted the idea of a universal church and defined it as "the whole body of the redeemed, whose names are written in heaven; and shall finally meet in that grand assembly which will surround the throne of God and the Lamb, when 'there shall be one fold, and one shepherd.'" This church consists of "glorified spirits, . . . visible saints on earth," thousands who are "yet in their sins, not having experienced the effectual call of the gospel," and, Furman added, "innumerable multitudes unborn." All of these manifest those gracious qualities irresistibly implanted by God's Spirit: repentance, faith, love to God, subjection to His authority and government, zealous concern for the honor of divine majesty. He who possesses those qualities "in whatever connection or denomination he is found, has a right and title to the character and privileges of a member of the church of Christ."[103] Those of this character Furman denominated "visible saints."

The visible church should be composed only of visible saints. Baptism, therefore, should be administered only to those who have the necessary qualifications required in the Scriptures. Infants must be excluded from baptism. They are not necessarily excluded from salvation but often recipients. Those who die in infancy are saved "in a sovereign gracious manner," but few if any other than those are "subjects of renewing grace."[104]

The officers of the church are pastors and deacons. Apostles, prophets, and evangelists served specific historical functions in the apostolic age, but their calling and divine credentials have ceased, and they, thus, cannot be succeeded. A pastor must be qualified in both teaching and governing, that is "an ability to perform the sacred work." In addition, he must have a sense of "duty, or call to it, by the grace and providence of God." Also, he must show a "willingness to comply with disinterested and holy views."[105] The minister should be truly acquainted with experimental religion and deeply affected with its reality and importance."[106]

Churches are not national bodies. The objections against such are virtually insuperable. Rather, they are congregational, having with themselves the power of admitting persons to membership and office, watching over and admonishing those who are its members and "excluding such as become scandalously wicked and obstinately impenitent."[107]

In all the actions of the congregation, its officers take the lead. The leadership, according to Furman, must always be united to the "consent and authority of the church . . . for the perfecting any act of public concernment." Furman appears to grant the officers, elders, and deacons, a power of objection (perhaps veto) when he says, "They may be justifiable in objecting to such acts, in which they cannot accord with the church."[108]

One function of the church most insisted on by Furman is the duty of church discipline: "to bring the notorious, or presumptuous sinner under the discipline of the church: and finally exclude the impenitent from the communion of saints."[109] Preservation of unity and purity in the church informs and defines the purpose of discipline. For the peace of the church, proceeding with decision, yet, with prudence and tenderness, is important. "Immoralities should be faithfully reproved, weaknesses pitied, and impartial conduct mark every proceeding."[110] In doubtful cases "candid enquiries" must be pursued so that action passes on the basis of clear truth rather than calumny and misrepresentation.

All of these experiential and ecclesiastical truths culminate in Christ's reception of the church to Himself as a bride spotless, blameless, and holy. The last doctrinal area considered is the eternal state.

Eternal state.—The eternal state for the regenerate consists of the final perfection of human nature in the immediate presence of the Triune God. Furman can speak of life as the "seed-time for eternity."[111] The unregenerate go into eternal punishment, where their ruin will be "certain and awful."[112] It is not a ruin which culminates in annihilation "for the soul is declared to be immortal." It is, therefore, the "total loss of happiness—of all which makes life, life." This death includes two elements, one a removal of common grace, and another, the aggressive infliction of wrath. The first comprehends "all that is lost by exclusion from the regions of light and gracious presence of God." The second comprehends "all that is to be suffered by guilty, despairing Immortals under the frowns and vengeance of the Almighty in a state of fixed, unutterable woe."[113]

How different for the redeemed! "Everlasting rest and blessedness with God, perfection in holiness, triumphant joy, and glory in the heavens" is theirs. The image of God is restored. That which began in regeneration, was being perfected in sanctification, and tested and tried unto perseverance, is perfected finally in the reception of final conformity to Christ in soul and body. Mind, will, and affections unite knowledge, purpose, and joy in the beatific vision and freedom from moral pollution; and the body, now vigorous, spiritual, immortal, and glorious,[114] becomes suited perfectly for the enjoyment of the incorruptible spiritual world. One's knowledge of and enjoyment of earthly acquaintances, as well as the events of all epochs, is a constituent part of that overall knowledge and immediate enjoyment of God.[115] Satisfaction will be complete, happiness perfect, and joy triumphant.[116]

At that time, unity with the people of God will be complete. No difference in sentiment, practice, or knowledge will separate. "All disagreement from imperfect knowledge and discordant passions will forever cease."[117] Furman pulls together all his theological understanding and rhetorical powers in describing the blissful reconciliation of the eternal state for the redeemed.

> The powers of the soul will be expanded, to comprehend much of the glory of Immanuel; it will enjoy the open vision of his face; see the beauties of his sacred person, and discern the wonders of his grace. Mysteries, which now appear dark and intricate, concerning the nature, decrees and providence of God; will then be unfolded, with light and glory, to its view. The splendor and glories of the heavenly world will stand disclosed to its astonished mind; and, perhaps, it will pass from world to world, to gain new discoveries of the wonderful works of God, displayed through the illimitable tracts of space. The mind, now in infancy, will then be grown up to a state of manhood: According to the measure of Christ's stature, or the fulness that is in him. The fulness of grace in Christ will bring his saints into this state of holy, conformity to him; or, they will be fully conformed to that state of moral excellency, glory and happiness, to which he, as their elder brother, forerunner and savior is advanced. O, glorious state! O, happy souls! Thus united in indissoluble bonds of love; cleansed from all their pollutions; advanced to the highest rational and divine improvement; their bodies as well as their souls made glorious and immortal; admitted to the open vision of the divine glory, and satisfied with the full and immediate communication of divine love.[118]

This vision of worship permeated the thinking and preaching of Furman and made him one of the most profound and intense of Baptist "experimental" theologians.

Bibliography

Works by Furman
America's Deliverance and Duty. Charleston: W. P. Young, 1802.

Constitution and Order of the Christian Church. Charleston: Markland & McIver, 1791.

Conversion Essential to Salvation. Charleston: J. Hoff, 1816.

The Crown of Life Promised to the Truly Faithful. Charleston: Wm. Riley, 1822.

Humble Submission to Divine Sovereignty the Duty of a Bereaved Nation. Charleston: W. P. Young, 1800.

Rewards of Grace Conferred on Christ's Faithful People. Charleston: J. McIver, 1796.

Unity and Peace. Charleston: Markland, McIver & Co., 1794.

Works About Furman

Baker, Robert Andrew, and Craven, Paul. *Adventure in Faith: The First 300 Years of the First Baptist Church of Charleston, S.C.* Nashville: Broadman Press, 1982.

Cook, Harvey Toliver. *Biography of Richard Furman*. Greenville, SC: Baptist Courier Job Press, 1913.

Rogers, James A. *Richard Furman: Life and Legacy*. Mercer University Press, 1985. This work contains an excellent bibliography of Furman materials as well as eight appendixes constituting a variety of Furman treatises, proposals, and addresses. Included are: "An Address to the Residents Between the Broad and Saluda Rivers Concerning the American War for Independence November, 1775;" "Exposition of the Views of the Baptists Relative to the Coloured Population of the United States in a Communication to the Governor of South Carolina;" "Rules of the General Committee for forming, Supporting, and Applying a Fund amongst the Baptist Churches united in the Charleston Association"; "Plan of Education"; "Circular Letter Pertaining to Columbian College"; "Constitution of the Baptist Convention [Triennial], May 1814"; "[Letter from] The Delegates of the Baptist Associations . . . in the State of South Carolina . . . to the Other Baptist Associations"; and "Address to the Churches."

Notes

1. William B. Johnson, "Richard Furman" in *Annals of the American Pulpit*, vol. 6. "Baptist," ed. William B. Sprague (New York: Robert Carter & Brothers, 1865; reprint New York: Arno Press, 1969), 166.

2. James A. Rogers, *Richard Furman: Life and Legacy* (Macon, Ga.: Mercer University Press, 1985), 1-3.

3. Ibid., 11-17. See also Robert A. Baker and Paul J. Craven, Jr., *Adventure in Faith: The First Three Hundred Years of First Baptist Church, Charleston, South Carolina* (Nashville: Broadman Press, 1982), 185.

4. Rogers, 18.

5. Baker and Craven, 186.

6. Ibid.

7. Ibid., 187.

8. Richard Furman, *America's Deliverance and Duty* (Charleston: W. P. Young, 1802), 9-10.

9. Ibid., 11.

10. David Benedict, *Fifty Years Among the Baptists* (New York: Sheldon & Co., 1860), 48-49.

11. William Cathcart, ed., *The Baptist Encyclopedia* (Philadelphia: Louis H. Everts, 1881). S.v. "Furman, Richard."

12. *Encyclopedia of Southern Baptists,* 2 vols. (Nashville: Broadman Press, 1958), 2:1223.

13. Baker, 242.

14. Richard Furman, "Oliver Hart," in *Annals of the American Pulpit,* ed. William B. Sprague (New York: Robert Carter & Brothers, 1865; reprinted New York: Arno Press and the New York Times, 1969), 6:49.

15. Ibid., 66.

16. Baker and Craven, 189.

17. Rogers, 16.

18. Baker and Craven, 156.

19. See Baker and Craven, 113-14.

20. This can be seen clearly from several of the confessions written by the Separate Baptists. The "Principles of Faith of the Sandy Creek Association" state a belief in the impotence of man to restore himself by his own will as well as "election from eternity, effectual calling by the Holy Spirit of God" and perseverance "through grace to the end." William L. Lumpkin, *Baptist Confessions of Faith* (Valley Forge, Pa.: The Judson Press, 1969), 358. Also see my discussion of John Leland in *By His Grace and for His Glory* (Grand Rapids, Mich.: Baker Book House, 1980). Those who tended toward Arminianism were sometimes found to have other doctrinal errors. Benedict records that the Arminian element of Separate Baptists imbibed the Universalism and Unitarianism of Elhanan Winchester. In addition, one must not forget that in its first stages Separate Baptist life arose from Congregationalism. Their confession was the Savoy Declaration, identical in its theology of salvation to the Second London Confession used so unanimously by the Regular Baptists. The "aversion to creed" felt by the Separates came from the sad situation in New England in which Congregationalism, because of several factors, had identified confessional orthodoxy with true Christianity. The First Great Awakening pointed this out as a great danger and set before all people the necessity of a radical change of heart which could be brought about only by the Spirit of God.

21. Fanny E. S. Heck, *In Royal Service* (Richmond: Foreign Mission Board, 1926), 25-27.

22. Richard Furman, *Unity and Peace* (Charleston: Markland McIver & Co., 1794), 13.

23. Richard Furman, *The Crown of Life Promised to the Truly Faithful* (Charleston: Wm. Riley, 1822), 6-7. This is a funeral sermon for the Reverend Edmund Botsford and is a marvelous example of the intensely searching doctrinal style of Furman's preaching.

24. Richard Furman, *The Constitution and Order of Christian Church* (Charleston: Markland & McIver, 1791), 23.

25. Ibid., 26-27.

26. Furman, *Constitution,* 5.

27. Furman, *Rewards,* 5.

28. Furman, *Constitution,* 14-15.

29. Ibid., 16.

30. Ibid., 37.

31. Richard Furman, "Address to the Churches," *Minutes of the State Baptist Convention,* cited in Rogers, 309-10.

32. Furman, *Crown of Life,* 13.

33. Richard Furman, John M. Roberts, and Joseph B. Cook, *To the Different Associations of the State Baptist Convention of South Carolina,* November 8, 1820, 5.

34. Furman, *Crown of Life,* 36.

35. Ibid., 33.

36. Furman, *Rewards,* 8.

37. Richard Furman, *America's Deliverance and Duty* (Charleston: W. P. Young, 1802), 9.

38. Furman, *Constitution,* 39.

39. Ibid., 28.

40. Ibid., 20.

41. Furman, *Unity and Peace,* 10.

42. Furman, *America's Deliverance and Duty,* 9-10.

43. Furman, *Rewards of Grace,* 9.

44. Furman, *Unity,* 25.

45. Furman, *Deliverance,* 9.

46. Ibid., 16.

47. *A Confession of Faith,* 2nd Charleston Ed. (Charleston: J. Hoff, 1813), 15; ch. 3, part 1.

48. Furman, *Deliverance,* 7.

49. Furman, *Rewards,* 9, 16. Furman, *Deliverance,* 16.

50. Furman, *Constitution,* 8.

51. Furman, *Crown,* 33.

52. Furman, *Rewards,* 18-20, 35.

53. Furman, *Unity,* 22.

54. Furman, *Rewards,* 36.

55. Ibid., 35.

56. Furman, *Constitution,* 23.

57. Ibid., 27.

58. Furman, "Address," 4-5.

59. Furman, Appendix H in Rogers, 310-11.

60. Furman, *Rewards,* 7.

61. Furman, *Crown,* 8.

62. Furman, *Unity,* 25.

63. Ibid.

64. Furman, *Constitution,* 10.

65. *The Baptist Catechism* (Charleston: Hoff, 1813), questions 24 and 9.

66. Furman, *Conversion,* 14.

67. Ibid., 15.

68. Furman, *Rewards,* 19.

69. Furman, *Deliverance,* 17.

70. Richard Furman, *Conversion Essential to Salvation* (Charleston: J. Hoff, 1816), 7-8.

71. Ibid., 12.

72. Ibid., 10.

73. Furman, *Constitution,* 9.

74. Ibid., 27.
75. Furman, *Crown,* 35.
76. Ibid., 36.
77. Furman, *Rewards,* 17-18.
78. Furman, *Conversion,* 14.
79. Ibid., 7, 15.
80. Ibid., 15, 17.
81. Ibid., 11-12.
82. Ibid., 10.
83. Furman, *Conversion,* 3.
84. Ibid., 6.
85. Ibid., 8.
86. Ibid.
87. Furman, *Constitution,* 31.
88. Furman, *Rewards,* 8, 10.
89. Furman, *Crown,* 18, 20.
90. Ibid.
91. Ibid., 18-19.
92. Ibid., 15.
93. Furman, *Constitution,* 30, 32.
94. Furman, *Constitution,* 20-21.
95. Furman, *Crown,* 15.
96. Ibid., 21.
97. Ibid., 20.
98. Ibid., 20-21.
99. Furman, *Unity,* 20.
100. Furman, *Rewards,* 12-13.
101. Ibid., 12.
102. Furman, *Crown,* 28-29.
103. Furman, *Constitution,* 8.
104. Ibid., 10.
105. Ibid., 22.
106. Ibid., 23.
107. Ibid., 12.
108. Ibid.
109. Ibid., 29.
110. Furman, *Unity,* 13.
111. Furman, *Rewards,* 18.
112. Furman, *Constitution,* 40.
113. Furman, *Conversion,* 14.
114. Furman, *Crown,* 16.
115. Furman, *Rewards,* 15.
116. Furman, *Crown,* 16.
117. Furman, *Constitution,* 34.
118. Furman, *Constitution,* 34-35.

8

John L. Dagg

Mark E. Dever

Biography

John Leadley Dagg (1794-1884) was the first Southern Baptist systematic theologian to be read widely by Southern Baptists. He exercised a long, prominent, and influential ministry as pastor, administrator, and teacher in Virginia, Pennsylvania, Alabama, and Georgia. Over one hundred years after his birth, his *Manual of Theology* was still frequently cited and used in colleges and theological seminaries. Almost two hundred years after his birth, this comparatively unknown theologian's *Manual of Theology and Church Order* is again in print. In 1903 E. Y. Mullins wrote that Dagg "was one of the most conspicuous figures among the Baptists of the South during the nineteenth century. . . . His work on theology has exerted a widespread and powerful influence throughout the South as well as elsewhere. Truly his was a life rich in influence for good and these influences continue in power to the present hour."[1] Who was this man? What did he teach?

John L. Dagg was born on February 14, 1794, in Middleburg, Virginia.[2] Dagg's boyhood was largely uneventful. His formal education was scant. Religion was not a large part of the Dagg household during his earliest years. Although his mother was raised as a Presbyterian, neither of his parents claimed to be converted until Dagg's early teenage years. He recounts his own conversion as having occurred in 1809.

Once converted, Dagg undertook a study of the highly controversial doctrine of infant baptism. Surrounded by Presbyterian literature and friends, Dagg thought it his duty to investigate the claims of infant baptism. Coming to baptistic conclusions, Dagg was baptized into the Ebeneezer Baptist Church by William Fristoe in the spring of 1812. After a few years studying medicine, Dagg was ordained to the ministry in November 1817. He spent the next eight years in his native northern Virginia pastoring several smaller churches. A preacher of some ability, Dagg received calls to large, city churches.[3] He declined these calls, however, and continued serving the small churches.

The second chapter of Dagg's ministry began in January 1825 when he accepted the call to the fashionable Fifth Baptist Church of Philadelphia. This young congregation already boasted a sanctuary which could seat 1,300—the largest Baptist sanctuary in Philadelphia. During this time his involvement in larger denominational concerns naturally increased.[4] He was an ardent spokesman for missions work, whether in western Pennsylvania or among the Cherokees in Georgia. Dagg's successful pastorate in Philadelphia ended due to the failure of his voice in 1834. Wanting to retain his services in the area, the Baptists of the Philadelphia Association approached him about serving as president and professor of theology at a new school (the Haddington Institute) they desired to open. Dagg accepted the position and served there until 1836, when the school was dissolved.

Dagg spent the next eight years of his life in Tuscaloosa, Alabama, as president of the Alabama Female Athenaeum. He continued to be active in Baptist life, serving on many committees and as an officer in the Alabama Baptist Convention. He was not, however, able to attend national meetings easily due to his poor health and the difficulties of the journey.

Dagg left Tuscaloosa on January 29, 1844, to journey to Mercer University in Penfield, Georgia, where he had been called as president and professor of theology. Dagg went with high hopes that Mercer would become the "Theological Seminary for the Southern States."[5] As president (1844-54), Dagg labored to build the theological department of Mercer. By the early 1850s, it was perhaps the most celebrated theological school in the South.[6] As a professor (1844-55), he was held in high regard by his peers. Mercer enjoyed great prosperity during his presidency, with student enrollment, value of property, and endowment growing severalfold.[7] During his successful tenure at Mercer, Dagg was called upon for larger denominational service.[8] In 1856 he retired from teaching theology at Mercer.

Dagg continued to live in Georgia for the next fifteen years. During the first years of his retirement he wrote his four larger books. The first and most celebrated was his *Manual of Theology,* published in 1857.[9] Then followed his *Treatise on Church Order* (1858), *Elements of Moral Science* (1859), and *Evidences of Christianity* (not published until 1869). During this time, his infirmities greatly increased. In 1870 Dagg moved with his daughter, Mrs. Henry Rugeley, to Lowndesboro for a few months, then to Hayneville, Alabama, (near Montgomery) where he remained until his death on June 11, 1884, at the age of ninety.

Dagg attended the 1869 meeting of the Southern Baptist Convention in Macon, Georgia. Then seventy-five years old, Dagg's only involvement was to lead in the devotional exercises on the first morning of the Convention. While Dagg was never able to attend another Convention meeting, it is clear that his influence on the body endured. Through his long years of outstanding service in Virginia, Pennsylvania, Alabama, and Georgia, Dagg had developed many close relationships with the religious leaders of the day. His service at Mercer was well-known and greatly appreciated. His writings served to keep his thoughts before the minds of thousands of his fellow ministers. In 1879 during the meeting of the Southern Baptist Convention in Atlanta, W. H. Whitsitt moved that "a catechism . . . containing the substance of the Christian religion" be drawn up by the "venerable" J. L. Dagg. The resolution passed unanimously.[10] Such was the respect and influence of John Leadley Dagg.[11]

John L. Dagg (1794-1884)

Exposition

John L. Dagg's *Manual of Theology* reveals a theology both simple and profound. In the *Manual* itself, Dagg neither quoted nor mentioned any authors, other than the Author of Holy Scripture. "It has been my aim to lead the mind of the reader directly to the sources of religious knowledge, and incite him to investigate them for himself, without respect to human authority."[12] Dagg presented theology as *always* an expression of piety—a loving heart desiring to know more of its Beloved. To search out the nature of God, His will, and His works, was an obligation for every sincere believer. Theology was not the task of the theologian any more than it was the task of the pastor, the deacon, or the church member.

> The study of religious truth ought to be undertaken and prosecuted from a sense of duty, and with a view of the improvement of the heart. When learned, it ought not to be laid on the shelf, as an object of speculation; but it should be deposited deep in the heart, where its sanctifying power ought to be felt. To study theology, for the purpose of gratifying curiosity, or preparing for a profession, is an abuse and profanation of what ought to be regarded as most holy. To learn things pertaining to God, merely for the sake of amusement, or secular advantage, or to gratify the mere love of knowledge, is to treat the Most High with contempt.[13]

Sanctification and edification rather than mere illumination were the ends of all proper theology. Knowledge of God was presented as the vehicle which the Holy Spirit used to bring one to know God, and to be completely transformed by Him. Dagg therefore introduced each of the eight "books" of his *Manual of Theology* with a section on the duty arising from the doctrine discussed within the book. Knowledge, for Dagg, clearly involved responsibility.

God

How do we know about God in order to know Him personally? Dagg presented four valid means of religious knowledge—personal moral and religious feelings, the moral and religious feelings of society, the natural world, and divine revelation. The first three of these, Dagg wrote, led to "Natural Religion" which taught the "fundamental truths on which all religion is based . . . ." Among these fundamentals, Dagg included knowledge of the existence of God, that this God is to be worshiped, that the soul is immortal, some basic morality, and that all people are ultimately accountable for their actions. Yet, none of this was saving knowledge of God. For that, we are specifically given the unique Divine revelation of the Bible, the written word—"the perfect source of religious knowledge, and the infallible standard of religious truth."[14]

After exhorting his readers to the love of God, Dagg set out the doctrine of God in traditional terms. The existence of God is "demonstrated" by our own moral nature, the existence of the world, and the common consent of mankind to this fact. Yet ultimately, the existence and character of God can only be established beyond doubt by God's revelation of Himself in the Bible.

What do we learn about God from Divine revelation? From Scripture we learn that there is but one God. This God is a spirit who is everywhere, eternal, and who knows all things. He is free, all-powerful, infinitely benevolent, always truthful, perfectly just, immaculately holy, and infinitely wise. As was typical of Protestant thought into the nineteenth century, Dagg held that "holiness" was the essence of God's character, comprising in itself all the other characteristics of God. These attributes were to be seen as a unified whole, together reflecting the nature of God.

God is not a static, unmoved mover but is an active God. God has a plan for the world and actively pursues that plan to the delight of all true believers. In discussing the will of God, Dagg distinguished between the will of "command" and the will of "purpose." By the former Dagg intended simply that which God commands us to do. This will is that which He would require of us; it is our duty revealed in His statutes and judgments, revealed most clearly in the Bible. God's will of "purpose" is His free, self-conscious determination of what He in fact does.

The fact that God has so determined His actions should not be taken as destroying the free-agency of humans. Though He over-rules all things, God is not to be charged with the authorship of sin. Dagg distinguished the authorship of sin from the permission of sin. The first is clearly denied in Scripture (1 John 1:5; James 1:13,17), the second is clearly affirmed (Acts 14:16). This distinction, helpful as it has been in Christian theology, leaves much unanswered. Dagg recognized this in his treatment of the vexed question of the reprobate. Here, Dagg exhorted his readers simply to trust God and to know that the author of justice can never Himself be unjust.

> If right principles prevailed in our hearts, we would not presume to dictate to the Infinitely Wise, nor find fault with his plans, but wait with pleasure on the development of his will: and when we cannot see the wisdom and goodness of his works, we should, in the simplicity of faith, rest assured that his plan, when fully unfolded, will be found most righteous and most wise.[15]

What has God in fact willed? Dagg answered this with the traditional distinction of God's acts of Creation and Providence. Creation was God's action of creating all things out of nothing. His works of Providence include His continual preservation of all things by His power and His control of their changes, of nature, of the moral sense of humanity, and ultimately of human actions. God has providentially predestined all things. His design is, at points, mysterious (as in its provision for sin in the world) but is, nevertheless, certain. In this mystery human philosophy must always show its inadequacy for the task of theology.

Humanity

And what of humanity? The fact that God has called all to repent (Matt. 3:2; Acts 17:30) is evidence of the present sinful state of humanity. Originally, man and woman were created holy. Humans are not sinful by creation, but only by the great perversion—the Fall. Dagg taught that a literal, historical Adam and Eve had been created as the first humans by God, and that they personally had violated their obligations of obedience to God.[16] This single act of disobedience plunged their entire offspring—the human race—into a state of alienation from God. By the act of one, all became transgressors of the covenant of God.

In recounting his conversion, Dagg wrote, "I saw clearly its [sin's] tendency to dethrone God, and felt that by this tendency its guilt was to be estimated."[17] Dagg believed that this was the experience of all humanity. Adam and Eve had acted as holy representatives for all of their progeny; therefore their depravity entailed our own. Through them human nature became sinful. This total depravity did not mean that there are no "amiable affections" in the heart of the fallen person. Rather, it meant that

> The love of God dethroned from the heart, and therefore the grand principle of morality is wanting, and no true morality exists. A total absence of that by which the actions should be controlled and directed, is total depravity.[18]

Love of self replaced the love of God. The corruption and guilt of this ruling love of self came to all of Adam's descendants by their federal, moral, and natural unions with Adam. The federal union was that by which God constituted Adam the representative of all of his descendants. The moral union is the actual sin that all humans, Adam and his descendants, willingly commit. The natural union is the fact of the physical descent of all humans from Adam. Dagg was unclear about exactly how this sinful nature was transmitted, but he asserted that it was clear that it was transmitted. Depravity entails the corruption of the image of God in humanity—conscience, actions, and even our mental capacities. It does not, however, entail the loss of the human will. Yet since a person's will always follows his own nature (which is now sinful) the person will inevitably will to sin. All humans are, therefore, condemned, helpless, and—apart from the intervention of God's Holy Spirit— spiritually dead.[19]

Christ

The necessity of this intervention of the Holy Spirit leads into Dagg's treatment of Christ. The object of our belief—Christ—must be understood to be both a man and God. Following Anselm (though without mentioning him) Dagg argued that God had to become man in order for Him to be a suitable sacrifice for those whose places He would assume. And yet the man Christ Jesus is also presented in Scripture as God (Jn. 1:1,14; 20:28; Acts 20:28; Rom. 9:5; Heb. 1:8; 1 Jn. 1:3; Rev. 19:13). Names of God, attributes of God, works of God, Old Testament references to God, and worship of God are all ascribed to Jesus Christ in the New Testament. Without referring to Chalcedon, or using all of its language, Dagg taught Chalcedonian orthodoxy. The union of the divine and human natures in Jesus Christ was without confusion or dissolution.

Dagg clearly affirmed the pre-existence of Christ; His incarnation; and His resurrection, ascension, and intercession. He used the traditional tripartite distinction of the three offices of Christ—prophet, priest and king. As a prophet, Jesus Christ revealed God to humans. As a priest, He made "an efficacious sacrifice for the sins of his people, and intercedes for them at the right hand of God, and blesses them with all spiritual blessings."[20] Finally, as King, Christ has authority over all for the glory of God and for the good of His people. Dagg treated the office of priest most extensively. Dagg taught that Christ's sacrifice effected atonement between helpless sinners and God. Christ died as a substitute for those who had incurred God's wrath, thereby reconciling sinners and God. He rejected any idea of the cross as simply a stirring example. That Christ's death was actually an atoning sacrifice for our sins was, he wrote, the doctrine that was "essential to Christianity."[21]

> It was not Christ transfigured on Mount Tabor; not Christ stilling the tempest, and raising the dead; not Christ rising triumphantly from the grave, and ascending gloriously, amidst shouts of attendant angels, to his throne in the highest heavens: but Christ on the cross, expiring in darkness and woe, that the first preachers of the Gospel delighted to exhibit to the faith of their hearers. This was their Gospel; its centre, and its glory.[22]

Holy Spirit

Dagg's briefest "book" in his *Manual of Theology* was reserved for the Holy Spirit. This brevity is not evidence of a low, or undeveloped Pneumatology, but rather of an entire theology done "in tandem" with the Holy Spirit. Each doctrine is treated as a sanctifying tool of the Holy Spirit. Therefore, much of the work of the Spirit is discussed in other places throughout his *Manual of Theology*. Dagg taught that Christians are utterly dependent for their spiritual lives upon "a person, distinct from the Father and the Son"— the Holy Spirit. This third Person of the Trinity is no mere force, or influence, but clearly a Person. And this "person" is clearly God. In the formula for baptism, and in the Great Commission, the Holy Spirit is named along with the Father and the Son as God. The Holy Spirit is legitimately worshiped (1 Cor. 6:19) and can be sinned against (Acts 5:3-4). Furthermore, passages in the Old Testament applied to God are clearly applied in the New Testament to the Holy Spirit (Ex. 17:7; cf. Heb 3:9; Isa. 6:8; cf. Acts 28:25; Jer. 31:31-34; cf. Heb. 10:15-17). The Holy Spirit is eternal, omnipresent, omniscient. He created, performs miracles, and raised Christ from the dead. In short, the Holy Spirit is God. His work among Christians is to set us apart as God's special people and to comfort us. He has become our Emmanuel.

Salvation

Divine grace is very important in Dagg's theology. As a Baptist Dagg stood in the Reformed tradition of earlier Baptist theologians like John Bunyan, Benjamin Keach, John Gill, Andrew Fuller, and Isaac Backus. Dagg's theology emphasized God's grace and the human response of gratitude. One could almost say that for Dagg all of theology was a study in the grace of

God. It is not surprising, therefore, to find his treatment of the doctrine of the Trinity in his book on "Divine Grace." "The doctrine of a three-fold distinction in the Godhead, belongs especially to the economy of grace . . . ."[23] This is so because Dagg combined an orthodox, Nicene treatment of the Trinity (affirming that Father, Son, and Holy Spirit, are three persons in one divine essence) with the expressions of Covenant theology. This theology originated among the Reformers and was most clearly developed in the late-fifteenth and sixteenth centuries. Covenant theology taught that before the foundations of the world, the three divine persons of the Trinity had determined to cooperate in salvation according to an eternal, pretemporal, intra-Trinitarian covenant. Dagg, too, taught that this was the framework upon which the entire story of redemption was to be understood.[24]

"The salvation of men is entirely of divine grace."[25] Each aspect of our salvation—our pardon, justification, adoption, regeneration, sanctification, final perseverance, and ultimate perfection—is accomplished only by the grace of God. This is consistent with Dagg's teaching of the helplessness of depraved humanity. That salvation is due completely to the grace of God is seen most clearly in Christ's bearing our burden of sin for us. Only His blood could effectually remove our sins. Apart from His action, no one could be saved. His righteousness is imputed to those for whom He died. Believers obtain this benefit from Christ by means of their consensual, spiritual, and federal unions with Christ (paralleling humanity's three unions with Adam). The consensual union is that union of Christ and the believer by which Christ consents to be the believer's substitute, and the believer consents to be found in Christ. The spiritual union is that union of the spirit by which the believer's spirit is reborn by the Spirit of God. The federal union is that union by which the believer is incorporated into the covenant of grace, now taking Christ as his legal representative before God. By these unions with Christ, believers are justified before God. Adoption is accomplished, whereby God's love and discipline are freely given to the believer. Regeneration is made possible only through God's gift of faith.[26] Sanctification, too, is primarily the work of the Spirit of God. Perseverance of the regenerate is certain, by God's grace. Rejecting the doctrine of final perseverance placed the hope of salvation on human effort, not on the purpose and grace of God. From the work of election to glorification, Dagg resisted any notion which would transfer salvation from the responsibility of God to the responsibility of man.

This insistence on the priority of God in salvation arose, in part, from Dagg's understanding of the Scripture's teaching on election, particular redemption, and effectual calling. In these doctrines, the consistent, cooperative activities of Father, Son, and Holy Spirit could be seen, each working for the salvation of a great multitude of humanity. Before the foundations of the world, the Father elected some. Since the salvation of any was purely a matter of grace, exceeding mere human justice or dessert, the charge of injustice could not meaningfully be hurled at God in any of His saving actions. Dagg asserted an uncompromising eternal election by God as the basis of salvation. "All who will finally be saved, were chosen to salvation by God the

Father, before the foundation of the world, and given to Jesus Christ in the covenant of grace."[27] This election is taught in Scripture and is mandated by the fact that God will certainly distinguish between the righteous and the unrighteous at the day of judgment. If it is right for Him to so distinguish in judgment, then it was right for such to be His purpose from all eternity. Dagg specifically rejected the Arminian interpretation (although not by name) that God's election was based upon His foreknowledge of the faith and obedience of some. He insisted that God by His mere grace chose some from among all of those who were under just condemnation and elected them to be the objects of His mercy.

Dagg defined the practical implications of this doctrine. Instead of making human effort useless, election produces that ultimate trust in and dependence upon God which is most needful for us to continue living as believers. Instead of undermining morality and creating antinomianism, it encourages believers to live holy and obedient lives, knowing that the Scriptures teach that such lives are evidences of God's election. Rather than suggesting that God is unjust, it shows Him to be at once truly sovereign and just, yet also merciful and gracious. Rather than proving God to be a "respecter of persons" it demonstrates that those regenerated are not so blessed because of any superiority within themselves but simply by God's grace. Rather than rendering a "promiscuous" preaching of the gospel to all "insincere," such an understanding of the doctrine of election underscores the faithfulness of God to all, whether in judgment of their sins, or in gracious salvation to those who respond in trust to Him through the gospel message. Rather than diminishing the extent of God's love, it leaves the ultimate extent unchanged from the Arminian perspective yet increases its depth and height (i.e., from eternity to eternity). Rather than presenting God as a despotic tyrant because of His reprobation of a part of the human race to misery, God is shown to be just, yet gracious (cf. Matt. 20:13-15). And finally, rather than being the doctrine of those who assume that they are among the chosen, this doctrine is the teaching of Scripture, creating not pride and self-satisfaction among those who receive it, but humility and a recognition of their utter dependence upon God. God's favor can never be earned—not even by the believer's acceptance of the doctrine of election.[28]

The doctrine of particular redemption clearly followed from this doctrine of election. Those whom the Father elected, the Son redeemed. Jesus had a particular people in view when He laid down His life. Just as the Father's election was particular, not extending to every individual, so the Son died to redeem not every individual, but a particular people. The cross was not a divine gamble, but a divine triumph. This is consistent, Dagg insisted, with the idea of the existence of hell. For should any suffer in hell if Christ has already suffered for them? Would not this be unjust? And yet if Christ died as a substitute for all, surely none could be sent to suffer *again* for those same sins for which Christ has already suffered. Dagg maintained that the intent of the atonement was clearly that the elect should be redeemed. To object either that the death of Christ must have been infinitely valuable, or that He had to suffer a specific additional amount for each one of those who respond to the gospel was to go beyond the testimony of Scripture. Simple faith would dictate that Christ's death was of appropriate value for the end He intended for it. To say that it was more than that, or to try to evaluate it more specifically, is unwarranted by God's self-revelation in Scripture. All the Scripture clearly teaches is that "The Son of God gave His life to redeem those who were given to Him by the Father in the covenant of grace."[29]

The Holy Spirit's part in this covenant of redemption was to call effectually to repentance and belief all whom the Father had elected and for whom Christ had died. While all who hear the gospel are called externally, only those who have felt the distinguishing grace of God, the internal grace, have that external call made effectual. This effectual calling of the sinner by the Holy Spirit always results in regeneration. Again, God is the author of salvation. All are under the just condemnation of God for their willful rebellion, and yet God—Father, Son, and Holy Spirit—has acted to bring some graciously to new life to the praise of His glory. Such action by such a God toward such creatures is entirely beyond explanation apart from His supreme love to us in Christ.

Eschatology

What was to be the end of this grand drama of redemption? Dagg answered that for the soul and the body, and for the righteous and the wicked, the ends will be different. For the soul, Dagg taught that there was immortality. God created each soul immortal. This was not so because philosophically it must be so, but because biblically, God had revealed that it was so (2 Cor. 5:8; Luke 23:43; John 14:3). For the body, the Scriptures taught that the bodies of all who die "will be raised from the dead, and reunited to their spirits, for the judgment of the great day."[30]

Finally, there is to be a future day of judgment in which Christ will judge all people according to their works. This day of judgment will be at Christ's second advent. Dagg did not clearly state his position on the second coming of Christ along the division common today (pre, post, or a millennial). What was important to him was the certainty and the outcome of that event. The certainty of it was clear from Scripture—Christ would bodily return in power and great glory to judge the living and the dead. The outcome of that event was twofold. For the righteous, the outcome will be heaven and perpetual happiness in the presence and enjoyment of God. While much is untold in Scripture, it is certain that there will be the best possible society, the most delightful employment, the absence of all unhappiness and the presence of all true enjoyment. For the wicked, hell is their eternal destination. There they "will suffer everlasting punishment for their sins."[31] Wherever and whenever hell may literally be, Scripture clearly teaches that this is to be the nature of it. This misery is not for the sake of purification, so that all may ultimately be restored to God, nor is it ultimately annihilating. God's justice demands that each person is considered a moral agent, bound to love and obey Him, and that those who do not do so are justly guilty, and liable to, and even require punishment. This, Dagg taught, in no way mars God's benevolence to humanity, rather it ensures the existence of true morality in the world.

The Church

That doctrine which is most distinctive of Baptists, and yet which has been the most disputed within Baptist groups has certainly been the doctrine of the church. Questions of structure, of the forms of worship, of the nature of the church (local and/or universal) and, of course, of baptism have repeatedly formed, divided and defined Baptist groups. In the middle of the nineteenth century the American frontier was the arena of Alexander Campbell and J. R. Graves. Denominational strife and pride were unusually prominent. It is not surprising, therefore, that John L. Dagg would choose to write a separate book, almost equal in length to his *Manual of Theology,* which dealt solely with ecclesiology. This reflected not only Dagg's historical situation, but also his commitment to the reality and importance of obedience to Christ in all that is revealed. Dagg concluded his introduction to *A Treatise on Church Order* by writing that

> Church order and the ceremonials of religion are less important than a new heart; and in the view of some, any laborious investigation of questions respecting them may appear to be needless and unprofitable. But we know, from the Holy Scriptures, that Christ gave commands on these subjects, and we cannot refuse to obey. Love prompts our obedience; and love prompts also the search which may be necessary to ascertain his will. Let us, therefore, prosecute the investigations which are before us, with a fervent prayer, that the Holy Spirit, who guides into all truth, may assist us to learn the will of him whom we supremely love and adore.[32]

Dagg taught that a Christian church is "an assembly of believers in Christ, organized into a body, according to the Holy Scriptures, for the worship and service of God."[33] Unlike the "Landmarkists" of his day, Dagg used *church* to refer local assemblies of Christians, regardless of denominational distinctives. The members of a church are only those who profess saving trust in Christ. (Dagg recognized that this was not equivalent to saying that only the elect are members of the local church, but it was denying, among other things, the practice of infant membership.[34]) This church was by definition an *organized* assembly. It was also a distinct, independent assembly (the New Testament having nowhere taught that one church was to be supervised by any organization or individual outside of the local church). The guiding rule for contemporary churches must always be the practice of the New Testament church. While not implying that "every minute particular in the doings of a church" is regulated by following New Testament practice, in major matters the New Testament is meant as the church's pattern.[35] Thus, baptism is still a prerequisite to church membership because it was so in the New Testament church.

Dagg also taught that the word *church* was used in the New Testament to refer to a universal company of all of those who are saved by Christ. This position was stringently criticized in the new teachings of the "Land-markists." Yet, Dagg specifically defended this doctrine against Land-markism, even quoting from their own popular writings.[36] Dagg did not, however, equate the local/universal dichotomy with the visible/invisible dichotomy. He insisted that any who were to be truly considered members of either the local or universal church must be visible to the world. "Notwithstanding the errors which human judgment may commit in individual cases, it still remains true, that the light of piety is visible."[37] Nor did he equate the universal church with any organization. The church universal was united not by organization, but by its spiritual nature. It will be culminated at the end of the world and will continue eternally. The word *church* in Dagg's thought "applies to a local church, because the members of it actually assemble; and it applies to the church universal, because the members of it will actually assemble in the presence, and for the everlasting worship of God."[38]

Baptism was one of the earliest doctrines with which Dagg wrestled. His early struggle left him with clear opinions on almost every conceivable aspect of the doctrine and practice of baptism. Baptism with water was certainly an ordinance for the church until the kingdom of God should be consummated by the return of Christ. The Christian is not merely to seek a "spiritual" baptism but is obligated to seek water baptism by the command of Christ and the apostles. It may not be set aside as a matter of indifference to the modern Christian. Dagg went to great lengths to demonstrate that the only proper understanding of baptism, is, by the very nature of the word, "to immerse."[39] This is proved by the use of the Greek word, and by the symbolic purpose of the act of baptism in Scripture. To read *baptizo* any other way, is to deny the clear results of etymological, historical, and scriptural research. The only proper subjects of this baptism are those who repent of their sins and trust in Christ for salvation. "Baptism was designed to be the ceremony of Christian profession . . . ." with none but baptized persons properly being able to be admitted to membership in the church.[40] To forego this would be to allow clear disobedience to the Christ one claims to follow.

It is not surprising, therefore, to find Dagg adamantly opposed infant membership in the church. By this, Dagg did not mean to suggest that *children* were not to be admitted to the church. Anyone, adult or child, who gave credible profession of faith and was baptized was to be admitted to the church. Infants, however, incapable of faith and with only the claim of the faith of their parents, were not proper candidates for membership. "As the covenant of circumcision in its literal sense, admitted none into the covenant seed but literal descendants of Abraham; so in the allegorical sense, none are included in the spiritual seed but true believers."[41] Therefore, infant baptism was wrong. The fact that those dying in infancy may, in fact, be saved by the grace of God, is no argument for the unbiblical practice of infant baptism. Infant baptism is nowhere commanded in the New Testament. Those who were baptized in the New Testament were disciples, which infants cannot be. The analogy of baptism to circumcision in the Scriptures is an analogy made with the circumcision of the heart (conversion) and not with the circumcision of the flesh. Indeed, Dagg argued, infant baptism is not heard of earlier than the close of the second century.

If Dagg gave a somewhat unconventional answer to the question "Who may be baptized?" he did not give such an unconventional answer to the question "Who may baptize?" Admitting that his conclusion here was reached by a more subtle series of reasonings from Scripture and history, he suggested that "the authority to administer baptism is conferred in the ordinary course of the ministerial succession, when an individual, called by the Holy Spirit to the ministry of the word, is publicly set apart to this service."[42] Again arguing against the Landmarkers, Dagg insisted that unbaptized ministers be recognized as true, if erring, ministers, and treated with respect. George Whitefield, Jonathan Edwards, Samuel Davies, Edward Payson are all examples heralded by Dagg of men who were indisputably used of God as ministers of the gospel, even if they were in error on the matter of baptism. Baptists must know and proclaim the truth of baptism, yet realize that this is not the essence of Christianity. To make this error is to fall into a new type of "popery."

> It is our duty, while rendering punctilious obedience to all the commands of God, to regard the forms and ceremonies of religion as of far less importance than its moral truths and precepts. . . . Because we differ from other professors of religion in our faith and practice respecting the externals of religion, we are under a constant temptation to make too much account of these external peculiarities. Against this temptation we should ever struggle. If we magnify ceremony unduly, we abandon our principles, and cease to fulfill the mission to which the Head of the church has assigned us.[43]

The distinctives of our denomination must never be confused with the essentials of our faith.

Like baptism, communion is to be observed by the church until the end of the world because it was so instituted by Christ. While denying the automatic efficacy of the rite of communion, Dagg saw a fuller significance in communion than that which Baptists have often. This Supper is to be understood as a memorial of Christ, "a representation that the communicant receives spiritual nourishment from him, and a token of fellowship among the communicants."[44] This Supper is to be celebrated in local churches by baptized members of any recognized churches there present. Dagg defended the position known as "strict communion." That is, while welcoming Christians of any denomination to the table, Dagg would deny the table to any who had not been immersed as believers. He denied, however, that paedobaptist brethren should feel disowned by this restriction.

> . . . there are surely many modes of testifying and cherishing the warmest affection toward erring brethren, without participating in their errors. We may be ready, in obedience to Christ, to lay down our lives for our brethren—though we may choose to die, rather than, in false tenderness to them, violate the least of his commandments.[45]

The rest of Roman Catholicism's "seven sacraments," and the foot washing some fellow Baptists considered as an ordinance, Dagg specifically rejected.

Only baptism and the Lord's Supper were ordered by Christ to be perpetually observed in His church.

Dagg dealt briefly with the rest of the external matters of the church. Public worship should be held on Sunday, the Christian sabbath. The church's regular meeting should be characterized by "prayers, songs of praise, and the reading and expounding of God's word."[46] Prescribed forms of prayers are objectionable, yet the use of hymnbooks is not. Those ministering the Word should be those who have been specifically called by God to do so. They should be set apart specifically for the work of the preaching of the Word. Although the apostolic ministry has ceased, God has continued to give His church ministers and missionaries to spread the gospel. Dagg taught that the prophetic gift, too, had ceased, and that this was simply one more attestation of the sufficiency of the revelation of Scripture. The one called to the ministry should especially study the Scripture, and should have his call corroborated by the larger body of Christ in his church; because, "every man who believes alone, that he is called of God to the ministry, has reason to apprehend that he is under a delusion. If he finds that those who give proof that they honor God and love the souls of men, do not discover his ministerial qualifications, he has reason to suspect that they do not exist."[47] Deacons, too, are to be recognized by the local church, as necessity demands. Ordination is appropriate, but not obligatory (not being ordered in Scripture). From among these ministers of the Word, the church is to choose bishops, or pastors, for their local congregation. Such deacons and bishops (pastors) are the only offices mandated for the local church in Scripture. Members should labor carefully for the edification of all their brothers and sisters in Christ through punctual and regular attendance of preaching, Bible study, religious reading and discussions, good works, and prayer meetings. Even excommunication must be used by the local church as a tool for the sanctification of the body of Christ.

Evaluation

To evaluate the theology of John L. Dagg, one must first recall his purpose in his theological writings. His *Manual of Theology* and all of his expressly theological writings were

> designed for the use of those who have not time and opportunity to study larger works on theology. In preparing it, my aim has been to present the system of Christian doctrine with plainness and brevity; and to demonstrate, at every point, its truth, and its tendency to sanctify the heart. Men who have inclination and talent for deep research, will prefer more elaborate discussions; but if the novice in religion shall be assisted in determining what is truth, and what the proper use to be made of it, the chief end for which have written will have been attained.[48]

Thus Dagg makes no attempt to reproduce Gill's massive *Body of Divinity* (a work influential in his own theological formation). Dagg's *Manual of Theology* can only imperfectly be compared to Boyce's *Abstract of Systematic*

Theology (a text of Boyce's lecture notes, in which discussion of historical theological debates is given prominence). Dagg's approach could better be compared with J. M. Pendleton's *Christian Doctrine* or E. Y. Mullins' *The Christian Religion in Its Doctrinal Expression*. Neither of these later volumes were renowned for their complex discussion of classical theological problems. Rather they, like Dagg's *Manual of Theology,* served as simple expositions of Christian truth from a Baptist perspective. And, it may be noted, their very simplicity has given them much of the wide influence they have known in the denomination's thought and practice.

Yet Dagg's *Manual of Theology* was not only simple and therefore accessible (like the written theologies of Pendleton and Mullins). It was written specifically as an exercise in theological edification.

> It has been no part of my design, to lead the humble inquirer into the thorny region of polemic theology. To avoid everything that has been a subject of controversy, was impossible, for every part of divine truth has been assailed. But it has been my plan to pursue our course of investigation, affected as little as possible by the strife of religious disputants, and to know no controversy, but with the unbelief of our own hearts.[49]

As part of this plan, Dagg decided to appeal to no authority but Scripture itself. Therefore, while Dagg goes into careful exegeses of passages, and at points deals extensively with the original languages, he nowhere *expressly* engages in the historical debates which have done so much to shape contemporary Christian theology. Nicea and the Reformation, the Council of Trent, and the Westminster Assembly nowhere appear by name in his theology (although many of his expressions and arguments are formed by the discussions which took place in these contexts). Dagg has, as it were, re-created many of the debates of the history of Christian theology (he was certainly not ignorant of them), yet in the context of simple, apparently contemporary discussions about the Scriptures. This has the advantage of re-creating in the reader that which was always the fundamental theological issue for Dagg—"What sayeth the Scripture?" Yet, it must also be said that however helpful this may be for the layperson, it is not an adequate introduction to the theological science for the student of theology. Ideally the student should be supplied not only with Dagg's reading of the text and the problems, but with exact historical theological definitions and disputes and the circumstances in which they arose.

This is not to say that Dagg's theological method was wrong. His attempt to be *ultimately* dependent upon Scripture alone is laudable. That should be goal of every biblical theologian. Too, his concern for the sanctification of the heart *via* theological inquiry is very fitting (and, it must be added, is sadly lacking today, especially in the midst of much contemporary unbelieving "theology"). Dagg's concern for the knowing of God which permeates his discussion of the knowledge of God is searching and singularly appropriate. To combine this zeal for remembering the presence of God throughout the discussion of God, with a careful notation of histories of the discussions would be an admirable goal for any written theology.

Dagg's chief concern may well be said to be the holiness of God—not simply God's moral rectitude, but His God-ness. All of His attributes are thereby seen to be a unity in the Divine character, not separable units. Everything is to be done to the glory of God. Everything is to be known to the glory of God. Everything *is* to the glory of God. Thus we are to search after, love, obey, believe, and thank God. The introductory sections in his *Manual of Theology* are the practical summary of Dagg's theology. This is also the basis for Dagg's discussion of that thorniest of theological issues—theodicy. God is, by His nature, to be trusted. He may be misunderstood by us in what He does or allows, but He cannot be declared wrong. Ultimately, Dagg would answer with the apostle Paul, "who are you, a man, to answer back to God?" (Rom. 9:20).

To some, Dagg's devotional manner may seem to be in striking dissonance with his uncompromisingly Reformed presentation of God; yet, it could be argued that these two are perfectly complementary—a "high" view of God, matched by a strong devotion to Him. This God was not to be condemned so much for the problem of evil as praised for the unmerited love that He shows in Christ. Election shows God not to be a despotic tyrant, but a determined lover. Morally, humanity stands rightfully condemned by its choice of disobedience. The only justice to be demanded is humanity's condemnation. God's love, shown to us in Christ, is a matter for tremendous praise exactly because God was not obligated to treat us so. In all of this Dagg could well be a teacher to contemporary Christianity in the English-speaking world. To both Arminian evangelicals and many more "progressive" theologians, Dagg might well ask uncomfortable questions: How can one assert biblically that God champions the greatest good of each person at all times regardless of their actions? Such an idea surely would be popular, but how does it conform to the more uncomfortable realities of the biblical text, and of the real world? Here Dagg's theology, antiquated as it may seem to some by its style and its substance, may address some basic difficulties that the modern, egalitarian person has in comprehending and "allowing" there to be an absolutely sovereign, righteous, loving, and self-existent God.

It is, however, exactly at this point that we should also note Dagg's ethical teachings—the source of his infamy in some circles today. Dagg's *Elements of Moral Science* (1859) was the last major defense of slavery published in book form. While Dagg's ethics deserve a more extensive treatment, such must be left to the reader through perusing the work for oneself. Dagg asserted that the moral quality of an act lay in the intention behind it. He also taught that there should be no equality of rights apart from equality of condition.[50] Social rights were always unequal in society (as in the recognition of private property, or of the rights of parents over children). It was proper of the government to restrict the liberties of some more than the liberties of others if it were intended for their own good. Also, Dagg defended slavery as an institution condoned and not condemned in Scripture. Finally, Dagg argued pragmatically that while slavery had many grievous evils, God, by His overruling providence, had actually prospered the Africans through it.

The sources of Dagg's conservatism in social issues are matters of speculation. Some have attributed his satisfaction with the status quo to his Calvinism, perhaps thinking that Dagg assumed that all about him was the perfect will of God.[51] While his Calvinistic theology could be an indirect source, filtering through attitudes or priorities, it certainly would not be a direct source of his social conservatism. Dagg himself was painfully aware of the fallenness and imperfection of the present world. Too, he was active for change in other social affairs. He was an early leader among Baptists in issues of temperance, education, and dealing with the problems of the native American Indians.

Dagg clearly conceded that slavery as it was practiced was accompanied by great evil. Yet he reacted against the calls for radical change in the culture which he had known for half a century. There was certainly ample material in Scripture from which to draw a defense of slavery, if that were one's intent. Many of his more educated contemporaries (R. L. Dabney, J. H. Thornwell) had long before taken up a defense of slavery. Dagg reacted with a natural and lamentable defensiveness when the faults of his own culture (clear to us) were presented to the nation. The fact that these faults were presented most loudly and dramatically by those who were most opposed to slavery simply made it all the easier to caricature his cultural assailants. Too, the Baptists (and Methodists) had become established in the South and evident spiritual good had been accomplished among the slaves. Often, it must have seemed, the Northern rationalists and liberals would not admit this, and therefore perhaps evidenced their widely differing values from the more orthodox, scriptural concerns of the South. Despite his efforts, we cannot conclude otherwise than that at this point Dagg's culture molded his Christianity in a most perverse direction.

Dagg's chief theological distinction among Baptists was his clear maintenance of what *had* been Baptist orthodoxy in the South—Calvinism—and his clear rebuttal of what was replacing it as Baptist orthodoxy on the frontier—Landmarkism. The Landmarkism of J. R. Graves, A. C. Dayton, and J. M. Pendleton, was a theology which accepted Calvinism, yet deemphasized it. The Baptists of the seventeenth, eighteenth, and nineteenth centuries whose theologies were distinctively Calvinistic were often those who stressed their essential unity with other evangelical Protestants. The central doctrines of God, humanity, Christ, and grace were those around which groups formed, by which they were defined, and over which they divided. By the middle of the nineteenth century, the emphasis on the American frontier was increasingly shifting from those central issues which united evangelical Christians, to those issues which distinguished one body of Christians from another. Landmarkism was the dominant form that this emphasis took among Baptists. Dagg was courageous, courteous, and uncompromising in his defense of an earlier version of baptistic Christianity—uncompromisingly Baptist, but clearly fundamentally Christian—over against the unwarranted claims of the Landmarkists. Dagg rightly taught that God had owned the ministry of those who were in error in varying ways, including in their doctrine of baptism. Dagg rightly taught that *church* was used in the Scriptures in a local and universal sense, and that it could rightly be used even of those local assemblies which misunderstood baptism. In all of this Dagg was writing "against the stream" but did so in such a clearly orthodox fashion that even the Landmark champion J. M. Pendleton would later commend Dagg's *Manual of Theology and Church Order* and use it as a text at Union College in Tennessee.

In conclusion, it would be fair to say that Dagg makes no distinctive contributions to those engaged in the theological task today. His expositions of doctrine were typical of historic Christian positions formulated initially by others. However much it may be felt that the biblical orthodoxy of Dagg's theology must be recovered today if theology is to avoid suicide and to express the true gospel of Christ, it must be admitted that, in most ways, it is better learned from others with more searching presentations of Scripture, doctrine, history and reason.[52] Dagg's writings are inadequate for use as the theology text in a modern seminary. Having said that, it must be stated that if Dagg is not a particularly notable doctor in the content of theology, he is almost unsurpassed among Baptists as a doctor in the purpose of theology. Dagg would teach that if the pursuit of theology is to be legitimate, its purpose must be clear. To pursue knowledge of the biblical God can only properly be done by seeking to know the biblical God. To be captivated by the knowledge of God is idolatrous unless one is captivated by God Himself. That Dagg was so captivated is clear; that he may so teach us is his enduring contribution.

Bibliography

Works by Dagg

Autobiography of Rev. John L. Dagg, D.D. Rome, Ga.: J. F. Shanklin, Printer, 1886.

"Effectual Calling." *The Christian Index,* 31 (May 11, 1863): 1.

The Elements of Moral Science. New York: Sheldon and Co., 1859.

The Evidences of Christianity. Macon, Ga.: J. W. Burke and Co., 1869.

"The Fallen State of Man." *The Christian Index,* 32 (March 20, 1863): 1.

A Manual of Theology. Charleston: Southern Baptist Publication Society, 1857.

A Treatise on Church Order. Charleston: Southern Baptist Publication Society, 1858.

Works Related to Dagg

Brantley, W. T., Sr. "The Doctrines of Grace." *The Columbian Star,* 1 (Aug. 8, 1829): 91.

Cline, C. W. "Some Baptist Systematic Theologians." *Review and Expositor,* 20 (1923): 311-316.

Cuttino, Thomas E. "A Study of the Theological Works of John Leadley Dagg." Th.M. thesis, The Southern Baptist Theological Seminary, 1954.

Dever, Mark E. "Representative Aspects of the Theologies of John L. Dagg and James P. Boyce: Reformed Theology and Southern Baptists." Th.M. thesis, The Southern Baptist Theological Seminary, 1987.

Gardner, Robert G. "The Alabama Female Athenaeum and John Leadley Dagg in Alabama." *The Alabama Baptist Historian,* 5 (July, 1969): 3-32.

_____. "The Bible . . . A Revelation from God, Supplying the Defects of Natural Religion." *Foundations,* 4 (July, 1961): 241-58.

_____. "John Leadley Dagg." *Review and Expositor,* 54 (April 1957): 246-63.

_____. "John Leadley Dagg in Georgia." *Baptist History and Heritage,* 3 (Jan. 1968): 43-50.

_____. "John Leadley Dagg, National Leader." *The Quarterly Review,* 33 (April-June 1973): 48-53.

_____. "John Leadley Dagg: Pioneer American Baptist Theologian." Ph.D. dissertation, Duke University, 1957.

_____. "Men Under the Dominion of the Lower Propensities." *The Chronicle,* 20 (July 1957): 115-30.

_____. "A Tenth-Hour Apology for Slavery." *The Journal of Southern History,* 26 (Aug. 1960): 352-67.

Holifield, E. Brooks. *The Gentleman Theologians.* Durham, NC: Duke University Press, 1978.

Humphreys, Fisher, ed. *Nineteenth Century Evangelical Theology.* Nashville, Broadman Press, 1983.

Loftis, John. "Factors in Southern Baptist Identity as Reflected by Ministerial Role Models, 1750-1925." Ph.D. dissertation, The Southern Baptist Theological Seminary, 1987.

Lumpkin, William L. *Baptist Foundations in the South.* Nashville: Broadman Press, 1961.

Mallary, C. D. Review of *A Manual of Theology,* by John L. Dagg. *The Christian Index,* 36 (Oct. 14, 1857): 162-63.

Matheson, Mark. "Religious Knowledge in the Theologies of John Leadley Dagg and James Petigru Boyce: With Special Reference to the Influence of Common Sense Realism." Ph.D. dissertation, Southwestern Baptist Theological Seminary, 1984.

Moody, Dwight A. "Doctrines of Inspiration in the Southern Baptist Theological Tradition." Ph.D. dissertation, The Southern Baptist Theological Seminary, 1982.

Mueller, William A. "Southern Baptists and Theology." *The Theological Educator,* 1 (Oct. 1970): 49-62.

Nettles, Thomas J. *By His Grace and for His Glory.* Grand Rapids: Baker Book House, 1986.

Patterson, L. Paige. "An Evaluation of the Soteriological Thought of John Leadley

Dagg, Baptist Theologian of Nineteenth-Century America." Ph.D. dissertation, New Orleans Baptist Theological Seminary, 1973.

Pendleton, J. M. *Christian Doctrines: A Compendium of Theology.* Philadelphia: American Baptist Publication Society, 1878.

Phillips, Charles D. "The Southern Baptist View of the Church: As Reflected in the Thought of J. L. Dagg, E. C. Dargan, and H. E. Dana." Th.M. thesis, The Southern Baptist Theological Seminary, 1957.

Reviews of *A Manual of Theology,* by John L. Dagg, in *The Baptist Family Magazine,* 1 (Oct. 1857): 310; *The Commission,* 2 (Jan. 1858): 223; *Mississippi Baptist,* 1 (Oct. 8, 1857): 2; *The Southern Baptist,* 12 (Sept. 29, 1857): 2; and *Western Recorder,* 24 (Oct. 7, 1857): 154.

Sands, William. Review of *A Manual of Theology,* by John L. Dagg. *The Religious Herald,* 26 (Oct. 1, 1857): 2.

Straton, Hillyer Hawthorne. "John Leadley Dagg." M.A. thesis, Mercer University, 1926.

Notes

1. E. Y. Mullins, "A Southern Baptist Theologian," *The Baptist Argus* 7 (May 7, 1903): 1.

2. Other than in brief articles, Dagg has never been the subject of a published biography. His life must be pieced together from his sketchy autobiography, correspondence, and dissertations written on some aspect of his theology.

3. The Baptist church at Alexandria, Virginia, was interested in him in 1822, but he declined to consider the matter. First Baptist of Richmond, then the largest Baptist congregation in the nation, extended a call to Dagg in December 1824, which he also declined.

4. Dagg was an officer in the Philadelphia Baptist Missionary Society (1825-27) and one of the founders of the Pennsylvania Baptist Missionary Society (forerunner of the Pennsylvania Baptist Convention). Dagg also served on the board of managers of the Triennial Convention (1826-36), as a vice-president of the Triennial Convention (1838-45), on the board of directors of the American Baptist Home Missionary Society (1832-36), as vice-president of the American and Foreign Bible Society (1837-43), and as president, vice-president, and other positions of the Baptist General Tract Society (1824–43). He also served as the host pastor for the 1829 Triennial Convention.

5. Dagg, "Mercer University," *The Christian Index,* August 8, 1844, 3.

6. Dagg's close friend, Basil Manly, Sr., had suggested Dagg for the presidency of Mercer after Manly himself declined the appointment. Dagg had earlier turned down an offer of the Chair of Theology at the Howard Institute in Birmingham. At Mercer Dagg not only served as professor and president, but he was also the only officer of the institution ever to serve on the board of trustees (1848-55).

7. While a student at Mercer, W. L. Kilpatrick was asked what he thought of President Dagg. Referring to Dagg's physical infirmites, Kilpatrick replied, "He can neither read nor write, he can neither walk nor talk, but he is a very good President," B. D. Ragsdale, *Story of Georgia Baptists* (Atlanta: Foote and Davies Co., 1932), 1:101.

8. After moving to Georgia, Dagg became active in the Georgia Baptist Convention. He served on the Executive Committee (1844-55). Dagg was one of ten people appointed to meet on April 28, 1845, in Providence, Rhode Island, to arrange for the dissolution of the American Baptist Home Missions Society. One month later, while attending the organizational meeting for the Southern Baptist Convention, Dagg was appointed as one of the vice-presidents of the new Domestic Missions Board of the Southern Convention. He also was appointed to the committee to draw up the constitution for the new convention. Dagg again attended the Southern Baptist Convention in 1849. His activities there included chairing a committee on the China mission, delivering its report to the Convention, and addressing the Convention as a corresponding messenger from the American Sunday School Union.

9. Laudatory reviews were published in Baptist papers and magazines across the nation. See *The Southern Baptist* 12 (Sept. 29, 1857): 2; *Western Recorder* 24 (Oct. 7, 1857): 154; *Mississippi Baptist* 1 (Oct. 8, 1957): 2; *The Commission* 2 (Jan. 1858): 223; *The Baptist Family Magazine* 1 (Oct. 1857): 310; *The Religious Herald* 26 (Oct. 1, 1857): 2. C. D. Mallary's review in *The Christian Index* even suggested that "this would be a good Book to have read in our churches—especially those which are not regularly supplied with preaching. The volume could be easily divided into about 25 portions of from 12 to 18 pages—each portion supplying rich matter for a Sabbath day's meditation." Mallary, *The Christian Index* 36 (Oct. 14, 1857): 162-63. Although he strenuously disagreed with Dagg's ecclesiology, J. M. Pendleton assigned Dagg's *Manual of Theology* as his textbook at Union College in Tennessee (1857-61). James P. Boyce made some use of Dagg's *Manual of Theology* during the first two years of The Southern Baptist Theological Seminary's existence.

10. J. B. Jeter, P. H. Mell, E. T. Winkler, J. B. Gambrell, and J. P. Boyce were requested to assist Dagg and to take the task on themselves if he was unable. There is no record of the results of this request of the Convention. It is interesting to note that Whitsitt's colleague, Boyce, chairman of the faculty at the seminary, and president of the Convention that year, currently had a catechism in print.

11. Considering the widespread use of his *Manual of Theology* throughout the rest of the nineteenth century and his many students, listeners, and friends, Dagg's influence has certainly been underestimated. An aspect of Dagg's life which has been completely overlooked is the influence that he exerted beyond his own person, not merely through his preaching, teaching, writing, and denominational service, but through his family. His son, John F. Dagg served as pastor of the Baptist church at Milledgeville, Georgia (1847-1851); editor of the Georgia Baptist paper, *The Christian Index* (1851-1857); clerk of the Georgia Baptist Convention (1855); pastor of the Cuthbert Baptist Church (1857-1866); professor (1857-1866) and president (1861-1866) of Cuthbert Female College in Cuthbert, Georgia; and president of Bethel Female College, Hopkinsville, Kentucky (1866-1872). Dagg's stepson by his second wife's first marriage was Noah K. Davis. Since Davis's father died when he was only a few months old, Dagg was the only father that Davis ever knew. Davis graduated from Mercer in 1849. He served as president of Bethel College in Russellville, Kentucky (and in that capacity actively opposed Boyce's idea to move the seminary to Louisville). He later became widely celebrated as professor of Moral Philosophy at the University of Virginia. (In this capacity, Davis delivered one of the first series of Gay Lectures at The Southern Baptist Theological Seminary in 1901.) Dagg's daughter Elizabeth married S. G. Hillyer, a prominent Baptist minister in Georgia who served successively as professor of Belles Lettres and Theology, and as president of Mercer University. Another daughter of Dagg's, Mary Jane, married

Rollin D. Mallary, son of the well-known Georgia Baptist, C. D. Mallary. R. D. Mallary graduated from Mercer in 1851, and served as president of Southwestern Baptist College, Cuthbert, Georgia; Shorter College, Rome, Georgia; and Shelby Female College, Shelby, North Carolina.

12. Dagg, *Manual of Theology,* v.

13. Ibid., 13.

14. Ibid., 21, Dagg held the prevalent notion of an inerrant Scripture—". . . the Scriptures were originally penned under the unerring guidance of the Holy Spirit, . . ." 24.

15. Dagg, *Theology,* 110.

16. That this was not universally taught among evangelical Baptists of the time is evidenced by the sermons of President Francis Wayland of Brown University. Wayland dismissed the issue of the historicity of the Fall narrative as unimportant. Francis Wayland, *University Sermons* (Boston: Gould, Kendall and Lincoln, 1849), 87-88. Cf. Dagg, *Theology,* 144.

17. John L. Dagg, *Autobiography of Rev. John L. Dagg, D.D.* (Rome, Ga.: J. F. Shanklin, Printer, 1886), 8.

18. Dagg, *Theology,* 152.

19. "In our natural state we are totally depraved. No inclination to holiness exists in the carnal heart; and no holy act can be performed, or service to God rendered, until the heart is changed. This change, it is the office of the Holy Spirit to effect." Dagg, *Theology,* 277.

20. Dagg, *Theology,* 152.

21. Ibid., 213.

22. Ibid.

23. Ibid., 246.

24. Ibid., 253-57.

25. Ibid., 258.

26. Dagg has a careful discussion of that faith which precedes regeneration, and that living faith which can only be the result of regeneration in *Theology,* 279-85.

27. Ibid., 309.

28. Dagg's discussion of this doctrine is a good model of a sensitive pastoral discussion, appropriate for a committed church member. See Dagg, *Theology,* 309-23.

29. Ibid., 324. Dagg cites Ephesians 5:25-27; Titus 2:14; John 10:11; Revelation 1:5-6; Acts 20:28; Hebrews 10:14; Isaiah 53:5,11. As strange as this doctrine may sound to many evangelicals today, Dagg held what had clearly been considered the biblical position among Southern Baptists and Presbyterians throughout most of the eighteenth and nineteenth centuries.

30. Ibid., 345.

31. Ibid., 364.

32. John L. Dagg, *A Treatise on Church Order* (Charleston: Southern Baptist Publication Society, 1858), 12.

33. Ibid., 71.

34. Ibid., 97-99.

35. Ibid., 88.

36. Dagg's *Treatise on Church Order* has lengthy treatments of specific arguments used by Landmarkers to deny that "church" has a universal reference in Matthew 16:18 and Ephesians 1:22; 3:21. (Dagg, *Church Order,* 100-21). Dagg's willingness to quote human authorities in his *A Treatise on Church Order* suggests

that Dagg realized that he was dealing with issues less clearly taught by Scripture and less central to the gospel.

37. Dagg, *Church Order,* 124.

38. Ibid., 143.

39. Therefore, Dagg insisted (at some length) on baptism by immersion even in cold climates. See Dagg, *Church Order,* 308-12.

40. Ibid., 70.

41. Ibid., 174.

42. Ibid., 257.

43. Ibid., 301-2

44. Ibid., 209.

45. Ibid., 218.

46. Ibid., 238.

47. Ibid., 248.

48. Dagg, *Theology,* iii.

49. Ibid., iv.

50. John L. Dagg, *Elements of Moral Science* (New York: Sheldon and Co., 1859), 170.

51. Cf. E. Brooks Holifield, *The Gentlemen Theologians* (Durham, N.C.: Duke University Press, 1978), 153.

52. Dagg's treatment of theology, though, provides unusually clear, simple explanations of many biblical doctrines in ways which show much pastoral sensitivity to the questions often asked by church members.

9

James Madison Pendleton
Keith E. Eitel

In 1861 the United States was in the early stages of a life and death struggle to preserve a union that had held together for two generations. The nation divided along regional lines causing deep fractures that have yet to heal. James Madison Pendleton, a Southern Baptist leader, lived in the midst of this sociological trauma. He represented an unusual mixture of conservative and progressive ideas, each of which was rooted in strong convictions. In the summer of 1861, Pendleton watched the Stars and Bars rise over the courthouse in Murfreesboro, Tennessee. That symbol of the Southern Confederacy stayed in place for nine months. Pendleton rarely saw it. He "was unwilling to look at it, because it was usurping the place of the flag of the United States—the flag of my heart's love. The 'stars and bars' were utterly distasteful to me."[1] Pendleton was willing to stand adamantly opposed to prevailing opinion to corroborate principles he believed to be true. He was a unionist and an emancipationist who disagreed strongly with his peers.

Pendleton's unyielding commitment to his convictions helps explain his involvement in the Landmark movement.[2] Was Pendleton indeed a Landmarker of the J. R. Graves type, or was he a more moderate influence? This chapter ascertains the degree to which he warrants the label of an "Old Landmarker." Pendleton's primary contribution to Baptist theology was his attempt to establish a biblical ecclesiology. An analysis of his theology, therefore, will necessarily involve an estimation of his impact on Baptist social development, particularly that of the Southern Baptist Convention. A biographical sketch and an evaluation of his theology provide the bases for conclusions.

Biography

John and Frances Pendleton married in 1806, and they eventually brought eleven children into this world. James Madison Pendleton, their fourth child, was born on November 11, 1811, as frontier optimism stimulated people to leave the restricted boundaries of thirteen Eastern colonies and pour into the expanse of a vast continent. Pendleton's parents named him after President James Madison. His parents had settled in Spottsylvania, Virginia. Shortly before he was born, his parents had conversion experiences and each was baptized. Prior to John Pendleton's conversion, he had studied with Andrew Broaddus. In 1812 the Pendleton family left Virginia and moved to Kentucky.[3]

James Madison Pendleton (1811-91)

Photo courtesy of Southern Baptist Historical Library and Archives

J. M. Pendleton remembered his own conversion experience vividly. He did not readily make a decision to become a Christian. He recalled that when he was fifteen years old there was a boyhood friend "with whom I had enjoyed the pleasures of sin." He was astonished when this friend told him that he no longer desired to do the same things because now he wanted "to be a Christian."[4] Pendleton mused over the fact that all the religious influence he had been exposed to had not affected him. Rather, Christ worked in and through a friend. His matured theological reflection on the circumstances surrounding his conversion led him to conclude that there is a major difference between believing in Christ and considering oneself to be a Christian. He determined to evaluate his life on a continual basis to bring every part of his character in line with truly Christian character found in the New Testament.[5] Even at such a young age, Pendleton sensed the need to live consistently with the New Testament's patterns. Later in life, he applied his desire for consistency to corporate church life.

After an extended revival meeting in his home church, Pendleton grew more aware of the need for committed involvement in the affairs of the church. He tried his hand at several duties and even led Wednesday evening prayer meetings on occasion. The members of the Bethel church licensed him to preach in February 1830. He stated that he "thought it quite uncalled for," and he "did not believe it possible" for him to preach.[6] In November 1833 Pendleton successfully underwent examination by an ordination council in Hopkinsville, Kentucky.[7]

His professional ministerial career began on January 1, 1837, when he assumed the pastorate of the Baptist church in Bowling Green, Kentucky. He held that post for twenty years. When first assuming the pastorate, the church paid him the then progressive salary of $400 per year. He noted that this allowed him to devote himself to the full-time ministry. "I was the first man in Southern Kentucky who abjured all secular avocations, giving myself wholly to the ministry of the word."[8]

While at Bowling Green, some of Pendleton's ideas about affairs in the political arena surfaced. Under the heading "A Southern Emancipationist," he wrote more than twenty articles for *The Examiner,* a paper which stood opposed to slavery. His motivation for this act was a concern for the injustice of the institution of slavery. He wrote, "I was deeply interested in the subject of Emancipation, for all the pulsations of my heart beat in favor of civil liberty. . . ."[9] In 1849 he supported efforts to revise the state constitution in Kentucky and to include emancipationist measures. To his dismay, the state mood grew colder regarding emancipation. Pendleton wrote, regarding his feelings at the time, "My spirit sank within me and I saw no hope for the African race in Kentucky, or anywhere else without the interposition of some Providential judgment."[10] Pendleton's degree of conviction regarding this issue is evident in the fact that during the Civil War his opinions placed him in opposition to his own son. When his son, John Malcom, enlisted in the Confederate Army, he strongly disagreed with him, but their relationship never ceased being a loving one. A stray bullet struck his son in battle; he died for the Confederate cause in October of 1862.[11] This was the same son Pendleton had baptized when the boy was young, and rebaptized in 1859 when John Malcom sensed he had never been saved. "I therefore did not hesitate to baptize him a second time, considering his first baptism, so-called, a nullity."[12] Circumstances did not take precedence over convictions. Pendleton's views regarding emancipation and baptism held firmly in spite of the ebb and flow of events.

Pendleton returned to his pastorate in Bowling Green after a sabbatical leave to help a pastor in Green River, Ohio. In February 1852, Pendleton invited J. R. Graves of Nashville, Tennessee, to preach revival services at his church. Graves had already formed rather strong opinions about alien immersion, but Pendleton had not yet considered the issue in any detail. Shortly after Graves's arrival, it became apparent that there was a substantial disagreement on this issue between the two men. Graves argued his case, and Pendleton remained unconvinced. Graves offered to leave prior to the start of the revival, but Pendleton encouraged him to stay. He desired to hear more about Graves's opinions.[13] Pendleton recalled,

> . . . the meetings went on from day to day and from week to week until about seventy five persons, young and old, were baptized and added to the church. Truly it was a time of refreshing from the presence of the Lord. Our old meeting-house was not large, but the members of the church now filled all the seats at the Lord's Supper, and we began to plan for a new house of worship.[14]

Apparently sometime during the meetings, Graves convinced Pendleton to embrace his opinion about alien immersion. The meetings aroused the contrary sentiment among some of the Pedobaptists in the area. Methodist and Presbyterian ministers used their pulpits to inveigh against the flurry of ideas stimulated by the meetings. Later Pendleton preached at the dedication ceremony at the Baptist church in Logan County. In this message he outlined the rationale for being a Baptist rather than being part of any other denomination. Eventually, he expanded the theme into a book entitled *Three Reasons Why I Am a Baptist*. Pendleton sold the rights to Graves, who then published it in 1853. Twenty-nine years later, after the copyright period ran out, Pendleton revised and expanded the book. In 1882 the American Baptist Publishing Society republished it under the title *Distinctive Principles of Baptists*. The original version was Pendleton's first of several books.[15]

Graves's revival meetings with Pendleton at Bowling Green in 1852 proved to be historic in that a working relationship between the men soon developed. Graves invited Pendleton to write a series of articles aimed at resolving a very pragmatic question of the day, "Ought Baptists to Recognize Pedobaptist Preachers as Gospel Ministers?" Graves published this series in the *Tennessee Baptist,* a popular paper which conveyed Graves's ideas on ecclesiology to a wide readership. This series of articles had even wider circulation when it appeared as a pamphlet entitled, *An Old Landmark Reset*. Pendleton noted, "Bro. Graves furnished the title, for he said the 'Old Landmark' once stood, but had fallen, and needed to be 're-set.' So much for the name." Pendleton understated the impact of this book in his autobiography. He said, ". . . the discussions connected with it have modified the views of many Baptists in the South, and of some in the North."[16] The title of the book provided a defined focus for a major movement which is partly responsible for the identity and character of the Southern Baptist Convention today.

In January 1857, Pendleton joined the faculty of Union University in Murfreesboro, Tennessee. He comprised the entire theology department when he started. While on the faculty, he and A. C. Dayton became joint editors, along with Graves, of the *Tennessee Baptist*.[17] Pendleton also was one of the editors for *The Southern Baptist Review,* which functioned for six years prior to the Civil War.[18]

During this period of close collaboration with Graves and Dayton, Pendleton's views on two political subjects surfaced and proved to be divisive, possibly causing the abrupt discontinuation of the relationship between the "Triumvirate" of Landmark leadership. Emancipationist activities were not new to Pendleton. He had been involved in clandestine literary efforts to support the cause as early as 1849. While at Union University, his emancipationist views led peers to label him an abolitionist. The latter was a much more serious charge in his particular social context. Pendleton's own definition of the distinction between the two terms makes it clear he favored the gradual dismantling of slavery as a legal, social institution. He was amazed that his accusers did not differentiate between the two terms.

> . . . he made no distinction between an "Abolitionist" and an "Emancipationist." The latter was in favor of doing away with slavery gradually, according to State Constitution and law; the former believed slavery to be a sin in itself, calling for immediate abolition without regard to consequences. . . . I was never for a moment an Abolitionist.[19]

Much to Pendleton's dismay, legal circumstances forced him into participation in the institution he wished to see abolished gradually. His mother died in 1863, and he inherited a female slave. State law prohibited him from setting her free. He tried to make the situation the best for her that he could. He hired her out as a laborer, gave her the wage earned for the particular job, and added 10 percent to the wage in order to treat her fairly. When slavery ended, he gladly set her free. He said of the whole experience, "I was not a slave-holder *morally,* but *legally*."[20] Pendleton offered to resign from Union University any time the trustees deemed it necessary. They never requested it, and he stayed on the faculty until the university suspended operation in 1861 because of the war.[21]

The prevailing tendency of the people that Pendleton came in contact with was to support the efforts of the Confederacy. He not only supported emancipation, but he was in favor of preserving the union of the United States. This latter point proved to be a source of serious conflict between Pendleton and both Graves and Dayton. He wrote of Graves's concern over this issue, "My friend Graves visited me and spent hours in trying to persuade me to declare myself in favor of the Confederacy. He thought my influence and usefulness would be greatly increased if I would do so, and would be ruined if I did not."[22] Many of Pendleton's contemporaries considered his views tantamount to treason. His views were bold, given the Confederate loyalty in Murfreesboro. He stated that the Confederacy "had no right to exist, I had no sympathy with it, and heartily wished its overthrow by the Army and Navy of the United States."[23]

These major differences may have produced enough tension, during a time of national crisis, that the "Triumvirate" could not bear the strain. In July 1861, Pendleton's services as associate editor of the *Tennessee Baptist* became a liability. He noted that the publishers, "owing to the financial embarrassment of the country have 'resolved' to dispense with my services . . . ."[24] On the same page, the remaining editors, Graves and Dayton, seemed compelled to explain that Pendleton's departure was not under duress.[25]

The pressures of these circumstances forced Pendleton and his family to migrate to the North in August 1862. He served briefly as pastor of a church in Hamilton, Ohio. From 1865 until 1883, he pastored the Upland Baptist Church in Upland, Pennsylvania. This was his last pastorate, and he retired from full-time ministry when he left that church.[26] During this period, Pendleton published mature works on a wide range of subjects. His most significant contribution to Baptist theology is his ecclesiology. While he provided much of the thoughtful development of Landmark ideology, his opinions were less extreme than those of Graves and Dayton and constituted a moderating influence.

Exposition

Pendleton's most noteworthy contribution to Baptist theology is in the area of ecclesiology. His definition of a New Testament church, and the consequent ramifications, are extrapolations of more foundational theological assumptions. Pendleton's primary epistemological base was the *a priori* information found in the Bible. He was a biblicist. He opened his *Christian Doctrines* with a discourse on the existence of God. Following Thomistic categories, he argued for the reality of God with keen Aristotelian logic patterns. Admitting the eternality of matter, which leaves humans subject to chance determinism, was unacceptable to Pendleton. He concluded that design required a designer to maintain meaning and purpose for life.[27] The existence of a personal God being reasonable, it naturally follows that this God revealed Himself to His creatures. He argued that the Bible has a theocentric origin. The uniqueness of the Bible authenticates its acclaimed status of revelational truth.[28] Scripture shows that humankind is fallen in nature, separated from the Creator God who is responsible for human existence. The occurrence of a separation was directly related to man's purposed disobedience and fall from the will of God. Adam represented the federal head of humanity, and his decisions affected the relationship of the entire human race to the Creator God. Pendleton noted, "The truth is as resistless as an axiom, that the effects of Adam's sin were not restricted to himself, but have been transmitted to his posterity. By this posterity I mean every human being—beginning with Cain and Abel—that has lived or is now living on the face of the earth."[29]

The helpless and depraved state of mankind required divine intervention in order to rectify the situation. Thus, the focus of written revelation is the exposition of God's solution to the great human dilemma of sin and depravity. God effected the offer of salvation through the Person and work of Jesus Christ—the God-Man. Christ's finished work on the cross provided the sufficient substitutionary atonement necessary to heal the breach between God and man.[30]

Repentance and faith constitute the balanced response to God's grace. Man recognizes his sinful condition and trusts the act of Christ on his behalf for his eternal well-being.[31] Christ established the church to convey the truth about man's lost condition and the offer of salvation throughout the world until His return. Pendleton adopted the then controversial opinion held by postmillennialists in the close of the last century. He stated, "My belief that the millennium will precede the personal coming of Christ has been sufficiently indicated."[32]

Church purity is essential to the effective progress of the gospel. True converts alone should comprise the body of Christ. Faithful converts ought to take church responsibilities seriously. What constitutes the true church? What are its responsibilities and functions? These questions provide the frame of reference for discussing Pendleton's ecclesiology.

All Landmarkers believed tenaciously in the authority of the local church. Only the visible institutional church inherited a mandate from Christ to evangelize the world. More extreme Landmarkers asserted that the kingdom of God was coextensive with the aggregate of Baptist churches, and that Baptist churches have an unbroken line of historical succession from the time of Christ.[33] Pendleton's thorough delineation of a Baptist ecclesiology provided the foundation for the less extreme form of Landmark ecclesiology.

The reader will recall that Pendleton did not agree with Graves about alien immersion when the two first met. After the revival meeting at Pendleton's church, Graves invited him to write a series of articles addressing a single question, "Ought Baptists to invite Pedobaptists to preach in their pulpits?" This series of articles makes up the content of *An Old Landmark Re-Set,* Pendleton's first systematic attempt to work out a biblical ecclesiology.

Pulpit exchange was not only a convenient practice in the frontier areas of the United States during the last century, it was often necessary when rural pastorates were vacant for extended periods. Whether this practice was, indeed, in agreement with biblical injunctions, became a vital issue. Graves called on Pendleton to provide logical analysis of its legitimacy among Baptists.

Pendleton embarked on this venture by pointing out that he was primarily writing for internal polemics. He was not trying to convince Pedobaptists of their doctrinal error, rather he wrote to convince Baptists that they should not endorse Pedobaptist error by offering them the right to function as New Testament ministers in Baptist pulpits. He clearly distinguished the entire discussion from the legitimacy of Pedobaptist salvation. Whether they were true Christians depended on other concerns and not on how they formed themselves into biblical churches.[34] Pendleton's argument followed these lines. Responsible church membership required baptism as prescribed in the New Testatment. Faith is the necessary prerequisite for administration of the rite of baptism. Faith is a cognitive human function. Volitional cognition is not possible for infants. Therefore, Pedobaptists administer baptism to subjects who are not believers at the time of baptism. In addition, the mode of baptism is not in keeping with New Testament precedents. On both counts, Pedobaptists fail to administer baptism properly. Their assemblies, therefore, do not constitute New Testament churches.[35]

Pastors in religious organizations, according to Pendleton, have no authority through which they can administer gospel acts like preaching.[36] Pastors in other denominations easily took offense at such restrictive definitions. Primarily, they argued that such views regarding baptism were novel, even among Baptists. Pendleton reasoned that if there were no such beliefs extant among earlier Baptists, the Puritans would not have been insistent on making a distinction between themselves and the Baptists during the time of Separatist struggles in England, even to the point of advocating persecution of Baptists. Pendleton responded,

My position is that, according to the gospel, authority to preach must, under God, emanate from a visible church of Christ. Hence members of a visible church alone are eligible to do the work of the ministry; for a church has no control of those who do not belong to it. But Pedobaptist Societies are not visible churches of Christ. How then can they confer gospel authority to preach?[37]

Pendleton developed his views further as the controversy over Landmark exclusivism grew. He treated the issues raised by providing concise principles which distinguished Baptists from all other denominations. In *Three Reasons Why I Am a Baptist with a Fourth Reason Added,* he provided exegetical and pragmatic justifications for Baptist distinctiveness. Pendleton felt he, "must show why Baptists differ from other religious denominations."[38]

Insistence on baptizing only adult believers was Pendleton's first reason for being a Baptist. He argued his point by attacking the traditional position of Pedobaptists for infant baptism. Pendleton saw no exegetical evidence for infant baptism. Those who practiced the rite appealed to the parallel practice of circumcision found in the Old Testament. The weight of all the New Testament evidence lent itself to his conclusion that faith is the basis for receiving baptism, and that faith involves intellectual and volitional elements. The issue depends on whether an infant is capable of exercising such cognitive functions. Pendleton concluded that infants could not "believe;" thus they should not be candidates for baptism. "No man can, in obedience to this commission, baptize an unbeliever or an infant. The unbeliever is not a penitent disciple, and it is obviously impossible for the infant to repent and believe the gospel."[39]

Pendleton's second rationale for being a Baptist was that New Testament precedent established immersion as the only acceptable mode of baptism. Immersion is "so essential that there is no baptism without it."[40] His argument for immersion rests on three basic lines of reasoning. He carefully laid out the exegetical evidence regarding the use of the New Testament word for *baptism*. Realizing that the lexical testimony rested on the use of the term in classical Greek, Pendleton went beyond the lexicons and demonstrated that the classical meaning assigned to the term was the same. Phenomenologically, immersion best represents the symbolic meaning of baptism. Death, burial, and resurrection are not concepts which imply partial participation. Pendleton appealed to the ante-Nicean practice of immersion as the final evidence for the practice.[41]

The third reason Pendleton endorsed Baptist practices was that Baptists adhered to a congregational form of church government. He noted that Episcopal and Presbyterian forms of government assume some degree of collective authority. This practice leaves the local church, and the individual believer, with little control over the administration of church responsibilities. Congregational government guaranteed three essential truths. Power over church affairs remained in the hands of the laity, or the individual believer. The majority of members determine the will of the local church. Local church action is final and cannot be transferred to another agency.[42]

Pendleton's fourth reason for being a Baptist was that Baptists alone observe the Lord's Supper in a true and scriptural way. The Lord's Supper, like baptism, is intrinsically linked to the symbolic meaning of the essential truths of the gospel. "These two ordinances of the church symbolically proclaim the three great facts of the gospel. These facts, as Paul teaches, (1 Cor. 15:3,4,) are that Christ died, was buried, and rose again."[43] A natural corollary of the concept of the Lord's Supper is the ground for admission to the rite. As with baptism, Pendleton maintained that there are requirements for a subject to be worthy to participate in the Lord's Supper. Essentially, the rite is meaningless to anyone except baptized members in good standing in a local church. Since the local church members alone know whether someone is in good standing, the administration of the Supper would necessarily be done so as to protect the purity of the rite.[44]

Pendleton was fully willing to admit that the "Church of Christ is either a local congregation of saints, or it is the aggregate of the redeemed."[45] Salvation itself is not restricted to those who are Baptists, but the visible church is a divinely instituted social entity which requires proper administration. Responsible church membership requires guarding and protecting the biblical injunctions regarding the ordinances and polity of a local church.[46]

Pendleton's arguments for the distinctive nature of the Baptist denomination raised still other issues. If the local church is autonomous, are churches to cooperate with each other? If so, how can it be done without jeopardizing the essential concept of independence? If administration of the Lord's Supper requires members to be in good standing, how is church discipline defined and implemented?

Pendleton's lasting influence is most clearly seen in the Baptist emphasis on the autonomy of the local church. The administration of ordinances, preaching, discipline, and support of Christ's kingdom throughout the world are each gospel functions which require faithful and biblical application. Responsibility for the purity of these rites and practices rests on individual believers and is not transferable to other entities without risking the compromise of biblical precedent. Hierarchies through which authority and power are transferred from local churches to administrative representatives dissolve the link between the local church and its ability to supervise the gospel functions it is held accountable for by God. Pendleton concluded, "I affirm with strongest emphasis that the independent form of government cherishes a sense of individual responsibility. These who have to decide great questions by their votes are in a responsible position."[47]

Evaluation

In an era when epistemological doubt emerged to challenge the idea of certainty, Pendleton's opinions appeared anachronistic. The Enlightenment forged a new direction for the nineteenth century. Absolutist ideas were successfully challenged at least as early as the Renaissance. The inherent capability of human reason replaced confidence in *a priori* based truth claims. The Bible was not immune to rationalistic attacks and suffered under the scrutiny of higher critics. Pendleton shows little awareness of biblical criticism. He presupposed the absolute nature of the Bible. In fairness to Pendleton, it is necessary to note that he had no formal theological training and lived during the time that critical theories were novel and just beginning to influence American theological schools.

Presupposing the reliability of the Bible enabled Pendleton to set about defining his theological ideology. He utilized Aristotelian logic and systematized biblical data into a cogent argument for a pure New Testament church. When inclusivistic trends were becoming the new standard, authoritarian exclusivism set Pendleton's theology apart from the broader religious world. The entire superstructure of his ecclesiology revolves around the authority to claim to be and to function as a New Testament church. Administration of ordinances, to Pendleton, required authority from the founder and head of the Church. Christ alone can build His church, but He has commissioned His disciples to make converts, induct them into the visible church through baptism, provide spiritual instruction through preaching, maintain moral discipline, and memorialize His redemptive death until He returns to earth. The question is whether some sort of organic authority is necessary to perform these gospel acts. Pendleton's Pedobaptist peers saw this as the crucial point of disagreement. His critics contended that administration of ordinances rested in ministerial authority and not in the authority of any specific church.[48] Likewise, they asserted that the administration of ordinances had no bearing on the constitution of a church. The only requirement for a local church to exist was the collection of believers into a functioning whole. This concept would extend to the aggregate of believing assemblies.[49] Pendleton also seemed to ignore the ramifications of his theology, especially when one considers that he never dealt with the intricate issues surrounding the use of the Bible as a normative propositional source book. Is the New Testament model of ecclesiology intended to be supracultural and transtemporal? Pendleton left such questions for later generations to answer.

As restrictive as epistemological certainty might be to moderns, it accommodates the idea of logical consistency, a sense of purpose and meaning, and an objective criterion for judging faith and practice. This set of presuppositions allowed Pendleton to erect a systematic and orderly understanding of a New Testament church. The definition he forged for Southern Baptists in the last century had a preserving effect. Reacting against the exclusive claims of Alexander Campbell and Roman Catholicism regarding baptismal regeneration, Pendleton provided Baptists with a biblically rooted raison d'etre in a society moving toward religious pluralism.

The historical significance of Pendleton's theology is closely tied to the impact of Southern Baptist Landmarkism. Graves, Pendleton, and Dayton comprised the Landmark "Triumvirate." Collectively their leadership forged the movement. Pendleton was, however, an independent thinker whose contribution to the movement ceased in 1862 when he moved to the Northern United States. Hence, the "Triumvirate" dissolved before the Civil War ended. Dayton died during the war, leaving Graves to carry on the polemic.

Pendleton never modified his views and focused on the issues arising from the legitimacy of Pedobaptists claiming the right to function as New Testament ministers.[50] Graves and Dayton, however, took their ecclesiological assumptions further than Pendleton. There are at least four points of clear disagreement between Pendleton and the other members of Landmark's "Triumvirate." Pendleton believed that the only physical church is a local one, but he was willing to admit the existence of a spiritual church. The aggregate or universal church existed in Pendleton's system because non-Baptists could indeed be regenerated believers. Pendleton could not endorse the idea that the kingdom of God is coexistent with all Baptist churches of all times. He refused to subscribe to the extremes of Baptist successionism and thought that disallowing intercommunion between Baptist churches was trivial.[51] Graves established a list of basic beliefs as the criteria for determining whether someone was truly an "Old Landmarker." The items Graves enumerated showed substantial differences between Pendleton and orthodox Landmarkism. James E. Tull, a later student of Landmarkism, sensed that the differences between Pendleton and Graves were so substantial that, "one of the members of the 'Great Triumvirate' was never able to 'make the grade.'"[52]

The schisms within the leadership of the Landmark movement forced a splintering of its various emphases. The movement's excesses stimulated controversies within the Southern Baptist Convention. Each issue drew the best minds of the Convention into polemical debate and actually helped define the ethos of the Convention. The major controversial issues centered around the basis for Convention representation, decentralized control over its foreign mission ventures, and whether the practice of immersion was indeed historically true for all Baptist churches.

Landmarkism's emphasis on the local church operating through a congregational polity was in conflict with the Convention's practice of allowing representation based on financial support of particular agencies within the Convention's operational umbrella. Tull noted that Landmarkism was responsible for the shift to a church-based representation.[53]

Gospel Missionism was an effort to decentralize control over mission work and return it to the local church or local associations of churches. This was an issue because Landmarkers concluded that federalized national control of missionary efforts tended to distance the work from the local church, which was the only agency commissioned biblically for such work.

William H. Whitsitt, professor of Church History at The Southern Baptist Theological Seminary from 1872 to 1896, contested Landmarkism's more extreme concept of Baptist successionism. He denied that immersion was always practiced by Baptists, hence he undermined the basis for successionist claims. He contended that early Baptists asserted believer's baptism first and later settled on the mode of immersion as the New Testament standard. After prolonged original research at the British Museum, Whitsitt concluded that the practice first appeared in the records in 1641.

Extreme Landmarkers reacted and vied for control over the seminary. Pressures mounted and Whitsitt submitted his resignation in 1898. In his farewell speech he concluded that, "The doctrine of the universal, spiritual church is one of the most important tenets of Baptist orthodoxy; it is also one of the most ancient."[54] The only member of the Landmark "Triumvirate" to espouse a similar view was Pendleton.[55] Pendleton probably influenced Whitsitt's opinions because he was one of Pendleton's students at Union University. In 1891 he attended Pendleton's funeral to "offer his tribute of respect and veneration to his departed friend and instructor."[56] These major controversies defined the future of the Southern Baptist Convention.

Landmarkism's influence is evident in the form and function of the Convention even to the present day. Tull noted that the strong local church emphasis of the Landmark movement had a lasting impact. In 1933 the Convention altered its representation system and rooted it in the numerical status of local churches.[57] In the midst of a global ecumenical trend, Southern Baptists reacted by forming a worldwide alliance of only Baptists. Southern Baptists also channeled their ecumenical energies into the formation of a devoted denomination.[58] The restraining influence on Southern Baptists during the move toward organizational ecumenism was the Landmark view of the local church, largely Pendleton's ecclesiology.

Likewise, the Convention did not involve itself in the Fundamentalist controversy which ensued in the first half of this century because theological alignment based on a particular view of the Bible tended to undermine denominational loyalties. Southern Baptists of the day, while conservative in theology, remained aloof from the squabble on ecclesiastic grounds. J. Frank Norris and his followers attempted to raise the same issues within the Convention, and the perceived threat to the denominational structure rallied Landmarkers and their counterparts to quell the tide of Norris's influence. In effect, Landmark influence both protected the Convention from exposure to the channels of liberal influences and forced a withdrawal from the debate over the nature of the Bible because of ecclesiological principles.[59]

J. M. Pendleton was the most logical mind in the "Triumvirate" of Landmark Baptist leadership. He was not an "Old Landmarker," according to the definition given by Graves. Pendleton's desire to restrict Landmark ideology to the central issue of the authority and function of the local church, his atypical Southern opinions regarding slavery, and his desire to preserve the union of the United States led to a serious relational breach between Pendleton and the other two leaders, Graves and Dayton. He never contributed to Graves's efforts to solidify Landmarkism after the Civil War. He pastored in the North; wrote expounding his more moderate Landmark views; and died on the eve of a major controversy over Baptist successionism involving Whitsitt, his most well-known student. The Southern Baptist Convention owes much of its own self-understanding to the Landmark emphasis on the local church, and consequently, to Pendleton for forming a biblical definition of a local New Testament church and its legitimate functions. Through Pendleton's indirect influence, therefore, the Southern Baptist Convention gained a sense of identity which issued forth in a strong denominational loyalty. During the Modernist-Fundamentalist controversy earlier this century, Landmark emphasis on the local church encouraged Southern Baptist unity along ecclesiological lines rather than epistemological ones. Southern Baptist withdrawal from the debate to defend the absolute and normative nature of the Bible postponed the inevitable, and today the Convention struggles over the issues Pendleton presupposed, while it maintains tenaciously his conclusions regarding the local church.

Bibliography

Works by Pendleton

Books

The Atonement of Christ. Philadelphia: American Baptist Publication Society, 1885.

Christian Doctrines: A Compendium of Theology. Philadelphia: American Baptist Publication Society, 1906 [1878].

Church Manual: Designed for the Use of Baptist Churches. Philadelphia: American Baptist Publication Society, 1867.

Distinctive Principles of Baptists. Philadelphia: American Baptist Publication Society, 1882.

Notes of Sermons. Philadelphia: American Baptist Publication Society, 1886.

An Old Landmark Re-Set. Walker: Truth Publications, n.d. [1854].

Questions to the Impenitent. St. Louis: St. Louis Baptist Publishing, 1857.

Reminiscences of a Long Life. Lousiville: Baptist Book Concern, 1891.

Short Sermons on Important Subjects. St. Louis: National Baptist Publishing, 1859.

Three Reasons Why I Am a Baptist with a Fourth Reason Added on Communion. St. Louis: National Baptist Publishing, 1856.

Articles

"Able Ministry." *The Southern Baptist Review* 5 (June 1859): 321-32.

"Dr. Alexander's Doubts on the Propriety of Infant Baptism." *The Southern Baptist Review* 1 (Jan. 1855): 31-39.

"Astronomy and Redemption." *The Southern Baptist Review* 1 (Aug. 1855): 449-57.

"The Atonement of Christ." *The Southern Baptist Review* 2 (Jan.-Feb. 1856): 41-61.

"Breckinridge's Theology." *The Southern Baptist Review* 4 (April 1858): 300-14

"Campbellism Examined." *The Southern Baptist Review* (Feb. 1855): 84-142.

"Christianity Susceptible of Legal Proof." *The Southern Baptist Review* 4 (Jan. 1858): 14-33.

"Extemporaneous Preaching." *The Southern Baptist Review* 1 (April-May 1855): 261-75.

"Faith—Justification by Faith." *The Southern Baptist Review* 2 (March-April 1856): 149-63.

"Fuller's Sermons." *The Southern Baptist Review* 6 (June 1860): 263-78.

"Fuller's Sermons." *The Southern Baptist Review* 6 (Oct. 1860): 554-69.

"A Good Minister of Christ." *The Southern Baptist Review* 3 (Oct. 1857): 573-89.

"Importance of Ministerial Piety." *The Southern Baptist Review* 2 (Sept.-Oct. 1856): 497-507.

"In Obeying The Dictates of Conscience, Do We Necessarily Do Right?" *The Southern Baptist Review* 2 (May-June 1856): 290-303.

"Life and Times of Elder Reuben Ross." *The Southern Baptist Review* 6 (Sept. 1860): 395-419.

"The Life of Spencer H. Cone." *The Southern Baptist Review* 2 (May-June 1856): 304-19.

"Peter Edwards on Baptism." *The Southern Baptist Review* 4 (June 1858): 419-34.

"Plea for Thorough Female Education." *The Southern Baptist Review* 2 (July-Aug. 1856): 369-84.

"The Scriptural Meaning of the Term Church." *The Southern Baptist Review* 1 (Jan. 1855): 6-17.

"The Scriptural Meaning of the Term Church." *The Southern Baptist Review* 1 (Feb.-Mar. 1855): 65-125.

Works Related to Pendleton

Borum, Joseph H. *Biographical Sketches of Tennessee Baptist Ministers.* Memphis: Rogers and Co., 1880.

Burnett, J. J. *Sketches of Tennessee's Pioneer Baptist Preachers,* vol. 1. Nashville: Marshall and Bruce Co., 1919.

Compton, Bob. "J. M. Pendleton: A Nineteenth-Century Baptist Statesman (1811-1891)." *Baptist History and Heritage* 10:1 (Jan. 1975): 28-35.

Eaton, T. T. "The Life of Rev. James Madison Pendleton." First annual meeting of the *Kentucky Baptist Historical Society* (June 14, 1904). Louisville: Baptist Book Concern, 1904.

Hill, James Emmett, Jr. "James Madison Pendleton's Theology of Baptism." Th.M. thesis, The Southern Baptist Theological Seminary, 1958.

Huddleston, William Clyde. "James Madison Pendleton, A Critical Biography." Th.M. thesis, The Southern Baptist Theological Seminary, 1962.

Taylor, W. C. "James Madison Pendleton: World Landmark of Baptist Devotion To Truth and Loyalty To New Testament Churches." Louisville: The W. C. Taylor Letters, n.d.

Notes

1. J. M. Pendleton, *Reminiscences of a Long Life* (Louisville: Baptist Book Concern, 1891), 122. There are several biographical sketches which exist, but all appear to be summaries of Pendleton's autobiography. See T. T. Eaton, "The Life of Rev. James Madison Pendleton" in *Kentucky Baptist Historical Society* (Louisville: Baptist Book Concern, June 14, 1904), 13-35; Joseph H. Borum, *Biographical Sketches of Tennessee Baptist Ministers* (Memphis: Rogers and Co. Publishers, 1880); and J. J. Burnett, *Sketches of Tennessee's Pioneer Baptist Preachers,* vol. 1 (Nashville: Marshall and Bruce Co., 1919).

2. Landmarkism was a provincial and reactionary movement. It was provincial in that it made a particular ecclesiology the test of fellowship. Its leaders reacted against the successionism espoused by both Roman Catholics and the followers of Alexander Campbell. It was an attempt to define and clarify Baptist distinctives amid a growing religious pluralism. J. R. Graves was its most extreme proponent. See H. Leon McBeth, *The Baptist Heritage: Four Centuries of Baptist Witness* (Nashville: Broadman Press, 1987), and James E. Tull, "The Landmark Movement: An Historical and Theological Appraisal," *Baptist History and Heritage* 10 (January 1975): 3-18 for a general assessment of the movement.

3. Pendleton, *Reminiscences,* 4-8, 12.

4. Ibid., 24.

5. Ibid., 28-29.

6. Ibid., 31-33.

7. Ibid., 47.

8. Ibid., 48-49.

9. Ibid., 93.

10. Ibid., 94.

11. Ibid., 67-68.

12. Ibid., 66-67.

13. O. L. Hailey, *J. R. Graves: Life, Times and Teaching* (Nashville: n.p., n.d.) 73-74. Pendleton did not include this incident in his autobiography. Hailey was Graves's son-in-law and based his information on Graves's diaries and records.

14. Pendleton, *Reminiscences,* 102.

15. Ibid., 102-3.

16. Ibid., 103-4.

17. Dayton was the third member of the Landmark "Triumvirate." He was trained as a physician and disseminated his ideas through numerous books and articles.

18. For a list of the major articles Pendleton wrote for this periodical see the bibliography for this chapter.

19. Pendleton, *Reminiscences,* 112-13.

20. Ibid., 127-28.

21. Ibid., 112-13.

22. Ibid., 119.

23. Ibid., 121.

24. *Tennessee Baptist,* July 13, 1861. Pendleton did not explain in his autobiography why he left the paper.

25. Ibid.

26. Regarding Pendleton's literary development see the observations made in Eaton, "James Madison Pendleton." 26-29.

27. J. M. Pendleton, *Christian Doctrines: A Compendium of Theology* (Philadelphia: American Baptist Publication Society, 1906, 1878), 11-22.

28. Ibid., 23-41. Pendleton based his conclusions on these assumptions without showing any awareness of the attacks of higher criticism. However, critical innovations were then new to the American academic setting.

29. Ibid., 169.

30. Ibid., 221-45, and J. M. Pendleton, *The Atonement of Christ* (Philadelphia: American Baptist Publication Society, 1885).

31. Ibid., 256-73, and J. M. Pendleton, *Questions to the Impenitent* (St. Louis: St. Louis Baptist Publishing, 1857).

32. Ibid., 383.

33. James E. Tull, "A Study of Southern Baptist Landmarkism in the Light of Historical Baptist Ecclesiology" (Ph.D. diss., Columbia University, 1960), 2-3.

34. J. M. Pendleton, *An Old Landmark Re-Set* (Walker, W. Va.: Truth Publications, n.p. 1854), 7, 13.

35. Ibid., 13-14.

36. Ibid., 15-16.

37. Ibid., 34-35. Pendleton indicated that Baptists could, however, invite Pedobaptist pastors to pray in their pulpits because that is not a gospel act requiring authority. The only prerequisite to prayer was that one be a Christian. He was willing to admit that non-Baptists were Christians through faith by grace also. Interestingly, Graves added a footnote to this later edition explaining that he disagreed with Pendleton's point and that even praying would constitute recognition of Pedobaptist pastoral authority.

38. J. M. Pendleton, *Three Reasons Why I Am a Baptist with a Fourth Reason Added on Communion* (St. Louis: National Baptist Publishing, 1856). 5.

39. Ibid., 11-12.

40. Ibid., 82.

41. Ibid., 83-127.

42. Ibid., 148-51.

43. Ibid., 105.

44. Ibid., 178-79.

45. J. M. Pendleton, *Notes of Sermons* (Philadelphia: American Baptist Publication Society, 1886), 78, and Pendleton, *Church Manual*, 5.

46. J. M. Pendleton, *Short Sermons on Important Subjects* (St. Louis: National Baptist Publishing, 1859), 338-39, and Pendleton, *Church Manual*, 64-65.

47. J. M. Pendleton, *Distinctive Principles of Baptists* (Philadelphia: American Baptist Publication Society, 1882), 211-24, and Pendleton, *Church Manual*, 117-46. In the latter reference, Pendleton delineated his view of church discipline. In essence, proper gospel functions require a pure church. Discipline is, therefore, necessary to urge correction and restoration of the offending member and to purge the body of Christ of those who may not be genuinely converted.

48. In the second edition of Pendleton's *An Old Landmark Re-set*, 23-36, he responded to criticisms of the first edition. In the appendix he has a "Reply to Dr. Hill" and therein argues for the precedent of adult baptism by citing the basis for the differences between English Presbyterians and Baptists.

49. Ibid.

50. T. A. Patterson, "The Theology of J. R. Graves, and Its Influences on Southern Baptist Life" (Th.D. diss., Southwestern Baptist Theological Seminary, 1944), 139-42.

51. Tull, "Southern Baptist Landmarkism," 259-60.

52. Ibid., 260.

53. Ibid., 564-68.

54. *The Seminary Magazine*, May 1899, as cited by Tull, "Southern Baptist Landmarkism," 615.

55. Pendleton, *Church Manual*, 5, and *Notes of Sermons*, 78-81.

56. Pendleton's son closed his autobiography and noted that Whitsitt represented both The Southern Baptist Seminary and J. M. Pendleton's former students at his funeral. Pendleton, *Reminiscences*, 198.

57. Tull, "Southern Baptist Landmarkism," 632.

58. Ibid., 666-68.

59. Ibid., 677-80, and Patterson, "The Theology of J. R. Graves," 287-88.

Patrick Hues Mell

Paul A. Basden

Biography

Patrick Hues Mell was born July 19, 1814, in Liberty County, Georgia.[1] Both of his parents died while he was a teenager. Mell began his education at an English and classical academy in his native town of Walthourville. Soon afterwards he enrolled in another academy in a neighboring town. He paid for his tuition at both schools by teaching some of the elementary classes.[2] He was baptized at the age of eighteen at North Newport Baptist Church in Liberty County in 1832.[3]

The following year, George W. Walthour, a rich benefactor, volunteered to pay for the young Mell's college education. Mell chose Amherst College and at nineteen enrolled as a freshman. Following numerous actions which bordered on insubordination to faculty and administration, Mell dropped out in 1834. He taught a few years in secondary schools in Massachusetts before returning to Georgia in 1837. Two years later, he accepted the principalship of a newly organized women's seminary in Oxford, Georgia. The dream for the new school never materialized, but Mell was elected principal of the Oxford Classical and English school, a preparatory school for Emory College.[4]

In 1839 Mell sensed a call to the Christian ministry and was subsequently licensed by his home church. The following year he married Lurene Howard Cooper. In early 1841 Mell was elected to the chair of ancient languages at Mercer University in Penfield, Georgia. Following his ordination to the ministry in 1842, Mell was called to be pastor of the Baptist church at nearby Greensboro, a service he performed for ten years. In 1848 he accepted a second pastorate, the Bairdstown church in Greene County. In 1852 Mell resigned the Greensboro pastorate to lead the Antioch church in Oglethorpe County. He held all three of these pastorates while serving on the faculty at Mercer.[5]

Mell's dynamic leadership abilities attracted the attention of numerous agencies, institutions, and churches. In 1851 he was offered the position of secretary of the Southern Baptist Publication Society. The trustees of Wake Forest College called him as their new president in 1854. The following year he was offered the presidency of the Baptist College of Mississippi, the principalship of the Female Institute in Montgomery, Alabama, and the pastorate of First Baptist Church in Savannah, Georgia. Mell declined each of these esteemed positions in order to continue teaching at Mercer.[6]

When John L. Dagg became president of Mercer in 1844, he and Mell began a close professional relationship and a lasting personal friendship.[7] Following Dagg's unexpected resignation in 1854, N. M. Crawford, professor of theology, was elected new president of the college. He and Mell disagreed over a number of administrative matters. Their dispute became serious enough for both men, along with two other faculty members, to resign in 1855.[8]

The following year Mell accepted the position of professor of ancient languages at the University of Georgia, while continuing as pastor at both Antioch and Bairdstown. In recognition of his keen academic abilities, Furman University awarded Mell an honorary Doctor of Divinity degree in 1858. Within a year, he was elected professor of ethics and metaphysics at the University of Georgia. He was simultaneously named vice-chancellor of the school.[9]

In addition to his teaching and pastoral responsibilities, Mell also assumed an active role in Baptist denominational affairs. He was first elected moderator of the Georgia Baptist Association in 1855, a position he held for twenty-nine years. He was then elected president of the Georgia Baptist Convention in 1857 and reelected for twenty-five of the next thirty-one years. He served as president of the Southern Baptist Convention for fifteen years. His expertise in the field of moderating and presiding over Baptist bodies earned him the title "Prince of Parliamentarians."[10]

The trustees of Georgetown College in Kentucky offered Mell the presidency of their institution in 1870, but he declined. In 1878 he was shocked at his election to the office of chancellor at the University of Georgia. After initially refusing the offer, he finally accepted the post but chose to resign his two pastorates in order to fulfill his increased responsibilities.[11]

Almost thirty years after the unfortunate resignation of Mell and three of his colleagues from Mercer University, the trustees of the school determined to endow a new chair of theology in the religion department. After considerable discussion, they offered the chair to Mell in 1882. Despite dozens of personal contacts and letters which encouraged him to accept this opportunity, Mell graciously declined the offer on the basis of his commitment to the University of Georgia.[12] He retired in December 1887 and died January 26, 1888.[13]

Exposition

Soteriology[14]

Mell never wrote a work on systematic theology. His publications consisted primarily of popular tracts and essays written at the request of various Baptist bodies. Two of these short works were designed to defend the Calvinistic view of soteriology, especially predestination. The first, published in 1851, was entitled *Predestination and the Saints' Perseverance, Stated and Defended from the Objections of Arminians, in a Review of Two Sermons, Published by Rev. Russell Reneau.*[15] This tract first appeared in installments

Patrick Hues Mell (1814-88)

Photo courtesy of Southern Baptist Historical Library and Archives

in periodic issues of *The Christian Index*. At "the request of many brethren," Mell expanded and republished the critical essay in bound form.[16]

Mell was grieved that certain Southern ministers had refrained from preaching "the doctrines of Grace" in their churches. So he wrote this tract in an attempt "to counteract the tendencies in our midst to Arminianism." His immediate aim was to answer the critiques of Calvinism offered by Russell Reneau of Oxford, Georgia, in two popular sermons which he preached throughout the state in 1849. The sermons were blatant attacks on the Reformed doctrines of predestination and perseverance. Mell sought to rebut these charges with typically Calvinistic arguments.[17]

A second document which Mell wrote contains a more general defense of Calvinism as a system, with particular reference to the doctrine of predestination. The tract was entitled *Calvinism: An Essay Read Before the Georgia Baptist Ministers' Institute, at Marietta, Ga., August 13, 1868, by P. H. Mell.*[18] Mell defined Calvinism as "a system of doctrine believed to be contained in the Bible, developed first more elaborately and consistently by John Calvin, and therefore called by his name." Its central characteristic is "God's sovereignty over all things, sin not excepted."[19]

What attracted Mell most about Calvinism was its concept of God. He appreciated the presentation of "God in a dignified and honorable aspect. It is surely a worthy view of God, to represent him as a sovereign and efficient ruler, who accomplishes all his pleasure, and is never thwarted." Mell contrasted this view with the "anxious and impotent" God of Arminianism. His rationale was simple: "Such a God, impotent, and subordinate, and changeable, dependent on contingencies that he does not ordain, and distracted by confusion that he cannot control, is not the God of Calvinism."[20]

Where did Mell learn about this God? His ultimate authority was a hybrid of human reason and the Bible. It was in the pages of the Sacred Scriptures that Mell claimed to find his doctrinal beliefs. Yet the truth he discovered there always seemed to support and be supported by his logical thinking. In his own mind, "the scriptural support to the Calvinistic system is ample and entire, and reason can furnish the most irrefragable arguments, from admitted premises, to sustain it."[21]

Mell's view of the Bible is that it is straightforward and uncomplicated. Its message is written "in plain and intelligible language." Common sense demands that God's "system of heavenly truth [be] harmonious and consistent; and revealed with perspecuity and precision."[22] But Christians throughout history have discovered that the "plain" language of the Bible is susceptible of many and varied interpretations. What is the reason for such diversity in understanding? Mell attributed the numerous variations to differing personal presumptions held by the interpreters. Mell noted: "Professing Christians (sometimes unconsciously) not infrequently form in advance an idea in their own minds—drawn from the teachings of others or from their own reflections—of the character of God and of the doctrines which he ought to promulgate and then afterwards consult the Bible to prove that their views are correct."[23] What Mell failed to realize was that not even he was exempt from presuppositional interpretation of the Scriptures.

In light of his view of God and his application of rigorous logic to biblical doctrines, Mell necessarily based his understanding of predestination on the nature and purpose of God's creation, foreknowledge, and decrees. God's first work was the creation of the world *ex nihilo*. This action was neither spontaneous nor unexpected but was the consequence of an eternal and immutable purpose, "according to the good pleasure of his will." The purpose of creation was for the "infinitely wise and reasonable" God to attain "some ultimate object, well-defined, and specific." Because of His infinite knowledge, God knew all certainties past, present, future and even all unrealized possibilities. Therefore He decreed to create this world, "composed as it is, and peopled as it is," to fulfill His purpose. In order to attain exactly what He intended for creation, He

> not only fixed, from eternity, all the forms, positions, relations, and motions of matter, . . . but he "fixed from eternity all the circumstances in the life of every individual or mankind and all the particulars which will compose the history of the human race from its commencement to its close."[24]

Whatever exists in time God decreed to exist from eternity.[25] The world, therefore, "is just as God designed it to be."[26] This concept of God is the foundation for Mell's doctrine of predestination: "The doctrine [of predestination] . . . necessarily grows out of the character of God, and his connection with the universe as its creator, upholder, and governor."[27]

Through his own free choice, yet consistent with the sovereignty of God,[28] man sinned. Because Adam was the federal head of the race, the consequences of his rebellion were so severe that all humankind is now "totally depraved, utterly destitute of any remaining natural good, or any communicated spark of grace." Such depravity is so great that "none, without divine influence," seeks the remedy of salvation.[29]

Out of His abundant mercy, God in eternity ordered a "covenant of redemption" which would be worked out in history as salvation through Jesus Christ. Trinitarian in design, the covenant originated with the Father, was executed by the Son, and was applied by the Spirit. The scope of the covenant included unconditional election, preterition, limited atonement, effectual calling, and perseverance.[30] Perseverance is important because it reveals that the end of salvation is as dependent on divine grace as is its beginning. If God is perfect, His decrees immutable, the Trinitarian covenant eternal, Christ's death redemptive, Christ's intercession for the elect profitable, and the Spirit's indwelling certain, then surely the elect will persevere in grace to final salvation.[31] Even if they sin, they will neither finally nor totally fall from grace.[32]

The heart of the covenant, though, was predestination. Surprisingly, Mell never defined predestination in his own words. He appealed neither to Calvin nor to the Westminster Confession nor to the Philadelphia Confession. Instead, he took a direct quotation from Jerome Zanchi's *The Doctrine of Absolute Predestination:*[33]

> Predestination is that eternal, most wise, and immutable decree of God, whereby he did, from before all time, determine and ordain to create, dispose of, and direct to some particular end, every person and thing to which he has given, or is yet to give, being; and to make the whole creation subservient to, and declarative of, his own glory.[34]

Predestination, then, is identical to God's eternal, absolute, immutable, unconditional, sovereign, personal decree. The basis of this decree, which comprehends both "election and rejection," is God's "will, sovereign, and infinitely wise; and this, too, for the manifestation of his glorious perfections."[35]

Predestination is bipartite. The positive side is election; the negative side is nonelection. After God "decreed to create a world and to people it with beings who would voluntarily sin against him, he determined from eternity to save some and to leave others to perish in their sins."[36] In order to fulfill this eternal purpose, He elected some to salvation through the redemption wrought by Jesus Christ. This election is based not on foreseen faith or good works in the elect, but on God's "sovereign will."[37]

Mell rejected conditional predestination for two reasons. First, if election were based on foreseen faith or works, then logically the only difference between the elect and the nonelect would be the higher moral character of the former. This would give the elect a reason a boast.[38] Second, to believe in conditional election is to "make the sinner take the initiative in his election, . . . and then introduce the Supreme Being as his coadjutor."[39] For Mell, election was the basis rather than the result of faith and good works.

While the elect are chosen for salvation in Jesus Christ, the nonelect "are simply passed by, and permitted to follow the inclinations of their own hearts." God forced them to do nothing evil. Yet their lives of sinfulness fulfilled the divine purposes of the decree, though "unconsciously and wickedly."[40] God does not predestine the nonelect to damnation: "Those not chosen are . . . simply passed by . . . without any invincible influence adequate to make them willing in the day of his power."[41]

The threefold proof of predestination is obvious, almost tautological. First, God knows intimately all His works: He upholds all His creation, provides for and sustains all His creatures, and "disposes and governs" the same.[42] Second, God's acts in time always correspond to an eternal decree. He acts in accord with His plan. One might even say that "God governs Himself by a determinate plan."[43] Third, this plan is eternal and immutable. Logic demands this, else He would have "a plan in time which he had not in eternity," and then He would be mutable.[44] Once these premises are accepted, then predestination "comes in like a flood." For what is predestination but God's immutable decree and His eternal plan?[45]

Not all Christians, however, embrace Calvinistic predestination as true to biblical teaching. Mell noted six of the most common arguments against predestination and then refuted each of them to his own satisfaction. The first objection is that predestination makes God the author of sin. Mell contended that such reasoning is absurd: Only the one who commits sin is the author of sin. This does raise a legitimate question, however: "Does not God then approve sin?" The existence of sin is beyond dispute. Arminians allow that God permits sin in time. Calvinists trace the permission of sin back to God's eternal decree. Both arguments deal with the age-old issue of theodicy, but one views it temporally and the other eternally.[46] Consequently, since not even Arminians deny that it does no violation to divine honor for God to save some and to bypass others in time, then it certainly does no violence to His honor to decree the same from eternity.[47] One may easily recognize that Arminianism is "just as liable" as Calvinism to the accusation that God is the author of sin. This entire problem finds resolution only in the paradoxical twin truths of divine sovereignty and human freedom. Though the Bible teaches both, they are never reconcilable.[48]

A second objection to predestination is that an eternal, immutable decree ultimately exonerates the sinner from blame for his own sin. This question is merely an extension of the first objection, therefore the counterattack is the same.[49]

Third, some critics claim that predestination makes man a mere machine. Mell rejected this idea, however, on the basis that it misunderstands the nature of human freedom. Man is free to act according to his own inclinations, whether he is elect or reprobate. In fact, predestination establishes rather than denies this freedom. The opposite of freedom is not necessity but compulsion. God compels no man to act in any particular way. Every man freely and necessarily acts according to his own predestined nature.[50] What Mell failed to mention is that personal inclinations depend completely on one's status as elect or nonelect, which, in turn, depends solely on God's absolute decision.

A fourth objection is that predestination makes God a respecter of persons. Mell contended that such a statement is patently false. Conditional predestination might allow such an objection, but election apart from foreseen works or faith silences it.[51]

Fifth, many have argued that God must be cruel and unjust if He eternally condemns some to damnation. Mell's response was a more detailed explanation of nonelection. Even as predestination is bipartite, so is nonelection itself bipartite. The first step, preterition, is passive. God simply passes by certain of His fallen creatures and leaves them in their sins. The active step is condemnation, in which God condemns and punishes those whom He has passed over for their own sins. Mell's contention was that God is neither cruel nor unjust at either point. He is fair in bypassing some because they neither deserved nor desired salvation.[52] God "was under no obligation to create us nor to destine us for one end rather than another.[53] He is free to treat His own in any fashion. God is likewise just in condemning evil and sin in every form, for His holy nature is always opposed to sin.[54]

Finally, a sixth objection is that predestination denies the uses of means in man's salvation. Mell answered simply by asserting that God has foreordained both the end, eternal life, and the means, hearing and believing the gospel.[55]

Although stubborn and unrepentant persons object to the doctrine of predestination, Mell believed that those who quietly submit to it and gladly believe it realize its inherent benefits. First, predestination produces humility. The profound awareness that no one deserves or attains anything in life outside of the plan and execution of God should silence every form of human pride. Moreover, predestination spurs on the elect to more diligent labor in the kingdom of God. Only one who knows his election can have total confidence that God is in control and that his purposes are sure. In addition, belief in predestination fortifies the suffering believer. He knows that nothing in life is accidental or purposeless. Last, predestination ought to instill in the believer gratitude to God, for he knows that salvation is all of grace and not of works.[56]

Ecclesiology

Other than soteriology, the only other doctrinal theme which Mell addressed in writing was ecclesiology. He always carefully delineated the two meanings of *church* in the New Testament. The first usage of the word is found in Matthew 16:18, where Jesus referred to the church as "the whole company of those who are saved by Him."[57] This notion of the church as all of the "redeemed people in heaven and in earth"[58] is commonly referred to as the universal church. Mell treated this meaning of *church* only in passing.

His real interest was the local church, which he described as "a company of believers called out of the world, and baptized, upon a profession of their faith, and associated together to maintain the worship of God and the ordinances of Christ."[59] This usage of the word is found in Matthew 18:17, where Jesus pictured the church as "a local society."[60] Each local church possesses "independence and sovereignty"[61] and maintains its government "in the hands of the membership."[62] Consequently a church, by definition, is not the same as a religious denomination. Only an "organized body" at a particular geographical location is a church.[63]

The sole basis or qualification for a group to be a church is that it follow the New Testament pattern of ecclesiology. This is the Baptist view. The apostolic succession of ministers is not necessary for a religious group to qualify as a church.[64] According to Mell, "Baptists maintain that the only apostolical succession consists in holding the doctrines and the practices of the apostles." Churches are successors to the apostolic church if they "operate according to the pattern given in the New Testament."[65]

To apply this test to Baptists is to discover that Baptists have always existed, but under different names. Over the centuries they have been called "Disciples, Christians, Montanists, Novatianists, Paulicians, Paterines, Waldenses, and Albigenses; Mennonites, or German Anabaptists; . . . Lollards, Wickliffites, and Baptists."[66] Baptists owe their origin to no one person such as Luther, Calvin, or Wesley. Rather, "Baptists are made so by a belief of the truths of God's Word, and a literal obedience to the commands of the King in Zion."[67] The sole origin of Baptists is the Word of God: "Every Baptist church . . . obtains its existence not from a long line of ancestry—it receives its vitality and authority . . . from God's truth."[68] As a result, anywhere "the seeds of unadulterated gospel truth are sown and take root, there spring up Baptist churches."[69]

If the origin of the church is God's Word, then the purpose of the church is to "maintain the worship of God, and the ordinances of Christ."[70] Mell concluded that the majority of evangelical Christians numbered the ordinances as two and identified them as baptism and the Lord's Supper. He also believed that the majority of evangelical churches required baptism as a condition of membership. The problem was the varied opinions which these churches registered regarding "the form and the design of this ordinance."[71] The only solution was to study the Scriptures to see what Christ taught on the matter and how His followers practiced baptism.[72] Mell's hope was that a detailed exposition of the biblical teachings on baptism would clear up the problem.[73]

Mell took such action in 1852, while he was pastor of the Antioch Baptist Church. In August the Antioch church experienced a "season of refreshing" that resulted in numerous conversions and subsequent baptisms. In fact, Mell baptized new believers daily for almost two weeks. At each of these baptismal services, he explained the meaning of the ordinance, "going over, in a hasty and superficial way, nearly all references to the ordinance in the Scriptures."[74]

Mell's riverside devotionals caused quite a stir in the community, particularly among pedobaptists. A local Methodist pastor preached on baptism at the October "Quarterly Conference," defending pedobaptist views. Mell responded immediately with two more sermons which defended the Baptist view of the ordinance. He apparently thought the "*quasi* controversy" had ended, until November 6 when his church unanimously voted to ask him to write a book on baptism.[75]

The book itself centers in on two subjects: the act of baptism and the subjects of baptism. First Mell treated the act of baptism. He argued that the only legitimate means or mode of baptism is immersion. This is seen first when one studies the meaning of the word in the original language. According to Mell, "all the Greek scholars" concluded that the primary meaning of *baptizo* is immerse or dip. Since the general rule of hermeneutical theory is to take a word in its "ordinary and literal sense" unless forced to reject it, then one can safely assume that Jesus used the word to mean the same.[76]

A second argument that baptism is immersion focuses on examples of baptism in the New Testament. Consider the baptism of Jesus by John the Baptist. John was baptizing *at* the Jordan River, "not in a house, or at a spring, or by a rill," because he needed enough water to immerse, not simply to sprinkle.[77] Furthermore, John was baptizing *in* the Jordan River for one reason: to immerse people in water. Neither sprinkling nor pouring would require those people to go into the river and get their clothes wet. Only immersion explains these two facts adequately. After being baptized, Jesus came up out of the water, indicating again that baptism is immersion.[78] Mell concluded that the details of Jesus' baptism demand that "all who read [it] with an unprejudiced mind, . . . must come to the conclusion that he was immersed."[79]

Mell continued this line of reasoning by examining closely the records of the mass baptisms at Pentecost;[80] the baptism of the Ethiopian eunuch;[81] and the baptisms of Cornelius, Lydia, the Philippian jailer, and Saul.[82] He concluded that, in each instance, the act of baptism was immersion.

A third argument for immersion as the only proper mode of baptism is the significance of the act itself. The form reveals the significance: "the design of baptism is to show the death, burial and resurrection of Christ—to exhibit, by an expressive emblem, the faith of the believer in the atonement of Christ, and of his union with him in his death, burial and resurrection."[83] Only "immersion in the 'liquid grave'" communicates the true significance of baptism.[84]

Early church history provided the fourth argument for Mell. He noted that no reference to sprinkling, pouring, or infant baptism existed until the end of the second century. Yet "immersion can be traced back to the very time of the apostles and primitive christians [sic]."[85] Mell reasoned that believers followed the teachings of the apostles more closely in the earliest centuries of Christianity, while "it required a lapse of time" for their teachings to be corrupted.[86]

Although Mell never treated the Lord's Supper in detail, he did relate the two ordinances by the practice of close communion. He claimed that Baptists practiced close communion not because of a perceived superiority to all other Christians, but because the "Lord's Supper is a church ordinance."[87] He believed that Baptists and non-Baptist believers could and should enjoy both ministerial and Christian fellowship, but not church fellowship. He allowed "only . . . those who have been baptized and been united to the church" to share in the Lord's Supper.[88] To state it simply, "baptism is a prerequisite" to the Lord's Supper.[89] At this point, Mell could find no biblical support for his claim. He merely responded with an argument based on majority opinion: "This proposition we need not stop to prove, since all grant it."[90]

While Mell regarded baptism as a prerequisite to partaking of the Lord's Supper, he rejected the notion that people were saved by the act itself. Baptism is "a means of professing a belief that they have been spiritually united to Christ."[91] Nevertheless, having said this, Mell stressed the absolute importance of baptism by claiming that it "is essential to salvation." His logic ran like this:

Baptism is essential to obedience, and obedience is essential to salvation. All those who deliberately refuse to be immersed, though they are convinced that God commands it, can have no reason to expect eternal life; and this, not because there is anything in the mere watery rite which is efficacious in securing salvation, but because that principle in their hearts, which prompts them to disobey God, utterly disqualifies them for a place at his right hand.[92]

Mell's defense is certainly not impregnable. How is it that baptism does not save, yet one may not be saved without baptism? Is the rejection of baptism by immersion the one unforgivable sin in the eyes of God? Can a person find salvation in Christ through faith, only to forfeit it by failing to submit to immersion? This is certainly the least sound theological statement made by Mell in his discussion of the act and importance of immersion.

Another topic which Mell treated concerned the subjects of baptism. He roundly rejected the practice of infant baptism, claiming that it was the origin of the Papacy. He asserted, "Infant baptism finds no warrant in God's Word."[93] The biblical subject of baptism is a believer only: "The Scriptures furnish, in precept and example, no baptism but that of a believer, upon a profession of his faith in Christ."[94]

Mell's denial of the validity of infant baptism centered in his inability to substantiate its practice in the New Testament. Pedobaptists argued that the Great Commission implies that the church should baptize everyone, including infants. Mell countered that the Great Commission in fact forbade infant baptism in the two accounts which mention baptism specifically. Mark 16:15 commands the church to baptize believers, yet no infant can repent of sin and actively believe in Christ. Similarly, Matthew 28:19-20 stresses baptizing disciples, yet no infant can follow and obey Jesus in a disciple-teacher relationship.[95]

Pedobaptists argued that Jesus encouraged infant baptism when He blessed the children on various occasions. Those passages, according to Mell, refer simply to Jesus' desire to bless children, not to the church's responsibility to admit children into its membership by baptism.[96] Pedobaptists also claimed that the many household baptisms recorded in Acts indicate the practice of infant baptism in the early church. But, Mell debated, not one household-baptism passage mentions a child by specific name or even by general allusion, and all who were baptized in these settings first believed in Christ, which infants manifestly cannot do.[97] His final conclusion is that the only fit subjects for New Testament baptism are believers.

Once believers are baptized and enter the church, they still may yield to sin or stray from their faith. How, then, should the church protect itself? Mell answered the question in a book on church discipline.[98]

A true understanding of church discipline depends upon a true understanding of the church. Mell believed that the church should be composed only of sincere believers in Jesus Christ. He asserted, "It is the Saviour's will of precept that the constituents of His churches shall be regenerated persons." The only legitimate members of a New Testament church are "those who believe with the heart that [Jesus] is the Son of God."[99]

Although the church is made up of believers only, these believers are not morally perfect. Their "infirmities" and "prejudices" lead them to commit offenses, even in the church. In spite of God's grace, "alienation" and "discord" occasionally replace "brotherly love, order, and harmony" in the local body of believers.[100]

The church is not left to itself, however, to determine the wisest way of handling these offenses. God foreknew the inevitability of sin within the congregation, so He specified certain types of correction for certain types of offense. According to Mell, the only remedy is simply "to perceive clearly the Divine discrimination, and to carry out implicitly the Divine prescription."[101]

Mell believed that the New Testament spoke of two distinct types of offenses: private and public. *Private offenses,* addressed by Jesus in Matthew 18:15, are not necessarily secretive in nature. They are, however, committed specifically against an individual and his private "rights, interests, or feelings."[102] Mell explained this definition by noting that "*the act* is not a crime against religion and morality, and *the object of the act* is a brother."[103]

By contrast, a *public offense,* which Paul describes in 1 Corinthians 5, occurs when "*the act* is essentially a crime against religion and morality, or *the object of it* is the Church in its organized capacity."[104] The first class of public offenses are "crimes exclusively against religion and morality," such as "drunkenness, profanity, lewdness," and other like sins.[105] The second class of public offenses are those committed "against the Church in its organized capacity."[106]

Mell noted four specific examples of public offenses against the organized church. The first is open apostasy and opposition to the teachings of the church. For a church member to renounce the faith is a public offense. Interestingly, Mell included in this example a church member's rejection of the church's practice of close communion.[107] A second example is nonattendance of regular church meetings.[108] Mell regarded apathy in the church as an offense "against the authority of the Church, which the member is bound and pledged to regard."[109] Third, a church member commits a public offense against the church when he rejects the church's authority over his life by refusing to listen to and obey its demands on him.[110] Fourth, intentionally causing divisions within the body is a public offense against the organized church.[111]

For both types of offense, private and public, the Bible prescribes a specific treatment. If the offense is private, Jesus gives a fourfold solution. First, the one who is offended should go to the offender privately, face to face. Second, the one offended should tell the offender how he has been offended. At this point, the offended one must allow the offender to explain or apologize for the offense. If the offender refuses to be reconciled, the third step is for the one offended to take one or two people with him to serve as mediators or witnesses. If all else fails, then the final step is to take the offense to the church and make it public. The goal at every step along the way is to reclaim the offender.[112]

If the offense is public, the church should conduct a trial to investigate the charges against the offender. If the offender is found to be guilty, the church must follow Paul's advice in 1 Corinthians 5:11, 13 and expel the offender immediately. Although this solution may seem harsh, in reality it has great value. It protects the reputation of the church, it seeks the good of the offender, and it serves as a warning to other church members.[113]

Behind the theory and practice of church discipline is one overarching principle: the sovereignty of the local church. Mell wrote, "Local churches have exclusive jurisdiction over their members."[114] The church "has no legislative power" over its members." Such power is the sole prerogative of Christ. Yet "Christ has invested [the church] with *judicial and executive powers*." With its juridical power, the church has total authority "to arraign and try its members."[115] The church, then, decides guilt and innocence, inasmuch as she "is the only judge of the law and the fact; her decision is final."[116]

In addition to juridical power, the church also holds executive power. Executive power entails the authority to "expel all whom she tries and condemns."[117] The decision is executed by a formal vote. If the vote is not unanimous, then majority vote rules. Mell claimed that it is the *"right of the majority to rule, and the duty of the minority to submit."*[118]

Evaluation[119]

Theological Influences

The most obvious influence in Mell's soteriological thought is the distinct brand of Calvinistic theology which he espoused. It is almost identical to that in the 1647 Westminster Confession of Faith. Where and when did Mell learn this statement of Presbyterian orthodoxy? According to one of his close friends from his early school days, Mell's mother was a godly Congregational woman who was, "no doubt, perfectly familiar with the Westminster Shorter Catechism, which was thoroughly taught in old Midway church in ancient and in modern times."[120] The Midway church was the Congregational church which his mother attended prior to joining the Baptist church in Liberty County.[121] It appears that young Mell learned Westminster theology during his formative years from his mother, who was thoroughly indoctrinated in her home church. Such familiarity with seventeenth-century Calvinistic orthodoxy[122] naturally led Mell to adopt a theological system which included absolute predestination, total depravity, limited atonement, effectual calling, and final perseverance.

He also studied strict Calvinism in an educational setting or on his own initiative. That would logically explain his quotation of Zanchi's work. Who was the man whose definition of predestination Mell accepted *en toto?*

Girolamo Zanchi (1516-90) was ejected from his native-born Italy because he would not deny his Reformed faith.[123] Zanchi learned Calvinism at the feet of Peter Martyr Vermigli, the Reformed thinker who was most responsible for wedding the philosophical method of Aristotle with the doctrinal teachings of Calvin. More specifically, he "tended more to proceed from the divine decrees down to particulars in a deductive fashion."[124] His view of predestination began with God's unlimited and eternal foreknowledge. He believed "that everything—and not only the eternal destiny of human beings—has been predestined by God."[125] Presupposing that predestination centered in the divine attributes of foreknowledge, will, immutability, omnipotence, justice, and mercy, Zanchi reasoned that both salvation and damnation must be eternal decrees.[126] Zanchi altered "Calvin's doctrine of predestination . . . [by] making it a doctrine that can be inferred from the nature of God rather than one by which the theologian attempts to express the experience of grace."[127] This is the strain of Calvinism to which Mell adhered in his soteriological thought.

It is far more difficult to discern any major influence in Mell's ecclesiological thought. In his two books on baptism and church discipline, he seemingly relied exclusively upon the kind of biblical exegesis which was peculiar to Baptists of his day. Therefore, no obvious influences on his understanding of the church may be readily discerned.

Critique

Patrick Hues Mell was not a creative thinker in the field of theology. In reference to soteriology, he merely popularized the orthodox Calvinism which was prominent in his day. He borrowed ideas from the writings of a sixteenty-century Italian Reformer and from the standard confession of seventeenth-century English Puritanism. At times, he interpreted and updated the language to correspond more closely to nineteenth-century vernacular, but often he simply paraphrased the original words.

His doctrine of predestination reflected an uncritical acceptance of Reformed orthodoxy. He began with a God who eternally foreknew all that would eventually occur and who acted effectually to cause or allow those very things to come to pass. Simple logic guided him to his conclusion of personal, absolute, eternal, immutable, irresistible, infralapsarian predestination.

In reference to ecclesiology, Mell was no more imaginative in his approach. He was essentially a popularizer of orthodox Baptist thought on the subject of the church. He relied primarily on logical argument and strict exegesis of Scripture to make his case.[128]

His concept of believer's baptism as somehow essential to salvation derived from his overwhelming desire to refute pedobaptism. His argument for the necessary role of baptism in regeneration comes dangerously close to the sacramental notion of baptism which he abhorred. Here we see Mell at his weakest as either a logician or an exegete.

Mell uncritically accepted the prevailing notion of close communion, defending it as true to Scripture. Yet, he neither cited biblical evidence nor offered cogent argument for his opinion. Again we see him holding on to an untenable position for the sake of defending the theological status quo.

Perhaps these critiques provide the final word on Patrick Hues Mell as a theologian. He succeeded masterfully at defending the doctrinal orthodoxy of his day, arguing from both logic and Scripture to prove his points. However, he seldom challenged the views which he so readily accepted and then so clearly promoted. In short, he was merely an uncritical popularizer of nineteenth-century conservative Baptist theology.

Bibliography

Works by Mell

Baptism in its Mode and Subjects. Charleston: Southern Baptist Publication Society, 1853.

Calvinism: An Essay Read Before the Georgia Baptist Ministers' Institute, at Marietta, Ga., August 14, 1868. Atlanta: Geo. C. Connor, 1868.

Corrective Church Discipline: With a Development of the Scriptural Principles Upon Which It Is Based. Charleston: Southern Baptist Publication Society, 1860.

A Manual of Parliamentary Practice: Rules for Conducting Business in Deliberative Assemblies. Rev. ed. New York: John R. Anderson, 1876.

Predestination and the Saints' Perseverance, Stated and Defended. n.p., 1850; reprint ed., n.p.: Wicket Gate, n.d.

Works Related to Mell

Basden, Paul. "Theologies of Predestination in the Southern Baptist Tradition: A Critical Evaluation." Ph.D. dissertation, Southwestern Baptist Theological Seminary, 1986.

Mell, P. H., Jr. *Life of Patrick Hues Mell, By His Son*. Louisville: Baptist Book Concern, 1895.

Worrell, A. S. *Review of "Corrective Church Discipline."* Introduction by N. M. Crawford. Nashville: Southwestern Publishing House, 1860.

Notes

1. Substantial portions of this biographical section come from Paul A. Basden, "Theologies of Predestination in the Southern Baptist Tradition: A Critical Evaluation" (Ph.D. diss., Southwestern Baptist Theological Seminary, 1986), 98-102.

2. P. H. Mell, Jr., *Life of Patrick Hues Mell, By His Son* (Louisville: Baptist Book Concern, 1895), 9-12.

3. Ibid., 15. Mell's father was not a member of any church. His mother was a Congrgationalist-turned-Baptist. See ibid., 11.

4. Ibid., 16-31.

5. Ibid., 43-47, 54.

6. Ibid., 76, 82.

7. Ibid., 48.

8. Ibid., 76-77.

9. Ibid., 105-7.

10. Ibid., 81, 100, 106. A tabular summary of Mell's official responsibilities among Southern Baptists may be found in ibid., 151.

11. Ibid., 176, 187-88.

12. Ibid., 207-12.

13. Ibid., 247-49.

14. The majority of the section on soteriology comes from Basden, "Theologies of Predestination," 103-14.

15. P. H. Mell, *Predestination and the Saints' Perseverance, Stated and Defended from the Objections of Arminians, in a Review of Two Sermons, Published by Rev. Russell Reneau* (N.p., 1850; reprint ed., n.p.: Wicket Gate, n.d.).

16. Ibid., 15.

17. Ibid., 15-19.

18. P. H. Mell, *Calvinism: An Essay Read Before the Georgia Baptist Ministers' Institute, at Marietta, Ga., August 14, 1868* (Atlanta: George C. Connor, 1868).

19. Ibid., 3.

20. Ibid., 13.

21. Ibid., 10.

22. Mell, *Predestination*, 23.

23. Ibid., 24.

24. Ibid., 29.

25. Ibid., 29-30. Mell did not mean that only the physical world was according to God's plan. Cf. *Calvinism*, 3: "The world, therefore, in all its physical *and moral* details, is just as he designed it to be" (emphasis added).

26. Mell, *Predestination*, 30.

27. Ibid., 29.

28. Ibid., 31.

29. Mell, *Calvinism*, 4.

30. Ibid., 5. Cf. also *Predestination*, 37, for Mell's belief that the effectual call of the Spirit extends only to a definite and exact number of persons.

31. Mell, *Predestination*, 67.

32. Ibid., 61.

33. Jerome Zanchi, *The Doctrine of Absolute Predestination*, trans. Augustus M. Toplady, reprint ed. (Grand Rapids, Mich.: Baker Book House, 1977), 83.

34. Mell, *Predestination*, 28-29.

35. Mell, *Calvinism*, 5.

36. Mell, *Predestination*, 31.

37. Ibid.

38. Ibid., 59.

39. Ibid., 56-57.

40. Ibid., 32.

41. Mell, *Calvinism*, 5. Mell contradicted this view of preterition by elsewhere clearly implying predestination to damnation: "it follows that some were before of old (i.e. from eternity), ordained to condemnation (Jude 4)" (*Predestination*, 38). Mell failed to resolve this contradiction in any of his writings.

42. Mell, *Predestination*, 35.

43. Ibid., 36.

44. Ibid., 37.

45. Ibid.

46. Ibid., 38-40.

47. Ibid., 32.

48. Ibid., 43.

49. Ibid., 43-44.

50. Ibid., 45.

51. Ibid., 45-46.

52. Ibid., 46.

53. Ibid., 32.

54. Ibid., 46.

55. Ibid., 48.

56. Ibid., 48-50.

57. P. H. Mell, *Corrective Church Discipline: With a Development of the Scriptural Principles Upon Which it is Based* (Charleston: Southern Baptist Publication Society, 1860), 48.

58. P. H. Mell, *Baptism in its Mode and Subjects* (Charleston: Southern Baptist Publication Society, 1853), 175.

59. Ibid., 199.

60. Mell, *Discipline,* 53-54.

61. P. H. Mell, *A Manual of Parliamentary Practice: Rules for Conducting Business in Deliberative Assemblies* (Rev. ed., New York: John R. Anderson, 1876), 15. Mell taught courses in parliamentary law at the University of Georgia when he wrote this book.

62. Ibid., 10.

63. Mell, *Baptism,* 175.

64. Ibid., 176.

65. Ibid., 177.

66. Ibid., 182.

67. Ibid., 179.

68. Ibid., 181.

69. Ibid., 180.

70. Ibid., 175.

71. Ibid., 1.

72. Ibid., 3.

73. Ibid., 4.

74. Ibid., v.

75. Ibid., v-vi.

76. Ibid., 8-10. Mell went even further to assert that *baptizo* has no secondary meaning. It means immersion "and nothing else" (p. 15). Mell reached this verdict by collecting and analyzing every use of the Greek word in pre-Christian Greek literature, the Old Testament Septuagint, the Greek New Testament, and the works of Josephus. He concluded that, "in every case, [immersion] is their proper and only meaning" (p. 16).

77. Ibid., 46.

78. Ibid, 47-48.

79. Ibid., 49.

80. Ibid., 104-15.

81. Ibid., 80-81.

82. Ibid., 115 *ff.*

83. Ibid., 127.

84. Ibid., 130.

85. Ibid., 160.

86. Ibid., 161.

87. Ibid., 192.

88. Ibid.

89. Ibid., 194.

90. Ibid., 192.

91. Ibid., 195.

92. Ibid., 196.

93. Ibid., 200.

94. Ibid., 201.

95. Ibid., 202-4.

96. Ibid., 215-17.

97. Ibid., 239-57.

98. *Corrective Church Discipline.* For a Landmarkist critique of Mell's book, see A. S. Worrell, *Review of "Corrective Church Discipline,"* intro. N. M. Crawford (Nashville: Southwestern Publishing House, 1860).

99. Ibid., 7.

100. Ibid.

101. Ibid., 7-8.

102. Ibid., 9.

103. Ibid., 9-10.

104. Ibid., 14.

105. Ibid., 10.

106. Ibid.

107. Ibid., 11.

108. Ibid., 12.

109. Ibid., 13.

110. Ibid.

111. Ibid., 14.

112. Ibid., 16-24.

113. Ibid., 25-29.

114. Ibid., 62.

115. Ibid., 68.

116. Ibid., 69.

117. Ibid., 76.

118. Ibid., 77.

119. Much of the section on evaluation comes from Basden, "Theologies of Predestination," 114-17.

120. Mell, Jr., *Life,* 11.

121. Ibid.

122. Justo L. González, *A History of Christian Thought,* vol. 3, *From the Protestant Reformation to the Twentieth Century* (Nashville: Abingdon, 1975), 272.

123. Norman Shepherd, "Zanchius on Saving Faith," *The Westminster Theological Journal* 36 (Fall 1973): 31.

124. González, 244.

125. Ibid., 245.

126. Cf. Zanchi, for a listing of the divine attributes most relevant to predestination.

127. González, 246.

128. Thomas J. Nettles, *By His Grace and for His Glory: A Historical, Theological, and Practical Study of the Doctrines of Grace in Baptist Life* (Grand Rapids, Mich.: Baker Book House, 1986), 181.

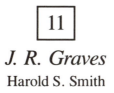

J. R. Graves

Harold S. Smith

In any discussion of Baptist theologians, J. R. Graves is "Mr. Baptist." For almost half a century—from 1845 when the Southern Baptist Convention was born until 1893 when he died—Graves was a dominating force among Baptists in the South. Although the name of J. R. Graves might no longer be mentioned frequently in theological discussions, some of his teachings remain with us—almost as a fulfillment of the inscription on his tombstone in Elmwood Cemetery in Memphis, Tennessee. Whether requested by family or Graves himself, the words are prophetic: "Brethren I will that ye remember the words that I spake unto you while I was present with you." Who was this remarkable, gifted man?

Biography

"The Rev. J. R. Graves, of Lexington, Ky., has arrived in Nashville, and wishes to conduct a Classical School the next session. He may be found at the City Hotel."[1] This unpretentious announcement was the first time Graves's name appeared in *The Tennessee Baptist*. Within two months, his first article was published in that paper. Interestingly enough, the article appealed for all Baptists to support the denominational paper.[2] By action of the General Association of Baptists in Tennessee in late 1846, Graves was named assistant editor of the paper, and the November 21, 1846, issue printed his name for the first time as one of the editors. Graves became sole editor on June 29, 1848. He remained in an editorial capacity with the paper until his death. Graves used the paper as a platform in his efforts to revive and restore the "old landmarks" of the faith and to establish a rigid, exclusive Baptist ecclesiology. Through his work with the paper, other religious publications, and an engaging pulpit manner, Graves's views became the dominant doctrinal influence among Baptists in the South.

James Robinson Graves was born April 10, 1820, in Chester, Vermont. He was the youngest of three children. The oldest child was a boy, Zuinglius Calvin, and his sister's name was Louisa Maria. Their father died when Robinson was only two or three weeks old, leaving his widow and their children to struggle for existence on a small, unproductive farm. These early hardships may have instilled a spirit of self-reliance in Graves that sustained him through many trying experiences in later years.

Graves published only one observation about his early years: "That I was a lively and jocose youth—and too much so—I admit, and it is still my constitutional failing."[3] Perhaps Graves's reluctance to comment on his childhood was an effort to suppress his northern background, an obvious area of sensitivity with him. For example, when charged with having sympathies with the North, he indicated that he did not choose the place of his birth and affirmed his loyalty to the South. He added: "We left as soon as we could obtain means to get away, and what more could we have done."[4] One of the interesting puzzles of Baptist heritage continues to be that a "Vermont Yankee" not only was accepted in the South, but he also achieved such a wide sphere of influence.

Graves shared information about his conversion only when someone suggested that he might not have been converted and properly immersed. He remembered: "We united with the Baptist Church in Springfield, (North) Vt., in our 15th year, and was [sic] baptized—immersed—by its then pastor, Elder Hodges, now deceased."[5] Church records verify that a Robinson Graves was received by baptism November 9, 1834.[6] Graves came from a Congregational background and did not indicate why he joined a Baptist church.

Opportunities for formal schooling were limited; nevertheless, Graves pursued a program of individual study. By studying eight hours a day, he completed the equivalent of a college course in four years. This lack of formal education might have been responsible for some of the objectionable elements in Graves's theology, but he should be commended for his initiative. J. J. Burnett said that "he was notably a self-educated, self-made man."[7] On the positive side, this lack of formal education might have inspired Graves's consistent interest in and appeal for a good education for all people. He devoted special attention to education for ministers and for women.

Apparently Graves expressed an interest in the ministry while at the North Springfield church. He was dismissed from the church by letter March 6, 1836. The pastor commented in the minutes: "Another member of the church, Robinson Graves, started to school this morning, with a *view* of finally preparing for the ministry—He is a youth of fair talents and of boyant [sic] spirits—May the Lord keep him from falling."[8] Graves rarely referred to his call to the ministry.

When Graves was nineteen, he moved from Vermont to Kingsville, Ohio, where he became principal of an academy. His strenuous schedule of self-study and daily work with the academy impaired his health, and he moved to Kentucky. There he became principal of the Clear Creek Academy in the Mount Freedom Community just outside the present town of Wilmore. Graves united with Mount Freedom Baptist Church by letter and examination during a revival meeting in May 1842. He was active in many areas of the life of the church, including serving as clerk pro tem. Several yellowing pages of church minutes are recorded in his handwriting.

The direction of Graves's future ministry began to take shape in this brief Kentucky period. Information about this time is sketchy and raises as many questions as are answered. For example, the minutes which record Graves's acceptance into Mount Freedom Baptist Church also record that he was li-

J. R. Graves (1820-93)

Photo courtesy of Southern Baptist Historical Library and Archives

censed to preach by the congregation. "The church on motion of brother Owens preceded to Licenses Brother Robt. Rowland and bro. James Graves to Exercise their gifts of preaching and Exhortation."[9]

While a member of Mount Freedom Baptist Church, Graves was ordained, but the records are not entirely clear. In August 1858, after Graves had become quite prominent as a leader of the Landmark movement, the congregation of Mount Freedom discovered that his ordination had not been recorded. Steps were taken to correct this oversight. In October 1858 a report was received by the church which set the ordination date as October 1842.[10]

Graves left Kentucky in 1843 and returned to Kingsville, Ohio, to study and to continue his preparation for the ministry. He told J. L. Waller, later editor of *The Western Baptist Review,* that he could not remain in a slave state and maintain silence about the evils he observed. Waller advised him to move to a location where his views would be more acceptable.[11] Later in his ministry Graves supported the institution of slavery, indicating that if slavery were wrong, then marriage was wrong—since both institutions were inaugurated by God the Creator.

In June 1845 Graves settled in Nashville, Tennessee. His work as pastor, editor, and writer became the context in which Graves developed his theology. On Sunday evening, June 13, 1845, Graves was received into the fellowship of First Baptist Church by letter from the First Baptist Church of Kingsville, Ohio. His wife, Lua, was received by application.[12] R. B. C. Howell was pastor of the Nashville church and editor of *The Tennessee Baptist*. The most serious personal controversy of Graves's life was with Howell. Apparently, they began as friends and colleagues, but serious differences (with a measure of jealousy and competition added) finally separated them.[13]

In November 1845 Graves became pastor of Second Baptist Church in Nashville and remained in that role until 1849. The church had been divided by Campbellism.[14] In all likelihood, his experiences with this congregation provided fertile soil for his strong anti-Campbellite concepts. In addition to Graves's pastoral duties, he became assistant editor of *The Tennessee Baptist* in November 1846. Following Howell's resignation from the paper and First Baptist Church, Graves became sole editor on June 29, 1848. He also was asked to fill the pulpit at the church. The paper was the primary platform from which Graves presented his theological viewpoints. That Graves would become a dominant force among Baptists in the South was almost inevitable with the outlets available to him for theological persuasion. The paper grew rapidly under Graves's direction, and his views found ready followers through his preaching, writing, and editing. Even the conflict with Howell and Graves's subsequent expulsion from First Baptist Church only seemed to multiply his popularity and make his views more appealing. He was victor even in defeat.

Graves was the father and most articulate spokesman of the Landmark Movement which arose among Southern Baptists in the mid-nineteenth century. This movement sought to identify, restore, defend, and preserve distinctive, historic Baptist doctrines—the "old landmarks." Ecclesiology was the primary focus of this movement. Graves was joined by other strong leaders who used their abilities to persuade large numbers of Baptists in the South to adopt the Landmark viewpoint.

In January 1859 Graves announced that a subscription list of more than thirteen thousand made *The Tennessee Baptist* the largest Baptist weekly in the world. In his judgment, this achievement was an obvious indication of God's approval and blessings.[15] Graves was joined in his work by J. M. Pendleton and A. C. Dayton. These men became "The Great Triumvirate" of the Landmark Movement. W. W. Barnes commented: "Pendleton was the prophet, Graves the warrior, and Dayton the sword-bearer in the campaign."[16] Their success waned as people grew weary of constant denominational strife and became preoccupied with the growing conflict between North and South. Graves left Nashville when it fell into Union hands; however, he continued to be active in seeking to provide literature for the soldiers. The Civil War, with all of its destruction and misfortune, probably prevented Graves's views from totally dominating Baptists in the South. To that point, nothing else had stopped the rapid spread of his doctrinal affirmations.

After the war, Graves settled in Memphis, Tennessee, and on February 1, 1867, published the first post-war issue of *The Baptist*. A more moderate Graves now sought to lead Baptists. Graves continued to pursue his major interests and wanted to make Memphis a denominational center for Baptists.[17] Nevertheless, he was unable to duplicate his pre-war achievements. Success seemed just beyond his grasp. He was a poor financial manager, and he lost money and influence in publication ventures that were unpopular and unfruitful. During this period he continued to write and published his maturing doctrinal position in book form.

Graves suffered a stroke while preaching in the First Baptist Church in Memphis on August 17, 1884.[18] Although permanently restricted, he was able to write, travel, and deliver his "chair talks"—sermons preached while sitting in a chair. All financial interests in the paper were relinquished to his son-in-law, O. L. Hailey, in August 1889.[19] The paper was moved to Nashville on August 22, 1889, and was issued as the *Baptist and Reflector*. Even a casual reader could detect that the paper no longer bore the image given to it by Graves. The paper became more denominational and less theological. Graves was injured in a fall in his yard on August 11, 1890, and did not walk again. He died June 26, 1893. The last issue of the paper to carry his name as an editor included a succinct biography. "He was an important factor in the Baptist denomination in the South for more than half a century and one of the ablest exponents of Baptist faith in the world. He was a great warrior in the cause of truth."[20] What an understatement!

Exposition

Issues in Graves's Theology

The life, work, and thought of J. R. Graves were so closely interwoven that separating one from the other results in an artificial abstraction. Most of Graves's theology was born in the heat of controversy as he labored to fulfill his calling from God through his editorial/writing ministry. Graves did not write a theology as such, so his thinking must be gleaned from books and hundreds of articles.[21] Several issues were primary for Graves as he developed his doctrinal affirmations.

Religious press.—Graves had a deep commitment to the power of the religious press as a formidable weapon against error. The printed word has potential to develop and to govern minds and opinions. He wrote in 1848: "A religious paper, read by at least ten thousand persons, is an engine of inconceivable power, bearing upon the mind, sentiments and opinions of men . . . . What the die is to the plate of silver, or gold, is the press to the public mind,—and it gives to it its impress, the image of Cesar [*sic*] or of Christ."[22] Graves validated his high estimation of religious publications by appealing to God's use of this means to give His revelation—a series of sixty-six inspired tracts. The religious press is obligated not only to proclaim biblical truth but to expose error.[23] Consequently his paper was

> designed to be the exponent of true Baptist faith and consistent Baptist practice, and to reflect the leading aspects of the "Great West" and the present times, and to meet and discuss the great issues of the day. "Principles cannot be compromised," ceaseless war with error, whether advocated by Papists, Protestants or Campbellites, "Progressive truth is truth aggressive"—are its mottoes.[24]

Graves used the printed word—his books, edited works, and paper—as an effective tool to indoctrinate his readers with what he believed to be vital doctrines so they might be well grounded in the gospel.

Controversy.—Graves's evaluation of the power of the religious press created an environment in which controversy was inevitable. Interestingly enough, his first editorial conflict was in defense of editor R. B. C. Howell.[25] How much controversy might have distorted his theological perspective or caused him to overstate his position cannot be determined. Nevertheless, Graves was not shy about standing firm and entering into theological battle, maintaining all along that he did not *issue challenges*—he only defended himself. He was aware that controversy might jeopardize denominational growth, but the assets far outweighed the liabilities since religious errors and corruptions had to be exposed. When asked his opinion regarding church gains, he replied:

> We answer, *Controversy,* CONTROVERSY, *Agitation,* discussion, and debates, Bold spirits, intellectual Great-Hearts, have risen up in the church, and reared the colors of truth, they found trailing in the dust, and nailed them to the mast head, under which they have contended earnestly for the faith, (while they have been decried and denounced by the same class of brethren,) and have repeatedly vanquished the opposers of truth, they are not carrying the war before the very gates of the citidel [*sic*] of error. The war must go on.[26]

Recognizing that Graves's theology was formulated largely in the crucible of controversy is essential for understanding his thought.

Baptist identity.—Early in his ministry Graves observed that Baptists frequently received alien immersion and freely participated in the practices of pulpit affiliation, union Sunday Schools, and union church meetings, all of which, he believed, departed from primitive Baptist principles and undermined Baptist distinctives.[27] Furthermore, he was troubled by the strength of the Methodists, who operated a vigorous and successful publishing house in Nashville, and by the aftermath of the Campbellite controversy. All of these elements led Graves to question whether Baptists would survive as a distinct group and to fear that they might lose all characteristics of self-identity. Hence, he sought to underscore an individuality that belonged uniquely to Baptists.

This uniqueness Graves discovered to be the continuity and identity of Baptists with the church founded by Jesus Christ Himself. Rather than being dominated or possibly absorbed by some other denomination, Baptists are the sole inheritors of New Testament Christianity. Therefore, participation in joint meetings must cease, since such activity only sanctions erroneous practices and recognizes other denominations as genuine churches of Christ rather than religious societies. Also, to ensure survival and identity, a publishing house to surpass the Methodist establishment must be organized so that by literature with sound doctrine, errors and deficiencies in other groups might be reviewed and rejected.

The importance of this issue must not be overlooked by anyone who desires to understand the theology of J. R. Graves. The possibility of the loss of identity was a determining factor in his ecclesiology as well as other doctrinal elements. This fear was significant in Graves's understanding and interpretation of church history. In his judgment, history discloses which of the competing denominations is the only heir to the church of Christ and which group has been faithful to the practices ordained in the New Testament. Following this methodology, Graves discovered Baptists with Landmark doctrines in each of the first nineteen centuries. Graves edited and issued G. H. Orchard's *A Concise History of Foreign Baptists* to support his view of church history.

Indeed, J. R. Graves is Mr. Baptist. He wrote: "I am a Missionary Baptist, as was John, Christ, Paul, as were all the apostles, and as were all *Baptists* until within the last century,—and he alone is truly a primitive Baptist who is a scriptural missionary Baptist."[28] While Graves did not argue that every idea he discussed was distinctly Baptist, he approached all theology as a convinced Baptist—believing that if Baptists were right, then all other denominations were wrong.

Not only does being a faithful Baptist lead to correct theology, being a Baptist also enables a person to reach his highest glory as a Christian and a citizen. Graves inquired:

> Would you be a *true Christian?* Have a Baptist heart. Have no other. It has ever beat for Christ for his uure [pure] word—for his church, to preserve it uncorrupted down thro' the track of ages. Baptists have circled the church like a wall of fire—and thro' centuries of blood have preserved it in its prestine [*sic*] virgin

purity—its laws, its ordinances and all its glorious principles—that have blessed and are destined ultimately to bless the world.

Show me a Christian with a genuine Baptist heart throbbing in his bosom, and we look upon a man who is an honor to his race and the pride of Christianity and a blessing to the world. We look upon a man who loves Christ—loves his government—his Church—his laws and ordinances for conscience sake with a pure heart fervently,—we look upon a martyr, wanting nothing but the occasion to lay down his life in testimony of Jesus.

Have a real Baptist heart, my brother, a good *round* heart—not a flat, slobby, sobby one—but a *firm* round one whose every throb is from principle— and every pulsation for the honor of Christ's persecuted cause. He who has a real Baptist heart within him will be a Baptist *everywhere,* and under all circumstances. No scoffer can shame, no opposition appal [*sic*] him. To be a full Baptist is the highest glory of man—is to be all that man can be—a christian in its sense—a patriot, a republican—the friend of God and a friend to man.[29]

Elements in Graves's Theology

God.—Graves's treatment of the doctrine of God is fragmentary and incomplete. His primary concern was to present enough information to convince any candid reader of the reality of God's existence and to examine those features which most related to redemption. The only extensive comments on the doctrine of God in Graves's writings are in the context of his study of the work of Christ.[30]

The existence of God can be established through logical arguments. These arguments include the universal belief of men in God, the being of man (the fact of man's existence is irresistible proof that something has always existed, namely the Great First Cause or the biblical God), and the design of the universe.

God's sole purpose in creating the universe was to manifest His glory. This purpose means that God left the imprint of Himself within the created order so that anyone who honestly investigates the available evidence will be convinced of His reality. Nothing more than rational, logical analysis of the created order is necessary for a recognition of the God who brought it into being. By the operation of reason on God's revelation in creation, man can know that God created the universe and that He is almighty, wise, beneficient, and self-existing. These qualities are the extent of man's knowledge through creation. Consequently, if man's understanding is to go beyond what can be learned through nature, God must reveal Himself more fully.

Revelation.—Knowledge of God depends on revelation. Graves's concept of revelation was related to his understanding of creation and the Bible. Although he did not use the terminology of general and special revelation, the distinctions he observed are parallel to the meaning of these terms.

On the basis of three facts "too self-evident to need proof," Graves declared that he was "forced to conclude" that this revelation has been given. The three indisputable facts are: (1) man absolutely needs a written revelation; (2) man intensely desires a written revelation; and (3) God is able to provide a written revelation of His will. "Therefore," Graves wrote, "we must as undoubtedly conclude that the Creator has made such a revelation to the race, as that such a Being exists."[31] In this discussion, Graves neglected to explain how he made the easy transition of the revelation in creation to the necessity for a *written account* of God's will for man. Obviously, he was preparing for the second stage in his understanding of revelation—the place of the Bible.

An ambiguity can be detected in the way in which Graves related the Bible and revelation. On the one hand, he proposed that the Bible itself *is* the revelation, for it is "a revelation from God to man."[32] On the other hand, the Bible is a book which "contains" God's revelation to man.[33] Graves did not attempt to reconcile this inconsistency; perhaps he saw no ambiguity.

Graves advocated the plenary-verbal theory of inspiration. This theory is to be distinguished from simple plenary inspiration which says that God infused ideas into the writers and permitted them to choose their own mode of expression. The simple plenary theory makes the Bible "man's production assisted by God"—"inspired matter in uninspired words." In reality, Graves believed, this theory is impossible, since thoughts cannot be expressed without words. The Bible is its own best witness to its plenary-verbal inspiration. Using a logical, axiomatic proposition—*"the whole includes the sum of its parts"*—Graves argued that every section of the Bible is fully and equally inspired. He wrote:

> If the whole is God's word, each and every portion and part of it, every paragraph and period, every sentiment and sentence and *word* is equally God's word. To intimate that the least sentence or allusion of the Scriptures is inaccurate or false, is to make God a liar.[34]

Could the Bible as a religious book possibly contain secular and scientific inaccuracies in the areas of geology, astronomy, geography, or history? Graves answered: "I can not accept this proposed betrayal of the Word of God. I accept no compromise. It is all God's Word, or none of it is God's Word."[35]

Finding one falsehood would jeopardize the entire Bible because the interpreter is then placed in the position of not knowing what is true and what is not. Graves clarified his position with a statement that has a contemporary flavor. He wrote: "There may be errors in the transcription of the ancient manuscripts; there may be errors in translation, and errors many in interpretation, but that *the original Scriptures* are *the words of the living God,* He most explicitly declares them to be."[36]

Nevertheless, he expressed an unwavering confidence in the total plenary-verbal inspiration of each section of the Bible.

Since the Bible is intended to enhance knowledge of God, Graves was convinced that the Scriptures could be understood by anyone willing to engage in careful, prayerful, diligent study. Otherwise, God would have been tantalizing humans by commanding them to know something that they could not comprehend. Consequently, he assigned a definite theme to the figurative passages that he discussed. For example, Jesus' parables are primarily an effort to persuade men to believe truths that probably would be rejected if spoken plainly, for the truths condemned those who listened.[37] Figures are not intended to hide truth.

Graves was motivated by an all-embracing principle of interpretation. He explained:

> We plant ourself upon one plain unquestioned rule of interpretation, which no sane, certainly no sound interpreter will presume to gainsay, i.e.:
> *THAT NO LANGUAGE CAN BE CONSIDERED FIGURATIVE, UNLESS IT CONTAINS A FIGURE; OR SYMBOLIC, UNLESS IT CONTAINS A SYMBOL.*[38]

Therefore, the literal meaning is always the proper meaning of a passage unless a figure occurs in the passage and requires a figurative interpretation. A figurative interpretation, however, will never conflict with plain, literal passages.[39] Graves was not ignorant of critical methodology, but he was suspicious of most critical analyses of the Bible. For example, he believed that no estimate could be made of the evil consequences which would result from the work of C. H. Toy.[40]

The major features of Graves's theology depended primarily on his understanding and interpretation of the New Testament. He wrote: "We take the New Testament as the rule of our religious faith and practice, endeavoring to conform our belief and our practice to its divine teachings."[41] Hence, his approach to theological essay depended upon an adherence to a scriptural norm. The New Testament is not a book of general principles but a book of specific laws which are to be followed with little flexibility. This viewpoint is obvious in Graves's writings and his use of prooftexts in theological debate.

Trinity.—Graves was confident that the Bible teaches the eternity of the Godhead, and at no point in his writings does he ever question the eternal existence of the Trinity. However, Father, Son, and Holy Spirit *are not* eternal relationships. Rather, these designations belong to the covenant of redemption and are relevant only to the Trinity's activities in time and history. Time, which began with creation, is the only proper context for measuring and describing relationships and orders of activity. Therefore, a description which belongs to time and its function must not be used of a relationship in eternity. In a frequently misunderstood passage, Graves wrote:

> Independently of creation there certainly was not, and there could *not* have been an idea of relationship that implied *order* of existence. Therefore, before the birth of creation there could have been no relationships existing as that of Father and Son, for these are terms of *relationship,* and imply *order* of being, and consequently demand *time*. If this be so, then evidently the phrases "Eternal Father," and "Eternal Son," are inadmissible, since they involve a manifest contradiction. As certainly as the Creator must exist before the thing created, the begetter must exist before the begotten—Father before Son. And it is no less contradictious to say that Father and Son eternally self-existed in these relations; we may as consistently affirm that the creature and its Creator co-eternally existed. . . . The phrases "Eternal Son of God," "The Eternal Father," are manifestly of human coinage,—not the selection of the revealing

Spirit. . . . The relationship, expressed by the terms Father and Son originated with the conception of the Covenant of Redemption and Work of Christ, and when that work is consumated, the relationship and its practical inferiority will cease.[42]

In spite of the apparent implications of this statement, Graves was not denying the eternity of the Trinity. Rather he was distinguishing very precisely the historical and eternal relations within which the persons of the Trinity function. The Bible does not disclose the functional relationship of the Trinity in eternity, but it does reveal the consequences of the covenant of grace in creation and redemption. In eternity, therefore, theologians should limit their interpretation to the fundamental statement that three infinite, coequal persons exist as a Trinity in unity. On the other hand, when the Trinity is examined in its historical manifestations, an order of existence and a sphere of relationships can be detected which do not belong to a perfect, eternal Godhead with three coequal persons. In history, authority and subjection are recognized in the theological assumption of first, second, and third persons—an impossibility with infinite, coequal beings. To say that the idea of an Eternal Son is "inadmissible" is not to deny the Trinity or the incarnation. Rather, this interpretation maintains that a finite description of time must not be applied to an infinite community of eternal persons.

Creation.—Graves's understanding of God's work in creation is based on a literal exposition of the biblical statements regarding the origin of the universe. Creation was designed as an arena in which God might declare His glory. In seeking to manifest His glory, however, God is absolved from any selfish motivations because the declaration of His glory also secures the highest good of all His creatures. The biblical phrase, "in the beginning," means that God's creative activity began at a specific point in time. Otherwise, creation would be co-eternal with God. Creation instituted time as a means of measurement. Time will exist only as long as creation exists.

Graves was interested in geology, but he was quite impatient with any scientific study which was contrary to the literal interpretation of the Bible. With complete confidence that competent biblical exposition and sanctified science are not contradictory at any point, he commented:

> We believe that the God of Reason, and of Nature, is the God and author of Revelation also, and if we observe the proper laws of symbolization and figures, where the language is symbolic or figurative, and sound laws of interpretation where it is literal, we have no fears that the voices of Revelation and Science, or Reason, will be discordant or contradictious.[43]

This statement does not leave as much friendly room as it might seem, for scientists were the objects of stern judgments from Graves when questions were raised about the flood or if any statements in Genesis were described as myth.

The problem of evil is an integral part of the doctrine of creation. Rejecting an eternal dualism, Graves located the origin of evil after the creation of the heavenly hosts and before the creation of man. The source of evil is the created order itself, for creation is finite and to be finite is to be inherently imperfect. Graves observed:

> Every created person or thing is finite, and therefore inherently and essentially imperfect; and it only requires time and opportunity for the creature to develop its weakness and imperfection—if a person, in error and sin; if a thing, in decay and dissolution. There is, therefore, a latent evil in every thing created, even in that which God pronounced "very good . . . ."[44]

Even Satan's fall was the natural result of the finitude of a created being. Graves confessed that he did not comprehend why God created as He did, but he was persuaded that God cannot be charged with wrong or sin.

Into this kind of world, humans were created by an immediate act of God. The creation of Eve came months or even years later, since Adam's task of naming the creatures would have consumed quite some time. Graves eliminated evolution as a possible means of creation. He believed this system of thought to be such an absurd form of error that "it would end by a self-explosion."[45] In a statement lacking in clarity, Graves commented: "The theory is utterly irrational—opposed to reason as well as to universal observation. Evolution and Involution are equal. It is self-evident that nothing more can be evolved than has been or is *in*volved, and that ends the whole question in our mind."[46]

This argument may have settled things for Graves, but it probably left his readers more confused.

Different races resulted from God's creative work. Although Noah was white, through the purpose of the Creator he became the father of sons of different complexions. Japheth was white; Shem was copper-colored; and Ham was black. Each son became the father of a major ethnic division in the family of nations. This idea undergirds Grave's interpretation of slavery as part of creation.

The man created to dwell in paradise was invested by his Creator with certain endowments which were integral to his character. He was to live in *sinless contentment and peace*. Perhaps as many as one hundred years passed before exposure to the tempter and the entrance of sin. The first man was placed under the *covenant of works*. This covenant endowed him with the responsibility of determining the spiritual direction of his entire posterity. In this covenant, Adam was the representative of all his descendants. Since he disobeyed, he bequeathed a corrupt nature to all his children. Had Adam not sinned and had someone sinned in a later age, that person would have been responsible for his own iniquity, and none of his children would have been involved. Only Adam (not Eve) was under the covenant of works. The *duty of worship* is an obligation given as an endowment from the creator. Man, however, does not have the right to worship God according to the dictates of his conscience. Rather, this duty must be fulfilled with a *good* conscience. God tells man how He wants to be worshiped. Man also was given *freedom of choice*. This endowment is quite significant for Graves in several areas—civil government, church government, and salvation. He preferred to call man a "free moral being" rather than a "free moral agent." Agent implies that instructions are coming from another and is contradictory to the idea of freedom. Graves, however, used both terms in his writings.

A final endowment is *the beard*. Yes, the beard. Graves maintained that shaving was contrary to God's laws. The God who placed the beard upon man's lips, jaws, and face did not intend for it to be shorn any more than the eye brows or the hair on man's head. Shaving originated in Canaan as an act of idolatrous worship. Beyond breaking God's laws, shaving is detrimental to man's well-being. For example, optic nerves extend into the upper lip, and constant shaving causes poor eyesight. Shaving the throat causes frequent colds, hoarseness, and baldness. Graves judged that deaths by consumption could be reduced by one-half if men stopped shaving.

Graves wrote a series of five articles on the beard that were published in *The Tennessee Baptist*. Sadly, these articles appeared in 1861 and 1862—a time when the nation was being torn asunder within—a time when he could have used his influence and the influence of his paper to deal with the more significant issue of war. One wonders how many of Graves's children still walk among us—those who major on issues of their choosing but who have a head-in-the-sand approach to many of the weightier matters facing Evangelical Christianity.

Even with these endowments, man fell. Satan approached Adam and Eve at their weakest points. Eve was tempted by her curiosity and her impulse of rivalry. She yielded, and as a fallen finite being influenced Adam. Adam was not deceived by the temptation; he sinned willfully and knowingly because he was moved by his emotional nature—love for his wife. By his fall, Adam brought depravity and woe to all his descendants as representative federal head of the race through the covenant of works. Eve's sin affected only herself, for she had no representative role. As a direct consequence of the fall, both man and creation have been subjected to the bondage of sin.

A final element in Graves's doctrine of creation is slavery. Graves was both a slaveholder and an advocate of the institution of domestic slavery.[47] The central biblical passage is the curse on Canaan in Genesis 9:25-27. Races originated when God determined that the sons of Noah would have different complexions. The color of a race, therefore, did not begin with the curse; the curse was imposed upon an already existing racial family. Domestic slavery, however, was not an original condition or intention of creation but was imposed because of sin. Hence, men are no longer born free and equal, for freedom and equality are characteristics of an innocence which no longer exists. By this reasoning, Graves maintained that slavery was a divine institution ordained by God. If slavery was a sin, then God was the author of sin.

Although the fall of man provided the general context for the inauguration of slavery, its institution was delayed until the days following the flood when the immediate provocation was the sin of Ham. Because of this sin, God saw fit to dispossess and disinherit all of Ham's descendants who, at that time, were represented in his oldest son, Canaan. The curse involved servitude, inferiority, and the absence of social equality. The colored descendants of

Ham were punished for his sin with perpetual slavery and inferiority to all other races. Furthermore, the prediction in the curse that Japheth would be enlarged and dwell in the tents of Shem was a clear announcement of the superiority of the white race. Even the New Testament did not question the propriety of slavery. Christianity did not condemn servitude but made it into a blessing by teaching slaves to be satisfied and content with their lot and to make no effort to escape from bondage.

Graves maintained this position before and after the Civil War. He always believed that his position was determined by the Bible and that slavery was intended to be a permanent social institution. He wrote:

> *The descendants of Canaan will ever be an inferior race; though the scenes of his servitude may change, he will still be a slave, in its essential sense, somewhere, and to somebody, until the dawning of the Second Advent,* when, for the first time, every curse of sin will be removed, and every yoke and distinction it has imposed be broken.[48]

Nevertheless, Graves was opposed to the abuses which often accompanied domestic slavery and warned abusing masters of God's coming wrath.

Redemption.—Graves's discussion of redemption has a dual focus. On the one hand, he dealt with *The Work of Christ in the Covenant of Redemption; Developed in Seven Dispensations,* meaning that all of God's works have redemptive ramifications. On the other hand, he approached redemption more narrowly in its specific relation to the activities of the incarnation. This section will describe the latter approach.

In his discussions of the atonement, Graves revealed a likeness to Anselm's theory of satisfaction, although Anselm was not mentioned. Man's sins have offended the honor, laws, and justice of God to the extent that legal satisfaction is required to redeem man. Simple repentance and reformation do not fulfill the demands of God, so a medium of satisfaction must prepare a way for man to approach God. Since neither Adam nor his descendants is able to achieve the required satisfaction, a third party—the incarnate, second person of the Godhead—was chosen to satisfy the penalty of violated justice through his vicarious suffering. Graves application of the satisfaction theme caused him to interpret the atonement in a legalistic framework that obscured elements of God's love and grace. His view might be called a sacrificial-substitutionary-satisfaction theory with a decided emphasis on the legal aspects of atonement.

The heart of Graves's doctrine of atonement is the covenant of redemption. This covenant is an agreement in which the Persons of the Trinity voluntarily and mutually covenanted to redeem fallen man and to complete God's purpose of self-manifestation in the created order. Conceived in eternity and fulfilled in history, this gracious plan of God allows man to escape the dreadful consequences of rebellion, conciliates God's honor, and does not infringe upon any of the divine perfections. When the covenant is finally fulfilled, the earth and man will be restored to the original state of perfection—a paradise peopled by sinless beings. In agreeing to restore man, each person of the trinity consented to perform specific functions. The functions inherent in the redemptive relationship are described by the terms *Father, Son,* and *Spirit.*

Only the persons of the Godhead are involved in the covenant of redemption. One member of the trinity "voluntarily, and by consent of all" undertook the office of representing the claims of the offended Godhead. He is called the first person and is officially superior to the other members of the trinity. Because of covenant relations with another person of the Godhead, he also is called Father. Under the terms of the covenant, another person of the Godhead "became" the Son. He fulfilled his functions through vicarious suffering. Graves was less specific about the work of the Spirit in the covenant. The Spirit seems to have assumed a relation of inferiority to Father and Son. His official role is to quicken the dead sinner by convincing him of sin. However, salvation is the work of the entire Godhead, not any one person. Each works with the other but does not violate the respective functions of the other. The person and work of Jesus Christ will be the focus for this summary.

S. H. Ford remarked that Graves had "peculiar views" of the person of Jesus Christ.[49] By accepting the obligations of the covenant of redemption, the second person of the trinity *became* the Son of the first person. The Son of God is literally begotten, for an eternal Son does not exist, only an eternal member of the trinity. This interpretation means that there was a time when the Son was not, questions the divinity of the Son, and led to Graves's being charged with Arianism. He denied this accusation and affirmed his belief in the incarnation of a divine being in the Son of God. However, in the incarnation, the divine person assumed human form but only in a limited way. The human nature of the Son was impersonal, for the true person of Jesus Christ was divine and only relatively human. Jesus Christ did not have a human soul, for the mind or soul was the dwelling place of the deity. In reality, for Graves the incarnation seems to be a divine person residing in and animating a human form. His God-man seems scarcely more than a Nestorian dichotomy of divine and human. The reason for this view appears to be Graves's insistence that divinity suffered on the cross. If Christ had a human soul, then divinity did not suffer, and salvation came through a finite being.

The work of Christ in the covenant of redemption was defined through a series of descriptive images, largely drawn from the Old Testament. These images include Kinsman-Redeemer; surety of the covenant; priesthood; and death, burial, and resurrection. Christ's death on the cross was not the atonement but only the sacrifice of the sin offering. By being resurrected, He was able to transport the blood offering to the right hand of God to complete His atoning work. This work of Christ is appropriated by faith.

Graves believed in a limited atonement. This position is based primarily on a logical syllogism. Graves wrote:

> Now, will not, must not, all *unprejudiced* Bible-read Christians agree to the following propositions?
>
> 1. That the Son undertook and will save all the Father, in the Covenant of Redemption, gave him to save.

2. Since all are not saved, as all evangelical Christians admit, we must conclude that *all were not given to the Son.*

3. That the Father, in the Covenant of Redemption, gave *some* of Adam's race to his Son to be redeemed.[50]

By His foreknowledge, God knew from the beginning who would believe. He determined to save those in all ages who would believe, and Christ died for these. God is willing to save all sinners, but some sinners are not willing to submit to God. Christ did die for all men in the sense that He removed every barrier so salvation by grace could be offered to humans. But God will not infringe upon freedom of choice. Therefore, if a person requests salvation by faith, Christ died for him. If this request is not made, then Christ did not die for the one who refuses to believe.

Those who believe have the assurance of salvation. Graves criticized the term *perseverance* because it implied that continuance in salvation depends on the believer. He preferred the security of the believer or the salvation of the believer.[51] To deny that salvation is permanent, in Graves's theology, means that regeneration depends on man's work instead of the work of God. Any church that believes in apostasy, consequently, cannot be a regular Baptist church and should not be recognized as such.[52] At no point in his writings did Graves vacillate on this position.

Ecclesiology.—The church was always Graves's primary concern, and he wrote more on this theme, particularly the ordinances, than any other theological subject. Every book and numerous articles touched in some way on ecclesiology. Given Graves's obsession with Baptist identity, one would expect this to be the case.

What is the church? Simply stated, "We define it as a body of voluntarily associated believers organized according to the pattern of the Church at Jerusalem."[53] A gathering of Christians in itself, however, is not a church, for a true church has definite, recognizable characteristics; a unique relation to the kingdom; and understands the distinction between church fellowship and Christian fellowship.

The characteristics of a true church are divine origin, perpetual existence, visible institution, local organization, biblical practices, and a Baptist body. The true church has a *divine origin* because its Founder, Jesus Christ, was divine, and the church He instituted was an expression of His divine intentions. In the covenant of redemption, He obligated Himself to establish an organization on earth. "By *Perpetuity,* I mean that Churches of this character, constituting the visible Kingdom of Christ, must have existed, unbroken and uncorrupted, and therefore needing no Reformation, as respect to anything affecting their true identity, from the days of the Apostles until this day."[54] This position, however, should not be confused with apostolic succession since the apostles had no successors. Hence, a succession of churches is required. Christ's body had only one beginning and has existed from that time until the present. He believed that documents to prove this succession might be locked in the Vatican.[55] Graves rejected the idea of an invisible church which includes all saints and maintained that a true church is a *visible institution*. A true church is a *local organization* that can be assembled in one place. Graves's interpretation of the term *ecclesia* led to this conclusion. No passage in the New Testament teaches a universal church. Even those passages that are figurative have a local meaning when the figure is interpreted correctly. The primary *biblical practice* that Graves emphasized was that the membership of a church must be composed of people who have been redeemed by faith in Jesus Christ. Infant baptism and sacramental salvation are eliminated in this position.

That the true church is also a *Baptist body* should come as no surprise. Only one denomination can be identified with the church in Jerusalem. Graves concluded that Jesus founded a Baptist church, and Baptist churches have existed in every age of Christian history. "The church denominated Baptist, *is the only Scriptural Church organization* . . . hence, when we preach Baptist doctrines, we preach the *Gospel*."[56] During the history of the church, Baptist have sometimes been called Montanists, Donatists, Paterines, Paulicians, and Albigenses. If these groups were not true churches, then Christ had no church in the world during such times.

The relation between church and kingdom is one of the fascinating issues in Graves's ecclesiology. *Churches* and *kingdom* are synonymous terms. This equation is based on his assumption that Matthew 16:18 was the fulfillment of Daniel 2:44. Jesus Christ used the word *church* in place of *kingdom* and, by so doing, equated the two terms.[57] The kingdom is a visible institution located on earth. No kingdom exists in Heaven as the home of all saints. Graves wrote: *"The kingdom of Christ, of God, of heaven, in constituted of the sum total of all his true visible churches as constituents, which churches are the sole judges and executives of the laws and ordinances of the kingdom."*[58] The multiplication of true churches, therefore, expands the kingdom.

Membership in this kingdom is contingent on membership in a local church. The only valid visible church is a local Baptist church. Therefore, membership in the kingdom must be preceded by union with a local Baptist church. Union with a local Baptist church depends upon a profession of faith followed by baptism. While salvation does not depend on baptism, church and kingdom membership does. Therefore, in order to enter the kingdom of God, the subject must be a Christian who has been baptized into a local, visible Baptist church. Are only Baptists saved? By no means. Membership in the kingdom and redemption from sin are two entirely different relations. A person can be a Christian without being in the kingdom.

If such is the case, how can the practical problem of relations between denominations be managed? This problem is solved by distinguishing between *church fellowship* and *Christian fellowship*. Graves did not castigate the Christian membership of a religious society and affirmed that Christian fellowship was possible between all believers regardless of denominational affiliation. Church fellowship is an altogether different matter and has narrowly defined limitations.

> It is the fellowship of *forms, faith, and facts or practices, and it has no reference to, and is no expression of, the personal feelings of the individual members of the communing bodies toward each other*. Church fellowship can only

exist between those churches that are constituted upon the same principles and forms of government, having a common faith and discipline.[59]

All Christians could engage in Christian fellowship, but church fellowship was restricted to members of a true church.

Baptism and the Lord's Supper are the only ordinances instituted by Jesus Christ to be observed by His church. Graves deliberately used the term *ordinance* instead of *sacrament* because he believed that sacrament had connotations which implied that grace was conveyed through participation. He rejected footwashing as an ordinance because the commandment of footwashing was directed exclusively to the apostles and was not intended for the church.

Graves wrote more on baptism than any other ecclesiological theme. "Of all ecclesiastical questions," he wrote, "it is the most important. It is so related to other questions that its answer answers more questions than any other known to us."[60] Immersion is the only form of baptism, and Graves rejected a cause-effect relationship between baptism and salvation. Through baptism a candidate declares that he has been redeemed by faith in Jesus Christ, meaning that it has a figurative significance only. Since immersion is the proper form, the figure intended is death, burial, and resurrection. Although only figurative, the importance of baptism must not be depreciated. For example, baptism unites the believer to the organization to which the administrator belongs. The candidate, therefore, does not profess a private faith, but his baptism is a confession of the faith of the denomination into which he is baptized.

What makes a valid baptism was an important question for Graves. He gave a specific answer. A valid baptism has three characteristics.

1. A scriptural subject, which is a *believer* in Christ. 2. A scriptural mode, which is immersion of the subject in the name of the Trinity. 3. A scriptural administrator, who must be an immersed believer, acting under the authority of a *gospel* church.[61]

Using these three elements as his standard of judgment, Graves examined the ordinances of other denominations and concluded that their baptisms were invalid. The fact that the administrator of baptism was obligated to act under authority of a gospel church disqualified every immersion except that performed in a Baptist church, for only Baptists are true churches.

The Lord's Supper is exclusively a church ordinance, and its significance is commemorative only. Jesus instituted the Supper by eating it with his disciples who constituted the first visible church and by commanding the observance of this practice in all later churches. Since this initial activity took place in a church setting, the Lord's Supper is clearly a church ordinance which indicates church relations rather than Christian fellowship. *Communion* is a fitting name for the Lord's Supper because this term emphasizes that the service is a memorial in which the fellowship is between God and man, and not man and man.[62] This concept was important for Graves.

Throughout his ministry Graves was opposed to denominational intercommunion or open communion. The nature of the church was the decisive issue which separated Baptists from other groups. Graves expressed two opinions about intercommunion between Baptist churches. These viewpoints do not coincide with distinct periods in his life. Rather, they overlap until he reached a definitive position. In 1847 Graves was moderator of the Concord Association when the group voted unanimously to celebrate the Supper in all future meetings. By 1854 a new theme appeared in Graves's writing, namely that the Supper should be preceded by the exercise of local church discipline and should be restricted exclusively to those over whom the church can exercise such discipline. He stated firmly, "Let it be considered an axiom, that *each church must have the Disciplinary power over all she is warranted to invite to partake of the Supper*."[63] However, in 1856 Graves visited his home church in Vermont and administered the Lord's Supper, and in 1860 all Baptists in good standing with their own churches were invited to participate in communion at the Spring Street Church where Graves was pastor. His definitive position followed the opinion he expressed in 1854. The Lord's Supper should be restricted to members in good standing in the church in which the ordinance was being observed. To extend the supper to Baptists in other churches is a clear violation of the autonomy of the local church. A church does not invite visiting Baptists to participate in business meeting, and these same Baptists should not be asked to take part in the Lord's Supper.

Eschatology.—Graves's eschatology was based on a literal interpretation of the Bible and was formulated according to a dispensational framework. Within this format, he categorized biblical narratives into a definite sequence of events which required that certain incidents take place before others can occur. The central issue in his eschatology is the return of Jesus Christ. Graves's use of dispensational themes probably accounts for the fact that eschatology was the only doctrine he organized carefully.

Christ's coming will be in two stages. His first coming will be secret and *will not* include all saints; the faithful ones who are gathered will be taken from the earth because of the coming tribulation. Approximately seven years later Christ will come in power and glory, and all remaining Christians will be gathered. The Millennium will be followed by the consummation, and the new earth will be established in the sabbatic age.

Evaluation

Evaluating the theology of Graves is difficult because of the temptation to judge him by current theological statements. In fairness, he must be interpreted as a person of his times and not by late-twentieth-century standards.

Identifying influences which shaped the development of Graves's theology is a difficult if not impossible task. Little information is available about his early years. Long hours of private study obviously influenced his thinking, but what he studied other than the Bible is not known. Also, Graves did not carefully document his early writings, leading to the charge of plagarism—perhaps with some justification. J. L. Burrows, a contemporary opponent of Graves, probably overstated the situation when he noted:

> It is useless then for us to look for these dogmas in previous Baptist history, creeds or usages. It is needless to search for its principles in the New Testament. It began, has continued, and we hope will end, with J. R. Graves, LL.D. We recognize it as his own peculiar pet hobby, and no one can deny that he has ridden it vigorously.[64]

Graves lived during a period when ecclesiology was a primary concern. His preoccupation with this theme demonstrates that he was a nineteenth-century thinker—a child of his times. This theme is closely akin to his concern for achieving a unique identity for Baptists. According to S. H. Ford, "in Nashville, more than any spot on the continent, religious discussion was constant, bitter, and personal, and with Baptists it was a battle of existence."[65] Graves's personality and approach to theology were compatible with this environment. Personal experiences, reading, and the times in which he lived were all significant factors in the development of Graves's theology.[66]

Graves's theology was unsystematic and practical. In his most theological writing, he stated that he did not propose "to write a system of Theology."[67] He wrote within a dynamic context of denominational competition and controversy and responded to issues as they arose. At the same time, he dealt with very practical issues not often discussed in doctrinal statements. For example, he wrote about church finances, care of the preacher's voice, education, and the place of honorary degrees. He was a practical thinker who sought to relate his understanding of the Bible to the church.

The idea of the covenant of redemption is the closest Graves came to having a unifying theme. However, the central issue in his theology is the ordinance of baptism. Without the proper administration of baptism, the true church would cease to exist, for church and kingdom membership depend on baptism. Without a true church, no agency has been commissioned to preach the gospel and preserve the truth. To remove baptism from Graves's theology would be tantamount to removing the "keystone" idea from his doctrinal formulations.

Graves's methodology and conclusions are vulnerable at several points. He was selective in his use of evidence. For example, Graves rejected Roman Catholicism, but his arguments for the existence of God could have appeared in a Roman Catholic treatise on theology. Likewise, he rejected Campbellism, but in his efforts to restore the "old landmarks" of biblical faith, he might have been influenced by Alexander Campbell more than he would admit. His absolute separation of eternal person and historical function in the trinity is suspect in that he does not allow function to influence person. Graves's attitude toward slavery is an untenable position and is based on a marginal (at best) exegetical methodology. His Christology is a hybrid of Arian, Apollinarian, and Nestorian elements. The equation of church and kingdom and the implications thereof are difficult, if not impossible, to support. Does baptism deserve the place Graves gave it? Is the Lord's Supper limited to church fellowship as opposed to Christian fellowship? His views of eschatology lacked the distinctive imprint that Graves gave to other doctrines and have the same weaknesses as other dispensational views. In any case, readers are invited to enter into dialog with Graves and to make their own judgments about his theology.

One significant element which must not be overlooked is how Graves understood and evaluated his own work. He was convinced that God had assigned him the task of proclaiming truth and defeating error. Persuaded that by God's grace he had discovered the truth, he intended to promote its acceptance to as many people as possible through every available means. Whatever specific influences might have shaped his doctrinal affirmations, his theology cannot be understood without realizing how he interpreted his own calling. "We are set for the defence of the truth," he wrote, "a watchman upon the walls, and our commission is, when we see danger coming, to sound the alarm, else blood will be found upon us."[68] Usually Graves did not consider the possibility that he might have misunderstood his calling or misjudged God's revelation of truth in the Bible. Consequently, no matter how much he might have been influenced by the times in which he lived, the experiences in which he was involved, or the materials he borrowed from others, the final theological form bore the express image of Graves himself. All influences were filtered through his evaluation of the work given to him by God. He was an able, capable thinker who should receive credit for having the skill to formulate a doctrinal position according to his own understanding.

What is the significance of the theology of J. R. Graves? He performed valuable services for nineteenth-century Baptists by helping awaken them to a needed self-consciousness when the loss of denominational identity was a real possibility. He reminded Baptists that they had a contribution to make to American Christianity in the areas of church government, a regenerated church membership, and the biblical meaning of the ordinances. When Baptists were primarily an ignorant, "backwoods," frontier group, he emphasized the need for education and encouraged the organization of schools. The theological dimension which he gave to his Baptist paper illustrated the need for and the broad possibilities of doctrinal publications, making them more than promoters of denominational enterprises. In the early years of the Southern Baptist Convention, he modeled that the quest for truth is far more significant than the preservation of an institution. One might not agree with his conclusions, but his quest was commendable.

Some of the words Graves used are still heard among Baptists. While he might not be exclusively responsible for all of these elements, his influence is significant as a primary source. These areas include: an anti-scientific bias; plenary-verbal inspiration and a distaste for biblical criticism; pragmatic understanding of the will of God; attitude toward women; weak Christology; exclusive ecclesiology supported by "a trail of blood" interpretation of Christian history; close communion; and dispensational eschatology. Are these influences negative or positive? Readers must make a personal determination at that point. For many, the theology of J. R. Graves (though this name might not be known) is the "historical Baptist position." Some have no idea that Baptists or Christians ever believed otherwise.

Being true to our Baptist heritage means that we will examine all of our past and those who contributed to it in light of our understanding of biblical truth. Particular attention must be given to the contexts in which this heritage developed. Those who might reject anything that has the flavor of Graves need to remember the positive elements that helped preserve Baptist identity in a rapidly changing society. Some of his contributions are genuine and transcend his time and place. Those who might be inclined to accept as a total package all of the theology of Graves need to remember that much of his theology was formulated in the atmosphere of denominational survival, development, and growth. A changing context should allow for alterations in theological affirmations.

In reality, J. R. Graves was not a formally trained theologian. He was an effective Baptist preacher, editor, and writer with a particular theological outlook that he expounded religiously. Let us be true to our heritage and study Graves's life, work, and thought. Then, also true to our heritage, let us *move beyond* the unsatisfactory, no-longer-relevant elements in his Landmark theology and *embrace* those positive contributions that are needed for the fulfillment of the work God has given to us.

Bibliography

Books by Graves

The Act of Christian Baptism. Memphis: Baptist Book House, 1881.

The Bible Doctrine of the middle Life, as Opposed to Swedenborgianism and Spiritism. Texarkana: Baptist Sunday School Committee, 1873, 1928.

Campbell and Campbellism Exposed. A Series of Replies. Nashville: Graves & Marks, 1854.

Christian Baptism, The Profession of the Faith of the Gospel. Memphis: Baptist Book House, 1881.

The Desire of All Nations. Nashville: Graves & Shankland, 1853.

The Dispensational Expositions of the Parables and Prophecies of Christ. Second edition. Texarkana: Baptist Sunday School Committee, 1887, 1928, 1939.

The Great Iron Wheel; or, Republicanism Backwards and Christianity Reversed. Seventeenth edition. Nashville: Graves, Marks and Rutland, 1856.

Intercommunion Inconsistent, Unscriptural, and Productive of Evil. Memphis: Baptist Book House, 1881.

John's Baptism: Was It From Moses or Christ? Jewish or Christian? Second edition. Texarkana: Baptist Sunday School Committee, 1887, 1928, 1939.

The Lord's Supper a Church Ordinance. Memphis: Baptist Book House, 1881.

The New Great Iron Wheel. An Examination of the New M. E. Church South. Texarkana: Baptist Sunday School Committee, 1884, 1928.

Old Landmarkism: What Is It? Second edition. Texarkana: Baptist Sunday School Committee, 1880, 1928.

The Relation of Baptism to Salvation. Memphis: Baptist Book House, 1881.

Satan Dethroned and Other Sermons. Edited by Orren L. Hailey. New York: Fleming H. Revell Co., 1924.

Spiritism. A Lecture. Memphis: South-Western Publishing Company, 1869.

The Trilemma; or, Death by Three Horns. Second edition. Texarkana: Baptist Sunday School Committee, 1881, 1928.

The Watchman's Reply. Nashville: Graves & Shankland, 1853.

What Is Conscience? Have You a Good Conscience? Memphis: The Baptist Book House, 1882.

What Is It to Eat and Drink Unworthily? Memphis: Baptist Book House, 1881.

The Work of Christ in the Covenant of Redemption; Developed in Seven Dispensations. Texarkana: Baptist Sunday School Committee, 1883, 1928, 1963.

(With John C. Burruss). *A Discussion on the Doctrine of Endless Punishment Between Rev. J. R. Graves, D.D., L.L.D., and Rev. John C. Burruss.* Atlanta: J. O. Perkins & Co., 1880.

(With John C. Burruss). *Restorationism Refuted. The Last Letters of the Written Discussion Between J. C. Burruss of Alabama, and J. R. Graves, Editor of The Baptist, Memphis, Tenn.* Memphis: Baptist Book House, 1880.

(With Jacob Ditzler). *The Graves-Ditzler: or, Great Carrollton Debate.* Memphis: Southern Baptist Publication Society, 1876.

Books about Graves

Burnett, J. J. *Sketches of Tennessee's Pioneer Baptist Preachers.* Nashville: Press of Marshall & Bruce Company, 1919.

Hailey, Orren L. *J. R. Graves, Life Times and Teachings.* Nashville: n.p., 1925.

Inman, W. G. *Planting and Progress of the Baptist Cause in Tennessee.* Edited by Orren L. Hailey. MSS in the Historical Commission of the Southern Baptist Convention, Nashville, Tennessee.

Patterson, T. A. "The Theology of J. R. Graves and Its Influence on Southern Baptist Life." Th.D. diss., Southwestern Baptist Theological Seminary, 1944.

Smith, Harold S. "A Critical Analysis of the Theology of J. R. Graves." Ph.D. diss., Southern Baptist Theological Seminary, 1966.

Tull, James E. *Shapers of Baptist Thought.* Valley Forge: Judson Press, 1972.

Notes

1. "[Announcement]," *Tennessee Baptist,* June 28, 1845, 720. The same notice was published in the city paper. Sources do not indicate why Graves was identified as being from Lexington. Hereafter, TB is used to designate *The Tennessee Baptist* and *The Baptist,* names of the paper with which Graves was associated.

2. J. R. Graves, "Our Paper," TB, August 30, 1845, 19. The origin of Graves's interest in religious journalism and his evaluation of the importance of religious literature are unknown.

3. Graves, "Reaction of Injury," TB, July 10, 1858, 2.

4. Graves, "This Paper and the Southern Baptist; or Ourself and J. B. Tustin," TB, June 13, 1857, 2.

5. Graves, "Reaction of Injury," 2.

6. Letter from Helen Clark, clerk of North Springfield Baptist Church, January 30, 1965. Graves explained that he was called Robinson in his boyhood at the request of James Robinson after whom he was named.

7. J. J. Burnett, *Sketches of Tennessee's Pioneer Baptist Preachers* (Nashville: Marshall & Bruce Co., 1919), 184.

8. Letter from Helen Clark. She explained that the word *view* was not entirely legible.

9. "Minutes," Mount Freedom Baptist Church, May 1842. The church from which Graves moved his membership was not identified in the minutes.

10. "Minutes," Mount Freedom Baptist Church, October 1858. Some biographers place the date as 1844. Since Graves left Kentucky in 1843, the 1842 date is probably correct.

11. J. L. Waller, "The Charges of the South-Western Baptist Met by Mr. Henderson's Own Witness," TB, September 4, 1858, 4.

12. "Minutes," First Baptist Church, Nashville, Tennessee, July 13, 1845.

13. For a summary of the conflict, see Homer L. Grice and R. Paul Caudill, "Graves-Howell Controversy (1857-62)," *Enclyclopedia of Southern Baptists,* 1958, 1:580-85.

14. Graves, "Extract from the Anniversary Sermon of 1848," TB, February 8, 1849, 3.

15. Graves, "The Goal Won at Last," TB, January 8, 1859, 2.

16. W. W. Barnes, *The Southern Baptist Convention, 1845-1953* (Nashville: Broadman Press, 1954), 103. The three men were first named as co-editors in the May 15, 1858, issue of the paper.

17. Graves, "Memphis as the Denominational Center of the Southern States," TB, June 6, 1874, 4.

18. J. S. Mahaffy, "Paralyzed in His Pulpit," TB, August 23, 1884, 7.

19. Graves, "Dr. Graves Gives His Blessing," *Baptist and Reflector,* October 31, 1889, 8.

20. "Recent Events," *Baptist and Reflector,* June 29, 1893, 9.

21. The most concise information about the life, thought, and theology of Graves is in Harold S. Smith, "A Critical Analysis of the Theology of J. R. Graves," (Ph.D. diss., The Southern Baptist Theological Seminary, 1966).

22. Graves, "Address: To the Readers of the Baptist," TB, October 19, 1848, 2.

23. Graves, "Beware of Impostors!!," TB, October 22, 1853, 2.

24. This statement was part of a standing announcement for the South Western Publishing House which was first printed on September 15, 1855.

25. Graves, "Detraction," TB, November 20, 1847. Howell planned to ignore the charges, but Graves said that his sense of justice would not allow him to be silent.

26. Graves, "A Chapter on Controversy," TB, February 8, 1849, 2.

27. Graves, "Queries," TB, October 15, 1870, 4.

28. Graves, "Querist," TB, April 4, 1857, 2.

29. Graves, "The Hearts You Should Have," TB, November 11, 1854, 3.

30. See Graves, *The Work of Christ in the Covenant of Redemption; Developed in Seven Dispensations* (Texarkana: Baptist Sunday School Committee, 1883, 1928, 1963).

31. Ibid., 21.

32. Graves, "The Scriptures, No. 4, *Virtual Infidelity Advocated by Modern Christians, by Interpreting Literal Language Figuratively—and Figurative or Symbolic Language Literally,*" TB, December 17, 1853, 2.

33. Graves, *The Work of Christ,* 21.

34. Ibid., 24.

35. Ibid.

36. Ibid., 24.

37. Graves, "The Querist," TB, February 21, 1850, 2.

38. Graves, "The Gospel in Ezekiel," *The Southern Baptist Review and Eclectic.* November and December 1856, 745. This article was a review of a book by Thomas Guthrie.

39. Graves, *The Dispensational Expositions of the Parables and Prophecies of Christ,* 2d ed. (Texarkana: Baptist Sunday School Committee, 1887, 1928, 1939), 17, 49.

40. Graves, "One Sinner Destroys Much Good, Eccl. IX, 18," TB, December 17, 1881, 436.

41. Graves, "Querist," TB, March 22, 1884, 8.

42. Graves, *The Work of Christ,* 61-62.

43. Graves, "The Scriptures, No. 4."

44. Graves, *The Work of Christ,* 47.

45. Graves, "Brevities," TB, February 5, 1881, 536.

46. Graves, "Evolution," TB, February 16, 1884, 5.

47. Graves's ownership of slaves is verified in J. R. Graves, ed., *The Little Iron Wheel, A Declaration of Christian Rights and Articles, Showing the Despotism of Episcopal Methodism,* H. B. Bascom (Nashville: South-Western Publishing House, 1857), 267. See ibid., 8-18, for a summary of his position on slavery.

48. Graves, *What Is Conscience? Have You a Good Conscience?* (Memphis: The Baptist Book House, Graves & Mahaffy, 1882), 20.

49. S. H. Ford, "Life, Times, and Teachings of J. R. Graves," *Ford's Christian Repository and Home Circle,* June 1900, 350.

50. Graves, *The Work of Christ,* 96.

51. Graves, "The Christian Saved," TB, May 3, 1873, 4. This use of security of the believer is one of the earliest among Southern Baptist writers—if not the first.

52. Graves, "Querist," TB, January 31, 1857, 2.

53. Graves, "Querist," TB, February 4, 1854, 2.

54. Graves, *The New Great Iron Wheel. An Examination of the New M. E. Church South* (Texarkana: Baptist Sunday School Committee, 1884, 1928), 28.

55. Graves, "Able Latitudinarians," TB, June 7, 1837, 4.

56. Graves, "Address to the Baptists of Tennessee. Number 3. Defects in the Appropriations and Instruction of Our Executive Boards—Tract Distribution—Sabbath Schools—Porters Work—Policy of Our Executive Boards," TB, July 12, 1849, 3.

57. Graves, *Intercommunion Inconsistent, Unscriptural, and Productive of Evil* (Memphis: Baptist Books House, 1881), 134.

58. Ibid., 160.

59. Graves, *Old Landmarkism: What Is It?,* 2d ed., (Texarkana: Baptist Sunday School Committee, 1880, 1928), 159-65.

60. Graves, "The Irrepressible Conflict," TB, June 22, 1867, 4.

61. Graves, "Remarks," TB, February 1, 1849, 2.

62. Graves, *Intercommunion,* 235-37.

63. Graves, "Querist," TB, August 12, 1854, 2.

64. J. L. Burrows, "Old Landmarkism," TB, March 5, 1881, 594.

65. S. H. Ford, "Life, Times, and Teachings of J. R. Graves," *Ford's Christian Repository and Home Circle,* October 1899, 613-14.

66. See Smith, 93-121.

67. Graves, *The Work of Christ,* 15.

68. Graves, "A Chapter on Controversy."

12

James Petigru Boyce
Timothy George

Biography

James Petigru Boyce was born on January 11, 1827, in Charleston, South Carolina.[1] Charleston, a city of some thirty thousand, was a flourishing center of commerce and culture where two ideals of civilization converged: the cavalier and the Puritan. The spirit of the jolly cavalier, brought from France and England, exemplified in fox-hunting parsons and state-sponsored Anglicanism, resulted in a culture of civility and urbanity which left its mark on young Boyce. His father, Ker Boyce, was one of the wealthiest men in South Carolina. Being a banker and business magnate, he desired his precocious son to follow in his steps. Like the father of Martin Luther centuries before, Boyce's father had wanted his son to study law and was bitterly disappointed when he opted for the ministry instead. One of his father's business partners, upon hearing that "Jimmy Boyce" meant to be a preacher, said: "Well, well, why don't he follow some useful occupation?"[2] Although he was to pursue a different path, Boyce did inherit his father's penchant for business success. His life's work, the founding of the first theological seminary among Baptists in the South, would not have been possible without his extraordinary acumen in business and financial affairs.

The cavalier culture was also reflected in Boyce's marked concern about manners. At the seminary, Boyce taught the students not only about the doctrine of justification and the eternal decrees of God, but also how to eat properly with a fork and knife, how to help a lady into her seat, how to stand in a pulpit, how to dress correctly for class, and how to make pastoral visits with propriety and discretion. It is not surprising that Boyce appears on Brooks Holifield's list of "gentlemen theologians" who had a decisive effect on Southern culture in the nineteenth century.[3]

However, it was not the cavalier but rather the Puritan ideal which was to shape Boyce's destiny. His mother, Amanda Jane Caroline Johnston, descended from strict Presbyterian stock. She had been converted under the ministry of Basil Manly, Sr., who came to be pastor of the First Baptist Church of Charleston in 1826. Early in his life, Boyce came under the tutelage of this great Baptist leader who was both an able exponent of Calvinistic theology and one of the first proponents of a common theological seminary for Southern Baptists. He was later to serve as chairman of the first board of trustees of Southern Seminary. At his funeral service in 1868 Boyce recalled the formative influence Manly, Sr., had exerted in his young life.

> After a lapse of more than thirty years I can yet feel the weight of his hand, resting in gentleness and love upon my head. I can recall the words of fatherly tenderness, with which he sought to guide my childish steps. I can see his beloved form in the study, in the house on King Street. I can again behold him in our own family circle . . . . I can call to mind his conversations with my mother, to whose salvation had been blessed a sermon preached on the Sunday after the death of one of his children on the text, "If I be bereaved of my children, I am bereaved." And once more come to me the words of sympathy which he spake while he wept with her family over her dead body, and ministered to them as it was laid in the grave.[4]

From his mother and from his pastor Boyce gained a sense of the transcendent. He became attuned to the life of the spirit and the life of the mind. His "barrel-shaped" figure, as one of his contemporaries described it, prevented him from engaging in the popular schoolboy sports, such as baseball or shinny. More often, he was sequestered in a corner reading a book. Throughout his entire life, he was an omnivorous reader and a bibliophile without peer.

After studying for two years at the College of Charleston, Boyce moved to Providence, Rhode Island, where he enrolled at Brown University, the first college founded by Baptists in America. Here he came under the influence of Francis Wayland, renowned Baptist statesman and educator and one of the formative leaders of the Triennial Convention. Wayland required his students to memorize a given lesson in advance and stand to recite it when called upon in class. Boyce later used this method of teaching by "recitation" in his own courses at Southern Seminary.

It was also under the influence of Francis Wayland that Boyce was converted to Christ. The Second Great Awakening had begun with a powerful revival at Yale College under Timothy Dwight. A similar outpouring of the Spirit occurred at Brown when Boyce was a student there. Dr. Wayland prayed for the students who had never professed faith in Christ and preached in chapel on the importance of spiritual welfare as well as intellectual advance. When Boyce returned to Charleston for spring break in 1846, he was under deep conviction. Despite his wealthy status, his promising future, his polish, and education, Broadus says "he felt himself a ruined sinner and . . . had to look to the merits of Christ alone for salvation."[5] He was saved and baptized during a protracted meeting conducted by Richard Fuller. Boyce returned to Brown a changed man. He became greatly concerned for his fellow classmates who were as yet unconverted. He began to pray for them and to share the gospel with them. "Two or three," he wrote home, "who had been brought up on the doctrines of Universalism [came] to look to Jesus as the author and finisher of our faith." Again, he wrote, "May God make me instrumental in his hands in the salvation of many!"[6] From his conversion in 1845 until his death in 1888, Boyce lost neither his devotion to God nor his dedication to disciplined study which was for him an expression of devotion to God.

Boyce received his formal theological training at Princeton Theological

James Petigru Boyce (1827-88)

Photo courtesy of The Southern Baptist Theological Seminary

Seminary where he studied from 1849 to 1851 under Archibald Alexander, his son Addison Alexander, and—above all—Charles Hodge, whose three-volume *Systematic Theology* would later serve as a model for Boyce's own *Abstract of Systematic Theology*. By the mid-nineteenth century, Princeton had become the theological center of Calvinist orthodoxy in America, and Boyce drank deeply from the wells of his great Reformed teachers. At Princeton, Boyce was exposed to the classic writings of Reformed Scholasticism including the *Institutio theologiae elencticae* by Francis Turretin, Calvin's successor as city pastor and theologian in Geneva. Boyce later adopted this book as a required text in his course on "Latin theology" at Southern Seminary, where it influenced an entire generation of Southern Baptist ministers. Boyce also thought highly of the Scottish Presbyterian John Dick whose *Lectures on Theology* he used repeatedly as a text in his systematic theology classes. Despite the formative role his Princeton experience had on his theological development, one should not think that Boyce was somehow seduced by an influence alien to his indigenous Baptist background. W. O. Carver, whose own theology was of a different bent than that of Boyce, put it succinctly: "I think that it was under Hodge's teaching that he formulated his theological views but these views did not differ from the theological atmosphere in which he had grown up."[7] Princeton provided Boyce with a systematic framework in which to cast the Calvinist theology he had imbibed from Basil Manly, Sr., and his other Charleston pastors.[8]

After completing his work at Princeton, Boyce served for two years as pastor of the First Baptist Church of Columbia, South Carolina. At his ordination council, Dr. Thomas Curtis asked Boyce whether he proposed to make a lifelong matter of preaching. "Yes," he replied, "provided I do not become a professor of theology."[9] In 1855 Boyce was elected to teach theology at Furman University. In July 1856 he delivered his inaugural address, entitled "Three Changes in Theological Institutions." By all accounts, this was a virtuoso performance, the more remarkable when one considers that it was delivered by a young man only twenty-nine-years old. A. M. Poindexter, secretary of the Southern Baptist Foreign Mission Board, declared Boyce's address to be "the ablest thing of the kind he had ever heard."[10] "Three Changes" was a virtual manifesto for a common theological seminary for Baptists in the South. Boyce suggested three ideals which such a school should embody. The first was *openness,* a seminary for everybody called by God regardless of academic background or social status. This was unheard of in the nineteenth century when it was universally agreed that a thorough grounding in the classical disciplines was an essential prerequisite for theological education. Boyce had two concerns in proposing this change. First, he knew that the majority of Baptist preachers did not have, and many could not acquire, the advantages of a classical education, yet they and the churches they served would be enhanced by their exposure to theological study. He also hoped that the experience of students from diverse backgrounds mingling together in a common community of learning and piety would engender mutual respect and lessen the jealousies and resentments which frequently flared up among Baptist pastors.

His second ideal was equally important—*excellence*. Boyce was intent upon establishing an advanced program of theological study which in its academic rigor would be on a par with the kind of instruction offered at Princeton, Andover, Harvard, Yale, or anywhere else in the world. He envisioned, as he put it, "a band of scholars," trained for original research and committed to accurate scholarship, which would go out from the seminary to contribute significantly to the theological life of the church by their teaching and writing as well as by their preaching and witness in the world.

The third ideal was *confessional identity*. Boyce proposed that the seminary be established on a set of doctrinal principles which would provide consistency and direction for the future. This, too, was a radical step in the context of nineteenth-century Baptist life. Newton Theological Institute, the first seminary founded by Baptists in America, had no such confessional guidelines. Nor, indeed, did the Southern Baptist Convention, organized in 1845. However, Boyce firmly believed that it was necessary to protect the seminary from doctrinal erosion. From his student days in New England, Boyce was aware of the recent currents in theology: Unitarianism, Transcendentalism, the New Divinity. In particular, he spoke against the "blasphemous doctrines" of Theodore Parker, who had denied that Christianity was based on a special revelation of God. At the same time he was concerned about populist theologies in the South, and warned against the "twin errors of Campbellism and Arminianism."[11]

In setting forth the rationale for Southern Baptists' first theological seminary, Boyce insisted that each professor subscribe to a set of doctrinal principles. Moreover, he declared, "his agreement with the standard should be exact. His declaration of it should be based upon no mental reservation, upon no private understanding with those who immediately invest him into office."[12] Boyce was well aware that there were those who felt that such a policy of strict subscription was a violation of academic freedom and liberty of conscience, but he urged its adoption nonetheless:

> You will infringe the rights of no man, and you will secure the rights of those who have established here an instrumentality for the production of a sound ministry. It is no hardship to those who teach here, to be called upon to sign the declaration of their principles, for there are fields of usefulness open elsewhere to every man, and none need accept your call who can not conscientiously sign your formulary.[13]

Boyce related the reluctance of some Baptists to adopt a specific doctrinal standard to the influence of Alexander Campbell whose slogan of "no creed but the Bible" had lured many Baptists away from their traditional confessional moorings.[14] Campbell had decried the use of confessions as an infringement upon the rights of conscience. Boyce, however, in a brilliant rebuttal, traced the history of confessional statements from New Testament times down to his own day. He showed that Baptists in particular had been prolific in promulgating confessions, both as public declarations of their own faith and as a means of testing the true faith in others. Following these guidelines, Basil Manly, Jr., drafted an Abstract of Principles which were incorporated into the Fundamental Laws of Southern Seminary. Since the founding of Southern Seminary in 1859 every professor who has served on the faculty of that institution has signed this original document, pledging thereby to teach "in accordance with and not contrary to" its provisions.[15] The Abstract of Principles was intentionally modeled on the Philadelphia Confession of Faith, which was based on the Second London Confession, which, in turn, was a Baptist adaptation of the Westminster Confession. Robert Lynn has said of the ideal of confessional identity that, while it has sometimes been a point of controversy, it has also provided "a thread of continuity which links past, present and future."[16]

Boyce's hopes for the seminary soon fell victim to the convulsions of the American Civil War. In 1862 the seminary disbanded. Although Boyce had been a vocal opponent of secession, both he and his colleague John A. Broadus ministered as chaplains among the Confederate troops. During this time, Boyce also served in the South Carolina state legislature. He so distinguished himself in that body that he was urged on all sides to give himself entirely to political life. On December 5, 1862, Broadus discouraged his friend from following such an alluring career:

> You have doubtless been told already that such capacities for public usefulness ought to be permanently devoted to the public good, and all that. My dear fellow, don't listen to it. Your mission is to bring theological science into practical relation to this busy world, and if God spares your life and grants the country peace, this seminary which was founded by your labors shall yet shine in conspicuous usefulness.[17]

Broadus's advice prevailed, and after the war, the four original founders of the seminary—Boyce, Broadus, Manly, and William Williams—gathered at the Boyce home in Greenville, South Carolina. They joined in prayer and a deep seeking of the will of God. At the end of the day Broadus said, "Suppose we quietly agree that the seminary may die, but we will die first."[18] All heads were silently bowed, and the matter was decided.

Boyce not only conceived and birthed the seminary but also nurtured it and kept it alive when for good reason nearly everyone else expected it to die. Time and again he gave generously out of his own dwindling estate to help needy students through another semester or to pay the salaries of the other professors. Once when the Southern Baptist Convention met in Nashville, Boyce was pleading so earnestly on behalf of the seminary that he actually burst into tears and began to weep profusely. "I would not beg for myself, or for my family like this, but for our beloved Seminary I am willing to beg." Boyce was repeatedly offered the presidency of railroads and banks and great universities, including Brown and Mercer. He declined them all to stay at Southern Seminary and fulfill his life's work.

In the summer of 1888, with his health failing, Boyce sailed for Europe in what would be his first and last trip abroad. He died in Southern France in December 1888. Had he lived two more weeks, he would have been sixty-two years old. His body was brought back to Louisville where, on a snowy January day, he was buried in Cave Hill Cemetery. Soon thereafter an impressive monument was erected over his grave which bears this inscription: "James P. Boyce, to whom, under God, the Seminary owes its existence." At the funeral, John A. Broadus, his closest friend and fellow laborer in the founding of the Seminary, gave the following eulogy:

> Oh Brother beloved, true yokefellow through years of toil, best and dearest friend, sweet shall be thy memory 'til we meet again! And may there be those always ready, as the years come and go, to carry on, with widening reach and heightened power, the work we sought to do, and did begin![19]

Exposition

Boyce served for thirty years as a professor of systematic and polemical theology. It was one of the great regrets of his life that due to the burdens of his office he was never able to give himself fully to the discipline he loved so dearly. Yet his theology had a profound and long-lasting influence on Southern Baptists. E. Y. Mullins, whose theology of experience led to a different paradigm, nonetheless had great respect for Boyce as a theologian and continued to use his *Abstract of Systematic Theology* as a required text for the first seventeen years of his own teaching career at Southern Seminary. In reviewing the central themes in Boyce's theology, we shall focus on his treatment of the doctrines of grace and his views on the authority of Scripture.

The Doctrines of Grace

Boyce defined *theology* as "the science which treats of God." His *Abstract* is a true *the*-ology in terms of its emphasis on the doctrine of God. The first sixteen chapters deal with the being, attributes, and decrees of God. The meatiest sections of the book deal with the various "moments" in the *ordo salutis:* the Fall, atonement, election, calling, regeneration, repentance, faith, and so forth. On all disputed points of soteriology, Boyce took pains to present opposing views with fairness, but in the end he invariably came down as a consistent, if somewhat benignant, Calvinist. E. E. Folk, one of his former students, once remarked: "Although the young men were generally rank Arminians when they came to the Seminary, few went through the course [in systematic theology] under him without being converted to his strong Calvinistic views."[20]

The Calvinist cast of Boyce's theology derived from his conviction that "a crisis in Baptist theology" was fast approaching. This crisis could only be avoided, he believed, by returning "to the doctrine which formerly distinguished us."[21] In his inaugural address at Furman, he had lamented the fact that the principles of Arminianism "have been engrafted upon many of our churches; and even some of our ministry have not hesitated publicly to avow them."[22] In the first decade of the nineteenth century the Baptist historian

David Benedict made an extensive tour of Baptist churches throughout America. He gave the following summary of the Baptist theology he encountered:

> Take this denomination at large, I believe the following will be found a pretty correct statement of their views of doctrine. They hold that man in his natural condition is entirely depraved and sinful; that unless he is born again—changed by grace—or made alive unto God—he cannot be fitted for the communion of saints on earth, nor the enjoyment of God in Heaven; that where God hath begun a good work, he will carry it on to the end; that there is an election of grace—an effectual calling, etc. and that the happiness of the righteous and the misery of the wicked will both be eternal.[23]

Despite a persistent Arminian strain within Baptist life, for most of their history most Baptists have adhered faithfully to the doctrines of grace as set forth by the mainline reformers. For example, the Philadelphia Confession of Faith, first published in 1742, was adopted verbatim by the Charleston Association whence it exercised a profound influence on Baptist life in the South.[24] Boyce emphasized the sovereignty of God and the gratuity of salvation as a corrective to what he perceived as a growing laxity about these vital themes.

In his *Abstract* Boyce clearly affirmed all five "points" of doctrine set forth in the famous Canons of the Synod of Dort (1618-19). In keeping with the Reformed tradition, Boyce asserted the federal headship of Adam and the totality of depravity which had passed to all his descendants. The inheritance of a fallen, sinful nature entailed not only corruption, but also condemnation. In his *Catechism* Boyce asked: "What evil effects followed the sin of Adam?" "He, with all his posterity, became corrupt and sinful, and fell under the condemnation of the law of God."[25] Boyce did not believe that all people were equally sinful, nor that the image of God had been totally effaced by the Fall. However, he did stress the "total" incapacity of fallen human beings to contribute anything toward their salvation apart from the interposition of divine grace.[26]

Boyce's complete definition of election, with manifold qualifications to prevent misunderstanding, presents a strong predestinarian doctrine of salvation.

> God (who and not man is the one who chooses or elects), of his own purpose (in accordance with his will, and not from any obligation to man, nor because of any will of man), has from Eternity (the period of God's action, not in time in which man acts), determined to save (not has actually saved, but simply determined to do so), and to save (not to confer gospel or church privileges upon), a definite number of mankind (not the whole or a part of the race, nor of a nation, nor of a church, nor of a class, as of believers or the pious; but individuals), not for or because of any merit or work of theirs, not of any value of him of them (not for their good works, nor their holiness, nor excellence, nor their faith, nor their spiritual sanctification, although the choice is to a salvation attained through faith and sanctification; nor their value to him, though their salvation tends greatly to the manifested glory of his grace); but of his own good pleasure (simply because he was pleased so to choose).[27]

Central to Boyce's soteriology was the doctrine of atonement. Through the sufferings and death of Christ, He "incurred the penalty of the sins of those whose substitute he was, so that he made a real satisfaction to the justice of God for the law which they had broken. On this account, God now pardons all their sins, and being fully reconciled to them, his electing love flows out freely towards them."[28] While teaching particular redemption, Boyce, like Calvin, could say that Christ's death was sufficient for all, but efficient only for the elect. The salvation of the believer is due to the overcoming grace of God, displayed in the elect through the regenerating power of the Holy Spirit, who enables them to persevere in faith and holiness unto the end.

Boyce was well aware that there were some who emphasized the sovereignty of God to the exclusion of human responsibility. In the nineteenth century a powerful hyper-Calvinist movement arose among Baptists in the South. Known variously as Primitive or Hardshell Baptists, these groups opposed organized missionary work, evangelism, Sunday Schools, and, especially, theological seminaries. Boyce had no truck with this perspective. His zeal for preaching the gospel began in his student days and continued throughout his life. He had a great burden for missions and organized a monthly Missionary Day at Southern Seminary, a tradition which continued until the 1960s. When D. L. Moody brought his evangelistic campaign to Louisville in 1887, Boyce permitted him to erect his five-thousand-seat tabernacle on seminary property, while seminary professors and students served as counselors in the inquiry room.[29] For Boyce the doctrines of grace were not inhibiting but rather motivating factors in the witness of the church. They underscored the fact that while we are called to be colaborers with God, all of the glory belongs to Him alone.

A final word should be said about Boyce's Calvinism: While he was a doughty defender of a high-predestinarian theology, he was not intolerant of other evangelical Christians who disagreed with his precise formulations of the doctrines of grace. He recognized that the shape of one's theology was largely a matter of emphasis and that the differences between a Wesley and a Whitefield, for example, "are not due to any contrariety of teaching the word of God, but to human failure to emphasize correctly."[30] Doubtless he would have agreed with the following statement of the great missionary statesman Luther Rice:

> How absurd it is, therefore, to contend against the doctrine of election, or decrees, or divine sovereignty. Let us not, however, become bitter against those who view this matter in a different light, nor treat them in a supercilious manner; rather let us be gentle towards all men. For who has made us to differ from what we once were? Who has removed the scales from our eyes?[31]

The Authority of Scripture

In his inaugural address of 1856, Boyce signaled the vital role a reverent approach to the study of the Bible would play in the seminary he envisioned.

> It has been felt as a sore evil, that we have been dependent in great part upon the criticism of Germany for all the more learned investigations in biblical

criticism and exegesis, and that . . . we have been compelled to depend upon works in which much of error has been mingled with truth, owing to the defective standpoint occupied by their authors.[32]

The heavy emphasis placed on biblical studies in the seminary curriculum, including a strong commitment to both biblical languages, assured a tradition of disciplined scholars committed to the centrality of Holy Scripture in theological education. Broadus's *Commentary on Matthew* (1886), A. T. Robertson's *Grammar of the Greek New Testament in the Light of Historical Research* (1914), and John R. Sampey's work as chairman of the Old Testament section of the American Standard Bible Revision Committee (1930-38) are evidence of the scholarly erudition and biblical emphasis which established the reputation of Southern Seminary as a leading center of evangelical biblical scholarship.[33]

Boyce clearly expressed his own views concerning the inspiration and authority of the Bible. In the preface to his *Abstract of Systematic Theology,* he declared his belief in the "perfect inspiration and absolute authority of the divine revelation" which alone among the world's literature is untainted with "the liability to error which arises from human imperfection."[34] In his *Brief Catechism of Bible Doctrine,* Boyce devised the following questions and answers:

Q: How came [the Bible] to be written?
A: God inspired holy men to write it.
Q: Did they write it exactly as God wished?
A: Yes; as much as if he had written every word himself.
Q: Ought it, therefore, to be believed and obeyed?
A: Yes; as much as though God had spoken directly to us.[35]

Boyce devotes little attention to the doctrine of Scripture in his *Abstract* because this theological topic was covered in the course on Biblical Introduction. However, he does refer to the Bible as "infallible" and divinely secured "from all possibility of error."[36] His hearty endorsement of the explicitly inerrantist views of his colleague Basil Manly, Jr., (whose *The Bible Doctrine of Inspiration Explained and Vindicated* [1888] was written at Boyce's behest) confirms the recent conclusion of Dwight Moody that Boyce "favored a conservative doctrine of the inspiration of Scriptures, generally known as the plenary verbal theory, which produces an inerrant manuscript containing infallible truth."[37]

For all that, however, Boyce was neither impervious to the difficult questions raised by the critical study of the Bible, nor indifferent to scholarly efforts to face such problems fearlessly and honestly. For example, he freely admits that the Scriptures use the language of appearance and observation to describe natural events, just as even today, long after Copernicus, we still speak of the sun as "rising" or "setting." Had the Bible been written originally in the language of true science, "age after age would have rejected it as false."[38] While Boyce was well aware of incipient theories of evolution, and even admitted the possibility of a pre-Adamite race, he strongly maintained the unity of the "race of men now existing," and traced their origin to the special creation of Adam and Eve as recorded in the opening chapters of Genesis.[39] The universal sinfulness of human beings, together with the New Testament analogy of Christ to Adam, requires such an affirmation which is, after all, the clear and obvious meaning of the scriptural text.

It is sometimes claimed that Boyce, with his Princeton background, held to a stricter doctrine of inerrancy than his great colleague Broadus who was trained at the University of Virginia. There is no evidence, however, to support this supposition. Both Boyce and Broadus published catechisms which were intended to be taught and memorized by new converts. If anything, Broadus's interrogations on Scripture are more comprehensive and precise than those of Boyce. For example, in a section of "Advanced Questions" Broadus presents the following concerns:

> Did the inspired writers receive everything by direct revelation? The inspired writers learned many things by observation or inquiry, but they were preserved by the Holy Spirit from error, whether in learning or in writing these things.
>
> What if inspired writers sometimes appear to disagree in their statements? Most cases of apparent disagreement in the inspired writings have been explained, and we may be sure that all could be explained if we had fuller information.
>
> Has it been proven that the inspired writers stated anything as true that was not true? No; there is no proof that the inspired writers made any mistake of any kind.[40]

W. H. Whitsitt once described Boyce and Broadus as Southern Baptists' great pair of twins, on the order of Luther and Melanchthon or Calvin and Beza.[41] Doubtless, both were equally committed to the Bible as the unique source of religious authority, just as they were united in guarding the seminary they had cofounded against an erosion of this commitment.

One of the most painful episodes in Boyce's life was the controversy over Crawford H. Toy, who had joined the faculty of Southern Seminary in 1869. At that time, Toy's commitment to the total truthfulness of Holy Scripture was explicitly stated in his impressive inaugural address: "The Bible, its real assertions being known, is in every iota of its substance absolutely and infallibly true."[42] Over the years, however, Toy gradually moved away from this position as he came more and more under the influence of Darwinian evolutionism and the theory of Pentateuchal criticism advanced by the German scholars Kuenen and Wellhausen. Enamored by the heady theories of "progressive" scholarship, Toy came to deny that many of the events recorded in the Old Testament had actually occurred. Moreover, he also questioned the Christological implications of many messianic prophecies, including Genesis 49:10 which the New Testament (Rev. 5:5) specifically applies to Christ. In 1876 Boyce wrote Toy a "gentle remonstrance and earnest entreaty" concerning his views on inspiration.[43] During the 1878-79 academic year, Toy's teaching became a matter of concern to the seminary trustees, chaired at that time by the venerable Baptist leader J. B. Jeter. Boyce requested Toy to refrain from espousing his radical critical views in the classroom. The latter agreed, but found that he could not do so. In the spring of 1879 Toy, under considerable pressure, tendered his resignation acknowledging that it has "become apparent to me that my views of inspiration differ considerably from those of the body of my brethren."[44]

Broadus spoke for Boyce, the faculty, and the trustees (with the exception of two dissenting members) when he characterized the painful necessity of Toy's removal from the seminary community: "Duty to the founders of the institution and to all who had given money for its support and endowment, duty to the Baptist churches from whom its students must come, required [Boyce] to see to it that such teaching should not continue." Boyce took no joy in the departure of Toy. In a poignant scene at the railway station, Boyce embraced Toy and, lifting his right arm, exclaimed: "Oh, Toy, I would freely give that arm to be cut off if you could be where you were five years ago, and stay there."[45] Toy subsequently became a professor at Harvard University where he affiliated with the Unitarian church and embraced even more radically critical views on the inspiration and authority of the Bible.[46]

Doubtless, the departure of Toy contributed to the conservative reputation which Southern Seminary enjoyed within the denomination and beyond. Once on a trip for the seminary, Boyce heard about certain students from Crozier Theological School who were trying to dissuade young preachers from coming to Southern because of the "antediluvian theology taught at Louisville." To which Boyce replied, "If my theology were not older than the days of Noah, it wouldn't be worth teaching!"[47]

On October 1, 1888, just two months before he died, Boyce wrote to his colleague, Basil Manly, Jr. With an eye to the Toy controversy which was just beginning to subside, he said:

> I greatly rejoice in the certain triumph of the truth. I feel that nothing but our own folly can prevent the success of the seminary. If we keep things orthodox and correct within and avoid injudicious compromises while we patiently submit and laboriously labor, we shall find continuous blessing. So much do I feel this that I look back on my life's work without any apprehension of future disaster.[48]

Evaluation

The legacy of James Petigru Boyce, like that of his younger contemporary, B. H. Carroll, is incarnated in the seminary he founded and into which he unstintingly poured his life. In Baptist history, Boyce stands as a link between an earlier generation of theological giants, the Gills, Fullers, and Furmans, and newer voices who sought to restate Baptist orthodoxy in a "world come of age," the Strongs, Mullinses, and Conners of the early-twentieth century. As we have seen, Boyce was both a strict (though not hyper-) Calvinist and a biblical inerrantist. It would be a mistake, however, to interpret him as a protofundamentalist, at least in the more recent, pejorative sense that label has assumed. If by fundamentalist we mean narrow-minded, mean spirited, obscurantist, sectarian, then Boyce was no fundamentalist.

His training at Brown and Princeton, his wide reading and extensive contacts all contributed to a broad and sympathetic spirit. In what may be his finest piece of theological reflection, Boyce wrote an extensive essay on "The Doctrine of the Suffering of Christ," which was published in England in *The Baptist Quarterly* in 1870. As his apology for entering into this well-worn topic, he wrote:

> It is manifestly important . . . that . . . definitions of doctrine should frequently be restated and re-examined. . . . . It is well that they should be tested in the crucible of every age and every mind, that if there be any error it may be detected and the correction applied.[49]

These are not the words of a rigid ideologue, locked in a closed system. Boyce believed in an error-free Bible, but he did not presume an unrevisable theology. For this reason, the task of theology is a never-finished one in the life of the church.

One of the major functions of the theologian is to help the church distinguish between evangelical essentials and matters of tolerable diversity in the realm of doctrine. Boyce faced this issue squarely when he established strict confessional guidelines for the seminary faculty. While the Abstract of Principles was intended to be "a complete exhibition of the fundamental doctrines of grace, so that in no essential particular should they speak dubiously," they were at the same time loudly silent on some specific points of Calvinistic doctrine which had been spelled out plainly in the Philadelphia Confession of Faith. Thus nothing was included about the scope of the atonement nor the doctrine of reprobation. As promulgated, the articles of faith represented a consensus of what Boyce called "the common heritage of the whole denomination."[50] This later became a matter of controversy not with reference to the strong Calvinism of the articles, but rather in connection with their laxity on points of Landmarkist ecclesiology. Although Boyce himself did not approve of the practice of "alien immersion," he defended his colleague William Williams who had been criticized for holding this view. Within his own faculty, then, Boyce was forced to make a distinction between doctrinal views which—however much he might personally disagree with them—were acceptable within the commonly agreed upon confessional standard, and others which clearly undermined confidence in the essential evangelical commitment of the school. Thus he protected Williams against the Landmarkers, while he urged, with gentle firmness, the resignation of Toy.[51]

Boyce's theology has been characterized as a form of scholastic rationalism, philosophically derived from Scottish common sense realism, and issuing in authoritarianism and even anthropocentrism.[52] Doubtless, Boyce borrowed much, both methodologically and substantially, from his Princeton mentors. He valued highly the role of reason and allowed for a robust natural theology. He was saved from the extreme dangers of this tendency, however, by his recognition that human fallenness encompassed the mind as well as the will and by his refusal to follow a speculative trajectory in theology. We might well wish that Boyce had studied Calvin more closely than Turrentin, and that he had emphasized the internal witness of the Holy Spirit as strongly as the objective content of revelation. However, in an age seduced by uncritical subjectivism and relativist moralism, Boyce stood as an uncompromising witness on behalf of the living God who speaks and acts and redeems. Far from countenancing a human-centered approach in theology, Boyce was consumed with the vision of the greatness, majesty, and grace of the Sovereign God, the Lord of heaven and earth. David M. Ramsay recalled the following incident about "Jim Peter," as the students fondly called Boyce.

> One Sunday at the seminary dinner, a bunch of students came in from church saying,
> "We heard the greatest sermon of our lives today."
> "Who preached it?"
> "Jim Peter."
> "What was his text?"
> "God."
> "What was his theme?"
> "God."
> "What were the divisions of the discourse?"
> "God."
> That was the man.[53]

Boyce still stands as an important model for the theological revitalization of the Baptist tradition. He calls us back to a vision of the true and living God, the God who meets us in judgment and mercy, the God whose favor we can never merit, but who in His sheer grace has called us to Himself, through a baby in a manger, and a man on a cross.

Bibliography

Works by Boyce

Abstract of Systematic Theology. Philadelphia: American Baptist Publication Society, 1887.

A Brief Catechism of Bible Doctrine. Rev. ed. Louisville: Coperton and Cotes, 1878.

"The Doctrine of the Suffering Christ." *The Baptist Quarterly* 4 (1870): 385-411.

"The Good Cause." *Louisville Courier Journal* 3 (September 1877). Introductory lecture given at the opening of The Southern Baptist Theological Seminary.

Life and Death the Christian's Portion. New York: Sheldon & Co., 1869.

Sermon Manuscripts of James Petigru Boyce. The Southern Baptist Theological Seminary Library, Louisville.

Three Changes in Theological Institutions: An Inaugural Address Delivered before the Board of Trustees of the Furman University: Greenville, S.C.: C. J. Elford, 1856.

The Uses and Doctrine of the Sanctuary. Columbia, S.C.: Robert M. Stokes, 1859.

Works Related to Boyce

Broadus, John A. *Memoir of James Petigru Boyce*. New York: A. C. Armstrong, 1893.

Cody, Z. T. "James Petigru Boyce." *Review and Expositor* 24 (1927): 145-66.

George, Timothy. *James Petigru Boyce: Selected Writings*. Nashville: Broadman Press, 1989.

_____. Review of *Abstract of Systematic Theology* by James Petigru Boyce, *Review and Expositor* 81 (1984): 461-64.

_____. "Systematic Theology at Southern Seminary." *Review and Expositor* 82 (1985): 31-47.

Hinson, E. Glenn. "Between Two Worlds: Southern Seminary, Southern Baptists, and American Theological Education." *Baptist History and Heritage* 20 (April 1985): 28-35.

Honeycutt, Roy Lee. "Heritage Creating Hope: The Pilgrimage of The Southern Baptist Theological Seminary." *Review and Expositor* 81 (1984): 367-91.

Mueller, William A. *A History of Southern Baptist Theological Seminary*. Nashville: Broadman Press, 1959.

Nettles, Thomas J. *By His Grace and for His Glory: A Historical, Theological, and Practical Study of the Doctrines of Grace in Baptist Life*. Grand Rapids, Mich.: Baker Book House, 1986.

Ramsay, David Marshall. "James Petigru Boyce, God's Gentleman." *Review and Expositor* 21 (1924): 129-45.

Sampey, John R. *Southern Baptist Theological Seminary: The First Thirty Years, 1859-1889*. Baltimore: Wharton, Barron & Co., 1890.

Notes

1. The standard life of Boyce remains John A. Broadus, *Memoir of James Petigru Boyce* (New York: A. C. Armstrong and Son, 1893). Other studies include: Lansing Burrows, "James Petigru Boyce," *Review and Expositor* 4 (1907): 173-89; Z. T. Cody, "James Petigru Boyce," *Review and Expositor* 24 (1927): 129-66; David M. Ramsay, "James Petigru Boyce—God's Gentleman," *Review and Expositor* 21 (1924): 129-45. A. J. Holt's unpublished address, "Christ the Builder, Boyce the Builder," (1923) is on file in the Boyce Centennial Library of The Southern Baptist Theological Seminary, Louisville, Kentucky. Other biographical details may be gleaned from the "Boyce Family File" and "Story Recollections of Dr. Boyce" by his daughter Elizabeth F. Boyce, both on deposit in the Boyce Centennial Library. Some of the material in this chapter has been adapted from the Founder's Day address, "'Soli Deo Gloria!' The Life and Legacy of James Petigru Boyce," delivered by Timothy George in the alumni chapel of Southern Seminary on February 2, 1988. It appears as the opening chapter in Timothy George, ed., *James Petigru Boyce: Selected Writings* (Nashville: Broadman Press, 1989), 14-27.

2. Broadus, *Memoir,* 54.

3. E. Brooks Holifield, *The Gentlemen Theologians* (Durham: Duke University Press, 1978), 218.

4. Broadus, *Memoir,* 17.

5. Ibid., 51.

6. Ibid.

7. Letter of W. O. Carver to Robert Soileau, January 20, 1954.

8. Manly, Sr., was pastor of the First Baptist Church of Charleston from 1826 until 1837. He was succeeded by W. T. Brantly, Sr. (1837-44) and N. M. Crawford (1845-47). All of these men were staunch Calvinists however much they may have nuanced their adherence to that position in slightly different ways. On this point see Walter Wiley Richards, "A Study of the Influence of Princeton Theology upon the Theology of James Petigru Boyce and His Followers with Special Reference to the Works of Charles Hodge," (Th.D. diss., New Orleans Baptist Theological Seminary, 1964).

9. Broadus, *Memoir,* 88.

10. Ibid., 120.

11. George, *Boyce,* 20. The complete text of "Three Changes in Theological Institutions" is given in this volume on pp. 30-59.

12. Ibid., 50.

13. Ibid., 56.

14. Ibid., 51-52. Thomas J. Nettles, "Creedalism, Confessionalism, and the Baptist Faith and Message," *The Unfettered Word,* ed. Robison B. James (Waco: Word Books, 1987), 138-54, has shown how deeply rooted in Southern Baptist history is the appeal to clear confessional guidelines. For example, he quotes B. H. Carroll who declared, "The modern cry, 'Less creed and more liberty,' is a degeneration from the vertebrate to the jellyfish, and means less unity and less morality, and it means more heresy. . . . It is a positive and very hurtful sin to magnify liberty at the expense of doctrine." Ibid., 148. Walter B. Shurden, on the other hand, has interpreted the growing confessional consciousness in Southern Baptist life as a threat to traditional Baptist freedoms. See his "The Problem of Authority in the Southern Baptist Convention," *Review and Expositor* 75 (1978): 219-33.

15. See Danny M. West, "The Origin and Function of the Southern Baptist Theological Seminary's 'Abstract of Principles,'" Th.M. thesis, The Southern Baptist Theological Seminary, 1983.

16. Robert Lynn, Southern Seminary Founder's Day Address (1982). Quoted, George *Boyce,* 20.

17. Letter of John A. Broadus to James P. Boyce, December 5, 1862.

18. Broadus, *Memoir,* 200.

19. Ibid., 310.

20. Ibid., 265. Another student, A. W. Middleton from Mississippi, proved less tractable. One of his fellow students recalled his classroom controversy with Boyce: "Not infrequently would Middleton raise a breeze in the lecture room when Dr. Boyce held forth from the professorial chair in Systematic Theology. He could not endure the perpendicular 'Calvinism' inculcated therefrom . . . . Boyce was no stranger to the fiery zeal for dogma which usually inheres in men whose minds and hearts are thoroughly inbred with this school of theology. He did not take very patiently the dissent which the good brother from Mississippi sometimes ventured to express quite emphatically." A. J. Dickinson, "Parrotic Theology," *The Seminary Magazine,* 1 (1888): 74.

21. George, *Boyce,* 49.

22. Ibid.

23. David Benedict, *A General History of the Baptist Denomination in America*

(Boston: Lincoln and Edmands, 1813), 2:456. Compare also the statement of Francis Wayland written in 1861: "The theological tenets of the Baptists, both in England and America, may be briefly stated as follows: they are emphatically the doctrines of the Reformation, and they have been held with singular unanimity and consistency." Francis Wayland, *The Principles and Practices of Baptist Churches* (London: J. Heaton and Son, 1861), 16.

24. H. A. Tupper, ed., *Two Hundred Years of the First Baptist Church of South Carolina* (Baltimore: R. H. Woodward and Co., 1889), 85.

25. Tom J. Nettles, ed., *Baptist Catechisms* (n.p., 1983), 232.

26. Cf. Mark E. Dever, "Representative Aspects of the Theologies of John L. Dagg and James P. Boyce: Reformed Theology and Southern Baptists," (Th.M. thesis, The Southern Baptist Theological Seminary, 1987), 53-72. B. B. Warfield criticized Boyce for his attribution of the imputation of sin to both the natural and federal headship of Adam. See his review of Boyce's *Abstract of Theology* in *Presbyterian Review* 10 (1889): 502-3.

27. James P. Boyce, *Abstract of Systematic Theology* (Philadelphia: American Baptist Publication Society, 1887), 246.

28. Ibid., 317. While Boyce criticized Andrew Fuller's presentation of the atonement as providing merely a means for redemption, rather than actual reconciliation, he too spoke of a universal reference of the atonement in a way not entirely dissimilar from Fuller. On this inconsistency in his thought, see Dever, "Representative Aspects," 92-102, and Thomas J. Nettles, *By His Grace and for His Glory* (Grand Rapids, Mich.: Baker Book House, 1986), 201-2.

29. *The Seminary Magazine,* 1 (1888): 29-31.

30. Boyce, *Abstract,* "Preface," viii.

31. James B. Taylor, *Memoir of Rev. Luther Rice, One of the First American Missionaries to the East* (Baltimore: Armstrong and Berry, 1840), 332-33.

32. George, *Boyce,* 45.

33. On the curriculum of Southern Seminary, see William A. Mueller, *A History of Southern Baptist Theological Seminary* (Nashville: Broadman Press, 1959), 112-18. E. Glenn Hinson acknowledges the conservative biblical orientation of the seminary's founding fathers while frankly admitting "that our theology would not agree with theirs." See his "Between Two Worlds: Southern Seminary, Southern Baptists, and American Theological Education," *Baptist History and Heritage* 20 (1985): 28-35.

34. Boyce, *Abstract,* "Preface," vii.

35. Nettles, *Catechisms,* 230.

36. Boyce, *Abstract,* 48.

37. Dwight A. Moody, "Doctrines of Inspiration in the Southern Baptist Theological Tradition" (Ph.D. diss., The Southern Baptist Theological Seminary, 1982), 77.

38. Boyce, *Abstract,* 173.

39. Ibid., 190-94. On Boyce's efforts to harmonize scriptural truth with contemporary scientific evidence, see L. Russ Bush and Tom J. Nettles, *Baptists and the Bible* (Chicago: Moody Press, 1980), 203-11.

40. Ibid., 226. Edgar V. McKnight, "A. T. Robertson: The Evangelical Middle Is Biblical 'High Ground,'" *The Unfettered Word,* ed. Robison B. James (Waco: Word Books, 1987), 96, cites as evidence to the contrary an 1883 sermon by Broadus as well as a statement from his commentary on Matthew that one should be "cautious in theorizing as to verbal inspiration." In the sermon, Broadus distinguishes truth in

substance from truth in statement, but he assumes that the scriptural writings are true—"thoroughly true," as he puts it—in both areas. The caution against theorizing is simply a good Reformed principle: theology must not give way to "vain speculation," but stay within the limits of revelation alone. Broadus's comments concerning the harmonizing of synoptic questions and the loose citation of scriptural sources are fully compatible with a nuanced doctrine of inerrancy as set forth, for example, in the *Chicago Statement on Biblical Inerrancy* (1978).

41. A. T. Robertson, *The Life and Letters of John A. Broadus* (Philadelphia: American Baptist Publication Society, 1901), 434.

42. C. H. Toy, *The Claims of Biblical Interpretation on Baptists* (New York: Lange and Hillman, 1869), 13.

43. Robertson, *Broadus*, 301.

44. Quoted, Bush and Nettles, *Baptists*, 233.

45. Taylor, *Memoir*, 263-64.

46. On the Toy Controversy, see Mueller, *History*, 135-42; Billy G. Hurt, "Crawford Howell Toy: Interpreter of the Old Testament," (Th.D. diss., The Southern Baptist Theological Seminary, 1965); Pope A. Duncan, "Crawford Howell Toy: Heresy at Louisville," *American Religious Heretics*, ed. George H. Shriver (Nashville: Abingdon Press, 1966), 56-88.

47. George, *Boyce*, 23.

48. Ibid.

49. J. P. Boyce, "The Doctrine of the Suffering of Christ," *The Baptist Quarterly* 4 (1870): 386.

50. J. P. Boyce, "Two Objections to the Seminary," *The Western Recorder*, June 20, 1874.

51. Compare the following letter of James P. Boyce to John A. Broadus: "I am anxious for Williams to go to Mississippi. If they should treat him badly I shall be sorry on his account and their's, but it will help us. Soul liberty is worth more than alien immersion, even with Landmarkers." Quoted, Mueller, *History*, 105.

52. See Mark E. Matheson, "Religious Knowledge in the Theologies of John Leadley Dagg and James Petigru Boyce: With Special Reference to the Influence of Common Sense Realism," (Ph.D. diss., Southwestern Baptist Theological Seminary, 1984), 192-209, especially page 191, n. 105.

53. David M. Ramsay, "Boyce and Broadus, Founders of the Southern Baptist Theological Seminary," 4.

13

Charles Haddon Spurgeon
Lewis A. Drummond

During Charles Haddon Spurgeon's thirty-seven-year ministry at the New Park Street Baptist Church in London, 14,000 members joined the congregation, making this the largest Protestant church in the world. Over 300 million copies of his sermons and books have been sold.* He is probably the most-read minister of all time. At any rate, there are still today more of Spurgeon's books in print than of any English author. He was not only a great preacher and pastor, he was a good thinker.

Why this unusually remarkable popularity? Many ministers have been prolific. Why did people all over the world seemingly hang on his ministry—verbal and written—during his lifetime, and many, it appears, to this present day?

The answer to these queries are varied and complex. Yet, certainly the theological and spiritual matrix of Spurgeon's life constitutes a major factor in the tremendous impact of his service. And what was that matrix of his work? The answer is plain: theological Puritanism. The London pulpiteer was an avowed and proud nineteenth-century Puritan. William Gladstone, the "Grand Old Man" of British politics, called Spurgeon, "The Last of the Puritans." Whether the prime minister was correct in the chronology of this statement or not, the moniker stuck and does provide an insight to the foundational approach of Spurgeon as a theologian. This chapter contends that the Puritan legacy is evident throughout his entire ministry. Further, and not incidentally, it may provide something of an insight to the development of an effective ministry in any age.

Biography

The life of Spurgeon is a constant testimony to the Puritan legacy and its influence in his entire service to Christ. On June 19, 1834, when the cries of Thomas and Eliza Spurgeon's firstborn were heard, little did the young couple realize what destiny had in store for their newborn son. That he should be a pastor perhaps would have been expected; Thomas was a Congregational pastor, as was the baby's paternal grandfather, James.

Due to rather stringent economic conditions, at eighteen months of age Charles was sent to live with his grandparents in Stanbourne, Essex. He was doted on by his "Aunt Anne," the spinster daughter of the grandparents, perhaps he was even a bit spoiled. At the age of six, little Charles happened one day into an old musty room in the manse at Stanbourne. The single window had been sealed off many years earlier because of the illogical window tax. The room exuded the odor of old leather-bound volumes. Most six year olds would have made a hasty exit, but Charles thought he had discovered a gold mine! There were old, well-worn Puritan theological folios. He could already read well and loved books. Delving into his newfound treasure, he picked up a copy of Bunyan's *The Pilgrim's Progress*. It fascinated him, and he read it more than 100 times. It became something of the pattern of his own pilgrimage.

A few years later Charles returned to his parents' home in Colchester. His education was somewhat above average for a boy of his time. He was what we would call a "bookish" boy. Young Charles was always rather awkward physically; sports were not his forte. So he became an avid reader and student. A fair portion of his reading centered in Puritan theological works. Further, his father and grandfather, being evangelical Congregationalists, were Calvinistic in their understanding and approach to Christian doctrine. They fulfilled to the letter the model set up by Richard Baxter in *The Reformed Pastor*. Such was the atmosphere in which Charles's early spiritual experiences took place.

In this setting, it is understandable why by the age of fifteen, Charles was deeply under conviction of sin and desperately seeking salvation. His conversion story, which he loved to tell, is typical of the Puritan approach. It culminated one Sunday morning in January 1850.

The snow was pelting down as the swordlike wind howling off the frigid North Sea cut him to the bone. Trudging with head down into the gale, young Charles tried vainly to ignore the miserable weather. He stopped, shivered, and looked down the swirling white street. At that moment he remembered his mother had told him about a Primitive Methodist chapel on old Artillery Street. "I'll go there," he reasoned, "it's right near, and the church where I intended to go is still a long way off."

Charles had determined he would attend every church in his hometown of Colchester, a small community some forty miles north of London. He had to find *the answer*. Of course, it was not unusual for a young man to go to church in 1850; the Victorians were notoriously religious. As one historian put it, "No one will ever understand Victorian England who does not appreciate that among the highly civilized . . . , it was one of the most religious that the world has ever known." *The answer* Charles sought was Christ. But seek as he would, salvation's peace eluded him. He had struggled long, just like Bunyan's Pilgrim, but he kept seeking forgiveness and relief. His Puritan upbringing had given birth to guilt, remorse, and misery in his very soul.

So to church after church in Colchester Charles went, hoping the burden on his back would fall away "at yonder wicket gate," as did Pilgrim's. Down Artillery Street he trudged, thinking he might find his *answer* there.

When Charles timidly entered the little church building, not more than fifteen people had assembled. He quietly slipped in and sat down about five

Charles Spurgeon (1834-92)

Photo courtesy of Southern Baptist Historical Library and Archives

or six pews from the rear, on the preacher's right, somewhat hidden under the small gallery. With head bowed—not because of the miserable weather now, but because of the miserable storm in his soul—he hardly looked up as the service progressed.

Charles previously nursed a few misgivings about worshiping in a Primitive Methodist church. That group had a reputation for splitting one's eardrums with their vociferous singing. Most people called them the "Ranters." But Charles was hardly aware, he felt so terrible. He did notice, nonetheless, that the pastor had not arrived when the service began. So a simple man, as Charles viewed him, took charge of the worship. It all proved quite different for the young seeker with his Congregational, Puritan background; he felt very much alone. The sermon began as the Primitive preacher took his text: "look unto me, and be ye saved, all the ends of the earth." He appeared to Charles more primitive than just in name; the preacher did not even pronounce the words correctly. Charles remembered the old preacher's actual words:

> My dear friends this is a simple text indeed. It says, Look. Now lookin' don't take a deal of pains. It ain't lifting your foot or your finger. It is just "look." Well, a man needn't get to college to learn to look. You may be the biggest fool and yet you can look. A man needn't be worth a thousand pounds a year to be able to look. Anyone can look: even a child can look. But then the text says, "Look unto me" . . . many of ye are lookin' to yourselves, but it's no use lookin' there. You'll never find any comfort in yourselves. Some look to God the Father. No, look to Him by and by. Jesus Christ says, "look unto *me*." Some of ye say, "We must wait for the Spirit's workin'." You have no business with that just now. Look unto *Christ*. The text says, "Look unto me."

Charles went on in his description of the dramatic moment:

> Whether he, the old Essex preacher, had reached the end of his tether having spun out about ten minutes or whether he was lifted out of himself and spoke words given to him at that moment, he fixed his eyes on the "stranger," [young Charles], easily distinguished amidst the company, and said, "Young man, you look very miserable." I was miserable. It was a blow struck right home, and although the young man had never had such a personal word from the pulpit before, he was too much in earnest to resent it. He continued, "you always will be miserable—miserable in life and miserable in death if you don't obey my text; but if you obey now, this moment you will be saved." Then lifting up his hands he shouted, as only a Primitive Methodist of Essex could, "Young man, look to Jesus Christ! Look! Look! Look! You have nothing to do but to look and live." I had been waiting to do fifty things, but when I heard the word Look, I could have almost looked my eyes away . . . I could have risen that instant and sung with the most enthusiastic of them of the precious blood of Christ, and the simple faith that looks alone to him. I thought I could dance all the way home. I could understand what John Bunyan meant when he declared he wanted to tell the cows on the plowed land all about his conversion. He was too full to hold. He must tell somebody. At such a time, clang went every harp in heaven. . . . Between half past ten, when I entered the chapel, and half past twelve, when I returned home, what a change had taken place in me.[1]

The answer had come. Charles Haddon Spurgeon had been graciously saved. In that little Primitive Methodist chapel, under the preaching of an unlettered man, a pilgrimage of ministry began, the universality of which no one there on that miserable Sunday could have imagined.

Spurgeon soon became convinced he should be baptized by immersion, leaving his Congregational background, at least on that point. When he announced this decision to his mother, she said, "Charles I have often prayed for your conversion, but *not* that you would become a Baptist." Charles replied, "That shows, dear mother, that God has done exceeding abundantly above all you asked or thought." After baptism in the River Lark, he joined the St. Andrews Baptist Church in Cambridge where he was attending school. He remained a Baptist throughout his days.

Four years later, at the age of nineteen, Charles Spurgeon was called as pastor of the historic and prestigious New Park Street Baptist Church in Southwark, South London. John Rippon, Benjamin Keach, and theologian John Gill had been his illustrious predecessors at the church. When Charles was only five years old, it had been prophesied by Richard Knill that he would become a preacher. The well-known prophecy had come to pass. Yet, it seemed a very young age to begin a ministry. But, he had already served for two years as pastor of the Waterbeach Baptist Church in Cambridge-shire—and that with unusual success. Moreover, his theology was pretty well fixed. He said he learned all this theology from an old, maidservant in Cambridge. That was probably an exaggeration. Still, he felt himself rooted in the doctrine of Puritan-Calvinism. From that theological stance Spurgeon never really departed in any measurable degree, as his preaching demonstrates. Some have argued he would have been a broader man theologically had he been formally educated in the theological disciplines—all know he never attended a theological school. Yet, that is doubtful. Spurgeon was strong-willed and strong-minded, and Puritan-Calvinism was so deeply ingrained in the very fabric of his personhood that he could hardly have been substantially moved. As Kruppa put it, "Intellectually, he remained captive to the evangelical Calvinism of his youth."[2] The Downgrade Controversy, the theological battle of his last years which caused him to leave the Baptist Union, seems to support such a contention.

So the "boy preacher of the Fens" (the "Fens" being Essex and parts of Cambridgeshire) began his London ministry of nearly four decades. His first sermon at the New Park Street Baptist Church was heard by a mere eighty people. In six months, two thousand were being crammed into the old church building while one thousand a Sunday were turned away unable to get in. Soon the Metropolitan Tabernacle was constructed, and he preached to 6,000 every Lord's Day. And although Spurgeon died in Mentone, France, at the relatively young age of fifty-seven, the world has rarely seen a more productive ministry. Notables like Prime Minister Gladstone, missionary David Livingstone, philanthropist Lord Shaftesbury, even it was reported, Queen Victoria in disguise, not to mention the thousands of common folk, flocked to hear his magnificent oratory. He started over twenty different social and evangelistic ministries through the Tabernacle. Two hundred new churches emerged out of the ministry. The Pastor's College to this day trains men and women for service. The Stockwell Orphanage also continues. Above all, the personal appeal of Spurgeon's writing converts and blesses many to the present hour. And permeating it all: The Puritan legacy. If Spurgeon were not "The Last of the Puritans," he certainly was one of the best.

Exposition

Puritan Theology

Charles Haddon Spurgeon exercised an effective, widespread pastor-evangelistic ministry because he saw himself as just that: a pastor-evangelist. Moreover, Spurgeon held strong theological convictions. This is obvious to everyone who knows his writings. Understanding his doctrinal base is essential in the attempt to grasp the insight that explains Spurgeon's powerful ministry.

Spurgeon stood as an avowed Calvinist, perhaps not a "high Calvinist," but he certainly held tenaciously to the basic position of the Geneva Reformer. Spurgeon said concerning the influence of his Puritan Calvinistic grandfather: "I sometimes feel the shadow of his broad bring (Puritan hat) come over my spirit." He confessed, "I have been charged with being a mere echo of the Puritans, but I had rather be the echo of truth than the voice of falsehood." What did that mean for Spurgeon?

If any theme of traditional Calvinism emerged as central in Spurgeon's Puritan theology, it would be the thought contained in the Calvinistic phrase "free grace." Spurgeon said concerning the concept, "What an abyss is the grace of God! Who can measure its breadth? Who can fathom its depth? Like all the rest of the divine attributes, it is infinite."[3] Spurgeon saw grace as ingredient to the very nature of God. Therefore, the bestowal of grace was purposed in the heart and mind of God long before our Lord ever freely poured it out on the sinner.

Moreover, Spurgeon stressed that this grace of God is *free*. It cannot be purchased, earned, or acquired by any mere human effort. He believed people were dead in trespasses and sin and therefore totally incapable of doing anything to please God or ever be worthy of grace. In other words, grace is bestowed by the *sovereignty of God*. That is, God freely grants this grace upon whom He pleases when and how He alone pleases. And on whom is that grace bestowed? Spurgeon made it very clear: It is the *elect* who receive free grace. There was no room for any Pelagianism.

The doctrine of election in Spurgeon's theology revolves around the concept that God in His sovereignty, according to His own purpose of grace, has foreknown and elected to salvation a certain number of individuals. This election took place before the foundation of the world. God will call those elected through the Holy Spirit and bring them to Christ for salvation. This number was given to Christ, who stood for them and died and paid their sin debt. They are the predestined ones.

For Spurgeon election and predestination meant virtually the same thing. Still, he did make a subtle distinction. He said:

> In one sense election is the result of a previous predestination, that is, during the past ages of eternity, before the creation of the world, and prior to human history the triune Godhead determined and designed a plan of redemption in which fallen mankind would be raised to a higher position than that which Adam had attained before he fell into sin.[4]

Furthermore, God calls the elect with an effectual call; those whom God calls to Christ will always respond. Moreover, Spurgeon forthrightly preached the doctrine. He did not downplay the idea, thinking it would offend people. Taking 2 Thessalonians 2:13 as his text, he said:

> By the word "calling" in Scripture, we understand two things—one, the "general call," which in the preaching of the gospel is given to every creature under heaven; the second call is the special call—which we call the effectual call, whereby God secretly, in the use of means, by the irresistible power of his Holy Spirit, calls out of mankind a certain number whom he himself hath before elected, calling them from their sins to become righteous, from their death in trespass and sins to become living spiritual men, and from their worldly pursuits to become the lovers of Jesus Christ.

Although Spurgeon felt that these concepts should be clearly preached, he did warn preachers to handle them with special prudence and care. The preaching of these ideas was to bring praise, reverence, adoration, and glory to the sovereign God. And when one is called and saved, that is exactly what happens; God is magnified. After all, Spurgeon would argue, the angels rejoice over just one sinner who repents.

To stop at this point, however, would be to picture Spurgeon as a typical high Calvinist. That is an error. Calvinistic as he claimed to be, Spurgeon never slipped into a "hyper" supralapsarian stance in his reformed Puritan views. Most of Spurgeon's contemporaries realized this; for example, *The World Newspaper* on September 18, 1818, reported: "Mr. Spurgeon is *nominally* a Calvinist." Actually, there were churches that would not have him in their pulpit because his Calvinism was not "high" enough. Others, of course, rejected him because he stood a far distance from Arminianism. Probably, Spurgeon saw himself as an example of John Calvin himself, primarily a biblical exegete. He was not a systematic theologian of the later Calvinistic school as were the second generation of thinkers like Theodore Beza of Geneva and William Perkins of Cambridge. It was this systematizing that precipitated what came to be called high Calvinism. But Spurgeon walked the razor's edge. He firmly believed in Divine election and predestination. He was convinced the Bible taught it, so he preached it. At the same time he tenaciously held to the necessity of human response—and human responsibility to respond. He firmly believed that people must repent and believe. The Bible taught that too, he argued. Thus he also declared that truth. He said:

> Saving repentance is an evangelical grace, whereby a person, being led by the Holy Spirit made sensible of the manifold evils of his sin, doth, by faith in Christ, humble himself for it with godly sorrow, detestation of it, and self-abhorrency, praying for pardon and strength of grace, with a purpose and endeavor, by supplies of the Spirit, to walk before God unto all well-pleasing in all things.

Further, Spurgeon believed faith was the other necessary side of repentance. He stated in a sermon: "True faith is reliance. It does not merely mean to believe, but to trust, to confide in, to commit to, entrust with, and so forth; and the marrow of the meaning of faith is confidence in, reliance upon."

This saving faith thus brings one, in Spurgeon's words, into an "immediate relation to Christ, accepting, receiving, and resting upon him alone for justification, sanctification, and eternal life, by virtue of the covenant of grace." This act of faith humans are *required* to do. Perhaps Spurgeon's own dramatic, "Arminian-style" conversion contributed to that insistence, as well as his commitment to the biblical call to repentance and faith.

Yet, it is only correct to say Spurgeon believed that no person could exercise repentance and faith apart from the inner work of the Holy Spirit. Those graces cannot be worked up by mere human generation. Faith is always a gift of God. But he constantly called people to repentance and faith. Thus, he kept the tension between the two concepts of predestination and human responsibility and walked the razor's edge in his preaching. Perhaps that is why he is reported to have prayed in the Metropolitan Tabernacle, "Lord, call out your elect, and then elect some more." Well known is his pungent retort to a person who asked him how he reconciled the ideas: "I do not try to reconcile friends."

Spurgeon saw the reception of God's marvelous free grace as possible because of the all-sufficiency of Jesus Christ and His work on the cross. Concerning Christ's person, Spurgeon said:

> Oh marvelous sight! . . . a Child of a virgin, what a mixture! There is the finite and the infinite, there is the mortal and the immortal, corruption and incorruption, the manhood and the Godhead, time married to eternity, God linked with a creature . . . He who fastened the pillars of the universe, and riveted the nails of creation, hanging on a mortal breast, depending on a creature for nourishment.

Spurgeon was happy with the so-called Chalcedonian formulation of Christology.

Further, the purpose of the good news of Christ's coming centered in his substitutionary atoning passion. He said in a sermon: "There is no preaching the gospel if the atonement is left out. No matter how well we speak of Jesus as a pattern, we have done nothing unless we point Him out as the substitute and sin-bearer." The passion of Christ was *always* central in the preaching of Spurgeon. He said, "I take my text and make a bee-line to the cross." Because Christ suffered *vicariously,* he saw in that act the penalty of sin paid.

Spurgeon found himself absolutely committed to the substitutionary view of the atonement. Actually, this became one of the key issues in the Downgrade Controversy for which Spurgeon put his entire ministry on the line. *Substitution* and *satisfaction* became key words for the preacher.

This emphasis in Spurgeon's theology grew out of his deep conviction concerning human need. He saw the human race as ruined and totally depraved because of sin (i.e., human rebellion to God's control of life). He took the concept of the Fall very seriously indeed. In Spurgeon's view, in the original act of rebellion against God, Adam as humanity's representative brought the judgment of God upon the whole human race and upon the entire earth. That opened the race to sin. He said:

> There is much to sadden us in a view of the ruins of our race . . . . When we behold the ruins of that godly structure which God has piled, that creature, matchless in symmetry, second only to angelic intellect, that mighty being, man, when we behold how he is "fallen, fallen, fallen, from his high estate," (he) lies in a mass of destruction . . . . The fall of Adam was our fall; we fell in and with him; we were equal sufferers. It is the ruin or our own house that we lament.[5]

Spurgeon believed firmly that the Fall precipitated the "total depravity" of all. As a result of Adam's sin, all are born with an innate tendency to sin. This does not mean that men and women are mere depraved beasts or that they are utterly corrupt in all their ways. It means that the original sin of Adam is imputed to all his descendants, affecting them with rebellion in every part of their mind, soul, and body. The Anglican Shorter Catechism, which Spurgeon accepted, states:

> The sinfulness of that estate whereinto man fell, consists in, the guilt of Adam's first sin, the want of original righteousness, and the corruption of his whole nature, which is commonly called original sin; together with all actual transgressions which proceed from it.

At the point of sin, the power of salvation is gloriously exercised and a radical transformation takes place. Spurgeon viewed salvation in a very broad sense. Salvation gives more to the believer than mere deliverance from the guilt and condemnation of sin. It encompasses sanctification, preservation, and glorification; the kingdom of God no less. These blessings take place through the power of the Triune God: Father, Son, and Holy Spirit. Thus there comes about a total transformation of the Christian into a holy being and a partaker with Christ of the heavenly glory. And in that transformation, one is secure.

It must be granted nothing "new" is found in Spurgeon's theology; it was truly an echo of mainline Puritanism. The edicts of Dort were his ministry. But it served him well, and when it all came together in his preaching, it is understandable why he was utterly committed to evangelism and urgent in presenting the gospel of free grace to all. Although it had been said of some, "they lost their evangelism, because they failed to prevent their theology from slipping away," Spurgeon could never be accused of guilt on that score. He really believed, as all the Calvinistic Puritans before him, that everyone needed Christ and he was absolutely convinced the Lord Jesus Christ stood as sufficient for all the elect. That was the core of his theology.

Puritan Evangelism

Spurgeon's ministry grew out of his basic theology. For Spurgeon, theology was a "theology of the road" (i.e., it must "work" in practical ministry). Spurgeon the pastor always stands as the "Prince of Preachers." The fact is, however, he was not only a great pastoral preacher, he was an extremely effective evangelist. That is true not only as a pastor-evangelist, but as an itinerant proclaimer of the gospel as well. Every week, as schedule and health permitted, he traveled about, preaching what we today would probably call evangelistic rallies. The impact he made in that arena is a story in itself. Untold numbers were converted in that setting. It is exemplified in his warm relationship to D. L. Moody and the British crusades. He would often invite such evangelists to his own pulpit. Ira D. Sankey actually sang at Spurgeon's funeral in 1892.

Spurgeon said about evangelistic preaching and its impact, "The revealed Word awakened me; but it was the preached Word that saved me; and I must ever attach peculiar value to the hearing of the truth." With this conviction it is understandable why he would then state, "I now think I am bound never to preach a sermon without preaching to sinners. I do think that a minister who can preach a sermon without addressing sinners does not know how to preach." He always saw the pulpit as his primary evangelistic tool. He went so far as to say in *The Sportman* in September 1890, "The ordinary sermon should *always* be evangelistic." And that evangelistic ministry emerged from his strong theological understanding.

Strange perhaps is the fact that Spurgeon was not particularly warm to planned, protracted series of evangelistic services in his own church, although he did affirm Moody and others and did use some such methods at times on a limited scale. He feared the "low" after the "high" of a high pressure crusade in his church. Yet, he could say, "I am not very scrupulous about the means I use for doing good. I would preach standing on my head, if I thought I could convert your souls." That sounds not too Calvinistic, but he was a preacher above all. The romance of his effective preaching at the Metropolitan Tabernacle and his itinerant ministry is ample evidence of his effectiveness in pulpit evangelism. His pungent evangelistic preaching to the common people possessed a power seldom seen in London. He baptized over ten thousand new converts in the Tabernacle.

His theological understanding and faithful preaching of the gospel undergirded his evangelism. But there were two other vital factors at work; one obvious, the other not quite so well known.

The obvious element along with his preaching of Christ is the fervent heart and burden for people Spurgeon personified. No one is useful in ministry until there is a burning compassion to reach people for Christ. Spurgeon had that spirit; hear him in *The Word and Work,* February 1891, "When a dog is not noticed, he doesn't like it. But when a dog is after a fox, he does not care whether he is noticed or not. If a minister is *seeking for souls,* he will not think of himself." Perhaps that accounts for a significant measure of Spurgeon's success.

But there is another factor, not so widely known, which is a most important element in Spurgeon's contagious influence—at least in the opinion of this writer. We must look to the Puritan legacy for an answer. Puritanism, because of its Calvinistic theology, constantly affirmed the absolute necessity of God's sovereign act in effecting personal redemption. Therefore, there was a constant seeking for the moving of the Holy Spirit to come upon the preaching of the Word to bring people to Christ. In other words, they were constantly seeking a reviving, an awakening, an outpouring of power. Simply put, they fervently prayed for revival. Spurgeon's pneumatology moved him in that basic direction.

Spurgeon was no exception. He too sought the "outpouring" of power. Nor was he disappointed. Revival came to the New Park Street Baptist Church almost simultaneously with his arrival in London. Actually, Spurgeon was something of a harbinger of the so-called Prayer Revival of 1858 that finally reached Britain by 1860 after its inception in America.

Few biographers, it seems, have realized this Puritan revival principle in the early ministry of Charles Haddon Spurgeon. So often his success is explained merely on the grounds that he was a great preacher and social worker. Great preaching and service alone simply cannot explain such a phenomenal ministry. Spurgeon recognizing this said, "the times of refreshing from the presence of the Lord have at last dawned upon our land. Everywhere there are signs of aroused activity and increased earnestness. A spirit of prayer is visiting our churches, and its path are dropping fatness. The first breath of the rushing mighty wind is already discerned, while on rising evangelists the tongues of fire have evidently descended."

An awakening of such magnitude as the 1858 Prayer Revival always encompasses vast areas. The spirit of prayer had moved across the Atlantic from America and initially touched Ireland. In 1858 the Presbyterian Church of Ireland dispatched observers to the United States to investigate the prayer revival that had now engulfed the entire nation. They returned home thrilled. Soon Belfast, Dublin, Cork, and all the countryside fell under the impact of the prayer revival. The nation was on its knees.

As the continuing news and thrilling stories of the American awakening spread through the British Isles, before long, Scotland became aroused. Prayer meetings sprang up in Glasgow, Edinburgh, and all the cities and towns of the country. By 1859 the United Presbyterian Church reported that one fourth of its members were regularly attending a prayer meeting for spiritual awakening.

Wales also came under the power of God—almost simultaneously with Ireland. Before long all Wales caught on fire with awakening power.

Finally, England began to be warmed by the conflagration. A united prayer meeting was held in the Throne Room of the Cosby Hall, London, in 1859. Soon attendance reached one hundred at the noon hour service. By the end of the year, twenty-four daily and sixty weekly prayer meetings were being held in the London area. In a matter of days, the number grew to 120; then it exploded all over the land.

In 1860 the Fortune, the Garrick, and Sadler Wells theaters opened their doors for Sunday evangelistic services. Even Saint Paul's and Westminster Cathedrals conducted special revival services. In Dorset, people were flocking to hear Evan Hopkins of later Keswick Convention notoriety. Charles Finney, the great American revivalist, was preaching with great effect in Bolton. William and Catherine Booth of Salvation Army fame were ministering with fresh power. Oxford and Cambridge Universities commenced special prayer meetings. All England, it seemed, was looking up in prayer.

As can be imagined, the awakening had its critics. Members of the secular press raised their voices in chorus to negate the positive impact of the movement. But historians now realize the awakening left a legacy of blessing extending even to this day. During the revival one million new members entered the churches of Britain. The Salvation Army, the Children's Special Service Mission, the China Inland Mission, and a host of new institutions were founded. As Spurgeon put it,

> It were well . . . that the Divine life would break forth everywhere—in the parlor, the workshop, counting house, the market and streets. We are far too ready to confine it to the channel of Sunday services and religious meetings; it deserves a broader floodway and must have it if we are to see gladder times. It must burst out upon men who do not care for it, and invade chambers where it will be regarded as an intrusion; it must be seen by wayfaring men streaming down the places of traffic and concourse, *hindering the progress of sinful trades,* and surrounding all, whether they will or no. Would to God that religion were more vital and forceful among us, so as to create *a powerful public opinion on behalf of truth, justice and holiness* . . . . A life which would *purify the age.* It is much to be desired that the Christian church may yet have *more power and influence* all over the world for *righteousness* . . . . *Social reform and moral progress.*

That is how Spurgeon understood revival, and that is what Britain was experiencing by 1860. Actually, the Prayer Revival became one of the last great spiritual awakenings experienced by all of Great Britain.

But notice, Spurgeon had been in the grip of real revival at the New Park Street Baptist Church for several years before the British Prayer Revival of 1860. That is vital to an understanding of the Spurgeon phenomenon. In 1860 Spurgeon said, "For six years the dew has never ceased to fall, and the rain has never been held. At this time the converts are more numerous than hither-to-fore, and the zeal of the church groweth exceedingly."

The foundation for the fresh move of the Holy Spirit in revival at New Park Street had been laid by the faithful praying members of the church. Spurgeon described those early days:

When I came to New Park Street Church, it was but a mere handful of people to whom I first preached, yet I could never forget how earnestly they prayed. Sometimes they seemed to plead as though they could really see the Angel of the Covenant present with them, and as if they must have a blessing from him. More than once we were all so awe-struck with the solemnity of the meeting that we sat silent for some moments while the Lord's Power appeared to over-shadow us; and all I could do on such occasions was to pronounce the benediction, and say "Dear friends, we have had the Spirit of God here very manifestly tonight; let us go home and take care not to lose His gracious influence." Then down came the blessings; the house was filled with hearers, and many souls were saved.

Spurgeon knew that revival explained his outstanding ministry, and he deeply desired it for all of England.

The awakening deepened and for three years 1,000 people were turned away every Sunday from the 10,000-seat capacity Surrey Gardens Music Hall where Spurgeon preached before the construction of the Tabernacle.

Some quite amazing occurrences took place in those revival days. For example, one Sunday in the Music Hall a man sat listening intently to Spurgeon preach. In his sermon Spurgeon said, "There is a man sitting here, who is a shoemaker; he keeps his shop open on Sundays, and it was open last Sunday morning; he took in nine pence and there was a four pence profit; he sold his soul to Satan for four pence." The man listening so intently felt cut to the heart. He actually was a shoemaker and he had kept his shop open the previous Sunday and had taken in nine pence and he did make a profit of four pence. He trusted Christ immediately. Dozens were saved in similar dramatic circumstances and joined the great Baptist church. The simple statistics of conversions during those years were phenomenal.

What was back of this profound spiritual awakening? What did Spurgeon get hold of that precipitated revival even before the emergence of the general awakening of 1860? If revival is one of the key answers to Spurgeon's staggering evangelistic success, why did it happen to him at that time? Three factors seem dominant. The primary foundation stone, as already implied, rested on the sacrificial, fervent prayers of the New Park Street people. Young Spurgeon inherited that blessed gift. Moreover, that spirit of prayer continued through the years into the decades of the great Metropolitan Tabernacle ministry. Often repeated is the well-known anecdote of Charles Haddon Spurgeon taking visitors through the Metropolitan Tabernacle and showing them the prayer room in the basement and remarking, "Here is our power house." Genuine spiritual awakening is always spawned in prayer.

Spurgeon expressed another central feature in the revival:

Sound doctrine and loving invitation make a good basis of material, which, when modeled by the hand of prayer and faith, will form sermons of far more value in the saving of souls than the most philosophic essays prepared elaborately, and delivered with eloquence and propriety.

The revival had its birth and was carried on in the context of "sound doctrine" (i.e., good theology, presented with "loving invitation"). Biblical theology presented in love cannot be divorced from revival. The great Puritan-pietistic movement that engulfed Britain and the continent beginning in the last decades of the sixteenth century has spawned many awakenings. No doubt one of the prime reasons for the spiritual impact of that powerful thrust centered in its insistence that orthodox, biblical theology and preaching must be at the core of one's ministry.

That theological approach made "The Last of the Puritans" critical of any sort of humanism that downplayed the sovereignty of God in evangelism. He would have been appalled at what goes under the name of evangelism in some circles today. There often seems little doctrine and theology in it. Human, psychological persuasion appears to be the central motif. Like his Puritan models, Spurgeon believed a lasting revival is born only through the power and sovereignty of God accompanied by prayer and the plain declaration of the essential truths of orthodox theology. Thus he filled his sermons with rich biblical, theological truths that some modern evangelists consider too "heavy" for the lighthearted crowd in today's world.

So through prayer, sound theology, and the preaching of Christ with loving invitation the revival flamed to life. The spiritual atmosphere of London crackled with excitement as hundreds of thousands thronged to hear the young man of God.

In that general setting, the fires of evangelism burned in Spurgeon's heart. Moreover, his evangelistic methods were done with integrity. For example, there was no superficial taking in of members in the Tabernacle. Everyone of the converts were personally counseled by a team of spiritually perceptive laypersons. Their report was given to the church in business session. The candidates for baptism then at times appeared before the congregation to give a personal testimony to demonstrate "the evidence of a work of grace in their lives," as they expressed it. Then they were approved for baptism and church membership. And if they did not persevere, they were excommunicated. Redemptive discipline was enforced.

Now note, much of this effective ministry was accomplished in an urban setting among common working people. The church in Britain has always tended to be a middle-class institution, often leaving the urban masses largely untouched. Spurgeon broke that spiritual syndrome. He spoke the language of the working class. He identified with them in their South London crush. His social ministries touched them where they hurt. His unconventionality in the pulpit communicated to them. He broke through their prejudices against the middle-upper class mentality of the established church. Somehow they knew he loved them and they responded. That is a lesson we desperately need to learn today.

What made Spurgeon that sort of a minister? Much of the answer is found in his spirituality and personal devotion to Jesus Christ.

Puritan Spirituality

Once again, Spurgeon reflects his Puritan theological orientation as one examines his spirituality. This is essentially true, in the first place, because of the London preacher's concept of the *source* of life in the Spirit. For Spurgeon it was the Bible, the Holy Scriptures. His spirituality was essentially a biblical spirituality which emerged out his Calvinistic theology, for Calvin was a biblicist if anything. Spurgeon could not be numbered among the mystics. But that does not mean he was a biblical legalist. It would be best to say that the source of Spurgeon's spirituality was objectively in the Bible, and experientially in the Christ of the Bible. Thus he combined the objective Scriptures with the existential experience of the living Christ as the sole source of true spirituality. This principle meant several things for Spurgeon.

First of all, spirituality demanded Bible study. In his early days as a new Christian, he developed a keen discernment concerning scriptural exegesis and its relation to spiritual life. Spurgeon grasped that principle the next Sunday after his conversion,

> I went to that same chapel, as it was very natural that I should, but I never went afterwards, and for this reason. That during my first week as a Christian, the new life that was in me had been compelled to fight for its existence. And the conflict with the old nature had been vigorously carried on. Now, I knew this fight within to be a special token of the indwelling grace within my soul. But in that same chapel, I heard a sermon on the text "Oh wretched man that I am, who shall deliver me from the body of this death?" And the preacher declared that Paul was not a Christian when he had that experience. Babe as I was, I knew better than to believe so absurd a statement. What but divine grace could produce such a sighing and crying after deliverance from indwelling sin? I felt that a person who could talk such nonsense knew little of the life of a true believer. He may be a good exhorter to sinners, but he cannot feed believers.

Spurgeon always rejected the antinomian belief in perfectionism. But the point is this: It is really quite remarkable that a young man of fifteen had grasped those biblical issues, had thought them through, and had arrived at his own understanding and interpretation of who the "wretched man" of Romans 7 is. Moreover, he had enough knowledge of the Scriptures to discern what at least he felt was best for him as a young believer. He said, "When I was but a child, I could have discussed many a knotty problem of controversial theology."

For Spurgeon, the Bible imparts life. But it is not just a question of knowing the words of the Bible; rather, it is being so filled with the message of the Scriptures that one can say with Jeremiah "Thy words were found, and I did eat them; and [they became] unto me the joy and rejoicing of [my] heart." Spurgeon said,

> There is a style of majesty about God's word, and with this majesty a vividness never found elsewhere. No other writing has within it a heavenly life which works miracles and even imparts life to its reader. It's a living and incorruptible seed. It moves, it stirs itself, it lives, it communes with living men as the living Word. Solomon says concerning it, "it shall talk with thee." You need not bring life to Scripture. You should draw life from Scripture.

Such was Spurgeon's theology of inspiration.

Typical of his biblical understanding, Spurgeon couched his spirituality in most personal terms. The principle of personal application of the Scriptures was vital to the Puritan reformed view of spirituality. Spurgeon readily agreed. He recalled a story which illustrates this point.

> I remember once feeling many questions as to whether I was a child of God or not. I went into a little chapel and I heard a good man preach. He was a simple working man and I heard him preach and I made my handkerchief wet with my tears as I heard him talk about Christ. When I was preaching the same things to others, I was wondering whether this truth was mine. But while I was hearing it for myself, I knew it was mine, for my very soul lived upon it. I went to that good man and I thanked him for the sermon. He asked me who I was. When I told him, he turned all manner of colors. "Why," he said, "Sir, that was your own sermon." I said yes, I knew it was. And it was good of the Lord to feed me with the food I had prepared for others.

Spurgeon maintained that if the Bible is to make an effective impact in human life and experience, listening quietly and sensitively and prayerfully to its message is a necessary spiritual discipline. As Raymond Brown points out:

> In this manner, as in so much else, he was essentially in the tradition of the Reformed as well as Puritan spirituality. The concept of meditation was of immense importance in Luther and in Calvin. Luther used to say that there were three things that make a preacher, meditation, prayer and suffering. John Calvin often spoke of the importance time and again, especially in his commentaries, of the importance of meditation, giving yourself quietly to its message. And I would not judge you when I say to my fellow preachers and say it with great love, it's so important for us.

This is most applicable to the preacher, for there is always the danger of becoming too technical in the study of the Bible, because of having the responsibility of facing the congregation on the next Lord's Day. Spurgeon said,

> The Spirit has taught us in meditation to ponder its message, to put aside, if we will, the responsibility of preparing the message we've got to give. Just trust God for that. But first, meditate on it, quietly ponder it, let it sink deep into our souls. Have you not often been surprised and overcome with delight as Holy Scripture is opened up as if the gates of the Golden City have been set back for you to enter? A few minutes silent openness of soul before the Lord has brought us more treasure of truth than hours of learned research.

But, Spurgeon argued, it must always be kept foremost in mind that the Bible—unique, inspired, and reliable—is always meant to point its readers to Christ. Spurgeon was not guilty of bibliolatry. The ultimate source of all rich spirituality is in the Living Word to whom the written Word points. And wisely, Spurgeon refused to separate, or confuse, the two. Without the Bible, he argued, Christ might be but the projection of one's own intangible dreams, the product even, of one's imagination. It is possible to build up a portrait of Jesus by taking selected passages of Scripture and to proclaim a Christ that suits us. A rich Christology must be found in a balanced study of all the Scriptures. Spurgeon loved to exalt the biblical Christ, but the Bible is not Jesus. Spurgeon's spirituality was drawn not only from the pages of Scripture, but from the presence of Jesus Himself.

That Spurgeon took his cue from the Puritans and their theological understandings is clear. In the introduction to his book, *The Saint and His Saviour,* which expounds more fully his spirituality than almost any other, he quotes the Puritan, Richard Sibbs, who says that the special work of the preacher is to lay open Christ, to hold up the tapestry and unfold the mysteries of Christ Himself.

Thus the Bible and the living Christ became the source of Spurgeon's spirituality. Yet, at the same time, there was a catholicity in his approach. Spurgeon contended there are many forms in which Christ and His gospel may be conveyed and experienced. In *The Saint and His Saviour,* he said,

> He who dares to prescribe one uniform standard of experience for the children of God, is either grievously ignorant or hopelessly full of self-esteem. Uniformity is not God's rule to spirituality. In grace as well as in providence, He delights to display the most charming variety.

So, there is a rich variety of experience in spirituality according to Spurgeon. His preaching clearly demonstrates the principle. In his sermons he quotes from Justin Martyr, Tertullian, Origen, the school of Alexandria, and Gregory of Nazianzus. The great Augustine, Gregory the Great, and Bernard of Clairvaux are cited. John Bunyan, George Fox, the Quakers, Richard Baxter, John Owen, John Howe, Joseph Allain, and Benjamin Keach are all quoted. We're not surprised to hear him quote from his favorite preacher, George Whitefield. Those other leaders in the evangelical revival, Roland Hill, Jonathan Edwards, David Brainerd, John Gill, Andrew Fuller, and John Newton all receive mention in his sermons. He even quotes F. W. Faber, one of the Tractarians in the Anglo-Catholic school. And all of that is just a small sample of the balanced catholicity of Spurgeon's search for spirituality.

At the same time there was nothing unreal or so "other worldly" about Spurgeon's spirituality that he retreated from life's harsh realities. Spurgeon's spirituality dealt with life's extremities. In his lovely *Pictures from Pilgrim's Progress* he wrote,

> If you will help others out of the slough of despond, you must have a bending back. You cannot draw them out if you stand bold upright. You must go right down to where the poor creatures are sinking in the mire. They're almost gone. The mud and the slime are well nigh over their heads so you must roll up your sleeves and go to work with a will, if you mean to rescue them. Learn to stoop.

A bubbly, effervescent, unreal spirituality did not appeal to him. He preached against the brand of spirituality that insisted on the novel, the dramatic, or spectacular. Spurgeon's realism taught him, "Grace grows best in the winter." In a sermon on Hebrews 12 he stated, "Nobody ever grew holy without consenting, desiring, agonizing to be holy. Sin will grow without sowing, but holiness needs cultivation. Follow it, it will not run after you." In that he reflected his innate Puritanism; spirituality is the result of realistic biblical discipline. And what he practiced he preached. That, too, is Puritan spirituality.

Spurgeon's Confidence in and Use of the Bible

If one seeks a summary of Spurgeon's tremendous power in ministry, one must look to his confidence in and use of the Bible. It is true, Spurgeon had great gifts. He had a photographic mind, a beautiful voice, a natural eloquence, a dramatic flair, and a great heart. His social sensitivity was outstanding. These factors were all positive contributions to his effectiveness. But, above all, his handling of the Word of God in the power of the Spirit was the real source of his effectiveness. And, again, the Reformed theological legacy shines forth in unmistakable bold relief.

In *The Greatest Fight in the World,* Spurgeon said:

> After preaching the Gospel for forty years, and after printing the sermons that I have preached for more than six and thirty years reaching now to the number of 2,200 in weekly succession, I think I'm fairly entitled to speak about the fullness and richness of the Bible as a preacher's book. Brethren, it is inexhaustible. No question about its freshness will arise if we keep closely to the text of the Sacred Volume. There can be no difficulties as to finding themes totally distinct from those we've handled before. The variety is as infinite as the fullness. A long life will only suffice us to skirt the shores of this great continent of light. In the forty years of my own ministry, I've only touched the hem of the garment of Divine Truth. But oh, what virtue has flowed out of it. The Word is like its author, infinite, immeasurable, without end. If you were to be ordained to be a preacher throughout eternity, you would have before you a theme equal to everlasting demands. Our Bible will suffice for ages to come for new themes every morning and for fresh songs and discourses, world without end.

Spurgeon admitted his utter reliance on the Scripture for his theology and his sermons. As one put it, "He knew only two subjects really well—the text of the English Bible and the writings of the Puritan divines . . . He measured everything he read against the yardstick of a verbally inspired Bible."

Regardless, His preaching and use of the Bible was formidable. *The Freeman,* an evangelical tabloid, stated concerning Spurgeon: "No other preacher in this age wields such power, and it may be questioned whether anyone else has ever done it in these Islands save John Knox in Scotland and Christmas Evans in Wales."

Moreover, Spurgeon was a "defender of the biblical, evangelical faith." He filled the role of "Mr. Valiant for Truth" in Bunyan's *The Pilgrim's Progress.* He was unaffected by any pressure from any source. He once said, "I will never modify a doctrine I believe to please any man that walks upon earth." But, he rarely launched a frontal assault upon the logic of a rational, empirical, epistemological hermeneutic, trying to prove, for example, that every jot and tittle of Genesis 1—11 was literally and historically true. He rejected the challenge of naturalistic science and history to the veracity of Scripture. He would point out that the very nature of the empirical, scientific method is merely a project of a hypothesis. He put all his trust in what he considered the unchanging, immutable truth of the Bible as he grasped it. Thus, he left his critics, at least as he saw it, with the sinking ship of experiment. He stated: "Is the thing called 'science' infallible? The history of ignorance which calls itself 'philosophy' is absolutely identical with the history of fools, except where it diverges into madness." Such a statement seems rather dogmatic today; yet, in Spurgeon's time the scientists and naturalistic critics were as dogmatic in their negative assertions about the Bible as he was in his attack on their presupposition.

What then was the one infallible rule of truth? The answer is obvious—the Holy Scriptures. Spurgeon was unwilling to make the slightest concession on any point which challenged this view of the Bible as the plenary, verbally inspired Word of God. He believed in the "all-or-nothing fallacy" (i.e., either everything was inspired or nothing was). He stated, "If the book of Genesis be an allegory, the Bible is an allegory all through . . . . We will never attempt to save half the truth by casting any part of it away . . . . We will stand by it all or have none of it. We will have a whole Bible or no Bible." He asked, "If this book be not infallible, where shall we find infallibility and unless we have infallibility somewhere, faith is impossible."

During the last years of Spurgeon's ministry, these issues came to a head in the famous Downgrade Controversy. Believing that the Baptist Union harbored ministers whose doctrinal views placed them outside the pale of evangelical Christianity, Spurgeon published a series of articles lamenting the "down grade" the church was on and calling for the adoption of a clear theological standard. In the end Spurgeon refused to name those he suspected of heresy because their names had been given to him in confidentiality. In 1887 Spurgeon withdrew from the Baptist Union rather than countenance what he called "wretched indifferentism" and doctrinal deviation. In the following year the Union passed a strong censure against Spurgeon. Although he might have formed a new denomination of disaffected Baptists, he urged others not to follow him out of the Union. Ironically, a large marble statue of Spurgeon greets the visitor to the Baptist Union building in London.

Not only did the Puritan legacy impact Spurgeon's theology as to the nature of the Bible, it largely determined his use of it in preaching. He learned from the Puritans the lesson of concise organization and structured subdivision of a text. For example, the following introduction to one of his sermons is an example of the typical Puritan approach to the use of the Bible in preaching. Spurgeon stated:

> The narrative before us seems to me to suggest three points, and these three points each of them triplets. I shall notice in this narrative, first, *the three*

stages of faith; in the second place, *the three diseases to which faith is subject;* and in the third place to ask *three questions about your faith.*

Through this analytical, Aristotelian approach, Spurgeon strove to make each of his sermons simple enough for a child to understand. And he usually succeeded.

He never tried to please "rationalistic" theologians and modern higher critics. Consequently, they were frequently appalled by his explication of texts. Horton Davies contended, "his exegesis could be capricious, idiosyncratic, and even grotesque." Whether this is true or not, we would probably all agree today he tended to play too much upon the meanings of words in the English text without a thorough grounding in the original language of the text. But then again, that was a common failure of Victorians; and he was certainly a Victorian. Still, in the face of it all, his preaching impact was tremendous and appreciated by most.

Because of the Victorian concern for the words of the text, Spurgeon became what today we would call a textual preacher. Rarely did he take a text and not turn it, digest it, and give it every twist possible. As a consequence, though at times he no doubt did too much with a verse, the people heard the Word, and in that they reveled and grew in the faith. Spurgeon was a biblicist in a theological and practical sense, and not much more needs to be said. Most evangelicals know of and have read him—and appreciate him profoundly.

Evaluation

So "The Last of the Puritans" made his contribution; and the legacy lingers on. The question is constantly raised: Would Spurgeon with his Calvinistic theology be effective in today's urban, secular world? The religious Victorian age is past, to be sure, and he was a man of that century. Yet, in the opinion of this writer Spurgeon would have been most effective in the present era—and for the very reasons he was effective one hundred years ago, as were the Puritans in their age. First, he was culturally a man of his day; hence, he knew how to communicate to it. Second, he had a firm grasp on the essential gospel. His theology held him in good stead. This is perennially important—and relevant. Third, he was a man of God with a contagious spirituality. People always respond to that in a minister. And he ministered to people in their real needs. Finally, he faithfully believed in and preached the "whole counsel of God"—the Holy Scriptures. And he did it all in an innovative fashion that ministered to people where they actually were in life. That sort of ministry is always alive, relevant, and responded to in any age.

Bibliography

Works by Spurgeon

All of Grace: An Earnest Word with Those Who Are Seeking Salvation by the Lord Jesus Christ. London: Passmore and Alabaster, 1892.

C. H. Spurgeon Autobiography vol. 1 rev. ed. Edinburgh: Banner of Truth Trust, 1962.

C. H. Spurgeon Autobiography vol. 2 rev. ed. Edinburgh: Banner of Truth Trust, 1973.

C. H. Spurgeon's Prayers. With an Introduction by Dinsdale T. Young. London: Passmore and Alabaster, 1905.

The Cheque Book of The Bank of Faith. London: Passmore and Alabaster, 1888.

Commenting and Commentaries: Two Lectures Addressed to the Students of The Pastors' College, Metropolitan Tabernacle, together with A Catalogue of Biblical Commentaries and Expositions. London: Passmore and Alabaster, 1876.

John Ploughman's Pictures; or More of His Plain Talk for Plain People. London: Passmore & Alabaster, 1880.

Lectures to my Students: A Selection from Addresses Delivered to the Students of The Pastors' College, Metropolitan Tabernacle. London: Passmore and Alabaster, 1890.

The Metropolitan Tabernacle Pulpit, 57 vols. London: Passmore & Alabaster, 1861-1917.

Morning by Morning: or, Daily Readings for the Family or the Closet. London: Passmore and Alabaster, n.d.

Morning by Morning. Grand Rapids, Mich.: Baker Book House, 1975.

The New Park Street Pulpit, 6 vols. London: Passmore and Alabaster, 1855-60.

The Soul-Winner; or, How To Lead Sinners to the Saviour. London: Passmore & Alabaster, 1895.

The Treasury of David: Containing An Original Exposition of the Book of Psalms; A Collection of Illustrative Extracts from the Whole Range of Literature; A Series of Homiletical Hints Upon Almost Every Verse; and Lists of Writers upon Each Psalm, 7 vols. London: Passmore and Alabaster.

Works about Spurgeon

Bacon, Ernest W. *Spurgeon: Heir of the Puritans*. London: George Allen & Unwin Ltd., 1967.

Davies, Horton. "Expository Preaching: Charles Haddon Spurgeon." *Foundations* 6 (1963): 14-25.

Day, Richard Ellsworth. *The Shadow of the Broad Brim: The Life Story of Charles Haddon Spurgeon Heir of the Puritans*. Philadelphia: The Judson Press, 1934.

Ferguson, Duncan S. "The Bible and Protestant Orthodoxy: The Hermeneutics of Charles Spurgeon." *Journal of the Evangelical Theological Society* 25 (1982): 455-66.

Fullerton, W. Y. *C. H. Spurgeon: A Biography*. London: Williams and Norgate, 1920.

Lorimer, George C. *Charles Haddon Spurgeon: The Puritan Preacher in the Nineteenth Century*. Boston: James H. Earle, 1892.

Murray, Iain H. *The Forgotten Spurgeon*. 2d ed. Edinburgh: Banner of Truth Trust, 1973.

Payne, Ernest A. "The Down Grade Controversy: A Postscript." *Baptist Quarterly* 28 (1979): 146-58.

Skinner, Craig. "The Preaching of Charles Haddon Spurgeon." *Baptist History and Heritage* 19 (1984): 16-26.

Notes

*A large portion of this chapter was taken from Lewis A. Drummond, *Charles Spurgeon* (Grand Rapids, Mich.: Kregel, 1990). Full bibliographical material can be found in this volume. The vast majority of quotations in this chapter are from Spurgeon's own sermons and autobiography. It is therefore not necessary that all these be noted as they have been published numerous times by various publishers over the past 100 years.

1. W. Y. Fullerton, *C. H. Spurgeon,* (London: Williams and Norgate, 1920), 30-31.

2. C. Kruppa, *A. Preacher's Progress,* (unpublished Ph.D. thesis).

3. Melton Mason, Jr., *The Theology of Charles Haddon Spurgeon,* (unpublished Ph.D. thesis), 155.

4. Ibid., 156.

5. Preached at Exeter Hall, April 1855.

14

Augustus Hopkins Strong

Kurt A. Richardson

Augustus Hopkins Strong is perhaps the most notable Baptist theologian of the nineteenth and early-twentieth centuries. His place in a compendium of Baptist theologians is central. In some cases he must be read in order to understand the theological writings of others. Strong taught and wrote his orthodox theology from a committed, reformed, Baptist perspective, while at the same time rigorously engaging intellectual developments within his cultural context. His death came on the eve of the Fundamentalist/Modernist controversy, a period whose resultant cleavages would render his theological contribution underappreciated. Strong's magnum opus, the *Systematic Theology,* embodied the best of his own theological reflection and of Baptist theological thought prior to this momentous crisis.

Widespread use of Strong's *Systematic Theology* has declined in the last generation, but the work is clearly among the finest products of the late-nineteenth and twentieth centuries in American religion. Perhaps for this reason it is no longer a primary textbook in the study of Christian doctrine. Due to its great popularity, Strong's book went through eight editions over more than a quarter century. Through the editions, especially the first to the fifth, we can trace the various changes in the ways he discoursed on Christian doctrine.

I begin this essay by mentioning Strong's theological transitions because he seems to have anticipated, so many years ago, how certain issues in modern thought would affect our Protestant and Baptist ways of thinking.[1] He was very attentive to currents of thought, both American and continental, which were having a profound impact within learned circles. His enthusiasm for every discovery or improvement in understanding which seemed to promote the truth of God is a distinguishing mark of his life's work. He was convinced that all true advancements in knowledge and artistic expression redounded to the greater glory of God and the truth of God, and he tried to convince his students and theological colleagues of this.

Strong was for more than forty years president and professor of theology at Rochester Theological Seminary. As chief administrator of the preeminent theological school of the era, Strong acquired an openness to diverse theological opinion. This openness was reflected in his faculty appointments which included: Walter Rauschenbusch and Albert Henry Newman and, in a number of cases, ranged beyond denominational ties. Among his close friends were those who accounted themselves "New Theologians" as well as conservatives like Alvah Hovey and A. J. Gordon. This is not to say that his own teaching, preaching, or writing exhibited a liberalizing tendency, or that he wanted Rochester Seminary to be liberal, rather, his was a commitment to the Christian pursuit of knowledge and ultimate truth and this meant a necessary openness to varied theological viewpoints.

Strong possessed a deep Christian conscience. In one respect, he found himself drawn to Rauschenbusch's critique of capitalism, and in another, to John D. Rockefeller's interests in funding religious endeavors and educational institutions. His own conspicuous wealth was merely a by-product of the widespread goodwill and trust which his personality engendered in the hearts of many very wealthy contributors to the seminary. Strong championed missions to the poor and the place of women in ministry (their graduate education and ordination). Strong was never neglectful of the thrice weekly services of his church or his own Sunday School teaching. On every life front, he set high standards of conscience for himself which won him broad admiration and affection.

Students benefited from his daily devotions at the seminary. They too were or became a theologically diverse group. Those who would count themselves as his disciples, some calling themselves "Strong's boys," fell into liberal and conservative groups. Maintaining the highest spiritual and intellectual commitment to the seminarians, Strong's imposing presence made him a pastor to the entire American Baptist denomination.

Biography

Strong was born August 3, 1836, in Rochester, New York, and died there, November 29, 1921. He was converted under the ministry of Charles Finney while a college student. Deeply impressed by the evangelist's penetrating logic and spiritual ardor, Strong soon felt called to the ministry. He completed his college study at Yale in 1857, seminary study at Rochester Seminary in 1859 and then took a year of study abroad (mostly in Berlin in 1860).

Strong then moved into a period of pastoral ministry during which he served two Baptist churches, first in Haverhill, Massachusetts, and then in Cleveland, Ohio. The young Strong's preaching was expositional and spiritually potent, and he quickly gained the esteem of the denomination. He refused to leave the pastorate to become president of Brown University. But when his mentor at Rochester, Ezekial Robinson, took that position, Strong accepted the seminary's invitation to become its president in 1872. As president and professor of biblical theology, Strong would serve at Rochester Seminary until his permanent retirement in 1912. During his tenure at Rochester he would be responsible for shaping what became one of the most respected and theologically diverse seminary faculties in America. Strong had become a pastor of pastors.

Strong took a very active part in denominational leadership as well, serving as president of the foreign mission society, of the General Convention, trustee and then board chairman of Vassar College. Strong's first wife and the mother of his six children, Harriet Savage, died in 1914, and the follow-

Augustus Hopkins Strong (1839-1921)

Photo courtesy of Southern Baptist Historical Library and Archives

ing year he married Marguerite Jones. His two sons, Charles and John, were highly intelligent men, the former, moving away from theology and the ministry as he found himself unable to hold to the orthodoxy of his father, the latter becoming professor in, but never president of, Rochester Seminary as his father had hoped.

Augustus Strong's publications: *Christ in Creation and Ethical Monism* (1899), *Philosophy and Religion* (1888), the *Systematic Theology* (1886-1909) in eight editions, *A Tour of Missions* (1918), and other lesser works, were some of the most influential theological pieces of the era. In our present treatment of the thought of Strong, we will focus our attention on the *Systematic Theology* and take special note of how his philosophical presuppositions, which he idiomatically termed "ethical monism," shaped its final form. These publications became the essentials of Strong's enduring legacy as "one of the preeminent conservative Protestant theologians of the period" (from 1880 to his death in 1921).[2]

Exposition

Philosophical Theology

Traditional reformed orthodoxy characterized the Baptist theology of the early Strong. In his lectures on Christian doctrine, Strong possessed much of the same orthodox rationalist approach that the great Princeton theologian Charles Hodge did. Strong always held to the scientific character of theology but his early philosophy of theology was common sense realism. The content of theology was strictly propositional whose objects have an "existence entirely independent of the subjective mental processes of the theologian."[3] The important point of Strong's approach here, which would hold for the rest of his theological development, was his commitment to the natural knowledge of God gained by intuition through the internally revealing Holy Spirit and its continuity with special or revealed knowledge. Strong did not produce a natural theology as such, but many aspects of his theological writings reflect a theology of nature or the world order. Strong saw this as an enhancement, not a compromise, of orthodoxy.

As the years went by, Strong's theologizing became more and more the enterprise of deducing propositions from the internal communication of the Holy Spirit in conjuncture with either the external revelation of God in nature or in Scripture.[4] This would never be in abstraction from the saving knowledge of God in Christ but rather on account of it. In union with Christ, a person is able to attune himself to revelations of Christ within the created order. In fact, Strong believed that ultimately everything revealed Christ, who is its Originator, Sustainer, and Redeemer.

By the time of his *Theology*'s seventh edition Strong would state clearly how his mind had changed in the doing of theology. Ethical monism, obviously a combination of two philosophical categories, was Strong's way of reconciling the view that the universe is of one substance with God (i.e., divine immanence) while maintaining the personal ("ethical") duality between creatures and the transcendent Creator. "Ethical monism" had "thrown new light" upon the old doctrines to which he still held. Drawing on such Scriptures as: "In him all things consist . . ."; Strong made assertions like: "Nature is the omnipresent Christ manifesting God to creatures;" "what we call uniformity in nature . . . is only the manifestation of an omnipresent mind and will;" and "Christ is the principle of evolution."[5] These assertions did not, for the most part, alter the substance of Strong's reformed orthodoxy, but they did represent a major shift in theological language and drew a flurry of criticisms from those who were otherwise in agreement with his theology.

Strong was clear about how pervasively philosophical monism, the doctrine that there is only one supreme reality, was being advanced in some universities of North America. This was, according to his reckoning, an advancement in knowledge and a latter-day product of the ever-illuminating Spirit of God. At stake was whether any moral or personal duality existed between the Creator and the creature or that a singular reality simply implied the relatively of all temporal conditions above the absolutely immanent God.[6] Strong's philosophy suggested "a monism which maintains both the freedom of man and the transcendence of God;" and yet "There is one substance— God." "The universe is Christ's finite and temporal manifestation of God . . . the partial unfolding of God's wisdom and power. . . ."[7] God and Christ are neither finite nor limited to any temporal manifestation. What is at issue is the relationship of nature to deity.

As much as Strong struggled to convince his readers that he was not adopting a pantheistic doctrine but affirming a transcendent personal God and a free humanity, he felt pushed to adopt language that bordered on paradox. In his article, "Ethical Monism Once More," he stated, "frankly and bluntly . . . ethical monism is *dualistic monism*."[8] Although Strong in many places seemed delighted that there was in his Christian version of monism an appropriation of evolutionary theory, he averred that he "accepts ethical monism because of the light which it throws upon the atonement . . . ."[9] Strong deflected the pantheism charge fairly effectively. He felt biological evolution, if it represented an important aspect of origins, need not be feared since nothing biblically is lost if God is the ultimate Originator.

Strong believed himself to have perceived a fundamentally new aspect for Christology. Since the creation is primarily the relatedness of Christ with humanity, the atonement was simply the ultimate—though not yet final— outworking of this total relatedness. This relatedness constituted an identification of Christ with humanity in the sense that human existence is mutually conditioned. God had determined from all eternity that the Son would be made man, thus making the being of humanity a direct consequence of Christ's human being. "I cannot think that this identification of humanity with Christ works anything but good in our interpretation of the atonement," wrote Strong as he sought to integrate his philosophical and theological convictions.[10] The atonement even transcends the death of Christ who

> as incarnate, rather revealed the atonement than made it. The historical work of atonement was finished upon the Cross, but that historical work only re-

vealed to men the atonement made both before and since by the extra-mundane
Logos. The eternal Love of God suffering the necessary reaction of his own
Holiness against the sin of his creatures and with a view to their salvation . . .[11]

Here we can detect Strong's enthusiasm over what he viewed as the successful synthesis of the current philosophical theism (in monism or idealism) and
his own orthodoxy.

Strong received numerous criticisms for his adaptation of the personal
idealism of philosophers such as Borden Parker Bowne, Edgar Sheffield
Brightman, and Hermann Lotze. By doing this he believed he was able to
come to grips with the continuities of evolutionary theory and the cataclysm
of eschatology. Evolution reflected, for him, the means of divine purpose for
creation as it moves towards its assigned goal.

Evolution is simply the ordinary method of Christ's working. . . . This method
is not exclusive. It leaves room for absolute creation, for incarnation, miracle
resurrection . . . . These are required either to precede, explain, or supplement
the evolutionary process.[12]

The process is secured by God's "involution" or immanent causation and
direction of it. The immanence of the eternal God with humanity in Christ
makes historical evolution possible and is the ordinary means of His working.

Working through the evolutionary process, human redemption will be realized and Christ's lordship progressively revealed. As a result the positive
civilizing process of humanity is everywhere evident in scientific discovery
and the dissimination of high artistic values and is inherently Christian,
though not an end in itself. Civilization will be caught up in a greater manifestation of Christ at His second coming. There will be a merging of two
types of eschatology in Strong's system: Christ's coming is "pre-millennial
spiritually, but post-millennial physically and visibly."[13] In Strong's view the
two eschatologies are not in conflict but simply indicate the marvelous teleol-
ogy of a God whose infinitely rich glory and grace is able to redeem the
time, both present and future, and all that it contains. The eschaton is already
present through the Holy Spirit who is unfolding the richness of the knowledge of God in the created order, and not yet, awaiting the glorious second
advent of Jesus Christ who will make all things new.

Doctrinal Theology

Strong's approach to Scripture was reverent and thoughtful. He imbibed
the attitude of his teacher, Ezekial Robinson, concerning the positive use of
historical criticism in biblical study. He preferred the orthodox Lutheran
European theologians to the Americans because he detected in the former a
thoroughness and comprehensiveness in handling problems of understanding
while in the latter he did not. Among his favorites were Isaac Dorner, Christian Thomasius, and F. A. Philippi. Through these he began to regard Scripture as as much a product of the historical circumstances and perceptions of
the writers as that of the Holy Spirit. In addition, Strong adopted their care in

acknowledging claims about the actual intrusion of the supernatural within history.

One contemporary review of the final edition of the *Systematic Theology* noted how Strong's views had changed from previous editions relative to miracle and inspiration. Of Strong's statement, "A miracle as an event inexplicable by the laws of nature, even if fully known, is omitted . . . miracle is . . . an evidence of the presence in nature of Christ." The reviewer wrote, "it leaves it possible that all miracles may have their natural explanations and may hereafter be traced to natural causes, while both miracles and their natural causes may be only names for the one and self-same will of God."[14] Certainly Strong would have protested against this construal of his method of interpreting miracle stories, but it is clear that some of his more liberal readers believed he had left them begging the question.

When Strong moved to a definition of Scripture, although his was a "high bibliology," the same reviewer observed that Strong had limited the scope of inerrancy due (apparently) to the term's connotation of scientific accuracy.

> Inspiration is that influence of the Spirit of God upon the minds of the Scripture writers which made their writings the record of a progressive divine revelation, sufficient, when taken together and interpreted by the same Spirit who inspired them, to lead every honest inquirer to Christ and to salvation.
>
> . . . inspiration did not guarantee inerrancy in things not essential to the main purpose of Scripture.[15]

Some were dissatisfied with what we might call "purposive inerrancy" because it left unclear how one is to distinguish those passages which convey the main purpose of Scripture and those which do not. These would have to rest content with the perpetual work of the Bible's spiritual author who always aids the discerning, searching reader.

For others who were worried that Strong had opened the door to a naturalistic or historicist assault upon Scripture he gave reassurance: "science has not yet shown any fairly interpreted passage of Scripture to be untrue." Human errors of a historical nature cannot detract it any way from the perfect inspiration of Scripture.[16] "Religious efficacy" rather than inerrancy of the Bible became Strong's positive stance. All of Scripture was the result of its writers being caught up in the movement of the Holy Spirit's inspiration but this had not suspended or removed their own perspectives and limitations on or in the world. That movement of the Holy Spirit, and His movement today, ensures that the Bible always effectively leads those who are being saved to true faith.

Strong recognized various proofs for the divine inspiration of Scripture, but the one he favored was the teaching and convincing that the Holy Spirit does in perpetually superintending the sincere reading of that Scripture. By this means, understanding the Scripture "as a whole and in all essentials," occurs so reliably that it must have God as its ultimate source and goal.[17] Scripture's inspiration was accomplished through the Spirit of God causing an interpenetration of fully divine and fully human characteristics.

Inspiration, therefore, did not remove, but rather pressed into its own service, all the personal peculiarities of the writers, together with their defects of culture and literary style.

Every imperfection not inconsistent with truth in a human composition may exist in inspired Scripture. The Bible is God's word, in the sense that it presents to us divine truth in human forms, and is a revelation not for a select class but for the common mind. Rightly understood, this very humanity of the Bible is a proof of its divinity.[18]

Moreover, because of the agency of the Holy Spirit, the Scripture is an "organic whole." And although it is an "imperfect mirror of Christ" because the words themselves are only feeble substitutes for His physical presence, believers and the church are able, by the same Spirit, to "distinguish the essential from the non-essential." The Spirit will lead each one into all the Truth, in actual fact, to Christ Himself, the authority to which the Scriptures point.[19]

More than dealing with inspiration, Strong's theological intent was to carry his readers into an extended contemplation of the Godhead and His works for humankind. Who God is in His innermost being and in relation to humanity needed fuller and fresher expression. We have already seen how open-minded Strong was when it came to sources for the knowledge of God. Strong wanted thought about God as revealed in Scripture and thought about God from experience to be seen in continuity. In the same way that Scripture is composed of a variety of literary forms, Strong asserted that there were a variety of ways that God is perceived. Direct revelation through theophanies, miracles, prophecies, or the unique incarnation of Christ could not be regarded as discontinuous to indirect revelation through various orders of spiritual experience ranging from mystical intuition to poetic imagination to rational thought about the world.[20] Strong's essential definition of God as "Spirit, Infinite and Perfect, the Source, Support, and End of all things" when delineated in his doctrinal theology drew as much upon experience of God as upon Scripture. This did not mean that Scripture was not primary in authority, indeed, Scripture was the source faith and the basis upon which our thinking about and experience of God was reoriented. In this way we could begin to experience God and to interpret that experience truthfully.

The love of God, according to Strong, is that scriptural attribute of God which surpasses the rigid philosophical notion of divine impassibility. On account of His love the infinite life of God—in perfect rationality and volition—is involved in the sufferings of the world. God has communicated Himself throughout history even to the point of suffering death in the completed work of the atonement. God's constant nearness to the world means He is willingly affected by it. "To know that God is suffering with it makes that suffering more awful, but it gives strength and life and hope, for we know that if God is in it, suffering is the road to victory."[21]

This suffering is realized especially in the self-limiting of God in the Incarnation in Jesus Christ. Once this reality of God's love in Christ is recognized, we then are led to knowing God in His Trinity.

Trinitarian doctrine is expressed by Strong with the word "tri-personality" though he denies tritheism. The names of the Holy Trinity, God the Father, God the Son, and God the Holy Spirit, convey the reality of three distinct personalities in God. Their unity or oneness is apparent in terms of the interrelation of one to the other.

> We are also warranted in declaring that, in virtue of these personal distinctions or modes of subsistence, God exists in the relations, respectively, first, of Source, Origin, Authority, and in this relation is the Father; secondly, of Expression, Medium, Revelation, and in this relation is the Son; thirdly, of Apprehension, Accomplishment, Realization, and in this relation is the Holy Spirit.[22]

Here one of the key attributes of the Son is that of Medium, whereby the immanence of God, as understood through Strong's ethical monism, is maintained. The Father as (evolutionary) Origin and the Spirit as Realization point to the active, guiding role that God has in the total process of history and the developing world order. It should be noted however that in Strong's consideration of tri-personality, the distinguishing characteristics are largely functional and less truly personal. Distinct personages within the deity constitute much more than functional relations to created reality. We ought to remember, however, that in any doctrinal theology of the Trinity at some point the effort to achieve precision in definition will tend more toward either the oneness of God or the threeness of God. In spite of Strong's use of the term "tri-personality" his Trinitarianism tends more toward the oneness of God.

We are not surprised then when Strong's discussion of God and His attributes is immediately followed by an extended treatment of the decrees of God. According to Strong's theology, the decrees of God constitute a single divine plan for originating, mediating, and realizing an order that reflects the majesty of His wisdom and the glory of His Person and purposes. All of the other doctrines of faith are vitally related by this preconditioning doctrine of the decrees (or doctrine of creation). The providence of God over all things, especially in the lives of Christians, is worked out purposively and intelligibly. Strong held

> . . . that God is continually near the human spirit by his providential working, and that this providential working is so adjusted to the Christian's nature and necessities . . .
>
> In interpreting God's providences, as in interpreting Scripture, we are dependent upon the Holy Spirit.[23]

Strong does not hedge in his commitment to the biblical understanding of God in His sovereignty so that all events serve His ultimate purpose and glory, even the reprobate in their destruction. Strong, however, is careful to avoid blind determinism and sets forth a compatibility between divine sovereignty and human responsibility.

The doctrine of man in Strong's *Systematic Theology* accepted the validity of a form of theistic evolution: a coworking of God and created developmental forces of nature. Theistic evolution, Strong claimed, was the means by which a human's physical being became the repository of the image of God: the "definite" moral nature of man. Strong marshals all of the current scientific understandings of the constituents of the truly human to illustrate the uniqueness of this object. His is a dualistic view of human nature which comprises material and immaterial parts. The first man was like God in his personality and moral qualities, though in no way possessed of a physical likeness to God.[24] In this way Strong avoided problems of forms of life preceding the "creation" of man. In order for any creature to possess humanness, the image of God had to be transferred to it. This transfer occurred only at a moment determined by God and thus, as interpreted by Strong, in no way runs against Scripture because Scripture does not disclose God's method of creation. To the extent that evolutionary theory corresponds to reality, it simply represents what God did in creation.

The harmony which originally existed between God and man is expressed through the law and grace of God. Sin is destructive of this relation because man has not, either by conscious disposition or action, remained in conformity with the will of God. The result is the universality of sin due to the possession of a corrupted nature and the depravity, guilt, and condemnation of the first humans imputed upon the rest. Strong adopts, after a long discussion of many possible interpretations, the Augustinian theory of Adam's natural headship:

> sin is imputed to us immediately, therefore, not as something foreign to us, but because it is ours—we and all other men having existed as one moral person or one moral whole, in him, and, as the result of transgression, possessing a nature destitute of love to God and prone to evil.[25]

This also means, of course, that condemnation is inherited and cannot be reversed by any means at man's disposal.

Here the man Jesus Christ is interposed, whose personality was also in union with the divine nature, and is the God-man. This union of deity and humanity is possible because "human nature is capable of the divine," especially perfected human nature renewed in the image of God.[26] By virtue of Christ's miraculous birth and the uniting of divine and human natures, His humanity was perfected. This individual unity of natures made it possible for Christ to have a general "organic unity" with the race so that it could be saved from "the whole mass and weight of God's displeasure."[27] Whenever the redeeming benefits of Christ's general unity with man are appropriated, salvation from God's righteous judgment is secured.

The coworking of God and nature in salvation is seen with respect to Strong's view of Christ in creation. Since the beginning of God's creating work, Christ has been at the center, originating its beauty and harmony and then winning it away from its captivity to corruption through incarnation, suffering, and death. Christ therefore, as incarnate, rather revealed the atonement than made it. The cross is the revelation of God's eternal suffering for sin.[28] This is how Strong gave expression to the substitutionary view of the work of Christ. The physical continuities of recent science had sparked

Strong's theological mind to perceive Christ as the heart of creation and the cross as the culmination of his work from the very beginning.

As to election, Strong was an advocate of the moderate-Calvinistic "sublapsarian" view. Election is the determination of God to save some out of the mass of fallen humanity and to pass over the rest. Grace and sovereign election are kept in close relation. Drawing deeply upon reformed theology at this point, the actual effects of election secure union with Christ prior to justification and regeneration in the *ordo salutis*. Strong's earlier assertions about Christ in creation set the context for this view of election. Union with Christ, while avoiding "a false mysticism" is emphasized because of the powerful reality that is signified by the doctrine.

> The Scriptures declare that, through the operation of God, there is constituted a union of the soul with Christ . . . a union of life, in which the human spirit, while then most truly possessing its own individuality and personal distinctness, is interpenetrated and energized by the Spirit of Christ, is made inscrutably but indissolubly one with him, and so becomes a member and partaker of that regenerated, believing, and justified humanity of which he is the head.[29]

Believers are elected to true spiritual union with Christ and, in turn, accrue to themselves all of the benefits of grace found in God through Christ.

We take special note of the phrase, "Union with life," where true life, in this case physical and spiritual, is identified with Christ Himself. In effect, Strong sought to turn romantic, naturalistic mysticism on its head through his scriptural insights on Christ. In other words, there is a proper biblical or Christological mysticism underlying our understanding of the redeemed relation with God. Union with Christ, which is union with Life itself, is the first step and ground of the order of salvation.

> Union with Christ brings about a fellowship of Christ with the believer,—Christ takes part in all the labors, temptations, and sufferings of his people; a fellowship of the believer with Christ,—so that Christ's whole experience on earth is in some measure reproduced in him; a fellowship of all believers with one another,—furnishing a basis for the spiritual unity of Christ's people on earth, and for the eternal communion of heaven. The doctrine of Union with Christ is therefore the indispensable preparation for *Ecclesiology,* and for *Eschatology.*[30]

From union with Christ, regeneration, conversion (including repentance and faith), justification, sanctification, and perseverance all follow in necessary and orderly relation.

Ecclesiology, according to Strong, stands on the twin pillars of a regenerate membership and voluntary association, whether at the local or universal level. Each member stands on equal footing with God, to glorify Him and to do His will. Christ is the sole Lord of the church, whose authority in doctrine and life must be kept pure. A helpful discussion of ordinances follows both supporting and defending the Baptist interpretation of relevant Scripture passages.[31]

The "doctrine of final things" of course concludes the *Systematic Theol-*

ogy as a discussion of the way in which God brings about the perfection of believers. After an extended discussion of what Strong regards as the false doctrine of annihilation of the unsaved, he posits a dichotomized intermediate state until the second coming of Christ after a millennium of the progressive realization of His kingdom with a simultaneous resurrection of the just and the unjust. Christ will then sit in judgment on both groups—one to perfect relation to Christ, the other to permanent degeneracy. Proclamation of the gospel must not ignore the reality of everlasting punishment, indeed, fear of punishment, wrote Strong, is a genuine motivating force in the renunciation of sin and commitment to following Christ. Although the material images of hell in Scripture should be spiritually and not literally interpreted, the issue must be treated with solemnity.[32]

Strong was criticized by his liberal contemporaries for not taking religious experience seriously enough. They believed that if he had, by allowing the human conscience fuller sway in the determination of the judgment and content of theology, he would have had a more scientific theology. But Strong was acutely aware of the dangers in this "New Theology" line of thought.

> Consciousness is in no case a new or collateral source of truth. Experience is only a testing or trying of truth already revealed. Intuition is not creative; it only recognizes objective realities that were already there to be recognized. . . . "The ethico-religious consciousness" is by itself utterly untrustworthy; it must ever be rectified, by comparison with express divine revelation; where revelation speaks, there Christian consciousness may safely speak; where that is silent, the latter must be silent: "To the law and to the testimony! If they speak not according to this word, surely there is no morning for them."[33]

In other words, the immanence of Christ did not mean that awareness of such by the believer could become a source of revelational authority. Life in God is immediate and free, but the revelation of God in Christ is final and limited to that certain deposit of knowledge in Scripture. This is not to say that no perception of the truth is attained apart from Scripture, because all truth derives from Christ who is everywhere present, but that our sinful attitude and bent of mind which pervert our ability to apprehend the truth must receive that saving knowledge of God which comes by the Scripture alone. The overbearing individualism of modern theology, according to Strong, fails to cope with the infirmities of the collective condition of humanity.[34]

Evaluation

By way of a few concluding remarks I wish to indicate, first of all, my sympathies with Strong's theological program. He could see that a new kind of metaphysic for theology was required in order to incorporate real advances—in some cases only apparent advances—in human knowledge, much like physicotheology had attempted to do following the discoveries of Isaac Newton in the eighteenth century. One need not look very far to find similar theological programs in our own day by people like Eric Mascall,

T. F. Torrance, Philip Hefner, and W. van Huysteen. If Strong's *Systematic Theology* is burdened down by his encyclopedic references or old school system of outlining theological questions and answers, we are certainly not the worse for reaping a treasury of theological insight, much of which we still propound today.

Certainly there have been some who thought that Strong had taken a first step upon a "slippery slope" toward liberalism. This is, however, a difficult call to make. Strong's visionary theological mind perceived Christ immediately present in all things and believed this to be fully compatible with what is uniquely revealed in Scripture about Christ. This was the essence of what he meant by ethical monism. But perhaps this Christology of creation and Strong's euphoria over general progress in science and the fruits of the fine arts meant that in certain practical cases, he came to tolerate what his better theological judgments would not have tolerated. His commitment to the advancement of real knowledge, wherever it might be found, inadvertently contributed to the development of a hard-line empiricist approach to the study of religion at places like the University of Chicago Divinity School. At Rochester Seminary, his departure basically spelled the end of the kind of badge orthodoxy he had represented at that institution. But then again, it seems Strong understood that to err on the side of encouraging free inquiry was less of a risk to the suppression of God's truth than in inhibiting the free pursuit of knowledge. This was the *liberality* of the man. Faith comes by hearing the Word of God and heeding the internal work of the Holy Spirit. Sound doctrine is basically a positive and not a polemical task—although there is polemic aplenty in the *Systematic Theology*.

Ethical monism never really took hold within evangelical theological circles or elsewhere. It was a product of the idealist thinking of the latter part of the nineteenth century which would soon give way to critical realism in the philosophy of science and phenomenology in the philosophy of mind. Interestingly, however, there are very definite trends in theological reflection on the physical nature of the universe where the boundary between the invisible and the visible, the material and the immaterial, form and being, is no longer regarded as something hard, but much more fluid and open. The search for a Grand Unified Theory of the universe one day may well have Christ at the center.

Augustus Strong's theology may, therefore, be due a rediscovery, not necessarily because it sets out a theological agenda which can be neatly transferred into our own contemporary theological setting, but because it so masterfully accomplished that in its own day, a day of our recent past.

In the generation following Strong and the denominational divisions which were suffered, there was not much of a place for his kind of theologizing. On the one hand, the *Systematic Theology* was far too conservative, on the other, it was too broad-minded. The orthodoxy of the fundamentalists and their neo-evangelical heirs could only slowly work their way back to taking the full range of human experience seriously. It was felt, that in the face of such monumental cultural losses, the one foundation, Holy Scripture, must be defended and propounded singly, and as never before. Thought and reflection in areas other than orthodoxy, and a rather truncated orthodoxy at that, were often stunted and isolated. Strong's theology continued to be read, but mainly as a source book for orthodoxy and not sensitively for all its masterful engagement with philosophy and culture. The soldier does not concern himself with worldly affairs.

It has been left to another generation to write theology with the breadth that Strong gave to his *Systematic Theology.*

Bibliography

Works by Strong

American Poets and Their Theology. Philadelphia: Griffith and Rowland Press, 1916.

[Annual Alumni Dinner Address (title varies)]. *Rochester Theological Seminary Record* 1 (1906)-7 (1912).

Annual Report of the New York Baptist Union for Ministerial Education. "Report of the President." Rochester NY: 1895-1912.

Appreciation [of William Rainey Harper]. *Biblical World* 27 (1916): 235-36.

Autobiography of Augustus Hopkins Strong [1896, 1906, 1908, 1917]. Edited by Crerar Douglas. Valley Forge, Pa.: Judson Press, 1981. (Handwritten and typed versions are on deposit at the American Baptist Historical Society, Rochester N.Y.)

Christ in Creation and Ethical Monism. Philadelphia: Roger Williams Press, 1899.

"Confessions of Our Faith." *Watchman-Examiner,* 9 July 1921, 910.

The Great Poets and Their Theology. Philadelphia: American Baptist Publication Society, 1897.

Introduction to *Control in Evolution: A Discussion of the Fundamental Principles of Social Order and Progress,* by George F. Wilkins. New York: A. C. Armstrong and Son, 1903.

Lectures on Theology. Rochester, N.Y.: Press of E. R. Andrews, 1876.

"Man a Living Soul." *Rochester Theological Seminary Record* 7 (May 1912): 12-16.

Miscellanies. 2 vols. Philadelphia: Griffith and Rowland Press, 1912.

"Modifications in the Theological Curriculum." *American Journal of Theology* 3 (1899): 326-30.

"My Views of the Universe in General." *Baptist* 1 (29 May 1920): 625-26.

One Hundred Chapel-Talks to Theological Students Together with Two Autobiographical Addresses. Philadelphia: Griffith and Rowland Press, 1913.

Philosophy and Religion: A Series of Addresses, Essays, and Sermons Designed to Set Forth Great Truths in Popular Form. New York: A. C. Armstrong and Son, 1888.

Philosophy and Religion. 2d ed. New York: Griffith and Rowland Press, 1912.

Popular Lectures on the Books of the New Testament. Philadelphia: Griffith and Rowland Press, 1914.

Review of *Theories of the Will in the History of Philosophy* by Archibald Alexander. *American Journal of Theology* 3 (1899): 344-46.

Systematic Theology: A Compendium and Commonplace Book Designed for the Use of Theological Students. Rochester, N.Y.: Press of E. R. Andrews, 1886.

Systematic Theology. 5th ed., rev. and enl. New York: A. C. Armstrong and Son, 1896.

Systematic Theology, 6th ed., rev. and enl. New York: A. C. Armstrong and Son, 1899.

Systematic Theology. 7th ed., rev. and enl. New York: A. C. Armstrong and Son, 1902.

Systematic Theology. 3 vols. 8th ed., rev. and enl. Philadelphia: Griffith and Rowland Press, 1907-09. Reprint (3 vols. in 1). Old Tappan, N.J.: Fleming H. Revell, 1970.

A Tour of the Missions: Observations and Conclusions. Philadelphia: Griffith and Rowland Press, 1918.

The Uncertainty of Life: A Sermon Preached in the First Baptist Church, Cleveland [OH], *January 28, 1866.* N.p.:n.d.

Union with Christ: A Chapter of Systematic Theology. Philadelphia: American Baptist Publication Society, 1913.

[Wilkinson Lectures.] "Five Lectures Delivered in 1921 on the Foundation of the William Cleaver Wilkinson Lectureship." Oak Brook, Ill.: Northern Baptist Theological Seminary, n.d.

What Shall I Believe? A Primer of Christian Theology. New York: Fleming H. Revell, 1922.

Works Related to Strong

"Augustus H. Strong Memorial Number." *Northern Baptist Theological Seminary Bulletin* 9 (December 1921): 6.

"Augustus Hopkins Strong Memorial Number." *Rochester Theological Seminary Bulletin* (supplement, May 1922).

Calvert, John B. "Dr. Strong, the Scholar and Friend." *Watchman-Examiner,* 22 December 1921, 1623.

Carman, Augustine S. "The Legacy of a Life." *Baptist* 10 December 1921, 1420.

Cleaves, Arthur W. "A Great Leader Has Passed." *Baptist* 10 December 1921, 1422.

"Dr. Strong Called Home." *Baptist Banner: The West Virginia State Paper* 15 December 1921, 6.

"Dr. Strong's Last Work." *Watchman-Examiner* 8 December 1921, 1551.

Heinrichs, Jacob. "Dr. Strong and Foreign Missions." *Watchman-Examiner* 22 December 1921, 1622.

"Immortality of Influence." *Baptist Observer: Official Paper of Indiana Baptists* 22 December 1921, 2.

Laws, Curtis Lee. "Dr. Augustus Hopkins Strong." *Watchman-Examiner* 8 December 1921, 1549.

"Rev. Dr. A. H. Strong Dead." *New York Times,* 3 December 1921, 13.

[Obituary]. *Democrat and Chronicle* (Rochester NY), 30 November 1921.

Taft, George W. "Augustus H. Strong." *Baptist* 10 December 1921, 1420.

Notes

1. Grant Wacker, *Augustus H. Strong and the Dilemma of Historical Consciousness* (Macon GA: Mercer, 1985), xiv, ". . . I was first attracted to Strong because the questions that troubled him are pretty much the same questions that trouble me. At the same time, the answers Strong eventually settled on, imperfect as they may be, are pretty much the answers that I, too, have come to accept."

2. Ibid., 4-6; cf. the very fine biographical sketch by S. Fraser Langford. "The Gospel of Augustus H. Strong and Walter Rauschenbusch," *The Chronicle* 14 (1931): 3-18.

3. Strong, *Systematic Theology,* 1:1-2; quoted in Wacker, 47; cf. Sydney E. Ahlstrom, "The Scottish Philosophy and American Theology," *Church History* 24 (1955): 259, regarding the eighteenth century ". . . it is more accurate to see the Scottish Philosophers as a liberal vanguard, even as theological revolutionaries, than to preserve the traditional picture of genteel conservatives bringing reason to the service of a decadent orthodoxy." The reading of the Scottish philosophers in American seminaries in the nineteenth century moderated strict doctrinal traditions time and again in order to destroy metaphysical heresies. Ahlstrom observes that even Charles Hodge was "caught up in the anthropocentrism of Scottish Philosophy" (266).

4. Strong, *Systematic Theology,* 7:13.

5. Strong, A. H. *Christ in Creation and Ethical Monism* (Philadelphia: Roger Williams Press, 1899), 7, 8, 10.

6. Ibid., 20-23.

7. Ibid., 25, 45.

8. Ibid., 53; italics mine; cf. 85, "My doctrine, then, is psychological dualism combined with metaphysical or philosophical monism."

9. Ibid., 78.

10. Ibid., 80-84.

11. *Systematic Theology,* 762.

12. A. H. Strong, *What Shall I Believe? A Primer of Christian Theology* (Westwood, N.J.: Revell, 1922), 49; cited in Irwin Reist, "Augustus Hopkins Strong and William Newton Clarke: A Study in nineteenth Century Evolutionary and Eschatological Thought," *Foundations* 13 (1970): 32.

13. Strong, *Primer,* 104. Cited in ibid., 36; cf. Strong's *Miscellanies* v. 1, 68 for his affirmation of a literal second coming of Christ.

14. By William Adams Brown in *The American Journal of Theology* 12 (1908): 152; citing Strong from *ST,* 119f. where Strong includes the virgin birth and resurrection of Christ as "none the less works of God when regarded as wrought by the use of natural means . . ."

15. *ST,* 104, 215; in ibid., 153 *ff,* where Brown is quite critical of Strong for not including religious experience in his prolegomena for theology and not consistently applying his philosophical commitments to his entire system of theology.

16. Ibid., 224; quoted in Carl F. H. Henry, *Personal Idealism and Strong's Theology* (Wheaton, Ill.: Van Kampen, 1951), 156. In an address to the mission societies in 1904, Strong said, "There have been changes in our Baptist views of the Scriptures . . . Nowhere does the Bible speak of itself as 'The Word of God.' That phrase designates the truth of which the Bible is the record. . . . in spite of imperfections, its authorship is divine, as well as human. . . . It is not intended to teach physical science or secular history; but it can lead us to Christ and the truth."

17. *ST,* 201.

18. Ibid., 212 *f.*

19. Ibid., 218 *f.*; cf. 220, "The unity and authority of Scripture as a whole are entirely consistent with its gradual evolution and with great imperfection in its nonessential parts." In contradistinction to some contemporary views regarding degrees of inspiration, "There are degrees of value, but not of inspiration. Each part in its connection with the rest is made completely true, and completeness has no degrees.

20. Strong even called Christ the greatest poet. See his *The Great Poets and Their Theology* (Philadelphia: Griffith, 1897) and *The American Poets and Their Theology* (1916), reprint ed. (Freeport, N.Y.: Books for Libraries, 1968); cf. Crerar Douglas, "The Hermeneutics of Augustus Hopkins Strong: God and Shakespeare in Rochester, *Foundations* 21 (1978): 71-6.

21. Quoting Alexander Vinet, *Vital Christianity.* 240 in Op. cit., 267; also 248, 266.

22. Ibid., 343; cf. 330; Strong avers that the Trinity is the proper theistic understanding of God because "Love is an impossible exercise to a solitary being" and "Without Trinity we cannot hold to a living Unity in the Godhead"; 347.

23. Ibid., 440, 397, 402.

24. Ibid., 465-513.

25. Ibid., 620, 622. "We regard this theory of the Natural Headship of Adam as the most satisfactory . . . It puts the most natural interpretation upon Rom. 5:12-21"; 554, 573-77, 593; cf. 635 where Strong refers to the "mystery of imputation" and prefers to stress the justice of God over His sovereignty. On 660 *f.* he states his belief that the penalty of God is eternal and entails spiritual and physical "positive retribution," though this will be spared infants through the grace of Christ and the compassion of God.

26. Ibid., 693, 673-84.

27. Ibid., 757. It is, however, only the guilt of Adam which Christ assumed, not personal guilt.

28. Ibid., 762, 198. In "Fifty Years of Theology," *Christ in Creation.* . . . cf. 771 where Strong also makes the point that the *atonement* is not limited but the *application* of the atonement through the work of the Holy Spirit.

29. Ibid., 795. "There is great need of rescuing the doctrine from neglect."

30. Ibid., 806.

31. Ibid., 887-980.

32. Ibid., 981-1056.

33. From "The New Theology," in his collection of essays, *Philosophy and Religion* (New York: Armstrong, 1888), 171.

34. Cf. ibid., 179.

Benajah Harvey Carroll

James Spivey

Biography

Benajah Harvey Carroll, the seventh of thirteen children, was born December 27, 1843, near Carrollton in Carroll County, Mississippi. His parents, Benajah and Mary Eliza (Mallad), raised twelve children to maturity and adopted twelve more on the meager income of a bivocational Baptist minister-farmer.[1] When Harvey was six, his family moved to Drew County, Arkansas, and he began school in Monticello. Though from a truly devout family, he felt strangely alienated from religion. At thirteen he was "converted" and baptized at a revival meeting, but realizing that this had been merely a catechetical exercise, he remained an avowed "infidel."[2] He imbibed Rousseau, Paine, Hume, and Voltaire, yet he also read the Bible several times and studied the great Christian theologians. He was no atheist, pantheist, or materialist; evolutionism he disregarded as "a godless, materialistic anti-climax of philosophy."[3] He explained ". . . my infidelity related to the Bible and its manifest doctrines. I doubted that it was God's book . . . . I doubted miracles. I doubted the divinity of Jesus of Nazareth . . . . I doubted his vicarious expiation . . . . I doubted any real power and vitality in the Christian religion."[4]

In December 1858 the Carrolls moved West. Riding the family mule, Harvey led the way and scouted the entire journey to Burleson County, Texas. At sixteen, after just six months of school in Caldwell, he entered old Baylor University at Independence as a junior. There he became a renowned debater aspiring to a legal career, but the war interrupted those plans—permanently.

Carroll debated persuasively against secession, but eventually his Southern loyalty caused him to enlist. In April 1861, only weeks before graduation,[5] he volunteered for McCullough's Rangers, the first regiment mustered into Confederate service. Soon, double tragedy struck. In November, Harvey was summoned from the Texas frontier to visit his dying father. While on emergency leave, he fell in love with a fifteen-year-old Caldwell girl, and they were married December 13, 1861. However, she refused to return to West Texas with him, and during the next two years she made it clear she had never loved him. The fact that a jury granted him a divorce because of her infidelity was no consolation to Harvey.[6] After this and his father's death, he lamented, ". . . it blasted every hope and left me in Egyptian darkness. The battle of life was lost. In seeking the field of war, I sought death. . . . I had my church connection dissolved, and turned utterly away from every semblance of Bible belief. In the hour of my darkness I turned unreservedly to infidelity.[7]

Immediately, he enlisted in the Seventeenth Texas Infantry Regiment which was deploying to Arkansas and Louisiana. Carroll threw himself into the heat of every battle. At the battle of Mansfield (April 8, 1864) a huge 'Minnie ball' grazed his femoral artery, and for weeks his life "hung upon a very brittle thread."[8] For him the war was over. While convalescing in Burleson County, he opened a school at Yellow Prairie and then moved it to Caldwell.[9]

In 1865 Reconstruction austerity crippled the skeptic with debt, and his confidence in secular philosophy evaporated on the blistering, drought-ridden Texas plains. As he desperately searched Scripture, Ecclesiastes and Job gripped him with "unearthly power": "and like Job, regarding God as my adversary, I cried out for a revelation."[10] Though he had vowed never again to enter church, that autumn his mother persuaded him to attend a Methodist camp meeting. The sermon left Carroll cold, but the closing appeal burned through his soul. The minister's exhortation "to make a practical, experiential test" of Christianity and his unique translation of John 7:17 opened Harvey's eyes: ". . . the knowledge as to whether doctrine was of God depended not upon external action and not upon exact conformity with God's will, but upon the internal disposition—'whosoever willeth or wishes to do God's will.'"[11]

He mentally committed himself to the "experiment," but his heart still hesitated. After the meeting, Carroll was overcome by a vision which accompanied his recollection of Jesus' invitation in Matthew 11:28. That evening Carroll became convinced that God was calling him to preach.[12] A few days later, he was baptized by his former Baylor schoolmate, W. W. "Spurgeon" Harris, in Caldwell.[13] Dove Baptist Church confirmed Carroll's call by licensing and ordaining him in 1866.[14]

Soon Harvey began to court seventeen-year-old Ellen Virginia Bell, whose family had moved from Starkville, Mississippi. On December 28, 1866, Carroll's college president and friend, R. C. Burleson, married them at the Caldwell church. Still burdened with debt, during the next three years Carroll barely provided for his growing family[15] as a schoolteacher, supply preacher, itinerant evangelist, and part-time pastor of Post Oaks Church in Burleson County. Finally, after a failed farming venture, he determined to make it as a full-time minister. In the fall of 1869 he was called as pastor of New Hope Baptist Church at Goat Neck, McLennan County. His reputation as a preacher spread rapidly. Early in 1870 he agreed to preach twice monthly at nearby First Baptist Church of Waco in the absence of the interim pastor, Dr. Burleson. After a year, that church called him as pastor, and he served there for twenty-eight years.

That year Orceneth Fisher, a highly reputed Methodist polemicist, was baiting Baptists from the pulpit of Fifth Street Methodist Church in Waco. Not to be intimidated, in April Carroll defeated Fisher at a well-publicized

Benajah Harvey Carroll (1834-1914)

Photo courtesy of Southwestern Baptist Theological Seminary

debate in Davilla. The *Texas Baptist Herald* printed accounts of this debate for the next eighteen months and made the young Waco pastor an instant Texas Baptist hero. Carroll gained notoriety throughout the Southern Baptist Convention.[16]

His growing reputation never equaled the man himself. He became one of those truly larger than life personalities who capture the attention of even casual observers. Strikingly handsome with his Moses-like beard, he was physically impressive. Standing six feet and four inches tall and weighing 250 pounds, his bearing was always erect and stately. His strong voice and persuasive oratorical style personified self-assurance. According to W. W. Barnes, he ". . . considered himself as much the agent of God as did any of the Biblical characters, with his abilities directed by a conscious knowledge of the mind of God and led by the Spirit he was irresistible. He had much of the mystic in his conscious contact with the Divine."[17]

Above all, B. H. Carroll was a great preacher and pastor. Comparing him with Chrysostom, George W. Truett described his former pastor as "the greatest preacher our State has ever known."[18] J. B. Cranfill claimed that his oratorical style equaled that of such giants as John Broadus, Henry Ward Beecher, William Jennings Bryan, and Woodrow Wilson.[19] But his real strengths were his practical teaching style and his biblical exposition.[20] His preaching influenced two generations of Baylor ministerial students, provided material for eighteen volumes of sermons, and laid the foundation for his exegetical summa, *An Interpretation of the English Bible*. Each week, many pastors eagerly awaited the delivery of their Baptist newspapers in order to glean from his latest published sermons.

Carroll did the entire work of a pastor: he indoctrinated, oversaw discipline, and managed all special collections. He conducted his own annual revival meetings, and with great results: the 1893 meeting resulted in hundreds joining the Waco church and the spreading of revival to every church in the city.[21] In an age when most Baptists disregarded organization, he efficiently marshaled church resources. First Baptist became a great church-planting institution. At one time, it provided half of the salaries of the Waco Association missionaries and one-third of all home, state, and foreign mission contributions in Texas. During his tenure, the church added 2,325 members and became one of the largest in the state.[22] J. M. Dawson, a successor, attested to his indelible influence: "B. H. Carroll's pastoral work abides . . . I have found his deep, abiding footprints everywhere about here. He hovers like a great, benign, inspiring spirit over us all."[23]

Carroll's ministry extended also to the social needs of Waco and Texas. During 1885-86, he led the McLennan County antiliquor forces to victory in a local option election. The following year he organized the state prohibition effort. During these campaigns he was a daunting opponent in debates against U.S. Senators Roger Q. Mills and Richard Coke and Governor L. S. Ross.[24] In 1894 he led the Waco ministers in opposing the Sunday opening of the Cotton Palace.[25] Neither pleas of economic necessity from his own members, nor Burleson's opposition,[26] nor personal threats could force his retreat.[27] He was ever a champion of civic righteousness. So powerful was his influence that one of his members, Governor Pat Neff, declared that Carroll lived vicariously in the governor's office during Neff's term.[28]

L. R. Scarborough's reference to Carroll as a "kingdom builder"[29] appropriately describes his denominational work. He served as chairman of several Waco Association committees and boards, the most important being his presidency of the Mission Board (1874-88 and 1889-92). For most of 1871-85 he was elected vice-president of the Baptist General Association of Texas under Burleson's presidency. As chairman of a BGA special committee (1883), Carroll began consolidating Texas Baptist work. During the next three years he influenced Texas Baptists to form the Baptist General Convention of Texas (BGCT) and to unify their newspapers, Sunday School conventions, women's work, and their two largest universities.[30] In 1894, when the Texas mission board was disintegrating financially, Carroll took a three-month furlough, and, with George Truett's aid, raised over $7,000 to keep the board solvent.[31]

A conspicuous figure in Southern Baptist life, for thirty years Carroll preached at almost every annual meeting, and in 1878 he delivered the Convention sermon. Besides his extensive committee work, he was the Texas member of the Foreign Mission Board for years and a trustee of The Southern Baptist Theological Seminary (1894-1911). Denominational leaders relied on his advice at almost every critical juncture: hence, John R. Sampey's comment to him, "you are now—since Broadus is gone—our natural leader in the Southern Convention."[32] He convinced Texas Baptists to align with the Southern Home Mission Board (HMB) rather than with the Northern Home Mission Society, which promised greater financial aid. In 1888 his Convention address at Richmond persuaded messengers to give the HMB their vote of full confidence instead of dismantling it. Two years later at Fort Worth, his oratorical skills helped J. M. Frost convince the Convention to establish its own Sunday School Board. Likewise, in Chattanooga (1906), he turned the tide in favor of establishing a Department of Evangelism in the Home Mission Board.[33]

Carroll's strong denominational position often led him into troubled waters. The evangelist Matthew T. Martin, whose theology already had been challenged in the *Texas Baptist and Herald* (1884), joined Carroll's church in 1886 and used it as his base of operations. In 1889, when it became apparent that his teachings were truly heterodox and that he presented a threat to Texas Baptists, Carroll used his influence to lift Martin's credentials and temporarily to disfellowship the Marlin Church when it restored his ordination.[34]

Next came the Landmark attacks on Texas missions. From the moment T. P. Crawford launched his independent Gospel Mission Movement (1892), Carroll recognized its subversiveness. He used his furlough (1894) to rally statewide support behind the Foreign Mission Board, and Crawford's momentum in Texas stalled.[35] That year Samuel Hayden, editor of the *Texas Baptist and Herald* began attacking the state mission board. His subsequent confrontation with Carroll resulted in Hayden's expulsion from the BGCT

(1897) and the formation of a rival organization, the Baptist Missionary Association (1900). Unfortunately, Carroll's close friend R. C. Burleson supported Hayden.[36]

Another controversy focused on William H. Whitsitt, professor of church history and president of Southern Seminary. Landmark sentiments were kindled against him in 1895 when he suggested his theory that American and English Baptists had not immersed prior to 1641. Though he disagreed with Whitsitt's "literary and historic criticism,"[37] Carroll avoided open confrontation until, as a trustee, he was pressured by his Texas constituency to take action. Advising restraint, he recommended that the trustees judiciously investigate the case at the Wilmington Convention (1897). When they glossed over the matter at that meeting, he believed his only alternative was to "go public" with the facts and to encourage renewed public discussion of the issue. From then he became identified as a leader of the anti-Whitsitt party which brought about the professor's resignation in 1898.[38]

Carroll said that his role in denominational controversy served one purpose: to promote unity. Facing Hayden in 1896, he exhorted Texas Baptists to affirm the purposes of their convention: harmony of feeling, concert of action, and a system of operative measures to promote missions.[39] He saw the real issue in the Whitsitt dispute as the threat of "breaking up of Southern unity, and the quite possible dismemberment of the convention."[40]

Carroll's most influential legacy was his gift of theological education. Though he never attended a seminary, he was a profound student of theology. A voracious reader, he read about 300 pages a day for over fifty years.[41] He did not have a photographic memory, but he could remember virtually every pertinent fact he had ever read and was able to cite its reference with phenomenal accuracy. J. B. Gambrell described him as having "the most capacious mind I have met in my life . . . He was an intellectual Colossus."[42] This was confirmed by his honorary degrees: M.A. from Baylor University, D.D. from the University of Tennessee, and LL.D. from Keatchie College, Louisiana.[43]

From his first days in Waco, he helped to educate other Baptist ministers. In 1871 he accepted the chairmanship of the General Association Committee for Schools and Education and began raising $30,000 for the endowment of Waco University.[44] Possibly as early as 1872 he assisted President Burleson in teaching ministerial students. They gathered in his study where he tutored them in the English Bible, J. M. Pendleton's *Church Manual,* and Robert's *Rules of Order.* Eventually, this developed into a well-rounded theological course of the university curriculum.[45]

When Baylor University at Waco was chartered, Carroll was elected president of the trustees—a position he held for over twenty years (1887-1907). In 1891 he enlisted the help of George Truett to liquidate Baylor's debt. Within two years they raised the required $90,000, enabling the university to expand. When a Bible Department was formed (1894) and Carroll was appointed to the Chair of Exegesis and Systematic Theology, he was in the unique position of working for the institution he governed. He also continued as pastor of First Baptist Church until shortly after his wife's death (1897). Just over a year later, his brother James prevailed upon him to resign the pastorate and to head the Texas Baptist Education Commission.[46] While in that office (1899-1902), he became the dean of the Bible Department and married one of his former parishioners, Hallie Harrison, the daughter of General Tom Harrison.[47]

Carroll's crowning achievement for theological education grew out of a vision he had in 1905 while traveling by train in the Panhandle of Texas. Believing Christ had commissioned him to establish a theological seminary in the Southwest, he immediately began to raise funds. In August he obtained the Baylor trustees' approval to constitute Baylor Theological Seminary and to start classes that fall. The faculty consisted of Carroll, A. H. Newman, L. W. Doolan, C. B. Williams, and Calvin Goodspeed. The state convention at San Antonio (1907) voted to separate the seminary from Baylor University, and it was chartered as Southwestern Baptist Theological Seminary in Waco on May 14, 1908. That year Carroll created the first Chair of Evangelism in any seminary. The "Chair of Fire," as he called it,[48] was filled by L. R. Scarborough. Finally, the seminary moved to Fort Worth, which had raised $100,000 for its support and provided a suitable site just south of the city: with a faculty of seven and 126 students, Carroll's dream was fulfilled when the doors of the new campus opened on Monday, October 3, 1910.[49]

B. H. Carroll died November 11, 1914, and was buried in Oakwood Cemetery, Waco, Texas. His deathbed commission to his successor, Scarborough, provides a succinct commentary on Carroll's theology:

> Lee, keep the Seminary lashed to the cross. If heresy ever comes in the teaching, take it to the faculty. If they will not hear you and take prompt action, take it to the trustees of the Seminary. If they will not hear you, take it to the Convention that appoints the Board of Trustees, and if they will not hear you, take it to the great common people of our churches. You will not fail to get a hearing then.[50]

Exposition

Carroll's concern for doctrinal purity was a driving force in his three ministerial roles. At the First Baptist Church of Waco, he used scriptural exposition to develop a biblical and pastoral theology. As a denominational leader, he employed sermons, editorials, addresses, debates, and private correspondence to propagate a biblical and confessional theology. Also employing a biblical and confessional approach in his teaching role, he used expository lectures, confessions, catechisms, and manuals as his instruments. He was essentially an expositor and polemicist with a biblical-pastoral theology who made little attempt to systematize doctrine. This exposition reconstructs Carroll's theology from his sermons, lectures, and addresses. For a more comprehensive view, it must be read in context with the New Hampshire Confession (revised 1853), which Carroll regularly employed.[51]

Revelation

Carroll acknowledged the traditional categories of general and special revelation. The first, the "revelation of wrath," was of two types: the influence of nature reveals God's providence, and intuitive light makes one cognizant of moral responsibility to God. Three forms comprise special revelation: unwritten, direct communication from God antedating Scripture; God's written Word; and the living Word, Jesus Christ. Though he called these "revelation from God," he also considered general revelation to be of divine origin.[52]

As a young skeptic, far from affirming scriptural authority, Carroll claimed to have detected almost one thousand apparent discrepancies in the Bible. But after conversion and diligent study, he resolved all except six "contradictions," which he attributed to own limited comprehension of God's truth, not to any scriptural fallibility.[53] He held a high view of divine inspiration: God's infallible[54] and inerrant word[55] does not just contain the word of God; it *is* God's very word.[56] He taught verbal, plenary inspiration: every word, not just the idea, is inspired—even down to the vowel points![57] This applies to the whole Bible: it is not inspired just in certain spots,[58] nor are certain passages less inspired than others. Yet, Carroll did not agree with some in his day who said that the entire text should be interpreted literally and that every passage was equally important. Though he conceded that only the originals were inspired, he believed that God had preserved the Bible "in a way that no other book has been preserved."[59]

He said Scripture has two purposes: to reveal salvation and to show Christians how to live.[60] Primacy must be given to the New Testament as the "Law of Christianity," which is God's fulfilled revelation. So Carroll refused to use the Old Testament as a model for Christian ethics or institutions.[61] He affirmed the perspicuity of Scripture: the unfettered, open Book is sufficiently clear to instruct all believers. Thus, he exhorted students, "The Book is open—who of you will read it?"[62] Carroll stood on four hermeneutical principles: (1) Since "the Bible is its own interpreter," view difficult passages in conformity with less ambiguous Scriptures; (2) appropriate biblical truths with faith and obedience in order to fulfill their practical purposes; (3) assurance of right interpretation comes through a maturing relationship with the Lord; (4) reverently appeal to the Holy Spirit for right understanding and application. While asserting that spiritually illuminated individuals should be able to interpret Scripture correctly and make competent decisions, he rejected exclusive, private interpretation.[63] Nor was Carroll a pure biblicist. For the sake of identity, unity, and doctrinal strength, he encouraged the use of covenants and confessions.[64]

The True God

The primary antecedent for all theology and morality is the fact that "God is."[65] Carroll explains this in Trinitarian terms. God is revealed in "three subsistencies," the essence (nature) of which is eternally immanent. This unified Godhead is "the key to every doctrine in the Bible." The distinction in the Trinity is between the persons, who, though equal in divine perfection, have different offices. Regarding office and personal relationships, the Holy Spirit is subordinate to the Son, as the Son is to the Father. He affirmed the "filioque clause" as the true relation of the Holy Spirit to the Father and the Son.[66] The Trinitarian idea is objective truth which is best appropriated by faith in Scripture: rationalistic, psychological explanations by themselves, being too subjective, inevitably yield erroneous doctrine.[67]

Regarding creation, Carroll affirmed that the Trinity made the universe from nothing. Though this was not done in a literal week, each day of creative activity was twenty-four hours long. He accepted Archbishop Usser's dating of the start of the human race at 4004 B.C. He opposed Darwinian evolutionism, but he accepted development within the species as biblical.[69]

Carroll described God's providence as His "direction, control and issue of all the events in the physical and moral universe." It goes beyond foreknowledge; God guides everything in order to accomplish His purpose without impinging on the freedom of moral creatures. Whatever God wills is best, for that will is an extension of Himself, who is the ultimate good.[70] He manifests this will in four ways: through preventive, permissive, directive, and determinative providence. Able to prevent evil, sometimes He permits it by withholding His preventive force. He directs/diverts evil actions, so as to frustrate sinners' intentions; and He determines boundaries which evil cannot transcend.[71] In all cases, God's will is never frustrated.[72] For each person He has a plan, and one's vision of this provides motivation for right action.[73] Man's response to divine providence should be humble, penitent prayer, whereby he discovers God's will on the "zig-zag" road leading to "his destiny on earth and in Heaven."[74]

Concerning the Son, Carroll disagreed with his friend W. C. Buck. Both maintained that the seed of life, as well as sin, comes from the male, not the female. They also agreed that Jesus, being of the Holy Spirit, did not inherit Adam's sin. However, while this led Buck to affirm the Apollinarian idea that Christ did not have a human soul, Carroll followed Broadus's lead in rejecting that heresy. Yet, this does not square with his traducianist anthropology, discussed below.[75] Unlike William Shedd, who distinguished Christ's humanity from His divinity by saying that the Logos exercised limited influence on his body and soul, Carroll argued that the Spirit controlled Jesus' entire being.[76] He emphasized the atonement to such a degree that he ascribed a fourth role to Christ: to prophet, priest, and king he added the "sacrifice."[77]

Carroll described the Holy Spirit's coming in two ways. First, at Pentecost, the Spirit came to "occupy" the existing church and to "accredit" it through miraculous signs. That "baptism of the Spirit" was for the whole church, not just individuals; it was for a limited time, though the "graces" of faith, hope, and love continued. Secondly, the Paraclete, or the "other Jesus" involved in every phase of salvation, came as the "vicar of Christ" with absolute sovereignty over His kingdom. Thus, Carroll exhorted Christians individually to receive the Holy Spirit: not as part of "regenerating grace," this is "a blessing of God entirely distinct from and subsequent to . . . repentance and . . . faith."[78]

Anthropology

Repudiating Darwinianism as a heathen doctrine, Carroll described its Christian advocates as "neither fish not fowl, neither pig not puppy."[79] Scriptural creationism and Darwin were irreconcilable: "There is no ground of compromise . . . The variance is radical, fundamental and vital. Both cannot be true and a mixture is less desirable than either."[80] Christian evolutionists such as Henry Ward Beecher reversed Scripture by saying the higher that man ascends, the more he needs God. Carroll said man needs salvation precisely because he has fallen away from God.[81]

The unity of humanity undergirds the plan of redemption: since all have descended from Adam, for whose descendants the gospel was sent, then to all the gospel must be proclaimed.[82] Rejecting the hyper-Calvinism of Daniel Parker, Carroll argued that the human race had not been divided into the "two seeds" of Eve. Parker's idea opposed Carroll's belief that Adam, not Eve, was ultimately culpable in the Fall. Also, "two-seedism" undercut the plan of redemption by withholding the gospel from the nonelect.[83]

Carroll said that Adam was created physically mortal, but with a provision for eliminating mortality "by continually eating of the tree of life."[84] Man is not a trichotomy. He is body (outer man) and soul (inner man): a dichotomous, yet unified, being. Carroll used the term "spirit," only to distinguish the higher (inner) from the lower (outer, body/soul) nature—thus he is still a dichotomy.[85]

Carroll believed the Fall was a historic event through which Adam became totally depraved; he lost the moral image of God but kept a deathless spirit.[86] Adam, the federal head, has conveyed "original sin" to all persons, who inherit their souls (traducianism) from male issuance, not from female conception. Carroll said that Christ, who had a human soul, did not inherit a depraved nature from an earthly father.[87] But the obvious problem remains unresolved: if the human soul is inherited through the male line, where did Christ get His human soul?

In one sense, Carroll noted, human sin is corporate. Angels are the only beings who sin only individually (i.e., apart from the federal head). Man's sin is also intensely personal, and individuals will be held accountable for their own actions.[88] Still, original sin alone is sufficient to condemn if Christ's grace is not operative; hence, dying infants must be, and by God's grace will be, regenerated.[89] With original sin comes the condemnation of death; with actual sin comes the condemnation of guilt.[90]

Satan is a personal being who, though limited in power, is incomparably stronger than man.[91] His motive for tempting Adam and Eve, Carroll reasoned, was to destroy the new race which had been created to have dominion over the angels.[92] Regarding adversity, Carroll said that temptation comes from Satan, while trials come from God, but often it is difficult to differentiate the two.[93]

Soteriology

Carroll distinguished between the legal (external) and the spiritual (internal) requirements for salvation. He used two formulae to explain this. First, the legal need is fulfilled by redemption, which is two-sided: having (1) made atonement, Christ (2) offers justification. Justification outwardly provides remission of sins; it inwardly expiates guilt. Second, the spiritual need, encompassing regeneration and sanctification, is fulfilled when divine grace evokes human response. The legal and the spiritual requirements meet with the intersection of divine remission and human trust.

Four elements comprise Carroll's soteriological scheme: redemption, atonement, justification, and adoption. Redemption, the buying back of the sinner, is achieved through the atonement and is applied through regeneration. In redemption the legal and the spiritual operations of salvation meet.[94] Christ's atonement was sacrificial, voluntary, vicarious, penal, and satisfactory.[95] It occurred in two stages. Christ paid an expiatory sacrifice to purge sin and to conquer Satan,[96] then He made propitiation before the Father, who reconciled sinners to Himself through the Son's blood.[97] The external application of the atonement is justification. The moment a sinner believes in Christ, he is instantly pronounced just by the Father and his sins are remitted; this is forensic justification.[98] The proclamatory imputation of Christ's righteousness does not mean the sinner is "made" personally righteous; that is done in the spiritual operation of salvation.[99] Carroll distinguished between expiation and justification. Apparently opposing antinomianism, he emphasized that sin also must be *actually* remitted: the cross made the provision, but the fact is not accomplished until the individual believes.[100] He distinguished between justification and pardon: "Justification comes from God's justice; pardon comes from his mercy." Justification is accomplished by payment of the debt, but the debt is still owed to the payee. Pardon results when the payee cancels the debt.[101] Justification, being irrevocable,[102] lays the foundation for adoption. Entry into God's family comes only with belief, but God had foreordained it in eternity.[103]

The spiritual fruit of salvation comes by regeneration and sanctification. Regeneration involves both human and divine action. God acts in two stages: He gives a "holy disposition" to the mind and then purges the defilement.[104] Cleansing begins at the point of belief, when remittance of sin, the legal product of justification, is applied. Cleansing continues throughout life. Preparatory to this, the "holy disposition" comes through divine conviction and prevenient grace. Man, formerly passive, awakens and responds: conviction brings contrition, and grace brings action. The order of action is: prayer, repentance, confession, conversion, and faith. As God's grace meets man's response, new birth occurs.[105] This is not a multistage regeneration. Against M. T. Martin, Carroll strongly repudiated regeneration as a "two-stage" process.[106] Instead, it is a single process which allows an "appreciable time-element between the several exercises."[107]

Each human "exercise" is a response to divine prompting. Contrition, the response to conviction, is godly sorrow which is the point of no return: once the sinner experiences this, God's irresistible grace will draw him to faith.[108] Repentance is the "change of mind toward God on account of sin."[109] Carroll realized that "conversion" is popularly equated with completed regeneration (i.e., to be "saved"). However, he defined it as "right about face," an action which *precedes* faith. Faith, which means "receiving and relying on Him," is the culminating human response in regeneration. Here justification and regeneration, legal and spiritual salvation, intersect.[110]

Sanctification is the other spiritual part of salvation. Regarding it as inseparable from regeneration,[111] Carroll repudiated John Wesley's idea of "second blessing."[112] Going beyond imputed righteousness, sanctification is the process of making the believer *personally* holy. It begins with regeneration and continues until death.[113] Here the contrast between the legal and the spiritual aspects of salvation is sharp. Justification is the forensic pronouncement by the Father which is done in heaven and certified on earth. Sanctification is the Holy Spirit making the believer actually holy; it is done on earth and certified in heaven. Justification is instantaneous and external. Sanctification is progressive and internal.[114]

Ecclesiology

Carroll rejected any concept of a universal church, whether visible or invisible. The church is neither parochial nor a denominational composite of local bodies. He defined it as the spiritual, visible, local assembly of believers who are called out of their homes to organize an autonomous, non-hierarchical, democratic body. Members are admitted through baptism and upon their confession, which give evidence of regeneration.[115] The church is not the kingdom of God. The kingdom is more comprehensive, and the church is an institution within the kingdom.[116] The purpose of the church is to fulfill Christ's mandates. Therefore, as the executive branch of His kingdom, it is first a missionary organization.[117] As the judicial arm, it maintains spiritual discipline.[118] This current, particular church is different from the "glory church," which will become a reality only when all the redeemed have been glorified.[119]

The two ordinances are the ceremonial aspects of salvation: baptism symbolizes regeneration; the Lord's Supper represents sanctification.[120] For baptism to be valid, four requirements must be met: (1) the proper authority, the church, administers it; (2) the proper subject is the penitent believer; (3) the proper act is immersion; and (4) the proper design is symbolic, with no trace of baptismal regeneration. Salvation precedes baptism, not vice versa. Though time may be allowed between the two events for catechizing, baptism is still a prerequisite for communion. Allowing no "alien baptism," Carroll accepted only members baptized in a Baptist church.[121] At the Lord's Supper he emphasized commemoration more than fellowship. Yet, he practiced "close communion," even to the point of forbidding communicants to sit with nonparticipants during the ceremony. Unlike Landmarkers, Carroll allowed Baptists from other churches to commune in Waco.[122]

The pastor and the deacons are the ordained officers of the church. Other unordained officers such as the clerk and the sexton may be employed. The deacons are not a ministerial order, a board of directors, a disciplinary body, or a pulpit committee. Their purpose is to assist the chief officer, the pastor, so that he has more time for ministerial functions. The deaconess is also a legitimate office, but she is not to be ordained; neither is a woman to be a pastor, to pray in open assembly, nor to teach in a position of authority over men.[123]

Under Christ as its head, the church is an autocracy. Its human government is a pure democracy, with all members being equal and sharing in autonomous rule. However, this does not mean the church can do anything it desires with majority approval. In as much as it is still subject to the law of Christ, Carroll agreed with J. R. Graves: "Principles, not majorities, constitute a church."[124]

Much of Carroll's ecclesiology resembled Landmarkism. He praised J. M. Pendleton, J. R. Graves, and A. C. Dayton as "the great Baptist trio of the South," and he used Pendleton's *Church Manual* as his text for ecclesiology lectures.[125] Carroll's definition of the church as a particular assembly and his rejection of the universal church are Landmark tenets. Though admitting it was impossible to verify, he believed in a succession of true churches since the apostolic era. He suggested these were Baptist churches and that John was the "first Baptist."[126] However, his disagreement with Whitsitt was not prompted by a strong advocacy of successionism. Furthermore, Carroll staunchly opposed Landmarkers like Crawford and Hayden because they threatened Baptist solidarity and the viability of organized missions. Certain of his practices opposed Landmarkism. He encouraged associational discipline and cooperation. His "close communion" was less restrictive, and he refused to equate the local churches with the kingdom of God.

Eschatology[127]

Carroll greatly emphasized this doctrine, especially the millennium. What seemed insignificant to others, he described as fundamental to all interpretation. He was a postmillennialist who said his position, being found in virtually every major Christian creed, represented the majority of Christendom. Though he respected certain premillennialists such as C. H. Spurgeon, D. L. Moody, A. J. Gordon, and J. R. Graves, he described their eschatology as dogmatic, complicated, stereotypical, and shallow. On the other hand, he opposed radical critics intent on minimizing the supernatural, prophetic element in the Book of Revelation. By his silence on the subject, Carroll disregarded amillennialism altogether.[128]

Carroll described postmillennialism as being remarkably simple. In heaven Christ reigns over His mediatorial kingdom and intercedes as High

Priest. His vicar, the Holy Spirit, applies salvation through preaching of the gospel by the churches. In the future, the millennium will be ushered in by the triumph of the gospel: Satan will be bound; the Jews will be converted in a day; a mighty outpouring of the Spirit will occur; and there will be universal peace and prosperity. This will conclude with the loosing of Satan, who, as the Antichrist will oppress Christians briefly. Then Christ will return victoriously with: one general resurrection of the just and the unjust; judgment, with degrees of reward and punishment pronounced from the great white throne; and the purging of wickedness from the world by a baptism of fire. Finally, the saints will inherit the new earth, and Christ will return the kingdom to the Father.[129] This scheme undergirds Carroll's soteriology and ecclesiology. Progressive sanctification points to the consummation of the kingdom.[130] Societal transformation and the reign of peace depend on the church fulfilling its missionary purpose—preaching the gospel.[131] He said premillennialism practically relegated the gospel to failure and undercut the motivation for missions.[132] Conversely, he criticized postmillennialists who deemphasized the Parousia. He avoided this error by teaching the "personal, real, visible, audible, palpable, tangible coming of the Lord Jesus Christ."[133]

Evaluation

"President Carroll, Bible in hand, standardized orthodoxy in Texas. He rallied the hosts of Baptists to the vital, ruling doctrines of the Holy Scriptures."[134] Thus J. B. Gambrell identified a common thread in Carroll's roles as pastor, denominational leader, and Christian educator. In each area, he championed Christian truth and Baptist unity, faith, and practice. Like Irenaeus, he was a pastor-polemicist who developed a strong, biblical theology to defeat heresy and schism. His doctrine of revelation developed in reaction to Christian modernists.[135] He developed soteriological responses to Martinism, the Methodist "second blessing," and Campbellite views on regeneration.[136] The antimissionism of Campbell and Daniel Parker evoked strong ecclesiological statements from Carroll,[137] as did the Whitsitt, Hayden, and Crawford controversies. Christian Science doctrine was targeted in his writings on pneumatology,[138] and his entire hermeneutical scheme was at variance with that of the premillennialists.[139]

Carroll's theology was influenced most by other conservative Baptists, especially Boyce, Strong, Spurgeon, and Broadus, whose catechism he recommended highly.[140] To say that he was a conservative evangelical is not adequate. Though the term was not yet in vogue, he could be described as a "Fundamentalist." His doctrine agreed with the basic tenets of *The Fundamentals* (1910-15), and he thoroughly disdained modernists as "cuckoos of infidelity." This antipathy was directed against Northern liberals when he encouraged a group of fundamentalist Illinois Baptists to seek admission to the SBC (1910). Led by Landmarker, W. P. Throgmorton, they had intended to align with Ben Bogard, a sympathizer with Carroll's nemesis, Samuel Hayden. In spite of strong resistance from some Southern Baptists, they were admitted partly because of Carroll's support.[141] The influence of Graves, Pendleton, and Dayton still embraced Carroll. Of "Landmarkish" convictions, he imbibed their ultraconservatism and much of their ecclesiology, but he could never abide their fissiparous spirit, especially regarding missions.

Carroll was a Calvinist in line with the moderate tone of the New Hampshire Confession. He said man, as totally depraved, has lost God's moral image but retains a "deathless spirit."[142] He held a supralapsarian view of single election: from eternity God unconditionally elected some for salvation. The nonelect were not chosen for reprobation; they simply have not been given grace efficient for salvation. The human race was never divided into two irrevocably predetermined lots.[143] On limited atonement Carroll was not rigid: Christ's death is certainly effective for the elect, and though He died for all, everyone will not be saved.[144] He made allowance for those who had not heard the gospel by stating that at the final judgment, "Each man is judged according to his light, privileges, opportunities, and environment . . . [and] one's attitude toward Christ in his gospel, his cause and his people."[145] The irresistibility of God's grace operates from the moment of contrition to bring the sinner to salvation.[146] Believers will surely persevere, and though assurance is not required for salvation, it is ascertainable.[147] This scheme eschewed any hint of antinomianism or hyper-Calvinism.[148]

J. W. Crowder described Carroll's written works as "A fine, juicy, comprehensive, Systematic Theology."[149] But Carroll systematized very little. Of the works published during his lifetime, all except two are on miscellaneous topics. Only *Baptists and their Doctrines* and *The Bible Doctrine of Repentance* resemble systematic studies. The nearest Carroll's work came to being "systematized" was through the editing of Crowder and J. B. Cranfill. They published 248 sermons by subject in eighteen volumes: these contain the essence of Carroll's pastoral theology. Their publication of his exegetical lectures in *An Interpretation of the English Bible* made his biblical theology available. Most of the truly systematic work is contained in the typewritten manuscripts edited by Crowder. These reveal that Carroll's main theological interests were ecclesiology, soteriology, eschatology, and revelation.

Carroll's great strength as a theologian was his conviction that ". . . doctrine must be so received by faith and assimilated by obedience as to become experimental knowledge. 'Whosoever willeth to do the will of God shall know of the doctrine whether it be of God.'" This was the Methodist revivalist's text from thirty-seven years before. Since that time Carroll had remained true to "experiential" religion and had urged his church members to do the same:

> Hence the prayer that the eyes of their understanding might be open to see the fullness [of God], their faith increased to grasp and appropriate it, their graces enlarged to corresponding strength to stand and work in that fullness. So fulfilled they realize in *experience* the fact that the Holy Spirit in all the fullness of God had already entered this particular body of Christ, and was only waiting to be recognized.[150]

W. T. Conner said the two ideals which controlled Carroll's life were "an authoritative Bible and the reality of Christian experience."[151] This completes the picture. For Carroll theology was a practical tool for edifying and equipping the church. His basis was the Bible, which shows, "first, how to be saved, and second, what saved people should believe and do."[152] From it he formulated a biblical-pastoral theology of practical value which called the church to evangelism and ethical responsibility.

Bibliography

Works by Carroll

Ambitious Dreams of Youth. Compiled by J. W. Crowder and edited by J. B. Cranfill. Dallas: Helms Printing Co., 1939.

Baptists and Their Doctrines. Compiled by J. B. Cranfill. New York: Fleming H. Revell Co., 1913.

The Bible Doctrine of Repentance. Louisville: Baptist Book Concern, 1897.

Christ and His Church. Compiled by J. W. Crowder and edited by J. B. Cranfill. Dallas: Helms Printing Co., 1940.

Christian Education and Some Social Problems, Sermons. Compiled and edited by J. W. Crowder. Ft. Worth: n.p., 1948.

Christ's Marching Orders. Compiled by J. W. Crowder and edited by J. B. Cranfill. Dallas: Helms Printing Co., 1941.

The Day of the Lord. Compiled by J. W. Crowder and edited by J. B. Cranfill. Nashville: Broadman Press, 1936.

Evangelistic Sermons. Compiled by J. B. Cranfill. New York: Fleming H. Revell Co., 1913.

The Faith that Saves. Compiled by J. W. Crowder and edited by J. B. Cranfill. Dallas: Helms Printing Co., 1939.

The Holy Spirit. Compiled by J. W. Crowder and edited by J. B. Cranfill. Grand Rapids, Mich.: Zondervan Publishing House, 1939.

Inspiration of the Bible. Compiled and edited by J. B. Cranfill. New York: Fleming H. Revell Co., 1930.

An Interpretation of the English Bible. 17 vols. Edited by J. B. Cranfill and J. W. Crowder. New York: Fleming H. Revell, Nashville: Broadman Press, 1913-1948.

Jesus the Christ. Compiled by J. W. Crowder and edited by J. B. Cranfill. Nashville: Baird-Ward Press, 1937.

Messages on Prayer. Compiled by J. W. Crowder and edited by J. B. Cranfill. Nashville: Broadman Press, 1942.

Patriotism and Prohibition. Compiled and edited J. W. Crowder. Ft. Worth: n.p., 1952.

The Providence of God. Compiled by J. W. Crowder and edited by J. B. Cranfill. Dallas: Helms Printing Co., 1940.

Revival Messages. Compiled by J. W. Crowder and edited by J. B. Cranfill. Grand Rapids, Mich.: Zondervan Publishing House, 1939.

The River of Life and Other Sermons. Compiled and edited by J. B. Cranfill. Nashville: The Sunday School Board of the S.B.C., 1928.

Saved to Serve. Compiled by J. W. Crowder and edited by J. B. Cranfill. Dallas: Helms Printing Co., 1941.

Sermons and Life Sketch of B. H. Carroll. Compiled by J. B. Cranfill. Philadelphia: American Baptist Publication Society, 1893.

Studies in Genesis. Nashville: Broadman Press, 1937.

Studies in Romans. Nashville: The Sunday School Board of the S.B.C., 1935.

Studies in Romans, Ephesians, and Colossians. By B. H. Carroll and E. Y. Mullins. Nashville: Broadman Press, 1936.

The Supper and Suffering of Our Lord. Compiled and edited by J. W. Crowder. Ft. Worth: n.p., 1947.

The Ten Commandments. Nashville: Broadman Press, 1938.

The Way of the Cross. Compiled by J. W. Crowder, edited by J. B. Cranfill. Dallas: Helms Printing Co., 1941.

Works about Carroll

Baker, Robert A. *Tell the Generations Following. A History of Southwestern Baptist Theological Seminary, 1908-1983*. Nashville: Broadman Press, 1983.

Cates, J. Dee. "B. H. Carroll: The Man and His Ethics." Th.D. diss., Southwestern Baptist Theological Seminary, 1962.

Cogburn, Keith Lynn. "B. H. Carroll and Controversy: A Study of his Leadership among Texas Baptists, 1871-1899." M.A. thesis, Baylor University, 1983.

Crowder, J. W., comp. and ed. *Dr. B. H. Carroll, the Colossus of Baptist History*. Fort Worth: By the editor, 1946.

Ray, Jeff. *B. H. Carroll*. Nashville: The Sunday School Board of the S.B.C., 1927.

Robinson, Robert Jackson. "The Homiletical Method of Benajah Harvey Carroll." Th.D. diss., Southwestern Baptist Theological Seminary, 1956.

Stewart, Wilson Lannin. "Ecclesia: The Motif of B. H. Carroll's Theology." Th.D. diss., Southwestern Baptist Theological Seminary, 1959.

Watson, Tom L. "The Eschatology of B. H. Carroll." M.Th. thesis, Southwestern Baptist Theological Seminary, 1960.

Notes

1. J. M. Carroll, "B. H. Carroll," in *Dr. B. H. Carroll the Colossus of the North,* ed. J. W. Crowder (Fort Worth: By the editor, 1946), 13. Hereafter *Colossus.*

2. B. H. Carroll, "My Infidelity and What Became of It," in *Sermons and Life Sketch of B. H. Carroll, D.D.,* ed. J. B. Cranfill (Philadelphia: American Baptist Publication Society, 1895), 13-17.

3. Ibid., 14-15.

4. Ibid., 15.

5. Jeff D. Ray, *B. H. Carroll* (Nashville: The Baptist Sunday School Board of the SBC, 1927), 15; W. W. Barnes, "Biography of B. H. Carroll," in Index of the Carroll Collection, Roberts Library, Southwestern Baptist Theological Seminary. Most sources say Carroll never earned a university degree. Ray and Barnes note that Baylor granted him the B.A. in absentia without requiring him to sit examinations.

6. The B. H. Carroll Personal Memorandum Book, 1, file 158 and miscellaneous files 157 and 167 of the Carroll Collection; M. V. Smith, "B. H. Carroll, Pastor of First Baptist Church, Waco," *Texas Baptist Herald,* July 25, 1878, 2; Robert A. Baker, *Tell the Generations Following* (Nashville: Broadman Press, 1983), 59, 105-6; Carroll, in *Colossus,* 13; Wilson L. Stewart, "Ecclesia: The Motif of B. H. Carroll's Theology" (Th.D. diss., Southwestern Baptist Theological Seminary, 1959), 5; Keith L. Cogburn, "B. H. Carroll and Controversy: A Study of His Leadership among Texas Baptists, 1871-1899" (M.A. diss., Baylor University, 1983), 7; Civil Minutes of the District Clerk, Burleson County, Caldwell, Texas; and the correspondence file of Dr. Leon McBeth of Southwestern Baptist Theological Seminary. The marriage license was issued December 11, 1861, to Carroll and O[phelia] A. Crunk, daughter of Nicolas S. Crunk. Harvey allowed his brother to bring suit for him in his absence, and the charges against Ophelia were confirmed November 9, 1863 (see Civil Minutes, Book C, 277). Two days later, she married B. D. Evans (see Burleson County Marriage Records, ii:100).

7. Carroll, "Infidelity," in *Sermons,* 17.

8. Carroll, in *Colossus,* 48.

9. Baker, 60.

10. Ray, 31.

11. Carroll, "Infidelity," in *Sermons,* 21.

12. Ibid., 22-23.

13. Baker, 63.

14. Dove Church Minutes (FBC, Caldwell) show he was to be licensed on the fourth Sunday (27th) of May and ordained on the fourth Sunday (15th) of November.

15. Ray, 46. Eventually they had nine children. Hassie, Ellen, Hallie, and Jimmie died in infancy. Guy Sears died in early adulthood. B. H. Jr., became a U.S. consular official. Charles taught at the New Orleans Baptist Theological Seminary. Kate was a missionary in Brazil. Louise was the wife of a New Mexico ranchman.

16. Cogburn, 16-24; Ray, 120. A similar incident occurred ten years later when Carroll defeated a Disciples opponent named Dr. Wilmeth.

17. Barnes, "Biography."

18. George W. Truett, "B. H. Carroll, The Titanic Champion of the Truth," in *Colossus,* 90.

19. J. B. Cranfill, "The Passing of B. H. Carroll," in *Colossus,* 105.

20. Ray, 74-75, 84-87.

21. Frank E. Burkhalter, *A World-Visioned Church* (Nashville: Broadman Press, 1946), 127-31.

22. Baker, 70-75.

23. Ray, 77.

24. Cogburn, 35-52. See B. H. Carroll, "Temperance Resolutions of *The First Baptist Church of Waco, Texas,* in "Defending the Faith," 113-43.

25. B. H. Carroll, "The Sunday Opening Question," in "Defending the Faith and Practice of Baptists," ed. J. W. Crowder, Roberts Library, Southwestern Baptist

Theological Seminary (typewritten manuscript, 1957), 265-69, gives the ministers' resolutions.

26. Cogburn, 110.

27. George W. McDaniel, "B. H. Carroll, the Colossal Christian," in *Colossus*, 160.

28. Pat M. Neff, "B. H. Carroll, the Champion of a Great Cause," in *Colossus*, 138.

29. L. R. Scarborough, "B. H. Carroll, a Kingdom-Builder," in *Colossus*, 127-29.

30. Robert A. Baker, *The Blossoming Desert, A Concise History of Texas Baptists* (Waco: Word Books, 1970), 134-52. The BGCT consolidated the Baptist General Association with the Baptist State, the East Texas Baptist, the North Texas Baptist Missionary, and the Central Texas Baptist Conventions. Baker, *Generations*, 76, 78-79.

31. Baker, *Generations*, 82-83; Ray, 101-2; Cranfill, *Sermons*, xi. For his sermon on this see B. H. Carroll, "The Indwelling Spirit of God," in *Saved to Serve*, comp. J. W. Crowder and ed. J. B. Cranfill (Dallas: By the editor, 1941), 175-91.

32. Carroll Collection, File 208-1, Letter to B. H. Carroll, August 24, 1896.

33. Ray, 97-101. Robert A. Baker, *The Southern Baptist Convention and Its People, 1607-1972* (Nashville: Broadman Press, 1974), 292-93. For his Chattanooga address (May 14), see B. H. Carroll, "Evangelism," in "Biblical Addresses," comp. J. W. Crowder, Roberts Library, Southwestern Seminary (typewritten manuscript, 1958), 226-44.

34. Cogburn, 54-73.

35. For an account of Crawfordism in one association see B. H. Carroll, "Concerning Grayson County Association (September 30, 1897)," in "Defending the Faith," 339-51.

36. Baker, *Generations*, 81-83; *Southern Baptist Convention*, 278-82; Cogburn, 98-129.

37. B. H. Carroll, "Back to the Realm of Discussion (May 27, 1897)," in "Defending the Faith," 326.

38. Cogburn, 74-97. See also Charles B. Bugg, "The Whitsitt Controversy: A Study in Denominational Conflict" (Th.D. diss., The Southern Baptist Theological Seminary, 1972), and Rosalie Beck, "The Whitsitt Controversy: A Denomination in Crisis" (Ph.D. diss., Baylor University, 1984).

39. B. H. Carroll, "Co-operation (1896)," in "Defending the Faith," 297-98.

40. B. H. Carroll, "The Real Issue in Whitsitt Case," *Texas Baptist Standard*, 5 (August 1897).

41. J. B. Cranfill, "The Passing of B. H. Carroll," in *Colossus*, 106.

42. J. B. Gambrell, "The Home-Going of President Carroll, An Appreciation," in *Colossus*, 101.

43. P. E. Burroughs, "Benajah Harvey Carroll," in *Ten Men from Baylor*, ed. J. M. Price (Kansas City: Central Seminary Press, 1945), 65.

44. Baker, *Generations*, 78; Cogburn, 26-27, 33. Carroll was also a member of the Central Baptist Education Commission of Texas, created to facilitate unification of Baylor and Waco Universities. His reasons for leaving the commission are given in B. H. Carroll, "Withdrawal from the Commission," in "Defending the Faith," 210-19.

45. Ray, 134; Barnes, "Biography."

46. Carroll Collections, File 14, Letter of Resignation (December 31, 1898).

47. Baker, *Generations*, 97-105; Ray 107-14, 127-28. They had one son, Francis Harrison, who became a journalist in Los Angeles.

48. B. H. Carroll, "A Chair of Fire (July 2, 1908)," in "Our Seminary or The Southwestern Baptist Theological Seminary, Fort Worth, Texas," Roberts Library, Southwestern Baptist Theological Seminary (typewritten manuscript, 1957), 307.

49. Baker, *Generations*, 111-59.

50. W. W. Barnes, *The Southern Baptist Convention, 1845-1953* (Nashville: Broadman Press, 1954), 209.

51. B. H. Carroll, "Baptist Church Polity and Articles of Faith," comp. J. W. Crowder, Roberts Library, Southwestern Baptist Theological Seminary (typewritten manuscript, 1957), 38, 95 *ff.*; Carroll Collection, File 73, "Safeguards of the Seminary," *Baptist Standard*, June 13, 1910.

52. Stewart, 55-60.

53. B. H. Carroll, *Inspiration of the Bible*, ed. J. B. Cranfill (New York: Fleming H. Revell Co., 1930), 121-22.

54. Carroll, *Inspiration*, 25.

55. B. H. Carroll, *Saved to Serve*, comp. J. W. Crowder and ed. J. B. Cranfill (Dallas: Helms Printing Co., 1941), 16.

56. B. H. Carroll, *An Interpretation of the English Bible*, ed. J. B. Cranfill and J. W. Crowder (Nashville: Broadman Press, 1947), 1:9.

57. Carroll, *Inspiration*, 84.

58. Ibid., 54.

59. Carroll, *Inspiration*, 26-27; Ray, 75.

60. Carroll, *Saved to Serve*, 35.

61. B. H. Carroll, *Baptists and Their Doctrines*, comp. J. B. Cranfill (New York: Fleming H. Revell Co., 1913), 9-10.

62. Carroll, "Biblical Addresses," 175.

63. B. H. Carroll, *Opening of the Course in the English Bible* (Waco: Kellner Printing Co., 1902), 2, 11-12; B. H. Carroll, *Jesus the Christ*, comp. J. W. Crowder and ed. J. B. Cranfill (Nashville: Baird-Ward Press, 1937), 99; Cates, 190.

64. "Baptist Church Polity," 35-38, 82-93.

65. "Biblical Addresses," 167-68; B. H. Carroll, *Ambitious Dreams of Youth*, ed. J. B. Cranfill (Dallas: Helms Printing Co., 1939), 136.

66. Carroll, "Baptist Church Polity," 112-23.

67. Carroll, "Defending the Faith," 292-94.

68. Carroll, *Interpretation*, 1:66, 156-57; B. H. Carroll, "Memorial, Meetings and Miscellanies," comp. J. W. Crowder; Roberts Library, Southwestern Baptist Theological Seminary (typewritten manuscript, n.d.), 75; B. H. Carroll, *Courses in the English Bible: Lectures III and IV. Creations, with Questions on Four Lectures* (Waco: Kellner Printing Co., n.d.), 25.

69. Carroll, *Interpretation*, 1:61-62, 79; 12:195.

70. B. H. Carroll, *Christ and His Church*, comp. J. W. Crowder and ed. J. B. Cranfill (Nashville: Broadman Press, 1940), 189.

71. B. H. Carroll, *The Providence of God*, comp. J. W. Crowder and ed. J. B. Cranfill (Dallas: Helms Printing Co., 1940), 21-24.

72. Carroll, *Saved to Serve*, 149.

73. Ibid., 249-50, 159-60.

74. Carroll, *Providence*, 17-29; Carroll, *Saved to Serve*, 152.

75. Carroll, "Baptist Church Polity," 130-31; Stewart, 44, 104.

76. Stewart, 44-45.

77. Carroll, "Baptist Church Polity," 120, 143-44.

78. B. H. Carroll, *The Holy Spirit,* ed. J. B. Cranfill (Grand Rapids, Mich.: Zondervan, 1939), 17, 20, 31, 40-45, 57-59, 76-79.

79. Carroll, *Inspiration,* 32.

80. B. H. Carroll, *Christian Education and Some Social Problems,* ed. J. W. Crowder (Fort Worth: By the editor, 1948), 14.

81. "Biblical Addresses," 38-39; Cates, 98.

82. Carroll, *Ambitious Dreams,* 59; Carroll, *Interpretation,* 1:63.

83. B. H. Carroll, *Southwestern Journal of Theology* 5 (October 1921); Carroll, "Defending the Faith," 80-81; Carroll, *Interpretation,* 1:105-6.

84. Carroll, *Southwestern Journal,* vol. 5; Carroll, "Baptist Church Polity," 126; Carroll, *Interpretation,* 1:81.

85. Carroll, *Interpretation,* 12:70; Carroll, *Christian Education,* 16-17.

86. Carroll, *Interpretation,* 1:117-19; 14:125; Carroll, "Baptist Church Polity," 185; Carroll, "Biblical Addresses," 38-39. Carroll uses the doctrine of total depravity as further proof against the theory of evolution.

87. Carroll, "Baptist Church Polity," 128-32, 156-57, 184; Carroll, *Interpretation,* 1:84, 136.

88. B. H. Carroll, *The Day of the Lord,* comp. J. W. Crowder and ed. J. B. Cranfill (Nashville: Broadman Press, 1936), 93, 96.

89. Carroll, "Biblical Addresses," 31-32; B. H. Carroll, *Ecclesia—The Church* (Louisville: Baptist Book Concern, 1903), 13-14.

90. Carroll, *Interpretation,* 3:37.

91. B. H. Carroll, *The River of Life and Other Sermons,* ed. J. B. Cranfill (Nashville: The Sunday School Board of the Southern Baptist Convention, 1928), 68-79.

92. Carroll, "Baptist Church Polity," 129.

93. Carroll, *Ambitious Dreams,* 69.

94. Carroll, *Interpretation,* 15:78-79; 16:206-7.

95. B. H. Carroll, *The Faith that Saves,* comp. J. W. Crowder and ed. J. B. Cranfill (Dallas: Helms Printing Co., 1939), 164. B. H. Carroll, *Evangelistic Sermons,* comp. J. B. Cranfill (New York: Fleming H. Revell Co., 1913), 74; Carroll, *Interpretation,* 2:310; 3:58; 4:122.

96. Carroll, *Interpretation,* 2:338-39; 11:393; 15:220.

97. Carroll, *Interpretation,* 11:395; 16:298, Carroll, *Evangelistic Sermons,* 62.

98. Carroll, "Defending the Faith," 83; Carroll, *Interpretation,* 14:92, 127.

99. Carroll, "Baptist Church Polity," 155. But he also understood justification in the sense of Christians' works justifying their faith. See Carroll, *Interpretation,* 13:29-30.

100. Carroll, "Defending the Faith," 86.

101. Carroll, "Baptist Church Polity," 161.

102. Carroll, *Interpretation,* 14:245; Carroll, "Baptist Church Polity," 156. 159.

103. Carroll, *Interpretation,* 15:78.

104. Carroll, "Baptist Church Polity," 188.

105. Carroll, "Baptist Church Polity," 181-83, 205; Carroll, "Biblical Addresses," 26-28; Carroll, *Interpretation,* 10:285-88.

106. Cogburn, 55-56, 66-67; Cates 65-66; Carroll, "Questions on Saving Faith and Assurance" and "Martin on Prayer," in "Defending the Faith," 92-102.

107. Carroll, "Baptist Church Polity," 209.

108. Ibid., 202-3, 208.

109. Ibid., 205.

110. Carroll, "Biblical Addresses," 39-40; Carroll, "Baptist Church Polity," 206-8.

111. Carroll, *The Providence of God*, 191.

112. Carroll, "Defending the Faith," 2-38.

113. Carroll, *Interpretation*, 13:140, 151. Carroll admitted that in a sense Christians are already sanctified as God sees them as complete in Christ.

114. Carroll, "Baptist Church Polity," 153-56.

115. Ibid., 5-20; B. H. Carroll, "Distinctive Baptist Principles, A Sermon Before the Pastors' Conference at Dallas, November 4, 1903," 9-14.

116. Carroll, "Biblical Addresses," 58-60.

117. Carroll, *The River of Life*, 136; Carroll, *Saved to Serve*, 39.

118. Carroll, "Distinctive Baptist Principles," 14-15.

119. Carroll, "Baptist Church Polity," 8.

120. B. H. Carroll, "Memorials, Meetings and Miscellanies," comp. J. W. Crowder, Roberts Library, Southwestern Baptist Theological Seminary (typewritten manuscript, n.d.), 194; B. H. Carroll, *The Supper and Suffering of Our Lord*, ed. J. W. Crowder (Fort Worth: Seminary Hill Press, 1947), 42.

121. Carroll, "Baptist Church Polity," 84, 267-68, 274; B. H. Carroll, *Baptism: Its Law, Its Administrator, Its Subject, Its Form, Its Design* (Waco: Baptist Standard Press Print, 1893).

122. Carroll, *The Supper and Sufferings*, 39; Carroll, *Baptist Church Polity*, 276, 345; Stewart, 137; B. H. Carroll, *Communion, from a Bible Standpoint: A Sermon* (Dallas: "Texas Baptist" Book and Job Printing House, 1876).

123. Cates, 197-98; Carroll, "Baptist Church Polity," 51-80.

124. Stewart, 138-39.

125. Carroll, "Baptist Church Polity," 2-4.

126. Baker, *Generations*, 94; Carroll, *Baptists and Their Doctrines*, 84; Carroll, "Distinctive Baptist Principles," 5.

127. For Carroll's explanation of this doctrine, see Carroll, "Biblical Addresses," 57-102; Carroll, *Interpretation*, vol. 17; and Carroll, *The Day of the Lord*. For studies, see Stewart, 146-68; and Tom L. Watson, "The Eschatology of B. H. Carroll" (M.Th. thesis, Southwestern Baptist Theological Seminary, 1960).

128. Carroll Collection, File 583, "New Testament English, Fall Term, 1912-1913," 2, 12; Carroll, "Biblical Addresses," 87-97; Carroll, *The Day of the Lord*, 177-78.

129. Carroll, "Biblical Addresses," 88-92; Carroll, *Interpretation*, 11:219; 17:274-75. Carroll believed the Jews would again become a nation and that most of them would be converted, but he did not identify this political nation as the "New Israel."

130. B. H. Carroll, *Jesus the Christ* (Nashville: Baird-Ward Press, 1937), 28.

131. Ray Summers, *The Life Beyond* (Nashville: Broadman Press, 1959), 124; Carroll, *The River of Life*, 148.

132. Carroll, *The Day of the Lord*, 177-78.

133. Carroll, *Interpretation*, 11:281.

134. Gambrell, "The Home-Going," in *Colossus*, 103.

135. B. H. Carroll, *The Theology of the Bible* (Fort Worth: Southwestern Baptist Theological Seminary, n.d.), 2; Carroll, *Inspiration*, 32.

136. Carroll, "Defending the Faith," 2-38, 92-102; Carroll, "Baptist Church Polity," 191.

137. Carroll, *Baptists and Their Doctrines*, 94-95.

138. Carroll, *The Holy Spirit*, 43.

139. Carroll Collection, File 583, Lecture Notes, 12.

140. Carroll, *Saved to Serve*, 22-24; Baker, *Generations*, 96-97; see Carroll, "The Death of Spurgeon," in *Sermons*, 24-44.

141. H. Leon McBeth, *The Baptist Heritage: Four Centuries of Baptist Witness* (Nashville: Broadman Press, 1987), 624-25; Baker, *Generations*, 500; Carroll Collection, File 76, "The Constitution of the Southern Baptist Convention and the Illinois Messengers." Later, Throgmorton served as a trustee of Southwestern Baptist Theological Seminary (1916, 1929).

142. Carroll, *Interpretation*, 1:135-36; 14-124.

143. Carroll, "Baptist Church Polity," 139, 167, 176, 214, 216; Carroll, "Defending the Faith," 80, 98-99; Stewart, 126.

144. Carroll, *Interpretation*, 15:86-92.

145. Carroll, *Interpretation*, 17:273.

146. Carroll, "Baptist Church Polity," 208.

147. Ibid., 156, 159, 163-64, 219-21; Carroll, "Defending the Faith," 93-94.

148. Ibid., 200; Ibid., 80.

149. Crowder, *Colossus*, 181.

150. Carroll, *Baptists and Their Doctrines*, 47.

151. W. T. Conner, *Southwestern Evangel*, December 1925, 6.

152. Carroll, *Saved to Serve*, 35.

16

E. Y. Mullins

Fisher Humphreys

Biography

Edgar Young Mullins was born in Franklin County, Mississippi, on January 5, 1860.[1] He was the fourth child and the first son of Seth Granberry Mullins and Cornelia Mullins. The senior Mullins was a farmer, a teacher, and a Baptist minister; he and his wife dedicated their newborn son to the Christian ministry, a commitment about which the son was told for the first time on his thirty-fifth birthday, after he had served as a minister for ten years.[2]

Shortly after General William T. Sherman's siege of nearby Vicksburg in 1863, S. G. Mullins moved his family to Copiah County in Mississippi, which was less directly affected by the war.[3] In 1869 the family moved to Corsicana, Texas, a frontier town, where Reverend Mullins established a school and a church, now the First Baptist Church of Corsicana.[4] He was a graduate of Mississippi College, and he encouraged his children to go to college. Edgar, at age fifteen, took a responsible position as a telegrapher for the Associated Press to contribute to the college expenses of his older sisters.[5] He was a member of the first class to enter Texas A & M in 1876, and he completed his basic college work there in 1879, continuing his work as a telegrapher during his college years.

E. Y. Mullins was preparing for a career in law. He had not yet made a profession of faith in Christ. He was converted at a revival meeting in Dallas and was baptized by his father in Corsicana at the age of twenty. He soon felt called to the Christian ministry, and he entered The Southern Baptist Theological Seminary in Louisville, Kentucky, in 1881. The trauma of the war, the fact that he had a strong family life, the quasi-military discipline of Texas A & M, and his years of working as a telegrapher combined to give Mullins a maturity beyond his years. He was elected by the student body to act as manager of the dormitory, Waverly Hall, a position he held until he completed the full course of work and graduated in 1885.

Mullins had intended to become a missionary, but his doctor advised against it. After graduation he accepted the position of pastor of the Harrodsburg Baptist Church in Harrodsburg, Kentucky. In 1886 he married Isla May Hawley. Mrs. Mullins later described her husband's appearance at this time as follows: "a slender, graceful figure of six feet, two inches, very erect . . . an abundant shock of very dark hair . . . a beard of soft fineness which was

E. Y. Mullins (1860-1928)

Photo courtesy of Southern Baptist Historical Library and Archives

then attractive and added much to his look of maturity."[6] The Mullinses eventually had two children, both sons, both of whom died young.

In 1888 Mullins went to Baltimore as pastor of the Lee Street Baptist Church, where he remained for seven years. He resigned from that position and worked for a few months for the Foreign Mission Board of the Southern Baptist Convention in Richmond, Virginia. In 1895 he accepted the pastorate of the Baptist Church in Newton Centre, Massachusetts, adjacent to Boston. Movement between churches affiliated with the Baptist conventions of the North and South was not as rare then as it later became.

In 1899 Mullins became president of The Southern Baptist Theological Seminary in Louisville. He held this position until his death in 1928. He was also professor of theology during this entire period. During his presidency the seminary experienced dramatic growth in its endowments and in the size of its faculty and student body, and was moved from a downtown location to a fifty-eight acre campus known as "The Beeches." The seminary also began publication of *The Review and Expositor* under Mullins's leadership, and Mullins contributed many articles and reviews to it over the years.

From his position as president of the seminary, Mullins exerted great influence on Baptist and public life. William E. Ellis says that Mullins acted as a kind of liaison between Baptists of the North and South. He also bridged other gaps. For example, he was asked by the organizers of the Federal Council of Churches to help bring the Southern Baptist Convention into the new organization.[7] In 1904 the Southern Baptist Convention rejected an invitation to join the Council and enthusiastically accepted an invitation to participate in the nascent Baptist World Alliance.[8] Following the First World War, Mullins and other leaders went to Europe to bring Baptists there greetings from the Southern Baptist Convention and to arrange for help for European Baptists who were suffering from the war and its aftermath. Mullins was president of the Southern Baptist Convention from 1921 to 1924 and president of the Baptist World Alliance from 1923 to 1928.[9] In 1923 the city of Louisville proclaimed an "E. Y. Mullins Day." The extent of Mullins's influence in Baptist life and public life may be gauged by reviewing the outpouring of appreciation for him when he died in 1928.[10] W. O. Carver described him as "the best known Baptist in the world" and said that he was "unsurpassed in influence for good by any man in his denomination."[11]

Exposition

Theological Issues

The three decades during which Mullins exercised great influence in Baptist life were turbulent ones. Mullins responded to a series of three theological issues which were polarizing Baptists.

First, the school to which he came as president in 1899 was of "a tenacious theological type,"[12] the Calvinism of its founder, James P. Boyce. Mullins continued to use Boyce's *Abstract of Systematic Theology* (1887) as a textbook in his theology classes for several years. But he also used other books, and his own book, *The Christian Religion in Its Doctrinal Expres-*

sion, became the textbook after its publication in 1917.[13] In the preface to *The Christian Religion in Its Doctrinal Expression,* a book dedicated to the memory of Boyce, Mullins positioned himself as follows:

> For example, Arminianism overlooked certain essential truths about God in its strong championship of human freedom. As against it, Calvinism ran to extremes in some of its conclusions in its very earnest desire to safeguard the truth of God's sovereignty. We are learning to discard both names and to adhere more closely to the Scriptures, while retaining the truth in both systems.[14]

Mullins consciously adopted a moderate position toward the Calvinist-Arminian polarity and also toward other polarities. He wrote:

> As usual the extreme parties are doing most of the harm. On one side is the ultra-conservative, the man of the hammer and anvil method, who relies chiefly upon denunciation of opponents, and who cannot tolerate discussion on a fraternal basis; on the other is the ultra-progressive whose lofty contempt of the "traditionalist" shuts him out from the ranks of sane scholarship and wise leadership. The really safe leaders of thought, however, are between these extremes.[15]

Mullins's consciously adopted moderation has been noticed by those who study him,[16] and it has been variously evaluated. Russell H. Dilday, Jr., praises Mullins for it and sees it as a good pattern for leaders today.[17] William E. Ellis seems to feel that, in the end, it was a position which was defeated.

> After 1925 he lost ground not only among his coreligionists but with other theists as well. Assailed on the right by fundamentalists within his own denomination and abandoned on the left by modernists who no longer had much patience with moderate evangelicals, Mullins was tormented by a loss of prestige and position in his last years.[18]

The moderation of Mullins did not prevail on every issue, but his moderate Calvinism did, in fact, prevail in Southern Baptist life.

A second theological issue which Mullins faced was the Landmark Baptist interpretation of Baptist history. Landmark Baptists believed that local congregations of baptized believers are the only ecclesiastical organizations which are authorized by the New Testament. They further held that a succession of such congregations has existed from the first century to the Baptists of today, a line which includes Montanists, Donatists, Waldenses, and others. William Heth Whitsitt, a church historian and Mullins's immediate predecessor as president of The Southern Baptist Theological Seminary, had written a book entitled *A Question in Baptist History* (1896) in which he said that believer's baptism by immersion cannot be shown on historical grounds to have existed prior to the seventeenth century in England.[19] Landmark Baptists' dismay at Whitsitt's conclusions led the trustees of the seminary to accept his resignation in 1899.

Mullins's handling of the Landmark concerns was conciliatory and diplomatic. He could refer to the same line of tradition that the Landmark Baptists did,[20] but "ultimately he rested the issue with historical scholarship."[21] Perhaps most interesting of all, he wrote very little about the doctrine of the church himself. For example, he did not include a chapter on the church in his systematic theology, *The Christian Religion in Its Doctrinal Expression*. He wrote: "Our present purpose does not contemplate a discussion of either church or kingdom in any of the controverted aspects of these great themes."[22] The basic reason seems to have been that the curriculum at the seminary was arranged so that systematic theology was a separate course from pastoral work, and ecclesiology was included with the latter.[23] This arrangement had been inherited by seminaries such as Princeton and Union in New York, from the German theological encyclopedia in which theological education comprised four parts: biblical, historical, theological, and practical.[24] When Mullins began to teach theology in 1899, the ecclesiology-pastoral work course was being taught by Edwin C. Dargan, who used as a textbook his own book, *Ecclesiology: A Study of the Church* (1897).

The third theological polarity which Mullins faced was the Fundamentalist-Modernist controversy. This controversy centered around a cluster of issues involving the implications of the critical study of history for the history reported in the Bible, of the natural sciences for the miracles reported in the Bible, and of evolution for the creation stories recorded in the Bible. One or more of these questions was on the theological agenda throughout the three decades of Mullins's teaching career. In each case, what was threatened was the Bible and the church's understanding of it; and in each case the threat came from the critical consciousness which had arisen in the Western world in the seventeenth century (science) and in the eighteenth century (history). As he did with Calvinism, once again he took a moderate stance—he adopted a position which resisted naturalistic reductions of Christian faith and the obscurantist rejection of the legitimate claims of history or science.

These polarities were all imposed on Mullins by circumstances in his denomination and world. They do not necessarily represent his own deepest concerns. To those concerns, and to the theology which he constructed, we now turn.

Writings

The faculty of The Southern Baptist Theological Seminary wrote a memorial of Mullins shortly after his death. In it they listed six of his books, with the comment: "These are not all of the books he wrote, but they show the ripeness and profoundness of scholarship that signalized his intellectual life."[25] The six are: *Why Is Christianity True?* (1905), *The Axioms of Religion* (1908), *Baptists Beliefs* (1912), *Freedom and Authority in Religion* (1913), *The Christian Religion in Its Doctrinal Expression* (1917), and *Christianity at the Cross Roads* (1924).

Why Is Christianity True? would today be called Christian apologetics. Written in four parts, it is a cumulative case for the truth of Christian faith and beliefs. First, Mullins demonstrates the superiority of theism as an explanatory hypothesis for our universe, to five alternative hypothesis: pantheism, idealism, materialism, agnosticism, and evolution. Next, Mullins presents Christ as the essence of Christianity and says that the Bible portrays Christ as a divine Savior as well as a great Teacher, and that He rose from the dead. Third, Mullins argues that the Christian experience of regeneration, including the moral transformation of life, verifies this New Testament portrait. Finally, Mullins argues "pragmatically" that Christianity has proven itself to be powerful and true through nineteen centuries of history. He also touches briefly on two other religions, Islam and Buddhism, finding that they both contain some truth but also they both are very inferior to Christianity.

Many of Mullins's great concerns are evident in this early book. He is an apologist who defends what will later be called "mere Christianity" or "plain Christianity" or "basic Christianity," against unbelief and disbelief on its left and other religions on its right.[26] He insists that science and religion are separate disciplines using separate methods to deal with separate facts. Christian experience is indispensable not only for Christian theology but also for Christian faith. While Mullins benefited greatly from the studies of religious experience by William James and others, and from the importance given to experience in the theology of F. D. E. Schleiermacher, his own mind turned naturally and consistently to the experience of conversion as preached and emphasized in churches influenced by revivalism. Mullins assumed that persons and personal life are appropriate and adequate categories for speaking of God and of human beings. Mullins was eloquent about Christian missions and evangelism, seeing their successes as indications of the truthfulness of their message, and he was optimistic about their future.

It is interesting to compare *Why Is Christianity True?* to a recent work of Christian apologetics, *On Being a Christian,* by the Roman Catholic Hans Kung. Both make Christ the center of Christianity, and both say that its truthfulness stands or falls with Christ. Both respond to unbelief on the left and to other religions on the right. Both accept a critical reading of the Gospels, though Kung is more explicit about this than Mullins. Neither feels that the traditional arguments for God's existence are compelling; but both think those arguments make a contribution. Mullins is more emphatic about the historicity of Jesus' resurrection than Kung, but both treat it as indispensable both for understanding and trusting Him. Mullins issues a call to conversion, to be followed by discipleship; Kung issues a call to a radically human life in the church.

Mullins's second great book, *The Axioms of Religion,* is subtitled "A New Interpretation of the Baptist Faith." It probably has done more than any other single volume to define Baptist identity in the twentieth century. Mullins says that the most distinctive and important of all Baptist beliefs is the belief in "soul competency," that is, in the freedom, ability, and responsibility of each person to respond to God for herself or himself. From this simple, universal "mother principle,"[27] Mullins derived six propositions, which are, he argued, axiomatic, that is, self-evidently true to all who accept Christianity and even to many who do not.

The theological axiom is that "the holy and loving God has a right to be sovereign." Mullins understands God as a sovereign Father rather than as sovereign omnipotence.[28] God asserts His sovereignty over human beings by personal and moral influences. "His sovereignty is holy and it is loving; it respects human freedom."[29]

The religious axiom is that all persons have an equal right to direct access to God.[30] Mullins wrote, "It is a species of spiritual tyranny for men to interpose the church itself, its ordinances, or ceremonies, or its formal creeds, between the human soul and Christ."[31] Mullins acknowledged that this axiom was not applicable to ancient Israel, and that it was lost by the church when infant baptism and the Constantinian settlement were accepted, but he insisted that it is the clear teaching of the New Testament.

The ecclesiastical axiom is that "all believers have a right to equal privileges in the church."[32] Mullins believed that democracy is the only church polity which is really true to this axiom. "No other polity leaves the soul free."[33] The autonomy of local congregations is not threatened by the existence of Baptist agencies or conventions, for these have no authority over local congregations.[34]

The moral axiom is that "to be responsible the soul must be free."[35] This axiom is the basis of all ethics, and it is the antithesis of all forms of determinism.

The religiocivic axiom is "a free church in a free state."[36] "When Roger Williams founded the commonwealth of Rhode Island, a new era in man's spiritual history began."[37] By their adherence to the separation of church and state, and their refusal to be content with mere toleration, Baptists "made a real contribution to the world's civilization."[38] But "there will, of course, remain a borderline where it will not always be clear how to discriminate and apply the principle correctly."[39]

The social axiom is, "you shall love your neighbor as yourself."[40] Christianity has emphasized two correlative truths: every individual has worth, and every human being is a social being. Social progress is the product of individual regeneration. The imitation of Christ does not link Christians to a single reform movement, but it does compel them to work for the welfare of all persons.[41] "The best service which Christianity can render to society is to produce righteousness in individual character and at the same time set the man free as an agent of righteousness in society at large."[42]

Mullins presents three chapters in which he applies the axioms to three sets of concerns. First, he says that the best denominational structure is that which respects the autonomy of churches, even though it may be frustrating when the churches do not cooperate as fully as they might. Second, he argues that the movement for church union—which will later be called the ecumenical movement—can proceed properly only if it accepts congregational polity; every effort to create church union along hierarchical lines must be resisted in the name of freedom.[43] Third, Mullins responds to critics who wish to be Christians without any commitment to institutional churches. They fail to take account either of the authority of Christ or of the realities of

Christian history, both of which indicate the need for institutional churches, baptism, and the Lord's Supper.

Mullins discusses the Baptist contribution to American civilization (it is the ideal of liberty) and also argues that the axioms are of incalculable value if the human race is to continue to make progress. In every area of human endeavor—the educational, the scientific, the philosophical, the political—progress will occur in direct proportion to the implementation of the truths of these axioms. "The axioms of religion derived from the gospel of Jesus Christ are fitted to lead the progressive civilization of the race."[44]

In some ways *The Axioms of Religion* bears the marks of its time. Many writers today would shy away from employing a vocabulary of "rights." Others might observe that Mullins asserted rather than demonstrated that individuals are really free. A historian might resist the assumption that authentic Christianity is always individualistic. Mullins's optimism about the future seems too facile.

And yet, many of Mullins's ideas made an impact on religion in America. Church and state are still separate. Many denominations emphasize the importance of a personal conversion experience. Historian Martin E. Marty has written of the "Baptistification" of American life, so Mullins's optimism was not totally unrealistic.[45] *The Axioms of Religion* may have been the most original book Mullins wrote. It was a very American book and a very Baptist book, and it went to the heart of Mullins's religious and theological concerns.

In *The Axioms of Religion* Mullins articulated for thoughtful readers the hidden assumptions underlying Baptist life; in *Baptist Beliefs* he interpreted for the general reader the beliefs which Baptists regularly confess. His method was to comment on the "excellent Baptist creeds" which are "now in existence in common use among us."[46] The topics with which Mullins dealt, and the sequence of the topics, reflect the New Hampshire Declaration, to which Mullins added comments on five topics—the kingdom of God, liberty of conscience, missions, education, and social service. Twelve years after the publication of this book, Mullins would become chairman of a committee to draw up a confession of faith for the Southern Baptist Convention; the committee began, as Mullins did, with the New Hampshire Declaration, and added to it articles on the same five topics Mullins had discussed along with articles on peace and war, cooperation, and stewardship.[47] In both these sets of additions, Mullins's theological and ecclesiastical concerns are evident.

Baptist Beliefs is folk theology at its best. It is readable. It addresses the real concerns of ordinary Christians. It explains but is not condescending. It argues but is not adversarial. It is coherent but not rationalistic. In some ways, what is most interesting is what is omitted; the emphasis on personal experience which characterizes *The Christian Religion in Its Doctrinal Expression* five years later is barely evident here, presumably because Mullins recognized that that emphasis was his own rather than characteristic of the Baptist confessions of which he was providing a fresh statement.

Freedom and Authority in Religion is unique among Mullins's books in that it has a single thesis, namely, that Jesus Christ is the religious authority for Christians and that He exercises His authority in such a way as to give Christians freedom rather than deprive them of it. The book might have been shorter than it is, but Mullins returns in it to themes in his earlier books. He also in this book carries on a sustained dialogue with many of his contemporary theologians.

The argument runs as follows. First, ours is an age which longs for freedom, which it understands as living and thinking without deference to any external authority. Second, Jesus claimed to be a unique and indispensable religious authority. Third, science is competent to deal with physical realities but not with spiritual realities such as the soul, freedom, immorality, and God; only religion is competent to deal with these. "Religion begins, therefore, exactly where science ends."[48] Fourth, philosophy, the quest for understanding which arose long after religion, the quest for redemption, produces an unsettled state of mind which is inadequate for religion.

Next Mullins begins his constructive work. Fifth, religious truth is assimilated through experience; it is a special form of personal knowledge which is arrived at by living as much as by thinking. It does not contradict logic or science, but it goes beyond them, to a direct encounter of the human will with the living God. Sixth, in every sphere of life, authority inevitably develops as truth is discovered and expressed. Seventh, religion is a universal human activity consisting of knowing about a supernatural personal spirit, and seeking a relationship with that spirit, and seeking deliverance from the human predicament. Christianity teaches that God takes the initiative in establishing the relationship and providing the deliverance. "God's revelation to us does mean that our experience religiously assimilates revealed truth and it becomes valid for us not as propositions imposed by sheer divine authority, but is recognized by us as the answer to our deepest needs and congruous with our highest aspirations."[49] Eighth, religious knowledge is given, not by inference, but empirically, that is, in the Christian experience of redemption. It is personal knowledge, that is, knowledge in terms of persons and personal relationships, not in terms of physical cause and effect. It is not subjective knowledge, for it is knowledge of an "object" outside oneself acting upon oneself. It is moral and spiritual knowledge, but it is just as cognitive as any other form of knowledge.

Ninth, "now we shall find, paradoxical as it may seem, that Jesus Christ while retaining the principle of authority combines it with the perfect ideal of human freedom. Christianity is as truly the religion of freedom as it is the religion of authority."[50] God is the supreme authority in religion; Jesus is the true revelation of God, and therefore the seat of religious authority. The New Testament and the Christian experience of redemption converge to affirm Jesus as the seat of religious authority. By putting us in touch with God, and providing redemption, Jesus gives us freedom. Christ gives His revelations to us in such a way that they become discoveries of truth by us. He exerts His authority over us precisely by making us free and by allowing us to accept it freely. His authority is the authority of a friendship.

Finally, Mullins turns his attention to the place of the Bible in Christianity. The Bible is "the literary expression of living experience in the religious life, the spontaneous and free output of that experience under the guidance of God's Spirit, (so that) it is precisely adapted to reproduce that experience in man to-day."[51] It is in that sense the final authority in religion, and this is perfectly consistent with Jesus Christ as the seat of authority in religion, because the Bible is the inspired interpretation of Christ which creates the possibility of his life being experienced by people today. "Christ as the Revealer of God and Redeemer of man is the seat of authority in religion and above and underneath and before the Bible. But the Bible is the authoritative literature which leads us to Christ."[52] It does this without coercion, and so it is an authority which respects human freedom and creates it, just as Christ does.

The Christian Religion in Its Doctrinal Expression is Mullin's largest and most constructive book. The first thing that strikes the reader of this systematic theology is the unusual title, and the second thing is the unusual sequence of topics. The title alerts us not to confuse the Christian religion—"religion" is a positive term for Mullins—with theology. The sequence of topics alerts us that Mullins will resist any effort to tear theology away from its roots in authentic religious life. The chapter titles are:

     I. Religion and Theology
    II. The Knowledge of God
   III. Preliminary Study of Christian Experience
    IV. Christian and Other Forms of Knowledge
     V. Revelation
    VI. The Supreme Revelation: Jesus Christ
   VII. The Deity of Jesus Christ
  VIII. The Holy Spirit and the Trinity
    IX. The God of Our Lord Jesus Christ
     X. Creation
    XI. Providence
   XII. Sin
  XIII. The Living Word of Christ
   XIV. Election: God's Initiative in Salvation
    XV. The Beginning of the Christian Life
   XVI. The Continuance of the Christian Life
  XVII. Last Things

The first four chapters would, in Germany, be called "Prolegomena," and the unusual thing about them is the emphasis on Christian experience. Mullins deals with Christian experience as prolegomena and then returns to it later in chapters 7, 15, and 16. The chapter on the Spirit and the Trinity seems contrived, since Mullins does not integrate it into the Christian experience; this is surely a missed opportunity. To speak of God only after speaking of Jesus is not really true either to experience or to chronology—we do, after all, have some knowledge of God before Christ. Five chapters intervene between Christ's person and work, and should not the emphasis on Christian experience lead one to deal first with Christ's work and then with his person?

We shall look briefly at what Mullins does in each chapter.

First, he distinguishes religion from theology, and attempts to justify his emphasis on Christian experience. He thinks the latter is intellectually justifiable, and it also prevents us from thinking of Christianity in exclusively intellectual terms. He defends the autonomy of religious experience; it is an experience which should not be reduced to other terms, and it puts us in touch with realities we cannot know in any other way. He carefully defends his emphasis on experience from the charge that it is a capitulation to subjectivism; Christianity, he says, "has to do with two great groups of facts: the facts of experience and the facts of the historical revelation of God through Christ."[53] Christian experience is made possible because God has graciously revealed Himself in a historical person, Jesus Christ. Christian theology is real knowledge, which uses appropriate methods to deal with its particular subject matter, God. The highest qualification for the study of theology is to be a person of religious faith. Scholarly and intuitive gifts are also helpful, as are moral qualities such as humility.

In the second chapter, Mullins defines religion and examines the sources of religious knowledge. Religious knowledge may be inferred from nature or man, or from the religious conscience, or learned from comparative religions, or accepted on the authority of the church or the Bible. But the supreme source of religious knowledge is the revelation of God given in Jesus Christ. Jesus was a historical person, and the New Testament tells what He was like, but He also transcends history and is active in human experience. We know God supremely through Christ, and we know Christ through the New Testament and through our experience of Him.

In chapter 3, Mullins lays down several general assumptions to prepare for his argument from experience. In his analysis of Christian experience, he says that God initiates or makes contact with man at the point of sin, and elicits a free response. This is possible because man is personal. God acts upon both the unconscious and conscious mind of man. Christian doctrine arises out of Christian experience; it is an experiential knowledge, but is none the less rational for that. It is knowledge with certainty; you cannot doubt what you learn from experience.

Chapter 4 traces the relationship of Christian knowledge to the knowledge of the physical sciences, of the psychology of religion, of ethics, of comparative religion, and of philosophy. Science and religion are separate spheres of knowledge and cannot conflict. The psychology of religion, as expressed by William James, for example, suggests the working of God in religious experience. The kingdom of God is, in fact, the highest expression known to us of the ethical ideal, and ethics finds its securest ground in God. Other religions are not wholly false, but they are moving upward toward an ideal which is already found in Christian religion. Philosophy is a quest for the true world view, which is natural for mankind, but it often arrives at false conclusions because it adopts too narrow a view of reality; false world views include agnosticism, materialism, and idealism, but personalism is much nearer the truth. Christian theism takes up where personalism leaves off. The traditional arguments for God's existence are less convincing to Christians than their knowledge of God from the revelation given in Christ, but they are welcomed as supplementary confirmations with cumulative force. The arguments help us to infer that God is, while an experience is a direct knowledge that God is. Mullins resists the charge of subjectivism with this argument:

> The charge of subjectivism may be brought by any objector to any conclusion in any sphere. All the data which we handle in our reasonings must pass through the human mold. Our intellect impresses its forms upon all facts, just as a dipper shapes the water it takes out of the bucket. But all truth becomes truth only on the supposition that our reason gives us reliable information. The fact that reason is satisfied and a religious need is met surely cannot be justly held to discredit it. It is rather the strongest of proofs that it is true. And when a form of experience like the Christian's, which belongs to a great order of experience running through nearly two thousand years, and embracing millions of other Christians, and which can be scientifically analyzed and explained— when such an experience is under consideration the charge of subjectivism loses all its force. If the experience were merely individual and exceptional there would be some point in the objection. But not otherwise.[54]

Chapter 5 begins by affirming that all religions consider revelation to be indispensable. The Christian claim that revelation was given in a Person, Jesus Christ, is unique. The Christian revelation "is primarily a revelation of God himself rather than of truths about God," "revelation is primarily salvation," and "revelation is 'acquaintance with' and not mere 'knowledge about' God."[55] "God's revelations can only become revelations when they become our discoveries."[56]

The Bible is the record of God's revelation. The biblical revelation is historical, experiential, morally transforming, progressive, purposive, congruous with life, and supernatural; it is also sufficient, certain, and authoritative for religion.

Jesus Christ is God's supreme revelation. We know Him through the New Testament; we also experience His redeeming work in our lives. The Deity of Christ is an essential article of Christian faith. Jesus reveals God as personal, and as loving, and He reveals the purpose of God in creation and the worthwhileness of human existence. Many efforts have been made to say how Christ can be both divine and human; we need to stress that He was one Person before we attempt to explain the two natures. Christ existed as God's Son before His birth, and He accepted self-imposed limitations in order to be a human being. The acceptance of those limitations is a great revelation of the self-sacrificing love of God. Jesus grew, as all human beings do; He grew intellectually and morally and in His consciousness that He was the Messiah. Mullins rejects the idea that Christ was merely human, or that He was merely filled with God's presence, or that He preexisted only ideally. He rejects William Sanday's proposal that Christ's consciousness was human and His unconsciousness divine as well as Albrecht Ritschl's suggestion that Christ has for us the value of God.

The Holy Spirit is a personal being distinct from Christ and the Father, who "makes the historical revelation in and through Christ morally and spiritually effective in the life of believers."[57] The one God is, both immanently and economically, Father, Son, and Holy Spirit.

The God of our Lord Jesus Christ is the supreme personal Spirit, perfect in all His attributes, the source, support, and end of the universe, who guides it according to the wise, righteous, loving purpose revealed in Christ, and who indwells in all things by His Spirit seeking to transform them and to create His kingdom. God is not immune to suffering. God's sovereignty is not that of an absolute and arbitrary Oriental monarch, but of a wise and loving Heavenly Father.

God created all that exists. His purpose is to make "a spiritual kingdom of free persons living together in eternal bonds of righteous love."[58] He is carrying out that purpose in His developing universe. Man is God's crowning work of creation; man is both physical and spiritual and bears the divine image.

God preserves His creation, that is, sustains its existence; and He rules providentially over it, that is, directs it toward the fulfillment of His purpose. His providence extends to individuals as well as to humankind as a whole. Sometimes He uses miracles—which are restorations rather than violations—to carry out his purpose. He answers the prayers of His children. It is presumptuous of human beings to assume that they are the only personal creatures made by God—angels are quite real, though we know very little about them.

God made men to be free; men freely chose to disobey God; in that choice is the origin of sin. Sin is universal, and each sinner is guilty and condemned for his or her sins.

Christ died for the sins of the world. The Bible provides numerous interpretations of that unique event. Although God's love and justice are never in conflict, the necessity of Christ's death is located in the moral nature of God as well as of man. Christ identified Himself fully with human beings, and so experienced God's wrath against sin—not an angry passion or vindictiveness, but the suffering and death which are the consequences of human sinning. "God of course did not really forsake Christ, but in his death there was, in some real sense, beyond our power to fathom, a clouding of his consciousness of God. He entered the region and shadow of death for human sin."[59] In so doing, He broke the reign of the principle of sin and death over human beings. In a profoundly personal and moral way, Christ became not only the head and representative of the human race but also its substitute. He died for all, not only for the elect.

Election is the sovereign initiative which God takes toward man in order to carry out His eternal purpose. If God did not take this initiative no one could ever be saved. Election does not eliminate human freedom but acts by inviting, persuading, and appealing.

The Holy Spirit reveals Christ and His salvation to men. He alerts men to their sin and calls them to repentance and to faith. Faith is knowledge of the gospel plus assent to the gospel plus a decision to trust Christ as Savior. The initial trust becomes a permanent attitude. Regeneration is the new life given at the moment of conversion. Justification is the legal acquittal of sinners by which God delivers them from condemnation and restores them to His favor. Adoption is God's taking sinners into His family. Regeneration, conversion, justification, and adoption are different expressions of a single great reality, which may be summarized as union with Christ.

God's purpose is to produce a community of holy men and women, and this means they must first be placed in a new relationship with God, and then a new character must be produced in them. Sanctification is God's inner transformation of sinners into persons of Christian character. It is both a gift and a task for the Christian, who must strive for it with the help of God. Christians reject antinomianism and perfectionism. Left to themselves, Christians would be in danger of falling from grace, so God preserves them in their salvation; they must cooperate with Him in every way they can, and this includes taking seriously the biblical warnings against apostasy. His preservation is not mechanical: "The personal God deals with personal man in a free personal manner."[60]

Eschatology is the attempt to describe the final carrying out of God's eternal purpose, and is an essential part of Christian theology. Following the death of the body, Christians enter a temporary intermediate state—not to be confused with purgatory or with soul-sleep—to await their resurrection and the final judgment, when they will enter heaven and receive their rewards. The end of history will occur when Christ returns personally to the earth. The millennium has been given too much prominence in recent theology, and none of the millennial views is fully satisfactory; what matters is the second coming of Christ and the resurrection of the body, which must not be confused with the immortality of the soul. Heaven and hell are very real, and denials of the latter are to be resisted. God cannot make men who freely choose to be bad, to be happy. "Christians to-day with practical unanimity hold that infants dying in infancy are saved. This means about one-third of the human race."[61]

Mullins's last book, *Christianity at the Cross Roads,* was published when Mullins was sixty-four years old and in poor health. The crossroads of the title was the Fundamentalist-Modernist controversy which was then at fever pitch in the churches.

In a chapter entitled "The Modern Spirit," Mullins criticizes modernity's lack of respect for the past, its one-sidedness, its loss of the sense of mystery, and its excessive simplification of reality.

In "Fundamental Issues," Mullins says that the issue is not between two forms of evangelical Christianity, or between science and religion, or between doctrine and culture. The issue concerns facts—the facts of Jesus Christ and of the supernatural in His life. It is about the rights of religion to deal with its facts. It is about what will really bring salvation to humankind.

"The Rights of Religion" include the right to reject the reductionism which eliminates the supernatural. It also includes the right to allow religious knowledge to be known religiously, by those with a personal relationship with God. Scientists as such are not equipped to evaluate religion, nor are religious persons as such qualified to evaluate science.

"Reducing Christianity: Modern Science" continues this line of thinking, and includes a paragraph which represents Mullins's position on evolution clearly. Mullins is describing an evangelical thinker:

> He is perfectly willing to admit that God made the world gradually through long eras of time, that there is progress and growth in the universe, that the world is dynamic with a great divine purpose which is moving towards a shining goal. Moreover he refuses to dogmatize in the scientific realm. He holds himself open to the acceptance of any established fact of science. He insists at the same time that science should practice the same modesty that it enjoins upon others. Let it assert only when the evidence warrants it.[62]

This chapter is a sustained polemic against the modernistic reduction of Christianity by the elimination of the supernatural in the name of science. The argument continues in chapter 5. Mullins writes:

> Religious experience knows more than biological science has discovered. It knows that a universe flattened down to the level of the law of continuity does not represent all the reality that is. It knows that any system which flattens out the personality of God and man to that biological level is contrary to the best attested items of our spiritual experience.[63]

Mullins says that the religion of biological science, represented by men such as E. G. Conklin, has collapsed because its God is not transcendent and personal, it does not see people as immaterial souls, and it restricts human hope to social progress. This religion is so empty that it attracts few followers, but, says Mullins, some are attempting to work out a compromise between it and Christianity. "The Compromise" (ch. 6) has a personal God, but Jesus is only a great teacher, not a redeemer, and the supernatural elements in the New Testament are rejected. The compromise position is mere theism, and it is always being pulled forward toward Christianity and backward toward naturalism, and must always fight for its life. "One is constantly surprised at the narrowness of vision, lack of sympathy and spiritual insight, and especially the lack of courage on the part of modern biologists who insist upon a thorough-going naturalism."[64]

Mullins next turns his attention to the reduction of Christianity by modern philosophy. Philosophy seeks to understand many ultimate problems on principles of rationality; religion seeks a relationship between God and man upon principles of personality.

> Christianity is primarily not a philosophy of the universe. It is a religion. It is not founded upon metaphysics. Like all things known to us, there is an implied philosophy. There is a certain view of God and nature and man and the world in the background of our faith. But Christianity is a historical religion, and a religion of experience. It is grounded in facts. The Christian world-view rests upon these facts.[65]

Philosophy cannot prescribe what religion ought to be, or to teach.

Then Mullins turns to the reduction of Christianity by means of historical criticism. The best way to study the New Testament is with "a sound historical criticism, combined with spiritual appreciation of its contents."[66] Historical criticism goes wrong when it eliminates some of the evidence—such as Jesus' miracles—or when it accepts one kind of evidence as if it were all there is, as when, for example, Harnack portrays Jesus as if He were only a teacher of morals or Schweitzer portrays Jesus as if He were only an apocalyptic prophet.

The last form of reductionism to which Mullins responds is "the latest theory," namely, the effort to account for Christianity by setting it in the context of other religions in the first century. Mullins welcomes the method of comparative religion, and he believes we have benefited from some of its conclusions. For example, Paul used terms found in mystery religions—but then, missionaries today also use terms taken from a non-Christian vocabulary. But the claim of, for example, Alfred Loisy, that Jesus was regarded by the church as a Savior-God only because the church was made up of people familiar with the mystery religions, is exaggerated and highly improbable; in fact, it is not even certain that the mystery religions existed as early as the first century.

The final four chapters of the book are Mullins's constructive work. They deal with "the irreducible Christ" and Christian experience, the New Testament, the spiritual life of the world, and Christian history, respectively. He summarized his view in these words:

> Christianity is at the cross roads. We face a great issue. The alternatives are clear. On the one hand we may listen to the voice of the New Testament, of a sound criticism, of a sound historical method, to the voice of a regenerating and redeeming Christian experience, to the voice of history during two thousand years and thus retain all the great elements in our historical faith. On the other hand we may listen to alien voices, that of physical science, philosophic speculation, subjective criticism, and comparative religion and thus reduce Christianity to the dimensions of an ethical movement or philosophic cult.[67]

In his earlier books, Mullins positioned himself carefully in a middle, moderate position, between the extremes. No doubt he thought of himself in a similar position in this book, between the extremes of fundamentalism and modernism. But the book itself is a sustained polemic against naturalism on his left, and against the versions of Christianity called modernism and liberalism which he regards as the thin edge of the naturalist wedge entering the church's life. For whatever reason, Mullins is here more than in any other of his books, the conservative defender of traditional views.

Evaluation

Mullins's greatest theological achievement may have been to guide Baptists, especially Southern Baptists, away from some of the more extreme expressions of Calvinism and Landmarkism. He was not able to do the same with fundamentalism. He established moderation as a virtue in theological work for many Southern Baptists. He helped many to move in their understanding of science and religion beyond the warfare stage to a separate-spheres understanding. He was not able to negotiate a similar movement regarding evolution in particular. He demonstrated the importance of the categories of persons, personal life, freedom, and Christian experience, for theological work by Baptists.

Mullins's theology could have been more balanced. He enthusiastically unpacked the meaning of his Protestant heritage, his revivalist heritage, and his distinctively Baptist heritage. But he seemed to think that the universal Christian heritage needed little or no exposition, only a strong defense. For example, the most universal, most distinctively Christian understanding of God is the Trinitarian. So far as I can tell, Mullins devotes, out of the 2,000 pages in his six major books, only nine pages to this great teaching. This is unbalanced.

Mullins was wise to insist that Christianity is about persons—about a personal God in interpersonal relationships with human persons. Mullins saw that science and philosophy threatened the personal categories, but he did not seem to notice the greater threat of the psychology of the unconscious to persons.

Nor did he deal very successfully with the social experience of Christianity. He formally assented to the importance of Christian community, but his mind turned instinctively and inevitably to the private experiences of conversion and moral transformation. He was intoxicated by personal freedom, even by personal rights—a category which owes more to the Enlightenment than to the New Testament—even to the loss of the indispensability of society and social relationships for personal life.[68]

His utilization of the category of experience was excellent. He successfully shielded himself from charges of subjectivism. The form of experience to which he referred was almost always that of conversion followed by moral transformation. This experience yields a knowledge—a certain knowledge—available in no other way. However, Mullins does not seem to have noticed the implications of the fact that that particular form of religious experience is widespread, in part, because it is carefully fostered in the revivalist tradition. Christian experience is possible because Christ acts in people's lives; the conversionist structure of experience is possible because it is managed by a church committed to it.

Mullins was a responsible, careful theologian; he read widely; he thought carefully; he was constructive; he spoke to the concerns of his time; he was not rationalistic, narrow, vague, or overly defensive; he was a great Baptist theologian.

Bibliography

Works by Mullins

The Axioms of Religion. Philadelphia: American Baptist Publication Society, 1908.

Baptist Beliefs. Louisville: Baptist World Publishing Co., 1912.

The Christian Religion in Its Doctrinal Expression. Philadelphia: Roger Williams Press, 1917.

Christianity at the Cross Roads. Nashville: Sunday School Board of the S.B.C., 1924.

Freedom and Authority in Religion. Philadelphia: The Griffith & Rowland Press, 1913.

The Life in Christ. New York: Fleming H. Revell Co., 1917. A collection of sermons, one of which was also included in *The Fundamentals*.

Spiritualism—A Delusion. Nashville: Sunday School Board of the S.B.C., 1920.

Studies in Ephesians and Colossians. Nashville: Sunday School Board of the S.B.C., 1913.

Talks on Soul Winning. Nashville: Sunday School Board of the S.B.C., 1920.

Why Is Christianity True? Philadelphia: The Judson Press, 1905; originally published by Christian Culture Press, Chicago.

Works about Mullins

Carver, W. O. "Edgar Young Mullins—Leader and Builder" *The Review and Expositor* (April 1929).

Dilday, Russell H., Jr. "E. Y. Mullins: The Bible's Authority Is a Living Transforming Reality." *The Unfettered Word*. Edited by Robison B. James. Waco: Word Books, 1987.

Dobbins, Gaines S. "Edgar Young Mullins." *Encyclopedia of Southern Baptists* II. Nashville: Broadman Press, 1958.

Ellis, William E. *A Man of Books and a Man of the People*. Macon: Mercer University Press, 1985.

The Faculty of the Southern Baptist Theological Seminary. *Edgar Young Mullins: A Study in Christian Character*. Louisville: n.p., n.d.

Mullins, Isla May. *Edgar Young Mullins: An Intimate Biography*. Nashville: Sunday School Board of the S.B.C., 1929.

_____. "Dr. Mullins as a Student." *The Review and Expositor* (April 1929).

Stubblefield, Jerry M. "The Ecumenical Impact of E. Y. Mullins." *Journal of Ecumenical Studies* (Spring 1980).

Thomas, Bill Clark. *Edgar Young Mullins: A Baptist Exponent of Theological Restatement*. Ph.D. diss., The Southern Baptist Theological Seminary, 1963.

Notes

1. Gaines S. Dobbins, "Edgar Young Mullins," in *Encyclopedia of Southern Baptists* (Nashville: Broadman Press, 1958) 2:930. Except where otherwise indicated, biographical information about Mullins has been taken from this article.

2. Isla May Mullins, *Edgar Young Mullins* (Nashville: The Sunday School Board of the Southern Baptist Convention, 1929), 9.

3. William E. Ellis, *A Man of Books and a Man of the People* (Macon, Ga.: Mercer University Press, 1985), 2. Ellis points out that S. G. Mullins owned four slaves in 1860.

4. Mullins, *Edgar Young Mullins*, 10. Isla May Mullins says the family moved when Edgar was eight years old. William E. Ellis (p. 4) says they began the move on November 16, 1869.

5. Isla May Mullins, "Dr. Mullins as a Student," in *The Review and Expositor* (April 1929): 142.

6. Mullins, *Edgar Young Mullins*, 15.

7. Ellis, *A Man of Books and a Man of the People*, 40.

8. Jerry M. Stubblefield, "The Ecumenical Impact of E. Y. Mullins," *Journal of Ecumenical Studies* (Spring 1980): 99.

9. Louie D. Newton, "Baptist World Alliance," *Encyclopedia of Southern Baptists* (Nashville: Broadman Press, 1958), 1:130.

10. See, for example, Russell H. Dilday, Jr., "E. Y. Mullins: The Bible's Authority Is a Living Transforming Reality," in *The Unfettered Word*, ed. Robison B. James (Waco: Word Books, 1987), 109.

11. W. O. Carver, "Edgar Young Mullins—Leader and Builder," in *The Review and Expositor* (April 1929): 128.

12. See the newspaper article appended to the biography by Isla May Mullins, *Edgar Young Mullins*, 214.

13. Bill Clark Thomas, *Edgar Young Mullins: A Baptist Exponent of Theological Restatement* (Ph.D. diss., The Southern Baptist Theological Seminary, 1963), 91.

14. E. Y. Mullins, *The Christian Religion in Its Doctrinal Expression* (Valley Forge, Pa.: Judson Press, 1917), vii.

15. E. Y. Mullins, *The Axioms of Religion* (Philadelphia: American Baptist Publication Society, 1908), 14.

16. "Moderation, indeed, remains a hallmark of Mullins' system of doctrine." Sydney E. Ahlstrom, "Theology in America: A Historical Survey" in *Religion in American Life*, vol. 1, ed. James Ward Smith and A. Leland Jamison, *The Shaping of American Religion* (Princeton: Princeton University Press, 1961), 306.

17. Dilday, "E. Y. Mullins: The Bible's Authority Is a Living Transforming Reality," 114.

18. Ellis, *A Man of Books and a Man of the People*, 218. Ellis is writing specifically of the evolution controversy, and generally about the Fundamentalist-Modernist controversy. See also 221-22.

19. The Whitsitt controversy antedates his presidency, and is traced by Gaines Dobbins to an encyclopedia article by Whitsitt which appeared in 1886. See Gaines S. Dobbins, "William Heth Whitsitt," in *Encyclopedia of Southern Baptists*, 2:1896.

20. E. Y. Mullins, *Why Is Christianity True?* (Philadelphia: The Judson Press, 1905), 354. It is not clear whether Mullins wrote this book before or after he returned to Louisville. Ellis (*A Man of Books and a Man of the People*, 74) and others report that he wrote it in response to a request which came after he arrived in Louisville. However, the book itself contains evidence that he wrote it before the close of the nineteenth century; see 376, where he refers to the nineteenth century as "the present century."

21. Ahlstrom, "Theology in America: A Historical Survey," 303-4.

22. Mullins, *The Christian Religion in Its Doctrinal Expression*, 425.

23. William A. Mueller, *A History of Southern Baptist Theological Seminary* (Nashville: Broadman Press, 1959), 113.

24. Robert Wood Lynn, "Notes toward a History: Theological Encyclopedia and the Evolution of Protestant Seminary Curriculum, 1808-1869" in *Theological Education* (Spring 1981): 118-44.

25. The Faculty of the Southern Baptist Theological Seminary, *Edgar Young Mullins: A Study in Christian Character* (Louisville: n.p., n.d.), 5. Bill Clark Thomas listed twelve books by Mullins in his bibliography; Mullins was a prolific writer; the list of all his writings given by Thomas is forty-three pages long! See Thomas, *Edgar Young Mullins: A Baptist Exponent of Theological Restatement*, 412-54.

26. The phrases are book titles by C. S. Lewis, J. B. Phillips, and John Stott, respectively.

27. Mullins, *The Axioms of Religion*, 59, 73.

28. Ibid., 79.

29. Ibid., 90.

30. Ibid., 92.

31. Ibid., 94.

32. Ibid., 127.

33. Ibid., 134.

34. Ibid., 147.

35. Ibid., 150.

36. Ibid., 185.

37. Ibid., 187.

38. Ibid., 194.

39. Ibid., 197.

40. Ibid., 201.

41. Ibid., 208-9.

42. Ibid., 210.

43. Ibid., 232.

44. Ibid., 307.

45. Martin E. Marty, "Baptistification Takes Over," *Christianity Today,* September 2, 1983, 33-36.

46. E. Y. Mullins, *Baptist Beliefs* (Valley Forge, Pa.: Judson Press, 1925; reprint of 1912 edition, published by Baptist World Publishing Co.), 5-6.

47. William L. Lumpkin, *Baptist Confessions of Faith* (Philadelphia: Judson Press, 1959), 391-98.

48. E. Y. Mullins, *Freedom and Authority in Religion* (Philadelphia: The Griffith & Rowland Press, 1913), 128.

49. Ibid., 257.

50. Ibid., 288.

51. Ibid., 402-3.

52. Ibid., 394.

53. Mullins, *The Christian Religion in Its Doctrinal Expression*, 18.

54. Ibid., 135-3.

55. Ibid., 141.

56. Ibid., 142.

57. Ibid., 211.

58. Ibid., 252.

59. Ibid., 323-4.

60. Ibid., 437.

61. Ibid., 503. Mullins's only two children died very young.

62. E. Y. Mullins, *Christianity at the Cross Roads* (Nashville: The Sunday School Board of the Southern Baptist Convention, 1924), 67.

63. Ibid., 97.

64. Ibid., 149.

65. Ibid., 163.

66. Ibid., 185.

67. Ibid., 233-4.

68. Mullins seems to have realized this sometime after the publication of *The Axioms of Religion* (1908); in *The Christian Religion in its Doctrinal Expression* he wrote, "Christianity emphasizes duties rather than rights," 427.

17

William Bell Riley
Timothy P. Weber

Historians of American religion have increasingly recognized the importance of William Bell Riley in the Fundamentalist-Modernist controversy. He has been called "the ablest executive that fundamentalism produced,"[1] "the ablest leader of orthodox reaction during the early part of the twentieth century" and the founder of "the only inclusive fellowship of fundamentalists in America,"[2] the "architect of fundamentalism,"[3] and "the organizing genius of American Fundamentalism."[4] But to date, no one has called him a theologian. Riley would probably be relieved. As the above list indicates, he was an activist, a doer, and a defender of the faith whose life was anything but that of a settled academic. In fact, theologians were among his least favorite people in the world. That was especially true for liberal theologians, but also included conservatives who refused to *do* anything about their convictions during controversial times.

Riley was a man of the people, not the academy. Nevertheless, his theological views exerted tremendous influence over thousands of people, inside and outside of his Northern Baptist Convention. In other words, he was one of those populist religious leaders who knew how to bypass educational and ecclesiastical elites to "storm heaven by the back door."[5]

Biography

William Bell Riley was born in Green County, Indiana, on March 22, 1861, to Branson Radish Riley of Kentucky and Ruth Anna Jackson of Pennsylvania. A pro-slavery Democrat and Southern sympathizer, Branson Riley moved his family across the Ohio River to Kentucky shortly after the Civil War began.[6] Riley grew up on his father's tobacco farm, "bathed," as his biographer-wife put it, "in the waves of the warm evangelical revival" that swept regularly over Kentucky. His parents were both committed believers, and William made his own profession of faith at age seventeen.[7]

By then, however, Riley had made up his mind to become a lawyer. In 1879 he used money he earned farming tobacco to finance a year's college preparatory course at Valparaiso Normal School in Indiana. In the spring of 1880 he left Indiana with a teacher's certificate, planning to start college in the fall. But financial difficulties forced him to spend the next year back on the farm. There, after considerable struggle, he yielded to the call to preach and never looked back.

In the fall of 1881 he entered Hanover College, a Presbyterian school in southern Indiana, where he excelled in debate and wrestling and, true to his new calling, pastored two small Baptist churches in Kentucky on the side. He graduated fourth in his class in 1885, then moved directly to The Southern Baptist Theological Seminary in Louisville. He finished the seminary program in three years, then held three small pastorates in Indiana (New Albany, 1887-88 and Lafayette, 1888-91) and Illinois (Bloomington, 1891-93). During his Lafayette ministry he married Lillian Howard with whom he eventually had six children.

In 1893 Riley moved to the newly organized Calvary Baptist Church in Chicago, full of ambition to reach the city for Christ. He was an energetic young pastor whose hard work got results. In four years the membership grew from sixty to five hundred, but Riley was not happy. The severe depression of 1893 kept the church from meeting its financial obligations to him, but even more troublesome was the way the city made him feel small and his work insignificant. He quickly concluded that "a big city is the poorest place in the world for any preacher except its most notable one. Its very extent suffices to reduce opportunity, to circumscribe influence, and even to destroy the reach of personality."[8] Riley decided that he would do better in a downtown church in a medium sized city. In 1897 he found his church and his city: the First Baptist Church in Minneapolis, where he stayed for forty-five years and built one of the most amazing ecclesiastical empires in the United States.

First Baptist Church was founded in 1854, and by the time Riley became pastor, it was famous for its beautiful facilities and its sophisticated membership. Never fond of elites of any kind, Riley decided to fill his church with ordinary people. He revised the church roll, eliminating all but active members; undercut the power base of the "old guard" by restructuring the church's boards; abolished pew rentals; and stopped the Ladies' Aid Society from raising money through bazaars and church suppers. He pushed the members to tithe their incomes; condemned worldly amusements, including theater-going, card-playing, and dancing; and changed the church's ethos by replacing the liturgical emphasis of his predecessor with rousing evangelistic preaching. The results were predictable. The clientele of First Baptist Church began to change. Of the 300 souls Riley added to the church during his first year in Minneapolis, nearly three-quarters were blue and white collar workers.[9] When people from the old power structure realized that the church was becoming lower middle class, they rebelled. For five years Riley fended off attempts to oust him, until finally 146 people withdrew to establish another church.[10] After Riley gained control, the church experienced steady growth, from 585 when he came to 3,550 when he retired.[11]

Riley always considered himself first and foremost a pastor, but he never failed to find other things to do too. In short order he established himself as a civic reformer, popular revivalist, Christian educator, and ecclesiastical politican of the first rank. From his earliest days in the ministry, Riley believed that urban pastors had to take public positions on social issues.[12] In both Chicago and Minneapolis he joined the Civic Federation, which fought

William Bell Riley (1861-1947)

against vice and the liquor industry, and spoke out against governmental corruption. Furthermore, after he moved to Minneapolis, the officials at First Baptist granted him permission to spend four months a year away from the church as an itinerant evangelist. After 1920 other responsibilities forced him to curtail his revival preaching, but for two decades he conducted scores of three- or four-week evangelistic crusades around the country and even overseas.[13] When he discovered that a third of the Baptist churches in Minnesota were without pastors, in 1902 he founded the interdenominational Northwestern Bible and Missionary Training School to supply pastors for small-town and rural congregations. In 1938 he established the Northwestern Evangelical Seminary to provide leaders for city churches, and in 1944 he opened Northwestern College as a liberal arts institution.[14]

Such activities earned Riley the reputation as an aggressive and effective leader with boundless energy, which he put to good use in the emerging Fundamentalist-Modernist controversy.[15] Born with a good nose for heresy and a temperament that loved a fight, Riley detected the liberal threat to orthodoxy early. He quickly gained credibility as a leader of militant conservatives through his participation in the Prophetic Conference movement that gained momentum around World War I. Converted to dispensational premillennialism in 1890, by the turn of the century Riley became a regular speaker at Bible prophecy conferences, where he made contacts, established his orthodox credentials, and watched the spread of theological liberalism with growing alarm.[16]

By the end of World War I, Riley believed the conservatives needed an interdenominational organization to meet the modernist challenge. Using millenarian leaders for support and the large prophetic conferences in 1918 as his platform, Riley announced a conference on Christian fundamentals for May 1919 in Philadelphia. When the time came over six thousand people showed up and voted into existence the World's Christian Fundamentals Association (WCFA). Riley was elected general secretary and editor of the organization's magazine, *Christian Fundamentals in School and Church*. Five standing committees were appointed to coordinate the efforts of the many fundamentalist organizations Riley was sure would join. He immediately put together a traveling squad of fundamentalist speakers and blitzed the nation, certain that modernism's days were numbered. Never one for understatement, he declared the founding of the WCFA to be "an event of more historical moment than the nailing up, at Wittenberg, of Martin Luther's ninety-five theses. The hour has struck for the rise of a new Protestantism."[17]

It was hardly that. Riley soon discovered that fundamentalism consisted of the loosest confederation of independent religious entrepreneurs who were not about to surrender their hard-won constituencies to him, who was probably the biggest entrepreneur of them all.[18] As a result, annual WCFA conventions produced more smoke than fire; and very little was ever accomplished. In 1920 Riley joined forces with William Jennings Bryan and turned the WCFA's attention to the crusade against evolution. For the next few years Riley campaigned hard in a number of states for anti-evolution legislation and conducted over two dozen public debates with evolutionists. But by the end of the decade he realized that he had failed to dislodge Darwinism from the schools.[19] In 1929 he resigned as general secretary, leaving the WCFA with very little to show for a decade of endeavor.[20]

At the same time he was directing the WCFA, Riley was deeply involved in the Northern Baptist Convention (NBC).[21] By 1920 conservatives were so concerned about liberalism in the Convention that they organized the Fundamentalist Fellowship, under the leadership of J. C. Massee, and called for a thorough investigation of Baptist schools and missionary agencies. When the Convention decided to do nothing about confirmed reports of liberalism here and there, the fundamentalists tried another approach. They proposed that the Convention adopt a binding statement of faith, which they hoped would drive liberals from the church. Since "creedalism" was anathema to most Baptists, the fundamentalists argued among themselves over how to sell the idea to the Convention. By 1922 Riley was tired of waiting for consensus and took matters into his own hands. He offered a resolution to make the New Hampshire Confession of 1833 the NBC's official creed. The liberals were ready; they countered with a resolution "that the New Testament is an all-sufficient ground for Baptist faith and practice, and we need no other statement." Not wanting to vote against the Bible, even conservatives supported the liberal resolution, 1,264 to 637. Riley kept fighting. Over the next few years he tried to exclude salaried employees of the NBC from voting in denominational matters and to make baptism by immersion a prerequisite for membership in NBC churches. He never won a vote.

Riley and other militant conservatives blamed such failures on weak leadership in the Fundamentalist Fellowship and called for a more aggressive behavior. In 1923 Riley, T. T. Shields of Canada, and J. Frank Norris of Texas organized the Baptist Bible Union, which sought to unite fundamentalists in the Northern, Southern, and Canadian Baptist Conventions. Under Riley and his two colleagues, the BBU did take a more militant stance but was no more successful than the Fundamentalist Fellowship at turning the tide in the NBC. When some in BBU threatened to leave the denomination, Riley squelched any talk of separation, utterly convinced that fundamentalists were close to regaining control of the church.[22] But Riley was wrong. By 1927 most fundamentalists had decided that they did not have the clout to change things. When what was left of the BBU finally decided to withdraw from the NBC in 1932 and form the General Association of Regular Baptists, Riley decided to stay behind, still convinced that the Convention could be saved.[23]

By 1930, then, Riley's well-publicized crusades to drive liberals from the NBC and evolution from the schools were over. Though he remained a fundamentalist leader with a national constituency, Riley concentrated on matters closer to home. In 1933, two years after his wife Lillian died, he married Marie Acomb, dean of women at Northwestern Bible and Missionary Training School. Probably as a reflection of his many disappointments, in 1934 Riley joined Gerald B. Winrod, Arno C. Gaebelein, and other dispensational leaders in promoting *The Protocols of the Elders of Zion,* an anti-Semitic forgery purporting to outline a plot to destroy Christian civilization, and the idea of an international Jewish conspiracy closely tied to communism.[24] The formerly optimistic crusader thus spent the last decade and a half of his life explaining in detail how the Great Depression, the New Deal, the movie industry, organized crime, and the success of modernism could be traced to a small group of Jewish conspirators.[25]

At the same time he dabbled in rightwing politics, he nurtured his church and schools. Graduates of his Northwestern Schools soon numbered in the hundreds and the Riley network crisscrossed the upper midwest. If he could not make the NBC safe for evangelical Christianity, he could at least save the Minnesota Baptist Convention. Riley became its president in 1944 and 1945 and broke all working relationships with the NBC. He favored the establishment of the Conservative Baptist Association of America in 1947, though his own congregation, from which he retired in 1942, decided to keep its ties to the NBC. Finally in May 1947, Riley resigned his personal membership in the denomination, convinced that it was beyond hope.[26]

There was still one thing left to do: find a successor to lead his Northwestern Schools. In August 1947, Riley summoned to his sick bed a twenty-eight-year-old evangelist named Billy Graham and told him, "Beloved, as Samuel appointed David king of Israel, so I appoint you head of these schools. I'll meet you at the judgment seat of Christ with them." Graham reluctantly accepted. Five months later, William Bell Riley, "a prima donna of fundamentalism,"[27] died. Harry Ironside, pastor of Moody Memorial Church in Chicago, wrote of his departed friend: "We need to remember that God never repeats Himself. . . . He will raise up others to carry on, but there will never be a second man of Dr. Riley's stamp."[28] According to C. Allyn Russell, "Riley's disciples lamented this fact; his enemies rejoiced that it was true."[29]

Exposition

Theologically, in many respects Riley was a typical Baptist traditionalist. He never stopped believing in the New Hampshire Confession of 1833, the most popular Baptist "creed" of the nineteenth century. His first major book was an exposition of the Confession,[30] and, as we have seen, in 1922 he tried to get the NBC to adopt it as its binding statement of faith. But hundreds of other Baptist traditionalists never supported Riley or his programs, which probably means that Riley was not as traditional as he thought he was. As a fundamentalist, Riley stretched his Baptist theology between the poles of biblical inerrancy and dispensational premillennialism.

According to the New Hampshire Confession, "the Holy Bible was written by men divinely inspired, and is a perfect treasure of heavenly instruction . . . it has God for its author, salvation for its end, and truth, without any mixture of error, for its matter." Twentieth-century traditionalists still affirmed this statement, but many of them wondered how far they could press it in light of the new biblical scholarship. Though most conservatives probably understood "truth without any mixture of error" as "inerrancy," many of them did not feel it was prudent to insist on it, as Presbyterian conservatives at Princeton Seminary were doing.[31] In fact, Augustus Strong, the North's leading conservative Baptist theologian, strenuously avoided inerrancy language in his doctrine of Scripture and warned that it was an indefensible position.[32]

Not so William Bell Riley. In light of the assault of biblical higher criticism, he believed that the doctrine of inerrancy was the *sine qua non* of orthodoxy. In 1891 he affirmed the New Hampshire doctrine of Scripture and pressed it as far as he could in the direction of inerrancy. Though humans actually recorded the words, they were only "the mediums of divine communication, and at times, like reporters of less important thought, wrote better than they themselves knew." In the last analysis, God wrote "every book, chapter, verse, sentence, and even word," which is why it is impossible—and dangerous—to try to distinguish between the Bible's religious statements and its historical and scientific ones. For Riley the Bible "[is] infallible, inerrant; . . . its integrity extends to history as well as to morals and religion, and involves expression as well as thought."[33] Riley knew that through transmission and translation errors had crept into the text, but insisted that they did not "cast any discredit upon the genuineness of the Word, nor indeed create a dread in the devout mind."[34] The original manuscripts were inerrant; the current texts were close enough. Here was the Princeton doctrine of inerrancy in Baptist clothes.[35]

According to Riley, denying inerrancy had produced two of modernism's most serious errors, higher criticism and evolution, whose advocates had chosen speculation over scholarship and skepticism over science. Riley's big objection was that these movements were not truly scientific: their conclusions were really unproved assumptions and none of their "assured results" could stand up to the inductive scientific method. In fact, Riley had a hard time understanding how anyone with common sense and an open mind could believe such nonsense. "Who, outside of themselves, have been convinced by their array of arguments, except it be some of the students who have sat at their feet, and whose mental furniture was so scarce that even doubt found greedy reception?"[36] He claimed to have proof that no student who graduated from seminary with an eighty per-cent or higher had ever succumbed to modernist propaganda.[37] To gain converts, modernists must have to deceive or bully their students. It was immoral, Riley declared, to take students fresh off the farm and throw them into the classrooms of such unscrupulous teachers. "To justify the destruction of the faith in which one was born . . . before he becomes capable of deciding whether he should surrender or retain the same, is a piece of robbery beside which the work of highwaymen is a minor incident."[38]

Riley said he was not against hard nosed biblical and scientific scholarship, only the anti-supernatural presuppositions that led modernists to their outrageous conclusions. Was it possible to be theologically orthodox and believe in some kind of evolution? Not as far as Riley was concerned: "There are men who hold to the evolutionary theory who are still 'theists,' or so they say; but without exception they are not worshippers of the God of the Bible, nor do they in any sense accept the essential Deity of Jesus Christ."[39]

Did Riley understand the ideas that he so soundly rejected? We will never know because he never attempted a scholarly critique of them. Many of his major books were transcribed sermons, a medium not usually suited to academic discourse;[40] and even those that Riley did not preach first were written for popular audiences. He did not engage the thought of his opponents; he characterized it. In a sense, even his most serious books rarely reached higher than his public debates with evolutionists during the 1920s. Such encounters were never intended to be high-level discussions of scientific issues. They were public spectacles where the already-convinced could be confirmed in their beliefs, and everyone could have fun at someone else's expense. These debates were never academic exercises for Riley; they were opportunities to engage an audience and build a clientele.[41]

This observation is not intended to impugn Riley's abilities or his motives. As a popular religious leader, his first obligation was to show people where modernism led, not how it was put together. Riley wanted his audiences to understand that modernism was bad for theology, bad for religion, and bad for morals.[42] He was absolutely convinced that common people were smarter than the so-called experts, and that if empowered and encouraged, they could figure out the Bible and the Christian faith pretty much by themselves.[43] Such views demonstrate that Riley, like other fundamentalists, held on to Common Sense philosophy long after it ceased to be the foundation for American education and science.[44]

Though it was hard for most people to arrive at dispensationalism on their own, Riley insisted that it stood with biblical inerrancy as a bulwark against modernism. Dispensational premillennialism came out of Great Britain in the 1830s, the brain child of John Nelson Darby, one of the founders of the Plymouth Brethren. It was essentially a complicated hermeneutic that sought to divide all of history into eras or "dispensations" and distinguish between the two separate peoples of God, Israel and the church, and their separate divine programs. By "rightly dividing the word of truth" in this way, dispensationalists believed that they had the key to unlock biblical prophecy: Before a great apostasy sweeps over the earth, Christ will secretly return to rapture his church and the anti-Christ will be revealed. Following the Great Tribulation, during which God's elect are persecuted, Christ will return with His raptured saints, fight again the anti-Christ and his supporters at the Battle of Armageddon, bind Satan for a thousand years, and set up His millennial kingdom. For dispensationalists, then, the Bible presented "history before it happened," which kept them looking for "signs of the times."

Dispensationalism came to the United States after the Civil War and spread through Bible and prophetic conferences, Bible institutes, and most importantly, the *Scofield Reference Bible,* whose textual notes helped people read the Scriptures dispensationally.[45]

As we have seen, Riley accepted the doctrine in the 1890s and became a popular speaker at prophetic conferences. His views were so typical of the dispensational establishment that he was asked by C. I. Scofield to contribute to his *Reference Bible* but had to decline because of other duties.[46]

Not all dispensationalists were alike, and Riley was more optimistic than most about what might be accomplished before the eventual demise of human civilization. While some dispensationalists were wringing their hands about the hopeless state of the world, Riley urged increased effort to slow the slide toward Armageddon. Because of his success as a revivalist and a social reformer, he knew that the Devil could be beaten. In 1922 Riley told the annual convention of the WCFA that "if Christ delay, the defeat of Modernism is certain."[47] Because he expected one more mighty revival before Christ's second coming, he could remain in the NBC and fight when other fundamentalists despaired and mount an aggressive political campaign to drive evolution out of the schools.[49]

This optimism in the 1920s makes his espousal of anti-Semitic conspiracy theories in the 1930s even more remarkable. By then, it must be remembered, Riley was in his seventies and had lost every major battle he had fought. The modernists and evolutionists were still in control and now, finally, the world seemed to be moving quickly toward its predetermined end. Dispensationalism, after all, is a conspiracy theory of cosmic proportions whose broad outlines could easily embrace wild theories of apostate and communistic Jews who had undercut the noble efforts of good people like Riley.[50] Even when he was criticized by other fundamentalists for his anti-Semitism, he refused to back down. The old war horse would not apologize, even to his friends.[51]

In retrospect Riley's theology was a blend of Baptist orthodoxy and fundamentalism, which became more extreme over the years. It was built on a straight-forward reading of the Bible, which some have correctly called "proof-texting,"[52] and aimed at common people. One must finally conclude that though his theology was ridiculed by his liberal opponents, it expressed the deeply felt convictions of millions, which for Riley spelled success and vindication. For popular religious leaders with a mass following, the audience is sovereign.

Evaluation

By what standard should William Bell Riley's work be judged? As a thinker, Riley has left no legacy. Fundamentalists today still hold his memory sacred,[53] but with the exception of an occasional sermon reprinted in the *Sword of the Lord,* they rarely read him. His books were, after all, "tracts for the times," not tomes for the ages. Because his theology was more polemical than constructive, it stayed useful only as long as the war raged and the enemy stayed the same. Even today's "creationists" who share his hatred of evolution are not likely to turn to his *Inspiration or Evolution* for help. In the 1990s the battlefield looks different and there is better ammunition available. Though they may admire the passion and persistence of his written work, most theological conservatives today probably feel about Riley's theology the same way most of us do about the furniture in our grandparents' parlor: we know it used to be the "latest thing" and served its purpose well, but we just don't want to live there anymore.

All that does not change the fact that Riley probably was the best leader fundamentalism ever produced. It is on that basis, then, that he should be judged. Riley was not great because of the books he wrote but because of the people he led.

The key for understanding Riley's real legacy can be found in Nathan Hatch's *The Democratization of American Christianity* (1989). The author argues that during the period of the early republic, American religion experienced a seismic reorientation along democratic lines. Dynamic young leaders without formal training or any sense of their own limitations "went outside normal denominational frameworks to develop large followings by the democratic art of persuasion. These are inherently interesting personalities, unbranded individualists, who chose to storm heaven by the back door."[54] These leaders empowered common people by taking their deepest longings at face value and helping them overthrow the authoritarian structures that tried to control them.

Hatch believes that twentieth-century fundamentalism is an example of the recurring populist impulse in American Christianity. By the turn of the century, American society was on a desperate search for order.[55] Business, government, and even the churches shifted sharply toward bureaucratic order and centralized authority. Liberal Christianity endorsed this need for rational study, efficient planning, and the learned professional. In such circles leadership was defined in those terms; and the experts were allowed to have the final word.

Many people resisted these efforts to consolidate and rationalize their churches and fought back with those populist techniques that had served American popular Christianity for over a century. They discovered that "their power in the modern world lies in their character as democratic persuasions."

Fundamentalism emerged because scores of self-appointed and independent-minded leaders knew how to tap in to the frustrations of common people who opposed the centralizing of ecclesiastical authority and resented being told that their faith was now ridiculous in light of modern scholarship. Locked out by the educational and bureaucratic elites, fundamentalist leaders bypassed the establishment by mastering the public media, founding their own churches and schools, and keeping theology and the Bible accessible to common folks. The more the modernist people in power belittled them, the more pronounced the leaders' populist instincts became.[56]

William Bell Riley was precisely this kind of leader. He was not trying to compete with the modernist theologians and ecclesiastical bureaucrats, whom he despised. He took his stand over against them, on the side of the common people. His resentments were the same as theirs; and he was successful as a fundamentalist leader because he knew what to do with them.

Riley identified with outsiders: "I am the son of a farmer whose fortune was not far removed from poverty. . . . By birth and breeding, I am a friend not alone of the manual laborer, but more especially of the poor and oppressed."[57] Such people never hatched heresies; that was the work of learned scholars in seminaries and universities whose salaries were paid by the people they ridiculed.[58] In 1921 Riley declared that Christian education was in peril because it was under "corporate control." Modernistic educators and their institutions formed an "academic octopus" that stretched from coast to coast and consciously excluded traditional Christian values and teachings.[59]

Riley was equally disgusted with the bureaucrats in charge of the denominations. Many conservative Baptists had opposed the formation of the Northern Baptist Convention in 1907 because they feared the effects of centralization on local church autonomy. Consequently fundamentalists interpreted every effort at increased efficiency and every call for a more professional ministry as an attempt to take away their prerogatives. In 1936 Riley complained that modernism had commandeered the ministry so that only those trained under its auspices were considered "professional" or worthy of advancement within the system. What ever happened to the call of God and the divine outfitting for ministerial service? Riley wanted to know. The ecclesiastical bureaucracy had ruined the training of ministers; that is why fundamentalists like Riley had to establish their own schools, so that common people could get a proper education.[60]

If the ecclesiastical and educational elites denied Riley a platform for his views, he knew how to get around them. Over the years Riley published over sixty books, wrote countless articles, and edited his own magazines (*Baptist Beacon, Christian Fundamentals in School and Church,* the *Christian Fundamentalist,* and the *Northwestern Pilot).* At the time of his death, 70 percent of the pastors in Baptist churches in Minnesota were products of his Northwestern Schools, whose alumni numbered over two thousand.[61] Modernism may have had the denominational and educational power, but Riley nearly had more people than he could handle.

As a populist leader, then, Riley was a roaring success. His independence, his unlimited energy, his extensive administrative skill, and his ability to seize the moment and mobilize the masses made him a standout in a field crowded with fundamentalist entrepreneurs. Ironically, his inability to defeat modernism did not hurt his reputation as a fundamentalist leader. According to Hatch, such leaders need big enemies; and they need to maintain their status as outsiders. In fundamentalism, losing sometimes means winning.

Bibliography

Works by Riley

Ten Sermons on the Greater Doctrines of Scripture. Bloomington, Ill.: Leader Publishing, 1891.

The Seven Churches of Asia. New York: Christian Alliance Publishing Co., 1900.

Vagaries and Verities. Minneapolis: Hall, Black, and Co., 1903.

Messages for the Metropolis. Chicago: Winona Publishing Co., 1906.

The Finality of the Higher Criticism. Minneapolis: n.p.,1909.

The Evolution of the Kingdom. New York: Charles C. Cook, 1913.

The Crisis of the Church. New York: Charles C. Cook, 1914.

The Menace of Modernism. New York: Christian Alliance Publishing Co., 1917.

Inspiration or Evolution. Cleveland: Union Gospel Publishing Co., 1923.

Christ the Incomparable. New York: Fleming Revell, 1924.

The Bible of the Expositor and the Evangelist, 39 vols. Cleveland: Union Gospel Press, 1925-35.

Ten Burning Questions. New York: Fleming Revell, 1932.

Protocols and Communism. Minneapolis: L. W. Camp, 1934.

Pastoral Problems. Westwood, N.J.: Fleming Revell, 1936.

Wives of the Bible: A Cross-Section of Femininity. Grand Rapids: Zondervan, 1938.

Seven New Testament Soul-Winners. Grand Rapids: Eerdmans, 1939.

Wanted—A World Leader! Minneapolis: n.p. 1939?

Re-thinking the Church. New York: Fleming Revell, 1940.

The Preacher and His Preaching. Wheaton, Ill.: Sword of the Lord Publishers, 1948.

The Conflict of Christianity with Its Counterfeits. N.p., n.d.

Riley's periodicals included the *Baptist Beacon, Christian Fundamentals in School and Church,* the *Christian Fundamentalist,* and *The Northwestern Pilot*.

Works about Riley

Hull, Lloyd B. "A Rhetorical Study of the Preaching of William Bell Riley." Unpublished Ph.D. diss., Wayne State University, 1960.

McBirnie, Robert S. "Basic Issues in the Fundamentalism of W. B. Riley." Unpublished Ph.D diss., University of Iowa, 1952.

Riley, Marie Acomb. *The Dynamic of a Dream*. Grand Rapids: Eerdmans, 1938.

Russell, C. Allyn. "William Bell Riley: Architect of Fundamentalism," *Minnesota History* (Spring 1972) 14-30.

Szasz, Ferenc M. "Three Fundamentalist Leaders: The Roles of William Bell Riley, John Roach Straton, and William Jennings Bryan in the Fundamentalist-Modernist Controversy." Ph.D. diss., University of Rochester, 1969.

Trollinger, William V. *God's Empire: William Bell Riley and Midwestern Fundamentalism*. Madison: University of Wisconsin Press, 1990.

Notes

1. Stewart G. Cole, *The History of Fundamentalism* (New York: Richard Smith, 1931), 325.

2. Robert S. McBirnie, "Basic Issues in the Fundamentalism of W. B. Riley" (Ph.D. diss., University of Iowa, 1952), 132.

3. C. Allyn Russell, "William Bell Riley: Architect of Fundamentalism," *Minnesota History* (Spring 1972): 14-30.

4. Ferenc M. Szasz, *The Divided Mind of Protestant America, 1880-1930* (University, Ala.: University of Alabama Press, 1982), 89.

5. Nathan O. Hatch, *The Democratization of American Christianity* (New Haven: Yale University Press, 1989), 210-19.

6. For basic biographical information see Marie Acomb Riley, *Dynamics of a Dream* (Grand Rapids: Eerdmans, 1938); William Trollinger, *God's Empire: William Bell Riley and Midwestern Fundamentalism* (Madison: University of Wisconsin, 1990); and Russell.

7. M. A. Riley, 31-33, 43-44; W. B. Riley, "My Conversion to Christ," *Watchman-Examiner,* May 6, 1937, 432.

8. "Four Anniversaries of a Great Christian Statesman," *The Northwestern Pilot* 27 (March 1947): 167.

9. Walter Ellis, "Social and Religious Factors in the Fundamentalist-Modernist Schisms among Baptists in North America, 1895-1934" (Ph.D. diss., University of Pittsburgh, 1974), 110-19.

10. M. A. Riley, 85-86.

11. Russell, 16.

12. William B. Riley, *Messages for the Metropolis* (Chicago: Winona Publishing House, 1906); Szasz, 60-61, 65.

13. Russell, 20-21; M. A. Riley, 172-82.

14. M. A. Riley, 146-60.

15. George M. Marsden, *Fundamentalist and American Culture* (New York: Oxford University Press, 1980).

16. On American dispensationalism, see Norman Kraus, *Dispensationalism in America* (Richmond: John Knox Press, 1958); Ernest R. Sandeen, *The Roots of Fundamentalism* (Chicago: University of Chicago Press, 1970); and Timothy P. Weber, *Living in the Shadow of the Second Coming: American Premillennnialism. 1875-1982* (Chicago: University of Chicago Press, 1987).

17. William Bell Riley, *Inspiration or Evolution* (Cleveland: Union Gospel Publishing Co., 1923), 181.

18. M. A. Riley, 128; Willard B. Gatewood, *Controversy in the Twenties* (Nashville: Vanderbilt University Press, 1969), 17-18.

19. Edward J. Larson, *Trial and Error: The American Controversy Over Creation and Evolution* (New York: Oxford University Press, 1985).

20. Russell, 24-28; Cole, 298-317.

21. Norman Furniss, *The Fundamentalist Controversy* (New Haven: Yale University Press, 1954), 104-18; George Dollar, *A History of Fundamentalism in America* (Greenville, S.C.: Unusual Publications, 1974), 145-58.

22. David O. Beale, *In Pursuit of Purity* (Greenville, S.C.: Unusual Publications, 1986), 211; Cole, 281-83.

23. Robert G. Delnay, "A History of the Baptist Bible Union" (Th.D. diss., Dallas Theological Seminary, 1963).

24. William B. Riley, *Protocols and Communism* (Minneapolis: L. W. Camp, 1934); William B. Riley, *Wanted—A World Leader!* (Minneapolis: Privately printed, 1939?).

25. Trollinger, chapter 3; Leo Ribuffo, *The Old Christian Right* (Philadelphia: Temple University Press, 1983).

26. See Beale, 393-95, for his resignation letter.

27. Dollar, 112-22.

28. Harry A. Ironside, "Dr. W. B. Riley, Defender of the Faith," *Northwestern Pilot* 28 (January 1948): 120.

29. Russell, 15.

30. William B. Riley, *Ten Sermons on the Greater Doctrines of Scripture* (Bloomington, Ill.: Leader Publishing, 1891).

31. Norman Maring, "Baptists and Changing Views of the Bible, 1865-1918 (Part I)," *Foundations* 1 (July 1958): 52-75.

32. Augustus Strong, *Systematic Theology,* 8th ed. (Old Tappan, N.J.: Revell, 1907), 196-242.

33. Riley, *Ten Sermons,* 3-10; William B. Riley, *The Finality of the Higher Criticism* (n.p., 1909), 21.

34. Riley, *Ten Sermons,* 5; William B. Riley, *Ten Burning Questions* (New York: Fleming Revell, 1932), 9-29.

35. Martin E. Marty, *Modern American Religion, Vol. I: The Irony of it All, 1893-1919* (Chicago: University of Chicago Press, 1986), 232-37; Sandeen, 103-31.

36. Riley, *The Finality of Higher Criticism,* 31.

37. Ibid., 43.

38. Ibid., 33.

39. William B. Riley, *Inspiration or Evolution* (Cleveland: Union Gospel Publishing Co., 1923), 71.

40. For example, *Ten Sermons on the Greater Doctrine of Scripture, The Finality of the Higher Criticism, The Crisis of the Church, Inspiration or Evolution, The Blight of Unitarianism, Vagaries and Verities,* and *Ten Burning Questions.*

41. See Gatewood, 157-61, for an example of Riley's debating style.

42. William B. Riley, *Vagaries and Verities* (Minneapolis: Hall, Black and Co., 1903).

43. Timothy P. Weber, "The Two-Edged Sword: the Fundamentalist Use of the Bible," in *The Bible in America,* eds. Nathan Hatch and Mark Noll (New York: Oxford University Press, 1982), 101-20.

44. T. D. Bozeman, *Protestants in an Age of Science: The Baconian Ideal and Antebellum American Religious Thought* (Chapel Hill: University of North Carolina Press, 1977); Marsden, 14-18, 110-16.

45. Kraus; Sandeen; and Weber, *Living in the Shadow of the Second Coming.*

46. William B. Riley, *Re-Thinking the Church* (New York: Fleming Revell, 1940), 81; William B. Riley, *The Evolution of the Kingdom* (New York: Charles C. Cook, 1912).

47. Quoted in Cole, 303.

48. Riley, *Inspiration or Evolution,* 231-32.

49. Marsden, 161, 169-70.

50. Weber, *Living in the Shadow,* 154-56, 185-91.

51. William B. Riley, "Cohn vs. Riley," *The Pilot* 15 (May 1935) 218; "Joseph Cohn Again," *The Pilot* 15 (June 1935): 249-50.

52. Russell, 17.

53. Dollar, 112-22; Beale, 279-87.

54. Hatch, 13.

55. Robert H. Wiebe, *The Search for Order, 1877—1920* (New York: Hill and Wang, 1967).

56. Hatch, 212-19.

57. Riley, *Inspiration or Evolution*, 91-92.

58. Riley, *The Menace of Modernism*, 136.

59. Riley, *Inspiration or Evolution*, 161-78.

60. William B. Riley, *Pastoral Problems* (Westwood, N.J.: Fleming Revell, 1936), 19-23.

61. Russell, 28.

18

Walter Rauschenbusch

Stephen Brachlow

Biography

August Rauschenbusch was a sixth-generation German Lutheran pastor who came to America in 1846 to do mission work among German immigrants. A zealous pietist, August eventually discarded his Lutheran ecclesiology in favor of Baptist views and was baptized in 1850 by immersion in the Mississippi River. It proved to be a costly act that alienated him from family and friends in Germany. In later years, Walter would cite his father's ecclesial independence as an important influence on his own highly independent theological spirit.[1]

Three years prior to Walter's birth, the Rauschenbusches had settled in Rochester, New York, where August helped inaugurate a department for German-speaking Baptists at Rochester Theological Seminary. Walter was born on October 4, 1861, in the warm religious milieu of a German pietistic seminary and a home where Bible reading and prayer were part of the daily routine. But the pious atmosphere in the Rauschenbusch household was often marred by marital disharmony, which the seminary's president, Augustus Hopkins Strong, described as "a shocking alienation" between husband and wife that eventually led to a four-year separation.[2]

Although Walter blamed his father for the domestic unhappiness, his father's fervent piety along with his love for classical learning powerfully shaped Walter's life. At the age of seventeen, Walter experienced a pietistic conversion in which, as he put it, "I got my own religious experience," an event he would later describe as "a tender, mysterious experience" that "influenced my soul to its depths." While sometimes highly critical of the narrow individualism that Pietism bred in the American church, he never abandoned the essentially pietistic orientation of his theological reflection, finding even his social activism continually nurtured by an inner, almost mystic experience of the living God. Indeed, his own conversion ignited a resolve to, as he said, "be a preacher and to help save souls," an evangelistic commitment which remained at the center of all his reforming activities.[3]

In 1879 Walter's father sent him to Germany to study under a classical curriculum at the Gutersloh gymnasium in Westphalia, a conservative pietistic school of the Reformed tradition opposed to the liberalism that dominated much of German theology. Four years later he returned to finish the A.B. degree at the University of Rochester and pursue theological studies at Rochester Theological Seminary, where he graduated at the head of his class in

Walter Rauschenbusch (1861-1918)

1886. He distinguished himself not only by his superior scholarship, but also through the increasingly progressive turn of his theological perspective. For example, he departed from the conservative path of his Old Testament professor, Howard Osgood, when he concluded that Osgood's notion of scriptural inerrancy was an untenable, "man-made" theory. He also troubled August Hopkins Strong, his theology professor, by discarding Strong's more traditional views of the atonement in a manner that his professor believed subverted biblical authority.[4]

His abandonment of several orthodox tenets of conservative evangelicalism proved to be a painful decision of conscience for him. They "cost me a hard struggle," he once said. They would also cost him an appointment as president of the Telugu Theological Seminary in India; Professor Osgood apparently convinced the Baptist Mission Union to drop Rauschenbusch's name because of his unorthodoxy. The decision to follow his conscience away from the conservative theology of his own heritage was never an easy matter for Rauschenbusch, and he always felt deeply the alienation and antagonism he occasionally encountered from religious conservatives.[5]

His social awakening initially occurred not through theological studies but, significantly, in the midst of ministry, after he became pastor of a small congregation of German immigrants on the west side of New York City in 1886. He came to New York, as he said, with "no idea of social questions." But the deplorable living conditions he encountered in the slums surrounding his church eventually affected the entire focus of his ministry. The church sat on the edge of a seedy tenement district known as Hell's Kitchen. There he ministered for eleven years, sometimes in near poverty himself, among masses of the city's poor. Witnessing as he did firsthand the grim face of poverty among exploited and often destitute immigrant workers of his neighborhood, Rauschenbusch came to recognize the inadequacy of what he called the old individualized gospel of Pietism. The gospel, he now believed, should address social as well as individual ills by applying the teachings of Jesus and the prophets to what he understood to be the structural injustices of capitalism.[6]

Two Christian laymen helped Rauschenbusch grasp the economic sources of the poverty he saw around him: the first was Henry George, a reformist mayoral candidate in New York City; the second was Richard Ely, an economist and an Episcopalian lay leader, who established much of the ideological framework for Rauschenbusch's future vision as a social ethicist. The works of other Christian social reformers would also be influential, especially those of Frederick Denison Maurice, W. P. D. Bliss, Josiah Strong, and Washington Gladden, along with the writings of Leo Tolstoi.[7]

But perhaps the most formative influence came through the intimate friendship he formed with two young Baptist ministers in New York City. In 1887 Leighton Williams, pastor of the Amity Baptist Church, and Nathaniel Schmidt, a Swedish Baptist pastor, joined with Rauschenbusch to form what Williams called "a new society of Jesus," an informal association born of their mutual longing to live a holy life and engage in effective forms of social ministry. They met weekly, sharing together in the Lord's Supper, offering one another support through prayer, and encouraging one another's efforts to minister to the social needs of people. The creative energy released by these gatherings eventually helped spawn a new publication in 1889, *For the Right,* a periodical designed to address the needs and concerns of the working class from the perspective of Christian socialism.[8]

In 1891 Rauschenbusch discovered that he was going deaf, an ailment that would leave him feeling lonely and often isolated from students, friends, and even family. In an effort to obtain medical treatment from a European ear specialist, Rauschenbusch took a year's sabbatical from pastoral duties and traveled first to England, then Germany. The journey failed to provide any hope for his hearing impairment, which was diagnosed as permanent, but the trip helped solidify his vision and sense of call to the social gospel. In England he was impressed by the efforts of the Salvation Army to combine revivalism and social ministry; but he was also critical of their work because he believed they treated only the symptoms and not the causes of poverty. At the same time, he was equally troubled by the narrow fanaticism he encountered among socialists in Germany. Nevertheless, he returned to New York the following year with a greater sense of commitment to the social mission of the church, which he now understood as "God's special work" for himself.[9]

His next major effort to organize and promote a comprehensive social vision of the gospel occurred in 1892, when Rauschenbusch and eight other Baptists formed the "Brotherhood of the Kingdom," a loosely knit organization of socially sensitive Christians seeking both spiritual communion and a deeper understanding of how Christianity might "Christianize" the social fabric of America. The Brotherhood met annually for more than twenty years in retreat at Leighton Williams's family farm, located high above the Hudson River. There Rauschenbusch and a cadre of like-minded friends gathered for fellowship. They sang hymns and gospel songs, prayed, shared in the Lord's Supper, and read papers on the theme of the kingdom of God and its implications for the ministry of the church in their world. These retreats on what Rauschenbusch once described as "this hilltop of the Spirit," fostered a profound consciousness of spiritual comraderie in the Brotherhood. It was there, more than anywhere, that Rauschenbusch delighted in the spiritual communion and sense of God's presence that he experienced in their shared vision for the kingdom and the spirit of worship that characterized their gatherings.[10]

Rauschenbusch married Pauline Rother in 1893. They remained in New York until 1897, when Rauschenbusch accepted the invitation of August Strong to teach New Testament in the German department of Rochester Seminary. Five years later he became professor of church history in the English division when the German Baptists, having become financially independent, established a separate institution elsewhere in Rochester. His decision not to move with the seminary founded by his father was difficult because he felt strongly the ties of loyalty that bound him to his immigrant community. Although formally associated with Rochester Theological Seminary, he never-theless remained active in German Baptist life, where he was always warmly welcomed for his pious and prayerful spirit, if somewhat less enthusiastically for his support of progressive social programs.[11]

Although he never wrote a book on church history, Rauschenbusch viewed himself professionally as a historian of Christianity rather than as a theologian or even as social ethicist. But the pressing needs of the poor and his desire to awaken the church to the social applications of the gospel drove him to write outside his academic discipline. Most of his vast literary output, from the countless articles and essays to the seven books he authored in English, focused almost entirely upon the social dimensions of Christian life and practice. His first major work on the issue, *Christianity and the Social Crisis,* appeared in 1907. Realizing the potential backlash this "dangerous book" might create, he wrote it, he said, "with fear and trembling" but also with a sense of spiritual compulsion as a "part of my Christian ministry."[12] He was surprised, then, when the book turned into a publishing success that merited the acclaim of August Strong, Harry Emerson Fosdick, and others, and propelled him into national prominence.

Six more books followed in the next decade. Together they would help make him into what Reinhold Niebuhr called "the real founder of social Christianity in this country" and "its most brilliant and generally satisfying exponent."[14] Having explored the conditions which constituted the social cri-sis of his day and the challenge it raised for the church in his first book, Rauschenbusch turned to the publication of a small book of prayers he enti-tled *For God and the People.* Reprinted in 1912 as *Prayers of the Social Awakening,* he came to regard it as his favorite book and as "one of the best gifts of God to me."[15] Two other slim volumes soon appeared, *Unto Me* in 1912, and *Dare We Be Christians?* in 1914.

His next major publishing venture, however, came in 1912 with the issue of *Christianizing the Social Order.* The book offered a constructive analysis for a host of contemporary social problems and proposed a variety of practi-cal solutions. He called upon the church to help redress the inequities in American society by engaging in the prophetic task of identifying the struc-tural evils and promoting a more Christian social vision that embraced ideals of social solidarity and democratic reform. The reviews were, again, largely favorable. August Strong praised it as "a great book" and Rauschenbusch soon found himself in demand as a public lecturer across the nation.[16]

In 1916 a brief, though highly popular study manual, *The Social Princi-ples of Jesus* was released. But by this time, Rauschenbusch had become increasingly melancholy over the tragic events of the Great War, which by then had been in progress for nearly two years. As a sign of mourning, he wore a piece of black crepe in his lapel, and a mood of despair—so uncharac-teristic of his compassionate character—settled over him for the few remain-ing years of his life: "Since 1914 the world is so full of hate," he wrote near the end, that "I cannot expect to be happy again in my lifetime."[17]

His profound grief, however, did not prevent him from publishing his last and perhaps finest book, *A Theology of the Social Gospel,* 1917. Originally prepared as the Taylor Lectures at Yale Divinity School, the book interpreted several traditional theological motifs from the vantage point of social Christianity.

By the time the book appeared in November, Rauschenbusch was suffering from cancer. He died on July 25, 1918, at the age of fifty-six.[13]

Exposition

Theological Methodology

Walter Rauschenbusch was not a systematic theologian. "I must confess," he wrote in a personal letter of 1912, "that I am not a theologian and never shall be. . . . The God of the stellar universe is a God in whom I drown. Christ with the face of Jesus I can comprehend, and love and assimilate. So I stick to him, and call him by that name."[19] The focus of his theological writings were almost entirely ethical. To the extent that he wrote theologically at all, he was less interested in speculative, or dogmatic theology than he was in the moral import of classical doctrinal themes. As Francis J. McConnell observed about Rauschenbusch's methodology, he "did not trouble himself overmuch about the requirements of systematic logic . . . . He made the fundamental human needs both his starting point and his point of arrival."[20] This entirely inductive approach to the theological enterprise resulted in the social orientation of his work. His social conscience "did not come from the church," Rauschenbusch once explained. "It came through personal contact with poverty . . . . In that way gradually social information and social passion came to me.[21]

In order to understand Rauschenbusch's peculiar theological orientation, it is necessary therefore to grasp the significance of his biography.[22] The impressionable son of immigrant parents, who inherited their warmhearted piety and yet endured the painful contradiction of their domestic quarrels, Rauschenbusch was always sensitive to the suffering of the weak and victimized, especially in the misery he encountered in his New York pastorate among the immigrant poor.[23] Thus, his theology grew not out of academic study but rather out of his efforts to address the appallingly desperate conditions of the urban poor with the same gospel he had learned to love from childhood.[24] And what he discovered was that the old, individualized Pietism of his youth was not sufficient for the overwhelming needs of the neglected, impoverished people of Hell's Kitchen.

The Social Gospel

Disturbed by the intolerable conditions of New York's west side, Rauschenbusch gradually came to understand through the social critique of Henry George and the writings of Christian socialists like Richard Ely and Fredrick Denison Maurice, that the gospel of Christ had implications not only for individuals but societies as well. Witnessing firsthand the hardships of the losers in the Industrial Revolution, Rauschenbusch became an advocate of the destitute and a tireless critic of the excesses in capitalism. He also became a standard-bearer of Christian socialism, a somewhat vague vision for the political order that made a biblically oriented concern for social equality and justice more important than the amassing of capital for the profit of a few. The great aim of Christian socialism was the abolition of class privilege and the creation of a free, just, and equitable social order.[25]

To this end, Rauschenbusch immersed himself in advocacy work on a wide variety of public policy issues such as public ownership of the railroads, city transit lines, and the utility companies. He also sought a more equitable system of taxation, safer and better working conditions in factories, the abolition of child labor, the institution of social security insurance, and the development of public parks, playgrounds, and libraries. He campaigned against the abuse of alcohol, for educational reform in the schools, and for the equal rights of women and minorities. When the Great War broke out in 1914, he inaugurated a "Peace Group" at Rochester Theological Seminary and criticized the war effort on grounds that the conflict was fueled primarily by the profit motive rather than fundamental issues of justice.[26]

Although Rauschenbusch worked in this way to further the goals of Christian socialism, he was never a thoroughgoing, ideological Socialist, nor a member of a Socialist political party.[27] He did, however, admit that "for working purposes I am myself a Socialist," and he participated in the Christian Socialist Society of New York City, a movement that repudiated the atheism and materialism of Marxism while maintaining that the social teachings of Jesus point to a form of economic democracy in the public realm.[28]

Rauschenbusch turned to the Bible to support his vision of a social system based on a Christlike love for the poor and the oppressed. According to Rauschenbusch, one of the central themes of the Scriptures reveals that God is socially biased. God takes the side of the wretched of this world while turning a cold shoulder to profit-hungry capitalists. This is especially evident, Rauschenbusch believed, in the preaching of Jesus as well as the prophets of the Old Testament, his two favorite sources. "As with the Old Testament prophets," he wrote in *Christianity and the Social Crisis,* "the fundamental sympathies of Jesus were with the poor and oppressed . . . . His healing power was for social help, for the alleviation of human suffering. It was at the service of any wretched leper, but not of doubting scribes."[29]

The social orientation of Jesus' ministry, Rauschenbusch believed, stood in sharp contrast with the values of capitalism, an economic system which offered the most efficient system for the creation of enormous material wealth for a powerful minority and offended the spirit of the gospel by its blatant materialism. By placing profit for a few industrialists, who controlled the means of production, above the common good of the masses of industrial workers, who possessed little or no power within the system in which they labored, the structure of capitalism was fundamentally "nonmoral or immoral, non-Christian or unchristian."[30] Rauschenbusch characterized capitalism as a "covetous machine" that was indifferent to human life, to the joy of human play, the value of the family and the stewardship of God's creation.

He believed that the "largest evangelistic and missionary task of the church" was, therefore, to awaken the nation to the sinfulness of unbridled capitalism and to help create a more Christian economic order based on principles of service and fraternity. He sought to replace capitalism with a form of "economic democracy" that gave the people control over the means of their own livelihood and emphasized values of the common good rather than individual competition and private profit.[31]

The Individual Gospel

Early in his career as an advocate of social reform, militant conservative Baptists, such as James Willmarth and W. B. Riley, charged Rauschenbusch with accusations of communism and heresy. They claimed he played into the hands of godless Marxists under the guise of Christian socialism, and, equally distressing for them, he promulgated the theologically dubious dogmas of nineteenth-century German liberalism.[32] In the minds of his conservative critics, the Social Gospel was inextricably tied to a form of theological liberalism that effectively reduced the life-transforming, divinely inspired gospel to mere sociological principles and substituted personal regeneration with social change. The Social Gospel, it was assumed, effectively divested Christianity of its true spiritual character.[33]

There is little question that Rauschenbusch was indebted to theological liberalism, especially—though not uncritically so—to the three patriarchs of the German tradition, Friedrich Schleiermacher, Albrecht Ritschl, and Adolf Harnack.[34] However, the essentially pietistic character of Rauschenbusch would be entirely missed if his association with the Social Gospel movement was taken to imply that he had forsaken the personal dimension of salvation of nineteenth-century evangelical revivalism in favor of social transformation. Rauschenbusch was indelibly marked by the stamp of Pietism.[35] He was invariably remembered by contemporaries as a prayerful, pious individual, whose social conscience was stirred as much by the almost mystic communion he shared with the living Christ he discovered in Scripture as it may also have been by his economic critique of capitalism.[36] "The main thing is to have God," Rauschenbusch wrote, "to live in Him; to have Him live in us . . . to realize His presence; to feel His holiness and to be holy."[37] This was the spirit that characterized Rauschenbusch. As Henry Robins recalled, he possessed "a passionate yearning for genuine kinship of spirit and experience with Jesus Christ which suffused his whole bearing with an unfailing quality of reverence."[38] Rauschenbusch once described with poetic imagery this sense of divine presence in life which came to him as "a faint and far call, sweeter than the rhythm of the spheres, the voice of the Father of spirits calling to his child. Our souls give answer by eternal longing and homesickness."[39]

Rauschenbusch's view of the authority of Scripture also stemmed directly from his religious experience. He rejected conservative arguments for biblical inerrancy as a "human tradition" because, he believed, they depended upon outward authority rather than "the self-evidencing power of God's living word" authenticated by the Spirit of God in the heart of the believer.[40] Rauschenbusch recognized the Bible alone as the "sufficient authority for faith and practice."[41] Moreover, he claimed that his most serious desire was "to perceive and believe in the whole truth of Jesus Christ and the entire Word of God" which, in classic language of the pietist, he said he believed "with all my heart."[42]

At the same time, Rauschenbusch was painfully aware of the destructive threat of indifference to personal holiness, prayer, and revivalism that the Social Gospel seemed to foster in many of his contemporaries.[43] More significantly perhaps, he was sensitively aware of the pitfalls that German liberalism had at times left in its tracks. He was wary of what he called "the rational substractions of liberalism" that, in his words, "snuff out the flame" of living faith.[44]

Although Rauschenbusch imbibed deeply in theological liberalism, he also empathized greatly with those who longed to preserve the heritage of orthodoxy. It was always his desire to "clasp hands"—to use his own metaphor of solidarity—with the conservatives of his day, as he did when he dedicated his last book with gratitude and respect to his friend and theological mentor, Augustus Strong.[45]

For Rauschenbusch the Social Gospel represented nothing more (nor less) than an expansion of the old evangelical message of individual salvation. Rauschenbusch confessed in *A Theology for the Social Gospel:*

> I have entire sympathy with the conservative instinct which shrinks from giving up any of the dear possessions which have made life holy for us. We have none too much of them left. It is a comfort to me to know that the changes required to make room for the social gospel are not destructive but constructive. They involve addition and not substraction. The social gospel calls for an expansion in the scope of salvation and for more religious dynamic to do the work of God. It requires more faith and not less. It offers a more thorough and durable salvation. It is able to create a more searching sense of sin and to preach repentance to the respectable and mighty who have ridden humanity to the mouth of hell.[46]

Despite his interest in changing what he believed to be the corrupt and corrupting structures of society, Rauschenbusch never belittled the importance of a personal experience of conversion in the old revivalistic sense. Even after he became committed to the cause of social justice, he nevertheless always cherished his own evangelical conversion as a profound and divinely formative experience that set the religious tone of his life for the remainder of his career. Throughout his writings as a social prophet Rauschenbusch made it clear that, while social structures needed to be redeemed, the salvation of the individual was always paramount. Without spiritual rebirth in the lives of individuals, all the finest social transformation in the world would ultimately prove ineffective and meaningless. For this reason, Rauschenbusch maintained that

> spiritual regeneration is the most important fact in any life history. A living experience of God is the crowning knowledge attainable to a human mind.

Each one of us needs the redemptive power of religion for his own sake, for on the tiny stage of the human soul all the vast world tragedy of good and evil is re-enacted. In the best social order that is conceivable men will still smolder with lust and ambition, and be lashed by hate and jealousy as with the whip of a slave driver. No material comfort and plenty can satisfy the restless soul in us and give us peace with ourselves. All who have made test of it agree that religion alone holds the key to the ultimate meaning of life, and each of us must find his way into the inner mysteries alone. The day will come when all life on this planet will be extinct, and what meaning will our social evolution have had if that is all? Religion is eternal life in the midst of time and transcending time.[47]

For Rauschenbusch the regeneration of an individual was entirely a mystery of Christ's divine grace, "who imparts His spirit to those who believe in Him and thereby redeems them from the domination of the flesh and the world, and their corruptions and transforms them into spiritual beings, conformed to His likeness and partaking of His life.[48] Rauschenbusch never lost this sense of the primacy of personal religious experience. In a letter written in 1918, the year he died, Rauschenbusch explained:

My life would seem an empty shell if my personal religion were left out of it. It has been my deepest satisfaction to get evidence now and then that I have been able to help men to a new spiritual birth. I have always regarded my work as a form of evangelism which called for a deeper repentance and a new experience of God's salvation.[49]

If Rauschenbusch was influenced by modern German theology it is also clear that he was equally disposed to embrace the American revivalist tradition. Early in his career, Rauschenbusch was moved personally by the preaching of Dwight L. Moody. The hymnody of the Moody songwriters, Fanny Crosby and Ira Sankey, captured for Rauschenbusch the heart and soul of the individual gospel that remained dear to him. He translated into German more than a hundred of their gospel songs, including "I Need Thee Every Hour," "What a Friend We Have In Jesus," "Rescue the Perishing," and "Onward Christian Soldiers."[50]

What Rauschenbusch strenuously objected to, however, was a revivalism and a personal piety that turned away from the world and became self-centered and self-serving. The experience of regeneration in Christ, if authentic and healthy, turned one not only from self to God but also to the service of humankind. The gospel of Christ had profound implications for individual salvation, Rauschenbusch believed, but it also drives us into a caring concern for the world. This was a holistic view of salvation, something he thought had been lacking in the individualistic style of evangelism. As he expressed it in *Christianizing the Social Order:*

Christianity must offer every man a full salvation. The individualistic gospel never did this. Its evangelism never recognized more than a fractional part of the saving forces at work in God's world. Salvation was often whittled down to a mere doctrinal proposition; assent to that, and you were saved. Social Christianity holds to all the real values in the old methods, but rounds them out to meet all the needs of human life.[51]

In Rauschenbusch, then, social concern was integrated with personal evangelism.[52] For him this was a new, more well-rounded gospel, "a distinct type of personal religion" as he explained it, "that in its best manifestations . . . involves the possibility of a purer spirituality, a keener recognition of sin, more durable power of growth, a more personal evangelism, and a more all-round salvation than the individualistic type of religion which makes the salvation of the soul its only object."[53]

Kingdom Theology

If any single theological motif governed Rauschenbusch's theology it was the kingdom of God. This theme provided a unifying and guiding principle that integrated his commitment to the individualism of Pietism with the social demands he discovered in Scripture. The kingdom of God motif was widely used by Rauschenbusch's contemporaries, especially among German intellectuals and American Protestants.[54] Although it had already become a popular concept in theological circles by the turn of the century, Rauschenbusch described his discovery of the idea as "a new revelation." He compared it to the awe-inspiring experience of watching the summit of a great Alpine mountain "come out of the clouds in the early morn and stand revealed in blazing purity."[55] The reason his discovery proved so powerful was that in kingdom theology he struck upon a solution to the uncomfortable dilemma he struggled with between the personal piety of the old faith and the social Christianity he embraced while laboring among the poor. Rauschenbusch recognized that the kingdom of God motif was large enough to embrace and synthesize these two seemingly opposing sides of his religious life. In a 1913 address at the Cleveland, Ohio, YMCA Rauschenbusch explained that the biblical concept of the kingdom provided a theological theme

> so big that absolutely nothing that interested me was excluded from it. Was it a matter of personal religion? Why the Kingdom of God begins with that! The powers of the Kingdom of God well up in the individual soul; that is where they are born and that is where the starting point must necessarily be. Was it a matter of world-wide mission? Why that is the Kingdom of God, isn't it—carrying it out to the boundaries of the earth. Was it a matter of getting justice for the workingman? Is not justice part of the Kingdom of God? Does not the Kingdom of God consist in this—that God's will shall be done on earth, even as it is done in heaven? And so, wherever I touched, there was the Kingdom of God. That was the brilliance, the splendor of that conception—it touches everything with religion. It carries God into everything that you do, and there is nothing else that does it in the same way.[56]

The kingdom of God was understood by Rauschenbusch's contemporaries in a variety of ways: within the revivalist tradition, many understood the concept as primarily an inner, spiritual reality that saved the individual soul for eternity; conservative evangelicals with a more clearly delineated premillennial eschatology defined it in purely future and otherworldly terms that would be realized at the end of human history; within the framework of German liberal theology, the kingdom was cast as a present, ethical reality to be realized within history through human progress. For Rauschenbusch each of these three conceptions contained fragments of truth, but none of them alone grasped the multidimensional character of kingdom theology. In his own exposition, Rauschenbusch embraced elements of all three: the kingdom of God was present yet future, an inner spiritual reality while also a social, historical force.[57] The kingdom of God begins as an individual reality in the heart of each believer but, Rauschenbusch said, it does not stay there. Its impact moves from the personal realm into the social and makes a tangible impression upon the social order. Thus, any time human beings live according to the will of God, there the kingdom of God becomes visible and historically present.[58]

While the kingdom of God is in this way realized in the world, its perfection was reserved for a future epoch.[59] Although Rauschenbusch at times shared in the utopian optimism that characterized the social Christianity of many of his contemporaries, he nevertheless carefully avoided the popular evolutionary notion of "inevitable progress." He was keenly aware of the problem of sin and what he called "the super-personal forces of evil" that were created by systemic or structural sin.[60]

Rauschenbusch believed that the coming of the kingdom depended in part on the obedient efforts of Christians to live by kingdom rules.[61] But its coming was, all the same, fundamentally a mystery of divine grace rather than a human effort. Rauschenbusch believed that the emergence of the kingdom of God in both its present manifestation and future fulfillment was "miraculous all the way."[62] God, not human effort, he said, "is the real creator of the Kingdom."[63] Thus the kingdom of God is both present and future. "Like God it is in all tenses, eternal in the midst of time. It is the energy of God realizing itself in human life. Its future lies among the mysteries of God."[64]

Although Rauschenbusch believed that the final perfection of the kingdom lay entirely in the future at the end of history following the return of Christ and the final judgment,[65] he nevertheless rejected the wholly future vision of the kingdom in premillennialist eschatology on grounds that it was an "unscriptural" abdiction of the ethical demands of the gospel. Premillennialism, he believed, stymied the social conscience of Christians. By placing the kingdom outside history and relegating the present age to eventual but certain destruction, premillennialists eliminated any hope that the redemptive efforts of believers in the public realm could be considered meaningful or effective kingdom work. But for those like himself who in faith viewed the kingdom as not only future but also a present possibility, kingdom theology offered a compelling and joyful invitation to work for justice and peace in human affairs for the very sake of God's coming kingdom. "Every human life is so placed that it can share with God in the creation of the Kingdom, or can resist and retard its progress. The Kingdom is for each of us the supreme task and the supreme gift of God. By accepting it as a task, we experience it as a gift. By laboring for it we enter into the joy and peace of the Kingdom as our divine fatherland and habitation."[66]

Evaluation

From the perspective of contemporary evangelicalism, the writings of Walter Rauschenbusch reveal at numerous points a theological kinship with the more liberal traditions of nineteenth-century Protestantism that many evangelicals today would find disconcerting. His decidedly subjective notion of biblical authority, his failure to affirm more clearly doctrines about the transcendence and the righteousness of God, as well as the Deity of Christ and the vicarious atonement, along with what some critics have perceived to be his almost naive optimism about Christian socialism and "building" the kingdom of God on earth, have all been cited as major inadequacies of Rauschenbusch's theology.[67] But from the perspective of the believers' church tradition—a tradition he avidly embraces as a Baptist—Rauschenbusch's theology exemplifies the emphasis on visible discipleship that characterized the focus of radical Protestantism.[68] For Rauschenbusch, the essence of Christianity revolved not so much around embracing certain orthodox propositions about Christ as it did in living out a Christlike life in the world.[69] Rauschenbusch was less concerned with the classical dogmas of academic theology (which he claimed were often too esoteric and elitist to be relevant to the real needs of common people) than he was in the ethics of biblical theology. His theology was practical and life oriented rather than speculative.[70] Radical discipleship, not orthodoxy, was the very essence of the Baptist heritage he embraced. It was, as he put it, "one reason I am a Baptist, because by being a Baptist I am a radical Protestant. . . . [and] I can help bring humanity to that simple, ethical, spiritual worship which Jesus taught."[71]

While some evangelical Christians today would feel uncomfortable with his radical brand of Christianity despite the warmth and zeal of his piety, there are others who have in recent years embraced a similar commitment to personal faith and social activism. The most dramatic evidence of a social conscience among evangelicals similar to Rauschenbusch's emerged early in the 1970s among a handful of students and faculty at Trinity Evangelical Seminary who, together with Senator Mark Hatfield, organized the People's Christian Coalition. Committed to an evangelical prophetic voice in American politics and to a ministry of solidarity with the urban poor, the group began publishing a quarterly periodical, *The Post American,* now better known as *Sojourners.* In one of the earliest issues, the concerns of the Coalition were articulated in words so reminiscent of Walter Rauschenbusch:

> We fault theological liberalism which neglects man's need of personal transformation, distorts the historic content of the Christian faith and retreats to ecclesiastical hierarchies. We fault a narrow orthodoxy that speaks of salvation but is often disobedient to the teachings of the prophets, the apostles, and Christ Himself, who clearly states that faith divorced from a radical commitment to social justice is a mockery.[72]

There have been other tributaries that have fed what has become an ever widening stream of evangelical social concern, from the 1974 Lausanne

Covenant which affirmed that "evangelism and socio-political involvement are both part of our Christian duty,"[73] to the Chicago Call of forty-one American evangelical leaders who, in their 1977 manifesto, deplored "the tendency of evangelicals to understand salvation solely as an individual, spiritual and other-worldly matter to the neglect of the corporate, physical and this-worldly implication of God's saving activity."[74]

Contemporary evangelicalism is a broad and widely diverse movement. Not all evangelicals share the same enthusiasm for social justice exemplified by Walter Rauschenbusch. But there are many, including, for example, Ron Sider and Evangelicals for Social Action[75] and, among Baptists, the Baptist Peace Fellowship of North America,[76] who take seriously not only the personal implications of the gospel but also what they see as the biblical imperative to help rectify inequitable social structures that marginalize some while unduly enhancing the lives of others.

It is this new social consciousness within the evangelical wing of the church that resonates so deeply with the concerns of Walter Rauschenbusch. While many Social Gospelers at the turn of the century tended to substitute almost entirely the work of social transformation for personal faith, Rauschenbusch "represented a unique blend of evangelical commitment and social consciousness."[77] He gave to American protestantism, as Martin Luther King, Jr., has said, "a sense of social responsibility that it should never lose,"[78] but he did so as a deeply evangelical Christian.[79] With all his interest in social reform and his frankly socialistic critique of capitalism, he was nevertheless "ever and fundamentally a spiritual prophet."[80] For Rauschenbusch, the new social order he envisioned sprang from personal communion with God, from a heart redeemed and transformed by Christ. In the last analysis, the social gospel was not merely a matter of changing the structures of society for the better; it was essentially a spiritual matter. "No outward economic readjustments will answer our needs," he said.

> It is not this thing or that thing our nation needs, but a new mind and heart, a new conception of the way we all ought to live together, a new conviction about the worth of a human life and the use God wants us to make of our own lives. We want a revolution both inside and outside.[81]

Bibliography

Works by Rauschenbusch

Neue Lieder, with Ira D. Sankey. Authorized translation of *Gospel Hymns Number 5.* New York: Biglow and Main, 1889.

Das Leben Jesu: Ein sytematisher Studiengang fur Jugendvereine und Bibelklassen. Cleveland: P. Ritter, 1895.

Evangeliums-Lieder 1 und 2, with Ira D. Sankey. New York: Biglow and Main, 1897.

Evangeliums-Sanger 3, 150 Neue Lieder fur abendgottesdienste und besondere versammlungen, with Ira D. Sankey. Kassel: J. G. Oncken, 1907.

Christianity and the Social Crisis. New York: Macmillan, 1907.

For God and People: Prayers of the Social Awakening. Boston: Pilgrim Press, 1910.

Unto Me. Boston: Pilgrim Press, 1912.

Christianizing the Social Order. New York: Macmillan, 1912.

Dare We Be Christian? Boston: Pilgrim Press, 1914.

The Social Principles of Jesus. New York: Association Press, 1916.

A Theology for the Social Gospel. New York: Macmillan, 1917.

The Righteousness of God. A previously unpublished manuscript reconstructed by Max L. Stackhouse. Nashville: Abingdon Press, 1968. Includes the most complete bibliography of works by Rauschenbusch.

Works about Rauschenbusch

Bodein, Vernon P. *The Social Gospel of Walter Rauschenbusch and Its Relation to Religious Education*. New Haven: Yale University Press, 1944.

Handy, Robert T., ed. *The Social Gospel in America, 1870-1920*. New York: Oxford University Press, 1966. Part 3 provides an introductory essay along with selections of Rauschenbusch's writings.

Hopkins, C. Howard. *The Social Gospel in American Protestantism*. New Haven: Yale University Press, 1940. Chapter 13 deals with Rauschenbusch.

Hudson, Winthrop S., ed. *Walter Rauschenbusch: Selected Writings*. New York: Paulist Press, 1984.

Landis, Benson Y., comp. *A Rauschenbusch Reader: The Kingdom of God and the Social Gospel*. With introductory essay by Harry Emerson Fosdick. New York: Harper and Brothers, 1957.

Mays, Benjman E., comp. *A Gospel for the Social Awakening: Selections from the Writings of Walter Rauschenbusch*. New York: Association Press, 1950.

Minus, Paul M. *Walter Rauschenbusch: American Reformer*. New York: Macmillan, 1988.

Sharpe, Dores R. *Walter Rauschenbusch*. New York: Macmillan, 1942.

Notes

1. Paul M. Minus, *Walter Rauschenbush: American Reformer* (New York: Macmillan, 1988), 53.
2. Ibid., 12; Klaus Juergen Jaehn, *Rauschenbusch: The Formative Years* (Valley Forge, Pa.: Judson Press, 1976), 13.
3. Dores Robinson Sharpe, *Walter Rauschenbusch* (New York: Macmillan, 1942), 43; Minus, *Walter Rauschenbusch,* 17. Near the end of his life, Rauschenbusch confessed: "I have always regarded my work as a form of evangelism." Winthrop S. Hudson, ed., *Walter Rauschenbusch: Selected Writings* (New York: Paulist Press, 1984), 46.
4. Minus, *Walter Rauschenbusch,* 40-44.
5. Ibid., 41; Hudson, *Walter Rauschenbusch,* 45-46.

6. Sharpe, *Walter Rauschenbusch*, 232.

7. Ibid., 11, 194-97; Minus, *Walter Rauschenbusch*, 61-64, 69.

8. Hudson, *Walter Rauschenbusch*, 13-19.

9. Jaehn, *Rauschenbusch*, 41-44; Minus, *Walter Rauschenbusch*, 71-82.

10. Hudson, *Walter Rauschenbusch*, 27.

11. Minus, *Walter Rauschenbusch*, 101, 117.

12. Sharpe, *Walter Rauschenbusch*, 233.

13. Minus, *Walter Rauschenbusch*, 161-62.

14. Reinhold Niebuhr, *An Interpretation of Christian Ethics* (New York: Harper and Brothers, 1935), preface.

15. Minus, *Walter Rauschenbusch*, 168.

16. Ibid., 169-74.

17. Sharpe, *Walter Rauschenbusch*, 448.

18. Minus, *Walter Rauschenbusch*, 194.

19. Letter to William Gay Ballantine, January 24, 1912, quoted in Sharpe, *Walter Rauschenbusch*, 322.

20. Ibid., 410.

21. Ibid., 429.

22. Ernest P. Clipsham, "An Englishman Looks at Rauschenbusch," *Baptist Quarterly* 29 (1981): 113.

23. Minus, *Walter Rauschenbusch*, 16.

24. F. W. C. Meyer, "Walter Rauschenbusch, Professor and Prophet," *The Standard* 3 (1912): 662.

25. Sharpe, *Walter Rauschenbusch*, 91-93.

26. Minus, *Walter Rauschenbusch*, 177-84.

27. Ibid., 92, 182; Sharpe, *Walter Rauschenbusch*, 157; Carl E. Johnson, "The New Present and the New Past: Some Timely Reflections on the Rauschenbusch Legacy," *Perspectives in Religious Studies* 14 (1987): 141.

28. Ibid., 91-92; Minus, *Walter Rauschenbusch*, 92. For Rauschenbusch's criticism of doctrinaire socialism, see Walter Rauschenbusch, *Christianizing the Social Order* (New York: Macmillan, 1912), 397-405.

29. Rauschenbusch, *Christianizing the Social Order*, 82-83; Walter Rauschenbusch, *A Theology for the Social Gospel* (New York: Macmillan, 1917), 168; 184.

30. Rauschenbusch, *Christianizing the Social Order*, 238.

31. Ibid., 323, 363, 376.

32. Minus, *Walter Rauschenbusch*, 90-91, 190.

33. A. C. McGiffert, "Rauschenbusch Twenty Years After," *Christendom* 3 (1938): 98-109.

34. Donovan E. Smucker, "The Origins of Walter Rauschenbusch's Social Ethics," (Ph.D. diss., University of Chicago, 1957), 189; Glenn C. Altschuler, "Walter Rauschenbusch: Theology, the Church, and the Social Gospel," *Foundations* 22 (1979): 145-47.

35. Smucker, "The Origins of Walter Rauschenbusch's Social Ethics," 62-79.

36. Minus, *Walter Rauschenbusch*, 113.

37. Walter Rauschenbusch, "The Culture of the Spiritual Life," *The Rochester Baptist Monthly* (November 1897); in Hudson, *Walter Rauschenbusch*, 98.

38. Quoted in Sharpe, *Walter Rauschenbusch*, 433.

39. Walter Rauschenbusch, "Religion: The Life of God in the Soul of Man," in Hudson, *Walter Rauschenbusch*, 132-33.

40. Ibid., 45.

41. Walter Rauschenbusch, "Why I Am a Baptist," *Rochester Theological Seminary Bulletin: The Record* (November 1918): 23.

42. Quoted in Minus, *Walter Rauschenbusch*, 53.

43. Rauschenbusch, "Religion: The Life of God," in Hudson, *Walter Rauschenbusch*, 123.

44. Rauschenbusch, *A Theology for the Social Gospel*, 11; Minus, *Walter Rauschenbusch*, 146.

45. Rauschenbusch, *A Theology for the Social Gospel*, foreward.

46. Ibid., 5, 10-11.

47. Rauschenbusch, *Christianizing the Social Order*, 104.

48. Walter Rauschenbusch, "Conceptions of Missions," *The Watchman* 24 (November 1892); in Hudson, *Walter Rauschenbusch*, 67.

49. Walter Rauschenbusch, "Letter to Lemuel Call Barnes," in Hudson, *Walter Rauschenbusch*, 46.

50. Minus, *Walter Rauschenbusch*, 56-57. See also his positive remarks about Moody in Rauschenbusch, *A Theology for the Social Gospel*, 97.

51. Rauschenbusch, *Christianizing the Social Order*, 114.

52. Vernon Parker Bodein, *The Social Gospel of Walter Rauschenbusch and Its Relation to Religious Education* (New Haven: Yale University Press, 1944), 157.

53. Rauschenbusch, *Christianizing the Social Order*, 117.

54. Minus, *Walter Rauschenbusch*, 27.

55. Rauschenbusch, *Christianizing the Social Order*, 93.

56. Quoted in Sharpe, *Walter Rauschenbusch*, 222.

57. Henry French, "Walter Rauschenbusch and Kagawa Toyohiko's Rediscovery of the Kingdom," *The Japan Christian Quarterly* (Summer 1987): 144.

58. Rauschenbusch, *A Theology for the Social Gospel*, 142.

59. Sharpe, *Walter Rauschenbusch*, 129.

60. Rauschenbusch, *A Theology for the Social Gospel*, 69-94; Johnson, "The New Present and the New Past," 137-40, 42-44.

61. Max L. Stackhouse, ed., *The Righteousness of the Kingdom* (Nashville: Abingdon Press, 107-8.

62. Rauschenbusch, *A Theology for the Social Gospel*, 139.

63. Walter Rauschenbusch, *Christianity and the Social Crisis* (New York: Macmillan, 1907): 63.

64. Rauschenbusch, *A Theology for the Social Gospel*, 140-41.

65. Stackhouse, *The Righteousness of the Kingdom*, 106; Minus, *Walter Rauschenbusch*, 91.

66. Rauschenbusch, *A Theology for the Social Gospel*, 141.

67. These and other criticisms are raised in William M. Ramsay, *Four Modern Prophets* (Atlanta: John Knox Press, 1986), 25; Clipsham, "An Englishman Looks at Rauschenbusch," 119; Minus, *Walter Rauschenbusch*, 188; Robert T. Handy, "Walter Rauschenbusch: An Introduction," in *The Social Gospel in America, 1870-1920* (New York: Oxford University Press, 1966), 261-62; C. Howard Hopkins, "An American Prophet, A Biographical Sketch of Walter Rauschenbusch," in Benjamin E. Mays, comp., *A Gospel for the Social Awakening* (New York: Association Press, 1950), 20.

68. Smucker, "The Origins of Walter Rauschenbusch's Social Ethics," 80-95; For the significance of discipleship in radical protestantism, see Donald Durnbaugh, *The Believer's Church Tradition* (New York: Macmillan, 1968), 209-25.

69. Minus, *Walter Rauschenbusch*, 46-47.

70. Rauschenbusch, *A Theology for the Social Gospel,* 15-17, 42.

71. Rauschenbusch, "Why I Am a Baptist," 17.

72. Quoted in Richard Quebedeaux, *The Young Evangelicals* (New York: Harper & Row, 1974), 120-21.

73. "The Lausanne Covenant," in J. D. Douglas, ed., *Let the Earth Hear His Voice* (Minneapolis: World Wide Publications, 1975), 5.

74. "The Chicago Call: An Appeal to Evangelicals," *Christianity Today* 21 (1977): 1036.

75. Evangelicals for Social Action, 5107 Newhall Street, Philadelphia, Pa. 19144.

76. Baptist Peace Fellowship of North America, 499 Patterson Street, Memphis, Tn. 38111.

77. W. Morgan Patterson, "Walter Rauschenbusch: Baptist Exemplar of Social Concern," *Baptist History and Heritage* 7 (1972): 136.

78. Martin Luther King, Jr., "Pilgrimage to Nonviolence," *The Christian Century* 77 (1960): 439.

79. Sharpe, *Walter Rauschenbusch,* 192.

80. C. Howard Hopkins, *The Social Gospel in American Protestantism* (New Haven: Yale University Press, 1940), 218.

81. Rauschenbusch, *Christianizing the Social Order,* 458-59.

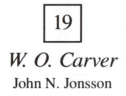

19

W. O. Carver

John N. Jonsson

Biography

William Owen Carver (1868-1954) grew up on a fifty-seven acre farm between Nashville and Lebanon, Tennessee. He was the second in a family of eleven children. Carver's mother died young, leaving him, the eldest surviving child, in charge of the family. His writings and memoirs indicate his deep affection for his mother. He saw her as one worn out by childbearing and household drudgery. To him she was a saintly, uncomplaining person, and in his reverence for her "saw himself as needing to serve as her surrogate."[1] His father, a Confederate veteran who suffered severe injury during the war, taught Carver from an early age to think for himself. Carver, in turn, applied the same philosophy to his children. To him education was more than the mechanics of formal training. "Education is the growth of personality in an environment. . . . Every truly educated person is self-educated. . . . Our ultimate environment is God."[2]

The resources of Carver's early public education were limited, but as a prolific reader he excelled in mathematics, Latin, and physics. At the age of eighteen he entered Richmond College as a ministerial student, and graduated with an M.A.[3] In October 1891 Carver began his theological education at The Southern Baptist Theological Seminary, Louisville, Kentucky, and graduated in the spring of 1896 with both the Th.M. and Th.D. degrees.[4] His dissertation for his doctorate in New Testament is entitled, "Gentile Opinion of the Jews in the First Century A.D." The brilliant twenty-eight-year-old graduate was immediately appointed as assistant professor of New Testament Interpretation and Homiletics at the seminary. In the same year Dr. H. H. Harris, who for many years had been president of the Foreign Mission Board, SBC, was invited to join the faculty of Southern Seminary. He introduced a new course in the study of missions. Unfortunately due to ill health, Harris had to terminate his stay at the seminary before the year was out.[5]

Quite clearly Harris made a profound impression on Carver's life and thought. Carver regarded Harris as one of the greatest teachers of his time and the greatest teacher he had ever had.[6] The blend of academic excellence and mission commitment made Carver the obvious choice to further the mission course at Southern. Accordingly, in May 1898 the trustees confirmed the appointment of Carver to take direction of the missions course in addition to New Testament Interpretation and Homiletics.[7] In his choice of a topic for his inaugural address, Carver turned aside from the two main departments in

W. O. Carver (1868-1954)

which he had been elected to teach, and spoke on "Missions and the Kingdom of Heaven." He gave the reason for this.

> I was impelled by my love for the subject; by a wish to make even a side issue, when it is missions, appear important, and to attract attention to its study; and by feeling that the heart of the department of the New Testament Interpretation is located in the study of Missions, and that the burden of the preacher's homily is "the kingdom of our Lord and His Christ."[8]

In 1899 Southern Seminary established a professorship in Comparative Religion and Missions under Carver's leadership. This is the oldest surviving department of missions in any seminary in North America and possibly in the world.[9] In 1867 Alexander Duff had been appointed to take the chair of missiologist at New College, Edinburgh, but within a year Duff had relinquished the position and the course in missions was discontinued.[10] In 1884 Claiborne H. Bell had founded a chair in missions at Cumberland University, Kentucky, but the course was dropped in 1909 when he died.[11] It was not until 1918 that Union Theological Seminary in New York appointed Daniel J. Fleming as its first full-time professor in the science of missions, to be followed by Yale and McCormick using part-time personnel.[12] The introduction of the teaching of missions in a theological institution at the turn of the century was innovatory for theological education.[13] Significantly, therefore, Carver was paid the tribute by Southern Baptists as being "the best informed man in Missions in America" or "in the world."[14]

W. O. Carver's tenure as a member of the faculty of Southern Seminary spans forty-five years (1898-1943). During this period he made a unique contribution to the lives of his students from his understanding of "missions in the plan of the ages," as "a purpose of the ages which God made in Christ Jesus" (Eph. 3:11). He developed a theology of missions that became determinative and foundational for missions both in his own denomination and beyond.[15] Missions was so central to Carver in his biblical hermeneutic that he had the strong conviction that no professor, in whatever department of a theological seminary, should evade teaching missions. In his inaugural address in October 1898, he wrote:

> Nowhere has this feeling been more emphatic than in the Southern Baptist Theological Seminary. Nor has the establishment of a Department of Missions lessened at all the emphasis everywhere given this fundamental Christian teaching. But we are sure the continuous, consistent, specific, and directed study is as necessary for a correct and comprehensive view of Missions as for any other phase of Biblical studies."[16]

Carver closely identified himself with the Foreign Mission Board of the Southern Baptist Convention. He served on the Board for two three-year terms (1917-23). At that time, James Franklin Love (1915-28) headed the administration of Southern Baptist foreign mission strategy. Love's basic premise was one of Anglo-Saxon supremacy, rooted in the idea that God had called Paul to go to Europe rather than to Asia.[17] This meant for Love that it was necessary for the white races to be Christianized first in order that they evangelize the world. Carver was quick to denounce Love's policies, stating that it was necessary for Southern Baptists to move away from such enculturated mission policies, which were "a rationalized justification of the racial pride, the economic greed, and the ambition of power which are the unconfessed urges of imperialism."[18]

Carver was ecumenical in spirit and identification, and refused to confine his mission parameters to Southern Baptist parochiality.[19] He had extensive experience as a member of the "Board of Missionary Preparation" established by the Foreign Missions Conference of North America. When the Foreign Missions Board, SBC, withdrew from the Foreign Missions Conference in 1919, Carver remained an affiliate of the interdenominational organization, much to the displeasure of J. B. Gambrell, the president of the SBC.[20] Undeterred, Carver took part in the process of formation of the World Council of Churches during the years 1938 to 1948. Although he was unable accept an invitation to serve on the committee which met in Utrecht, the Netherlands, in 1938, in 1939 he was appointed to the American Theological Committee, a subsidiary of the World Conference on Faith and Order.[21] Carver's contribution included a paper entitled, "The Importance of a Functional Study of the Church." He stressed the functionality of the church as the basis of ecumenical discussion, and not union in terms of the church as institution. To him Baptists were too diversified to be institutionalized as "a church." To Carver the church must be viewed in relationship to Christ, as the continuation of the incarnation."[22]

W. O. Carver's life as missiologist covers a period from the founding of the Foreign Missions Conference of North America in 1893, through to the founding of the World Council of Churches in 1948, and the National Council of Churches of Christ in the U.S.A. in 1950. During this period the Baptist World Alliance came into being in 1905; the great World Missionary Conference of Edinburgh took place in 1910; the International Missionary Council was founded in 1921; two World Wars shattered the Western world; and the United Nations organization was established in 1945. Throughout this period Carver expounded his biblical insights on mission. This found its fullest expression in the publication of his study of Ephesians in 1949, under the title, *The Glory of God in the Christian Calling*.[23] Carver had a growing conviction of the importance of the Book of Ephesians. "This supreme epistle," as he called it, spoke of both the timeless revelation of the grace of God unto salvation, and the need to apply it to the conditions of his time.

Carver did not serve in any missionary appointment abroad, but in 1900 and in 1907-08 he visited Europe in the interest of missions. In 1922-23 he toured Latin America and the Orient in order to be in touch with mission praxis abroad.[24] Two of his children spent extensive periods abroad in mission appointments. Dr. George A. Carver, his son, was appointed by the Foreign Mission Board, SBC, and served on the faculty of the University of Shanghai, China, during the period 1931-41. He also spent ten years (1953-63) as professor of Missions and dean of the Carver School of Missions and

Social Work at The Southern Baptist Theological Seminary.[25] Carver's daughter, Dorothy, served from 1935 for nearly forty years as a missionary in Japan.[26] Akiko Endo Matsumura, who later became a leader of Baptists in Japan and a vice-president of the Baptist World Alliance, had been led to Christian commitment through the ministry of Dorothy Carver Garrott, and spoke in glowing terms of W. O. Carver.[27]

Carver's broad-ranging scholarship and his inspiring, disciplined teaching produced a flow of scholars from his classroom. One such was Hugo H. Culpepper, who went as a missionary to China, Chile, and Argentina, and then taught missions and world religions at Southern Seminary for two periods, interspersed with a five-year stint as director of the Missions Division of the Home Mission Board, SBC. Culpepper pictures Carver's scholarship as "characterized by originality of insight, breadth of interests and depth of understanding." His range and brilliance led to his becoming something of a "handy-man" on the faculty, teaching for various lengths of time in the whole range of the seminary's curriculum.

Carver published fairly broadly, including eight books in the field of missions. Though somewhat difficult in style, his works sold well; some remained in print over forty years. He was justifiably looked upon by his contemporaries in Southern Baptist life as their greatest missiologist, a judgment that can stand to this time.[28]

Exposition

Philosophy of Life

Carver's philosophy of life was tempered by his early home training in which education was intended to provide the resources to students to think for themselves. W. Bryant Hicks, missionary to the Philippines, and presently M. Theron Rankin Professor of Foreign Missions at Southern Seminary, recalls the impression Carver left on him. In a chapel service the venerable scholar was giving advice to the new students commencing seminary training. Carver said:

> You will be offered many new ideas and options by those who will be your professors. These will often sound exciting and convincing, but take care. Do not discard any part of your present theological furniture. It has been tested by years of life and has proved serviceable. If you find some new piece of furniture that seems more attractive and superior, bring it in with your present furnishings and let it be well tested by time. Only then can you make an adequate judgment as to whether it is better. Then you can make a sound judgement as to what shall be kept and what, discarded."[29]

This advice expresses Carver's basic stance toward all of life, which was always some form of biblical injunction to *test all things and hold to that which is good.* For this great missiologist/teacher all such sage counsel—in fact, all Christian thought and life—issued from the glory of God, from what God eternally is.

Dale Moody regards Carver as a philosopher and theologian. To him

Carver was captive to God's word that exhorted, "Prove all things; hold fast that which is good" (1 Thess. 5:21). Moody further characterizes Carver as having "too much integrity to be evasive and too much courage to be silent," insisting that in any issue of significance, one might not know how this professor would react, but that it was certain that he would react. Carver, as philosopher and personalist, was basically a biblical theologian, who focused strongly on the kingdom of heaven, and on the church as the body of Christ. These elements strongly governed his thought and his writings. Generations of students, Moody declares, learned to be captive to the Word of God through Carver's courses and personal example. This great scholar in his opposition to Landmarkism, Fundamentalism, and Dispensationalism demonstrated his masterly biblical scholarship.[30] When he entered into controversy with issues in his time, he did so because of his profound spiritual insights and Christian conviction that the eternal purposes of Scripture had been violated.

Carver's philosophy of life contributed to his interdisciplinary perspective of academics, making him possibly the greatest scholar Southern Seminary has ever produced. He is remembered as a faculty member most able to walk into any classroom on a moment's notice and do a creditable job of teaching in any discipline in the curriculum. Carver himself had a far more modest self-image:

> While I had from 1895, when I began as a tutor, been nominally associated with only the two departments, New Testament and homiletics, then with Comparative Religion and Missions, as a matter of fact I was from time to time asked to undertake work in other departments. I really became a sort of handyman, teaching for longer or shorter periods in Theology, Biblical Introduction, Ecclesiology, indeed in the whole range of the curriculum except for Hebrew in which I met classes now and then. Through the years I continued to share emergency demands, especially during the period of the first World War when I had to share with others almost all of Mullins' teaching load [in Theology]. Scattering my energies over such a wide range, I was able to maintain a rather comprehensive interest along with a limited knowledge of the entire theological field. But the price of this was that I never was able to become an actual expert and authority even in my own chosen field. While I made real progress here I never felt that I deserved the tribute which was too often paid to me by Southern Baptists as "the best informed man in Missions in America" or "in the world." I knew that these gracious brethren were very little acquainted with the actual authorities in the field of missions and especially in the field of comparative religion.[31]

In making the New Testament his ultimate standard Carver was careful to distinguish between what was essential and accidental in the text of Scripture. To him the essential belonged to what is inherent to the nature of humankind and of the gospel, and arises out of them. This he considered to be the exposition of principle, a perspective of conduct for all time. Jesus "went about doing good," and this is the principle to apply for all people for all time. "What was essential—springs out of the inherent nature of man (humanness) and of the gospel, the same yesterday and today and forever—and what was accidental, and therefore changing with time and clime and civilization."[32] Carver's philosophy of life was molded within a biblical hermeneutic which stressed the inviolability of the gospel and the recognition of the dignity and worth of human life.

Biblical Perspective of Missions

Perhaps the key to W. O. Carver's greatness is found in what H. Cornell Goerner calls his deep conviction "of the inspired quality of the scriptures." He contends that Carver approached the study of the Bible "with a reverence which amounted almost to awe."[33] As a theological educator, Carver inspired his students with numerous insights from Scripture. One example was his insistence that God's choice of Israel (and of the church) was both instrumental and conditional. Election was for service and was conditioned by obedience. This concept became for Carver's students a key to understanding the Scriptures. Carver made clear to his classes that the choice of Abraham and the Hebrew people was not an act of favoritism on God's part. They were chosen, not for salvation, but for service.[34] Even more general, according to Goerner, was Carver's emphasis on God's "plan of the ages" (Eph. 3:11). Generations of students left his classes to share the urgency of God's "purpose with a plan." Through such insights as this, Goerner declares, Carver "above all others met my needs as a hungry-hearted, disoriented, seeking student; and I know he did the same for many others."

To Carver missions ultimately originates in the heart of God. Carver considered that there was elaborate evidence in the Old Testament to show how God moves in universal love to all humankind. But the origin of missions is vested in the work, life, and commands of Jesus Christ and projected in the lives of His followers. For this reason, the Bible is the missionary textbook. The New Testament must be understood to be the product of missions, and it is only in the light of this missionary idea that we can truly interpret it.

For Carver the kingdom of God may be said to be the formative concept of Jesus' ministry. God's ideal expressed in Christ is that His kingdom shall rule *within* all, and that all shall know God from the least to the greatest. Missions is the agency through which this becomes possible. The value of Christ's incarnation depends upon the believing acceptance of human beings, which means that His incarnation is incomplete until all peoples have been made aware of it, and have accepted or rejected it in their lives.[35] While we need to make much of the second coming of our Lord, the missions obligation is to make known this primary incarnation. Jesus identified Himself so closely with His servants, that in missions "Jesus continues doing and teaching in His Spirit-filled followers."

Carver gives his fullest attention to the role of the Holy Spirit in the mission of Jesus' followers in his book, *The Acts of the Apostles,* published in 1916. He agreed with those who called the Book of Acts "the Acts of the Holy Spirit."[36] For this reason Carver thought it appropriate to provide a commentary which was "practical" rather than "critical." In the preface of his book he wrote: "I have long had the conviction that, as the gospel of the Holy Spirit, Acts is at once supremely fascinating and in importance a counterpart of the gospel of Jesus Christ."[37]

Missions and Social Involvement

The work of heralding and witnessing unto all nations needed to be succeeded by "teaching them to observe all things." This had special implications. Though he questioned the legitimacy of the theories of sociology, he affirmed that sociology was a province of Christianity. False theories would prove their futility; however, Carver felt the church should learn from the sociologists who were dealing with issues at the grass root level in society. The churches should awaken to their opportunity, with lands being Christianized and not merely evangelized. Carver spoke of Christianization as a kind of "social revolution" which should become "an aim of the Christian effort." This he considered to be the aim of regenerated lives.

> People must be regenerated, not organized, into the kingdom of heaven. We are to save society, but by means of sending saved and sanctified people into society. The failure of the church to recognize, or even to admit, that it is to introduce the kingdom into the world, has led social reformers too generally to despise the church. We say that people must be regenerated into the kingdom, but do not seek to regenerate them, nor generate the kingdom in our own lives and churches.[38]

The Carver School of Missions and Social Work, which grew out of the Woman's Missionary Training School founded in 1907, is a tribute to the development of Carver's thesis of the kingdom of heaven, propounded so early in his career on the faculty of Southern Seminary.[39] In 1907 the purpose of the WMU Training School had been to prepare young women for Christian service in home and foreign mission fields. At the time the training of young women in the United States to serve as Christian workers was a new departure from the traditional, with no precedents or patterns to follow. In 1953 with the naming of the Carver School of Missions and Social Work, the purpose of the school was redefined, for the preparation of women and men in the areas of specialized missionary training and church social work. This was the outcome of a new social awareness involved in evangelical concerns relating to the kingdom of heaven. The naming and establishment of the Carver School of Church Social Work, under the deanship of Anne C. Davis in 1984, marks another development in the directions Carver prescribed in 1898 for missions and social involvement.[40]

Carver stressed the human dimension as part of the interpretation of the texts of Scripture. In his inaugural address in 1898, he spoke of his biblical hermeneutic in terms of "the inherent nature of human life and of the Gospel."[41] His genius is reflected in his understanding of the incarnation of Jesus Christ which we must share with the world. In the words of Duke McCall at Carver's memorial service in May 1954:

> He lifted the motive of missions above sentimental concern . . . . He brought it back and centered the motive of missions in the privilege of co-operation with

God in God's plan of the ages. . . . he did not do something eminently worth while in only one aspect of the kingdom of God, but he rather called us back to the central purpose of God himself in the work.[42]

Carver's perception of the gospel of the kingdom of heaven is reflected in a manner of life which was not discriminatory to women. Akiko Matsumura, a Japanese student who was accepted into the Carver family, stressed that Carver's greatest contribution to her was the manner in which he related to her in a normal and healthy manner, never making derogatory remarks about women. He demonstrated to her by life and word that each person had eternal value in God's sight, regardless of sex, race, or any other human factor. This, she said, enabled her to "be natural around him with no pretense or defense."[43]

Catherine Allen highlights Carver's career as being based on the premise that women, and not only men, are obligated to spread the gospel, for "all who are saved are constituted agents of salvation."[44] This firm conviction sustained Carver in his faith in the Women's Missionary Union. As an educator he pioneered opportunities for women to receive theological training at the Woman's Missionary Union Training School. When fifty years later (in 1957) this program was named the "Carver School of Missions and Social Work," the semicentennial brochure at the inauguration had this tribute from the women in Southern Baptist life:

Much of the history of Christian Missions learned under the tutelage of the late Dr. W. O. Carver, missionary statesman and scholar unexcelled, has escaped our memory, but the compulsion of the missionary purpose and plan of God through his missionary message of the Bible shall never escape its command upon our lives.[45]

Catherine Allen points out that as a creature of his time, Carver used masculine terms in the neuter as generic sense. He often, however, made a point of saying "men and women" in order to stress the inclusiveness of women in their elected role in the kingdom.[46]

Although Carver did not ally himself with the feminist movement, he acknowledged that feminist movements had been tempered by Christian ideals, goals, and motivation. He held that the churches, in opposing the entire issue of women's rights, had "antagonized the legitimate full autonomy of woman as a unit in every social organism."[47] Carver further contended that women in society in general had legal and political powers they were not exercising to their full potential. He considered this to be due to the check the community was making against their greater involvement.

Ecumenism and the Functioning Church

Carver contended that William Carey was not the founder of modern missions but was the father of organized missions, the father of the modern missionary society. Carey's idea of the individual responsible to God for the world's evangelization had molded the missionary enthusiasm of a century into practical results. To Carver, the best means of discharging this obligation is through cooperation with other individuals who share in the same consciousness of their responsibility.

Carver cited the Moravians as the only denomination that had approximated this idea in beginning not as a "church" but as a society for the evangelization of the world. He also noted that if this emphasis of modern missions was turning on individual responsibility, thus bringing us back to the New Testament unit in endeavor, we should also open ourselves to the possibility in our missions involvement to learn yet other concepts of New Testament Christianity for future extension of the kingdom. It is through missions that God leads His people back to primitive Christianity. "(In this) journey through the road of the world-wide Missions to primitive Christianity; an important feature of this work is making the Bible a new book and greatly reinforcing our faith in it."[48]

From this beginning Carver grappled with the issues relating to the responsibility of the individual in relationship with Christ; the church as a missionary society for the evangelization of the world; and the involvement in missions which would transform the Bible into a new book for Christian faith. In a return to primitive Christianity, Carver was convinced that we would need to go beyond the dominant idea of evangelization to that of Christianization, a kind of "social revolution."

During Carver's term of office on the Foreign Mission Board of the SBC (1917-23), the Board in 1919 withdrew from the Foreign Missions Conference of which it had been a member since the Conference came into being in 1893.[49] Carver, however, refused to sever his connection with interdenominational movements. He believed that from those in other communions many Baptists could learn a more rounded and effective emphasis on worship, more orderliness and beauty in the physical aspects of our corporate life, and a more adequate ministry to world leaders. E. Luther Copeland points out that Carver thought we might acquire more appreciation for the continuity of Christian life and faith and,

> recover the sense of community of all believers which we largely lost in the centuries of our struggles for freedom under the persecutions . . . inflicted by Catholics and Protestants, and from which our people still suffer in some countries.[50]

Carver provided a Baptist bibliotheological perspective on the American Theological Committee (a subsidiary of the World Conference on Faith and Order) on which he served from 1939 to 1948. In his written presentation he stressed that ecumenical discussion should center on the function of the church. He could not subscribe to union in terms of the church as an institution. He was opposed to attempts "to unite, the churches in one great organic union," as being the ecumenical aim and objective. Such union could only be achieved by coercion, destroying "the voluntary unity of the spirit" mediated by our relationship to Christ.[51]

Copeland shows how Carver sought to encourage Southern Baptists to respond to the ecumenical challenge by (1) a thorough knowledge of the facts and the rejection of "prejudice, ignorance, arrogance or indifference"; (2) by a loyalty to Jesus Christ, to His person, to His truth, to His plan, to His people; (3) by cherishing and developing "a genuine ecumenical Baptist fellowship"; (4) by magnifying the actual unity in spirit and in fellowship of all believers, and (5) by accepting our full share of world responsibility, not merely in theory and in principle, but actually by taking it over and doing it.[52]

Carver summarized his ideas in an appeal to the Baptist World Family in 1949. Cooperation in the World Council, or in any other form, should not be purchased at the cost of breaches in the Baptist fellowship. The best service in the present and in the immediate future should be along the lines of the completest possible unity of spirit and fellowship in service of all the Baptist peoples of the world. Along with this there also should be fellowship and cooperation with other bodies of Christians within suggested limits. The fact that any body of Baptists should feel led to participate in the World Council, as in the case of the Northern Baptist Convention, should not constitute a breach of fellowship or confidence on the part of other Baptists.[53]

The Church as the Continuation of the Incarnation of Jesus Christ

As Carver anticipated the publication of his study of the Book of Ephesians in 1949, *The Glory of God in the Christian Calling,* he told how enthusiastic he had become over this remarkable epistle. He shared his growing conviction of its importance for the gospel and the kingdom of our Lord Jesus Christ. Throughout his study of "this supreme epistle," Carver had been conscious of both the timeless revelation of the grace of God unto salvation, and the need to apply it to the needs and conditions of his time.[54]

Whereas Carver rightly recognized that the entire Book of Ephesians starts and proceeds from God's standpoint, with the focal point being "God's glory," equally outstanding and important is the experiential nature of the book. It is this relationship between God's glory and human experience which develops the ethical emphasis so inherent in the entire concept of the Christian calling. Impressively prominent throughout Ephesians is the exaltation of Jesus Christ and the concept of the church as Christ's body, the continuation of His incarnation.[55]

Carver felt that the manner in which we handle the framework of this "treatise" is important. He rejected the procedure which attempted to divide the Book of Ephesians into "doctrinal" and "practical" sections. He could find no such sharp distinction between these two aspects of truth and experience in its originality. If doctrine is not practical and practiced, it is unreal, delusive, and useless. This artificial division Carver considered to be one of the major sources of confusion and weakness in Christian history and practice.

Carver considered the authentic framework of Ephesians to be the manner in which God and humankind are found in living encounter with each other throughout, for the good of humankind and for the glory of God.[56] For this reason, Carver rejected John S. Lidgett's understanding of "glory" in the doxology of Ephesians 3:20-21, as being an Alpine point in the great chain of primary Christian concepts. To Lidgett the Book of Ephesians could be epitomized in the slogan, "The Glory of God in Jesus Christ."[57] This thesis Carver was forced to reject.

The significance of Carver's discovery is that he was able to detect the relationship to be between God and human beings. Though in chapters 1—3 our experience is viewed from God's perspective, it is set in the context of His relationship with human beings. Carver pointed out that by reducing Ephesians to "The Glory of God in Jesus Christ," Lidgett had omitted part of Paul's idea, namely that the glory of God was both "in the church and in Jesus Christ"[58] It is this crucial point of the relationship between God and human beings which evokes in Carver the discovery of "The Glory of God in the Christian Calling." Carver concluded: "Jesus did not call human beings first of all to follow him into heaven but to enter into the kingdom of heaven, into its service and sacrifice, its righteousness and redemption."[59]

Evaluation

W. O. Carver's incorporation of the study of missions and world religions into the parameters and framework of institutional theological training is a much needed corrective to mind-sets which wedge a cleft between theology and missions.[50] Among Carver's great contributions was the manner in which he wedded the studies of missions, theology, and the Bible. Carver was neither an enthusiastic missions activist, lacking theological reflection on the biblical intent of missions, nor the kind of theologian for whom the doctrines of the Christian faith have little or nothing to do with the missions enactment in the world. Nor is there a dichotomy between Christian commitment to missions and the academic excellence of his penetrating theological inquiry into the biblical intent. Carver did not discard the quality of his training in the classics in order to become involved in missions. Missions was a pervasive theme in the Bible, necessitating a scholarly articulation with other disciplines. For Carver, missions and the best of scholarship belong together, and scholarship is best served in the cause of missions.

Carver's first real book, *Missions in the Plan of the Ages,* (1909) must be evaluated within the first decade of the twentieth century. While in seminary training in London in 1949 I remember a discussion with an aging Baptist minister. He recalled how at the turn of this century it seemed as though the millennium was just about to begin on earth. When the first world missionary conference convened in Edinburgh in 1910, optimism was at its peak, and the disintegration of non-Christian religions was still being envisaged. This optimism dwindled in the years that followed, particularly as a consequence of the shattering blow of World War I (1914-18). Any possibility of a symbiosis between culture and religion was viewed with cynicism from this point onwards.

It would be unfair to minimize the importance of Carver's missiological thought on the grounds that he shared something of the Western optimism at the time of the publication of his first book. Carver was aware of certain limitations in his book, and in its fifth edition in 1951, he made it clear that he would have to arrange the book differently if he were to write a new book, and he would differ in a few places from the interpretation of certain Scriptures he had developed in his original work. His thought predates our contemporary missions emphasis on the commonality of the world's humanness, its dignity and inherent worth, yet Carver before his time gave recognition to human life as being essential in the interpretation of the texts of Scripture. His genius is reflected in his understanding of the incarnation of Jesus Christ which we must share with the world.[61]

Carver's translation of Ephesians 3:11 as "the plan of the ages" seems to be somewhat static when analyzed in isolation from the Christian calling. Carver, however, wedded "the Glory of God" to "the Christian calling," thus engendering the dynamic reflected in the experiential nature of the Book of Ephesians. The manner in which he reacted so strongly to John S. Lidgett's understanding of "glory" is a key to the matter. "The Glory of God in Jesus Christ," as expounded by Lidgett merely related to God's character. This Carver viewed as only half the idea, stating that Ephesians 3:21 viewed "the glory of God" as being both "in the church and in Jesus Christ." In this notion, the nature of God's glory is coexistent with the glory of God in the mission engagement of the church.

The dignity with which human life is regarded by Carver in this relational concept of "the glory of God" and "the Christian calling" has profound implications in missions understanding today, possibly beyond anything Carver could have envisaged in his day. This acknowledgment of the enduring worth of human life and the gospel so foundational to Carver in 1898, stresses what is "essential" to the interpretation of Scripture. All else in Scripture is "accidental" and must be treated as such.[62]

Whereas Lidgett related the dignity of "glory" solely to the character of God, with doctrinal interest; Carver related the dignity of God's character to both the church and to Jesus Christ, with missions significance. This gives recognition to the dignity of Christ's incarnation and to the value of human life. This also gives full weight to the mission role of those incorporated by God's spirit into the body of Christ. Here missions, in terms of the Christian calling, relates to our regeneration, to our incorporation into Christ's body, to the church as the continuum of the incarnation of Jesus Christ.

Bibliography

Works by Carver

The Acts of the Apostles. Nashville: Broadman Press, 1916.

All in the World in All the Word. Nashville: The Sunday School Board of the SBC, 1918.

Baptist Opportunity. Philadelphia: American Baptist Publication Society, 1907.

The Bible a Missionary Message. New York: Fleming H. Revell Co., 1921.

Christian Missions in Today's World. New York: Harper & Brothers, 1942.

The Course of Christian Missions. New York: Fleming H. Revell Co., 1932.

The Furtherance of the Gospel. Nashville: The Sunday School Board of the SBC, 1935.

The Glory of God in the Christian Calling: A Study of the Ephesian Epistle. Nashville: Broadman Press, 1949.

God and Man in Missions. Nashville: Broadman Press, 1944.

How the New Testament Came to Be Written. New York: Fleming H. Revell Co., 1933.

"If Two Agree." Nashville: Broadman Press, 1942.

Missions and Modern Thought. New York: Macmillan Co., 1910.

Missions in the Plan of the Ages: Bible Studies in Missions. New York: Fleming H. Revell Co., 1909.

Out of His Treasure: Unfinished Memoirs. Nashville: Broadman Press, 1956.

The Rediscovery of the Spirit. New York: Fleming H. Revell Co., 1934.

Sabbath Observance. Nashville: Broadman Press, 1940.

The Self-interpretation of Jesus. Nashville: The Sunday School Board of the SBC, 1926.

Thou When Thou Prayest. Nashville: The Sunday School Board of the SBC, 1928.

Why They Wrote the New Testament. Nashville: The Sunday School Board of the SBC, 1946.

Works about Carver

Ellis, Curtis Ray. "The Missionary Philosophy of William Owen Carver." Nashville: Historical Commission, Southern Baptist Convention, 1969. Microfilm copy of a thesis, New Orleans Baptist Theological Seminary, 1968.

Forehand, Robert Vernon. "A Study of Religion and Culture as Reflected in the Thought and Career of William Owen Carver." Th.D. diss., The Southern Baptist Theological Seminary, 1972.

Goerner, H. C. "Kingdom Statesman: An Appreciation of William Owen Carver." *The Commission* (Dec. 1943): 346 *f*. Published on the occasion of his retirement from teaching at age 75.

Jonsson, John N., ed. *God's Glory in Missions*. Louisville, Ky.: Nilses, 1985.

Smith, William Cheney, Jr. "A Critical Investigation of the Ecclesiological Thought of William Owen Carver." Th.D. diss., The Southern Baptist Theological Seminary, 1962.

Notes

1. Catherine Allen, "Concerns Beyond Feminism," in *God's Glory in Missions*, ed. John N. Jonsson (Louisville: Nilses, 1985), 61-62.

2. Cf. Hugo Culpepper, "The Scholar and Missiologist," in *God's Glory in Missions*, 2; W. O. Carver, *Out of His Treasure: Unfinished Memoirs* (Nashville: Broadman Press, 1956), 15 *f*.

3. Richmond College is now the University of Richmond, Virginia.

4. Carver, *Unfinished Memoirs*, 129.

5. Cf. John N. Jonsson, ed., *God's Glory in Missions*, 101 *f.*

6. Carver, *Unfinished Memoirs*, 132.

7. W. O. Carver, *Mission and the Kingdom of Heaven: The Inaugural Lecture* (Louisville: John P. Morton, October 1, 1898), 3.

8. Ibid., 3.

9. Cf. Olav Guttorm Myklebust, *The Study of Missions in Theological Education*, 2 vols. (Oslo: Forlaget Land og Kirke, 1955), 1:376 *f.*

10. William Paton, *Alexander Duff: Pioneer of Mission Education* (London: SCM Press, 1923).

11. Myklebust, 375.

12. J. Verkyl, *Contemporary Missiology* (Grand Rapids, Mich.: Eerdmans, 1978), 15.

13. Jonsson, *God's Glory,* 101-6.

14. Cf. W. O. Carver, "Recollections and Information from other Sources Concerning The Southern Baptist Theological Seminary" (Louisville: Unpublished manuscript in SBTS Library), 62 *f.*

15. Cf. H. Cornell Goerner, "The Greatest Teacher I Ever Knew," in *God's Glory in Missions*, 14-24; E. Luther Copeland, "The Ecumenical Participant and Spokesman," in *God's Glory in Missions*, 65-84; Hugo H. Culpepper, "The Scholar and Missiologist," in *God's Glory in Missions,* 1-13; Dale Moody, "Holding Fast that Which Is Good," in *God's Glory in Missions*, 85-95.

16. Carver, *Missions and the Kingdom of Heaven*, 4.

17. J. F. Love, *The Mission of our Nation* (New York: Fleming H. Revell, 1912), 15.

18. W. O. Carver, *Christian Missions in Today's World* (Nashville: Broadman Press, 1942), 37.

19. Carver, *Unfinished Memoirs*, 72-73.

20. Ibid., 73.

21. Cf. *Christendom* 9:2 (Spring 1944), 263.

22. Ibid., 266, 284. Cf. R. Newton Flew, ed., *The Nature of the Church* (London: SCM Press, 1952), 243.

23. W. O. Carver, *The Glory of God in the Christian Calling* (Nashville: Broadman Press, 1949).

24. Cf. George A. Carver and H. C. Goerner, "William Owen Carver," *Encyclopedia of Southern Baptists* (Nashville: Broadman Press, 1958), 1:236.

25. Jonsson, *God's Glory,* 110-11. Personal discussion with Dr. George A. Carver.

26. Dorothy Carver Garrott, *Japanese Youth Faces the Future* (Nashville: Broadman Press, 1940).

27. Akiko Endo Matsumura, "The Man with a Heart for the World," in *God's Glory in Missions*, 25-45.

28. Cf. W. Bryant Hicks, "Introduction" in *God's Glory in Missions*, i-ii.

29. Ibid.

30. Cf. Moody, "Holding Fast that Which Is Good," in *God's Glory in Missions*, 85-95.

31. Cf. Culpepper, "The Scholar and Missiologist," in *God's Glory in Missions*, 5.

32. Carver, *Missions and the Kingdom of Heaven*, 5.

33. H. Cornell Goerner, "The Greatest Teacher I Knew," in *God's Glory in Missions*, 14-15.

34. Cf. Ibid., 14-24.

35. W. O. Carver, *Missions in the Plan of the Ages* (New York: Fleming H. Revell, 1909), 71.

36. Ibid., 215.

37. W. O. Carver, *The Acts of the Apostles* (Nashville: Broadman Press, 1916), 3.

38. Carver, *Missions and the Kingdom of Heaven*, 15. ("People" has been substituted for "men" in Carver's book.)

39. Alma Hunt, *History of Woman's Missionary Union* (Nashville: Convention Press, 1964), 190, and Bobbie Sorrill, *Annie Armstrong: Dreamer in Action* (Nash-

40. Cf. John N. Jonsson, *God's Glory in Missions*, 110-11.

41. Carver, *Missions and the Kingdom of Heaven*, 5. (Human life has been substituted for "man" in Carver's book.)

42. Carver, *Unfinished Memoirs*, 157.

43. Matsumura, "A Man with a Heart for the World," in *God's Glory in Missions*, 25-45.

44. Catherine Allen, "Concerns Beyond Feminism," in *God's Glory in Missions*, 51.

45. *Semicentennial Brochure*, The Southern Baptist Theological Seminary Library Restricted Area (378.992c .256se), 9.

46. Allen, 61.

47. Allen, 60.

48. Carver, *Missions and the Kingdom of Heaven*, 26.

49. Cf. W. W. Barnes, *The Southern Baptist Convention, 1847-1953* (Nashville: Broadman Press, 1954), 276-77, 280-83.

50. R. Newton Flew, ed., *The Nature of the Church* (London: SCM Press, 1952), 293-98.

51. Cf. *Christendom* 9:2 (Spring 1944): 266.

52. *The Commission* 7:1 (January 1944): 6.

53. Baptist World Alliance, *Sixth Baptist World Congress, Atlanta, Georgia, USA, July 22-28, 1939*, 136; Cf. E. Luther Copeland, "Ecumenical Participant and Spokesman," *God's Glory in Missions*, 65-82.

54. W. O. Carver, *The Glory of God in the Christian Calling* (Nashville: Broadman Press, 1949).

55. Cf. Jonsson, *God's Glory in Missions*, 115-18.

56. Ibid., 21. Carver, *The Glory of God in the Christian Calling*, 21.

57. John Scott Lidgett, *God in Christ Jesus; A Study of Paul's Epistle to the Ephesians* (London: C. H. Kelly, 1915), 16-17.

58. "His Glory" in Ephesians 3:16 is defined in Ephesians 3:21 in terms of "Glory in the Church in Christ Jesus."

59. Carver, *The Glory of God in the Christian Calling*, 38.

60. Nils Alstrup Dahl, *Studies in Paul* (Minneapolis: Augsburg, 1977), 70.

61. Carver, *Missions and the Kingdom of Heaven*, 5.

62. Ibid.

20

H. Wheeler Robinson

Duane A. Garrett

Biography

When H. Wheeler Robinson was born in Northhampton, England, on February 7, 1872, his father, George Robinson, had already abandoned the family for South America; Robinson met him only once. He was timid and solitary as a boy, but was known to be intelligent and disciplined. He grew up with his mother in the home of her uncle and with them attended College Street Church, a Northhampton Nonconformist fellowship. He professed faith there and was baptized on March 28, 1888.

Robinson graduated from Edinburgh University in Arts in 1895 and proceeded to Mansfield College at Oxford University. There he studied under Karl Budde, Theodor Nöldeke, S. R. Driver, and, especially, George Buchanan Gray, and learned the methods and conclusions of higher criticism. His dissertation, "The Psychological Terms of the Hebrews," won the Senior Kennicot Hebrew Scholarship at Oxford.

He graduated in 1900, married Alice Ashford, and took a pastorate in Pitlochry in Perthshire. In 1903 he moved to St. Michael's Baptist Church in Coventry. The congregation grew significantly during his three years of service there.

Robinson began his academic career in 1906 when he took a teaching position at Rawdon Baptist College in Yorkshire, where he remained until 1913. His first significant publication, a commentary on Deuteronomy and Joshua, was released in 1907 in the *Century Bible*. His reputation within his own denomination and beyond grew during this period. During the war years he returned to the pastorate, the supply of students having diminished.

He became principal of Regent's Park College in London in 1920. The school moved to Oxford in 1927, and Robinson held the principal's post until retirement in 1942. In addition, he was from 1934 reader in biblical criticism in the university. Through all this time he not only produced a steady flow of scholarly writings, but was also a devoted servant of the Baptist Union and wrote many popular works in defense of Baptist theology and polity. He deeply impressed his students with his personal piety in his Friday evening communion services and Saturday morning sermon classes. In addition, he occasionally preached over the radio.

Robinson continued writing after retirement and planned to write a major Old Testament theology. These plans, however, were cut short by his death on May 12, 1945.[1] Nevertheless, Robinson had already made significant

H. Wheeler Robinson (1872-1945)

contributions to biblical and theological scholarship. The corpus of his writings, although somewhat redundant, is enormous.

Exposition

Robinson as Baptist Apologist

Robinson published two significant books in defense of Baptist doctrine and polity, *Baptist Principles*[2] and *The Life and Faith of the Baptists*.[3] He wrote them to explain Baptist doctrine to Christians of other traditions and to strengthen Baptists in their convictions.[4] *The Life and Faith of the Baptists* is the more complete study of the two, *Baptist Principles* being a defense of adult baptism by immersion.[5]

The Life and Faith of the Baptists includes forty-four pages of "Studies in Baptist Personality"[6] consisting of biographical vignettes of early English Baptists which are meant to serve as examples of Baptist teachers, pastors, reformers, and families. The stories, as Robinson tells them, are quaint and almost Dickensian, and serve as historical testimonies to the Baptist faith. After this, Robinson discusses four areas in which Baptists hold distinctive positions: baptism, the church, missions, and liberty.

Baptism.—In both his books, Robinson works from the position that "The baptism of the New Testament is the immersion of intelligent persons, as the expressive accompaniment of their entrance into a new life of moral and spiritual relationship to God in Christ."[7] He asserts that this practice manifests three Christian beliefs. These are the necessity of conversion by conviction, the importance of submission to New Testament rules of practice, and the concept of the Church as a community of the converted.[8] In addition, the act of immersion itself implies cleansing from sin, the gift of the Holy Spirit, administration to believers only, and union with Christ. The passivity of the infant in paedobaptism contradicts the ethical necessity of personal conversion.[9]

Like many Baptists, he attempts to find support for this position not just in the New Testament but in church history as well. He argues that the earliest postbiblical witness to the mode of baptism, in Justin Martyr, supports the Baptist position and he claims that the advent of infant baptism eroded the demand for conversion and corrupted the moral character of the Church.[10] He also finds examples of Baptist-like positions in the pre-Reformation church.[11]

The church.—For Robinson, the three fundamental principles of ecclesiology are: "(1) the diversity in unity of the Catholic Church of all believers, (2) the right of the local Church to be self-governing, (3) the sole authority of Christ within the Church."[12] The church is thus not a hierarchical institution but a body of believers. A convert does not join a church but "constitutes" it.[13]

He admits that Baptist worship is often lacking in reverence and seems more like a social occasion than a worship service but asserts that the homeliness of Baptist worship befits the fact that Baptists consider the church to be their spiritual home.[14] In this way Robinson counters the complaints of high

Anglicanism and Roman Catholicism, which see the Baptist worship as a paltry affair devoid of grandeur. Where two or three are gathered, he says, and Christ is with them, "there is ample room for veneration and awe and faith."[15]

Discussing a matter of controversy among Baptists, he rejects "closed" communion and says the Lord's table should be open to all who consider themselves true Christians. He supports "the larger logic of the essential unity of the Church over against the narrower logic that a man is not fully a Christian unless he has been baptized according to what Baptists regard as the New Testament baptism."[16]

Missions.—For Robinson, the traditional Baptist emphasis on missions and evangelism is one of the strongest vindications of Baptist doctrine. It demonstrates the Baptist adherence to New Testament Christianity. He lists Andrew Fuller, William Carey, and Timothy Richard, among others, as examples of Baptist missionary zeal.[17]

Liberty.—Robinson asserts that passion for liberty is a dominant characteristic of Baptists. He notes that John Smyth, Thomas Helwys, and Roger Williams were among the first champions of the Baptist contention that governmental authority only extended into secular matters of government and not into the realm of religious beliefs.[18]

Robinson extends the principle of liberty, however, beyond freedom of religion within the body politic to freedom of thought within the Body of Christ. He is particularly uncomfortable with theological dogmatism based on a conservative view of the Bible.[19] He asserts that the Baptist love of liberty ought to make them open to biblical criticism: "Baptists, of all people, ought to welcome that criticism which takes men back beyond the letter to the living spirit, which unbares the experience which was first creative of the literature."[20]

Evaluation.—Robinson's work here, if in many points not original, is a very able presentation and defense of the Baptist perspective. Some of his opinions, on the other hand, are not necessarily expositions of the traditional Baptist position. Despite extensive use of quotations from Helwys, Smyth, and other Baptist founding fathers, for example, it is noteworthy that he provides no citation which supports the concept of extending religious liberty within the state to theological liberty within the church.

Still, he is a worthy apologist for the Baptist faith. Although Robinson argues his case in a straightforward and direct manner, he is never belligerent. He was free of doctrinal arrogance and desired to see both "catholicity through conviction" and "recognition of individual liberty of conscience and judgment."[21]

Robinson as Old Testament Scholar

Old Testament introduction and history.—Robinson describes his views on Old Testament introduction in *The Old Testament: Its Making and Meaning.*[22] This book is a summary and popularization of the views of the higher critical scholarship of the early-twentieth century. Although it does show some awareness of the most recent developments of that time, such as the form-critical studies of Gunkel and Mowinckel and the theories of oral tradition history, it scarcely deviates from the classic Wellhausen model as adopted and propagated in England by S. R. Driver[23] and others. His analysis of the major problems of the Pentateuch, Isaiah, Psalms, Daniel, and other texts is in line with the classic critical positions.

Much the same can be said of Robinson's historical survey, *The History of Israel.*[24] He considers Genesis 1—11 to be essentially "myth" and the patriarchs to be the stuff of "legend," with many of the stories being retrojections from the monarchial conditions.[25] He considers Moses to have led an exodus of the Joseph tribes.[26] From the monarchy to the postexilic, he generally follows the biblical narrative although he often attempts to separate the "earlier" and "more credible" documents from the later, legendary accretions to the stories.[27] Robinson is well within the mainstream of the documentary approach to Israelite history.

Old Testament theology.—Robinson's understanding of Old Testament theology informed the theological emphases of his entire literary career. In one of his earliest books, *The Religious Ideas of the Old Testament,*[28] he set forth the major concepts that would dominate his theology. His emphases and interpretations had scarcely modified when his last book, *Inspiration and Revelation in the Old Testament,*[29] was posthumously published. Throughout his writings, a number of key ideas repeatedly appear.

Hebrew psychology.—Robinson frequently stresses that to the Israelites, a person was an animated body and not an incarnate soul. The human *nephesh* is not a "soul" in the Greek sense but God's gift of life itself. For this reason, the Old Testament conceives of a person as a unity, not a dichotomy or trichotomy. More importantly, the Hebrew *nephesh*, unlike the Greek *psyche*, emphasizes human dependence on God for existence.[30]

Robinson also deals with the concept of the *ruach* ("spirit"). He asserts that through a period of development it became the term for the aspect of human nature that partakes of something of the Divine nature. The *ruach* is the realm of the human personality which deals with God, and it must draw upon the *ruach* of God.[31]

Robinson contends that the Israelites ascribed psychological functions to various internal organs of the body and even asserts that they were thought to possess a quasi-consciousness of their own. For this reason the Hebrews, more readily than we, could accept the idea of a person being controlled by an alien spirit, be it divine or demonic.[32]

Robinson doubts whether much positive evidence for a doctrine of afterlife can be found in the Old Testament. Sheol is gloomy and uninviting, and a clear idea of resurrection is found in only two late texts (Isa. 26:19 and Dan. 12:2).[33] He notes, however, that in the Old Testament the key idea is not the afterlife itself so much as the idea that people are in relationship with God. "The hope of a future is made to depend on the relation of the soul to God."[34] Also, the Hebrew idea of resurrection evolved from their conception of the unity of body and soul, in contrast with the Greeks, whose doctrine of body and soul dualism gave rise to the idea of the immortality of the soul.[35]

Corporate personality.—Robinson's seminal study of corporate personality[36] was, in the words of Brevard Childs, a "brilliant essay" the impact of which "was immediate and widespread, affecting even German scholarship."[37] In this analysis, Robinson seeks to demonstrate, first, that the Israelites had an idea of corporate personality that extended both into the past and the future. The Hebrews believed that in burial in the family tomb, one was "gathered to his ancestors" in a real sense of uniting with them and that one's existence in the world was perpetuated through sons. This also explains the election of the people of Israel in the persons of their ancestors.

Second, he asserts that for the Hebrews this was a reality and not merely a personification. Rachel's weeping for her children was not a poetic device but an assertion that she died in the deaths of her children. Third, Robinson sees an aspect of this in the fluidity of the Hebrew text in moving between the singular and the plural in referring to the people. For them, the transition from the one to the many and from the many to the one was psychologically easy. Fourth, he argues that a major advance in the discovery of the individual came in the prophecies of Jeremiah and Ezekiel, although even they continued to maintain the corporate concept.[38]

The concept of corporate personality enables Robinson to explain a number of difficult problems in the Old Testament. He argues that in the "I" of the Psalms, the entire community is never far from view. This is not because the psalmist imagined himself the representative of the community or its personification, but that the "collective sense is so much a part of himself" that "he can never detach himself from the social horizon."[39] He also interprets the Suffering Servant of Isaiah collectively as Israel.[40] This becomes crucial in Robinson's theological writings.

Nature, humanity, and history.—Robinson argues that Old Testament revelation functions in the three realms of nature, human personality, and history. Nature, he asserts, is not treated in the Old Testament as a mechanistic object which functions according to "natural law." Instead, all of nature, even inanimate objects, is understood to be living and vital.

Nature is not, however, handled in a pantheistic or mythological way. It is a creature dependent on God and thus a revelation of God. For this reason the animals are studied not for biological classification but for moral lessons (e.g., in Proverbs). The mountains and seas and skies are presented as either praising God or trembling before Him. Miracles, moreover, are not regarded as examples of suspension of natural law. "There is no such Hebrew separation between the natural and the supernatural as that definition implies; Nature is already supernatural, though it can be raised to new meaning."[41] Nature is above all "the unique utterance of a unique being."[42]

Robinson also deals with hamartiology as part of his anthropology. Sin is the polar opposite of God's holiness, although Israel had to go through a religious evolution from a primitive concept of holiness governed by the taboo to an awareness of the central place of morality and the motives of the heart. But as the moral nature of God came to be recognized the Hebrew conception of repentance came to expression: it is not so much a feeling of remorse over guilt as a return to God.[43]

For Robinson, the recognition of God's moral nature means that "The most characteristic feature of the religion [of Israel] was its moral emphasis."[44] This arises from both God's demand for justice and the interdependence of the community. It ultimately leads to the recognition of God's fatherhood of all people, and to a universal (that is, not distinctively Israelite) presentation of moral principles in Wisdom Literature.[45]

It is in the sphere of history, however, rather than in nature or the human spirit, that Old Testament revelation finds its most dynamic expression. He credits the prophets with the discovery that history is the primary arena of God's activity and the proof of His moral character. They brought Israel to a consciousness of God's fulfillment of His redemptive purposes through human agents and political events.[46] The Israelite perspective is ever one of waiting on God to complete His plan even while the nation is swamped by calamities and hardship. The themes of retribution and deliverance, the Day of Yahweh, and the election of Israel all contribute to the prophetic interpretation of history.[47]

The evolution of Hebrew religion.—Robinson, with the documentary school, contends that Hebrew religion evolved over a prolonged period and that texts from each significant period can be isolated in the Old Testament. In one of the earliest extant texts, the Song of Deborah, Yahweh is essentially a tribal war God.[48] As the religion and the literature developed, however, three great movements of religious perspective emerged in Israel (viz., prophecy, the priesthood, and wisdom).

As mentioned above, the prophets are to Robinson the creative genius behind Israel's religion. Called and commissioned by God, as well as possessed by Him in the way that Hebrew psychology allowed, they preached a message that was "emphatically ethical."[49] This moral emphasis, together with their presentation of history as the primary sphere of the activity of God, justifies regarding them as the fountainhead of the spiritual and ethical monotheism which characterizes the purest understanding of religion.[50]

In the critical tradition, Robinson asserts that the priestly material was codified in the postexilic period and represents a late stage of cultic theology. Priestly theology primarily stresses the holiness and thus the moral nature of God and priestly "representation." As the priest represents the people, so the sacrifice is symbolic of the individual's return to God. The priesthood and cult was the "necessary complement to the prophet"[51] but the danger of falling into a religion of tradition and ritual was pronounced in priestly theology.[52]

"Hebrew Wisdom is perhaps the best historical example of ethical experience interpreted as revelation."[53] Profoundly influenced by foreign expressions of wisdom, biblical wisdom, although dominated by faith in Yahweh, generally avoids the distinctively Israelite emphases and is more practical and even utilitarian in tone. But Israelite wisdom is also quite profound, as when it wrestles with the issues of divine retribution and human suffering.[54] The moral emphasis of wisdom, however, is not original but is derived from the prophets. "We may, in fact, define the Wisdom of Israel as *the discipline whereby was taught the application of prophetic truth to the individual life in the light of experience*."[55]

Evaluation.—Robinson adhered to the classic theories of higher criticism without significant variation. Two important issues emerge from this. First, the classic critical theories explicitly assert that much of the Old Testament is legendary[56] or without historical basis,[57] is misguided in its theology,[58] or is reflective of conflict among the schools and sects in Israel that produced the present text.[59] Robinson, having adopted this model, had the task of building a theology compatible with historic Christianity on foundations which were at least new if not alien. A question yet to be considered is whether or not he succeeded.

Second, it is noteworthy that Robinson, publishing in 1937, adhered with only minor variation to views that Driver had expressed forty years earlier.[60] Form criticism, tradition history, and historical and literary research in conjunction with biblical archaeology, although still carried out at that time with a nod to the Documentary Hypothesis,[61] had already forced many to wonder whether the critical consensus could be maintained. S. H. Hooke, for example, in a volume which Robinson edited, admitted that archaeology implied that the Hebrews had written records earlier than the classic theory allowed and had given credibility to the patriarchal narratives; even so, he too asserted that the main lines of the Documentary Hypothesis were unscathed.[62] Later scholars both of the left and right would exploit the cracks in the foundation that had already been exposed.[63] Robinson's confidence in the castle his teachers had built seems anachronistic to the modern reader.

Robinson's contributions on biblical anthropology and corporate personality are helpful in understanding the Israelite perspective on life, and he has naturally provoked a good deal of discussion.[64] On the other hand, aspects of his approach are problematic. For example, his claim that the Israelites believed that parts of the body possessed quasi-consciousness is probably a misunderstanding of Hebrew synecdoche.[65]

The whole idea of corporate personality, moreover, is at least questionable. Robinson's contrast of the story of Achan's sin (Josh. 7) to the discovery of the "principle of individuality" in Jeremiah and Ezekiel is a case in point. Robinson says that in Joshua 7 the whole nation was "put in the wrong" by Achan's disobedience and that the nation and afterwards his entire family suffered accordingly. For Robinson, this is the "principle of corporate personality;" the many are guilty because of the sin of the one. By contrast, Jeremiah and Ezekiel enunciated the "principle of individual responsibility" in rejecting the proverb that the "fathers have eaten sour grapes and the children's teeth are set on edge."[66]

It is not at all clear, however, that the Israelites of Joshua 7 held to corporate guilt. Their search for the guilty party indicates that they understood the "principle of individual responsibility." Even their execution of Achan's family does not mean that they believed that all the family members were corporately guilty. Instead, the family members were killed precisely in order to punish Achan himself by "cutting off" his name. He had forfeited the right to an inheritance in his name in the land.

The very term "corporate personality" is probably ill chosen. Instead, the Israelites displayed a strong regard for community and family identification. Israel was identified with the sin of Achan and his name was extended to his family. This was never done, however, at the expense of the recognition of Achan's personal responsibility. The cynical belief in corporate guilt that Jeremiah and Ezekiel opposed was aberrant. It never had a place in the "orthodox" Israelite faith.

Two further and more fundamental objections to Robinson's Old Testament theology have yet to be raised. First, Robinson's insistence that morality is at the heart of Old Testament religion tends to obscure the crucial place held by the themes of covenant and deliverance. It is surely true that Yahweh is a righteous God and demands righteousness from His people. But the distinctive *theological* emphasis of the Old Testament is that Yahweh was in covenant with Israel and delivered the nation in the Exodus.

Second, Robinson's contention that the prophets were the source and highest expression of the Israelite faith is arbitrary. This certainly is not the position of the Old Testament itself, which consistently looks to Moses to fill that role.[67] The definition of wisdom as the practical exposition of the prophets is questionable not only on chronological grounds[68] but because it obscures the profound differences between those divisions of the canon. The priesthood, moreover, cannot simply be placed in a supporting role behind the prophets.

At the same time, one can discover profound insights in Robinson's writings. He is certainly correct that the Hebrew position is not so much a doctrine of afterlife as it is dependence on the person of God.[69]

Robinson As Theologian

Humanity: morality, sin, and the will.—As described above, Robinson regards Christianity as above all a religion of morality. He therefore must interpret the issues of sin and the will. Robinson scarcely deals with traditional Christian assertions that sin and suffering are to a great degree the result of the Fall and the work of Satan and demons.[70] "To explain man's sinfulness by a 'Fall' either within or prior to the history of the world would really destroy moral responsibility, just as much as an evolutionary theory of sin, which would make it a necessary stage in man's development."[71]

Nevertheless, Robinson maintains the universality of human sin as a fact of experience and a biblical doctrine, and he criticizes the Pelagians for having obscured this and the necessity of grace. Robinson remains, however, very sympathetic with the Eastern emphasis on the freedom of the will (and on those grounds criticizes Augustine) and holds to a synergistic soteriology.[72] He does not hold to the concept of the bondage of the will.[73]

Suffering and redemption.—The problem of suffering is the axis on which many of Robinson's theological ideas rotate. So dominant is this concern that even many of his interpretations of critical problems of Old Testament, soteriology, and Christology are best treated under this heading.

The problem of suffering.—Suffering is not only the subject of a major book, *Suffering: Human and Divine,* and a number of individual studies,[74] it also emerges in many works not directly concerned with the question.[75] Nevertheless, Robinson's position on this issue can be succinctly summarized. Suffering is present in all realms of existence (viz., in nature, in history, and in the individual life). Various types of suffering can be categorized, including retributive, disciplinary, probationary (i.e., as a call to faith), and sacrificial.[76] Much suffering, therefore, but not all, is a result of sin.

The theological anchor, however, by which the Christian is able to withstand the storms of suffering is recognition that *"the actuality we call sin is existent within God only as suffering."*[77] Out of this divine suffering[78] comes the cross of Christ, and into this labor the believer is called to enter. Suffering is redemptive for the Christian because by it he or she is in "sympathy" with God. By interpreting suffering as something done in and with God, the Christian is in true fellowship with Christ the Redeemer.[79]

The messianic concept in the Old Testament.—This interpretation of suffering dominates Robinson's understanding of Christ the suffering servant. Nevertheless, he does not regard the Servant Songs of Isaiah (42:1-4; 49:1-6; 50:4-9; 52:13 to 53:12) as explicitly messianic. Instead, the servant is corporate Israel, and their suffering is the result of their having entered the suffering of God because of their special relationship to Him. This is the suffering in which the Maccabean martyrs understood themselves to be participants.[80]

Similarly, Robinson does not regard the Old Testament Messiah to be incarnate Deity. "Exalted to this high place, and vested with unique powers that he may worthily discharge his office, the Messianic king of the Old Testament still remains a man supreme among men, rather than the equal, in any sense, of God."[81] The New Testament revelation is new wine in a new wineskin, not just the fulfillment of an old hope.

From this background, how does Robinson interpret the Person of Christ? Robinson is, first of all, uncomfortable with the Chalcedonian formula of "two natures in one person" because he considers this to be Greek philosophy more than biblical teaching.[82] Instead, he explains the Deity of Christ from two concepts.

The first of these is his understanding of the "kinship" between God and man that he develops in his analysis of the term *ruach.* The human spirit is the point of contact with the Spirit of God and the link between humanity and infinity. Without it no incarnation would be possible. This does not mean, Robinson adds, that Jesus is to be understood as a man who has ascended to Deity; He is Deity descended to humanity. But the fact of divine-human kinship is essential for understanding how Jesus could be called God.[83]

Christ's suffering, however, most clearly presents His Deity and messianic character. The cross is the embodiment of divine suffering over sin. All are called to join in this divine pain over sin, but Christ, as the God-man, participated in a way none other could equal. A danger here is that Christ could simply be regarded as *primus inter pares* in suffering, and Robinson explicitly asserts such an understanding to be inadequate. "The redemptive suffering of Christ is unique, supreme and fully adequate because of His unique relation to God."[84]

The cross and the atonement.—How, therefore, does Robinson interpret the atonement? Once again, one must begin with Robinson's Old Testament studies. Old Testament sacrifices, he says, did not contain any notion of vicarious suffering or transference of guilt. Originally, they were animistic rites presented as meals for the god. By the time of the postexilic period, the Israelites abandoned the more primitive conceptions and the worshipers simply thought they had to fulfill the rituals in the required way and probably gave little thought to their effectiveness or meaning.[85]

In the New Testament, moreover, although various metaphors of redemption and atonement are applied to the work of Christ, no single theory is developed or advocated as the standard. Robinson, therefore, considers both the "subjective" and "objective" theories of atonement to be inadequate and misleading if pressed. Instead, the real meaning of the cross is that it is the manifestation of divine suffering over sin. It was "the earthly counterpart of a divine and eternal reality."[86] "God has always been transforming the fact of sin by His own attitude towards the suffering which it occasioned in Him."[87] From this, the Deity of Christ and the meaning of His work are clear. He is God suffering for sin and, thus, not only our Redeemer but the pattern we are to follow.

The Holy Spirit.—Robinson develops his understanding of pneumatology in *The Christian Experience of the Holy Spirit.*[88] Here, in an exhaustive treatment of the subject, he deals with the presence of the Spirit in the Old and New Testaments, in the experience of the individual, in the incarnation of Christ, as well as in the life of the church, the sacraments, and the inspiration of the Bible. He also examines in detail the question of the place of the Holy Spirit in the doctrine of God.

The real burden of the book, however, is that the message of Christianity is above all the creation of a new life through the presence of the Holy Spirit. Robinson here serves as a Christian apologist against the notion that the Christian's experience can be explained in sociological or psychological terms. He asserts that the Spirit raises the believer to a new consciousness of sin by a radical transformation of values whereby he or she comes to enter the experience of God. It is the Spirit which makes us true followers of Christ.[89] Robinson, as a Baptist, is very much a theologian of experience and the heart.

The canon.—The canonization of the Hebrew Scriptures was, for Robinson, a priestly work which was not an unmixed blessing. It not only placed many of the more primitive traditional ideas about God on an equal footing with the loftiest proclamations of the prophets, it also brought in a danger of a religion of the dead letter instead of a living relationship with the Spirit of God. Thus God was removed further from the worshiper, and the complex angelology of the intertestamental period was the result.[90]

This does not mean that Robinson wants to abandon the Bible. The Bible remains a treasure of inspiration and guidance for the Christian, and even the law has great value in this respect. Robinson is aware of the danger of falling into subjectivism with regard to biblical authority, but he feels this can be avoided by the "witness of the Spirit." By this he means not just the witness in the heart of the individual but in both the history of Christian doctrine and in the fellowship of believers.[91] Nevertheless, "there can be no hard and fast line at the margins" of the Bible.[92] Revelation is primarily in history and Christianity is primarily a living relation with the Spirit of God.

Evaluation.—Robinson's theology has obvious strengths. His emphasis on moral responsibility is badly needed in the present age, and his insistence that the Holy Spirit must be at the heart of the Christian experience eloquently protests against a religion of formal traditions and institutions. His analysis of suffering as participation in the pain and work of God is not only of great ministerial use but provides a needed balance in our theology and christology.

At the same time, problems in his theology are apparent. Just as his moral reading of the prophets obscures the central place held by covenant and deliverance in their theology, even so his synergistic anthropology misses the radical presentation of human sin and divine salvation found in biblical (especially Pauline) soteriology.

Robinson's understanding of the canon, moreover, can hardly be considered satisfactory. Despite his assertions that the Bible came to us by providence and is an inspiration to faith, it is very difficult to see how his model affords any meaningful statement on biblical authority. His exaltation of certain prophetic texts and denigration of other passages[93] is a crude and unhelpful application of the "canon within the canon" concept.

It is precisely in Robinson's greatest theological contribution, however, his analysis of suffering, that his positions are most troubling. A number of difficulties are present but two shall be mentioned here.

First, although Robinson himself insists on the centrality of the cross and an objective work, it is difficult to see how his theological base supports this conclusion. His theory begs the question of whether the cross itself really was necessary or if the actual means of our salvation is the timeless suffering of God. If the latter is the case, we can only ask again *Cur Deus Homo?* Similarly, Robinson's protests to the contrary, it is hard to see how Christ the sufferer is more than *primus inter pares*.

The New Testament, we might add, reverses Robinson's perspective. Instead of the cross being an earthly manifestation of an eternal reality, it is an earthly and temporal event with eternal and heavenly effects (Heb. 9:11-28).

The second question that arises from Robinson's presentation is whether a New Testament Christology that grossly misunderstands Old Testament messianic concepts can be regarded as valid. The problems of the New Testament's use of the Old are many, but it is beyond question that the New Testament not only holds to the Deity of Christ but understands the Old Testament to do the same. It is futile, moreover, to deny that the New Testament asserts Jesus to be the servant of Isaiah's songs. On Robinson's interpretation, however, it is hard to avoid the conclusion that Christ is something other than the Old Testament Messiah and that the Maccabees understood the Servant Songs better than Jesus and the apostles.

Conclusion

H. Wheeler Robinson believed that advances in science, biblical criticism, and philosophy made many of the traditional answers offered by the church untenable in the modern world. He tried to show, however, that the essential and important doctrines of Christianity could not only be maintained but were more clearly visible in the light of modern progress.

Did he succeed? He did if by that we mean that he was able to present in forceful and lucid terms significant aspects of Christian doctrine. On the other hand, many of his own analyses, if rigorously followed, detract from rather than build up the faith he was determined to maintain.

Bibliography

Works by Robinson

Robinson's literary output was enormous. In addition to his books and scholarly articles, he wrote a column for the *Baptist Times* from 1914 to 1924 and reviewed books for the *Critical Review, Times Literary Supplement, Church Quarterly Review, Journal of Theological Studies, Baptist Quarterly,* and others. The following is a bibliography of his books and other significant articles. For a chronological (but still partial) bibliography including many of his popular essays see E. A. Payne, "A Bibliography of the Writings of Dr. H. Wheeler Robinson," in *Studies in History and Religion Presented to Dr. H. Wheeler Robinson, M.A., on his Seventieth Birthday,* ed., E. A. Payne (London: Lutterworth Press, 1942), 254-58.

Books

Baptists in Britain. With J. H. Rushbrooke. London: Baptist Union, 1937.

Baptist Principles. London: Kingsgate Press, 1925.

The Christian Doctrine of Man. Edinburgh: T. and T. Clark, 1911. 2d ed., 1913, 3d ed., 1926.

The Christian Experience of the Holy Spirit. London: Nisbet, 1928.

Corporate Personality in Ancient Israel. Philadelphia: Fortress Press, 1964. Reprints the essays "The Hebrew Conception of Corporate Personality" and "The Group and the Individual in Israel."

The Cross in the Old Testament. London: SCM, 1955. This reprints *The Cross of Job, The Cross of Jeremiah,* and *The Cross of the Servant*.

The Cross of Hosea. Edited by E. A. Payne. Philadelphia: Westminster, 1949.

The Cross of Jeremiah. London: SCM, 1926.

The Cross of Job. London: SCM, 1916.

The Cross of the Servant. London: SCM, 1926.

Deuteronomy and Joshua. (Century Bible, Vol. IV) Edinburgh: T. C. and E. C. Jack, 1907.

The History of Israel. London: Duckworth, 1938.

Inspiration and Revelation in the Old Testament. Oxford: Clarendon Press, 1946.

The Life and Faith of the Baptists. London: Methuen, 1927.

The Old Testament: Its Making and Meaning. University of London Press, 1937.

Redemption and Revelation in the Actuality of History. London: Nisbet, 1942.

The Religious Ideas of the Old Testament. London: Duckworth, 1913.

Suffering, Human and Divine. London: SCM, 1939.

Two Prophets: Studies in Hosea and Ezekiel. Edited by E. A. Payne. London: Lutterworth, 1959.

The Veil of God. London: Nisbet, 1936.

Books Edited by Robinson

The Bible in Its Ancient and English Versions. Oxford: Clarendon Press, 1940. Includes "The Bible as the Word of God" by Robinson, 275-302.

Record and Revelation. Oxford: Clarendon Press, 1938. Includes two articles by Robinson, "The Philosophy of Revelation," 303-20, and "The Characteristic Doctrines," 321-48.

Articles and Essays

"The Christian Doctrine of Redemption," *The Christian Faith*, ed. W. R. Matthews. London: Eyre and Spottiswoode, 1936.

"The Eschatology of the Psalmists," *The Psalmists*, ed. D. C. Simpson. Oxford University Press, 1926.

"The Group and the Individual in Israel," *The Individual in East and West*, ed. E. R. Hughes, 1937.

"The Hebrew Conception of Corporate Personality," *Werden und Wesen des Alten Testaments*, ed. P. Volz, F. Stummer, and J. Hempel. Berlin: Alfred Töpelmann, 1936.

"Hebrew Psychology in Relation to Pauline Anthropology," *Mansfield College Essays Presented to the Reverend Andrew Martin Fairbairn, D.D. on the Occasion of his Seventieth Birthday, November 4, 1908*. London: Hodder and Stoughton, 1909.

"Hebrew Psychology." *The People and the Book*, ed. A. S. Peake. Oxford University Press, 1925.

"Law and Religion in Israel." *Judaism and Christianity*. vol. 3, ed. E. I. J. Rosenthal. London: Sheldon Press, 1937-38.

"The Old Testament Background." *Christian Worship: Studies in its History and Meaning*, ed. N. Micklem. Oxford University Press, 1936.

"The Religion of Israel." *A Companion to the Bible*, ed. T. W. Manson. Edinburgh: T. and T. Clark, 1939.

"The Social Life of the Psalmists." *The Psalmists*, ed. D. C. Simpson. Oxford University Press, 1926.

Notes

1. For an affectionate, uncritical biography see Ernest A. Payne, *Henry Wheeler Robinson: Scholar, Teacher, Principal* (London: Nisbet and Co., 1946). For a more succinct biography see John Reumann, "Introduction," in H. Wheeler Robinson, *Corporate Personality in Israel* (Philadelphia: Fortress Press, 1964), v-xiii.

2. H. Wheeler Robinson, *Baptist Principles* (London: Carey Kingsgate Press, 1925).

3. H. Wheeler Robinson, *The Life and Faith of the Baptists*, rev. ed. (London: Kingsgate Press, 1927; 1946). Robinson also penned numerous articles on various aspects of Baptist history and polity and, with J. H. Rushbrooke, published *Baptists in Britain* (London: The Baptist Union Publication Department, 1937), for which Robinson wrote "The History of Baptists in England," 9-34.

4. Robinson, *Life and Faith*, v.

5. *Baptist Principles* (pp. 56-65) contains a short history of the Baptists. The book was "popular" not only in the sense that it was intended for the lay reader but that it enjoyed several reprintings.

6. Robinson, *Life and Faith*, 44-68.

7. Robinson, *Principles*, 12. (Cf. *Life and Faith*, 69-70.)

8. Robinson, *Principles*, 17-27.

9. Robinson, *Life and Faith*, 70-73. Robinson also asserts the practical values of immersion. These are (1) psychological, as a reinforcement in the believer's mind to the fact of his or her conversion; (2) as an indication that conversion and the subsequent walk of faith is ultimately a private and individual matter; and (3) as an acted-out confession of faith in Christ (74-80).

10. Robinson, *Principles*, 31-39.

11. Ibid., 52-55. He discusses, for example, the Paulicians, a sect of the Eastern Church, and notes that their doctrine, as described in their catechism *The Key of Truth* (ca. 800), forbade infant baptism.

12. Ibid., 83.

13. Ibid., 85.

14. Ibid., 94.

15. Ibid., 88.

16. Ibid., 100-01.

17. Ibid., 108-22.

18. Ibid., 123-38.

19. Ibid., 137: "Baptists need to remember . . . that if there is an externalism of Church authority which has worked mischief in religion, there is also an externalism of the appeal of Scripture, not less alien to the living truth of Christ."

20. Ibid., 141-42.

21. Ibid., 66.

22. H. Wheeler Robinson, *The Old Testament: Its Making and Meaning* (Nashville: Abingdon Press, 1937).

23. For example, Robinson dates the "little apocalypse" of Isaiah 24—27 around 300 B.C. (*Old Testament,* 216), whereas Driver dates it earlier in the postexilic period. Compare S. R. Driver, *An Introduction to the Literature of the Old Testament* (2nd ed., 1913; reprint, Gloucester, Mass.: Peter Smith, 1972), 221. But these differences are so minor as to be insignificant. In every important problem of Old Testament introduction, Robinson essentially echoes Driver.

24. H. Wheeler Robinson, *The History of Israel* (London: Duckworth, 1938).

25. Ibid., 22-23.

26. Ibid., 40-41.

27. Ibid., 52.

28. H. Wheeler Robinson, *The Religious Ideas of the Old Testament* (London: Duckworth, 1913).

29. H. Wheeler Robinson, *Inspiration and Revelation in the Old Testament* (London: Oxford, 1946).

30. Robinson, *Religious Ideas,* 79-87, and *Inspiration and Revelation,* 69-70.

31. Robinson, *Religious Ideas,* 82-83, and *Inspiration and Revelation,* 76.

32. Robinson, *Inspiration and Revelation,* 71-77. See also H. Wheeler Robinson, *The Christian Doctrine of Man* (Edinburgh: T. and T. Clark, 1911), 11-27.

33. Robinson, *Religious Ideas,* 92-98, and *Inspiration and Revelation,* 92-102.

34. Robinson, *Religious Ideas,* 96.

35. Ibid., 96-97.

36. "The Hebrew Conception of Corporate Personality" first appeared in *Werden und Wesen des Alten Testaments,* ed. P. Volz (Berlin: Töpelmann, 1936), 49-62. References that follow are to the Fortress Press reprint of 1964.

37. Brevard S. Childs, *Biblical Theology in Crisis* (Philadelphia: Westminster, 1974), 46.

38. Robinson, "The Hebrew Conception of Corporate Personality," 3-10.

39. Ibid., 14.

40. Ibid., 16-17.

41. Robinson, *Inspiration and Revelation,* 37.

42. Ibid., 47. See pages 1-48 for a complete presentation of Robinson's views on the subject.

43. Ibid., 49-62.

44. Robinson, *Religious Ideas,* 26.

45. Robinson, *Inspiration and Revelation,* 78-91.

46. Robinson himself sees evidence of Divine activity in Israel's history. He notes that three salient features of Israel's history are: (1) a "remarkable series of foreign influences" (Egypt, Canaan, etc.); (2) major personalities who work from individual initiative (Moses, Samuel, Elijah, etc.); and (3) the consciousness of possessing a unique religion. These factors, Robinson says, when the remarkable manner in which Jewish history has been joined to that of Christianity is also considered, indicate the teleological or providentially governed character of Israel's history (*Religious Ideas,* 17-23). Even if Robinson's premises are granted, however, it is difficult to see how his conclusion necessarily flows from them.

47. Robinson, *Inspiration and Revelation,* 123-59.

48. Robinson, *Religious Ideas,* 55.

49. Robinson, *Inspiration and Revelation,* 174.

50. Ibid., 164-98.

51. Ibid., 230.

52. Cf. Robinson, *Religious Ideas,* 42-43.

53. Robinson, *Inspiration and Revelation,* 241.

54. Ibid., 231-61.

55. Ibid., 241. Emphasis Robinson's.

56. E.g., the patriarchs.

57. E.g., the tent of meeting legislation of P.

58. E.g., the abortive messianic revolution of Haggai 2:20-23.

59. E.g., the disputes over the priestly privilege among the Aaronite, Mushite, and Levitical groups.

60. The first edition of Driver's *Introduction* was completed in 1897.

61. E.g., in the form-critical work of Hermann Gunkel and archaeology of W. F. Albright.

62. S. H. Hooke, "Archaeology and the Old Testament," in H. Wheeler Robinson, ed., *Record and Revelation* (London: Oxford, 1938), 372-73.

63. For a definitive study of the unraveling of the Documentary Hypothesis and rise of alternative theories in modern scholarship see R. N. Whybray, "The Making of the Pentateuch," *JSOT Supplement Series* 53:13-219.

64. For an excellent though brief discussion of the issue and review of the literature up to his time, see Walther Eichrodt, *The Theology of the Old Testament* (Philadelphia: Westminster Press, 1961), 1:483, n.4.

65. Aubrey R. Johnson, *The Vitality of the Individual in the Thought of Ancient Israel* (Cardiff: University of Wales, 1942), 83, n.2, 102, n.2. Cited by John Reumann in *Corporate Personality,* 38.

66. Robinson, *Religious Ideas,* 88-89.

67. It has been shown, for example, that Hosea did not consider himself a leader in a new theological emphasis but an exponent of the Pentateuch. See Umberto Cassuto, "The Prophet Hosea and the Books of the Pentateuch" (1933; reprinted in U. Cassuto, *Biblical and Oriental Studies* [Jerusalem: Magnes Press, 1973], 79-100).

68. In the traditional chronology, much of wisdom antedates classical prophecy.

69. This is also the stance of Jesus, who affirms the resurrection not so much by a proof text as by an assertion that individual persons are in covenant relationship with God (Matt. 21:32).

70. Cf. H. Wheeler Robinson, *The Christian Doctrine of Man* (Edinburgh: T. and T. Clark, 1911), 97.

71. H. Wheeler Robinson, *Suffering: Human and Divine* (New York: Macmillan, 1939), 79.

72. See Robinson, *Man,* 178-94, 301-7. Cf. H. Wheeler Robinson, *Redemption and Revelation* (London: Nisbet and Co., 1942), 284.

73. This emerges most clearly perhaps in Robinson's last work: "We can assert its validity only if we are ready to admit that there is a real kinship between God and man, a kinship which makes possible both sympathy and understanding, the kinship which Hosea describes as that of Husband and of Father. Man is presented in the Old Testament as a spiritual being, and as such he is, notwithstanding all limitations, akin to God who is Spirit. The greatest of those limitations, the most serious of all the barriers between man and God, is again and again declared to be moral evil. If men persist in it, there can be no knowledge of God in them, no revelation of Him to them. But this does not mean, as some theologians down to our own times have asserted,

that the kinship of God and man has been broken by the sin of the first man for all his descendants. There is no exegetical warrant for reading back into the story of Eden the Christian dogma of 'original sin.' Man may individually sin himself away from the very capacity to know God, but there is no such inevitability and personal irresponsibility in this result as the dogma of original sin implies. Both the word which the prophets declare and their frequent appeals for obedience to it imply the capacity of man to understand and to obey. The kinship of God and man means the Yahweh is the kind of God who does reveal Himself to man, and that man is the kind of being that is capable of response to the revelation." (Robinson, *Inspiration and Revelation*, 190).

74. See especially H. Wheeler Robinson, *The Cross in the Old Testament* (Philadelphia: Westminster Press, 1955). This contains three monographs: "The Cross of Job" (1916), "The Cross of Jeremiah" (1925), and "The Cross of the Servant" (1926).

75. For examples, see H. Wheeler Robinson, "The Inner Life of the Psalmists," in D. C. Simpson, ed., *The Psalmists* (London: Oxford University Press, 1926), 56-65; Robinson, *The Veil of God* (London: Nisbet and Co., 1936), 72-104; Robinson, *Redemption and Revelation*, 245-80; and Robinson, *Religious Ideas*, 159-83.

76. Other forms of suffering are "revelational" (to bring one to a deeper awareness of God, as in Hosea's marriage) and "eschatological" (national suffering as prologue to final triumph, as in apocalyptic). See Robinson, *Suffering*, 31-48.

77. Robinson, *Suffering*, 178.

78. Robinson is aware of the problems involved in the idea of divine suffering (frustration of divine will, entanglement in the time process, and God as less than the absolute), but responds that self-limitation is not frustration but is the moral and spiritual suffering that is part of true sympathy, that the time process is in God rather than Him being entangled in it, and that we should not maintain the notion of God as the absolute over against the biblical concept that God is involved in history. See Robinson, *Suffering*, 146-55.

79. Ibid., 31-48, 65-224. See also Robinson, *The Cross in the Old Testament*, 111-12.

80. Robinson, *The Cross in the Old Testament*, 65-97.

81. Robinson, *Religious Ideas*, 111-12.

82. Robinson, *Redemption and Revelation*, 207-11. (On page 213 he says that we cannot regard Chalcedonian Christology as "sacrosanct.")

83. Ibid., 211-18.

84. Robinson, *Suffering*, 191. Cf. 163-84. Robinson, *The Cross in the Old Testament*, 98-114, and *Redemption and Revelation*, 262-63.

85. Robinson, *Religious Ideas*, 141-48.

86. Robinson, *Suffering*, 174.

87. Ibid., 183. Also, page 170: "This victory of Christ is not simply symbolic of the hidden victory of God; by being that part of the divine victory which we are permitted to see it becomes the supreme victory, the *instrumental* center of historical redemption. It is a temporal event, but it is also part of the eternal reality which the Gospel proclaims." Cf. Robinson, *Redemption and Revelation*, 271-80.

88. H. Wheeler Robinson, *The Christian Experience of the Holy Spirit* (London: Nisbet and Co., 1928).

89. See especially Robinson, *Christian Experience*, 199-220.

90. Robinson, *Religious Ideas*, 126-27.

91. H. Wheeler Robinson, "The Bible as the Word of God" in H. Wheeler Rob-

inson, ed., *The Bible in Its Ancient and Modern Versions* (Oxford: Clarendon Press, 1940), 294-96.

92. Ibid., 298.

93. Ecclesiastes, for example, is for Robinson a hopelessly skeptical piece of Hellenized Judaism that makes no positive contribution to Hebrew wisdom. See Robinson, *Inspiration and Revelation*, 257-58.

21

Walter Thomas Conner

James Leo Garrett, Jr.

Biography[1]

Birth and Boyhood

Walter Thomas, the second son of Philip Orlander Conner (1846-1896) and Frances Jane Monk Conner (? -1904), was born on January 19, 1877,[2] at Center, now called Rowell,[3] in Cleveland County, Arkansas. Orlander Conner had been born near Pontotoc, Mississippi, and three of his four brothers had died in the Confederate cause. He, his son born to his deceased first wife, and his second wife had moved from Mississippi to Center, twenty-five miles south of Pine Bluff.[4] After Walter's birth, Orlander bought on credit and moved to an eighty-acre farm on the road from Pine Bluff to Warren and near the present village of Rye.[5] In 1889 Orlander Conner moved his family to Kingsland, Arkansas, where he was employed in a sawmill.[6] Commenting in later years on his childhood, Walter T. Conner stated: "I was brought up in the dire poverty of the South after the Civil War."[7] His early education consisted of attending "ungraded country schools on an average of three or four months a year and some years practically none."[8]

In November 1892, when Walter was fifteen, Orlander Conner again moved his family, this time a far greater distance. The new home was to be a farm in West Texas, some eight miles southwest of Abilene in Taylor County, in a community then called Tebo but now known as Tye.[9]

Conversion, Call to the Ministry, and Early Preaching

The beginnings of the Christian motivation which was to dominate the life and ministry of W. T. Conner are recorded in his own words: "My earliest religious impressions go back to the [Enon] church where my parents and grandparents belonged in Cleveland County, Arkansas."[10] On one occasion in that church Walter was inclined to make a profession of faith in response to a gospel appeal, but his older brother caught his coat and held him back.[11] In the Kingsland community the Conner family was "not convenient to a Baptist church and . . . attended a country Methodist church." Walter Conner recalled his experience at about age fourteen of being in a Methodist service in which the young preacher had made "an intense and protracted appeal" for non-Christians to evidence some interest in becoming Christians, and he resisted that appeal.[12]

After the move to Texas, young Conner discovered that Baptist and Methodist preachers "were still talking about the cross and the love of God." His conversion occurred in the summer of 1894 when he was seventeen.

> I was converted in an old-time, horrah, Methodist meeting. . . . My conviction of sin gradually deepened until it became a very definite and heavy load. . . . I became deeply enough interested to begin to go forward for prayer and thus seek for help. . . . A number of people talked to me at what was then known as the mourner's bench but none of them seemed to give me any very definite help. . . . Finally, my load became so heavy, not knowing what else to do, I gave up. The expression "gave up" expresses my experience better than any other that I can think of. When I gave up, my burden was removed but I did not have any ecstatic joy or feel like shouting or anything of the kind. I simply felt that my burden was gone and I hardly knew what had happened. . . . Finally . . . it came to me that I was saved by putting my trust in Christ and not by any particular type of feeling that I had had.[13]

Both Conner's life and theology were grounded upon an abiding confidence in the validity of evangelical Christian conversion. He was baptized by W. M. Reynolds[14] and received into the fellowship of Harmony Baptist Church at Caps, Texas.[15]

According to Conner, his impression of a call to preach the gospel went "back to the time when I was a small boy, and became a definite conviction soon after I was converted."[16] In the small library in the Conner home there were books of a doctrinal nature. He participated in a young men's prayer meeting in the Caps community, from which came at least half a dozen Baptist and Methodist preachers. In a country debating society Conner learned to speak in public.[17] J. M. Reynolds, the brother of W. M. Reynolds, while preaching in evangelistic services at Caps in the summer of 1895, interrogated young Conner as to his conviction of a divine call to preach. When Conner answered affirmatively, Reynolds encouraged the church to license Conner, and the church did so.[18] Conner's first sermon was on the text, "Wist ye not that I must be about my Father's business?"[19] Through J. M. Reynolds's assistance Conner soon had preaching appointments in nearby Baptist churches.[20]

Conner's first pastorate was at Tuscola, Texas, during 1898-99.[21] In October 1899 the church at Caps ordained him,[22] and he served that church as pastor during 1899-1900. During 1903-04 Conner was resident pastor of Baptist churches in south Texas at Eagle Lake half-time and at Rock Island and East Bernard quarter-time,[23] having been recommended by B. H. Carroll.[24] Later, for a period ending in 1908, Conner was pastor of the Baptist churches at Blum and Rio Vista in Johnson County, south of Fort Worth.

Academic and Theological Education

Conner's determination to pursue an education which would equip him for his lifework may be seen in events which covered nearly two decades. His struggles for an education were made more difficult by the death of his father in 1896. During 1896-98 he was enrolled intermittently as a student at Simmons College (now Hardin-Simmons University) in Abilene, Texas. After

Walter Thomas Conner (1877-1952)

borrowing money he entered Baylor University, Waco, in the fall of 1898 but after one term had to withdraw in order to pay his debts. He returned to Baylor in the fall of 1901, but withdrew in January 1903, this time to make it possible for his brother John to continue as a student at Baylor.[25] Early in his Baylor days W. T. Conner came to the conviction that he should be a foreign missionary; this conviction was due to a large extent to the influence of Professor John S. Tanner, whose missionary zeal led to the founding of an organization of students committed to foreign missionary service.[26] In the fall of 1904 Conner again enrolled in Baylor and continued until he graduated with the B.A. degree in 1906.[27] Also in the 1906 Baylor graduating class was Miss Blanche Ethel Horne of Albany, Texas,[28] who became on June 4, 1907, Mrs. W. T. Conner. Both husband and wife, the latter a capable student of Latin and Greek, taught Latin at Baylor University during 1907-08.

Conner continued his studies at the Baylor Theological Seminary, which had received full seminary status in 1905 under the mentorship of its dean, B. H. Carroll. Its faculty included Albert Henry Newman, Charles B. Williams, Calvin Goodspeed, and L. W. Doolan.[29] In 1908 Conner received a Th.B. degree from the seminary, which in March had been chartered as Southwestern Baptist Theological Seminary, and an M.A. degree from Baylor University.[30]

During 1906-08 B. H. Carroll indicated to W. T. Conner that he "would be offered the position of teacher of theology in the seminary" if he "would make proper preparation." The original suggestion concerning Conner seems to have come from A. H. Newman. Conner went, therefore, to Rochester Theological Seminary, Rochester, New York, for two years of study with the understanding that he would return to teach theology at Southwestern.[31] He was graduated from Rochester in the spring of 1909, "no degree being given then on graduation." At the suggestion of Professor Walter Rauschenbusch he wrote a fellowship thesis on "Theodore Parker's Theological System." After one more year of study at Rochester on the fellowship, he received in 1910 the B.D. degree.[32] His teachers at Rochester included Rauschenbusch, A. H. Strong, William A. Stevens, and H. C. Mabie.[33] Conner studied for two weeks in the summer of 1910 under George B. Foster at the University of Chicago before returning to Texas.[34] In September he assumed his duties as a professor at Southwestern Seminary, which was in process of moving from Waco to Seminary Hill, Texas, now within the corporate limits of Fort Worth. Conner had been elected to succeed Calvin Goodspeed, whose title had been "professor of systematic theology, apologetics, polemics, and ecclesiology."[35]

During 1914 Conner was given a leave of absence for graduate study at The Southern Baptist Theological Seminary, Louisville, Kentucky. There he pursued a major in theology under Edgar Young Mullins and minors in philosophy of religion and psychology of religion under William O. Carver and B. H. Dement, respectively. In May 1916 Conner received the Th.D. degree, having written a thesis on "Pragmatism and Theology."[36] In the summer of 1920 he studied at the University of Chicago for six weeks, and during the same summer Baylor University conferred on him the honorary D.D. degree.[37] Later, when The Southern Baptist Theological Seminary granted the Ph.D. degree instead of the Th.D. degree, it gave to its alumni who held the latter degree the privilege of writing an additional thesis on the basis of which the Ph.D. degree would be conferred. Conner wrote another thesis on "The Idea of the Incarnation in the Gospel of John" and received the degree in March 1931.[38]

Professorship and Related Activities

Conner's teaching career at Southwestern extended from September 1910 to May 1949, when a stroke compelled his retirement from active service. From 1910 to 1913 he was "acting professor" and from 1913 to 1949 professor. During certain periods of his career it became necessary for Conner to assume the teaching of courses other than systematic theology, chiefly because of changes in personnel in the seminary faculty; these other disciplines included English New Testament (1921-22), biblical theology (1923-25), and Greek New Testament exegesis (1939-44).[39]

From 1910 until 1917 the Southwestern professor used as a text in his basic systematic theology course A. H. Strong's *Systematic Theology*. From about 1918 until 1922 he used *The Christian Religion in Its Doctrinal Expression* by E. Y. Mullins. In 1922 Conner began to use his own notes in mimeographed form and in 1926 shifted to his book, *A System of Christian Doctrine*. In later years he required the reading of his *Revelation and God* and *The Gospel of Redemption*.[40]

Conner's classroom technique enabled him to hold the attention of his students. A native Irish wit, a keen sense of the proper use of anecdote, and his concern that theological concepts should be applied were combined to create an interesting classroom lecturer.[41]

Conner was pastor of Baptist churches at Godley and Handley, Texas, and was the first pastor of the Seminary Hill Baptist Church, now the Gambrell Street Baptist Church of Fort Worth. Supply or interim pastorates were numerous. He often lectured at Bible conferences and summer assemblies and sometimes addressed Baptist conventions and preached in evangelistic meetings. Although Conner did not enter foreign mission service, he and Mrs. Conner had a distinctive Christian ministry among the Chinese in Fort Worth. A continuing interest in world missions characterized his entire career, and the Foreign Mission Board of the Southern Baptist Convention "relied upon" his counsel concerning candidates for appointment.[42]

In 1928 Conner addressed the fourth world congress of the Baptist World Alliance in Toronto on theological education.[43] He was an active member of the Southwestern Society of Biblical Study and Research, serving as chairman of its council in 1933 and 1942 and as president in 1941.[44] The Fort Worth professor delivered in 1946 the Wilkinson Lectures at Northern Baptist Theological Seminary, Chicago, on Johannine theology.[45]

Years of financial stringency both before and during the Great Depression were very difficult for Conner and his colleagues at Southwestern, especially since Conner's six children, all of whom became college graduates, were enrolled in college between 1925 and 1940. Conner also had several illnesses, including three cases of pneumonia.[46] He declined a professorship in philosophy at Baylor University about 1926 and the presidency of Kansas City Baptist Theological Seminary about 1937.[47] In his later years Conner's recommendation of young men for the Southwestern faculty was tantamount to their election.

Conner died on May 26, 1952, and was buried in Mount Olivet Cemetery, Fort Worth.[48]

Exposition

Investigation into the sources of and the influences upon Conner's theology, made more difficult by his practice of providing limited documentation of such, has been undertaken elsewhere[49] by the author and can only be summarized here. Probable sources or influences include the Baylor faculty,[50] the Rochester faculty,[51] the Louisville faculty,[52] the Chicago faculty,[53] Baptist denominationalism,[54] the Southwestern faculty and Fort Worth,[55] British evangelicals,[56] Baptists in the United States,[57] other American theologians,[58] American philosophers,[59] other British theologians,[60] Continental European theologians,[61] and classical theologians.[62]

Conner's work in New Testament theology came to fruition in *The Faith of the New Testament* (1940). Following the pattern laid down by George Barker Stevens[63] and Henry Clay Sheldon,[64] Conner organized his book according to the principal types of New Testament literature: Synoptic, Jewish Christian, Pauline, and Johannine. Conner recognized both unity and variety of teaching in the New Testament. In this volume, he emphasizes Jesus' wilderness temptations, explains His teaching about the kingdom of God and about prayer, reckons the Epistle to the Hebrews to be of Alexandrian method, and explicates Paul on the universality of sin and John on "eternal life."[65]

Conner also engaged in polemics and apologetics. His earliest major effort came in his short monographs providing a theological refutation of the teachings of Christian Science[66] and of what we now call Jehovah's Witnesses.[67] Beginning with his Rochester thesis on Theodore Parker and continuing in his books, he offered criticisms of Unitarianism. In various books and articles the Southwestern theologian refuted teachings of Baptist antimissions ("Hardshellism"), pedobaptism, the theology of Thomas and Alexander Campbell, theological modernism and liberalism, dispensational premillennialism, the theology of Karl Barth, Roman Catholic theology, Holiness and Pentecostal movements, and anti-Christian philosophies (materialism, pantheism, agnosticism, and anti-Christian theism).[68]

"It has come to pass again that men are not ashamed to be known as theologians." Those words Conner wrote in the preface to *The Gospel of Redemption* (1945),[69] as he noted that the "science of religion" was no longer prevailing. The rise of biblical theology and the renascence of systematic theology even affected Conner, who had never winced at being a theologian. His *The Gospel of Redemption,* a revision of the second half of *A System of Christian Doctrine* (1924), showed the impact of biblical theology to a degree not found in *Revelation and God* (1936), a revision of the first half of the same book.

Conner began his systematic exposition of Christian doctrine with the doctrine of revelation rather than with the doctrine of God. He paid particular attention to the human capability to receive divine revelation. Human beings by creation have the capacity to know God and a craving to worship and trust God, and despite their sin they are valuable in God's sight. Conner drew upon personalism rather than biblical theology to provide the characteristics of human beings as spiritual persons: intelligence, rational affection, free will, and conscience. In 1924 Conner treated the revelation of God in Christ prior to discussion of Old Testament revelation and revelation through nature, but in 1936 revelation through nature preceded biblical revelation. Conner stressed "man's religious consciousness" and restated the classic arguments for God's existence. Without specifying such, Conner basically agreed with the position of John Calvin and Emil Brunner that general revelation is not salvific but the basis for human accountability and preparatory for the revelation in Jesus Christ. Conner clearly differentiated revelation and the Bible, which is the product and record of unique and historic divine revelation and a book of religion. Following Strong, he did not attempt to espouse a specific theory as to the process of divine inspiration of the Bible, and, following Mullins, he utilized the concept of progressive revelation. The Bible's "central interest" is redemption, and its unity is found in Jesus Christ. Conner was accustomed to reply to a student who would ask, "But doesn't the Bible mean what it *says?*" by saying, "No. It means what it *means.*"[70] Revelation in Christ, which is "final" or ultimate, involves Jesus' own consciousness of God, His teaching about God the Father, His own character and life, His claims relative to His unique relationship with the Father, and His redemptive work. Paralleling the objective revelation in Christ is the subjective revelation through the Holy Spirit, and faith is the "venture" and "vision" necessary for receiving God's self-disclosure. For Conner "the authority of the Bible is the authority of Christ" so that there are not dual authorities.[71]

The doctrine of God in the inclusive sense meant for Conner the Person of Jesus Christ, the nature and relations of God the Father, the Holy Spirit, and the Trinity. In Conner's books the Person of Christ was always treated prior to the doctrine of God, probably because Christ was seen as the Revealer of God and so that the doctrine of God would "square with the character, work, and teachings of Christ."[72] For Conner the "person" of Christ embraced not only the interrelation of humanity and Deity in Him but also the virgin birth, sinlessness, miracles, and resurrection of Jesus. Conner was more emphatic than Mullins on the humanity of Jesus, and, unlike Strong and Mullins, related Jesus' sinlessness to His humanity.[73] Affirming both virgin birth and resurrection, both preexistence and ascension, Conner found Jesus' favorite self-designation to be "Son of man." The Deity of Christ received detailed treatment, and the incarnation was identified as a "mystery." Various kenotic theories were rejected, but a basic condescension or self-emptying was retained. Conner acknowledged that the application of personhood to God is analogical. What some theologians described as the "natural attributes" of God he treated as "the absoluteness" of God or His "infinity." From it can be inferred God's self-existence, unity, and supremacy. God is related to space/time in terms of omnipresence, eternity, and immensity. As omniscient God can foresee acts that are also free acts. The moral attributes for Conner were chiefly holiness, or transcendence, righteousness, and love. Conner taught both creation and sustenance, both natural law and miracle. The Holy Spirit is God's power at work in the world. The Fort Worth theologian became less certain that in the Old Testament the Spirit of God is hypostatically distinct from God but was sure that in the New Testament such distinction is clear. The Spirit enabled Jesus in His ministry, was bestowed at Pentecost, is to enable Christians, and gives charismata for the edification of the church. Conner deplored various modern substitutes for the working of the Holy Spirit. He did not find full-blown Trinitarian teaching in the Old Testament but was led by the Deity of Jesus and the personhood of the Holy Spirit to mainstream immanental Trinitarianism in which ancient heresies are avoided and the term "person" is used advisedly.[74]

Conner saw sin as a religious conception and as the result of the temptation of the personal Satan. He clearly rejected idealism's tendency to explain sin as being due to bodily appetites or man's possession of a physical body—or an evolutionary animal hangover—and naturalism's tendency to explain sin as due to human creaturely finitude. Instead, the nature of sin centers in willful rebellion and unbelief. For Conner there are degrees of guilt. Departing from Calvin's concept of depravity as hereditary corruption, he taught depravity as the inevitability of sinning. Conner refused to accept either the Augustinian or the federal theories as to "original sin" as human sharing in Adamic guilt and shifted the focus from Romans 5:12-21 to Romans 1:18 to 3:20. For him a historical Adam was no problem, but human beings, while perversely affected by the sin of Adam and Eve, are guilty only for their own sin. Conner developed the concept that suffering or natural evil could have been the "anticipative consequence" of sin. Sin separates the sinner from God, alienates him from his fellow humans, and destroys the true self; sin issues in death.[75]

Redemption, a major theme in Conner's theology, includes election, the work of Christ, becoming a Christian, the Christian life, the church, and last things. Election for Conner was definable in terms of God's purpose, not God's decrees. It embraces both the totality of God's people and individuals and is the unfolding of God's plan. But it is not the self-election of believers by repentance and faith or merely God's foreknowing who would repent and believe. God is responsible for faith but not for unbelief. Hence Conner has been classified under "modified Calvinistic predestination."[76] On the doctrine of the saving work of Christ, Conner shifted from his earlier commitment to a moderate form of the penal substitutionary theory in *A System of Christian Doctrine* (1924) and *Gospel Doctrines* (1925) to his later embracing of the Christ as victor theory in *The Gospel of Redemption* (1945) and *The Cross in the New Testament* (1954).[77] He favored the term "the cross" rather than the term "atonement." Christ's saving work must embrace His life and His resurrection as well as His death and cannot be separated from the person of Christ. Conner explored and criticized the Anselmic (satisfaction), the Grotian (governmental), the Abelardian (moral influence), the Socinian (example), the "commercial" or quantitatively penal, and A. H. Strong's eternal atonement theories.[78]

Rather than follow the classical Protestant pattern of justification, sanctification, and glorification Conner gave attention to the various New Testament terms used to describe one's becoming a Christian, although "salvation" (past, present, future) was used comprehensively. He successively expounded union with Christ, forgiveness, justification, reconciliation, adoption, new life, and sanctification. Conner was critical of the forensic doctrine of justification ("declared righteous") issuing from the Reformation and argued for a vital doctrine ("made righteous") which was devoid of Roman Catholic works-righteousness and closely joined to regeneration.[79] On sanctification Conner moved away from Protestant orthodoxy by insisting that the term had initial, continuing, and consummative uses, not merely the continuing. Identifying repentance and faith as "conditions of salvation," in 1925 Conner placed them prior to the discussion of the aforementioned terms and in 1945 after such discussion. The final rubric under becoming a Christian was assurance. The Christian life was interpreted under four themes: providence, prayer, perseverance, and growth. Objections to providence, including that arising from suffering, are answered, and a special providence affirmed. Prayer "is communion of the soul with God"; Conner noted its various moods and answered objections to prayer. Conner's doctrine of stewardship, including his objection to "storehouse tithing," was expressed in various articles. On perseverance Conner clearly remained a Calvinist with no disposition to allow apostasy, but his careful definition of perseverance has led to his being identified as a "modified Calvinist."[80] He advocated Christian growth but rejected perfectionism.[81]

Moving beyond Baptist Landmarkism, Conner found the term "church" to be used in the New Testament in a universal as well as local sense. The church as the body of Christ is primarily fellowship rather than organization. Conner favored democratic polity, basing it on the principles of New Testament Christianity rather than on proof-texts. In 1925 he stressed edification, evangelization, benevolence, and moral dynamism as the mission of the church, whereas in 1945 he contended that "the first business" of a church is worship. Emphatic about a divine call to preach, he reckoned baptism and the Lord's Supper to be pictorial and symbolic, rejected pedobaptism and "alien immersion," and held to close communion. Conner treated last things under the title "The Consummation of Salvation: The Coming of the Kingdom of God." Recognizing that there were unique difficulties vis-à-vis eschatology, he set forth a fivefold interpretation of the kingdom of God: universal sovereignty, the theocracy of Israel, the spiritual rule founded by Jesus, "a progressive power in the world," and the consummated or eternal kingship. In 1924 Conner taught one general resurrection of all humans at the time of the second coming of Jesus, whereas in 1945 he, following T. P. Stafford, inclined toward the view that resurrection bodies are received at death and resurrection itself will accompany the second coming. In 1924 Conner inclined toward postmillennialism, but in 1945 he identified himself generally with amillennialism. The final judgment will reveal human character, assign destinies, and vindicate God's dealings with humanity. Conner affirmed heaven and hell, rejecting restorationism and annihilationism.[82]

Evaluation

The theology of W. T. Conner has numerous elements of *strength* that can be recognized four decades after his work ended. For him Christian theology was to be closely related to Christian experience and the church and hence was not to be primarily speculative. Conner's writing style, marked by simplicity and an Anglo-Saxon vocabulary, made his teachings available to pastors and lay people.[83] Conner gave emphasis to the doctrine of revelation when it was receiving much attention from Protestant theologians. His anti-Barthian espousal of general revelation and his teaching of the finality in Christ are seen as strengths by this author. The attributes of God are to be interpreted so as to attain to the moral self-consistency of God, and the doctrine of God should be framed in the light of Jesus Christ. Conner was increasingly concerned with the doctrine of the Holy Spirit, especially the Spirit's work. Man is not worthy of salvation, yet worth saving. Man is personally responsible for sin, and hence Conner had no tolerance for theories of imputation of Adamic guilt. Late in life Conner made a major shift from penal substitution to Christ as victor. His departure from Protestant orthodoxy concerning sanctification is probably more persuasive than his departure concerning justification. Providence, for Conner, meant Romans 8:28-29. Moreover, the kingdom of God should be so interpreted as to be consistent with the mission of Jesus Himself.[84]

Weaknesses in the theology of Conner are also identifiable. Certain major topics treated by other theologians during the nineteenth and twentieth centuries were bypassed or treated only slightly by Conner; for example, theories concerning the divine inspiration of the Bible, the biblical doctrine of the image of God in man, and the relation of the doctrine of the creation of man to evolutionary science. Sometimes the readers of Conner's books may be inclined to want to press questions upon him. Have you mistakenly fused general revelation and theistic arguments for God's existence? Are there no clearer conclusions to be drawn concerning Chalcedonian Christology and kenoticism? Is not the Trinity more important for other doctrines and for one's total theology than you have specified? Have not your objection to "alien immersion" and your defense of close communion become anachronistic among Southern Baptists? A Southern Presbyterian criticized *The Gospel of Redemption* for its lack of "a sense of dialectic" and for its failure to "grapple seriously" with great contemporary issues confronting church and society.[85] Those who would identify Conner as a fundamentalist will fall short of proving their case, and those who would interpret him as a full-blown Synod of Dort Calvinist must face the fact that he clearly taught only two (election and perseverance) of the "five points."[86]

The *classification* of Conner as a theologian is a difficult task. Clearly he was a Southern Baptist theologian. Aspects of his theology agreed with classical Christian orthodoxy and with Protestant teachings, but he deviated at key points from Protestant orthodoxy. Philosophers of religion may classify him under "traditional supernaturalism."[87] Perhaps he can best be identified with conservative or constructive evangelicalism.

Conner's *influence* was almost exclusively limited to Southern Baptists, although some of his books were translated into Spanish, Portuguese, and Chinese. Nearly four decades of students were shaped in his classroom, and his books were widely circulated until the 1960s. In the 1980s his theological work has been found to be relevant to the problems confronting Southern Baptists and a field for intensive research.

Bibliography

Works by Conner

Christian Doctrine. Nashville: Broadman Press, 1937.

The Christ We Need. Grand Rapids, Mich.: Zondervan, 1938.

The Cross in the New Testament. Edited by Jesse J. Northcutt. Nashville: Broadman Press, 1954.

The Epistles of John: Their Meaning and Message. New York: Fleming H. Revell Co., 1929.

The Faith of the New Testament. Nashville: Broadman Press, 1940.

Gospel Doctrines. Nashville: The Sunday School Board of the SBC, 1925.

The Gospel of Redemption. Nashville: Broadman Press, 1945.

Personal Christianity. Grand Rapids, Mich.: Zondervan, 1937.

The Resurrection of Jesus. Nashville: The Sunday School Board of the SBC, 1926.

Revelation and God: An Introduction to Christian Doctrine. Nashville: Broadman Press, 1936.

A System of Christian Doctrine. Nashville: The Sunday School Board of the SBC, 1924.

The Teachings of Mrs. Eddy. Nashville: Broadman Press, 1926.

The Teachings of "Pastor" Russell. Nashville: The Sunday School Board of the SBC, 1926.

What Is a Saint? Nashville: Broadman Press, 1948.

The Work of the Holy Spirit. Nashville: Broadman Press, 1949.

Works about Conner

Allen, Arthur Lynn. "A Comparative Study of the Person of Christ in Selected Baptist Theologians: Augustus H. Strong, William N. Clarke, Edgar Y. Mullins, and Walter T. Conner." Th.D. diss., New Orleans Baptist Theological Seminary, 1979.

Basden, Paul Abbott. "Theologies of Predestination in the Southern Baptist Tradition: A Critical Evaluation." Ph.D. diss., Southwestern Baptist Theological Seminary, 1986.

Draughon, Walter D., III. "A Critical Evaluation of the Diminishing Influence of Calvinism on the Doctrine of Atonement in Representative Southern Baptist Theologians: James Petigru Boyce, Edgar Young Mullins, Walter Thomas Conner, and Dale Moody." Ph.D. diss., Southwestern Baptist Theological Seminary, 1987.

Garrett, James Leo, Jr. "The Bible at Southwestern Seminary during Its Formative Years: A Study of H. E. Dana and W. T. Conner." *Baptist History and Heritage* 21 (Oct. 1986): 29-43.

_____. "Conner, Walter Thomas." *Encyclopedia of Religion in the South*, ed. Samuel S. Hill. Macon, Ga.: Mercer University Press, 1984.

_____. "Conner, Walter Thomas." *Encyclopedia of Southern Baptists*. Vol. 1. Nashville: Broadman Press, 1958.

_____. "The Theology of Walter Thomas Conner." Th.D. diss., Southwestern Baptist Theological Seminary, 1954.

_____. "W. T. Conner: Contemporary Theologian." *Southwestern Journal of Theology* n.s. 25 (Spring 1983): 43-60.

Gray, Elmer Leslie. "The Ultimate Purpose of God." Th.D. diss., Southwestern Baptist Theological Seminary, 1951.

Hunt, William Boyd. "Southern Baptists and Systematic Theology." *Southwestern Journal of Theology* n.s. 1 (April 1959): 43-49.

Hurst, Clyde J. "The Problem of Religious Knowledge in the Theology of Edgar Young Mullins and Walter Thomas Conner." *Review and Expositor* 52 (April 1955): 166-82.

McClendon, James William. *Pacemakers of Christian Thought*. Nashville: Broadman Press, 1962.

Moody, Dwight Allan. "Doctrines of Inspiration in the Southern Baptist Theological Tradition." Ph.D. diss., Southern Baptist Theological Seminary, 1982.

Morgan, Darold H. "Traditional Supernaturalism and the Problem of Evil." Th.D. diss., Southwestern Baptist Theological Seminary, 1953.

Newman, Stewart Albert. *W. T. Conner: Theologian of the Southwest*. Nashville: Broadman Press, 1964.

Northcutt, Jesse James. "Walter Thomas Conner: Theologian of Southwestern." *Southwestern Journal of Theology* n.s. 9 (Fall 1966): 81-89.

Parks, Robert Keith. "A Biblical Evaluation of the Doctrine of Justification in Recent American Baptist Theology: With Special Reference to A. H. Strong, E. Y. Mullins, and W. T. Conner." Th.D. diss., Southwestern Baptist Theological Seminary, 1954.

Youngblood, Clark Richard. "The Question of Apostasy in Southern Baptist Thought since 1900: A Critical Evaluation." Ph.D. diss., The Southern Baptist Theological Seminary, 1979.

Notes

1. Much of this section has been taken with some modification from James Leo Garrett, Jr., "The Theology of Walter Thomas Conner" (Th.D. diss., Southwestern Baptist Theological Seminary, 1954), 1-23.

2. *Who's Who in America* (Chicago: A. N. Marquis Co., 1950), 26:547; Stewart A. Newman, *W. T. Conner: Theologian of the Southwest* (Nashville: Broadman Press, 1964), 19-20.

3. W. T. Conner, "Trip to Arkansas, January 1948," unpublished manuscript now deposited in the library of Southeastern Baptist Theological Seminary, Wake Forest, N.C., 1. Copy in A. Webb Roberts Library, Southwestern Baptist Theological Seminary, Fort Worth, TX.

4. Newman, 19.

5. Ibid.

6. Ibid., W. T. Conner, "Autobiographical Sketch," in *Southwestern Men and Messages,* ed. J. M. Price (Kansas City, Kan.: Central Seminary Press, 1948), 41.

7. Conner, "Trip to Arkansas," 5.

8. Conner, "Autobiographical Sketch," 41.

9. Conner, "Trip to Arkansas," 6; Newman, 19-20.

10. Conner, "Autobiographical Sketch," 41.

11. W. T. Conner, "My Religious Experiences," unpublished manuscript now deposited in the library of Southeastern Baptist Theological Seminary, Wake Forest, N.C., 1. Copy in A. Webb Roberts Library, Southwestern Baptist Theological Seminary, Fort Worth, TX.

12. Ibid., 2.

13. Ibid., 3-4.

14. Conner, "Autobiographical Sketch," 41.

15. L. R. Scarborough, *A Modern School of the Prophets* (Nashville: Broadman Press, 1939), 190; Newman, 29, based on the minutes of Harmony Baptist Church, Caps, Texas.

16. Conner, "Autobiographical Sketch," 41.

17. Conner, "My Religious Experiences," 5-6.

18. Conner, "Autobiographical Sketch," 41.

19. Conner, "My Religious Experiences," 7.

20. Conner, "Autobiographical Sketch," 41.

21. Ibid.

22. Scarborough, 190.

23. Conner, "Autobiographical Sketch," 42.

24. Conner, "My Religious Experiences," 12.

25. Conner, "Autobiographical Sketch," 41-42.

26. Conner, "My Religious Experiences," 10-11.

27. Conner, "Autobiographical Sketch," 42.

28. John S. Ramond, comp., *Among Southern Baptists* (Shreveport, La.: author, 1936), 1:106.

29. Conner, "My Religious Experiences," 14.

30. Conner, "Autobiographical Sketch," 42.

31. Conner, "My Religious Experiences," 14-15.

32. Conner, "Autobiographical Sketch," 42-43.

33. W. T. Conner, "Some Outstanding Men That I Have Known," unpublished

manuscript now deposited in the library of Southeastern Baptist Theological Seminary, Wake Forest, N.C., 10-15. Copy in A. Webb Roberts Library, Southwestern Baptist Theological Seminary, Fort Worth, TX.

34. Conner, "Autobiographical Sketch," 43.

35. *Second Annual Catalogue of the Southwestern Baptist Theological Seminary, 1908-1909,* 18.

36. Hugh R. Peterson, registrar, Southern Baptist Theological Seminary, to James Leo Garrett, Jr., September 28, 1953.

37. Conner, "Autobiographical Sketch," 43.

38. Peterson to Garrett.

39. For the documentation, see Garrett, "The Theology of Walter Thomas Conner," 12-13.

40. Ibid., 13-14.

41. "Connerisms," *The Southwestern News* 10 (November 1952): 6.

42. Frank K. Means, "Advocate of Missions," *The Commission* 15 (September 1952): 242.

43. W. T. Conner, "Theological Education," in *Fourth Baptist World Congress: Record of Proceedings,* ed. W. T. Whitley (London: Kingsgate Press, 1928), 286-91.

44. John W. Cobb to James Leo Garrett, Jr., September 17, 1953.

45. Charles W. Koller to James Leo Garrett, Jr., September 18, 1953.

46. Based on the author's conversations with Mrs. W. T. Conner, 1953.

47. W. T. Conner, "Here and There," unpublished reflections, December 18, 1931—December 31, 1939, deposited in the library of Southeastern Baptist Theological Seminary, Wake Forest, N.C. Copy in A. Webb Roberts Library, Southwestern Baptist Theological Seminary, Fort Worth, TX.

48. Newman, 143.

49. See Garrett, "The Theology of Walter Thomas Conner," 24-132.

50. John S. Tanner, S. P. Brooks, B. H. Carroll, A. H. Newman, and Calvin Goodspeed.

51. A. H. Strong, Walter Rauschenbusch, W. A. Stevens, and H. C. Mabie.

52. E. Y. Mullins and W. O. Carver.

53. George B. Foster, Shailer Mathews, and Gerald B. Smith.

54. Especially Landmarkism.

55. L. R. Scarborough, J. Frank Norris, Charles B. Williams, H. E. Dana, W. W. Barnes, et al.

56. James Denney, P. T. Forsyth, H. R. Mackintosh, A. B. Davidson, James Orr, James Moffatt, et al.

57. A. T. Robertson, John B. Champion, T. P. Stafford, E. C. Dargan, et al.

58. George B. Stevens, B. B. Warfield, J. Gresham Machen, James H. Snowden, Newman Smyth, E. Stanley Jones, E. F. Scott, James M. Campbell, A. C. Knudson, Nels F. S. Ferré, et al.

59. William James, Borden P. Bowne, et al.

60. John Baillie, A. E. Garvie, R. Newton Flew, Sydney Cave, et al.

61. Karl Barth, Emil Brunner, Gustav Aulén, et al.

62. Augustine of Hippo, John Calvin, et al.

63. *The Theology of the New Testament* (New York: Charles Scribner's Sons, 1899).

64. *New Testament Theology* (New York: Macmillan, 1922).

65. For a fuller treatment, see Garrett, "The Theology of Walter Thomas Conner," 294-319.

66. *The Teachings of Mrs. Eddy.* Conner had written articles about Christian Science prior to 1926.

67. *The Teachings of "Pastor" Russell.* Conner's monograph, though written during the presidency of Joseph F. Rutherford, was directed against the teachings of Charles Taze Russell.

68. For a fuller treatment, see Garrett, "The Theology of Walter Thomas Conner," 133-81.

69. Page ix.

70. James William McClendon, *Pacemakers of Christian Thought* (Nashville: Broadman Press, 1962), 54.

71. For documentation and a fuller treatment, see Garrett, "The Theology of Walter Thomas Conner," 182-205.

72. Conner, *Revelation and God,* 212.

73. Arthur Lynn Allen, "A Comparative Study of the Person of Christ in Selected Baptist Theologians: Augustus H. Strong, William N. Clarke, Edgar Y. Mullins, and Walter T. Conner" (Th.D. diss., New Orleans Baptist Theological Seminary, 1979), chapter 6.

74. For documentation and a fuller treatment, see Garrett, "The Theology of Walter Thomas Conner," 205-34.

75. Ibid., 234-41.

76. Paul Abbott Basden, "Theologies of Predestination in the Southern Baptist Tradition: A Critical Evaluation" (Ph.D. diss., Southwestern Baptist Theological Seminary, 1986), 173, 208-29.

77. See Walter D. Draughon III, "A Critical Evaluation of the Diminishing Influence of Calvinism on the Doctrine of Atonement in Representative Southern Baptist Theologians: James Petigru Boyce, Edgar Young Mullins, Walter Thomas Conner, and Dale Moody." (Ph.D. diss., Southwestern Baptist Theological Seminary, 1987), chapter 3.

78. For documentation and a fuller treatment, see Garrett, "The Theology of Walter Thomas Conner," 241-57.

79. Robert Keith Parks, "A Biblical Evaluation of the Doctrine of Justification in Recent American Baptist Theology: With Special Reference to A. H. Strong, E. Y. Mullins, and W. T. Conner" (Th.D. diss., Southwestern Baptist Theological Seminary, 1954), 147-57, 188-89, has contended that Conner went too far in abandoning the values of the forensic view.

80. Clark Richard Youngblood, "The Question of Apostasy in Southern Baptist Thought since 1900: A Critical Evaluation" (Ph.D. diss., The Southern Baptist Theological Seminary, 1979), chapter 2.

81. For documentation and a fuller treatment, see Garrett, "The Theology of Walter Thomas Conner," 257-76.

82. Ibid., 277-93.

83. Conner's deliberate decision not to write for scholars and not to include detailed documentation may be considered by some to be a basic weakness.

84. See Garrett, "The Theology of Walter Thomas Conner," 320-26.

85. Holmes Rolston, Review of W. T. Conner, "The Gospel of Redemption," *Interpretation* 1 (October 1947): 527-28.

86. James Leo Garrett, Jr., "W. T. Conner: Contemporary Theologian," *Southwestern Journal of Theology,* n.s. 25 (Spring 1983): 59-60.

87. H. N. Wieman and B. E. Meland, *American Philosophies of Religion* (Chicago: Willett, Clark, and Co., 1936), 61-76.

22

Herschel Hobbs

Mark Coppenger

Biography

By examining his beginnings, one could not have predicted the impact Herschel Hobbs would have on the Southern Baptist Convention. While his early home life was wholesome and clearly tied to the church, there was no family tradition of theological studies, writing, and strategic involvement in denominational affairs.

Herschel was born on October 24, 1907, in Talladega Springs, Alabama, the son of a farmer. When he was two, he lost his father to malaria, and, as One year later, his mother sold the farm and moved Herschel and his five sisters to Birmingham, where he would stay through college at Howard College (now Samford University). A succession of jobs, and not school, became his preoccupation. In fact, his mother had to push him to finish high school. But it all served to shape him admirably for the later yeoman service he was to render. One colleague put it this way:

Whether plowing the family's forty acres or serving in a restaurant with a railroad clientele, the young Herschel early learned to work. At the same time, his spiritual sensibilities were developing, and, at age twelve, he was converted. By this time, the family had moved from Talladega Springs to Ashland to Montevallo, and it was here that he was baptized at Enon Baptist Church.

One year later, his mother sold the farm and moved Herschel and his five sisters to Birmingham, where he would stay through college at Samford University. A succession of jobs, and not school, became his preoccupation. In fact, his mother had to push him to finish high school. But it all served to shape him admirably for the later yeoman service he was to render. One colleague put it this way:

> Take a farmer who has learned how God can grow a mighty oak from a tiny acorn; mix this with a portion of theatre usher, who found a ready smile and a warm sense of humor could overcome almost any predicament; add a dash of auto parts salesman who learned that sometimes the little things mean a lot; marry him to a quiet and graceful girl; send him to school where he will not only develop a mind which can trap knowledge but which hungers for the same and you will have a partial picture of the man, raised by a widowed mother and five sisters, who has preached his way into hearts surrounding the earth— Herschel Harold Hobbs . . . .[2]

Herschel Hobbs (1907-   )

Photo courtesy of E. C. Dargan Research Library
Sunday School Board of the Southern Baptist Convention

College did not follow high school immediately. The young parts department manager at the Buick dealership was getting on with what seemed a suitable life. At nineteen, he married Frances Jackson and found in her encouragement to grow in his commitment to the local church. Still there was a spiritual struggle. At one point, he surrendered to "special Christian service," but he backed away from this under the influence of rowdy friends who at times would have Herschel drive for them as they drank. The flame was not, however, extinguished, and Herschel reconfirmed his calling during a revival invitation.

As he grew as a Christian, he joined his wife in home prayer, became choir director, was elected deacon, and began tithing. His first opportunity to preach came as a volunteer substitute. His text was that in which Jesus said to Andrew, "Follow me" and the title he chose was "God's Universal Call to Humanity." Quoting R. G. Lee and exhibiting his characteristic humor, Hobbs said of this sermon, "In topic and text I laid a foundation for a skyscraper. Then I went ahead and built a chicken coop right on top of it."[3] Still, it was a beginning.

In preparation for ordination, he approached a seasoned pastor with the question, "Do you have a copy of the Baptist Creed?" Anticipating the argument Hobbs would make many years later in the preamble to the 1963 *The Baptist Faith and Message,* the man responded, "No, son, I've never seen one; the New Testament is our creed."[4]

Now that the course was set, Herschel and Frances wasted no time in moving forward. Pastoring all the while, they raced through Samford in two and a half years, receiving special dispensation from the president to graduate so quickly. From there, it was on to The Southern Baptist Theological Seminary in Louisville, Kentucky, where Herschel took the Ph.D. six years later. In the process, he was named valedictorian of his Th.M. class, even though he had borne the weight of seminary pastorates (American Baptist) in Southern Indiana.

The course of study at Southern was rigorous. Broadus had adapted and condensed an already challenging curriculum from the University of Virginia, and the seminary had assembled such forceful and gifted faculty as John Sampey, W. O. Carver, and the world-renowned Greek scholar, A. T. Robertson. Theologian E. Y. Mullins had died five years earlier, but his influence was still strong.

Of all the professors at Southern, Hersey Davis was most influential in Hobbs' life—

> I think Hersey Davis was one of the greatest New Testament scholars I ever knew. Robertson had an accumulative mind. He knew everything that anybody had ever said or written about anything in the New Testament. Davis had an incisive mind. He was more like Alexander the Great cutting the Gordian knot; he cut right through and went to the heart of the thing.[5]

In part through deference to A. T. Robertson, with whom he disagreed on certain points of interpretation, Davis published little. He planned to follow up after Robertson's death, but by that time he was onto new things and simply never got around to it. Hobbs, however, absorbed his teacher's thought and passed a great deal of it along in his own writing and teaching. He, of course, freely granted this debt to Davis, with whom he did his Ph.D. work.

Hobbs distinguished himself in Louisiana and Alabama pastorates in the years following seminary. But it was not until he came to First Baptist Church, Oklahoma City, that he began to play an unparalleled role in Southern Baptist life. He began his prodigious publishing career there and was selected as the "Baptist Hour" radio preacher, a post he held for eighteen years.

With this base of Bible teaching and writing, he enjoyed the trust of laypersons and pastors alike. From this base, he moved into a number of critical positions of leadership—board memberships (New Orleans Seminary; Oklahoma Baptist University; Foreign Mission Board; Executive Committee; SBC Peace Committee); presidencies (SBC Pastors' Conference; Baptist General Convention of Oklahoma; SBC); chairmanships (Oklahoma Baptist University Board; *The Baptist Faith and Message* committee); a vice-presidency (Baptist World Alliance).

He was a mediator in the Southern Baptist version of the Fundamentalist-Modernist struggle and generated a staggering amount of correspondence in the process. A vast body of Hobbs materials is in the keeping of the SBC Historical Commission in Nashville. In the archives of Oklahoma Baptist University in Shawnee, dozens of scrapbooks, prepared by his wife Frances, document his many travels, guest messages, and honors.

He likened his work to that of a transformer which reduces the force of electricity from the high tension wires so that it might be usable to the sixty-watt bulb. He took the theology of the "giants" and made it accessible to people in the pews. He was unapologetically biblical in his theology, and he charged that there were many philosophers posing as theologians. They wound up their minds as if they were toy airplanes, turned them loose to fly as they pleased and land where they would. Proper theology rather kept "one foot on base—the Bible."[6]

One observer of Southern Baptist theology held that in the first half of this century, E. Y. Mullins spoke for the denomination. In the 1960s and 1970s, it was Herschel Hobbs.[7] A great deal of this can be attributed to Hobbs' exposure as author and radio preacher. Certainly his humor, industry, and gift for plain communication were critical factors. Hobbs himself said that timing was of the essence in that a generation of leaders was passing from the scene just as his crop of seminarians came in. But the substance of his thought was essential to his prominence.

Exposition

The Baptist Faith and Message

Hobbs will likely be best and longest remembered for his work as chairman of the committee which produced the 1963 version of *The Baptist Faith and Message*. This version, as well as its 1925 predecessor, was born of controversy. The earlier statement came in response to the encroachment of evolutionary teachings upon the traditional biblical account of creation. In Hobbs's words, it served to "anchor the moorings" in the face of liberalism and modernism.[8] In the 1960s Hobbs's committee labored in the storm over faithfulness to the biblical account in seminary teaching. Midwestern Seminary professor Ralph Elliott, author of *The Message of Genesis,* was the proximate cause of concern.

The 1962 Convention in San Francisco rocked with indignation over and defense of Broadman's decision to publish Elliott's book, which questioned the historicity of a number of accounts in the early chapters of Genesis. A resolution affirming the accuracy of biblical reports passed. A motion to withdraw the book failed, leaving the decision to the Sunday School Board, which decided not to reprint the book. When Elliot persisted in seeking another publisher, the Midwestern Seminary Board asked him to leave. In the midst of this struggle, the Convention voted to appoint a committee to reconsider and/or reaffirm its 1925 statement. It was a collective and irenic decision to get their bearings.

The 1963 *Annual* of the Southern Baptist Convention presents the 1963 and 1925 versions side by side. There might well have been a third column displaying the text of the 1833 New Hampshire Confession, since significant passages were carried over from that document. The committee had to decide whether to readopt, replace, or revise the 1925 statement. They chose the third option, and the dual column display showed the great similarity of the two confessions. The Convention accepted their work and the 1963 version is today the leading expression of Southern Baptist theology.

In some sections Hobbs introduced concepts and phrases. In others he coordinated the thinking of the committee. Throughout, he was the writer, presenting successive drafts for committee approval.[9] His enthusiasm for the document in whole and in part is obvious in his explanation and defense of the text in a widely used study course book.

Calling the preamble "as important as any other part,"[10] Hobbs spent a great deal of time and energy pressing the point that *The Baptist Faith and Message* is not a creed. The introductory disclaimer speaks of *The Baptist Faith and Message* as a statement of faith, the product of a living faith. It affirms "the soul's competency before God, freedom in religion, and the priesthood of the believer."[11] His concern was that the document not serve as an instrument of coercion or as a litmus test for the true Baptist.

In his homespun way, Hobbs drew the distinction:

> . . . the difference between a creed and our position is the difference between the ways you let a cow graze. One way is to snub her to a post, and as she grazes around the post, the rope gets shorter and shorter, until she finally gets her head right up against the post and can't get away and graze either. That's a creedal faith. A living faith is where you build a fence around a pasture and turn the cow loose in there and say, "Now you eat anywhere in the pasture, but don't get outside the fence." The fence in this case is the Scriptures. We be-

lieve a person is free to read and interpret the Scriptures as he feels led of the Holy Spirit, but it must be within the framework of the entire Bible, not just a verse or an event in isolation.[12]

In his 1908 book, *The Axioms of Religion,* E. Y. Mullins identified soul competency as critical to all religion. By the 1960s, the book had fallen from currency. Hobbs discovered a copy in a secondhand book store and began to mention its notions. Encouragement came from the Sunday School Board to represent Mullins's ideas to the Convention, and in 1978 Hobbs came out with a revised edition of Mullins's work.

While Hobbs made it clear that Baptists have no business using *The Baptist Faith and Message* or similar documents as a test for church membership, he did defend the enterprise of distilling denominational beliefs for "general instruction and guidance" concerning who Baptists are. And he was adamant in his conviction that one cannot believe just anything and be a Baptist. That being said, Hobbs's strong commitment to soul competency should be underscored again:

> Baptists oftentimes forget that our basic Baptist belief is not the infallibility of the Scriptures as some call it. It is not even the deity of Jesus Christ, though I believe in the inerrancy of the Scriptures and believe in the deity of Jesus Christ without question. The basic belief of Baptists is the competency of the soul in religion. When we forget that, then we get into all kinds of trouble. When I mention that nowadays, young preachers look at me like a calf looking at a new gate.[13]

Moving from the preamble to the section on the Scriptures, we find an addition to the 1925 statement—"The criterion by which the Bible is to be interpreted is Jesus Christ." At the time, there was concern over Elliott's construal of Melchizedek as a priest of Baal. This seemed to many to stain Jesus in that He was likened to that ancient priest. Elliott defended himself on grounds that the biblical wording was not "like Melchizedek" but "after the order of Melchizedek."

This sliced things a bit thin, so the committee persisted in erecting a shield against using any part of Scripture to diminish the stature of Christ. As Hobbs explained it, "you have to interpret Jesus Christ not in the terms of Melchizedek, but Melchizedek in terms of Jesus Christ."[14]

The same principle works against those who would magnify the Holy Spirit above Jesus. If, for instance, one implies that "Jesus doesn't do it all," that "you need the second blessing from the Holy Spirit," then you've violated the standard of Christ as the key to all understanding of Scripture.[15] In short, all readings of the Bible must do justice to Jesus.

The 1925 *The Baptist Faith and Message* presented a short statement on God, the second sentence of which delineated the Trinity. The 1963 *The Baptist Faith and Message* gave a separate paragraph to each Person of the Trinity. Among the new statements on God, the Son, Hobbs took special note of two in his recollections. The first concerned the phrase "Yet without sin" and the second, the word "Mediator."

The drafts were circulated throughout the seminaries and Sunday School Board for comment. Wayne Ward of Southern Seminary took exception to the statement that Jesus identified Himself completely with mankind. This, he argued, would make Christ a sinner, in that all men were. All agreed to the qualifying clause, "yet without sin."[16]

In calling Christ the Mediator, Hobbs was intent that the committee avoid the picture "of God on one side and man on the other . . . mad at one another, and Jesus in the middle trying to pull them together."[17] Rather, as God-man, Jesus perfectly represents each to the other.[18] Reconciliation occurs within the nature of Christ, not as a result of the third-party machinations of Christ.

The 1963 statement on salvation was more concise than the 1925 version. Three aspects were given—regeneration, sanctification, and glorification. After getting committee approval for his oral sketch, Hobbs wrote this section on his own. Its most striking change concerned its treatment of sanctification. The earlier *The Baptist Faith and Message* called it a process. Hobbs, as he explains in the study course book on *The Baptist Faith and Message,* saw it as instantaneous, upon conversion. It is at that point that "one is set apart to God's service."[19] One develops then within the context or state of sanctification, not unto a state of sanctification.

The only section to face opposition on the floor of the Convention in Kansas City was the one on the church. The committee had added a sentence which recognized the sense in which the church "includes all of the redeemed of all the ages." "Landmark" Baptists insisted that "church" can only refer to the local church. Hobbs asked rhetorically which local church Jesus was naming when He said of Peter, "Upon this rock I will build my church." A messenger yelled "the First Baptist Church of Jerusalem," to which Hobbs replied, "He was at least seventy-five miles from where he built that church when he said it."[20] He also used a quote supplied him by Albert McClellan, from Landmarker J. M. Pendleton to strengthen his case. In that quote, Pendleton referred to the "redeemed in aggregate." The Landmark opposition did not prevail, and the entire *The Baptist Faith and Message* passed with ease.

Hobbs's thoroughgoing biblicism compelled him to sort carefully through the scriptural basis for each clause of *The Baptist Faith and Message.* He found the match in the 1925 version to be less than perfect and was determined that those given in 1963 would clearly support the theological assertions. He and committee secretary Dick Hall took on the task of checking them all, a job Hobbs called "the most tedious I ever had" and "nerve-wracking."[21] But, in the end, he was satisfied.

Mediation

Again and again, Hobbs spoke of a sort of wisdom in the middle. Along with this conviction came a populism, a belief that the great mass of folks will find and occupy this middle. And as he did theology, Hobbs played the pastor's role in gathering the flock on this lush temperate zone, away from the treacherous fringe regions.

Here are typical expressions of these opinions:

The greater body of Southern Baptists have always been a conservative people not given to extreme positions in theology either on one side or the other. They have been, so to speak, a middle-of-the-road people. At given times, the theological road has turned either to the right or to the left. But Southern Baptists have remained in the middle of the road. No Southern Baptist is justified in disturbing the fellowship by seeing how near the edge of the pavement on either side he can come and still remain on the road. A common road sign is applicable here, "Danger! Soft Shoulders!" Nor should Southern Baptists seek to widen the middle beyond reasonable proportions. If they get out of their lane, they may have a head-on collision with strange theological traffic headed in the other direction.[22]

Someone is going to shape and guide this new theology. And Southern Baptists are best fitted to do so. They are a "grass roots" people. Their success is due largely to the response given by the "grass roots" to the Gospel as Southern Baptists preach it. If Southern Baptists forsake their conservatively middle-of-the-road interpretation of the gospel, the "grass roots" will seek elsewhere for spiritual food and guidance.[23]

We have never been extremists in anything . . . Southern Baptists are about five percent to the right and five percent to the left of center . . . but ninety percent of them are right down the middle of the road where Southern Baptists have always been . . . I don't know whether you ever fed hogs or not. But you go out with a basketful of shucked corn and call up the hogs. You throw it down right together, and there is enough there for all hogs to eat, and more. Invariably, one old hog, usually an old sow, will grab up an ear of corn and run way off down to the corner of the hog lot and eat it, as if every other hog was trying to get its ear of corn, when there is more corn up there than they can all eat. So you have people that will take a doctrine, one little facet, and run off with it and go to an extreme one way or the other. But the masses of Southern Baptists have always been a middle-of-the-road people.[24]

Despite his love for the middle, he was not beyond putting in a good word for the extremes.

. . . our doctrine is like a muscle. If a muscle loses its tension, it loses its usefulness; and if our doctrines lose their tension, they lose their usefulness . . . . This theological tension is good for us, and I think these rights and lefts are good for us. They keep us on our toes.[25]

And in this spirit of appreciation for the full spectrum, he repeatedly spoke positively of Baptist "unity-in-diversity."

Baptists then should celebrate both their differences and the great conservative center which has held throughout the years. The common person, the simple Bible believer, will gravitate toward sweet reasonableness in faith and practice.

Armed with this conviction, Hobbs joined in countless committee deliberations. From the tensions of the Midwestern dealings with Elliott to the Peace Committee sessions of the 1980s, he optimistically and irenically sorted through the issues with the various disputants.

Biblical Inerrancy

Within the context of the Southern Baptist theological conflicts, Hobbs consistently distanced himself from the label, "fundamentalist." Choosing instead to call himself a conservative, albeit a "progressive conservative,"[26] he positioned himself as a center-of-the-road man. But he embraced the expression "inerrancy," which carried a good deal of the same emotional baggage as "fundamentalism." "I do believe in the inerrancy of the original manuscripts because of my faith in God who does not commit errors."[27]

In that inerrancy implies the accuracy of the historical narratives, some would prefer the word *infallible*. They maintain that whether or not this or that report is entirely accurate, the Bible succeeds in telling men how to find God to be saved. After all, the account goes, the Bible was never meant to be a book of science or history, so haggling over the number of Israelites in Sinai or the ability of a fish to house Jonah is petty.

"Infallible," however, was not adequate for Hobbs. In opposing its substitution in the 1963 *the Baptist Faith and Message,* he said,

> Infallible has two meanings; one is "without error," the other that "it fulfills its intended function." A dull knife can be an infallible knife if you use it to cut butter. You will weaken the statement by putting in that word. I know it's your pet word, and it's the pet word of a lot of people, but it isn't as strong as the words "without any mixture of error."[28]

Granting that the Bible was indeed intended to bring man to saving faith, he still affirmed that it was trustworthy where it spoke.

> The Bible is not a book of science. Yet it contains no proved scientific error. When both science and the Bible are understood, they do not conflict but rather compliment each other. The Bible is trustworthy history. There was a time when cynics pointed out supposed historical errors in the Bible. But the science of archaeology has changed the picture. Wherever it has thrown light on such problems, it has always substantiated the Bible.[29]

He made a point of repudiating the neoorthodox view of Scripture. "The Scriptures . . . do not *contain* the word of God. They are the word of God."[30] And he defended the inerrantist's citation of the original manuscripts: "We've never seen Jesus Christ either, but we believe in him."[31] In short, he made an unequivocal commitment to inerrancy in a time when there was serious pressure to hedge your words in the interest of peace.

There was, however, another side to Hobbs's treatment of Scripture that should be noted. He was very reluctant to call another's handling of Scripture "out of bounds." He defended *The Broadman Bible Commentary,* calling it a "very good work"[32] and found no serious theological problem with Ralph Elliott. After questioning him privately on his views on Genesis, Hobbs concluded "Dr. Elliott, you are not a heretic; you are a poor writer."[33] In Hobbs's view, it was intransigence rather than interpretive error that made Elliott's further employment impossible.

How is it then that Hobbs, an inerrantist, was so ready to accommodate the writings of those who would reject that label and whose treatment of the biblical text often fell short of the sort of thing inerrantists found acceptable? There were several reasons. First, Hobbs had great respect for scholarship. While he always kept his "down-home" touch, his lessons were clearly appreciative of archaeology and the biblical languages. Hobbs was well-read and devoted to the seminaries. And it was his interest to protect professors and studious pastors from the censorious raids of the unreflective.

He affirmed progressive revelation: "This refers not to God's ability to reveal, but to man's ability to receive the revelation. Thus we have a more exalted picture of God in John than in Genesis."[34] And he insisted upon broad reliance upon the grammatic-historical method. If, for instance, there seem to be difficulties in Chronicles, we may simply note that the text cites the chronicles of the kings as sources. And we know that they were braggers.[35] So the Bible itself gives us clues as to how literally we should take things.

While he ultimately championed Mosaic authorship of the Pentateuch, he did give respectful treatment to the documentary hypothesis.[36] He recognized a "D" document and suggested that Moses might well have worked from written sources. This, of course, was commonplace to many scholars, but it represented something of a stand for one calling himself an inerrantist. He chose to not only represent the laity to themselves and to the scholars, but also to represent the scholars to the laity.

His conviction that "theological thought is never static"[37] spurred him to grant theologians space to maneuver. And he was not at all alarmed that James P. Boyce would have found E. Y. Mullins a liberal.

> The unfolding of an increased knowledge of the universe demanded that Doctor Mullins seek to interpret the *Science of God* in the light of that greater unveiling of truth. Yet Doctor Mullins did not destroy the teachings of Doctor Boyce. He built upon their solid foundation a greater structure out of the truth held by both.[38]

Hobbs, of course, maintained the necessity of fixed theological points of reference and of faithfulness to the Bible, but his basic commitment to theological growing room was clear.

Soul competency figured prominently here: "If a man errs from the truth, God should judge him, not other finite and erring fellow-Christians. Each should declare the truth as he feels led to see it. But he should leave God to deal with himself and others as he sees fit."[39] It is perfectly in order to state your own convictions, thereby implying that others have missed the mark in their disagreement with you. It is quite another thing to suggest that the other has so thoroughly missed the mark that he is pernicious or apostate in his thinking.

Denominationalism provided another reason for tolerance. Hobbs's devotion to the structure and traditions of the Southern Baptist Convention was singular, and he opposed any movement which would jeopardize the working fellowship.

> A man expressed fear about passing a cemetery at night. Asked if he feared that the dead people would hurt him, he replied, "No, but I'm afraid they'll make me hurt myself." That is the greatest danger facing Southern Baptists. Not that outside forces shall hurt them. But that they may cause them to hurt themselves.[40]

You find in this quote both the conviction that the inerrancy dispute is dangerous and that it is essentially the product of thinking outside the warm cooperation of the Southern Baptist way.

Fear for the denomination's well-being was not the only reason for tolerance. Enthusiasm for its vitality also led him to eschew disciplinary action:

> We heard protests. Not many at first, but we heard some protests. But we didn't listen. I said *we* didn't listen. I'm a party to it just like anybody else who was more or less in the thick of things. Then we heard more, but we still didn't listen. After all, everything was going fine. The seminary enrollment was up. Cooperative Program was up. Evangelism up. New churches and all. You know the old saying that if it's working, don't fix it.[41]

This has a certain Gamaliel perspective—Leave it alone and truth will win. "Rabbits run in circles, but they'll come back to the Bible."[42] You only injure yourself when you let yourself get exercised over these matters. Speak the truth of inerrancy in love, and the grass roots folks will sort things out.

He closed his essay, "What Baptists Believe About the Scriptures" with a poem, whose last stanza read:

> And so, I thought, the anvil of God's word.
> For ages skeptic blows have beat upon:
> Yet, though the noise of falling blows was heard
> The anvil is unharmed—the hammers, gone![43]

Concerning Calvinism

Hobbs strengthened the hold of only one of the five traditional points of Calvinism. In his book on Hebrews, the "fall away" passage (6:4-6) is construed as touching only effectiveness and not salvation.[44] By his account, God's redemptive purpose runs through history; we are not going to stop it. But, on the model of the Exodus epic, some will lose their opportunity to join in it. They will, so to speak, die in the wilderness. They will, though saved, miss out on his world mission of evangelism. So each Christian must watch lest he squander his chances for strategic usefulness at his own Kadesh-barnea. Thus interpreted, the text cannot serve the Arminian in his struggle against the doctrine of the perseverance of the saints.

The doctrine of unconditional election does not fare so well at Hobbs's hand. Neither does its corollary, the doctrine of irresistible grace. To make his point, he advances the words of E. Y. Mullins, quoting from *The Christian Religion in Its Doctrinal Expression:*

> Election is not to be thought of as a bare choice of so many human units by
> God's action independently of man's free choice and the human means em-

ployed . . . To ignore man's free will is to see God arbitrarily electing some to salvation to the neglect of all others.[45]

If election is not a matter of God's choosing and winning, then what is it? Working from the Greek for "predestinated," Hobbs ventures,

It is like building a fence around a piece of land. In this case the fence is Christ . . . So God elected that all who are "in Christ" will be saved. All outside of Christ will be lost . . . God in his sovereignty set the condition. Man in his free will determines the result.[46]

As for "limited atonement," Hobbs maintained that "God's purpose in election is to save not a few but as many as possible,[47] suggesting that the only limitation comes at the point of man's choice and not at the point of God's decision. And finally, on the question of man's depravity, we find a softening in the language of the 1963 *The Baptist Faith and Message.* The 1925 statement said "whereby his posterity inherit a nature corrupt and in bondage to sin;" Hobbs' 1963 version read "whereby his posterity inherit a nature and an environment inclined toward sin."[48]

As Thomas Nettles has demonstrated in *By His Grace and for His Glory,* Southern Baptists have moved substantially from their early Calvinistic commitments. Whether Hobbs played a significant role in this or simply reflected Baptists back to themselves is hard to say. That his theology on these matters was different in tone from that of his seminary's founders (as expressed in Southern's *Abstract of Principles*) is undeniable.

Eschatology

Because of Hobbs's stature as an inerrantist and as a strong and palpable expositor, he was able to lend credibility here and there to less popular causes. Such was the case with amillennialism. He was not alone in his defense of this doctrine. Ray Summers's *Worthy Is the Lamb* and E. A. McDowell's *The Meaning of the Book of Revelation* carried a great deal of the weight. But among conservatives, premillennialism was the preferred stance in that generation, and those of the dispensationalist school at times suggested that amillennialists played fast and loose with Scripture.

In *The Cosmic Drama,* Hobbs argued that the key to interpreting Revelation lay in John's statement, "He signified it to me."[49] The word *signified* may be construed as sign-i-fied, underscoring the symbolic nature of the book. And once you commit to a symbolic reading, you have no business "changing horses." It is unfair to jump from symbolic to literal reading simply to suit your program.

By his account, amillennialism was something of a closet affair for many. When he came out with his arguments in print, its acceptability was enhanced and a number of people began to show their own amillennial colors.

Evaluation

Since he pastored a church as he wrote, communicated effectively with laypeople, and filled his writing with application, Hobbs was called a pastoral theologian, but there is another, larger, sense in which his theology has a pastoral flavor. Hobbs was concerned to keep the flock intact, the flock in this case being the Southern Baptist Convention.

Hobbs's conciliatory style, his great reluctance to cast folks out and his clear preference for common sense rather than the awkward extreme are hallmarks of his work. He loved to sand rough edges and solicit broad and tolerant consensus. Of course, this showed itself most notably in his committee work. But you find clear signs of this spirit in his biblical theology as well.

Consider his response to Calvinism and Arminianism. Both schools of thought have aspects that are harsh and disturbing to today's ear. The Calvinist speaks of God's choosing only some to be saved, consigning the rest to hell. The Arminian raises the specter of a saved man's losing his grip and sliding into hell. Hobbs' response was to generalize election and champion security of the believer. This solution is so much more amiable than either approach taken purely on its own.

Devotion to the "middle of the road" was another feature of Hobbs' amiable approach to theology. One works with the conviction that the great mass of saints is essentially healthy in its thinking and that one's main task is to keep the wanderers on either side from injuring themselves and spooking the flock.

One is reminded of Aristotle's account of the virtues. Each one lies between two vices of excess. For instance, the virtue courage lies between the faults of foolhardiness and cowardice. Moderation then is our watchword. Zealotry is to be shunned.

The biblical support for this conviction is not without its problems. For while there are words of appreciation for the body of Christians in the Epistles, there are also words of praise for awkwardness and fanaticism in the world's eyes and words of exasperation at the waywardness of the church. Biblical enthusiasm for the performance and judgment of the typical church member is, at best, mixed.

In *Axioms of Religion,* it is clear the expression "soul competency" was meant to distance Baptists from the sacramental and hierarchical convictions of Roman Catholicism. It was not intended to keep Baptists from policing themselves doctrinally. Hobbs made it clear that soul competency did not mean license, but Hobbs's irenic spirit restrained him from confronting those who wished to interpret the phrase in that manner.

Observers will sooner forget his treatment of Hebrews 6, his arguments concerning soul competency, and his amillennialism than they will his great love for the Bible. In a sense the focus of his life on Scripture was his most eloquent theological argument.

The greatest theological contribution Hobbs made lay not in the particulars of his exposition, but in his passion for understanding and presenting the biblical text. He modeled a set of priorities, the first of which was devotion to the teaching of Scripture. Through his Bible teaching on radio, in Sunday School periodicals, and by means of books, he made it clear that the Bible merits the most careful and extensive attention and devotion we can give. It is no mere jumping-off point for self-gratifying speculation, but rather is a chief instrument of the lordship of Christ.

Bibliography

Works by Hobbs

The Axioms of Religion. With E. Y. Mullins. Nashville: Broadman, 1978.

The Baptist Faith and Message. Nashville: Convention, 1971.

Christ in You: An Exposition of the Epistle to the Colossians. Grand Rapids, Mich.: Baker, 1961.

The Corinthian Epistles. Grand Rapids, Mich.: Baker, 1960.

The Cosmic Drama: Studies in Revelation. Waco: Word, 1971, 1987.

The Epistle to the Corinthians: A Study Manual. Grand Rapids, Mich.: Baker, 1960.

The Epistles of John. Nashville: Thomas Nelson, 1983.

An Exposition of the Four Gospels. Grand Rapids, Mich.: Baker, 1965.

An Exposition of the Gospel of John. Grand Rapids, Mich.: Baker, 1968.

An Exposition of the Gospel of Luke. Grand Rapids, Mich.: Baker, 1966.

An Exposition of the Gospel of Mark. Grand Rapids, Mich.: Baker, 1970.

An Exposition of the Gospel of Matthew. Grand Rapids, Mich.: Baker, 1965.

Fundamentals of Our Faith. Nashville: Broadman Press, 1960.

Galatians: A Verse by Verse Study. Waco: Word, 1978.

The Gospel of John: A Study Guide. Grand Rapids, Mich.: Zondervan, 1965.

The Gospel of John: Invitation to Life. Nashville: Broadman Press, 1988.

The Gospel of Mark: A Study Manual. Grand Rapids, Mich.: Baker, 1971.

The Gospel of Matthew. Grand Rapids, Mich.: Baker, 1961, 1979.

Hebrews: Challenge to Bold Discipleship. Nashville: Broadman Press, 1981.

The Holy Spirit: Believer's Guide. Nashville: Broadman Press, 1967.

How to Follow Jesus: The Challenge of Hebrews for Christian Life and Witness Today. Nashville: Broadman Press, 1971, 1981.

John: A Bible Study Commentary. Grand Rapids, Mich.: Zondervan, 1983.

A Layman's Handbook of Christian Doctrine. Nashville: Broadman Press, 1974.

The Life and Times of Jesus: A Contemporary Approach. Grand Rapids, Mich.: Zondervan, 1966.

Messages on the Resurrection. Grand Rapids, Mich.: Baker, 1959.

New Testament Evangelism. Nashville: Convention Press, 1961.

The Origin of All Things: Studies in Genesis. Waco: Word, 1975.

Revelation: Three Viewpoints. With George R. Beasley-Murray, Ray Robbins, and David C. George. Nashville: Broadman Press, 1977.

Romans: A Verse by Verse Study. Waco: Word, 1977.

Studies in Hebrews. Nashville: Convention Press, 1955.

Studying Adult Life and Work Lessons. Nashville: The Sunday School Board of the Southern Baptist Convention, 1968-

What Baptists Believe. Nashville: Broadman Press, 1964.

You Are Chosen: The Priesthood of All Believers. San Francisco: Harper and Row, 1990.

Works about Hobbs

Baker, James Donald. "An Examination of the Baptist Hour Preaching of Herschel H. Hobbs from 1958-1968." Th.D. diss., New Orleans Baptist Theological Seminary, 1972.

Ingleheart, Glenn Alle. "A Study of Radio Preaching as Represented by Four Speakers on the Baptist Hour, 1951-1960." Th.D. diss., The Southern Baptist Theological Seminary, 1964.

Notes

1. Herschel Hobbs, interview by Ronald Tonks, Hobbs Collection, Southern Baptist Historical Commission Archives, 1-8.
2. Stanton Nash, "Operation Baptist Biography Data Form for Living Persons," Hobbs Collection, Southern Baptist Historical Commission Archives, 4.
3. Tonks interview, 16.
4. Ibid., 18.
5. Ibid., 28.
6. Herschel Hobbs, personal interview, December 1987.
7. Walter Shurden, "The Pastor as Denominational Theologian," *Baptist History & Heritage* (July 1980): 21.
8. Herschel Hobbs, "Talk Back with Hobbs," Baptist Telecommunication Network teleconference (BTN), 1988.
9. Tonks interview, 272.
10. BTN teleconference.
11. Herschel Hobbs, *The Baptist Faith and Message* (Nashville: The Sunday School Board of the SBC, 1963), preamble.
12. Tonks interview, 286.
13. Ibid., 129.
14. Ibid., 286.
15. Personal interview.
16. Tonks interview, 274.
17. Ibid., 273.
18. Ibid.
19. Herschel Hobbs, *The Baptist Faith and Message* (Nashville: Convention Press, 1971), 61.
20. Tonks interview, 279.
21. Ibid., 275.
22. Herschel Hobbs, "President's Address," in *Southern Baptist Convention Annual* (Nashville: Convention Press, 1962), 86.

23. Ibid., 87.

24. Tonks interview, 270.

25. Personal interview, 278.

26. Hobbs, "Southern Baptist Convention: The Inerrancy Controversy," The Herschel H. and Francis J. Hobbs Lecture on the Baptist Faith and Heritage (Oklahoma Baptist University, October 14, 1987), 6.

27. BTN teleconference.

28. Tonks interview, 307.

29. Herschel Hobbs, "Questions About the Bible," Hobbs Collection, Southern Baptist Historical Commission Archives, 2.

30. Herschel Hobbs, "What Baptists Believe About the Scriptures," Hobbs Collection, Southern Baptist Historical Commission Archives, 3.

31. BTN teleconference.

32. Tonks interview, 309.

33. Ibid., 284.

34. Hobbs, "Scriptures," 3.

35. Personal interview.

36. Herschel Hobbs, "The Graf-Wellhausen Theory," Hobbs Collection, Southern Baptist Historical Commission Archives, 13-14.

37. Herschel Hobbs, "Are Southern Baptists Facing a Theological Revolution?" Hobbs Collection, Southern Baptist Historical Commission Archives, 2.

38. Ibid., 5-6.

39. Herschel Hobbs, "Southern Baptists' Greatest Danger," Hobbs Collection, Southern Baptist Historical Commission Archives, 1.

40. Ibid.

41. Personal interview.

42. BTN teleconference.

43. Hobbs, "Scriptures," 7.

44. Herschel Hobbs, *How to Follow Jesus: The Challenge of Hebrews for Christian Life and Witness Today* (Nashville: Broadman Press, 1971), 60-61.

45. Herschel Hobbs and E. Y. Mullins, *The Axioms of Religion* (Nashville: Broadman Press, 1978), 70.

46. Ibid., 72.

47. Ibid., 71.

48. Hobbs, *The Baptist Faith and Message*.

49. Herschel Hobbs, *The Cosmic Drama: Studies in Revelation* (Waco: Word, 1971), 24.

23

W. A. Criswell
L. Russell Bush III

Some say there have been two W. A. Criswells: (1) the platform personality, the convention speaker, the fiery controversialist; (2) the Spirit-filled pastor/theologian of his famous Dallas pulpit. I think such characterizations are simplistic, but perception is important. Unfortunately, many know Criswell only through his "conference preaching" or through his media representation. His critics see him as bombastic, loud, highly emotional, uncompromising, often unnecessarily controversial, and seemingly egotistical and brash. Many pastors and laypeople, however, enjoy his brand of enthusiastic preaching. Criswell, himself, always smiles about his tongue-in-cheek reputation as a "Holy-roller with a Ph.D.," whose sermons could be heard anywhere within five miles by anyone with an open window. In this chapter, I wish to write about the Criswell of more than six decades of ministry to people, the Criswell of integrity and theological insight, the Criswell of the pastor's study and of the weekly pulpit, W. A. Criswell, the pastor/theologian.

Biography[1]

Six days before Christmas, 1909, Anna Currie Criswell, a resident of Eldorado, Oklahoma, presented her husband, Wallie Amos, with a newborn son. In keeping with a tradition not uncommon in rural America, they named the boy by simply giving him the initials of his father.[2] At the age of four (1914), W. A. moved with his family to a small railroad servicing town known as Texline (located in the Texas panhandle on the border with New Mexico), where his father opened a barber shop.

Young Criswell loved the church. His family often invited guest preachers in for a meal after they held services at the little, white "cracker-box" church in Texline. Criswell fondly recalls sitting around the kitchen table listening to his mother talk about the Bible with these preachers. When he was nine years old, Criswell was attending a morning (10:00 a.m.) weekday service at the Texline church (1919).[3] The revival preacher was Brother John Hicks (who apparently was also staying in the Criswell's home at the time), and the message touched the young boy's soul. He stood during the invitation hymn and turned to look at his mother who had been sitting just behind him. Tears were streaming down her face as she asked him if "today" he would give his heart and life to the Savior. He never tells the story without tears

W. A. Criswell (1909-   )

welling up in his eyes, even many years later. "Yes, Mother! Today, I will accept the Lord Jesus as my Savior!"[4]

Criswell's mother did not push him into the ministry, however. She wanted him to become a physician. She feared the poverty and the fishbowl life of the minister. He was, nevertheless, in his own mind committed to a pulpit ministry at least since the age of twelve.[5]

Anna Criswell moved to Amarillo (leaving her husband behind temporarily) so that W. A. could attend high school there (and hopefully get a better education). She later did the same by moving to Waco to help him get started at Baylor University. He never disappointed her with his grades.

In 1928 the San Jacinto Baptist Church of Amarillo, recognizing the call of God in the young man's life, formed an ordaining council to examine him and to bring him before the congregation to be ordained by the church as a gospel minister at the age of seventeen. While attending Baylor he served as pastor for two small churches in the communities of Devil's Bend and Pultight.

In 1931 Criswell arrived in Louisville, Kentucky, to attend The Southern Baptist Theological Seminary. There, W. Hershey Davis deeply impressed the young preacher and instilled in him a love for the Greek New Testament.

He continued preaching throughout seminary days. While serving a church in Mount Washington, Kentucky, on a part-time basis, he met the pretty pianist, Betty Harris, whom he later married (1935).[6]

Finishing his Master of Theology degree (1934), he applied and was accepted into the Ph.D. program at Southern, eventually writing a dissertation on "The John the Baptist Movement in Its Relation to the Christian Movement" (unpublished, 1937).

Though the prestigious First Baptist Church of Birmingham, Alabama, wanted Criswell to come to be their pastor, the First Baptist Church of Chickasha, Oklahoma, had asked him first. Believing strongly in the sovereignty of God in such matters, Criswell accepted the smaller church in the lesser-known area (1937). Later he moved to the First Baptist Church of Muskogee, Oklahoma, where some of his happiest years (1941-44) were spent.

George W. Truett, the pastor of the First Baptist Church of Dallas, Texas, since 1897 and one of Southern Baptist's greatest statesmen, died on July 7, 1944, after an extended illness. Soon thereafter, Criswell had a dream in which he was attending the funeral, sitting in the old balcony of the Dallas Church, and Truett came over to sit beside him. The great pastor spoke to him and said, "Son, you must go down and preach to my people." Though some have expressed skepticism about this story, there is no doubt but that Criswell himself believes it.[7] Nor is there any doubt that he did soon move from Muskogee to Dallas at the invitation of the First Baptist Church.

Criswell's sixty-year ministry is by any standard astonishing. Not only was there consistently rapid growth (from about 7800 in 1944 to a total church membership of over 25,000 in the mid-1980s), but there were also hundreds of baptisms each year, dozens of mission churches started in many needy areas, social ministries for the poor, the establishment of a complete educational system (from elementary grades through college), radio and television ministries, growth from $250,000 in gifts in 1944 to more than a 10 million dollar annual church budget in the 1980s, and a rather extensive ministry through books and other Christian literature.

Exposition

The Pastor

W. A. Criswell is so meticulous about the details of the pastorate,[8] that it would have been hard for him not to excel. Criswell has no hobbies except watching the stock market. His priority, however, is always the church. He loves the work of the church, and he gives himself almost completely to it. He is a master at finding good men and women for his staff and for various leadership positions, and then letting them do their best for the church.

He spends his mornings in study and sermon preparation. Eventually the Dallas church built a library annex onto his Swiss Avenue home so that he could more easily get to his study early in the morning. Since his normal pattern was to preach verse by verse or section by section through a biblical book, he could leave his books open on his desk and study from the same commentary volumes over a period of several months. He also has an extensive library of sermon books, and he had all of those sermons indexed by text in the margin of an old hardback edition of the 1901 *American Standard Version* of the Bible.[9] He never gave up the *King James Bible* for pulpit use, but he loves to study from the original language texts and from the best of the modern translations of Scripture.

In the afternoons the pastoral duties of hospital visitation, counseling, and church administration would fill his time. For many years he also scheduled an exercise session at the YMCA (which at that time was located just across the street from the church). The evenings were given to the social ministries and committee meetings of the church. Criswell never really had or took much family time, nor did he ever take a day off, nor did he take a "for pleasure only" vacation. Even on holidays he was filling a pulpit somewhere, preaching.

Criswell is a convinced Baptist. His theology of baptism grew partly from his seminary work. One of his conclusions about John the Baptist was that John's uniqueness was not so much that he was immersing people but that he (John) was immersing them. In other words, the people were not dipping themselves (as was common in Qumran, for example), but they were being dipped by someone else (symbolizing that salvation could not be by self-effort or human works, but must be an act of God's grace). Moreover, the act of immersion itself was a clear depiction of the death and resurrection of the Savior. Thus baptism's form is crucial to its meaning.

Perhaps his greatest contribution to the practice of baptism is the manner in which this church ordinance is carried out under his direction. "Never do you see someone take the body of their loved one to the open grave and throw them down into the pit. That is unthinkable," he would say. "No! You lower your loved one gently and reverently into that grave. We respect the dead out of love for their memory and in the hope of the blessed resurrection. Thus in baptism, the ceremony is to be done with great dignity. You do not splash the water unnecessarily, nor do you rapidly plunge the candidate under! Rather, you lower the body gently and you seek to make the ceremony as worshipful as possible."[10] Though using similar baptismal formulas, Criswell often would say different things for each candidate as he publicly and personally baptized them one by one. And at the end of every baptismal service, Criswell would look pleadingly out into the gathered congregation and beyond to the lost world, and with arms open wide he would say, "And yet there is room for more."

The Theologian

"Our preaching needs depth, force, and doctrinal content, and the only way to get it is by long hours of study and prayer."[11]

Generally speaking Criswell's preaching is deep, forceful, and full of doctrine, and it arises out of long hours of study and prayer. As described, every morning was his sermon preparation time, every afternoon and evening his church activities. These mornings were filled with reading, with original language exegetical work, commentary work, and homiletical research.

Most of his books are edited transcriptions of his sermons. Altogether Criswell has over fifty titles in circulation.[12] The content of these volumes enables us to speak rather precisely about his theological ideas. The quantity of these published volumes allows us to speak rather confidently about his influence throughout Baptist and evangelical circles.

Criswell's theology is an exegetical theology. He typically published expository sermons on biblical books. However, *Did Man Just Happen?*[13] treats the subject of evolution quite effectively and shows not only a broad knowledge of science but demonstrates his theological grasp of biblical themes. *The Holy Spirit in Today's World*[14] is an explicitly theologically structured book (though it, too, is a sermon series). He prepared and delivered a history of the doctrine, an exposition of the biblical materials, and a practical theological synthesis for "today's world." Even those who disagree on some points of interpretation (such as his view that the silence of women in the church was a prohibition primarily against their public speaking in unknown tongues, or his limiting of significant kinds of spiritual gifts to the apostolic era—identifying the "perfection" of 1 Corinthians 13:10 with the finished canon of Scripture) may still find much of value in the book.

Criswell is dispensational, but he is not a dispensationalist. The seven-dispensation structure of biblical history seems perfectly logical to Criswell, and he believes it to be true. But to argue that salvation was ever offered to a sinner on the basis of human works or human merit is never a part of his presentations. Salvation is always and forever by grace through faith. Nevertheless, Criswell believes that it is essential to recognize the dispensation of the law as an entity unto itself, else we Christians would have to observe the

Sabbath.[15] Moreover, the prophets made promises to Israel and Judah, and God intends to fulfill those promises even in our day. Criswell sees modern-day Israel as a real fulfillment of prophecy (though, just as ancient Israel sometimes disobeyed God, modern Israel is not automatically right in all policies or actions just because God is working to bring them into the land so that He eventually can convert them and bless them as He promised through the prophets that He would).

Criswell strictly separates Israel and the church based on the newness of the church in Ephesians 3:2-13,[16] but he does not separate them eternally (as the real dispensationalists do). Criswell expects the church to be on the earth during the millennium as joint heirs (Eph. 3:6) with Israel of the kingdom.[17] We may have separate blessings, but these are temporal blessings, and in the eternal kingdom all will be one, in God's intended unity with Christ as the head over all. No Jew will ever be accepted simply because of his heritage or nationality. Jews must be saved by believing in Christ just as Gentiles must (John 3:3). Israel must be converted, just as Paul was converted (1 Cor. 15:8). The point is, however, that Criswell believed that by God's grace the Jews will be converted, at the second coming, in mass, so that a new converted Israel will be the nation "born in a day" (Isa. 66:8).

This expectation of eschatological conversion as a means of fulfilling biblical prophecy is a part of Criswell's Calvinism. All of us are converted strictly by the regenerating work of the Holy Spirit.[18] It is all of grace and divine sovereignty. His sermons on Ephesians 1 set these doctrines out in the most explicit terms.[19] He with Spurgeon was clearly committed to the sovereign elective purposes of God in all things, including salvation.[20] This is his basis for believing in the providential perseverance of the saints.[21] Not one of the elect will be lost. But Criswell, as if he were an old-time Methodist evangelist, pled for souls and urged sinners to respond to the love of God.[22] He has an exegetical theology (not a strictly logical systematic theology), and he is as comfortable with the tenth chapter of John as he is with the twenty-second chapter of Revelation.

Criswell is not a doctrinare Calvinist because (among other things) he never accepted the doctrine of limited atonement. Criswell affirms a robust general atonement theory. But at the same time it is absolutely clear that he is no universalist. The atonement is substitutionary, effectual, and complete in that all sin is paid for and original sin is completely judged in the death of Christ (the innocent second Adam). The blood of Christ is absolutely sufficient for the salvation of all people. But God commands that each one of us repent of our personal sins and in faith turn to Jesus as Christ and Lord. If we do not we will be eternally lost. Our salvation is now a "Son" question, because the "sin" question has been dealt with by the atoning death of Christ. We are lost not because we have sinned too much or even at all, and surely not because of Adam's sin, though we do still suffer the consequences of that sin and of our own personal sins. Our lost condition, however, has been overcome satisfactorily on the cross. If, however, we do not turn to that cross and plead the blood of Christ, we will be lost and perish in an eternal hell apart from life and light and God.

Along with this we can see that Criswell is a firm believer in creationism. He accepts the historicity of the Genesis material,[23] but the point being made here relates to his view of the origin of the soul. At the moment of birth, the breath of life enters the child's body, and a living soul is born. This is not for Criswell a denial of the value of the fetus. Jeremiah and John the Baptist both are biblical examples showing that God knows and relates to the preborn child. Criswell opposes modern abortion practices, but he nevertheless holds that the eternal soul is created in each one of us at our first breath upon birth. We do not therefore inherit the actual sins of our parents, though we do enter the world and suffer the consequences of their sinful actions. We are all born "outside of the Garden" and thus are inevitably separated from the tree of life. All people sin and come short of God's glory. The wages of sin is death. But the gift of God is life eternal. This doctrinal understanding of sin is consistent with his theory of general atonement and of salvation by God's grace alone. Human works have no part in the plan of salvation at all. All we can do is look and live,[24] that is, trust and receive the gift of God.

Criswell's sturdy defense of biblical infallibility seldom included antiintellectual reasoning. *Why I Preach that the Bible Is Literally True* made a more substantial case than its critics allowed. In that book Criswell begins with the power of the Word to convert. This experience calls attention to the Bible, but the next major step in his argument was Christ's attitude toward and use of Scripture. This argument is rational but not scholastic, because the test of faith is not human reason so much as it is trust in the personal authority of Christ. Having established that one who believes Christ is one who should also believe the Scriptures, Criswell quickly moves to the supporting evidence of the internal witness of the Bible (its unity, its self-explanatory character, its consistency) and the evidence of fulfilled prophecy. In this he is methodologically following the patristic apologists. Only then does he employ the external confirmation of archaeology and historical evidences. Representative "problem passages" are also treated to show how the inerrantist position can cope with the textual and content phenomena found in the canon.

Interestingly, Criswell was never guilty of actually holding a mechanical dictation theory of inspiration, nor did his understanding of verbal inspiration come anywhere close to a theory of verbal revelation as being the source of every word in Scripture. Consider this paragraph from *Why I Preach . . .*:

> Frequently we hear discussions concerning whether the Bible is the Word of God or only contains the Word of God. If, by the former, it is meant that God spoke every word in the Bible, the answer, of course, is no. But if it is meant that God caused every word in the Bible, true or false, to be recorded, the answer is, yes. There are words of Satan in the Bible; there are words of false prophets; there are words of the enemies of Christ; yet they are inspired as being in the Bible, not in the sense that God uttered them, but in the sense that God caused them to be recorded infallibly, inerrantly, and for our profit.

In this sense the Bible does not merely contain the Word of God; it *is* the Word of God.[25]

For Criswell, the object of inspiration was "to put correctly in human words the ideas that come from God." Thus there can be no inspiration of the Scripture if there is no inspiration of the human words that make up what Scripture is, and that kind of inspiration includes and accounts for the accuracy of the record. Verbal differences between Matthew and Luke in recording the Lord's Supper or the Model Prayer, for example, are seen by Criswell simply as examples of the freedom of the Holy Spirit of God to speak as He speaks and to choose His own way of expressing Himself through choosing and leading the various human authors to write.

Christian doctrine is Bible doctrine. Apart from a divinely inspired Scripture, Christian beliefs would be nothing more than devout opinions of sinful men. If the Bible is not literally (actually) true (that is, if its properly understood teachings do not truthfully represent authentic history, or if the Bible does not correctly set forth God's absolute moral standards or divinely revealed theological doctrines), then Christianity could never be *shown* to be true at all. Surely Christ could be trusted for salvation by someone unfamiliar with biblical criticism and/or even by some of those who are mistaken in some of their critical or hermeneutical views. (Salvation is not dependent upon one's belief in biblical inerrancy nor upon one's hermeneutical expertise.) However, even basic biographical information about Christ is drawn almost exclusively from the careful exegesis of biblical historical materials. There is no Christ to trust other than the Christ revealed (described) in Scripture. The Christ of human reason or human imagination or even of subjective human experience is not necessarily the Christ who offers salvation. Only the biblical Christ does that. For Criswell these were compelling reasons to affirm the doctrine of biblical infallibility.

Though without doubt Criswell is known for his defense of the authority and the inerrancy of the Bible, it is misleading to think that he treated that doctrine with any special emphasis from his pulpit. There were sermons preached explicitly on this subject,[26] but he is far better known for the fact that over an almost eighteen-year period he preached Sunday morning and Sunday evening (picking up in the next service where he left off in the previous one) beginning with Genesis 1:1 and continuing through Revelation 22:21.[27] This grammatical-historical, exegetical, verse-by-verse pattern (along with his acceptance of the straightforward truthfulness of the teachings of the Bible) is what he claims led him to become a premillennialist.[28] His eschatology certainly cannot be ignored in trying to understand his theological mind or his theological influence.[29] However, eschatology is not the basis of his theology.

Christology, not eschatology, is at the heart of all that Criswell does theologically.[30] Even his millennialism is centered on the King to whom the Kingdom belongs. His Genesis 1 literal creationism is focused not upon science but upon the Creator who became flesh. His dispensationalism is lodged upon the Lord whose plan for salvation history it was and is. The atonement is the great mystery in God's Word. Salvation is the Lord's greatest gift. The church is the new creation, the spiritual family, made up of those redeemed by the blood of the Lamb. The church was God's secret kept from the Old Testament prophets but was revealed to the apostles and to us. All of this centers upon Christ Himself who was, is, and ever shall be Lord.

Criswell argues that in our modern world there are two great theological issues that face the Christian thinker: (1) the inspiration of the Bible; (2) the virgin birth (the term by which he referred to the entire doctrine of the incarnation itself as well as to the underlying issue of the reality of miracles and thus of the existence of God).[31] He compares the incarnation to other interventions of God in human history such as creation, the great Flood in Noah's day, the calling of Abraham to establish a new nation, the appearance of Elijah as a new kind of prophet, the rise of John the Baptist to announce the dispensation of grace, and the consummation of the age. The incarnation, however, is the greatest of these "interventions" by God.[32] The virgin's conception was for Criswell one of the two great biological miracles of God (the first being the creation of Adam without biological parents). Jesus was genetically whole even though he had only the woman's "seed" from which to form His body. But why was a body formed at all? Hebrews 10 teaches that the Lord's body was prepared in order to be sacrificed.[33]

Gnosticism, ancient or modern, is a heresy. Christ Jesus is both fully God and fully man. This truth is absolutely essential to the gospel.[34] Christ truly identified Himself with us in His suffering. The atonement is God's provision for our redemption and is based upon the very nature of God. Because we are all created in His image, we all have a moral sensitivity, and we can all understand ransom and redemption. God's provision for our sins is a gift, because it is an actual substitution of His life for ours. This principle of substitution and atonement is found throughout the Old Testament and throughout human history.[35]

But how does the death of Christ save us? Criswell in his later years shifted from some of his earlier views on this, but his mature conclusion was that Christ actually destroyed Satan's power by literally invading and destroying the essential structure of Satan's kingdom. Upon His death, Christ (in Criswell's view) actually descended into hell itself where He confronted Satan and the spirits of darkness. He defeated them, taking their "power to triumph" away from them.[36] There in Hades itself He destroyed the power of death.[37] Upon His resurrection and ascension, He entered the heavenly tabernacle and offered His atoning sacrificial blood on the altar there. Even the heaven of heavens was defiled by the sinfulness of mankind, but Christ has now cleansed it with His blood. This is how Christ saves us, by blood, propitiation, atonement, and, thus, on that basis, forgiveness.[38]

Our Lord's resurrection is, for Criswell, fact and not fiction. In his sermon "Our Lord's Entrance into Resurrection Life,"[39] Criswell developed the message by claiming that the resurrection of Jesus was a philosophical fact, a pragmatic, empirical fact, a psychological fact, an ecclesiastical fact, a sote-riological fact, a literary fact, and an experiential fact. This last point was not lost on the congregation who often heard the "great fact." Jesus is alive![40] The disciples recognized Him as "the same Jesus." His presence was actually with them in tangible ways at first and in nonetheless real ways even after His ascension. And so is His presence yet with us.[41]

The single most characteristic teaching that Criswell's regular congregation would know from his years of preaching is this: the only God we will ever see, the only God there is, is Jesus. Jesus saves, and this I know, for the Bible tells me so.[42]

Thus Criswell set the stage for what was surely one of the greatest themes that he held before the people regularly. Christ, because of who He was and what He had done, could now be our sympathetic high priest, the intercessor, the mediator, the answer to our needs.[43] We all long for God (whether we know that is what we truly want or not). All the needs of the human heart are met in Christ Jesus, our great Savior and High Priest. The God of all the universe became a man. His death was not the end of His manhood. After His resurrection, He even asked for fish and honey to eat (Luke 24). Christ saved us and will keep us saved. It is His power all the way on which we must rely. And it is His intercession and His mediation that enables us to boldly go before the throne of grace. Moreover, it is His incarnation that allows Him to serve as our sympathetic High Priest. In Criswell's own words:

> He [Christ Jesus] is touched with our infirmities, and He is able to comfort and strengthen those who are tried. He is no different there in heaven than He was down here in this world in the days of His flesh. He was moved by the least cry. . . .
>
> He was that way in the days of His flesh, and the author of Hebrews says that He is that way still. He is moved with the feelings of our infirmities. When anyone prays or cries, He bows down from heaven to hear and to see.
>
> Can you imagine the great, mighty Lord God who stops to listen to pleas and cries of the least of His saints! "Whosoever shall call upon the name of the Lord shall be saved." He listens; He bows down His ear to hear when His people cry.[44]

Evaluation

Some say there are two W. A. Criswells. This is an oversimplification. There have actually been many W. A. Criswells. He was once an ardent segregationist, but his heart was one day changed. There is a pre- and a post-South American plane crash Criswell. There is a pre- and a post-heart attack Criswell. There is a pre- and a post-Vatican Criswell, and a pre- and a post-Moscow Criswell. There are many turning points in this man's life. He shared himself completely, pouring his very soul into his ministry. Out of that has come a renewed interest in biblical expository preaching and in premillennial eschatology within Baptist life in the South and Southwest. Out of that has come a deep concern on the part of laypeople and pastors for orthodoxy within denominational institutions. Out of his many years of preaching have come thousands of professions of faith and rededications to the Lord's work.

But beyond the encouragement that faith does not have to be antiintellectual, that there is real power in prayer, that the gospel is reality, that faith can and should be fun, and that the gates of hell really cannot stand against the onslaught of the true church; beyond the leadership shown in the days of racial strife in evangelical and Baptist church life;[45] beyond the sense of expectation that he was able to communicate concerning the nearness of the Lord's return; W. A. Criswell most clearly communicated a spirit of devotion to Christ. His eyes often glisten and shine when he speaks of the Lord. He is a man who truly loves the Son of God. He also loves his sons in the ministry. He is not perfect, and, like all of us, he has feet of clay. But he found grace in the eyes of the Lord.

Bibliography

Works by Criswell

Acts: An Exposition. Grand Rapids, Mich.: Zondervan, 1977.

The Bible for Today's World. Grand Rapids, Mich.: Zondervan, 1965.

Criswell's Guidebook for Pastors. Nashville: Broadman Press, 1980.

Did Man Just Happen? Grand Rapids, Mich.: Zondervan, 1957.

Ephesians: An Exposition. Grand Rapids, Mich.: Zondervan, 1974.

Expository Notes on the Gospel of Matthew. Grand Rapids, Mich.: Zondervan, 1961.

Expository Sermons on Daniel. Grand Rapids, Mich.: Zondervan, 1976.

Expository Sermons on Galatians. Grand Rapids, Mich.: Zondervan, 1973.

Expository Sermons on the Epistles of James. Grand Rapids, Mich.: Zondervan, 1975.

Expository Sermons on the Epistles of Peter. Grand Rapids, Mich.: Zondervan, 1976.

Expository Sermons on Revelation. Grand Rapids, Mich.: Zondervan, 1969.

Five Great Affirmations of the Bible. Grand Rapids, Mich.: Zondervan, 1959.

Five Great Questions of the Bible. Grand Rapids, Mich.: Zondervan, 1958.

The Gospel According to Moses. Nashville: Broadman Press, 1950.

Great Doctrines of the Bible. Grand Rapids, Mich.: Zondervan, 1982.

The Holy Spirit for Today's World. Grand Rapids, Mich.: Zondervan, 1966.

In Defense of the Faith. Grand Rapids, Mich.: Zondervan, 1967.

Isaiah: An Exposition. Grand Rapids, Mich.: Zondervan, 1977.

Look Up, Brother! Nashville: Broadman Press, 1970.

Passport to the World. Nashville: Broadman Press, 1951.

The Scarlet Thread Through the Bible. Nashville: Broadman Press, 1971.

These Issues We Must Face. Grand Rapids, Mich.: Zondervan, 1953.

Why I Preach that the Bible Is Literally True. Nashville: Broadman Press, 1969.

Works Related to Criswell

Leon McBeth. *The First Baptist Church of Dallas*. Grand Rapids, Mich.: Zondervan, 1968.

The Criswell Study Bible. Nashville: Thomas Nelson, 1979.

"Essays in Honor of W. A. Criswell." *Criswell Theological Review* 1: (Spring 1987).

Notes

1. The standard biographical sources are as follows: Billy Keith, *W. A. Criswell: The Authorized Biography* (Old Tappan: Revell, 1973), a well-intentioned, factual biography, but by no means an adequate scholarly source even for the period of life and ministry covered; H. Leon McBeth, *The First Baptist Church of Dallas* (Grand Rapids, Mich.: Zondervan, 1968), an excellent centennial history of the church which includes a biographical section on Criswell, but which is no longer up-to-date and, in fact, never attempted to be an intellectual history of the pastor and his theological beliefs; compare also R. W. DuCasse, "A History of the First Baptist Church of Dallas, Texas" (Th.M. thesis; Dallas Theological Seminary, 1964). The closest thing to an autobiography is the work of Thomas A. Charlton and Rufus B. Spain who recorded and transcribed an oral history under the auspices of the oral history program at Baylor University in Waco, Texas; see *Oral Memoirs of W. A. Criswell* (Waco: Baylor University, 1973). This is the best source available, but it is dated. An excellent evaluative biographical source is by Paige Patterson, "The Imponderables of God," *Criswell Theological Review* 1 (Spring 1987): 237-53.

2. Thus his real name is W. A. Criswell, not Wallie Amos Criswell, Jr. The practice of using initials for a legal name is not widespread in urban America, however, and under constant questioning about what the initials stood for, he finally declared his name to be Wallie Amos, and thus it is in the minds of most of his associates. In his later years he seems to have become more fond of the name Amos due to his sense of identity with the powerful preacher/prophet by that name in the Old Testament. Nevertheless, in all written correspondence or published materials, he remains always W. A.

3. Though I never heard Criswell mention it, I always supposed that this probably occurred during the traditional August "revival" meeting common in Baptist churches of that era.

4. Not long after this public profession of faith, Criswell was baptized (by immersion) by his pastor, Brother L. S. Hill.

5. It is to my mind odd that Criswell so often told the dramatic story of his day of decision, his conversion, his profession of faith, but to my knowledge never told of an experience of calling to the gospel (preaching) ministry. It seems that his call to the preaching ministry is something that grew within him from the day of his conversion. In fact, it may not be unfair to say that his call to faith and his call to ministry were one in the same. McBeth, however, reports a conviction by Criswell regarding a

preaching ministry at the age of six (*The First Baptist Church of Dallas*, 229). Criswell did make a public dedication of himself to full-time Christian service at the age of twelve. Supposedly his first sermon was a funeral message for a pet dog.

6. Betty Criswell raised their daughter Mable Anne and later their grandson Chris while at the same time giving herself to every aspect of church life. She in later years taught the largest Sunday School class in the church with a regular attendance exceeding 500 people.

7. A complete description of the dream is given in McBeth's history of *The First Baptist Church of Dallas*, 227 f. This mystical approach to seeking God's will is a characteristic of Criswell's devotional life that can be found again and again throughout the years. He was not reckless, but he did seek confirming signs, and he relied on intuitive insight. This aspect of his life has not been adequately recognized by those who view his biblicism as a rigid literalism. It should also be noted that every year on the anniversary of Dr. Truett's death, Criswell devoted a Sunday morning sermon to the life, ministry, and special interests of Dr. Truett. He kept Dr. Truett's memory alive long beyond the point of courtesy or respect. This continued affirmation of the former pastor is to me an indication that this reported dream actually did occur.

8. By far the best written source of information on Criswell as a pastor is his *Criswell's Guidebook for Pastors* (Nashville: Broadman Press, 1980). Though it may be one of his least known books, the 385-page volume may well be his best and most useful.

9. Criswell, *Guidebook*, 74.

10. In the huge Dallas auditorium, microphones were used so that the congregation could hear the pastor recite the candidate's name and a baptismal formula. He would raise his hand and in a prayerful tone express the meaning of the ceremony. He often used the phrase "in obedience to our Lord's command," and he always mentioned each member of the Trinity (though not always by the same terms). After he finished, the microphone would be turned off so that the sloshing and dripping water sounds would not be amplified.

11. Criswell, *Guidebook*, 74.

12. The most exhaustive bibliography available to date of Criswell's own published materials is the one prepared by Lamar E. Cooper, Sr., "The Literary Contributions of W. A. Criswell" *Criswell Theological Review* 1 (Spring 1987): 255-67 (though it does contain some errors). For more extensive bibliographical materials including secondary sources and articles, one should consult J. E. Towns, *The Social Conscience of W. A. Criswell* (Dallas: Crescendo, 1977); J. E. Townes, "The Rhetoric and Leadership of W. A. Criswell as President of the Southern Baptist Convention: A Descriptive Analysis Through Perspective and Public Address" (Ph.D. diss., Southern Illinois University, 1970); Harold T. Bryson, "The Expository Preaching of W. A. Criswell in His Sermons on Revelation" (Th.D. diss., New Orleans Baptist Theological Seminary, 1967); C. M. Roberts, "W. A. Criswell's Choice and Use of Illustrations" (Th.M. thesis, Dallas Theological Seminary, 1976); and G. Allison's dissertation (in process) at Mid-America Baptist Theological Seminary in Memphis, Tennessee, on the preaching of W. A. Criswell.

13. W. A. Criswell, *Did Man Just Happen?* (Grand Rapids, Mich.: Zondervan, 1957).

14. W. A. Criswell, *The Holy Spirit in Today's World* (Grand Rapids, Mich.: Zondervan, 1966).

15. Scripture clearly requires the descendants of Israel to keep the sabbath. Criswell consistently taught that Jews should still keep the sabbath today, but Chris-

tians are interdicted from keeping it, he said, and are to worship on the Lord's Day, the first day of the week. See Criswell, *Great Doctrines of the Bible,* ed. Paige Patterson (Grand Rapids, Mich.: Zondervan, 1972-   ), 6:56-74.

16. W. A. Criswell, *Great Doctrines,* 3:35 *f.*

17. Ibid., 3:110 *f.*, 121.

18. Ibid., 5:85-94. The Spirit's work of regeneration is accomplished through the power of the Word of God to convict and convert the sinner's mind and heart. Criswell's interpretation of John 3:5 ("born of water") is based on Titus 3:5 and Ephesians 5:26 so as to emphasize the place of Scripture in the spiritual process of conversion, the new birth. He does not accept the idea that "water" in John 3:5 could refer to the "flesh" of verse 6 and thus be the water of natural, physical birth.

19. W. A. Criswell, *Ephesians: An Exposition* (Grand Rapids, Mich.: Zondervan, 1974).

20. Criswell, *Great Doctrines,* 5:124-44. It should be noted that Spurgeon (rather than Truett) was Criswell's hero in the ministry. Criswell patterned himself after Spurgeon in many ways and read widely in Spurgeon's materials. He collected Spurgeon memorabilia. The Downgrade Controversy among English Baptists was for Criswell the pattern for what he feared would happen in Southern Baptist life if the problems were not addressed soon enough and effectively. Spurgeon's Calvinism was perhaps more central to Spurgeon's ministry, but when discussing election, predestination, and related themes, Criswell never backed away from Spurgeon's views. References to Spurgeon were less frequent in the sermons themselves than they were in the "out of pulpit" comments. For Criswell, Spurgeon was the greatest preacher who ever lived after Paul and Apollos (who Criswell believed wrote Hebrews).

21. Ibid., 5:115-23, 145-54.

22. Ibid., 5:41-84. See also, Criswell, *Guidebook,* 227-54.

23. Criswell held a rather sophisticated version of the old interval theory, the theory that Genesis 1 is a description of God's restoration of the original earth created in Genesis 1:1 and subsequently destroyed by the fall of Satan (between Gen. 1:1 and 1:2 and unmentioned in the text). For him the days are literal twenty-four hour days, but the age of the earth is actually quite vast and ancient. Genesis 1:1 is in the distant past, but Genesis 1:2 is in the relatively recent past (perhaps 10 to 20 thousand years ago, though Criswell believed it could be less). The Genesis narrative is an account of God recreating the earth for Adamic man (and thus for us and for Christ). Criswell was an ardent antievolutionist, but he was not a recent creationist.

24. The phrase "look and live" refers to the biblical type of the bronze serpent on the pole in Numbers 21 (cf. John 3), but Criswell's frequent use of this phrase seems to have been drawn more directly from Spurgeon's autobiographical account of his own conversion.

25. W. A. Criswell, *Why I Preach that the Bible Is Literally True* (Nashville: Broadman Press, 1969), p. 66.

26. See, for example, W. A. Criswell, *The Bible for Today's World* (Grand Rapids, Mich.: Zondervan, 1965). It is interesting and important to realize that this book did not receive the bitter attacks that were to come later against Broadman for publishing *Why I Preach that the Bible Is Literally True* (1969). The theological stance was the same, however. See also Criswell, *Great Doctrines,* vol. 1.

27. At the beginning he moved rather rapidly, completing the Old Testament in three and one-half years. September 12, 1948, with Matthew, he began to slow down and do a more thorough exposition of each book, finishing the Gospels in February 1953. He reached Revelation on December 4, 1960, and spent three years in that

book. (Church members often noted the date that they joined the church by identifying which text was in view the Sunday they joined.) Later he went back to do in-depth studies on Daniel, Isaiah, and Ezekiel (all of which were published). He also did more thorough studies of Acts, Ephesians, Galatians, James, and 1 and 2 Peter. Among his many sermon books *The Gospel According to Moses, Expository Notes on the Gospel of Matthew,* and *Expository Sermons on Revelation* are the only ones representative of the original "Through the Bible" series.

28. While it is true that Criswell never studied with an acknowledged premillennialist in college or seminary, it must be remembered that he read widely and that he must have been aware of the great success of the Bible Conference movement. His *Criswell Study Bible* is not explicitly or excessively dispensational, but it is premillennial. The great (early-twentieth century) theological leaders in the Southwest (Truett, Carroll, and others) were often postmillennial. That is, they believed in a historical kingdom that would be brought in through the preaching of the gospel prior to the return of Christ. This optimistic, triumphalistic theology was dealt a severe blow by World War I and was virtually crushed in Southern Baptist Convention life by World War II. The mainline reaction was to shift into an amillennial stance and give up the expectation of a literal kingdom historically manifested. The spiritualization of the prophetic passages required for this view seemed to Criswell to be nothing more than patristic and/or medieval allegorizing revived in modern dress. It is Augustinian and Catholic. The early church, however, often affirmed a millennial kingdom following Christ's return. That realization is the likely source of Criswell's premillennialism. He found that a moderate dispensationalism allowed him to read the straightforward normal meaning out of any text and simply accept it either as history, dogma, or prophecy.

29. Patterson claims: "Largely due to the influence and respect accorded to Criswell, premillennialism began once again to assert itself in the life of Southern Baptists and stands now on a more prominent footing than at anytime in the past twenty years. Though other influences added to this phenomenon, Criswell's preaching would have to be considered one such major contribution." Paige Patterson, "The Imponderables of God" 248.

30. See, for example, W. A. Criswell, *The Gospel According to Moses* (Nashville: Broadman Press, 1950); W. A. Criswell, *These Issues We Must Face* (Grand Rapids, Mich.: Zondervan, 1953); W. A. Criswell, *Five Great Questions of the Bible* (Grand Rapids, Mich.: Zondervan, 1958); W. A. Criswell, *Five Great Affirmations of the Bible* (Grand Rapids, Mich.: Zondervan, 1959); W. A. Criswell, *Christ and Contemporary Crises* (Dallas: Crescendo, 1972); W. A. Criswell, *Christ the Savior of the World* (Dallas: Crescendo, 1975); W. A. Criswell, *The Compassionate Christ* (Dallas: Crescendo, 1976); and W. A. Criswell, *The Christ of the Cross* (Dallas: Crescendo, 1977).

31. See, for example, *Great Doctrines,* 2:79.

32. Ibid., 2:83.

33. In fact, Criswell quite explicitly affirms that Jesus was miraculously given the necessary genetic substance to allow Him to have a real human body (implying forty-six chromosomes) even though no spermatozoon was involved. (Cf. Criswell, *Great Doctrines,* 2:83-86.) Criswell once spent six months preaching on the tenth chapter of Hebrews during his survey of the Bible.

34. Criswell, *Great Doctrines,* 2:115-22.

35. In fact these two principles, (1) the biblical illustration and (2) the illustration of the truth in human history, make up the basic preaching outline for almost every

sermon. His published sermons clearly demonstrate this. See also his own description of sermon preparation in *Guidebook*, 76 *f.*

36. See Criswell's sermons on 1 Peter 3:18-20*a* and Ephesians 4:7-10 in *Expository Sermons on the Epistles of Peter* (Grand Rapids, Mich.: Zondervan, 1976) and *Ephesians: An Exposition* (Grand Rapids, Mich.: Zondervan, 1974). See also *Great Doctrines*, 2:140-47.

37. Though Criswell does not spell this out, it is almost as if he thinks of death itself as if it were an evil entity that can be and was confronted, defeated, and, thus, will one day be finally and utterly destroyed. As an aside, I might note that if there is one major flaw in Criswell's understanding of human psychology it is his conviction that death is dreaded by all mankind. He often made the point that all of us feel the horror, dread, and terror of death. (See, for example, *Great Doctrines*, 2:148.) The truly depressed person (and even Christians can reach this state) may actually long for death, seeing only pain in living, and he may seek the end of life as the only hope of ending the sense of despair he feels about his life. Here Criswell has a marvelous answer in his rich understanding of the joy Christ can bring to the committed believer, but at times he tends not to consider this attitude that arises from extreme depression as being real. His own love for life and his boundless enthusiasm probably make it impossible for him to grasp fully the plight of the truly lonely whose self-image has been bruised and severely damaged by stress and by compromise with sin.

38. See Criswell, *Great Doctrines*, 2:188-96.

39. Ibid., 2:156-63.

40. Ibid., 2:164-71.

41. This practical application of every doctrinal truth to "us" is as typical as any other element in the expository preaching method practiced by W. A. Criswell. I have never been able to find out if this threefold (biblical, historical, personal) method was taught in his seminary classes on homiletics or if this is just Criswell's own contribution to the practice of preaching. The amount of research that goes into such messages is enormous, but the appeal to the people is also enormous. The sermon's introduction is usually exegetical and linguistic. Then each expositional point is developed using at least one if not two of these elements. Then the sermon will close with the personal application. Such application may be found earlier in the message as well, but it is always the manner of preferred closing. There were exceptions to this pattern, of course, most notably the times doctrinal points were allowed to make their own application. In later years, however, as the burdens of such a rigorous study schedule began to be felt, the applications became more and more the content of the sermon. Such might be expected, however, after multiple decades of preaching from the same pulpit, and after the extensive sermon ministry Criswell attempted (as reflected in his more than fifty books).

42. See Criswell, *Great Doctrines*, 2:68-77, 106-14. See also Criswell, *Expository Sermons on Revelation*, 1 vol. edition (Grand Rapids, Mich.:Zondervan, 1969); and Criswell, *Expository Sermons on Daniel*, 1 vol. edition (Grand Rapids, Mich.: Zondervan, 1976).

43. Criswell, *Great Doctrines*, 2:197-203.

44. Ibid., 2:202 *f.*

45. See Criswell, *Look Up, Brother* (Nashville: Broadman Press, 1970), 43-55.

24

Eric Rust

Bob E. Patterson

Biography

Eric Charles Rust was born at Gravesend, England, June 6, 1910. His parents, Charles Henry Rust and Ruth Wiles, were members of Sittingbourne Baptist Church in which his grandfather was an elder and his father a deacon "lay preacher." At age fourteen Eric was baptized into this church fellowship and, like his father, began preaching in small Baptist churches near his home.

Eric's father was a master bridge builder. At the outbreak of World War I the family transferred to Sheerness, where his father was made responsible for the construction of small naval craft by the British Admiralty. At age eight, Eric shifted from a private school to the public Borden Grammar School at Sittingbourne where he did his secondary education. At age sixteen, he took his 0-level exams and received "distinctions" on ten out of twelve exams, easily passing the examination to be an engineer officer.

Although Eric preached regularly in Baptist churches, a scientific vocation seemed to be opening for him. At eighteen (1928) he began to specialize in mathematics, physics, and chemistry. Because of his excellent academic record, he won one of the five Royal Scholarships at the Royal College of Science, one of England's finest schools. After two years he became a math instructor for his fellow students and began doing research. At age twenty, Eric received the Bachelor of Science with first-class honors and the ARCS from the Royal College.

During his two years at the College, he had preached regularly as a member of the London Baptist Preachers Association. He remained at the Royal College of Science for two more years until he received both the Master of Science from the University of London and the DIC from the Imperial College of Science. But his preaching and his work in science created a vocational tension for him. Many of his fellow Baptists took a hostile stance against science which Eric found puzzling and strange. He was finding silence from the pulpits on the correlation of faith with science in the increasingly secular England of the 1930s. In his efforts to reconcile his faith with his scientific training, he began to see how he could best serve his church by becoming a bridge builder between faith and science. Shaped as a scientist, he now began to seek ministerial and theological training.

Eric entered Oxford University in the fall of 1932 and enrolled at the Baptist school, Regent's Park College. H. Wheeler Robinson, a distin-

Eric Rust (1910-   )

guished Old Testament teacher who combined piety and scholarship in a remarkable way, was principal at Regent's Park. From Robinson (1872-1945) Eric received a reinforcement for his evangelical Christianity, his already deep love for the Old Testament, an interpretative method, an insight into the "salvation history" approach to the Bible, and a biblical realism. No teacher at Oxford added more to Eric's love for the Bible than Robinson, and when he came to the United States to work, he often confessed that he was a "Wheeleronian Robinsonian" in his understanding of the Hebrew Bible.

Oxford was alive with intellectual giants, and Rust profited from studying with them. His New Testament tutor, T. W. Manson, vigorously insisted upon the full significance of the Jesus of history, and Rust has followed his lead tenaciously. T. G. Collingwood showed him how to relate faith to history, and how to distinguish history from science. His other tutors included John S. Whale, a specialist in Protestant theology; C. J. Cadoux, an authority in church history; and Nathanial Micklem, principal at Mansfield College. He attended the lectures of such distinguished men as Austin Farrer, B. H. Streeter, Kenneth Kirk, C. J. Stone, R. H. Lightfoot, and R. G. Collingwood.

Eric Rust received his B.A. degree from Oxford in 1935, having taken first-class honors in the honors school. He also received the M.A. degree in 1938 and the B.D. degree in 1946. Rust also began his career as a minister in English Baptist churches in 1935, serving the Hay Hill Baptist Church until 1939. In 1940 he became minister of the Oxford Road Baptist Church in Birmingham, but this elite congregation was soon scattered to the countryside under the increasing Nazi blitz. As World War II began, Rust sustained his academic contacts while his theological interests increased. At the University of Birmingham he taught as an extension lecturer, and at King Edward High School he taught sixth form mathematics. At the high school he formed an after-school club for teenagers, and still preaches from a Bible given him by the group. During those war-torn years he wrote *The Christian Understanding of History,* the book which earned him an Oxford B.D. in 1946. His writing was interrupted many nights as he herded parishioners into shelters as a sector air-raid warden. He has often said that a theology which can't relate to life—that cannot be preached—has no meaning. His reputation as a minister-scholar was growing, and in December 1942 he became pastor of a large Baptist congregation, the New North Road Church, in Huddersfield. At the same time he became an extension lecturer at the University of Leeds.

In 1946, one year after the death of his teacher H. Wheeler Robinson, he became professor of philosophy and theology at Rawdon Baptist College. There he taught biblical theology, ethics, philosophy of religion, Old Testament, world religions, and systematic theology. His academic skills were widely recognized, and in 1947 he gave an address on "Science and Religion" at the Seventh Baptist World Congress held in Copenhagen. In 1952 he came to the United States to teach biblical theology as visiting professor at Crozer Theological Seminary in Chester, Pennsylvania. That year he gave the Norton Lectures at The Southern Baptist Theological Seminary in Louisville, Kentucky, and in May 1953 he joined the faculty at Southern and continued there until his retirement. I walked into the classroom of Eric C. Rust in Louisville in September 1954 and took my seat as one of his theological students. To me Eric Rust will always be the "Great Reconciler" because of the way that he reconciles the worlds of science, philosophy, Christian doctrine, and the Bible in a wholesome and winsome way.

For four decades Rust has had an immeasurable influence on Baptist life through his thousands of students. His doctoral students serve literally around the world—from Cali, Columbia, to Tokyo, Japan, to Ogbomosho, Nigeria, Africa. In the area of the relationship between the Bible and science, he has been of enormous help to Southern Baptists. His longtime colleague, Professor E. Glenn Hinson, has said of Rust: "In most of his career as minister, teacher, and scholar, he has wrestled with and addressed himself to the relationship of Christian faith to modern science, an issue which has increasingly taken a central place in Christianity."[1] It has been Rust's lifelong notion that the warfare between science and Scripture should come to an end.

Exposition

Science and the Bible

Why should I, a Baptist, along with other evangelical Christians, have had such difficulty in relating science and the Bible? The problem was there long before Rust, the reconciler, came on the scene to give me and others a helping hand.

Since Copernicus the biblical exegetes and the experimental scientists have been quarreling when they should have been acting in harmony. In 1605 Francis Bacon said in his *The Advancement of Learning* that God had two books, the Book of Scripture and the Book of Nature, and that we should strive to be proficient in both but that we should not unwisely mingle the two. Those since Bacon who have wanted to separate "Athens from Jerusalem" have made the most noise, fought the most battles, and steadfastly refused to sign a truce. They took only the side of Bacon which said "don't mingle the two." In our day, however, we have seen enough changes in science and in theology to note a thaw in the icy relationship. With the presumed status of scientific knowledge now in question, the scientist seems more willing to listen to the theologian, and the biblical exegete, with better tools at hand to understand the Bible in its original context, seems more open to what is going on in the laboratory.

Eric Rust preaches that each should listen to and look at the models for understanding the world presented by the other, with humility and sympathy. He says that it is time for a rapprochement between the two Books of God. Even though the advance of science will continue to raise urgent problems for religion, which must be frequently and fearlessly discussed, science and Christianity need never return to the open warfare that has marked their past relationship.

A review of the long conflict will help put Rust's reconciling contribution in perspective. Modern science had its birth in the seventeenth century. This "century of genius," giving us a new world-view, is epitomized for the physical sciences by Galileo's *Dialogues* (1632) and Sir Isaac Newton's *Principia* (1687). Galileo brought together mathematics and experimentation, and Newton fulfilled this revolution in scientific outlook by picturing nature as a law-abiding machine. The eighteenth century, the Age of Reason, or the Enlightenment, developed Newton's physics into a view of nature that was more and more deterministic and reductionistic. Lagrange, d'Alembert, Laplace, and others became spokesmen for a model of nature as a self-sufficient and impersonal machine, an inflexible cause-and-effect system governed by exact and absolute laws. God was either portrayed as the remote and impersonal Clockmaker of Deism, or He was omitted from the picture completely.

The nineteenth century continued many patterns of thought established in the two previous centuries, but the field of biology witnessed a change which is one of the major revolutions in intellectual history. Charles Darwin in biology was to the nineteenth century what Newton was to physics in the seventeenth. Both produced a unified scheme based on theoretical concepts—Newton gave an image of nature as an intelligently designed machine and Darwin depicted nature as a dynamic and progressive process. The publication of Darwin's *Origin of Species* in 1859 with its theory of evolution directly challenged the deistic assumptions of Newton's world-view. Evolution shifted the prevailing view of nature by pointing to the importance of change, the interacting character of organisms in a "web of life," the lawlike aspects of growth, and humans as biological creatures in nature. Evolution also influenced religion by destroying a naively simple form of the design argument, humanity's traditionally unique place of dignity in nature, long accepted moral understandings, and a literalist interpretation of the Bible. By 1900 some form of the evolutionary theory was accepted by virtually all scientists and by the majority of Christian theologians.

The twentieth century brought another major shift in our understanding of physics and biology, the two branches of science that have most radically reshaped our interpretation of the Bible. Before 1900 the "classical" scientific world-view regarded nature as simple in structure, and composed of a relatively few substances in variously combined patterns. Today we know it is infinitely varied and enormously complex. The universe consists of a hierarchy of levels of organization which stretch from the puzzling microworld of the subatomic through the equally baffling macroworld of our sense perceptions, to the megaworld of space, billions of light years across, with its exploding galaxies and its gravitational fields of "black holes."[2]

Before 1900 the natural world was regarded as mechanically determined and predictable, and the future state of all its systems could in principle be calculated from their present states. All laws seemingly could be derived from the laws governing a few kinds of particles and fields. Albert Einstein and the development of quantum theory during the 1920s, changed the picture. Now we view the world as the interplay of chance and statistics, with indeterminancy at the subatomic microlevel and unpredictability at the complex macrolevel.

In 1900, in spite of Darwin, the natural world was still thought of as static and basically closed to any radical change. Now we are told to think of it as dynamic, free, forever changing, subject to novelty, newness, spontaneity, creativity, and potentially ready for new emergents in the future.

At the opening of the twentieth century, the world seemed to be made up of very solid, readily intelligible, subunits of atoms. That simple view has vanished, and the bedrock on which the universe is built seems to be a mystery. Physicists are now aware of the infinite complexity of the subatomic world, and that not only is the atom more mysterious than they imagined, it is more mysterious than they can imagine. Also, as they understand better the universe they see that complexities are found at each smaller level.

The scientific world-view today no longer has an absolute space and time (thanks to Einstein), it no longer has an objective observer who can describe the world as it really is independently of his observations (thanks to Heisenberg's Uncertainty Principle), and it no longer has an absolute determinism with its corollary of predictability. We can only conclude for our time that scientific concepts are partial, abstractive, and symbolic; the whole is more than the sum of its parts so we need theories that deal with integrated systems at higher organizational levels; nature is a dynamic process of perpetual change and creativity; freedom is a constitutent part of the cosmos; scientific theories are not literal and objective replicas of the world; and humility is the quality most befitting the modern scientist. Our awareness of our ignorance is growing faster than our knowledge. Our ways of misconstruing nature in the past were not so much an error in our science, but a mistake in our philosophy of science. We had eyes to see, but we did not see.

Our ways of interpreting the Bible have changed along with our ways of interpreting the natural world. The change started as far back as the mental coming of age and spiritual emancipation of the Renaissance and Reformation. The individualism and toleration, the broader outlook that came with the opening of America and the East, and the scientific advances of the seventeenth century led to significant cultural, social, political, and religious changes in the eighteenth century. So it was the Enlightenment *(Aufklarung, L'Illumination)* that sent shockwaves through the Bible interpreters as nothing did before or after, and Christian Bible readers have never been the same since.

The Enlightenment was the cultural epoch that started in Europe with the Glorious Revolution of 1688 and prevailed until the defeat of postrevolutionary France in 1815 and the romantic reaction. Many of its methods, values, and ideas are still with us. "The approved concepts were reason, freedom, nature, utility, happiness, rights, tolerance, deism, rational Christianity, natural religion, social contract, science, autonomy, harmony, and optimism."[3] Paul Tillich says that the Enlightenment can be characterized by four concepts: human autonomy—the universal law of reason, which is the structure of reality, is within me; reason—the awareness of the principles of truth, justice, and goodness; harmony—there is a law behind us which has the effect of making everything come out most adequately; and tolerance—a toleration of everything but the intolerant.[4] The Enlightenment, as with many movements, declined by an overemphasis of its own principles.

However, many Enlightenment ideas did not die out and are a part of our thinking today. Its high evaluation of science, its emphasis that all truth claims must be reasonable, and its quest for freedom and tolerance are still with us. So is its skepticism about authority, the Bible, revelation, and theological ethics. It held that there was no reality transcending nature, and it was this mentality which has led to the four assumptions of our twentieth century secular culture. Our secular assumptions are, first, a comprehensive contingency: all reality has a provisional character. Second, the temporal is everything: a total transiency of reality and experience. Third, a radical relativity: there are no ultimate truths, morals, or authority. Fourth, the absolute autonomy of man: since man is self-sufficient he does not need God.[5] These standards of secularism cannot sustain our cherished Western values, so the "modern pagan," to escape nihilism, invests his life with other than Christian values.

The one idea of the Enlightenment that bore most directly on the interpretation of the Bible was the notion that all documents of the past, both secular and biblical, must be submitted to literary and historical criticism. This provoked a crisis for those who looked to the Bible as a source of authority, because the Bible was written in a prescientific age. This crisis is still with us and is not yet resolved. Biblical criticism in skeptical hands challenged the traditional interpretation of the Bible by questioning its divine origin and inspiration. Also, the development of science led to serious doubts about the Bible's historical integrity. For example, astronomy questioned the Bible's small universe, geology cast doubt on the Bible's short-lived earth, biology was skeptical of the Bible's picture of man's creation, and the scientific understanding of the nature of events hesitated over the miracles recorded in the Bible.

The question of the Enlightenment is still with us: How can a book (Bible) written in a prescientific, precritical age be interpreted as authoritative for us today? As we move into the twenty-first century we are becoming even more the disciples of science and technology. Must we capitulate to the Enlightenment and become modern pagans, or should we resort to obscurantism in matters of science and biblical criticism? Certainly there are better alternatives, and Eric Rust has presented one such alternative.

Trained in both science and biblical studies, holding that the God of creation and the God of the Bible are the same, Rust has felt a divine imperative to harmonize science and Scripture. He admits that scientists have made stupid blunders in pitting their views against the Bible, and that theologians have made equally bad mistakes in exegeting the Bible, but if each had listened attentively to the other there would have been no disharmony between them.

His 1967 book, *Science and Faith: Towards a Theological Understanding of Nature,* remains a good model of how to reconcile Bacon's "two books." In this volume Rust explored the historical, philosophical, and psychological bases of scientific and religious thought. To be able to speak to the scientist, he said, the Christian must be prepared to validate his faith in the analytical, empirical terms of today. The scientist, on the other hand, must recognize the value of the "synthetic and holistic aspects of human knowing"—the spark which connects the knowable with the possible. Rust said,

> I am convinced that the historical faith which the Church has treasured down the centuries is still relevant to our time. It needs to be re-expressed. The technique of biblical criticism, the contemporary concern with the nature of religious language, the scientific exploration into the origins of man and the universe, the increasing understanding of man's psychosomatic nature, the new attempts to understand divine revelation and to justify divine transcendence—all require that the ancient faith be poured into new·wineskins.[6]

In this book Rust shows how modern scientific thought is closely related to the biblical revelation and how the Christian revelation can relate to secular concerns. He holds that we can only understand God the Creator if we already experience Him as God the Redeemer in Christ. Rust argues that these two ways of knowing, science and faith, coalesce rather than conflict with one another. He happily, even if critically, reconciles Genesis 1 with biological evolution, the "image of God" with modern psychology, and the incarnation of Christ with the "sacramental universe" model of modern science. Modern science must always be looked at through the spectacles of biblical revelation. He says that only as we rediscover the immanence of God the Holy Spirit can we face the secular emphasis of our time. He puts it this way: "Thus we may describe the Holy Spirit as the immanence of God within his creation, effecting the divine intention of the Father as this is expressed in creative, sustaining and redemptive activity through the Son."[7] Thus Rust is thoroughly Trinitarian in relating God to the world of nature.

If Rust serves as a model for Baptists and other evangelical Christians on how to relate Bible and science, he also serves as a second model on how to relate positive critical scholarship to the doctrine of Revelation.

Revelation and Inspiration

Since 1980 the Southern Baptist Convention has been in a continuing struggle over the direction of the Convention, a battle centered around the questions of revelation-inspiration. This conflict has its roots back in the Enlightenment, which promoted the notion that all documents of the past (including the Bible) must submit themselves to literary and historical criticism. Nineteenth-century liberalism capitulated to the Enlightenment while fundamentalism ignored it. Liberalism so highlighted the humanity of the Bible that it gave up its divinity, while fundamentalism hedged the Bible's humanity by surrounding it with divinity.

Eric Rust taught his students how to accept both modern knowledge and the integrity of Scripture. Again, he proved to be for Baptists the "Great

Reconciler," showing that revelation-inspiration has both a Godward and a manward nature. To emphasize only the Godward aspect of revelation would result in a series of propositions far removed from the dynamic quality of the Bible. To stress only the manward side of revelation would shape God in man's image. Both the divine and the human must be blended between God's giving of himself and man's interpretative response. Both God's giving (revelation) and man's interpretation (inspiration) are God-directed. Rust has said:

> Such witnessing is at one and the same time a proclamation and a confession. It proclaims what God has said in the concrete confrontation of history, and it confesses the faith of the witness in the living God, his own recognition of and commitment to the God who has spoken. Such witnessing is inspired, for only God can open men's eyes to his presence, lift the veil in the historical mediating event, and only God can direct aright their testimony to what they have seen and heard. The human response to revelation is faith.[8]

Rust uses the expression "historical images" to describe both God's activity and man's receptivity in revelation-inspiration. "Historical" refers to the media that God uses to give revelation, and "images" refers to man's inspired response to God's activity. For Rust, the Bible's authority rests upon both God's activity in history and the inspired words which convey that activity. Rust says:

> Now these images are not arbitrary, or bound to the time and place in which they emerge, as Bultmann contends. This brings into view the association of divine inspiration with the imagination of the prophets and witnesses . . . in the case of the prophets and apostles, the imagination is so creatively controlled by the divine Spirit that the images and symbols have divine authority. The events and images are concomitant elements in the revelation, and without either there would be no revelation.[9]

Rust follows his teacher, H. Wheeler Robinson, when he says that God uses nature, man, and history as the three main types of media through which to reveal Himself.[10] Since nature was created by God, continues to be sustained by God, and someday will be transformed to fulfill God's purpose perfectly, it can be viewed as a medium of God's revelation. Rust says of the healing and nature miracles of Jesus:

> He who can order the storm to cease and bring back the dead to life; who declares that the Father clothes the lilies of the field and cares for the sparrow; who in His Person reveals the power over nature which the Old Testament ascribes to God alone; He confirms our faith that though nature is not to be identified with God, it is wholly sustained by Him and may become the medium of his revelation.[11]

Rust, trained in the modern sciences, sees that nature is much more open to a Christian interpretation than it was in the days of "unbreakable natural laws" and mechanistic causation. For Rust there should be no conflict between the language of science and the Bible; but if there is, he prefers the language of the Bible.

Theological language can embrace scientific language and interpret it. But the reverse is not the case, since science deals only with empirical "observables." Theological language describes a total view of reality, whereas scientific language describes only a partial view. In theology the universe is understood in personal terms, but science abstracts from the person and concerns itself with the impersonal.[12] In the Incarnate Christ the language of science and the language of the Christian faith should come together in a harmonious fashion.

Rust holds that the second main medium that God uses to reveal Himself is the human consciousness. Since man is pictured in the Bible as a body animated by the Spirit of God, man easily becomes a sphere in which revelation occurs. This is especially true of man's moral consciousness, made in the image of God. The Bible views man as a unity, a psycho-physical whole, and this is supported by modern scientific analysis.

> The psychosomatic nature of the human person has been borne out increasingly as science has progressed. Evidently our personality, our selfhood, has its roots deep down in the physical and physiological aspects of our bodily structure. More and more we are made aware of the interrelationship of a body chemistry and our personal characteristics, of the intimate bond between the brain and our mental activity, of the implications of our genetic structure for our personal development.[13]

The perfect picture of what we should be is found in Jesus Christ.

The third main medium that God uses to reveal Himself, says Rust, is history. The Bible shows that, because humans are free moral agents, history is dynamic, subject to change, creative of values, can be interpreted, and the perfect time frame in which the eternal God can meet humanity. Christ's life, death, resurrection, and second coming is the fullest expression of God's revelation of Himself in history. Because of his training in modern science, Rust views matter as energy, and consequently holds firmly to a historical revelation.

> Salvation history is grounded in historical actuality. Miracles are historically attested occurrences. The Virgin Birth is not myth, however difficult it may appear to modern man. The resurrection cannot be dismissed as the creation of faith. Rather it is the historical actuality that vindicates the cross and creates faith. Historical actuality as such must not be confused with pure symbolism even though the interpretation of it may involve us in historical imagery.[14]

This historical revelation will be completed only with the return of the ascended Christ at the end-of-the-ages accompanied by a general resurrection.

The prophet, priest, sage, and psalmist interpret God's giving of Himself in revelation in the Old Testament, while the apostles interpret God's revelation of Himself in nature, humans, and history in the New Testament. These people not only interpret the revelation, but they also became mediums of revelation in themselves. For example, Hosea interpreted God's word, and his personal domestic tragedy became God's word to Israel. Further, when Hosea's spoken word became the written Word (or Bible), God speaks again to me as I respond in faith. This human role in revelation is continued by the

New Testament apostles. The reason that we know Christ today is because of the words of the apostles.

> [Revelation] is a particular series of historical events which itself carried the meaning and redemption of all history. In the center of it stand the interpretative figures of the witnesses, the prophets and the apostles, and those who gathered around them. To them the revelation came. Indeed they belong to the revelation itself, for without the God-given insight which was granted to them, the Word of God which came to them within their historical situation, our own faith would be impossible.[15]

Evaluation

General revelation is the universal knowledge of God available to all of us at all times and all places, while special revelation is God's giving of Himself to prepared people at special times and in special ways. Rust's model of special revelation should be subjected to several traditional questions. Is his model faithful to the Bible? Is it plausible and free from internal self-contradiction? Does it illuminate all our other experiences, and does it enhance the quality of our moral and intellectual life? Does it help us to understand other religions and enter into dialogue with them? Neither liberalism nor fundamentalism could pass this test, but Rust's model does.

Rust's approach equally emphasizes God's deeds and words. The Bible is full of deeds in which God reveals Himself in historical events, through events, and by events. At the same time God's speech is mediated by Old Testament spokesmen and New Testament apostles. In Christ we meet the most complete form of God's revelation as Word-Deed.

Rust's model of revelation has several advantages. First, it balances the tension between revelation as event, doctrine, and experience. Second it leaves revelation to be initiated by God. Third, it leaves us responsible for accepting revelation by faith. Fourth, it opens up dialogue with others who have had a different experience of revelation from our own. And, fifth, it implies an inspired Bible.

An inspired Bible is necessary for me to have the same revelation of God as Moses, John, and Paul. The Spirit of God guided the biblical writers so that their account of revelation now becomes revelation to me. This implies that the Bible writers were so directed by the Holy Spirit that we have exactly the Scriptures that God wants us to have. The inspiration came from God, but the Holy Spirit used the unique talents of each writer. This avoids a dictation model of inspiration while stressing the trustworthiness and authority of the Bible. Inspiration, then, includes both the writer and the writing.

The Bible, when understood in its original context and with its original meaning, is fully inspired. To be understood properly it must be properly interpreted. When properly interpreted it becomes the final written authority for the Christian. It has the right to define what we believe and how we are to behave. When we rely upon the Holy Spirit to give us understanding, comprehension, and certainty, we hear the voice of God speak to us in the Bible.

Liberalism will not like Rust's model, and will accuse him of not recognizing that the Bible was written by fallible men who were wholly human in all they wrote. Fundamentalism will not like his model because he does not ignore the Enlightenment and is not militant against all higher criticism of the Bible. Rust is guilty neither of underbelief (liberalism) nor overbelief (fundamentalism).

Rust, then, has helped Baptists retain and reaffirm the historic doctrine of the church about revelation-inspiration by using rather than denying modern scholarship. God is the ultimate author of Scripture, guaranteeing its trustworthiness as a whole and in its parts. The text and images (language) of the Bible are divinely inspired, the humanity of the writers is affirmed, and the writers were given truths beyond their natural resources. Few Baptists have done more than Eric Rust to bring historic Christianity and modernity into creative dialogue. He has shown us how to use the Bible in boldly stepping across the stream to the modern world.

Bibliography

Books

The Christian Understanding of History. London: Lutterworth Press, 1947.

Covenant and Hope. Waco: Word, 1971.

Evolutionary Philosophies and Contemporary Theology. Philadelphia: The Westminster Press, 1969.

Judges, Ruth, 1 & 2 Samuel. Layman's Bible commentary, vol. 6. Richmond: John Knox Press, 1961.

Nature and Man in Biblical Thought. London: Lutterworth Press, 1953.

Nature: Garden or Desert? Waco: Word, 1971.

Positive Religion in a Revolutionary Time. Philadelphia: The Westminster Press, 1970.

Salvation History. Richmond: John Knox Press, 1962.

Science and Faith. New York: Oxford University Press, 1967.

Towards a Theological Understanding of History. New York: Oxford University Press, 1963.

Contributions to Edited Volumes

Articles on "Prophecy," "Man," "Sin," "Creation," "Grace." *Encyclopedia of Southern Baptists*. Nashville: Broadman Press, 1958.

"Does Science Leave Room for God." *Science and Religion*, ed. J. C. Monsma. New York: G. P. Putnam's Sons, 1962.

"History and Time." *The Teacher's Yoke*, ed. E. Jerry Vardaman. Waco: Baylor University Press, 1964.

"Science and Ethics." *Baker's Dictionary of Christians Ethics*, ed. Carl F. H. Henry, Grand Rapids, Mich.: Baker Book House, 1973.

Sermon: "The Challenge of a World Fellowship." *Younger Voices*, ed. Graham W. Hughes. London: The Carey Press, n.d.

Sermon: "The Hiddenness of God." *Professor in the Pulpit*, ed. W. Morgan Patterson and Raymond Bryan Brown. Nashville: Broadman Press, 1963.

"The Limitations of Science." *Official Report of the Seventh Baptist World Congress, 1947*. London: Baptist World Alliance, 1948.

Journals and Magazines

"The Apologetic Task in the Modern Scene." *The Review and Expositor* 56 (April 1959).

"The Atoning Act of God in Christ." *The Review and Expositor* 59 (Jan. 1962).

"The Bible and Revelation." Three articles. *Community, a Journal of Christian Interpretation* 14 (Nov. 1950, Jan. 1951, April 1951).

"The Biblical Faith and Modern Science." *The Review and Expositor* 71 (Spring 1974).

"The Church in the 1970's." *The Review and Expositor* 67 (Winter 1970).

"The Contemporary Theological Scene." *The Review and Expositor* 67 (Summer 1970).

"Creation and Evolution." *The Review and Expositor* 59 (April 1962).

"The Destiny of the Individual in the Thought of the Old Testament." *The Review and Expositor* 58 (July 1961).

"The 'God Is Dead' Theology." *The Review and Expositor* 64 (Summer 1967).

"Interpreting the Resurrection." *The Journal of Bible and Religion* 27 (Jan. 1959).

"The Nature and Problems of Biblical Theology." *The Review and Expositor* 50 (Oct. 1953).

"The Possible Lines of Development of Demythologizing." *The Journal of Bible and Religion* 27 (Jan. 1959).

"Theology and Preaching." *The Review and Expositor* 52 (April 1955).

"A Theology of Stewardship." *The Review and Expositor* 70 (Spring 1973).

"The Theology of the Lord's Supper." *The Review and Expositor* 66 (Winter 1969).

"Time and Eternity in Biblical Thought." *Theology Today* 10 (Oct. 1953).

Notes

1. E. Glenn Hinson, "Eric Charles Rust: Apostle to an Age of Science and Technology," Bob E. Patterson, ed., in *Science, Faith, and Revelation: An Approach to Christian Philosophy* (Nashville: Broadman Press, 1979), 13. See also Richard B. Cunningham, "The Concept of God in the Thought of Eric Rust," in ibid., 199-223.

2. See A. R. Peacocke, *Creation and the World of Science* (Oxford: Clarendon Press, 1979), 61-63; and Ian Barbour, *Issues in Science and Religion* (Englewood Cliffs, N.J.: Prentice-Hall, Inc., 1966), 15-137.

3. Bernard Ramm, *After Fundamentalism: The Future of Evangelical Theology* (San Francisco: Harper & Row, Publishers, 1983), 3.

4. Paul Tillich, *A History of Christian Thought* (New York: Harper & Row, Publishers, 1968), 287-93.

5. Langdon Gilkey, *Naming the Whirlwind: The Renewal of God-Language* (New York: The Bobbs-Merrill Co., 1969), 31-36.

6. Eric C. Rust, *Science and Faith: Towards a Theological Understanding of Nature* (New York: Oxford University Press, 1967), vii.

7. Ibid., 184.

8. Eric Rust, *Salvation History: A Biblical Interpretation* (Richmond: John Knox Press, 1962), 27.

9. Ibid., 42-43.

10. Max E. Polley, "Revelation in the Writings of H. Wheeler Robinson and Eric Rust: A Comparative Study," in *Science, Faith and Revelation,* 144-66.

11. Eric Rust, *Nature and Man in Biblical Thought* (London: Lutterworth Press, 1953), 263.

12. Rust, *Science and Faith,* 129.

13. Ibid., 207.

14. Eric Rust, *Salvation History,* 41.

15. Eric Rust, "The Authority of Scripture—The Word of God and the Bible," *Review and Expositor* 57 (January 1960): 38.

25

George Eldon Ladd
Molly Marshall-Green

Rigorous, tenacious, single-minded, thorough—these words are sprinkled generously in descriptions of Professor George Eldon Ladd (1911-82). A keen mind and a love of biblical proclamation drew this pastor-teacher to a lifelong explication of "faith seeking understanding." Few have wrestled with the implications of historical-critical methods for evangelical biblical studies as painstakingly as he; he believed that the truth of Scripture could be more clearly obtained by employing these refined critical tools. A deep love for the Scriptures, students, and scholarship shaped his contributions to scores of seminarians and lay persons who read his accessible works.[1] In the 1978 *Festschrift* for Ladd, President David Hubbard of Fuller Theological Seminary characterized Ladd's overarching motivation: "As much as anyone in our generation, he has sought consciously to make evangelical scholarship credible in the universities of the world."[2] As a teacher and writer, he would not avoid hard questions or confrontation. Texts and colleagues and students were often subjected to the glare of his probing inquiry; usually the result was a strengthened "reason for the hope that is within" (1 Pet. 3:15).

Biography

In God's providence George Ladd was born to Christian parents in Alberta, Canada, on July 31, 1911. His father's profession as a doctor moved the family first to New Hampshire and then to Maine. There, at age nineteen, George was converted in a Methodist church under the preaching of a young woman from Moody Bible Institute. As is often the case when a person accepts Christ at a more reflective age, he became quite concerned with the mandate of the gospel for proclamation and mission. These continued to be pulsating themes in Ladd's lectures and writing, as many former students testify.

Ladd completed his undergraduate work at Gordon College in Boston while serving as a student pastor in Gilford, New Hampshire. Christ's claim on his life would not let him defer participation in active ministry in order to pursue his love of academic studies without distraction. His life bore passionate testimony to his enduring will to combine study and service, both a "ministry of the Word." Ladd graduated with a Th.B. and was ordained as a minister in the Northern Baptist Convention (now the American Baptist Convention) in 1933. That year he married Winifred Phyllis Webber.

He completed his Bachelor of Divinity degree at Gordon Divinity School

George Eldon Ladd (1911-   )

Photo courtesy of Fuller Theological Seminary

in 1941, during another pastorate. The Ladds' devotion to pastoral ministry led them to First Baptist Church of Montpelier, Vermont, where they ministered from 1936 to 1942. But study and teaching were to comprise George's primary vocation, and thus the Ladds moved back to Boston in order for him to pursue doctoral studies. From 1943 to 1949 he engaged in vigorous work as a Ph.D. candidate in Classics at Harvard University; at the same time, he served as an instructor in Greek and New Testament at Gordon College, his alma mater.

After graduation they moved to the fledgling Fuller Theological Seminary in Pasadena, California, in 1950.[3] The attractiveness of this position was the promise of having ample time to write, in addition to classroom responsibilities. Ladd managed to juggle the demands of his academic post with discipline and determination. President Hubbard, his former student, commented on the impact of Ladd's work style: "We were encouraged by his example and forced by his requirements to work harder than we ever had before."[4] Indeed, Fuller gained a good measure of its academic notoriety because of the prolific pen of this committed scholar who was professor of New Testament Exegesis and Theology.

Ladd was faithful to his library and his lecturn. Persons engaged in teaching positions seldom approximate the balance between scholarly research and publication and insightful classroom presentations and graduate supervision that Ladd managed. Sabbatical study leaves spent in Heidelberg University and Basel University strengthened his ability to converse in the large world of scholarship. Ironically, appreciation for Ladd's contributions may have been greater in England and on the Continent than at home.[5] Distinguished lectureships at a variety of evangelical seminaries in America during the 1950s and 1960s furthered the impact of Ladd's scholarship. Those engaged in the task of constructive biblical theology knew that his questions about the nature of "salvation-history," the role of eschatology, the primacy of exegesis, and the centrality of the resurrection could not be ignored without peril. His advocacy for a critical yet loyal approach to Holy Scripture was quite influential.

When Ladd died in 1982, having previously suffered a debilitating stroke (although he could still recite Scripture from memory, according to one fellow teacher), his beloved school and colleagues around the world lost a friend and goad to ever more precise critical assessment of the teaching of the New Testament. His legacy through his students (many of whom are now teaching) and publications continues to bless Christ's church, for whom he offered his life.[6]

Exposition

George Ladd wrote during an epoch of confidence about the enterprise of biblical theology. Even after many scholars trumpeted the bankruptcy of this approach to the Scriptures,[7] Ladd contended for the propriety of attempting to construct the pattern of theology within the New Testament texts.

Ladd could not abide what he perceived to be obscurantism in many fundamentalist writers.[8] He tirelessly attempted to engage the broad range of critical insights so that his evangelical contribution to biblical exegesis and theology might be taken seriously.[9] Ladd firmly believed that the Fundamentalist-Modernist controversy of the 1920s was still raging in churches, divinity schools, and seminaries,[10] and he worked to assist conservative biblical scholars in getting beyond this impasse.

Approach to Biblical Criticism

Many dialogue partners helped shape the parameters of Ladd's investigations; to his credit, he carefully examined the implications of their positions before attempting an evangelical critique.[11] In his monograph, *The New Testament and Criticism,* he argued that the character of the Bible should determine the appropriation of critical methodologies. Because the Bible is "the Word of God given in the words of men in history,"[12] those who employ the tools of biblical criticism must acknowledge their limited compass of adjudication. One by one Ladd assessed the significance of the regnant approaches; textual criticism, linguistic criticism, literary criticism, form criticism, etc., were shown to be of constructive value for the evangelical understanding of the Bible as the Word of God.

Ladd was acutely aware, however, that many of his colleagues in the evangelical camp had neglected the reality that the Bible was also given in the words of humans. Thus, he insisted that an evangelical faith "demands a critical methodology in the reconstruction of the historical side of the process of revelation."[13] Attention to this concern could expect to bear good fruit; his contention that an objective approach to the Bible, undergirded by faith's recognition of certain "fundamentals" (i.e., the virgin birth, the Deity of Christ, the reality of His miracles, His vicarious death, His bodily resurrection, His second coming, and the plenary inspiration of the Scriptures),[14] would allow a coherent exposition of biblical theology is evident throughout the corpus of his writings.

As his useful textbook, *A Theology of the New Testament,*[15] demonstrates, Ladd had boldly investigated the various critical methodologies employed in New Testament exegesis and theology. Incisively Ladd saw that the crucial question must be the relationship between claims for biblical revelation and a historical approach to Scripture.[16] Avoiding this question would either render biblical faith a vacuous assertion, unrelated to historical inquiry, or would offer false affirmation of the historian's ability to "prove" the historicity of the foundational events for faith.[17]

Thus, Ladd's engagement of historical-critical approaches to Holy Scripture returned often to the question of the nature of "salvation-history" and the adequacy of the historian's methods (which bracketed out the supernatural) to treat such Christian claims as God's mighty acts of deliverance in the history of Israel and, ultimately, of course, the resurrection of Christ.[18] History cannot be treated as if it can conform to the methodological ideals of natural science, Ladd contended; Bultmann fell into this trap when he viewed history as a closed continuum which disallowed the verification of the action of God within it—or precluded the possibility of God acting within the natural order.[19]

Salvation-History

Ladd was an adherent of the *Heilsgeschichte* approach to Scripture and theology.[20] Like Karl Barth, Oscar Cullman, Reginald Fuller, Dale Moody, Eric Rust, and others, Ladd believed that the unique acts of God do occur in history but that these acts cannot be interpreted according to the naturalistic[21] or positivistic[22] methodologies of Troeltsch or von Ranke. They are revealed to the eyes of faith.

This view delineates two kinds of history, an affirmation some contemporary scholars find intolerable.[23] Proponents of salvation-history maintain a natural history which is accessible to the methods of secular historiography and a sacred history, or *Heilsgeschichte,* which affirms the possibility and reality of the supernatural activity of God in human history. This latter view of history readily affirms that "God has acted in history in ways that transcend ordinary historical experience."[24]

Further, within this rubric, Ladd argues for the historicity of miracle; it "is an event *in history* which has *no historical cause*."[25] Thus he clearly rejects any naturalistic interpretation of history which excludes *a priori* the possibility of resurrection or any other mighty act of God that transcends the historian's purview. Because he believed that the historian could not assess the realm of God's action, he maintained that the burden of coherent argumentation should be borne by the believer.[26]

"God's power is not limited by the world which is his creation . . ." Ladd boldly asserts.[27] Rather, God repeatedly discloses divine power in the natural order of things; this should not be interpreted as "violating" the laws of nature. Nor should this be regarded as "non-historical." Ladd describes his vision of the interpenetration of history and theology succinctly: "The supernatural, when it impinges upon the natural, becomes historical."[28] Only one who has experienced the gracious power of God can speak in an informed manner about the possibility of the confluence of the supernatural (i.e., transcendent action of God, within the realm of human concourse).

Eschatology as the Unifying Center of New Testament Theology

One of Ladd's most constructive contributions to the field of biblical theology was his attention to the eschatological fulcrum of the New Testament.[29] He was convinced that a fundamental unity[30] undergirded the writings of the New Testament. He insisted that the apocalyptic doctrine of the two ages, a tension unrelaxed by Jesus in His proclamation of the nearness yet future consummation of the reign of God, is the foundation for the theology of the entire New Testatment.[31] With his sustained reflection on the eschatological focus of the preaching and ministry of Jesus, Ladd presaged, in many respects, what was to become a burning issue in contemporary systematic theology.[32]

Ladd examined the varied perspectives on the pronouncement of the impending rule of God; he wrote with acute cognizance of the bifurcation in New Testament scholarship over the difference between "inaugurated" or "realized" eschatology.[33] It was his conviction that eschatology provides the basic unifying structure of New Testament theology in the following manner:

> a) the apocalyptic structure of two aeons is basic for the theology of the Synoptics, of Paul, and also of John; b) there is a contemporizing of eschatology in all three strata of New Testament theology; and, c) this contemporizing of eschatology in each case is to be understood as an anticipation, genuine though partial, of the future eschatological consummation.[34]

Ladd shares the view that the context of Jesus' preaching was the apocalyptic expectation of Jewish thought.[35] The unique element in Jesus' preaching about the kingdom, in contrast with Jewish apocalyptic, is his accentuation of the "mystery" of the kingdom. According to Ladd, the "mystery is a *further* disclosure of God's purpose: the Kingdom which is to come finally in apocalyptic splendour has in fact entered the world in advance in a hidden form to work secretly among and within men."[36] It is a partially present, dynamic reality. Ladd does not neglect the future consummation of the kingdom in his program of biblical eschatology. His understanding of the Scriptures places him in the category of "historical premillennialists."[37] With logical consistency and attention to detail in exegesis, he contends against those who believe the church's hope is in a "pretribulation rapture" (an inference drawn in nineteenth-century evangelical scholarship) rather than in the second coming of Jesus.[38] The "Blessed Hope is not deliverance from the Tribulation; it is union with the Lord at His coming."[39] The *Parousia* of Christ will be the realization of the salvation offered by God to sinful humanity. It is "an absolutely indispensable doctrine in the Biblical teaching of redemption."[40] Ladd feared the trend in modern scholarship of sacrificing the visible, bodily return of Christ; otherwise, he contends, salvation remains a purely private truth, unrelated to the salvation and judgment of society and the world as a whole. That "God's will be done on earth" demands Christ's glorious return to bring completion to God's work.[41]

The Relationship of the Kingdom and the Church

Ladd is fully aware of the difficulties engendered when there has been an identification of the kingdom with the church through relaxing the eschatological tension between the "already and not yet." Loisy's famous dictum "Jesus foretold the Kingdom, but it was the church that came,"[42] has put an improper dichotomy between the two, yet equally problematic has been the triumphalistic notion that the church *is* the present rule of God. This has led to skewed perceptions of the relationship of the church to Israel, among other problems. Ladd does not want the church to presume that it has *replaced* Israel, inheriting all the promises made to the nation in God's covenantal election. Thus, he will use the language of the church as the "true Israel" rather than the "new Israel."[43] A believing remnant comprised of Jesus' disciples receives the messianic salvation of God during the earthly ministry of Jesus; He forms an "incipient church" in the twelve gathered around Him.[44]

Ladd traces the relationship of the church and the kingdom at length in *A Theology of the New Testament*. He offers several theses to delineate the relationship between the two: 1) the church is not the kingdom; 2) the kingdom creates the church; 3) the church witnesses to the kingdom; 4) the church is the instrument of the kingdom; and, 5) the church is the custodian of the kingdom.[45] He does affirm that Jesus proclaimed the rule of God (i.e., the kingdom, which is the dynamic expression of God's authority and the realm where it is experienced).[46] The church has a particular role in bearing witness to the kingdom, proclaiming the rule of God. The church cannot establish the rule of God or "build up the kingdom"; that is the sovereign gift of God. The church is privileged to participate already in the present manifestation of God's realm and with the world, awaits its final and full expression.[47] Wisely, Ladd wants to guard against ecclesiastical presumption that arrogates to the institution the prerogatives of God alone.

The Accessibility of the Historical Jesus

Ladd wrote during the time of renewed interest in the recovery of the "historical Jesus." As has been well documented,[48] many of Bultmann's students were dissatisfied with his thoroughgoing skepticism about knowing anything of the life of Jesus. They objected to his claim that the Jesus of history was irrelevant for faith.[49]

Ladd recognized that the Gospels are products of faith; however, this does not "demand the conclusion that the Jesus of history has been lost, or that the Gospels do not present an essentially accurate portrait of Jesus and his message."[50] Of course, one can discern that a process of interpretation has taken place in the writing of these accounts, but one does not have to approach them in a spirit of radical skepticism. Ladd believed in a basic continuity between the Jesus who actually lived in history and the biblical Christ portrayed by the Evangelists.[51]

Once again, Ladd's primary dialogue partner on the matter of faith and history is Rudolf Bultmann. Convinced that few of his critics had understood the nuances and implications of Bultmann's magisterial New Testament contribution, especially the paradoxical role of Jesus,[52] Ladd undertook a clarification of this aspect.

He sharply disagreed with Bultmann over the means of speaking about an act of God. For Bultmann, to speak of an act of God is at the same time an existential statement—it is to reflect on a personal encounter with the Christ through the proclamation of the kerygma. Moreover, it is a statement of faith that does not rest upon external evidence. Ladd would not countenance the subjectivity of this assertion; faith must rely on certain objective events, such as the resurrection, he contended.[53] This event "is more than historical; it is an event within history, yet one which transcends history."[54]

It is at this point that Ladd pressed Bultmann most acutely and demonstrated the inconsistency of his position. The logical consequence to Bultmann's concept of faith is not utterly dispensing with the historical Jesus, as many have accused him; rather, he places priority upon the Word of Jesus which brought persons to a crisis of decision. The Word of God finds its beginnings in the historical Jesus, but one can only bear testimony to this in light of having been addressed by God through the kerygma.

Ladd criticizes Bultmann for mitigating the "once for all" nature of Jesus' life and, particularly, of God's act in Him.[55] Yet, Ladd contends that Bultmann's proposal still remains dependent upon some historical grounding because he does not dispense with the historical Jesus for the origination of the kerygma. The importance of the continuing word of proclamation for Bultmann clearly threatens to eclipse the uniqueness of Jesus, in Ladd's opinion.[56]

One is not forced to choose between the historical Jesus attested to in Scripture and the Jesus that meets one in the present proclamation of the gospel, Ladd insists. Such is Bultmann's false dichotomy; a "philosophy of religion which makes an absolute bifurcation between history and faith cannot do justice to the biblical witness."[57] In his willingness to allow a dimension within history which transcends historical control, Ladd basically follows the method of Karl Barth.[58]

Ethics and the Christian Life

Although he gave sustained attention to the issue of eschatology, Ladd did not neglect the centrality of ethical living in the present for the Christian. In a focal chapter on "The Ethics of the Kingdom" in his magnum opus,[59] he stresses Jesus' concern about human conduct.

Jesus' ethical teaching cannot be severed from His proclamation of the kingdom of God, Ladd argues.[60] He criticizes the old liberal interpretation for its attempt to disregard the apocalyptic elements in Jesus' preaching of the kingdom, clinging only to the ethical dimension.[61] Jesus does not offer only "interim ethics" (contra Schweitzer), according to Ladd. Jesus taught, rather, "absolute ethics" which derive from the reign of God.[62] This ethic will only be fully realized in the future; nevertheless, as is clear from the Sermon on the Mount, Jesus expected His disciples to practice His teachings in this present age. Jesus was not giving a new *torah* but intensifying the demand of the Mosaic law to fulfill the inner dimension. Yet, Jesus does not offer this ethical demand as the means of attaining righteousness; it is the practical and public demonstration of one living under the reign of God.[63]

Christian ethics, in the preaching of Jesus, is always related to the kingdom as both gift and goal.[64] The "very goal for which we strive also implies a pattern for ordering our lives";[65] such living is "both attainable and unattainable."[66] The primary description of the ethics of the kingdom is a life-style of righteousness in the present. This righteousness takes the form of self-humbling servanthood; readiness to forgive; indiscriminate love; tangible acts of charity; a radical, unqualified decision for Christ that takes priority over other relationships; and unflagging trust in the goodness of God.[67] One cannot fulfill the demand of the law; the rule of God is a gift of grace that allows one to live in the present in the faithfulness desired by God, in Ladd's understanding. Since one will not fully experience the righteousness of God until the end of the age, one is called to perseverance in the present.

Evaluation

In his constructive approach to biblical theology, Ladd offers a method of treating Scripture which he describes as "Biblical Realism."[68] It is an attempt to understand the Bible from within the minds of its authors rather "than to force the biblical message into modern thought forms."[69] This approach was counterpoint to many writing in the same epoch.[70] His methodology, relentlessly followed and articulately offered, produced substantive contributions to the discipline of New Testament theology. Ladd's writings were more than gauntlets to be defended in the academy, but a "source of faith and practice," in the testimony of a former student.[71]

Ladd believed that the primary task of the New Testament theologian was historical and descriptive. First, one must understand what the New Testament meant in the first-century context; second, only then can one use consistent heremeneutical principles in an interpretative effort to bring this message to contemporary understanding. The Bible can speak to all ages, Ladd averred; interpretation is dependent upon discovering what the inspired authors meant.

It is not surprising, given these convictions, that biblical theology claimed Ladd's attention throughout his teaching and writing career. He was little given to philosophical or systematic concerns in theological construction; exegesis and exposition formed the heart of his books and lectures. He believed (without equivocation) that demythologization was not necessary to understand the basic message of the New Testament if one did not presuppose that human-centered assessments are the measure of all reality.[72] The Christian believer must be open to "biblical thinking" which makes room for divine activity in the world (i.e., the realm of human history does not preclude the free action of God within it). Modern scientific thinking cannot mandate that Christians be permitted to speak of the redemptive acts of God only in existential terms.[73] Ladd sounds clear Reformation themes in his insistence on the priority of Scripture and the transcendent sovereignty of God.

Although he strove to maintain proper objectivity and balance in his analysis and critique of the writings of others, at times his own passion for a topic mitigated this methodological ideal.[74] Dispassionate scholarship was valued, but not more than zeal for truth mediated through Holy Scripture. This truth was, in Ladd's opinion, both timeless and historical; certainly it was accessible.

Ladd wrote during the decades when the theological specialization of biblical theology was not given to the degree of self-doubt that it is today. He believed that New Testament theology has the task of "formulating expressions of the living religious experiences of early Christianity understood in the light of the religious environment."[75] Rightly appropriating the tools of the historical-critical method and rightly dividing the word of truth go together, Ladd believed. In many respects, his life's work was that of interpretation. To his more conservative evangelical colleagues, he pointed the way forward in the critical study of biblical texts. To those whose confidence in the newest critical tools threatened to distort the revelation of God's salvific history with humanity, he reminded them that the Bible remains the Word of God.

The sphere of his influence has been remarkable. In a survey of evangelical biblical scholars, Ladd was ranked as "most influential" by scholars in the progressive evangelical organization Institute for Biblical Research and was second behind John Calvin as "most influential" among scholars in the Evangelical Theological Society.[76] His offering to God of scholarship, teaching, and ecclesiastical service was a worthy one, indeed. By God's grace, his legacy continues to shape those who long to read the Bible with greater understanding.

Bibliography

Books

The Blessed Hope. Grand Rapids, Mich.: Eerdmans, 1968.

A Commentary on the Revelation of John. Grand Rapids, Mich.: Eerdmans, 1972.

Crucial Questions About the Kingdom of God. Grand Rapids, Mich.: Eerdmans, 1952.

The Gospel of the Kingdom: Scriptural Studies in the Kingdom of God. Grand Rapids, Mich.: Eerdmans, 1959.

I Believe in the Resurrection of Jesus. Grand Rapids, Mich.: Eerdmans, 1975.

Jesus and the Kingdom: The Eschatology of Biblical Realism. New York: Harper and Row, 1964.

Jesus Christ and History. Chicago: Inter-Varsity Press, 1963.

The New Testament and Criticism. Grand Rapids, Mich.: Eerdmans, 1967.

The Pattern of New Testament Truth. Grand Rapids, Mich.: Eerdmans, 1968.

The Presence of the Future: The Eschatology of Biblical Realism. Grand Rapids, Mich.: Eerdmans, 1974.

Rudolf Bultmann. Chicago: Inter-Varsity Press, 1964.

A Theology of the New Testament. Grand Rapids, Mich.: Eerdmans, 1974.

The Young Church: Acts of the Apostles. New York: Abingdon Press, 1964.

Festschrift Articles

"Apocalyptic and New Testament Theology." *Reconciliation and Hope*, Robert Banks, ed. Exeter: Paternoster Press, 1974.

The Holy Spirit in Galatians." *Current Issues in Biblical and Patristic Interpretation*, G. F. Hawthorne, ed. Grand Rapids, Mich.: Eerdmans, 1975.

"The Parable of the Sheep and the Goats in Recent Interpretation." *New Dimensions in New Testament Study,.* R. Longenecker, ed. Grand Rapids, Mich.: Zondervan, 1974.

"Paul and the Law." *Soli Deo Gloria,* J. M. Richards, ed. Richmond: John Knox Press, 1968.

"Revelation and Tradition in Paul." *Apostolic History and the Gospel,* Ralph P. Martin and W. W. Gasque, eds. Grand Rapids, Mich.: Eerdmans, 1970.

"Why Did God Inspire the Bible?" *Scripture, Tradition, and Interpretation.* W. S. Lasor and W. W. Gasque, eds. Grand Rapids, Mich.: Eerdmans, 1978.

Articles

"Advent Song." *Anglican Theological Review* 56 (Oct. 1974): 431.

"Biblical Theology, History, and Revelation." *Review and Expositor* 54 (April 1957): 195-204.

"Christology of Acts." *Foundations* 11 (Jan.-Mar. 1968): 27-41.

"Consistent or Realized Eschatology in Matthew?" *Southwestern Journal of Theology* 5 (Oct. 1962): 55-63.

"Eschatology and the Unity of New Testament Theology." *Expository Times* 68 (June 1957): 268-73.

"History and Faith." *Foundations* 7 (Jan. 1964): 5-14.

"History and Theology in Biblical Exegesis." *Interpretation* 20 (Jan. 1966): 54-64.

"Israel and the Church." *Evangelical Quarterly* 36 (Oct.-Dec. 1964): 206-13.

"The Kingdom of God—Reign or Realm?" *Journal of Biblical Literature* 81 (Sept. 1962): 230-38.

"The Knowledge of God: The Saving Acts of God." *Basic Christian Doctrines,* Carl F. H. Henry, ed. Grand Rapids, Mich.: Baker Book House, 1962.

"The Life-Setting of the Parable of the Kingdom." *Journal of Bible and Religion* 31 (July 1963): 193-99.

"More Light on the Synoptics." *Christianity Today,* March 2, 1959, 12-16.

"Origin of Apocalyptic in Biblical Religion." *Evangelical Quarterly* 30 (Apr.-June 1958): 75-85.

"Paul's Friends in Colossians 4:7-16." *Review and Expositor* 70 (Fall 1973): 507-14.

"A Redactional Study of the Gospel of Mark." *Expository Times* 92 (Oct. 1980): 10-13.

"Resurrection and History." *Dialog* 1 (Autumn 1962): 55-56.

"Revelation and Jewish Apocalyptic." *Evangelical Quarterly* 29 (April-June 1957): 94-100.

"Revelation, History, and the Bible." *Christianity Today,* July 8, 1957, 5-8.

"The Revelation of Christ's Glory." *Christianity Today,* Sept. 1, 1958, 13-14.

"Revelation 20 and the Millennium." *Review and Expositor* 57 (April 1960): 167-75.

"Righteousness in Romans." *Southwestern Journal of Theology* 19 (Fall 1976): 6-17.

"The Role of Jesus in Bultmann's Theology." *Scottish Journal of Theology* 18 (March 1965): 57-68.

"RSV Reappraisal: New Testament." *Christianity Today,* July 8, 1957, 7-10.

"The Saving Acts of God." *Christianity Today,* Jan. 30, 1961, 18-19.

"The Search for Perspective." *Interpretation* 25 (Jan. 1971): 41-62.

"Unity and Variety in New Testament Faith." *Christianity Today,* Nov. 19, 1965, 21-24.

"Why Not Prophetic-Apocalyptic?" *Journal of Biblical Literature* 76 (Sept. 1957): 192-200.

Notes

1. See the bibliographical sketch by David Allen Hubbard, *Unity and Diversity in New Testament Theology: Essays in Honor of George Ladd,* ed. Robert A. Guelich (Grand Rapids, Mich.: Eerdmans, 1978), xi *ff*. While most of Ladd's books were meant for the scholarly community, others found a wide readership among nonspecialists as well. Included in this category are *Jesus Christ and History* (Chicago: Inter-Varsity Press, 1963); *The Young Church: Acts of the Apostles* (New York: Abingdon Press, 1964); *A Commentary on the Revelation of John* (Grand Rapids, Mich.: Eerdmans, 1972); and *I believe in the Resurrection of Jesus* (Grand Rapids, Mich.: Eerdmans, 1975).

2. Hubbard, *Unity and Diversity,* xiii.

3. See George Marsden's assessment of Fuller Seminary's character and unique contribution to evangelical thought in *Reforming Fundamentalism: Fuller Seminary and The New Evangelicalism* (Grand Rapids, Mich.: Eerdmans, 1987). A collection edited by Marsden, *Evangelicalism and Modern America* (Grand Rapids, Mich.: Eerdmans, 1984), is also helpful in gaining cultural and historical perspective on the evangelical movement in the twentieth century.

4. Hubbard, *Unity and Diversity,* xiii. George Marsden recounts (with humor) Ladd's attempt to "introduce New England culture" into the rather casual ethos of the student body of Fuller Seminary in the 1950s. (See Marsden, *Reforming Fundamentalism,* 128.)

5. See the list of contributors to *University and Diversity in New Testament Theology* as well as the *Festschriften* to which he was asked to contribute. He was not always well received beyond evangelical circles, however. Readers of Ladd are aware of the patronizing treatment he received at the hands of Norman Perrin in his review of Ladd's *Jesus and the Kingdom: The Eschatology of Biblical Realism* (New York: Harper & Row, 1964) in *Interpretation* 19 (April 1965): 228-31.

6. See the newsletter published for the Fuller Theological Seminary Alumni, *Theology, News, and Notes* 30:2 (June 1983), for the tribute by Robert P. Meye, dean of Fuller's School of Theology, and for the reflection of four of Ladd's students upon central themes in his scholarship. Not only did he inspire high standards among his students, he clearly "valued piety and lent a strong voice to the pervasive Fuller emphasis on missions," according to George Marsden in *Reforming Fundamentalism,* 120.

7. See Brevard Childs' *Biblical Theology in Crisis* (Philadelphia: Westminster Press, 1970). Compare the helpful analysis of Henning Graf Reventlow, *Problems of Biblical Theology in the Twentieth Century* (Philadelphia: Fortress, 1986).

8. George Eldon Ladd, "Why Did God Inspire the Bible?" in *Scripture, Tradition, and Interpretation*, eds. W. S. Lasor and W. W. Gasque (Grand Rapids, Mich.: Eerdmans, 1978), 49-59, is an example of his apologetic task to those to his right.

9. George Eldon Ladd, *The New Testament and Criticism* (Grand Rapids, Mich.: Eerdmans, 1967) is his *tour de force* for this concern. It would be hard to estimate how many evangelical students have been helped by this incisive work. See Mark A. Noll's analysis of Ladd's brand of "believing criticism" in *Between Faith and Criticism* (San Francisco: Harper and Row, 1986), 163-64, 113-14.

10. George Marsden, *Fundamentalism and American Culture* (New York: Oxford University Press, 1980). This book is particularly helpful in assessing the confluence of issues addressed in this controversy and its ongoing influence in the larger arena of American Protestantism.

11. Among these are Rudolf Bultmann (probably the most frequently cited), Oscar Cullmann, Joachim Jeremias, C. H. Dodd, and G. E. Wright, to name only a few of the more prominent.

12. Ladd, *The New Testament and Criticism*, 12.

13. Ibid., 215.

14. Ibid., 7-8; 216-17.

15. Ladd, *A Theology of the New Testament* (Grand Rapids, Mich.: Eerdmans, 1974). Reginald Fuller, in a modestly favorable review, characterized the book as "a conservative evangelical alternative to Bultmann, . . ." *Anglican Theological Review* 58 (July 1976): 381-84.

16. Ladd, "The Problem of History in Contemporary New Testament Interpretation," *Studia Evangelica* 5 (1968): 88-100.

17. See Ladd's articles "Biblical Theology, History, and Revelation," *Review and Expositor* 54 (April 1957): 195-204; "History and Faith," *Foundations* 7 (January 1964): 5-14; and "History and Theology in Biblical Exegesis," *Interpretation* 20 (January 1966): 54-64.

18. Ladd, *I Believe in the Resurrection of Jesus* (Grand Rapids, Mich.: Eerdmans, 1975), 16 *ff*. In this terse volume, Ladd offers an unflinching critique of many German scholars' use of the historical-critical method which, he asserts, "is not an open-minded inductive study of the evidence." Cf. Willi Marxsen, *The Resurrection of Jesus of Nazareth* (Philadelphia: Fortress, 1970); and Rudolf Bultmann's *Jesus Christ and Mythodology* (New York: Charles Scribner's Sons, 1958), 78.

19. Ladd, *Existence and Faith*, ed. Schubert M. Ogden (New York: Meridian Books, 1960), 291 *ff*. Cf. *Kerygma and Myth*, ed. H. W. Bartsch (London: S.P.C.K., 1953).

20. Gerhard Hasel offers a helpful review of this distinctive approach in his *New Testament Theology: Basic Issues in the Current Debate* (Grand Rapids, Mich.: Eerdmans, 1978), 111-32.

21. In his essay of 1900, "Historical and Dogmatic Method in Theology," Ernst Troeltsch emphasizes three aspects of historical method: "the habit of mind associated with historical criticism; the importance of analogy in the study of history; and the correlation or interaction obtaining among all historical events." This is cited in the introduction to a reprint of Troeltsch's pivotal *The Absoluteness of Christianity* (London: SCM Press, 1971), 8.

22. The famous expression "wie es eigentlich" occurs in the preface, dated October 1824, to von Ranke's *Geschichte der romanischen und germanischen Volker von 1494 bis 1535*. See also Leopold von Ranke, *The Theory and Practice of History*, eds. G. Iggers and K. V. Moltke (Indianapolis: Bobbs-Merrill, 1973), 137.

23. See Wolfhart Pannenberg's *Theology as History*, vol. 3 of New Frontiers in

Theology, eds. James M. Robinson and John B. Cobb, Jr. (New York: Harper and Row, 1967) and *Jesus—God and Man* (Philadelphia: Westminster Press, 1968), 13.

24. Ladd, *A Theology of the New Testament*, 29. Cf. G. Ernest Wright, *God Who Acts* (London: SCM Press, 1952).

25. Ladd, *I Believe in the Resurrection of Jesus*, 21.

26. See the article by Lee McDonald, "Historical-Critical Inquiry and the Resurrection of Jesus," *Theology, News, and Notes* (June 1983): 5-7.

27. George Eldon Ladd, "Biblical Theology, History, and Revelation," *Review and Expositor* 54 (April 1957): 198. The question of the extent of God's self-limitation through God's self-determination to be Creator is a continuing concern in contemporary systematic and biblical theology. See especially Langdon Gilkey, *Reaping the Whirlwind: A Christian Interpretation of History* (New York: Seabury Press, 1976) and David H. Kelsey, "The Bible and Christian Theology," *Journal of the American Academy of Religion* 48 (September 1980): 385-402; and Jurgen Moltmann, *God in Creation: An Ecological Doctrine of Creation* (London: SCM Press, 1985).

28. Ibid., 200.

29. See Ladd's article "Eschatology and the Unity of New Testament Theology," *The Expository Times* 68 (June 1957): 268-73.

30. His proposal differs greatly from James D. G. Dunn's later assessment in *Unity in Diversity in the New Testament: An Inquiry into the Character of Earliest Christianity* (Philadelphia: Westminster Press, 1977).

31. See the evaluation by Victor R. Gordon in his article, "Eschatology as the Structure of New Testament Theology," *Theology, News, and Notes* (June 1983): 12-14. Ladd's primary work detailing his understanding of eschatology is *Jesus and the Kingdom: The Eschatology of Biblical Realism* (New York: Harper and Row, 1964).

32. See Pannenberg's *Jesus—God and Man, The Crucified God* by Jurgen Moltmann (London: SCM Press, 1974); and Edward Schillebeeckx, *Jesus: An Experiment in Christology*, trans. Hubert Hoskins (New York: Seabury Press, 1979).

33. Ladd, "Eschatology and the Unity of New Testament Theology," 268-69.

34. Ibid., 269.

35. Interpreting the proclamation and ministry of Jesus through the lens of the apocalyptic expectation in first century Judaism is a signal contribution of the "eschatological theologians," Wolfhart Pannenberg and Jurgen Moltmann. Bultmann, on the other hand, dismisses the eschatological elements in Jesus' preaching as "secondary" in *Das Urchristentum im Rahmen der antiken Religionen* (1949), 242.

36. Ladd, "Eschatology and the Unity of New Testament Theology," 269. See also *A Theology of the New Testament*, 91-104; "Apocalyptic and New Testament Theology," *Reconciliation and Hope*, ed. Robert Banks (Exeter: Paternoster Press, 1974), 285-96; and *The Presence of the Future: The Eschatology of Biblical Realism* (Grand Rapids, Mich.: Eerdmans, 1974).

37. George Eldon Ladd, *Crucial Questions About the Kingdom of God* (Grand Rapids, Mich.: Eerdmans, 1952). Of Ladd's contribution, Dale Moody, *The Word of Truth* (Grand Rapids, Mich.: Eerdmans, 1981), writes: "the most scholarly writings on Historical Premillennialism have come from George E. Ladd . . ." who has ". . . created considerable consternation among those who realized that his challenge to Dispensationalism was solely on the basis of biblical exposition on which Dispensationalism thought it had a monopoly."

38. George Eldon Ladd, *The Blessed Hope* (Grand Rapids, Mich.: Eerdmans, 1956).

39. Ibid., 12. With this assertion, Ladd attacked one of the key points in C. I.

Scofield's notes in the *Scofield Reference Bible*. See Marsden, *Reforming Fundamentalism*, 151.

40. Ibid., 6.

41. Ibid.

42. *The Gospel and the Church* (1902), cited in Hans Kung, *The Church* (Garden City: Image Books, 1976), 69.

43. Ladd, *A Theology of the New Testament*, 108. See also his fine article, "Israel and the Church," *Evangelical Quarterly* 36 (Oct.-Dec. 1964): 206-13. In this article (212-13), Ladd expresses his belief without falling into the excesses of dispensationalism in the future salvation of literal Israel, which will take place on "fundamentally the same terms as the salvation of the Gentiles, viz., through saving faith in Jesus Christ as her crucified Messiah."

44. Ibid., 108-11.

45. Ibid., 111-19.

46. Ibid., 111. Cf. Ladd's article, "The Kingdom of God—Reign or Realm," *Journal of Biblical Literature* 81 (Sept. 1962): 230-38.

47. George Eldon Ladd, *Jesus and the Kingdom: The Eschatology of Biblical Realism* (New York: Harper and Row, 1964), 258 *ff.*

48. W. G. Doty, *Contemporary New Testament Interpretation* (Englewood Cliffs, N.J.: Prentice-Hall, Inc., 1972); Ernst Kasemann, *Essays on New Testament Themes* (London: SCM Press, 1964); and J. M. Robinson, *A New Quest of the Historical Jesus* (London: SCM Press, 1959).

49. Rudolf Bultmann, *Theology of the New Testament* (New York: Charles Scribner's Sons, 1951), 3.

50. Ladd, *Jesus and the Kingdom*, xii.

51. Ladd, *A Theology of the New Testament*, 19 *ff.*

52. George Eldon Ladd, "The Role of Jesus in Bultmann's Theology," *Scottish Journal of Theology* 18 (March 1965): 57-68.

53. George Eldon Ladd, "The Resurrection and History," *Dialog* 1 (Autumn 1962): 55-56.

54. Ibid.

55. Ladd, "The Role of Jesus in Bultmann's Theology," 62.

56. Ibid., 65.

57. Ladd, "The Resurrection and History," 57.

58. See the response of Rudolf Bultmann to Barth's position in *Philosophical Essays* (London: SCM Press, 1955), 260 *f.* Cf. Richard R. Niebuhr's *Resurrection and Historical Reason* (New York: Scribner's, 1957). For Ladd to confess his affinity for Barth's approach to history was a radical position in 1962 in the context of Fuller Seminary. (I am indebted to R. Albert Mohler, Jr., for this keen insight.)

59. Ladd, *A Theology of the New Testament*, 120-34.

60. George Eldon Ladd, *The Gospel of the Kingdom: Scriptural Studies in the Kingdom of God* (Grand Rapids, Mich.: Eerdmans, 1959).

61. A contemporary example of this approach, in Ladd's opinion, can be found in C. H. Dodd. See the following writings: "The Ethical Teaching of Jesus," *A Companion to the Bible*, ed. T. W. Manson (Edinburgh: T & T Clark, 1946), 378-81; and *History and the Gospel* (London: Nisbet and Co. Inc., 1938).

62. Ladd, *A Theology of the New Testament*, 128. Cf. his book, published in the same year, *The Presence of the Future: The Eschatology of Biblical Realism* (Grand Rapids, Mich.: Eerdmans, 1974).

63. Ibid.

64. Richard B. Gardner, "Matthew and the Kingdom," *Theology, News and Notes* (June 1983): 17.

65. Ibid.

66. Ladd, *A Theology of the New Testament*, 131.

67. Ibid., 131 *ff.*

68. Ladd, *Jesus and the Kingdom*, xiii.

69. Ibid.

70. See especially the analyses of contemporary trends and problems in biblical theology offered by Ernst Kasemann, "The Problem of a New Testament Theology," *New Testament Studies* 19 (1972-73) and Peter Stuhlmacher, *Historical Criticism and Theological Interpretation of Scripture* (Philadelphia: Fortress, 1977).

71. Robert A. Guelich, "On Becoming a Minister of the Word," *Theology, News, and Notes* (June 1983): 8.

72. George Eldon Ladd, *Jesus Christ and History* (Chicago: Inter-Varsity Press, 1963), 17. James M. Robinson holds to an oppositive view in *Kerygma und historicher Jesus* (Zurich: Zwingli, 1960); he believes that the possibility of miracles must be excluded from positivistic historiography because the consistency of the method demands it (14).

73. Ladd criticizes Bultmann's program of "demythologizing" the biblical materials at length in most of his writings. See Rudolf Bultmann, *The Presence of Eternity* (New York: Harper and Bros., 1957), for a succinct exposition of the Marburg scholar's attitude toward history.

74. See Norman Perrin's critique of Ladd's use of biblical criticism cited in Marsden's *Reforming Fundamentalism*, 249.

75. Ladd, *A Theology of the New Testament*, 17.

76. See Mark A. Noll, "Survey of Evangelical Biblical Scholars," appendix in *Between Faith and Criticism: Evangelicals, Scholarships, and the Bible in America* (San Francisco: Harper and Row, 1986), 209-14.

26

Frank Stagg
Robert Sloan

Biography

Frank Stagg was born on his grandfather's rice farm on October 20, 1911, in Acadia Parish, a few miles east of Eunice in southwest Louisiana.[1] Stagg's grandfather, Etienne Stagg, had been reared as a Roman Catholic, but when he and his brother, Adolphe, began reading the Bible, they became convinced Baptists. Adolphe (Frank Stagg's great-uncle) is still remembered by Louisiana Baptists as one of the earliest French preachers of the gospel among the Cajuns of southern Louisiana. The Adolphe Stagg Association in southern Louisiana is not only a memorial to the work of Adolphe Stagg, but an indication of the devout Baptist heritage to which Frank Stagg fell heir.

Stagg's father, Paul, was a Baptist deacon and Sunday School teacher who, though he lived and died as a rice farmer (except for a few years teaching in a one-room schoolhouse), had an educational background in Latin and mathematics. From his father Frank Stagg not only gained a devotional appreciation for the Bible, but also learned to be unafraid of the questioning process. At the age of eleven Frank received Christian baptism and some eight years later experienced a traumatic but decisive call to preach, a decision which he made public in the First Baptist Church at Eunice in 1930, about a year after graduation from high school.

Stagg then entered Louisiana College where his leadership abilities both on and off campus were often recognized. He was not only an outstanding student academically but was deeply involved in various college organizations. He was editor of the *Wildcat,* the college weekly; president of the Athenean Literary Society; and president of the Baptist Student Union of Louisiana in 1933-34. The year before graduation from Louisiana College, Stagg became the quarter-time pastor of the church at Dodson, and on September 10, 1933, he was ordained to the gospel ministry. Upon graduation from Louisiana College in 1934 Stagg gave an additional Sunday to the church in Dodson and also began to serve in two other part-time churches.

On August 19, 1935, Stagg married Evelyn Owen, a brilliant young woman whom he had met during his junior year at Louisiana College. Evelyn Owen Stagg would prove to be in the years ahead not only a devoted wife and mother to their two sons and one daughter, but also a significant participant in Frank Stagg's academic career, a role that came substantially to the foreground in the Staggs' collaboration on and coauthorship of the 1978 publication *Woman in the World of Jesus*. Evelyn Stagg's contribution to

Frank Stagg (1911-   )

Frank Stagg's academic career was grounded in the Owen family (her three brothers, for example, all served as university professors), and personally nurtured in her own academic pursuits as a student at The Southern Baptist Theological Seminary where she was enrolled in the WMU Training School, having a curriculum identical to that of her husband with the exception of Hebrew and preaching. Stagg graduated from Southern Seminary with the Th.M. in 1938 and the Ph.D. in 1943.

After serving the Highland Baptist Mission in Louisville during his seminary days, Stagg became pastor of the First Baptist Church in DeRidder, Louisiana, in 1940. While this was the only full-time pastorate in Stagg's years of ministry, throughout his academic career he struggled with the kinds of pastoral/ethical questions that he wrestled with during his years of pastoral ministry. Making the Bible and Christian theology relevant for the Christian life was and always has been primary to Stagg. During his pastorate in DeRidder, Stagg showed the kind of conscience, regarding issues of race and war, that would later develop more fully. Stagg's antipathy to racism became strikingly evident in the 1950s with the publication of his commentary on Acts; and with the advent of the Vietnam War in the 1960s, his views on the church, violence, and what he perceived to be the military-industrial complex would further develop.

While Stagg was at DeRidder, a seminary friend, Duke McCall, became president of the Baptist Bible Institute, which was later to become New Orleans Baptist Theological Seminary. McCall urged Stagg to come to New Orleans and fill the post of New Testament professor which, after some hesitation, he did beginning January 1, 1945. For nearly twenty years Stagg taught New Testament in New Orleans. Those years were not without struggle. His 1955 publication, *The Book of Acts: The Early Struggle for an Unhindered Gospel,* was clearly written with patterns of racial injustice in mind. The social pressure exerted upon those who in the 1950s and 1960s attempted to articulate both the dignity of all persons as creatures made in the image of God and the oneness of all Christians in Jesus Christ may be only a memory to the current generation, but it was very palpable to those brave souls like Frank Stagg who endured the pain and slander of epithets born of hatred and bigotry.

In 1964, while New Orleans Baptist Theological Seminary was still in the throes of controversy and a declining faculty morale, Frank Stagg received an invitation to join the faculty of The Southern Baptist Theological Seminary in Louisville, Kentucky. Apart from the negative factors abiding in the New Orleans situation, there was also the very positive pull to return to Southern and rejoin a college friend and New Orleans colleague, Penrose St. Amant, who was the dean of the School of Theology. McCall, who, as president of the Baptist Bible Institute, had originally brought Stagg to New Orleans, was now the president of Southern. Southern, too, had gone through a time of crisis involving the loss of a number of faculty members, and the addition of Stagg was part of the rebuilding process.

Stagg went to Southern as the James Buchanan Harrison Professor of New

Testament Interpretation, and until his retirement in 1981, his service as a teacher, preacher, and writer to the Christian world and the Southern Baptist Convention in particular proved nothing short of remarkable. In fact, considering the demands placed upon Baptist professors of religion in terms of classroom hours assigned and the number of students taught, Stagg's academic and professional feats appear herculean by today's standards. In addition to the normal work load of a seminary curriculum, Stagg served on the graduate faculty of Southern Seminary. Furthermore, his literary production, outspoken views, and academic excellence made him much in demand as a conference speaker and preacher. Stagg edited the *Review and Expositor* from 1965 through 1971 and from 1973 to 1975. With all these activities, Frank Stagg found still other ways to serve the denomination he loved. Not only did he produce an almost unceasing flow of curriculum materials for denominational publications, but he also worked as a consulting editor for *The Broadman Bible Commentary* and authored volumes on Matthew and Philippians. In 1976 Stagg became senior professor of New Testament Interpretation. After his retirement he and Mrs. Stagg moved to Bay St. Louis, Mississippi, where, at this writing, he continues to enjoy an active role in Southern Baptist church and denominational life.

As a teacher Stagg was greatly admired by his students. He was not known as a stimulating lecturer in terms of oratorical and/or charismatic style, but, for the attentive student, Stagg was always profoundly engaging with respect to course content. His students continue to bear witness to Stagg's academic determination and drive. He never ceased growing and learning. He threw himself wholeheartedly into every new area of research into which his love of the New Testament carried him.

Stagg exerted an enormous influence on Southern Baptist churches throughout the middle part of the twentieth century. Indeed, some would argue that Frank Stagg has been the premier New Testament scholar among Southern Baptists for the middle third of the twentieth century. Certainly the reading, learning, and academic expertise reflected in Stagg's writings serve as strong evidence to that claim. Though Stagg has certainly never been without his theological opponents, almost none would dispute that in Stagg one finds an unusual combination of Christian devotion and academic excellence.

Exposition

Historian-Grammarian-Exegete

Frank Stagg is never better as a scholar than when he is drawing together and summarizing historical, grammatical, or biblical materials. His *New Testament Theology,*[2] for example, is replete with the kind of historical and biblical summary that is most serviceable for the student and minister. In his chapter on the "Plight of Man as Sinner," Stagg summarizes some dozen New Testament terms for sin. In his chapter on "Baptism: Origin and Meaning," he summarizes the antecedents of and parallels to Christian baptism with respect to both Jewish proselyte baptism and the baptism of John, then surveys the various New Testament traditions regarding the practice and meaning of baptism. Examples of this sort could easily be multiplied.[3] Another illustration of Stagg's ability to summarize large blocks of material is in his 1962 article on "The Christology of Matthew." There Stagg offers helpful insight into the structure of Matthew and gives an excellent introductory summary on the importance and functional nature of New Testament Christology. Stagg's gift for summarization is evident in his discussion of the major Christological titles in Matthew such as Son of David, Son of God, Christ, Son of man, and Suffering Servant.[4]

In Stagg's 1966 article, "The Gospel and Biblical Usage," there is further evidence of his ability to draw together various biblical traditions under one theme. First, he presents a brief but fascinating history of the English term "gospel" and then gives a similar survey of the Greek noun *euangelion*. The term is traced through Acts, Mark, Luke, Paul, and Revelation. As is customary, Stagg summarizes the salient points derived from the historical survey and applies the historical and biblical material to Christian living.[5]

"The Holy Spirit in the New Testament," another 1966 article, is a marvelous survey of the function of the Spirit in the gospels and/or the ministry of Jesus. Utilizing the Book of Acts, Stagg synthesizes extensive amounts of material regarding the gifts of the Spirit, conditions for receiving the Holy Spirit, the Holy Spirit in baptism, the Holy Spirit in glossolalia, the work of the Holy Spirit, and the fruit of the Spirit. Not only has Stagg brought together great amounts of material under various topical headings, but he has assimilated the material according to issues that were particularly relevant for church life in the 1960s. The "charismatic movement" that spread across churches in America brought many instances of division and discord because of the unbiblical practices associated with the movement. Stagg, as always, sought to speak to the needs of the hour.[6]

Stagg shows himself familiar with currents in Lukan scholarship and yet retains readability in his 1967 article, "The Journey Toward Jerusalem in Luke's Gospel." This work is an excellent summary of Luke's so-called "Travel Narrative" (9:51 to 19:27). While providing a fine exposition of this entire midsection of the Gospel of Luke, Stagg does so in a way that is not only readable but also avoids superficiality.[7]

Providing an excellent survey of the various Lord's Supper traditions in the New Testament, Stagg published in 1969 "The Lord's Supper in the New Testament." He shows an uncanny ability, once again, to reflect contemporary scholarship and yet do so in a way that is enormously relevant to the life of the church. Questions related to "open" and "closed" communion have frequently been at issue for Baptists, and Stagg's survey of the biblical traditions with regard to the Lord's Supper does not fail to address such matters. Having taken the reader through the communion traditions in the Pauline literature, Stagg analyzes the relatively similar Markan and Matthean traditions and closes with a brief summary of the tradition in Luke. It must also be noted, however, that Stagg's popular relevance to issues in Baptist life and his capacity for summarization did not render him incapable of advocacy. Stagg is critical of those who (all too commonly in Baptist life) have reduced the meaning of the Supper to "remembrance" alone and have forgotten its other significant dimensions (i.e., covenant, sacrifice, hope, and fellowship). Stagg's writings reflect a recurring focus upon the centrality of *koinonia*/fellowship in Christian experience, and therefore, it is not surprising that Stagg spends the greater portion of the article dealing with the divisive forces in Corinth which—in the context of a fellowship meal—were actually destroying the unity of the church.[8]

Virtually all of Frank Stagg's academic output has been published by church-related organs, especially those of the Southern Baptist Convention. The great exception to this is his 1972 article, "The Abused Aorist," which appeared in the *Journal of Biblical Literature,* the professional quarterly of the Society of Biblical Literature. Though Stagg is best known by Southern Baptists for his publications in the *Review and Expositor* and/or through Broadman Press, this brief article on the nature of the aorist tense won Stagg his greatest acclaim in the professional guild of New Testament scholarship. The article is a superb treatment of the function of the aorist tense in New Testament Greek. With humor, incisive analysis, and abundant ancient and contemporary illustration, Stagg burst one of the great myths of modern-day scholarship, commentary, and preaching. The "decisive," "once for all," and/or "punctiliar" nature of the aorist, so often celebrated in sermon and commentary, is little more than scholarly or sermonic nonsense if, according to Stagg, one is arguing that it is the aorist tense *per se* that proves the nature of the action behind it.[9]

Stagg's gift for historical and exegetical summary is also clearly evident in his 1973 publication, *The Holy Spirit Today.* Though Stagg's Trinitarian views and his treatment of the role of demon exorcisms in the Gospels may not find agreement with all, Stagg's summary of New Testament material regarding the work of the Holy Spirit is not only still exegetically and historically rich, but extremely relevant in a day of widespread concern over the doctrine of the Spirit. Once again, one may see reflected Stagg's insistence that the fruit of theology be borne out in terms of its relevance for Christian living.[10]

Ralph Herring, Frank Stagg, and others published in 1974 an excellent work, *How to Understand the Bible.* The book is a surprising gold mine of information about the history and interpretation of the Bible. Stagg's gifts as a historian and a popularizer (I do not use the latter term pejoratively) are everywhere in evidence.

New Testament Theologian

No one's theology can be summarized in a few simple propositions, but it is fair to say that there are some leading concerns reflected in the writings of Frank Stagg. In all, it must be maintained that Stagg is, first and foremost, an exegetical theologian. However one may agree or disagree with his theology, it must be said that his is an attempt to derive a theology from Scripture.

Man as both free and responsible.—Stagg's *Polarities of Man's Exis-*

tence in Biblical Perspective is a book that was a long time in the making but, in many respects, represents the book that Stagg most wanted to write. As he states in the foreword, the book "is not intended to be a comprehensive review of biblical material on man. Rather, . . . it is concerned primarily with man in certain polar situations, where he is claimed from two sides at once and where he finds his authenic existence in the resulting tension."[11] Stagg's view is that man is neither God nor brute. On the one hand, he is made in the image of God and thus is more than other creatures, and yet, on the other hand, he is not God. Stagg believes that we live "in certain tensions, finding [our] being between what appear to be opposite claims made upon us." For Stagg, man is both complex yet holistic, aspective yet not partitive, individual yet part of a community. Man is both being and in need of becoming. He is both free and bound, both subject and object, a sinner and a saint, called both to deny and yet affirm self, and ultimately "called to a salvation that is absolutely free yet costing everything, as pure gift yet absolute demand.[12]

Stagg does not interpret man in terms of apocalyptic dualism or cosmological oppressors, and certainly not in terms of an inherited Adamic sin. Rather, being a creature made in the image of God, man is part of a universe that, in the nature of the case, involves certain polarities—a kind of existential dialectic—whereby man, living by faith in the tension of these polarities, discovers his authentic self. For Stagg, because man is created free, he is capable both of good and evil; but more than "capable" of evil, man is, even before the "Fall," inclined toward evil. Since man is created inclined toward sin, the Fall is the result and not the cause of this inclination.[13]

Stagg's doctrine of man is deliberately and even polemically articulated in contradistinction to what he would call "Augustinian" presuppositions. In his assertion of the freedom of man, Stagg tends to downplay any theological notions which seem to detract from man's freedom and/or its polarity, his responsibility. Views of man as somehow a participant in Adam's sin are expressly denied by Stagg. In his article, "Adam, Christ, and Us," Stagg's obvious goal is to minimize the role of Adam for biblical theology. He points out the relative infrequency of the appearance of Adam's name in the Bible and gives a lengthy treatment of Romans 5:12, the text which, being commonly misunderstood according to Stagg, forms the basis of the Augustinian theory that mankind has participated in Adam's sin. According to Stagg:

> . . . the Augustinian theory of inherited sin opens the way to a transactional view of atonement, by which we got lost and then got saved without having one thing to do with either, except in a passive and involuntary sense. This is to reduce theology to nonsense, and it is more imposed upon than derived from the Scriptures. This is Augustinian logic, not biblical theology.[14]

Stagg argues that the key phrase in Romans 5:12 is not, as the Vulgate reads, "in whom all sinned," but "because all sinned." Instead of referring mankind's sin to his participation in Adam, Stagg insists that sin involves the free and voluntary response of every individual.

Stagg's insistence upon man's freedom and individual responsibility is reflected throughout his writings.[15] Not only is sin not to be regarded as a result of mankind's participation in Adam, but neither does Stagg accord any particularly significant role to Satan and/or cosmic oppressors of evil, these being theological notions which detract from human responsibility. James 1:13-15 and Romans 1:18 to 3:20 are his primary scriptural models for understanding the nature of sin, wrath, and human responsibility.[16] Stagg interprets these passages as having no reference to Adam, Satan, or apocalyptic/cosmic powers. The blame for sin lies entirely within man and is a result of his misuse of freedom. For Stagg the gift of authentic freedom in creation involved not only the potential for both good and evil, but also an "inclination" toward evil, an inclination whose origin the Bible does not explain, but rather assumes by referring to its "activation."[17]

Salvation as authentic human existence based upon repentance and faith.—Stagg's anthropology is consistent with his soteriology. Since sin is an individual problem, not based upon either cosmic oppressors or participation in a fallen order, salvation itself, for Stagg, is not to be seen as a result of a historical event or a "transactional" atonement.[18] Rather, salvation is to be grounded in God, based upon repentance and trust in the God who has revealed Himself through Jesus Christ. Reflecting the character of God, who has always been willing to forgive, the work of Christ is thus primarily revelatory. Salvation does not finally depend upon some subsequent event in salvation history (like the cross or resurrection). Rather, the cross is the culmination and epitome of God's own vulnerability and self-denial as revealed in the person of Jesus Christ.[19] Thus, for Stagg, salvation is discovered in self-denial, not self-assertion. When man denies himself, he becomes authentically human. Using a psalm of contrition to illustrate his doctrine of salvation, Stagg writes:

> . . . it is false to subsume all Scripture under some scheme of *Heilsgeschichte*. This is obvious for the Psalms and wisdom literature but not less true for much else in Scripture which simply reflects the existence of man in the immediate presence of God, whether in despair or hope, in fear or faith, in guilt or forgiveness, in rebellion or worship. Psalm 51, for example, is not to be fitted into any transactional "plan of salvation." It is the anguish and faith of a man who believed himself to be addressed directly, and who addressed God directly, with the joy of salvation hanging in the balances, then and there. Salvation as a possibility then and there is grounded on the one side solely in God, with no contingency upon some subsequent transaction in salvation history, and on the other side in the sinner's contrition and openness of faith. It is that direct and simple.[20]

Then, in the following paragraph of the same article, Stagg writes concerning the theology of Jesus and comes to similar conclusions:

> When we turn to the Gospels we find Jesus portrayed as bringing God to men and men to God, then and there. God is seen as making Himself knowable to man, and man is called into God's presence and to decision in which he sees his existence as it is and is moved by the presence of God to his existence as it might be. This is salvation. To be saved is to become an authentic human

being. It is not to become an angel as in popular thought or divine as with some Gnostics. It is not to become a fraction, either in Gnostic reduction to a bodiless soul nor in secular reduction to a mere animal. It is for the whole man to be made whole (John 7:23) in his total ecological existence in the community of God and man and the world about him.[21]

For Stagg, salvation, like sin, is a matter of human decision. The individually responsible sinner may turn to God in faith and repentance and thus experience salvation, thereby becoming authentically human.

Christ the revealer.—Stagg's doctrine of salvation is, in turn, of a piece with his Christology. Opposed to any schema of salvation history which makes salvation dependent upon historical events, thereby robbing salvation of its immediacy and its foundation in God alone, Stagg illustrates his doctrine of salvation primarily by appeal to the theology of Jesus. It may be noted that Stagg finds little support for these views in the writings of Paul and thus makes virtually no attempt to ground his soteriology and/or Christology in Paul, except for his views of sin and human responsibility read primarily out of Romans 1:18 to 3:20 (i.e., read so as to minimize the role of Satan and/or other forces outside man's own will).[22]

For Christology, Stagg boldly turns to the Synoptic Gospels, which, though written after Paul, nonetheless reflect what he calls an authentic memory of the theology of Jesus. Stagg's appeal to the "Jesus material" is largely an appeal to selected scenes within the synoptic traditions, but not primarily to the passion and resurrection narratives. For Stagg, certain Synoptic episodes in the life of Jesus clearly illustrate the immediacy of salvation as a gift of God to all those who come to him in repentance and faith.

Stagg's February 2, 1971, faculty address given in alumni chapel at The Southern Baptist Theological Seminary, later printed in the *Review and Expositor* clearly sets forth his views; and his 1981 article, "Reassessing the Gospels," is a more detailed attempt to explicate the same basic thesis. Chronologically, the Synoptic Gospels obviously follow the Pauline Letters, but Stagg believes that Paul represents something of a departure from the theology of Jesus as reflected in the Gospels, particularly in certain Synoptic episodes. In fact, Stagg suggests that the memory of Jesus contained in these Gospel episodes is retained *in spite of* the theological development in the early church which, though it shaped the gospel narratives overall, is moving in "another direction than the theology of Jesus as reflected in the episodes themselves.[23]

Stagg's procedure is the exposition of various synoptic scenes beginning with Mark and moving through Matthew and Luke. The basic point made in each of the episodes adduced is that, without appealing to the contingency of salvation as something to be fulfilled by virtue of a subsequent "transactional" event, Jesus offered salvation immediately to those who would trust. The woman with the hemorrhage of Mark 5:25-34 is told, "Daughter, your faith has healed you; go in peace." To blind Bartimaeus in Mark 10:46-52 Jesus said, "Your faith has healed you." In Stagg's words:

There is no reflection in the story of any sense of problem as to "soteriology." The man is "saved" then and there simply in response to his cry for mercy. In the perspective of this story, the only ingredients required for salvation are the Savior and a person willing to submit his need to a willing Savior. This salvation occurred before Golgotha, and it is reported with no attention to the sophistications which came to be a preoccupation of a theologizing church.[24]

In Matthew 25:31-46 salvation

is determined by the criterion of response to such human need as hunger, thirst, alienation, nakedness, sickness, and imprisonment. . . . Nothing is said about salvation history. Nothing is said about the fall of Adam or any compensating "atonement." Nothing is said about sacraments or orthodoxy. Salvation is seen in terms of existence (disposition) and relationships.[25]

Stagg's view of salvation, as grounded in the theology of Jesus, is also well illustrated in his treatment of Luke 19:1-10, the story of Zacchaeus.

Luke's story of Jesus and Zacchaeus stands in sharpest contrast to sophisticated rationales as to how God finds a working plan by which he might save sinners. In the presence of Jesus, a "collector" became a "distributor;" and in this transformation, Jesus saw that salvation had come to Zacchaeus: "This day salvation has come to this house" (v. 9). Jesus did not say "Zacchaeus, I know that you have a problem and I am working on it; and when I have completed salvation history, I will be able to forgive your sins and save your soul." Then and there salvation came, the conversion of a man in the presence of Jesus.[26]

Stagg's understanding of the cross is primarily what would be called an exemplar theory of the atonement. For Stagg, the cross represents the revelation of the divine self-denial which was always at the very heart of God and thus demands that man find authentic existence as God's creature.[27]

Though Stagg rather dislikes the Nicene language of the three persons of the Godhead, he strongly affirms Christ as God incarnate. Christ, as God, is the complete presence and revelation of God, and, especially in His death on the cross, reflects the very character of God. The cross is thus "both a particular event at Golgotha" and something that belongs "eternally to the nature of God."[28] The cross reveals the way in which God has always dealt with man.

The cross is eternal and particular. Its eternality transcends its particularity at Golgotha and its particularly at Golgotha is not robbed of its meaning by its eternality. The cross belongs eternally to the being of God. The cross was in God and in God's action when in making man He gave up some of His freedom and power to man, enabling man to accept or reject, trust or distrust, love or hate. The cross was in God's action when the Word became flesh and lived among us exposed to our understanding or misunderstanding, love or hate. The Cross was in God's action when at Golgotha he spurned all self-defense and gave Himself to the fullest. When God created man free, He made it possible for man to defy Him. When God came in Jesus, He made it possible for man to crucify Him.[29]

Indeed, for Stagg, one could virtually say that the eternality of the cross is of more significance than its historical particularity.

> Jesus Christ was already the slain Lamb before men nailed him to the cross. Redemption is in what he is, not in what was done to Him. Salvation comes from the unchanging being of God, not out of some transaction in history, hence salvation is a possibility whenever man stands open to the presence of God: so for Abraham, the Psalmist, Zacchaeus, Saul of Tarsus, you, and me.[30]

Christian ethicist: the gift brings demand.—Though Frank Stagg was the full-time pastor of only one church, his entire writing and speaking career reflect the concerns of a pastor. The Christian life and the relevance of the Bible and Christian theology for Christian behavior have always been of great importance for him. Indeed, his career can be traced in terms of the great social issues of the times. Stagg was always concerned for the poor. Having grown up in relative poverty and having lived through the Great Depression and two world wars, Stagg never lost the ability to identify with the dispossessed and those who suffer. One need not read far into Stagg's *The Book of Acts: The Early Struggle for an Unhindered Gospel* to realize that racial concerns provided much of the ethical dynamic for that work.[31] One must also note that it was not only racial pride that concerned Stagg, but, in the days following World War II, the sins of national pride also provided impetus for his interpretation of Acts as teaching the universalism of Christianity over against the selfish particularisms of nation and race.[32]

The onset of the Vietnam War also influenced the ethical application of Stagg's theological exegesis. His two lectures at Baylor University on February 22-26, 1975, presented during the Lectures-Workshop on "Civil Religion" as jointly sponsored by the J. M. Dawson Studies in Church and State and the Christian Life Commission of the Baptist General Convention of Texas, declare his opposition to violence in no uncertain terms. As usual, Stagg appeals to the example of Jesus and is convinced thereby that "a part of his radicality was his rejection of violence as a means to revolution."[33]

In that connection, the social and theological conservatism of the church's stance toward American military involvement in Vietnam also raised for Stagg important political/ethical questions about the relationship of church and state. In his Baylor lectures Stagg declared that "civil religion" is "any political structure assuming the dimensions of religion, and it is contended that the church is *practicing* civil religion whenever it yields to the state what belongs alone to God."[34] It is clear for Stagg that the Christian owes allegiance to the governing authorities within their own due parameters, but:

> the claim of God must take priority over every other claim. . . . Man's own personhood is also at stake. One cannot be an authentic human being if he yields ultimate claim to any other human being or human structure. . . . The church must disassociate itself from all ideologies and crusades of the state.[35]

Questions related to the single person also concerned Stagg as evidenced in his 1977 article, "Biblical Perspectives on the Single Person."[36] Stagg's concern for the role of women and the issue of women's ordination found profound expression in the book he coauthored with his wife, Evelyn, entitled *Woman in the World of Jesus*.[37] This latter work is an outstanding collation of Jewish, Greek, and Roman texts on issues related to women in the ancient world. It proceeds by examining the theology and behavior of Jesus—always critical for Stagg—with respect to women and concludes with an analysis of women in the early church. For Stagg, the theology of Paul, with possibly the lone exception of Galatians 3:28, whereby Paul clearly declares, "There is neither Jew nor Greek, slave nor free, male nor female," is something of a step towards the arbitrary and restrictively regressive application of the gospel to women in the family and in the life of the church. By studying the various household codes reflected in the Pauline literature (including also 1 Pet. 2:13 to 3:7), Stagg became convinced that the theology of Paul represents the beginning of a significant departure from the theology and intention of Jesus with respect to the role of women. The subordinationist outlook of the household codes, in the early church, constitute, for Stagg, cultural "skins" that are not essential to the new wine of the gospel and, thus, may be corrected and/or come under review as necessary.[38]

In the early 1980s Stagg addressed the issue of aging and the role of the elderly in society. His book, *The Bible Speaks on Aging,* is a popular, but responsible, attempt to draw together biblical material relevant to the issues of age and/or the aging process.[39]

Living the Christian life was not a matter to be taken lightly. Stagg's writings are peppered with exhortation, a fact which reflects the moral demand that he insists is inextricably linked to the gracious gift of God. When reading Stagg, one repeatedly encounters his objection to any notion of "forensic" righteousness in the New Testament, especially in the Pauline literature. For Stagg, righteousness is never to be a legal fiction nor merely a matter of "perspective," but always a practical and realistic demand imposed upon those who dare to name the name of Jesus.

Evaluation

It must always be remembered that an evaluation says as much about the one doing the evaluating as the one being evaluated. Therefore, I offer the following remarks with no attempt whatsoever to hide my own theological preferences. Moreover, it is with the utmost respect for Stagg's historical, grammatical, and exegetical prowess that I offer the following criticisms, and I offer them in the same spirit of openness and theological rigor which Stagg so graciously and vigorously exemplified. One other proviso: though the lines of intellectual continuity are there in Stagg, what follows by way of evaluation is not as true of the early Stagg, the Stagg of *New Testament Theology,* as it is the later Stagg who wrote "Salvation in Synoptic Tradition," "Reassessing the Gospels," and "The Concept of the Messiah."

I fear that Stagg has ruptured the canon of the New Testament. This rupture is not a literary fissure so much as it is a theological one. It is very clear that Stagg's preference for the theology of Jesus over the theology of Paul finally led him to something of a break with the kerygmatic "cross and resurrection" theology of the apostle and, indeed, the entire New Testament. Stagg's attempt to isolate (i.e., separate) the theology of the historical Jesus from the rest of the New Testament, especially Paul and the overall cross-resurrection context of the Synoptic Gospels themselves, and to prefer that theology to what he would call the "transactional" kind of theology that grounded salvation in historical events, finally destroys the theological unity of the New Testament. Stagg himself has argued that the shape of the New Testament canon is partly a function of theology.[40] But, the theological discontinuity envisioned by Stagg between Jesus and Paul does not allow, it seems to me, for the kind of theological consensus historically required to explain the emergence of the New Testament canon. Though he disclaims any return to the new quest for the historical Jesus, Stagg's attempt to separate various Synoptic episodes from the larger cross-resurrection framework of the Gospel narratives, and from those episodes, so isolated, to extract a doctrine of salvation, has far reaching implications.

To be sure, Stagg rejects Bultmann's radical, and largely negative, historical conclusions regarding the reliability of the Synoptic Gospels as source material for the theology of Jesus. However, no amount of conservative historical handling of the various episodes can compensate for Stagg's ultimate rejection of the cross-resurrection theological consensus of early Christianity. His efforts to represent Pauline theology as a move away from the theology of Jesus, not only in terms of the domestic codes, but especially in his rejection of the cross and resurrection as the necessary culmination of God's objective saving activity through the person of Jesus Christ, can have only disastrous results for theology. Of course, Stagg clearly affirms the historical death of Jesus and His bodily resurrection, but that is not the point under discussion here. Stagg drives a wedge between Jesus and Paul that leaves the door open for the kind of canonical/theological reshuffling characteristic of Koester, Robinson, and Pagels.[41] They argue that the Pauline (and/or cross-resurrection) interpretation of the life of Jesus was only one among numerous competing interpretations of the Holy Man, Jesus. Stagg, of course, clearly affirms the true divinity of Christ and repeatedly maintains that He is the very revelation and presence of God. But the fact still remains that, for Stagg, the Synoptic "memory" of the precross Jesus and/or the theology represented thereby is very different from the kind of cross-resurrection preaching that was characteristic of the apostle Paul and the earliest communities whose theological concerns shaped the Gospel narratives. It is historical audacity indeed to claim, as Stagg does, that one can detect the authentic "Jesus material" in contradistinction to, and virtually in spite of, the overall theological direction of those who preserved the materials themselves. Indeed, Stagg's critically reconstructed theology of Jesus is apparently not only more primitive (earlier) than, but also to be preferred to, the cross-resurrection theology of the very communities in which (unknowingly?) the Jesus traditions were preserved and embedded in the Gospel narratives.

In the first place, it is difficult to understand how Stagg can justify the extrication of his chosen Synoptic episodes from the larger narrative structure of the Gospels in such a way as to shelter the interpretation of those Synoptic episodes from the overarching point of the Synoptic narratives (i.e., the death and resurrection of Jesus for our salvation). Of course, no one will dispute that the salvation already offered to Zacchaeus (Luke) and the woman with the hemorrhage (Mark) reflects Jesus' own gift of salvation to these two Gospel characters upon the basis of their trust. But surely these episodes, and the many others of like nature cited by Stagg, should not be interpreted in discontinuity with the kerygmatic nature of the gospels seen as narrative wholes. Such incidences, I would argue, are to be seen as historical and literary anticipations (and/or illustrations) of the way of salvation revealed as itself initially fulfilled in the cross and resurrection of Jesus (I say "initially" because even yet final salvation awaits the return of Christ; Romans 8:24f.; 1 Pet. 1:3-9). The salvation given to New Testament characters, prior to the death and resurrection of Jesus, would be of the same proleptic/anticipatory sort as that attributed in the New Testament to Old Testament heroes of faith. The author of Hebrews, for one, certainly makes the salvation of Old Testament saints dependent upon the kerygmatic events (cross-resurrection-exaltation) that have occurred in connection with Jesus (Heb. 11:31). New Testament theology and/or the theological/canonical unity of the New Testament can ill survive the wedge that Stagg has driven between the theology of Jesus and the theology of Paul.

It is also appropriate to note Stagg's rather resounding rejection of the cross as a "transactional" means of salvation. If by "transactional" all Stagg means is some ancient and/or Augustinian belief that the Father must somehow be propitiated or appeased by the Son before salvation can be accomplished, or that the Son had to pay a fee or ransom to the devil, we may all let the criticism stand; but, what Stagg ends up doing by his repeated (and pejorative) references to a "transactional" atonement is rather simplistically rejecting virtually every other view of the atonement save a kind of exemplar/repentance model. Stagg leaves the cross of Christ as little more than revelatory of the character of God. To be sure, the cross *does* reveal the nature of the God with whom we have to do (i.e., he is indeed the God of self-sacrifice and suffering). He is the kind of God who is very much unlike the capricious gods of the Greeks and Romans. There is little doubt that the cross of Jesus is both a marvelous and mysterious revelation of the serving, self-giving character of God. Indeed, the New Testament clearly points to the cross of Jesus as having exemplar value (Eph. 4:32 to 5:2); but none of that can dismiss what is also transparently evident in the New Testament: specifically, that the death and resurrection of Jesus actually accomplished something objective for our salvation. For all of Stagg's affirmations as to the historical particularity of the cross, it becomes clear in the end that the greater value of the cross for Stagg is in its essential eternality (i.e., its revelatory "intensity" as an example of the kind of suffering and self-giving that are at the very heart of God). While one may welcome Stagg's focus upon the revelatory nature of the cross, it is disturbing to note that, for Stagg, the cross and resurrection seem to lack objective and particular redemptive value.

Stagg's appeals over the years to Hebrews 6:6 as a basis for his subjectivizing/departicularizing of the cross ("they crucify *to themselves* the Son of God"), thereby making more palatable what he calls the universality and eternality of the cross, are based upon what sppears to be a questionable exegesis of what is a much disputed text.[42] Stagg's views virtually deny the saving value of the death and resurrection of Jesus as events. Indeed, Stagg does insist that salvation is grounded in God and *not* in historical events.[43] In fact, Stagg's attempts to isolate form-critically certain Synoptic scenes from the theologically decisive and literarily dominant cross-resurrection narratives reflect his own tacit admission that the New Testament does characteristically ground salvation in certain events, particularly the historical coming of Jesus and especially His coming as interpreted through His death and resurrection. Moreover, it is a strange procedure which separates the activity of God from historical events—especially, of course, the historical events of the cross and resurrection. To say that salvation is accomplished by the cross and resurrection does not separate those saving events from their saving function in the eternal purposes of God. I would argue that Stagg has, his own denials notwithstanding, virtually dehistoricized the cross and ultimately dehistoricized salvation. With faith thus separated from specific historical events, salvation becomes (as indeed it does for Stagg) little more than a doctrine of repentance.[44] We are indeed left wondering about the real necessity of the cross.

In a similar vein, I would argue that Stagg has deeschatologized large segments of Synoptic theology (especially what he calls "Jesus material") and selected portions of Pauline theology. Stagg's attempt to separate eschatology from apocalyptic is appropriate on a relative basis but cannot stand up absolutely.[45] To speak of the end of history in Jewish eschatology is normally to speak of a catastrophic/apocalyptic day of the Lord. The presence or absence of excessive apocalyptic symbolism or language does not, contrary to Stagg's apparent assumption, eliminate the apocalyptic features of eschatology. His efforts to deapocalpyticize New Testament eschatology are nonetheless consistent with his rejection of "transactional" theology (so construed) and his related attempts to downplay notions of salvation history (though Stagg's own admission, that New Testament theology is eschatological, is, itself, an admission that salvation history is, at least to some extent, both an appropriate and necessary model for doing New Testament theology) and to reduce the role of Satanic and/or cosmic oppressors in the drama of redemption.[46] Indeed, the very language "drama of redemption" is not at all welcome to Stagg.[47] But such efforts will not stand up to the pervasively cross-resurrection kind of theology/eschatology reflected in the New Testament's unapologetically apocalyptic thought world.

As far back as his *New Testament Theology,* Stagg's theological views caused him to minimize the role of Satan and cosmic powers. Stagg prefers to interpret sin on the model of James 1:13-15 and that in a way that does not, it seems to me, see the rather clear-cut allusions to the story of Adam. In this same connection, it may be observed that Stagg's selection of Romans 1:18 to 3:20 as the determinative core for Paul's views of sin and wrath is largely based upon Stagg's view that this particular passage in Romans makes no use of apocalyptic language, has no reference to Satan, and none at all to Adam.[48] In the first instance, I do not think one can read "for the *wrath* of God is *revealed from heaven* . . ." (Rom. 1:18, emphasis added) without seeing the apocalyptic horizon of Paul's thought.[49] Furthermore, given the highly personalistic terminology used to describe "sin" in contradistinction to the sphere of God through Christ, it is hard for this reader of Romans to believe that the single term "sin" in Romans 6 and 7 is not in some respect a reference to cosmic powers of darkness. Romans 7:7-25 cannot, it seems to me, be read apart from either the perception of references to Adam (see especially vv. 8-13) or salvation history (cf. 7:5 with 7:7-25; 7:6 with 8:1ff.).

Apart from Paul, however, I think Stagg's attempt to read the Synoptic Gospels and/or the theology of Jesus apart from Christ's battle with the powers of darkness, as reflected in the demon exorcisms and the preaching tours of the twelve and seventy, is misguided. The kingdom is manifested in the coming of Jesus and the reign of God inherent in His preaching, His miraculous/eschatological signs of the glorious age to come, and His demon exorcisms. Talk of conquering Satan and/or the defeat of demonic powers may not seem relevant to some moderns, but that has no bearing on the way in which the New Testament and/or the theology of the synoptics and/or the theology of Jesus is to be historically understood. I, for one, find a great deal of relevance in the New Testament view of principalities and powers who live and work under the aegis of Satan, for nothing short of such cosmic powers of evil can explain the despicable patterns of evil and injustice manifested in the world and against which Stagg so admirably lived, wrote, and preached. Quite apart from the abiding relevance of such an apocalyptic (New Testament) world-view, it seems historically impossible for a reader of the New Testament to call any theory of the atonement competent which, while trying to be historically descriptive of the theology reflected in the New Testament, does not reckon with Christ's defeat of the powers of darkness in his ministry, death, resurrection, and exaltation. To claim such is not to seek a return to any crude notions of Christ's paying a ransom to Satan, but it is to take seriously the commonly asserted Christian belief—widely reflected in the New Testament—that Christ came to "destroy him who holds the power of death—that is, the devil" (Heb. 2:14).

Stagg's Christology is strong with regard to his affirmation of the divinity of Christ, but his trinitarian views leave something to be desired.[50] It must first of all be said that Stagg is not always clear in his views on the subject of the trinity. He certainly sounds like what the historians of doctrine would call a "modalist," though Stagg himself denies this charge.[51] It is abundantly manifest that Stagg dislikes the language of Nicea and, though he speaks of Father, Son, and Spirit, does at times seem to question the tripersonality of

God.[52] Concerning passages where Christ prays to the Father, Stagg relegates these to the mystery of the incarnation[53] and thus leaves this reader both dissatisfied with and puzzled over his views. It must be said, of course, that Stagg's views cannot be called heretical because of his dislike of Nicene language. Indeed, Stagg is to be admired for his attempt to retain terminology that is as fully biblical as possible; but Stagg's views do not, it seems to me, take seriously enough the particularly Trinitarian language of the New Testament, given his hints that specifically *tri*-nitarian (as opposed to *bi*-nitarian or even other numeric models) language is not binding theologically.[54] One gets the feeling that, for Stagg, the difference, for example, between God the Father and God the Son is not a matter of essential distinction within God so much as it is a matter of functional perception on the part of the believer. In that regard there is no necessary or significant theological attachment to "three" in Stagg's discussions of the one God.

Finally, it must be noted that this reader was not always comfortable with Stagg's ethical applications of New Testament materials. Of course, the fact that Stagg consistently endeavored to make the New Testament relevant to Christian living is to be warmly applauded and deeply admired; but I do think that the political agenda of the more liberal side (relatively speaking) of American politics did not receive the kind of dispassionate analysis and criticism that the right wing of American politics in the 1960s and 70s received. All of us would do well to remember that the gospel can be tied to neither an ideology of the left nor the right.

Though one may not always agree strategically with Frank Stagg's ethical applications of the gospel, there can be little doubt that the New Testament he has so faithfully treasured calls us to a radical discipleship in the world. It is to Frank Stagg's great credit that he has not only courageously chosen to live his own life under the lordship of Jesus Christ, but as a minister/teacher of the gospel he has also called upon each of us to live in a way that is consistent with our calling in Christ Jesus. However one may disagree with Stagg's theological synthesis, we must all agree that both the confession and the living out of the lordship of Jesus Christ is not only a mandate from the Risen Lord Himself, but our mission to a lost and dying world.

Bibliography

Books

The Bible Speaks on Aging. Nashville: Broadman Press, 1981.

The Book of Acts: The Early Struggle for an Unhindered Gospel. Nashville: Broadman Press, 1955.

The Doctrine of Christ. Nashville: Convention Press, 1984.

Exploring the New Testament. Nashville: Broadman Press, 1961.

Galatians and Romans. "Knox Preaching Guides," edited by John H. Hayes. Atlanta: John Knox Press, 1980.

The Holy Spirit Today. Nashville: Broadman Press, 1973.

New Testament Theology. Nashville: Broadman Press, 1962.

Polarities of Man's Existence in Biblical Perspective. Philadelphia: Westminster Press, 1973.

Studies in Luke's Gospel. Nashville: Convention Press, 1967.

Woman in the World of Jesus. With Evelyn Stagg. Phildelphia: Westminster Press, 1978.

Contributions to Other Books

"Adam, Christ, and Us." In *New Testament Studies: Essays in Honor of Ray Summers in His Sixty-Fifth Year,* edited by Huber L. Drumwright and Curtis Vaughan. Waco: Baylor University, 1975.

"Authentic Morality and Militarism." In *Proceedings of the 1970 Christian Life Commission Seminar.* Nashville: Christian Life Commission of the SBC, 1970.

"Biblical Perspectives on Women." With Evelyn Stagg. In *Findings of the Consultation on Women in Church-Related Vocations,* edited by Johnni Johnson. Nashville: Southern Baptist Convention, 1978.

"A Continuing Pilgrimage." In *What Faith Has Meant to Me,* edited by Claude A. Frazier. Philadelphia: Westminster Press, 1975.

"Establishing a Text for Luke-Acts." In *1977 Seminar Papers, Society of Biblical Literature Book of Reports.* Missoula, Mont.: Scholars Press, 1977.

"Explain the Ending of the Gospel of Mark, Mark 16:17-18." In *What Did the Bible Mean,* edited by Claude A. Frazier. Nashville: Broadman Press, 1971.

"Glossolalia in the New Testament." With Glenn Hinson and Wayne E. Oates. In *Glossolalia: Tongue Speaking in Biblical, Historical, and Psychological Perspective.* Nashville: Abingdon Press, 1967.

"He that Judgeth Me." In *More Southern Baptist Preaching,* edited by H. C. Brown, Jr. Nashville: Broadman Press, 1964.

"How I Prepare My Sermons." In *More Southern Baptist Preaching,* edited by H. C. Brown, Jr. Nashville: Broadman Press, 1964.

"Matthew." In *The Broadman Bible Commentary,* vol. 8, edited by Clifton J. Allen. Nashville: Broadman Press, 1969.

"Philippians." In *The Broadman Bible Commentary,* vol. 11, edited by Clifton J. Allen. Nashville: Broadman Press, 1971.

"Playing God with Other People's Minds." In *Should Preachers Play God,* edited by Claude A. Frazier. Independence: Independence Press, 1973.

"Preaching from Luke-Acts." In *Biblical Preaching: An Expositor's Treasury,* edited by James W. Cox. Philadelphia: Westminster Press, 1983.

"Preaching from the Sermon on the Mount." In *Biblical Preaching: An Expositor's Treasury,* edited by James W. Cox. Philadelphia: Westminster Press, 1983.

"Rights and Responsibilities in the Teachings of Paul." In *Emerging Patterns of Rights and Responsibilities Affecting Church and State.* Washington D.C.: Baptist Joint Committee on Public Affairs, 1969.

"Understanding Call to Ministry." In *Formation for Christian Ministry*, edited by Anne Davis and Wade Rowatt, Jr. Louisville: Review and Expositor, 1981.

"What and Where Is the Church?" In *What Can You Believe?* edited by David K. Alexander and C. W. Junker. Nashville: Broadman Press, 1966.

"What Is Truth?" In *Science, Faith and Revelation, An Approach to Christian Philosophy*, edited by Robert E. Patterson. Nashville: Broadman Press, 1979.

"A Whole Man Made Well." In *The Struggle for Meaning*, edited by William Powell Tuck. Valley Forge, Pa.: Judson Press, 1977.

"Women in New Testament Perspective." With Evelyn Stagg. In *Encyclopedia of Southern Baptists*, vol. 4, edited by Lynn Edward May, Jr., Nashville: Broadman Press, 1982.

Journal Articles

"The Abused Aorist." *Journal of Biblical Literature* 91 (1972): 222-31.

"An Analysis of the Book of James." *Review and Expositor* 66 (1969): 365-68.

"Biblical Perspectives on the Single Person." *Review and Expositor* 74 (1977): 5-19.

"The Christology of Matthew." *Review and Expositor* 59 (1962): 457-68.

"The Concept of the Messiah: A Baptist Perspective." *Review and Expositor* 84 (1987): 247-57.

"The Domestic Code and Final Appeal: Ephesians 5:21-6:24." *Review and Expositor* 76 (1979): 541-52.

"Eschatology: A Southern Baptist Perspective." *Review and Expositor* 79 (1982): 381-95.

"Exegetical Themes in James 1 and 2." *Review and Expositor* 66 (1969): 391-402.

"The Farewell Discourses: John 13-17." *Review and Expositor* 62 (1965): 459-72.

"Freedom and Moral Responsibility Without License or Legalism." *Review and Expositor* 69 (1972): 483-94.

"The Gospel in Biblical Usage." *Review and Expositor* 63 (1966): 5-13.

"The Great Words of Romans." *Theological Educator* 7 (1976): 94-102.

"The Holy Spirit in the New Testament." *Review and Expositor* 63 (1966): 135-47.

"Interpreting the Book of Revelation." *Review and Expositor* 72 (1975): 331-43.

"Introduction to Colossians." *Theological Educator* 4 (1973): 7-16.

"The Journey Toward Jerusalem in Luke's Gospel." *Review and Expositor* 64 (1967): 499-512.

"The Lord's Supper in the New Testament." *Review and Expositor* 66 (1969): 5-14.

"The Mind in Christ Jesus." *Review and Expositor* 77 (1980): 337-47.

"The Motif of First Corinthians." *Southwestern Journal of Theology* 3 (1960): 15-24.

"The New International Version: New Testament." *Review and Expositor* 76 (1979): 377-85.

"The New Testament Doctrine of the Church." *Theological Educator* 12 (1981): 42-56.

"Orthodoxy and Orthopraxy in the Johannine Epistles." *Review and Expositor* 67 (1970): 423-32.

"The Plight of the Jew and the Gentile in Sin: Romans 1:18-3:20." *Review and Expositor* 73 (1976): 401-13.

"Prophetic Ministry Today." *Review and Expositor* 73 (1976): 179-89.

"The Purpose and Message of Acts." *Review and Expositor* 44 (1947): 3-21.

"Rendering to Caesar What Belongs to Caesar: Christian Engagement with the World." *Journal of Church and State* 18 (1976): 95-113.

"Rendering to God What Belongs to God: Christian Disengagement with the World." *Journal of Church and State* 18 (1976): 217-32.

"Reassessing the Gospels." *Review and Expositor* 78 (1981): 187-203.

"Salvation in Synoptic Tradition." *Review and Expositor* 69 (1972): 355-67.

"Southern Baptist Theology Today: An Interview." *Theological Educator* 3 (1977) 15-36.

"A Teaching Outline for Acts." *Review and Expositor* 71 (1974): 533-36.

"Textual Criticism for Luke-Acts." *Perspectives in Religion Studies* 5 (1978): 152-65.

"The Unhindered Gospel." *Review and Expositor* 71 (1974): 451-62.

Notes

1. For some extensive biographical information see Malcolm Tolbert, "Frank Stagg: Teaching Prophet," in *Perspectives on the New Testament: Essays in Honor of Frank Stagg,* ed. Charles H. Talbert (Macon, Ga.: Mercer University Press, 1985), 1-16. It will be evident to those familiar with Tolbert's excellent piece that I have been greatly helped by his work in this biographical section; see also Penrose St. Amant, "A Continuing Pilgrimage: A Biographical Sketch of Frank Stagg," *The Theological Educator* 8 (Fall 1977): 37-49; Ann Evory, ed., *Contemporary Authors,* New Revision Series, vol. 1 (Detroit: Gale Research Co., 1981), s.v. "Stagg, Frank," 623; Frank Stagg, "A Continuing Pilgrimage," in *What Faith Has Meant to Me,* ed. Claude A. Frazier (Philadelphia: Westminster Press, 1975), 146-56.

2. Frank Stagg, *New Testament Theology* (Nashville: Broadman Press, 1962).

3. See, for example, the very helpful survey of biblical terms and theological ideas in chapter 4, "The Doctrine of Salvation," 80-121.

4. Frank Stagg, "The Christology of Matthew," *Review and Expositor* 59 (October 1962): 457-68.

5. Frank Stagg, "The Gospel in Biblical Usage," *Review and Expositor* 63 (Winter 1966): 5-13.

6. Frank Stagg, "The Holy Spirit in the New Testament," *Review and Expositor* 63 (Spring 1966): 135-47.

7. Frank Stagg, "The Journey Toward Jerusalem in Luke's Gospel," *Review and Expositor* 64 (Fall 1967): 499-512.

8. Frank Stagg, "The Lord's Supper in the New Testament," *Review and Expositor* 66 (Winter 1969): 5-26.

9. Frank Stagg, "The Abused Aorist," *Journal of Biblical Literature* 91 (June 1973): 222-31.

10. Frank Stagg, *The Holy Spirit Tooday* (Nashville: Broadman Press, 1973), passim.

11. Frank Stagg, *Polarities of Man's Existence in Biblical Perspective* (Philadelphia: Westminster Press, 1973), 11.

12. Ibid., 16.

13. Ibid., 10; cf. Frank Stagg, *New Testament Theology* (Nashville: Broadman Press, 1962), 20.

14. Frank Stagg, "Adam, Christ, and Us," in *New Testament Studies: Essays in Honor of Ray Summers in His Sixty-Fifth Year,* ed. Huber L. Drumwright and Curtis Vaughan (Waco: Baylor University Press, 1975), 125.

15. See Frank Stagg, "Salvation in Synoptic Tradition," *Review and Expositor* 69 (Summer 1972): 355-367; Frank Stagg, "The Great Words of Romans," *The Theological Educator* 7 (Fall 1976): 94-102; Frank Stagg, "The Mind in Christ Jesus: Philippians 1:27—2:18," *Review and Expositor* 77 (Summer 1980): 337-47; Frank Stagg, "Reassessing the Gospels," *Review and Expositor* 78 (Spring 1981): 187-203; Frank Stagg, "Eschatology: A Southern Baptist Perspective," *Review and Expositor* 79 (Summer 1982): 381-95; Frank Stagg, "The Concept of the Messiah: A Baptist Perspective," *Review and Expositor* 84 (Spring 1987): 247-58.

16. For James 1:13-15 see, for example, Frank Stagg, "Exegetical Themes in James 1 and 2," *Review and Expositor* 66 (Fall 1969): 391-402; for Romans 1:18 to 3:20 see Frank Stagg, "The Plight of Jew and Gentile in Sin: Romans 1:18—3:20," *Review and Expositor* 73 (Fall 1976): 401-13; Stagg, "The Great Words of Romans," 94-102; and Stagg, *New Testament Theology,* 21 *ff.*

17. Stagg, "Salvation in Synoptic Tradition," 359.

18. Stagg's soteriology is most evident in "Salvation in Synoptic Tradition," passim; and "Reassessing the Gospels," passim.

19. Stagg, "The Concept of Messiah: A Baptist Perspective," 257.

20. Stagg, "Salvation in Synoptic Tradition," 358.

21. Ibid.

22. This by no means indicates that Stagg utterly ignores Paul; but he does clearly prefer to ground his theology in the Gospels. See Frank Stagg, "Southern Baptist Theology Today," *The Theological Educator* 8 (Fall 1977): 35.

23. Stagg, "Reassessing the Gospels," 189.

24. Ibid., 192-93.

25. Ibid., 194 *f.*

26. Ibid., 197.

27. See Stagg, "The Mind in Christ Jesus," passim; "Southern Baptist Theology Today," 36; and "The Concept of Messiah," 257.

28. Stagg, "Salvation in Synoptic Tradition," 366 *f.*

29. Ibid., 367.

30. Ibid.

31. Frank Stagg, *The Book of Acts: Early Struggle for an Unhindered Gospel* (Nashville: Broadman Press, 1955), viii, 123 *f,* 186.

32. Ibid., 18.

33. Frank Stagg, "Rendering to Caesar What Belongs to Caesar: Christian Engagement with the World," *Journal of Church and State* 18 (1976): 101.

34. Frank Stagg, "Rendering to God What Belongs to God: Christian Disengagement from the World," *Journal of Church and State* 18 (1976): 217.

35. Ibid.

36. Frank Stagg, "Biblical Perspectives on the Single Person," 5-19.

37. Frank Stagg and Evelyn Stagg, *Woman in the World of Jesus* (Philadelphia: Westminster Press, 1973).

38. Cf. Frank Stagg, "The Domestic Code and Final Appeal: Ephesians 5:21—6:24," *Review and Expositor* 76 (Fall 1979): 543 *f.*

39. Frank Stagg, *The Bible Speaks on Aging* (Nashville: Broadman Press, 1981).

40. Ralph Herring, Frank Stagg, et al., *How to Understand the Bible* (Nashville: Broadman Press, 1974), 132.

41. See an excellent summary and theological evaluation of these views in Raymond Brown's 1986 Presidential Address delivered at the Forty-first General Meeting of *Studiorum Novi Testamenti Societas,* printed in *New Testament Studies* 33 (1987): 321-43.

42. I read Hebrews 6:6 not as an actual reference to the subjective recrucifixion of Christ on the part of those who turned away from him, but as a hypothetical reference to something which cannot in fact happen; indeed, no other author in all the New Testament makes it more clear than the author of Hebrews that Christ has suffered but once and indeed cannot die again.

43. Stagg, "Salvation in Synoptic Tradition," 357; Stagg, "Reassessing the Gospels," 192 *f.*

44. Stagg, "Salvation in Synoptic Tradition," 357; Stagg, "Reassessing the Gospels," 192 *f.*

45. Stagg, "Eschatology," 382.

46. Ibid., 385.

47. Stagg, "The Mind in Christ Jesus," 340-43.

48. Stagg, *New Testament Theology,* 21; Staff, "The Plight of Jew and Gentile," 402 *f.*; Stagg, "Adam, Christ, and Us," passim.

49. Calvin Schoonhoven, *The Wrath of Heaven* (Grand Rapids, Mich.: Eerdmans, 1966), 17 *ff.*; for compelling arguments that Paul cannot be understood apart from the apocalyptic texture and core of his thought cf. J. Christaan Beker, *Paul the Apostle* (Philadelphia: Fortress Press, 1980).

50. Stagg, "Reassessing the Gospels," 190; Stagg, "Southern Baptist Theology Today," 23-28; Stagg, "The Concept of Messiah," 252-54; Frank Stagg, *The Doctrine of Christ* (Nashville: Convention Press, 1984), 90-99.

51. Frank Stagg, *The Holy Spirit Today* (Nashville: Broadman Press, 1973), 17-19.

52. Stagg, "Southern Baptist Theology Today," 26; Stagg, *The Doctrine of Christ,* 91-95; cf. Frank Stagg, "Matthew," in *The Broadman Bible Commentary,* ed. Clifton J. Allen, vol. 8 (Nashville: Broadman Press, 1969), 252 *ff.*; Stagg, "The Concept of Messiah," 254.

53. Stagg, "The Christology of Matthew," 461; Stagg, *The Doctrine of Christ,* 99.

54. See note 52.

27

Carl F. H. Henry

R. Albert Mohler, Jr.

In an age of declining theological vigor and few theological giants, Carl F. H. Henry has emerged as one of the theological luminaries of the twentieth century. His experience as journalist, teacher, theologian, editor, and world spokesman for evangelical Christianity ranks him among the very few individuals who can claim to have shaped a major theological movement.

Biography

Born January 22, 1913, to immigrant parents in New York City, Henry's life is in many ways a reflection of America in the early-twentieth century. His parents, Karl F. and Joanna (*nee* Vathroder) Heinrich, were both young German immigrants to the United States. The family name was changed to Henry due to the anti-German sentiment occasioned by the first world war.

The Henry family lived the lives of a typical immigrant family, with hardworking parents and little luxury. Though his mother was Roman Catholic by family tradition and his father a Lutheran, there was little evidence of religion in the Henry household.[1]

The family later moved to a farm on Long Island, where his father was eventually to purchase a small general goods store. The Henry children grew into adulthood in a spartan, but not impoverished setting, and Carl—the eldest of eight children—took a succession of part-time jobs to supplement the family's income.

Public schools provided Henry's early educational experiences, and as a high school student Henry seemed destined for a career in journalism. Graduating in the midst of the Great Depression, he sought and obtained work at *The Islip Press* on Long Island. He quickly became a working reporter and was later to write for the *New York Herald Tribune* and the *New York Daily News*. Just three years after assuming his first newspaper position, Henry became the editor of *The Smithtown Star,* a major weekly paper on Long Island. He was later to cover a large section of Long Island for *The New York Times*.

His newspaper experience put him into contact with a devout Christian woman and, through her, to members of the Oxford Group.[2] At age twenty, with ambitions and success in journalism, Henry was confronted with the claims of the gospel and became a believer.

Perceiving a call from God to a life of vocational Christian service, Henry left his promising newspaper career and enrolled at Wheaton College in the

Carl F. H. Henry (1913-   )

Photo courtesy of Word Books, Inc.

fall of 1935. Henry's experience at Wheaton shaped the course of his later life and thought. He was drawn to Wheaton by its reputation as the "evangelical Harvard" and because he had heard its president, J. Oliver Buswell, speak at a Stony Brook conference on the importance of the rational dimension of faith. At Wheaton, Henry found himself in the bosom of the evangelical movement—and at a very precipitous moment in the development of conservative Christianity in America. Henry was to establish friendships at Wheaton with individuals such as Billy Graham and Harold Lindsell. Most importantly, he was there introduced to Gordon Clark, professor of philosophy, who was to become perhaps the most important intellectual influence on Henry's thought. Clark was a conservative Presbyterian who stressed the inherent rationality of theology and belief in God.[3] By the time of his graduation in August 1938, Henry had determined to pursue graduate study in theology. He considered an invitation to join the Moody Bible College as director of promotion, but followed instead his sense that theology was to be his calling.

Wheaton was to introduce Henry to another significant influence on his life, Helga Bender. Married in 1940, they were later to have two children.[4]

Henry remained at Wheaton to complete his M.A. in theology, while engaged in the Bachelor of Divinity program at Northern Baptist Theological Seminary in nearby Lombard, Illinois. Northern Seminary had been founded as an alternative to the increasingly liberal direction taken by the University of Chicago Divinity School. Henry was to complete the Bachelor of Divinity and Doctor of Theology degrees at Northern, completing his work in 1942.[5]

Nine years after his conversion, Henry held a degree from Wheaton and three graduate degrees in theology. The shape of his early thought was already clear, with the battle for the rational and evangelical expression of Christian theism in the forefront. Already a published author, Henry was to release several small volumes on religious thought and theology which indicate his critical reading of contemporary theology and his call for a vigorous conservative offensive.

Henry began his teaching career at Northern Seminary, teaching theology at his alma mater until 1947, when he was invited to join the faculty of the young Fuller Theological Seminary in Pasadena, California. The seminary was the visionary project of evangelist Charles E. Fuller and Harold J. Ockenga, pastor of Boston's prestigious Park Street Church. Fuller was projected as a great evangelical seminary for the rapidly growing West Coast. Henry accepted Ockenga's invitation and moved to Pasadena in 1947. He began his tenure at Fuller while pursuing a Ph.D. in philosophy under personalist philosopher Edgar Brightman at Boston University. At Fuller Henry was to teach theology and philosophy, with a concentration in apologetics and ethics.

Fuller, though plagued by a difficult birth and an absentee president, made remarkable progress and Henry emerged as a key leader within the faculty.[6] Nevertheless, within a decade of his move to Pasadena he was to accept an invitation to serve *Christianity Today* as founding editor.

Theological conservatives had long yearned for a flagship vehicle for their evangelical perspective. *Christianity Today* was the brainchild of Billy Graham and Harold J. Ockenga and was intended as an alternative to the more liberal Protestant journal, *The Christian Century*. Henry was the logical choice as editor. With a background in journalism, impeccable academic credentials, and an unquestioned commitment to evangelical orthodoxy, Henry was uniquely poised to lead such an effort. *Christianity Today* was established with offices in Washington, D.C., and emerged in 1956 with an impressive appearance and solid content.

At the helm of *Christianity Today,* Henry exerted growing leadership over the larger evangelical movement and earned a worldwide reputation for serious engagement with modern thought. Nevertheless, his leadership at *Christianity Today* came to an end in 1967 following a disagreement over the direction of the magazine.[7]

Vacating the editorship at *Christianity Today,* Henry traveled to Cambridge, where he undertook study and research which formed the nucleus of his massive theological project, the six-volume *God, Revelation and Authority*.

Returning to the United States, Henry accepted a teaching post at Eastern Baptist Theological Seminary in Philadelphia. Later, he was to serve as Lecturer-at-Large for World Vision, an evangelical social action agency. He continues to lecture, write, and teach, and has held several visiting professorships. Though formal lectureships have been a part of his experience since the 1940s, the 1970s and 1980s have been a period of intensive and influential lectures at secular and evangelical universities. He delivered the prestigious Rutherford Lectures at Edinburgh in 1989.

Exposition

Carl Henry and the Evangelical Movement

The evangelical movement in America is notoriously difficult to define, its precise boundaries and constituencies varied and often blurred. The movement has been most easily identified in terms of specific institutions, agencies, and individuals. The evangelical movement, as it has developed after the second world war, has been represented by institutions such as Fuller Seminary, Gordon Conwell Seminary, Trinity Evangelical Divinity School, and World Vision. Publishing houses such as William B. Eerdmans, Baker Book House, and Zondervan release hundreds of evangelical volumes each year. But evangelicalism has been most readily identified by means of individuals. Billy Graham, the world-famous evangelist has epitomized the evangelistic commitment and orthodox preaching of the gospel. Carl F. H. Henry, however, has represented the intellectual and cognitive defense of evangelical truth so central to the evangelical movement.

The year of Henry's conversion, 1933, was also the year of the release of the Humanist Manifesto, the organized call of the intellectual elite to a humanist agenda. This coincidental timing has not been lost on Henry. This era was also colored by the continuation of the Fundamentalist/Modernist controversy, a battle assumed by most to have been lost by the fundamentalists. Henry's experience at college and seminary put him into contact with those who had decided to separate from the mainline churches, and with those who determined to remain within their denominations as agents of conservative witness.

By the conclusion of his doctoral studies at Northern Seminary, Henry was convinced that the fundamentalist movement would be required to change its anticultural stance if it was to be effective in the twentieth century. His concern that fundamentalism had ignored all social and ethical issues led to the publication of Henry's first epocal work, *The Uneasy Conscience of Modern Fundamentalism*.[8] The volume became a manifesto of a movement later to be known as the "new evangelicalism."

Henry was to become one of the founding fathers of the modern evangelical movement. As defined by these young conservatives, the new evangelicalism would combine a stalwart defense of the orthodox faith, buttressed by solid academic underpinnings, with careful attention to the social application of the gospel message.[9]

The character of this new evangelicalism was to shape Fuller Theological Seminary. Henry, though among the youngest of the founding faculty, was elected dean. His reputation as a premier evangelical thinker and spokesperson was enhanced by his considerable vision and organizational skills. In his decade at Fuller Henry would write eight books and numerous articles, complete his Ph.D. at Boston University, and emerge as a principal organizer behind such events as the annual Rose Bowl Sunrise Service.[10]

Henry's pivotal leadership at *Christianity Today* solidified his influence among the evangelical leadership. *Christianity Today* represented their hope for a fully respected vehicle for evangelical advance. His editorials and articles, though not lengthy, were known for solid content and indicate the optimism of the movement.[11]

The zenith of Henry's institutional and organizational influence in the evangelical movement was reached in 1966, when he served as chairman of the World Congress on Evangelism in Berlin. This conference, organized by Henry and Billy Graham, was another symbol of evangelical advance.[12] Yet, within two years Henry was no longer editor of *Christianity Today* and the magazine's direction and character was later to undergo significant change.[13]

Henry's role within evangelicalism has been unique and extensive. More than any other evangelical, he has given serious and sustained attention to the issue of evangelical identity and definition. The titles of his books, from *Evangelical Responsibility* in *Contemporary Theology, Evangelicals at the Brink of Crisis*, and *A Plea for Evangelical Demonstration* to *Evangelicals in Search of Identity* indicate his self-conscious intention to assist in the definition and mobilization of the movement.

The Uneasy Conscience of Modern Fundamentalism established Henry's call for cultural engagement by orthodox Protestants. That same year Ockenga coined the "new evangelicalism" and a movement was spawned. Henry differentiated the older conservatism (fundamentalism) from the new (evangelicalism) by a basic distinction in "moods" between the two approaches. Evangelicalism would embody the mood of engagement with broader theological movements and a recognition of the social and cultural dimensions of the gospel.

The new evangelicalism was to be fully orthodox but would cooperate across denominational lines, building a constructive theological movement out of the ruins of a fallen liberalism. The movement would avoid the excessive preoccupation on eschatology, spirit of separatism, and lack of engagement common to fundamentalism. The new evangelicals saw their responsibility in vivid terms, for the fall of the older liberal theologies could presage an even more dangerous theological context.[14]

The new evangelicalism would combine the manifest strengths of the older fundamentalism, but would reject its excesses and seek to meet the challenges of modernity as a full intellectual partner.[15]

Though the 1966 World Congress on Evangelism fixed Henry's stature among world evangelicals, it was the eventual publication of the six-volume *God, Revelation and Authority* which established Henry's stature as the primary proponent of an evangelical doctrine of revelation and scriptural authority. The publication of his *magnum opus* also marked Henry's growing sense that American evangelicalism was in grave danger of missing its greatest opportunity for intellectual and cultural influence.[16]

Henry's leadership in the evangelical movement has shifted in his later years from the institutional influence he wielded at Fuller and *Christianity Today,* to his current position as the acknowledged dean of evangelical theologians. Nevertheless, he has continued an organizational presence through such activities as his cochairmanship of the 1989 "Evangelical Affirmations" conference at Trinity Evangelical Divinity School.

Henry on Modern Theology

"This generation, with which we die," wrote Henry in 1946, "is a pivot point in world history."[17] This sense of urgency has marked Carl Henry's theological mission from its inception. With much of the world in literal ruins, Henry saw an opportunity to demonstrate the failure of liberal theology to deal with the problems of the age. Theology had reached "the mid-twentieth century impasse" between liberal revisionism and orthodox faith.[18]

Henry identified a "great divide" between evangelical and mediating or liberal systems of thought. Assuming the destruction of schools associated with the older liberalism of Harnack, Ritschl, and Hermann, he aimed his critiques at the "neo-supernaturalist" systems of the neoorthodox theologians and other more contemporary variants of thought.[19]

The basic pattern evident in Henry's critique of mediating systems can be traced to his Boston University dissertation on the Northern Baptist theologian A. H. Strong. Strong's attempt to forge a mediating system between orthodoxy and liberalism (based in his case upon a personalistic monism) was seen by Henry to end in failure on all fronts. Both conservatives and liberals found the attempted bridge inadequate and untrustworthy. The lesson provided Henry with a model of the failure of mediating systems, especially those based on modern critical philosophy and any post-Kantian epistemology.[20]

Henry's engagement with the theology of Karl Barth reveals his pattern of theological critique. Clearly, Barth was the dominant theological presence in postwar Europe, though Rudolph Bultmann's influence was growing swiftly. Henry understood Barth's theological system to be an attempt to mediate between the older liberalism of his teachers and the evangelical heritage of the Reformation. Though not completely unappreciative of Barth's program, Henry was quick to warn his fellow evangelicals against a hasty appropriation of Barth's thought.

Grounded in a Kantian epistemology, Barth's system was therefore based not in a rediscovery of full scriptural authority, but in a "neo-supernaturalistic" tradition "which has contributed as much to the theological confusion of our times as it has been a force corrective of some of the weaknesses of liberalism."[21] Henry saw Bultmann as the greater danger, but thought Barth to be insufficiently orthodox to stem Bultmann's tide.[22]

The fatal flaw Henry identified in Barth's system centered in the Swiss theologian's insistence on the nonpropositional character of special revelation. This, Henry lamented, led to a doctrine of revelation insufficient to provide a sturdy alternative to Bultmann's program of demythologization. Though Barth was refreshingly orthodox on many doctrinal issues, his system was unable to provide a workable mediation between modernity and theism.[23]

Few movements or theologians escaped Henry's critique. As the neoorthodox schools collapsed, a myriad of variant systems emerged, with the "death of God" movement receiving the most popular attention. Henry considered innovations including the theologies of hope represented by Jurgen Moltmann and Johannes Baptist Metz, the theology of Wolfhart Pannenberg, and the schools of thought associated with liberation and process theologies.[24] Each system was seen by Henry to be based in an inadequate epistemology and thus a faulty doctrine of revelation.[25]

Henry reserved his most forceful theological analyses for those systems which by their compromising nature posed a threat to evangelicalism itself. Thus, though Bultmann was far less orthodox than Barth, it was Barth who represented the greater danger to evangelicals, many of whom found hope in Barth's apparent conservatism. In the same manner he lamented the "hermeneutical relativism" of the narrative theologians and the cultural relativism of Charles H. Kraft as dangerous attractions to the evangelical faithful.[26]

Henry's Theological Method

The Fundamentalist/Modernist controversy set the terms for the theological development of the "new evangelicals." Though issues such as Christology and creation captured popular attention, the evangelicals realized that the most crucial issues were directly related to Scripture, and were thus epistemological questions at root. If the modernists' positions evolved from defective understandings of revelation and the resultant lack of commitment to biblical authority, then the evangelicals would have to reestablish an adequate epistemological basis for faith—and commit themselves to Scripture as divine revelation.

A basic divide appeared among the conservatives at this point. Agreed that the epistemological issues were paramount, they differed concerning an appropriate method of integrating faith and reason. This basic divide, between camps later known as evidentialists and presuppositionalists, continues to divide evangelicalism.

This cleavage in the conservative camps separates evangelicals who would seek to ground an apologetic approach in arguments from reason and evidence, from those who base their theological thinking in a basic *presupposition* of the authority, truthfulness, and divine inspiration of the Bible.[27]

Henry, while placing himself clearly within the presuppositionalist camp, nevertheless resisted any charge of fideism or irrationality. He saw three rival theological methods, and identified these with the figures of Tertullian, Aquinas, and Augustine. Tertullian, he explained, represented the triumph of irrationality, belief in absurdity (*credo quia absurdum*) while Aquinas ("I know in order to believe") so qualified revelation by his reliance on reason that faith lost its primacy. Augustine, on the other hand, was identified with a *via media* which established the primacy of faith and revelation, and constructed a theology based upon believing deduction.

The tradition of Tertullian, Henry suggests, was never a prominent option in Western theology until the rise of neoorthodox theology. The evidentialist tradition raised the possibility of a natural theology inferred from general revelation. The Augustinian tradition, on the other hand, identified as well with Anselm, Calvin, and Luther, presents a genuine alternative to an independent natural theology which places reason prior to revelation or to a theology of the absurd, which places faith outside the realm of rational discourse.

Henry's central method was thus deductive, a tradition he rooted in the tradition of the church from its first systematician, Origen. Though evidentialists caricature presuppositionalists as fideists, Henry sought to demonstrate that theology could be based in a prior commitment to revealed truth while remaining open to the questions raised by public reason.[28]

The foundation of Henry's theological system is therefore an affirmation of biblical theism and the authority of Scripture as the inerrant word of God. Neither axiom is held aloof from reason, but no apology is made for the a priori assertion of the revealed truth.[29]

Though Henry is first and foremost a theologian, he has not produced a systematic theology, choosing instead to concentrate upon the doctrines of revelation, God, and religious authority; the major points of compromise in twentieth-century theology.[30] Glimpses of what his systematic theology would look like are available in his shorter theological writings, and within the pages of *God, Revelation and Authority*. What appears is a thoroughly conservative theology in the evangelical tradition, yet fully conversant with competing schools of theological thought as well as the worlds of philosophy and science. Yet, any review of Henry's theological accomplishment must concentrate on the issues to which Henry dedicated his life and his major writing project.

Revelation

Though God is greater than, and ontologically prior to His revelation, Henry begins with revelation as the epistemological starting point for Christian theology. Revelation is, in his words, "the basic epistemological axiom," that is, the foundational principle for any theological investigation—or of any search for truth. As Henry stated:

> Divine revelation is the source of all truth, the truth of Christianity included; reason is the instrument for recognizing it; Scripture is its verifying principle; logical consistency is a negative test for truth and coherence a subordinate test. The task of Christian theology is to exhibit the content of biblical revelation as an orderly whole.[31]

Thus, the biblical revelation, given by God at his own gracious initiative, is the source from which all theological statements are to be drawn. "Had God insisted on remaining incommunicado," Henry reminds, "we would know nothing whatever about him."[32]

Henry's exposition of the doctrine of revelation stands as an awesome evangelical achievement. His stress on the actuality and trustworthiness of divine revelation serves to remind all evangelicals of the revelatory basis of all theological constructions.

Consistent with his epistemological method, Henry acknowledges the reality of natural revelation, but denies it a positive role within his dogmatic system. He affirms "the considerable variety in God's revealing activity"[33] and points to general revelation as part of any evangelical understanding of God's revelatory initiative. General revelation is foundational to understanding human sin and culpability before the divine Creator.[34] Nevertheless, Henry demonstrates that the creature did not move from general revelation to a "natural theology" based upon such revelation, but rather to a revolt against the Creator.

His system is based upon an unwavering commitment to divine revelation as found in Scripture, and ultimately in the incarnate Word, as recorded and proclaimed in that Scripture.

The Bible

The theological world, both evangelical and mainline, associates Carl Henry with a fervent and continuing defense of the authority and inerrancy of the Bible. Henry's theological system has given scriptural authority more attention than any other doctrinal issue.

Revelation is, in Henry's words, "rational communication" in "conceptual-verbal form." That is, God has revealed Himself in intelligible concepts, and thus through understandable language. His revelation comes as both act and deed, related in human language. Henry denies any role for revelation through the irrational.[35]

Henry defined the Bible as "the reservoir and conduit of divine truth, the authoritative written record and exposition of God's nature and will."[36] Though modern humans revolt against all authority, Henry articulated a doctrine of inscripturated revelation which allowed for no compromise on the issue of biblical authority. In so doing he set himself against the tide of twentieth-century theology, including neoorthodoxy, narrative theologies, and the contributions of Moltmann and Pannenberg. He also set himself against any compromise within the evangelical camp, and set out to refute the criticisms of revisionists such as James Barr.

This defense of biblical authority is tied to Henry's stress upon the validity of propositional revelation. Not all revelation, he asserts, is propositional, but any stance which denies the inherent propositional nature of much of the biblical revelation leads, he suggests, to a loss of biblical truth. A denial of propositional revelation, which Henry associates with neoorthodoxy, devolves into revelation as irrationality; the "Tertullian temptation" to assert faith in the absurd.[37]

Henry has not produced an elaborate theory of biblical inspiration, yet steers a middle course between the so-called "dynamic" and "dictation" theories. He affirms the role of the Holy Spirit in both the inspiration and illumination of the text, yet allows for a genuine role to be played by the inspired authors of the biblical text.[38] Henry asserts that the evangelical doctrine of biblical inspiration affirms that "the text of Scripture is divinely inspired as an objective deposit of language," thus protecting the verbal character of the revelation; that inspiration "is wholly consistent with the humanity of the prophets and apostles;" that divine inspiration was limited to the chosen biblical authors; that divine inspiration was not limited by the "natural resources" of the authors; that Scripture is inspired as a whole and in its parts; and, in conclusion, that God is understood therefore to be the ultimate author of Scripture.[39]

Biblical inerrancy also serves a role in the evangelical doctrine of Scripture. Henry roots the doctrine within the theological heritage of the church, and denies the claim that the concept of inerrancy is a modern (and thus unnecessary) innovation. The term is often misunderstood, and has been an issue of messy theological warfare, yet Henry asserts that the concept is vital to any consistent evangelical position.

Inspiration posits the divine authorship of the biblical text. Inerrancy serves to articulate the fact that this divine revelation is therefore free from error and untruth. Inerrancy "affirms a special activity of divine inspiration whereby the Holy Spirit superintended the scriptural writers in communicating the biblical message in ways consistent with their differing personalities, literary styles and cultural background, while safeguarding them from error."[40] Henry's defense of biblical inerrancy is one of the most thorough treatments in the evangelical literature. A reading of Henry's various writings on inerrancy, and especially the relevant sections in *God, Revelation and Authority*, reveals the depth of Henry's passionate commitment to the concept—and indeed to the Word itself—and yet also indicates that Henry is unwilling to allow the word to become a weapon of theological warfare. He declined to participate in the first meetings of the International Council on Biblical Inerrancy, and broke publicly with his former colleague Harold Lindsell by suggesting that inerrancy be a test of evangelical *consistency* rather then *authenticity*.[41]

In other words, *consistent* evangelicalism will maintain biblical inerrancy as a vital corollary. From this point Henry will make no further concessions. He defines inerrancy so as to protect its central claims of trustworthiness for the biblical text, while avoiding the excessive claims of modern technical precision or absolute verbal exactitude in New Testament quotations of Old Testament passages made by some proponents of the term. Neither will he claim that a commitment to biblical inerrancy guarantees evangelical orthodoxy on all other points of doctrine.

On the other hand, Hnery does suggest that inerrancy implies that the truthfulness of the text extends to scientific and historical matters, as well as ethical and theological teachings. Further, he maintains that inerrancy inheres in the actual words of Scripture; that inerrancy attaches *directly* to the autographs, and only *indirectly* to the copies; and that evangelicals must therefore strive to determine the most accurate text for study.

God

The Scriptures are not an end in themselves, but are the self-revelation of the Revealer God. Henry's attention to issues of revelation and biblical authority point toward his massive exposition of the reality, objectivity, and sovereignty of God. The two great divisions within *God, Revelation and Authority* are "God Who Speaks and Shows" and "God Who Stands and Stays." The former established the epistemological basis for the latter, his discussion of the doctrine of God.

In the face of modernity's flight from metaphysics (and the complicity of much modern theology) Henry speaks of the God who *is*, "not a god who *may be*, or a god who *was*, or is yet *to be*."[42] Modern revisionist renderings of God are thusly denied, along with logical positivism and existentialism.

In summary, Henry affirms the God revealed within the Bible, the father of Abraham and Isaac and Jacob, and the Lord and father of Jesus Christ. He affirms the Trinity as a vital biblical teaching, and articulates the divine attributes, and His sovereignty, and providence. Furthermore, he maintains the identification of the Creator as none other than the first person of the Trinity.

Refusing to define God by means of analogy, dialectic, or empirical data, Henry bases his treatment of the divine attributes on the biblical revelation. Scripture reveals the simplicity of God as "a living center of activity pervasively characterized by all his distinctive perfections."[43] His treatment of the doctrine defies summary, but is a stalwart defense and explication of classical Christian theism based thoroughly in the biblical revelation.

God is seen to be the divine Creator, who created the universe and all within it *ex nihilo* and exercises his providential care and direction over His creation. He defines God in terms of "incomparable love" and unconditioned holiness. He rejects universalism as an implication of this love, and provides a brief treatment of divine election.

Jesus Christ is "the personal incarnation of God in the flesh," the climax of revelation, in whom "the source and content of revelation converge and coincide."[44] Henry stresses the preexistence of the Logos, His historical incarnation and intelligibility, His incarnation as the focus of prophecy and expectation, and His role as the only divine Mediator between God and humanity. Jesus Christ, crucified, dead, resurrected, and now glorified, was the divine God/Man in His incarnation; and is now the Lord of the universe at the right hand of the Father.

Ethics

The Uneasy Conscience of Modern Fundamentalism, Henry's epochal volume of 1947, demonstrated his interest in Christian ethics, both personal and social. He was to produce *Christian Personal Ethics*, a work of massive dimensions, and *Aspects of Christian Social Ethics*, a much smaller volume limited by Henry's teaching load and responsibilities at *Christianity Today*. He was also to edit Baker's *Dictionary of Christian Ethics*, a major reference work for evangelicals.[45]

In recent years Henry has emerged as a potent opponent of abortion and a champion of other moral causes. His opportunities for lectures and occasional writings have granted his ethical writings much visibility and considerable influence in the evangelical world.[46]

Evaluation

Carl Henry has emerged as a major influence in twentieth-century theology. His influence, extended through his voluminous writings and public exposure, has shaped the evangelical movement to a degree unmatched by any other evangelical theologian of the period. His staunch defense of classical theism, biblical authority, and the role of the church in society have earned the respect of evangelicals and nonevangelicals alike.

One of his major achievements has been the reestablishment of theology as a vital concern of the Christian community. His theological vigor and force have often laid bare the latent antitheological attitudes among some evangelicals, and have reasserted the vital role of theology as a servant of the church.

The evangelical movement has also benefited from Henry's model of aggressive engagement with the broader theological community. Henry has been a master of the theological literature and has addressed variant theological systems with an acknowledged expertise. Yet, dialogue alone has never been his goal. As indicated most clearly in his dream for *Christianity Today,* Henry has always been committed to a missionary vision—a truly evangelical vision—of influence in the broader theological community. His mission has been to bring contemporary theology back to a firm commitment to biblical authority.

Evangelicals are in Henry's debt for his effective and thorough restatement of the evangelical doctrine of revelation and biblical authority. Critics have often painted him as a rationalist (or even a Thomist) and have lamented his scholastic approach to epistemological issues.[47] Nevertheless, his achievement in *God, Revelation and Authority* will stand as an encyclopedic *Prologomenon* to an evangelical theology.[48]

This function as *Prologomenon* (or methological introduction) to a full evangelical theology points to the fact that Henry's theological project has not included a complete systematic theology. As suggested above, this is tied to Henry's reading of contemporary theology and the critical points of theological compromise in the twentieth century. As such, Henry's work reminds evangelicals of the importance of methodological issues as the foundation of any systematic effort. The lack of a systematic expression has left several theological issues untouched or underdeveloped in Henry's system. He has given little attention to the Holy Spirit, and except for his work in personal ethics, to the Christian life and devotion. The most glaring omission in his theological project is the doctrine of the church (ecclesiology).

Henry's pilgrimage mirrors the emergence of the parachurch movement in conservative Protestantism. The evangelical movement itself, while including many within the established churches, was largely a parachurch movement. The momentum and defining characteristics of the movement came from the parachurch institutions which shaped the evangelical consciousness. Henry's biography includes a litany of evangelical parachurch organizations and institutions ranging from Wheaton College and Fuller Seminary to *Christianity Today* and World Vision. Indeed, his conversion experience came by means of a parachurch movement, and not through the evangelistic thrust of a local church. In this manner Carl Henry is symbolic of the evangelical movement as a whole.

This raises the important question of Carl Henry as a *Baptist* theologian. Concern for a biblical understanding of baptism led Henry into membership in a Baptist church during his days at Wheaton and Northern Seminary. Upon his call to the ministry he was licensed to preach by the Babylon Baptist Church on Long Island, having been baptized there just ten months earlier. In October 1940 he was called as student pastor of the Humbolt Park Baptist Church in Chicago and was ordained to the ministry there in 1941. The ordination service was performed with the Chicago Baptist Association, affiliated with the Northern Baptist Convention (now the American Baptist Churches).

Henry's involvement with the Northern Convention was marred by his ejection from the convention's annuity program after his move to Fuller Seminary. While at Fuller the Henrys attended a Baptist church and upon his move to *Christianity Today* they joined the Capitol Hill Metropolitan Baptist Church in Washington, D.C., an evangelical congregation affiliated with the American Baptist Churches and the Southern Baptist Convention.

These linkages notwithstanding, Henry's most critical involvements have been outside denominational life. Yet, he has played a part in theological discussion and debate within both the Northern and Southern conventions. His mission has been to call his fellow Baptists to the high ground of biblical authority, noting that "Baptist distinctives of rebirth, of resolution, of resource are fixed in the confidence that the New Testament revelation is the climax of divine disclosure."[49] Further, Henry chided Baptists for their "theological amnesia" seen in the fact that "Southern Baptists often close their theological history with E. Y. Mullins or W. T. Conner; Northern Baptists with A. H. Strong."[50] He called for a revival of vigorous theology among Baptists as well as an openness to cooperation with other evangelicals in common efforts, for "Arbitrarily to equate denominational, and in this case Baptist, affiliation with membership in the body of Christ is obviously theologically naive and increasingly theologically unrealistic."[51]

The 1987 Southern Baptist Pastors' Conference included Henry as a major speaker and honored him for his contributions to theology as a Baptist.[52] In the main, however, Henry is usually identified as an evangelical statesman and theologian.

Numerous honors and accolades have come to Henry. He has served as president of the Evangelical Theological Society and the American Theological Society, and has delivered many of the most prestigious lectureships in the world, among them the 1989 Rutherford Lectures at the University of Edinburgh, Scotland. He has been recognized by evangelicals and nonevangelicals as the premier theological representative of the evangelical movement in the last half of the twentieth century. As E. G. Homrighausen of Princeton Theological Seminary remarked, Henry "has championed evangelical Christianity with clarity of language, comprehensiveness of scholarship, clarity of mind, and vigor of spirit."[53] Baptists and their fellow evangelicals stand in his debt.

Bibliography

Books by Henry

Aspects of Christian Social Ethics. Grand Rapids: William B. Eerdmans, 1963.

Christian Countermoves in a Decadent Culture. Portland, OR: Multnomah Press, 1986.

Christian Personal Ethics. Grand Rapids: William B. Eerdmans, 1957.

Confessions of a Theologian. Waco, Tx: Word Books, 1986.

Conversations With Carl Henry: Christianity for Today. Lewiston, NY: The Edwin Mellen Press, 1986.

The Drift of Western Thought. Grand Rapids: William B. Eerdmans, 1951.

Evangelical Responsibility in Contemporary Theology. Grand Rapids: William B. Eerdmans, 1957.

Evangelicals at the Brink of Crisis. Waco, Tx: Word Books, 1967.

Evangelicals in Search of Identity. Waco, Tx: Word Books, 1976.

Faith at the Frontiers. Chicago: Moody Press, 1969.

Fifty Years of Protestant Theology. Boston: W. A. Wilde, 1950.

Frontiers in Modern Theology. Chicago: Moody Press, 1966.

God, Revelation and Authority, six volumes. Waco, Tx: Word Books, 1976-1983.

The God Who Shows Himself. Waco, Tx: Word Books, 1966.

Notes on the Doctrine of God. Boston: W. A. Wilde, 1948.

Personal Idealism and Strong's Theology. Wheaton, Il: Van Kampen Press, 1951.

A Plea for Evangelical Demonstration. Grand Rapids: Baker Book House, 1971.

The Protestant Dilemma: An Analysis of the Current Impasse. Grand Rapids: William B. Eerdmans, 1949.

Remaking the Modern Mind. Grand Rapids: William B. Eerdmans, 1946.

Twilight of a Great Civilization: The Drift Toward Neo-Paganism. Westchester, Il: Crossway Books, 1988.

The Uneasy Conscience of Modern Fundamentalism. Grand Rapids: William B. Eerdmans, 1947.

Books Edited or Co-edited by Henry

Baker's Dictionary of Christian Ethics. Grand Rapids: Baker Book House, 1973.

Basic Christian Doctrines. Grand Rapids: Baker Book House, 1962.

Christian Faith and Modern Theology: Contemporary Evangelical Thought. New York: Channel Press, 1964.

Contemporary Evangelical Thought. Grand Rapids: Baker Book House, 1957.

Evangelical Affirmations. Grand Rapids: Zondervan, 1990.

Fundamentals of the Faith. Grand Rapids: Zondervan, 1969.

Jesus of Nazareth: Savior and Lord. Grand Rapids: Baker Book House, 1966.

Quest for Reality: Christianity and the Counter Culture. Waco, Tx: Word Books, 1973.

Revelation and the Bible: Contemporary Evangelical Thought. Grand Rapids: Baker Book House, 1949.

Articles by Henry

"American Evangelicals and Theological Dialogue." *Christianity Today,* January 15, 1965, 27-29.

"Are We Doomed to Hermeneutical Nihilism?" *Review and Expositor* (1974).

"Between Barth and Bultmann," *Christianity Today,* May 8, 1961, 24-26.

"The Bible and the Consciousness of Our Age," in *Hermeneutics, Inerrancy, and the Bible,* edited by Earl Rademacher and Robert Preus.

"Biblical Authority and the Social Crisis," in *Authority and Interpretation: A Baptist Perspective,* edited by Duane Garrett and Richard Melick (Grand Rapids: Baker Book House, 1985), 203-20.

"The Cultural Relativizing of Revelation," *Trinity Journal* 1 ns (1980): 153-164.

"The Deterioration of Barth's Defenses." *Christianity Today,* October 9, 1964, 16-19.

"Evangelical," in *The New International Dictionary of the Christian Church,* ed. J. D. Douglas (Exeter: Paternoster Press, 358-359.

"Evangelicals and Fundamentals," *Christianity Today,* September 16, 1957, 20-21.

"Evangelicals: Out of the Closet But Going Nowhere?" *Christianity Today,* January 4, 1980, 16-22.

"Evangelism and the Sacred Book." *Christianity Today,* October 15, 1956, 22.

"Justification by Ignorance: A Neo-Protestant Motif?" *Christianity Today,* January 2, 1970, 10-15.

"Liberation Theology and the Scriptures," in *Liberation Theology,* ed. Ronald H. Nash (Milford, Mi: Mott Media, 1984), 187-202.

"Narrative Theology: An Evangelical Appraisal," *Trinity Journal* 8 (1987): 3-19.

"The Priority of Divine Revelation: A Review Article," *Journal of the Evangelical Theological Society,* 27 (1984): 77-92.

"The Stunted God of Process Theology," in *Process Theology,* ed. Ronald H. Nash (Grand Rapids: Baker Book House, 1987), 357-376.

"Theology and Biblical Authority: A Review Article," *Journal of the Evangelical Theological Society,* 19 (1976): 315-23.

"Where Will Evangelicals Cast Their Lot?" *This World* 18 (1987): 3-11.

"Wintertime in European Theology," *Christianity Today,* December 5, 1960, 12-14.

Works about Henry

Patterson, Bob E. *Carl F. H. Henry,* "Makers of the Modern Theological Mind," (Waco, Tx: Word Books, 1986).

Fackre, Gabriel. "Carl F. H. Henry," In *A Handbook to Contemporary Theology,* ed. Martin Marty and Dean Peerman.

Mohler, Richard Albert, Jr. "Evangelical Theology and Karl Barth: Representative Models of Response." (Ph.D. diss., The Southern Baptist Theological Seminary, 1989), 107-134.

Contributor's Note

Carl F. H. Henry's written contributions now total over thirty written volumes, numerous edited materials, and a constellation of articles on issues ranging from social and ethical issues to contemporary theology. This bibliography is only a brief introduction to Henry's published works. In particular, readers are advised to consult Henry's voluminous production of articles and editorials during his tenure as editor of *Christianity Today.*

Notes

1. As Henry recalled: "In respect to church participation we were Christmas and Easter Christians. My father was Lutheran by family heritage and my mother Roman Catholic. But we had no family prayers, no grace at table, no Bible in our home." See Carl F. H. Henry, *Confessions of a Theologian: An Autobiography* (Waco: Word Books, 1986), 17-18.

2. The Oxford Group was an evangelistic and devotional movement founded by Frank Buchman. The Group's emphasis on personal spiritual direction caused a considerable degree of controversy among evangelicals. Though members of the group were instrumental in his conversion, Henry was never to join the movement.

3. Clark's tenure at Wheaton came to an end when his Calvinism became an issue of controversy in the evangelistically charged community of the college and its supporters. He was later to teach at Butler University in Indianapolis and Covenant College in Tennessee.

4. Born to the Henrys were Paul Brentwood (1942) and Carol Jennifer (1944). Both children followed their parents in academic training. Carol was to become a musician and Paul, who taught political science at Calvin College for some years, was later elected to the U.S. House of Representatives, holding the Grand Rapids seat once held by President Gerald R. Ford.

5. Henry identified his mentors at Northern Seminary as Peder Stiasen, Julius R. Mantey, Ernest E. Smith, Faris D. Whitesell, William Emmett Powers, William Fouts, and J. N. D. Rodeheaver. In roughly the same period he was also to study at Indiana University under W. Harry Jellema and Henry Veitch. Jellema, a Calvinist, was to influence Henry and be honored as one of "three men of Athens" to whom Henry dedicated his first foray in theology, *Remaking the Modern Mind*. The other two so honored were Gordon Clark and Cornelius Van Til.

6. The history and development of Fuller Seminary is well documented by George M. Marsden in *Reforming Fundamentalism: Fuller Seminary and the New Evangelicalism* (Grand Rapids, Mich.: Eerdmans, 1987). Marsden's history is a model of interpretive historiography, and provides critical insights into the development of American evangelicalism as seen through the history of one of its primary institutions. The critical role played by Carl F. H. Henry in Fuller's early struggles is documented by Marsden.

7. See Henry, *Confessions of a Theologian,* 141-302.

8. Carl F. H. Henry, *The Uneasy Conscience of Modern Fundamentalism* (Grand Rapids, Mich.: Eerdmans, 1947). Henry lamented the loss of evangelical social concern and compared the fundamentalist movement to the priest and Levite of the parable of the good Samaritan, "by-passing suffering humanity." He called for a "New Reformation" to correct this failure in fundamentalism. Nevertheless, this prescription, matched with the lack of separatism among the "new evangelicals," brought on an eventual break with the older fundamentalist movement. See Farley P. Butler, "Billy Graham and the End of Evangelical Unity" (Ph.D. diss., University of Florida, 1976).

9. Others among the "new evangelicals" were Bernard Ramm, Edward John Carnell, Harold J. Ockenga, and Vernon Grounds. The exact origin of the term "new evangelical" is unclear, though it is generally attributed to Ockenga and linked to his 1947 convocation address at Fuller Seminary. See Harold J. Ockenga, "From Fundamentalism, Through New Evangelicalism, to Evangelicalism," in *Evangelical Roots,* ed. Kenneth S. Kantzer (Nashville: Thomas Nelson, 1978), 35-48. Though Henry

evidently did not coin the term, its popularization and conceptualization were largely due to his efforts. See especially Carl F. H. Henry, "The Vigor of the New Evangelicalism," *Christian Life and Times,* January 1948, 30-32, March 1948, 35-38, 85; April 1948, 32-35, 65-69.

10. Henry's experience at Fuller was mixed. Though fully in agreement with the vision of its founding, he was aware of a lack of consensus among the faculty concerning its future direction.

11. A review of *Christianity Today* under Henry's leadership reveals his commitment to evangelical orthodoxy paired with a missionary zeal to reach beyond the evangelical movement.

12. For Henry's evaluation of the congress, see his *Evangelicals at the Brink of Crisis: Significance of the World Congress on Evangelism* (Waco: Word Books, 1967). Henry's optimism was tempered by concerns that evangelicalism would miss a critical opportunity for influence and extension. He wrote of the event as indicative of evangelicalism's "new prominence," as well as "a brink of decision."

13. Under Henry's editorship the magazine was directed toward a readership of trained pastors and therefore dealt with a wide array of theological issues. The magazine is now marketed to a general readership, and has lost much of its intellectual content.

14. As Henry commented: "The masses are craving an *authoritative word*—not the discredited probability of the modernist mood. But the downfall of liberalism need not be the rise of evangelicalism; rather, it may be the forerunner of a secularism even worse than that of recent decades." See *Christian Life* (April 1948): 69.

15. Though liberalism was understood to be the foe, the evangelicals, and Henry among them, rejected the tendency of the fundamentalists to reduce theology "to simple cliches, without much thought of their profounder systematic implications." See Carl F. H. Henry, *Evangelical Responsibility in Contemporary Theology* (Grand Rapids, Mich.: Eerdmans, 1957), 33. Over twenty years later, Henry responded to James Barr: "American evangelicals have for a generation distinguished between what is desirable and what in undesirable in fundamentalism. We did not have to wait until 1977 [the publication of Barr's *Fundamentalism*] and Barr to realize that fundamentalist preaching is often exegetically shallow, that fundamentalism uncritically elevated certain prudish traditions to scriptural status, that not infrequently its spokesmen argue that historical criticism 'inevitably' tears apart the whole fabric of faith, and that many fundamentalists tend to appropriate selected bits of nonevangelical scholarship rather than to initiate creative studies, so that serious students all too often turn to mediating scholars for productive challenge." See Carl F. H. Henry, "Those Incomprehensible British Fundamentalists," *Christianity Today,* June 2, 1978.

16. This growing sense of a missed opportunity is evident throughout Henry's later writings, and can be traced to his indictment of evangelicalism's failure to fulfill the promise of the Berlin Congress. In the 1970s and 1980s Henry released a steady stream of jeremiads intended to invigorate the evangelical movement in both its theological commitments and its engagement with alternative theological systems. See, for example, Carl F. H. Henry, *Evangelicals in Search of Identity* (Waco: Word Books, 1976); *A Plea for Evangelical Demonstration* (Grand Rapids, Mich.: Baker Book House, 1971); and "The Evangelical Prospect in America," the concluding chapter to his *Confessions of a Theologian,* 381-407. See also the series of interviews with Henry published as *Conversations with Carl Henry: Christianity for Today* (Lewiston, N.Y.: Edwin Mellen Press, 1986).

17. Carl F. H. Henry, *Remaking the Modern Mind* (Grand Rapids, Mich.: Eerdmans, 1946), 19.

18. Carl F. H. Henry, *The Protestant Dilemma: An Analysis of the Current Impasse in Theology* (Grand Rapids, Mich.: Eerdmans, 1948).

19. Carl F. H. Henry, *Fifty Years of Protestant Theology* (Boston: W. A. Wilde, 1950); *The Drift of Western Thought* (Grand Rapids, Mich.: Eerdmans, 1951); *Notes on the Doctrine of God* (Boston: W. A. Wilde, 1948).

20. See Carl F. H. Henry, *Personal Idealism and Strong's Theology* (Wheaton, Ill.: Van Kampen Press, 1951). Though this pattern of thought is evident in Henry's earliest writings, its basis is most clearly seen in this study, the published version of his Boston University dissertation under Edgar S. Brightman.

21. Henry, *Fifty Years*, 37.

22. Carl F. H. Henry, "Between Barth and Bultmann," *Christianity Today*, May 8, 1961, 24-26; "The Deterioration of Barth's Defenses," *Christianity Today*, October 9, 1964, 16-19; "the Pale Ghost of Barth," *Christianity Today*, February 12, 1971, 40-43; "Wintertime in European Theology," *Christianity Today*, December 5, 1960, 12-14.

23. For a thorough analysis of Henry's interaction with Karl Barth, see Richard Albert Mohler, Jr., "Evangelical Theology and Karl Barth: Representative Models of Response" (Ph.D. dissertation, The Southern Baptist Theological Seminary, 1989), 107-34.

24. Carl F. H. Henry, "The Stunted God of Process Theology," in *Process Theology*, ed. Ronald H. Nash (Grand Rapids, Mich.: Baker Book House, 1987), 357-76; "Liberation Theology and the Scriptures," in *Liberation Theology*, ed. Ronald H. Nash (Milford, Mich.: Mott Media, 1984), 187-202.

25. His responses to alternative theological systems take many forms, among them the following: Carl F. H. Henry, "Narrative Theology: An Evangelical Appraisal," *Trinity Journal* 8 (1987): 3019; "Theology and Biblical Authority: A Review Article," *Journal of the Evangelical Theological Society* 19 (1976): 315-23 (a response to David Kelsey, *The Uses of Scripture in Recent Theology*); "The Priority of Divine Revelation: A Review Article," *Journal of the Evangelical Theological Society* 27 (1984): 77-92 (a response to Avery Dulles, *Models of Revelation*); "The Cultural Relativizing of Revelation," *Trinity Journal* 1 ns (1980): 153-64 (a response to Charles Kraft, *Christianity in Culture*).

26. Henry, "Narrative Theology" and "The Cultural Relativizing of Revelation." See also the interesting exchange between Henry and Mark Ellingsen. Ellingsen, a mainline Protestant, called for a dialogue and eventual merging of the evangelical and mainline movements based in a form of narrative theology. See Mark Ellingsen, *The Evangelical Movement: Growth, Impact, Controversy, Dialog (GRA)* (Minneapolis: Augsburg Publishing House, 1988), and Henry's response in "Where Will Evangelicals Cast Their Lot?" *This World* 18 (1987): 3-11.

27. This controversy is, of course, as old as Christian theology itself, but is of particular importance among the evangelicals. The most ardent and influential presuppositionalist of the twentieth century was Cornelius Van Til, who influenced generations of evangelicals with his unyielding rejection of evidentialist apologetics. The evidentialist tradition has also been a major influence in the evangelical movement, with neo-Thomists such as Norman Geisler and Reformed figures such as John Gerstner influencing large segments of conservative Protestantism.

28. See Henry, *GRA*, 1:181-87. See also his Rutherford Lecture, "Presuppositionalism and Theological Method."

29. Henry states: "Evidentialists who disparage the primacy of faith do no special service to evangelical theology. The fact is, that to affirm the priority of faith need not mean, as all presuppositionalists are charged with holding, that truth rests on faith alone *apart from, instead of,* or *over against* reason. The emphasis that faith precedes reason in establishing certain basic truths does not require that reason and evidence are not irrelevant to authentic faith." ("Presuppositionalism and Theological Method," 4.)

30. During his doctoral studies at Northern Baptist Seminary, Henry and his fellow graduate students had announced their intention to produce a systematic theology which would replace the work of A. H. Strong in Baptist seminaries.

31. Henry, *GRA*, 1:215.

32. Henry, *GRA*, 2:18.

33. Ibid., 79.

34. "Anyone who denies this doctrine places himself not only in unmistakable contradiction to the Bible and to the great theological traditions of Christendom that flow from its teaching, but also against the living God's disclosure in cosmic reality and in mankind to which Scripture testifies (Rom. 1:19-21)." (Henry, *GRA*, 2:83-84.) Further, "Since human beings are culpable sinners because of revolt against light, to deny general revelation would destroy the basis of moral and spiritual accountability." (Henry, *GRA*, 2:85.)

35. In so doing Henry places himself against certain strands of neoorthodoxy, modern language philosophy, and analytic philosophy, though he shows himself thoroughly conversant with these positions. See Henry, *GRA*, 3 and 4.

36. Henry, *GRA*, 4:7.

37. As Henry demonstrates, any denial of propositional truth requires a *propositional* denial. See his treatment of this issue in *GRA*, 3:455-81.

38. Note that Henry criticizes the Chicago Statement on Biblical Inerrancy (1978) which "strenuously disavows dictation, but unfortunately in some passages suggests divine causation of each and every word choice." See *GRA*, 4:141.

39. Ibid., 129-61.

40. Ibid., 166-67.

41. See Carl F. H. Henry, *Conversations with Carl Henry: Christianity for Today* (Lewiston, N.Y.: Edwin Mellen Press, 1986), esp. 23-30. Henry's careful distinction at this point should not be missed. While claiming inerrancy as a critical component of an evangelical doctrine of Scripture, Henry nevertheless recognized that inerrancy is not the *first* claim to be made for the biblical text. An affirmation of inerrancy should not, in his mind, be the *sine qua non* of evangelical identity. It is critical enough to function as a test of evangelical *consistency,* but cannot alone bear the weight of a test of evangelical *authenticity.* To allow this would be to identify critical allies in the fight for biblical authority as nonevangelicals. As Henry asserts: "I think it highly unfortunate that the *primary* thing that should now be said about men like F. F. Bruce and [G. C.] Berkouwer, men who have made significant contributions to the conservative position—even though we might have hoped for somewhat more from them—is that they are not authentic evangelicals because of their position at this one point." See *Conversations,* 24.

42. Henry, *GRA*, 5:21.

43. Ibid., 130.

44. Henry, *GRA*, 3:9.

45. Carl F. H. Henry, *Christian Personal Ethics* (Grand Rapids, Mich.: Eerdmans, 1956); *Aspects of Christian Social Ethics* (Grand Rapids: Eerdmans, 1964);

and ed., *Dictionary of Christian Ethics* (Grand Rapids, Mich.: Baker Book House).

46. See the collections of lectures, sermons, etc. in Carl F. H. Henry, *The Christian Mindset in a Secular Society* (Portland, Oreg.: Multnomah Press, 1978); *Christian Countermoves in a Decadent Culture* (Portland, Oreg.: Multnomah Press, 1986); and *Twilight of a Great Civilization: The Drift Toward Neo-Paganism* (Westchester, Ill.: Crossway Books, 1988).

47. Note, for example, the assessment offered by William Abraham of Southern Methodist University. Abraham, who represents the Wesleyan tradition within evangelicalism, charged that *God, Revelation and Authority* is "over three thousand pages of turgid scholasticism." See William Abraham, *The Coming Great Revival* (San Francisco: Harper and Row, 1984), 37. This statement indicates something of the great divide between those who define evangelicalism primarily by a set of theological commitments and those who point instead to an evangelical faith experience and concern for personal holiness. To be fair, Henry has evidenced a concern for both dimensions, but has given the cognitive dimension primary attention in his writings.

48. Thomas Reginald McNeal's doctoral dissertation at Southwestern Seminary identified Henry as a Thomist and termed his theological method "apologetic presuppositionalism." As he stated: "The thesis of this dissertation is that Henry's apologetic presuppositionalism represents a rationalistic theological methodology dominated by the priority of reason over faith." See Thomas Reginald McNeal, "A Critical Analysis of the Doctrine of God in the Theology of Carl F. H. Henry." (Ph.D. diss., Southwestern Baptist Theological Seminary, 1986), 1. Yet, Henry has always stressed that revelation is *prior* to both reason and faith, even as he has championed the role of reason and rationality in human thought. Henry has provided a key to understanding this issue through his models of Tertullian, Thomas Aquinas, and Augustine, with Augustine representing Henry's own position of reason working upon divine revelation. Henry may be *rationalistic,* if by this we indicate his reliance upon reason as an instrument of understanding; but he is not a *rationalist,* if by this he is thought to place reason prior to revelation. As Henry stated: "To be sure, evangelicals need not tremble and take to the hills whenever others charge us with rationalism, since not every meaning of the term is objectionable; those who glory in the irrational, superrational, or subrational ought to be challenged head-on" (Henry, *GRA* 3:480).

49. Carl F. H. Henry, "Twenty Years a Baptist," *Foundations,* 47.

50. Ibid., 53.

51. Ibid., 54. He continued: "Our century is surrounded and crowded, rather, by the insistent problem: in thought and in practice does the quantitative and qualitative value ascribed to the Word, incarnate and written, produce both a Christian and a Baptist? The turmoil over Baptist distinctives, within Baptist distractions, yields ambiguous Baptist directives."

52. Nelson Price, 1987 president of the Pastors' Conference, presented Henry a plaque celebrating his influence and claiming his identity as a Southern Baptist. Henry has also served as a visiting professor at The Southern Baptist Theological Seminary and has delivered lectureship at New Orleans Baptist Seminary and Southeastern Baptist Theological Seminary, among others.

53. E. G. Homrighausen, Review of *A Plea for Evangelical Demonstration* by Carl F. H. Henry, *Princeton Seminary Bulletin* 65 (July 1972): 96.

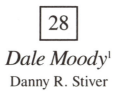

Dale Moody[1]

Danny R. Stiver

One of the last chapel addresses that Dale Moody gave at Southern Baptist Theological Seminary climaxed with Moody, at that time under heavy fire from critics on his views of Scripture, shouting the famous words attributed to Martin Luther at the Diet of Worms: *"Hier stehe ich. Ich kann nicht anders. Gott helfe mir!* Here I stand. I can do no other. God help me. . . . My conscience is captive to the Word of God."[2] Few words could better capture the essence of virtually a fifty-year career of preaching, teaching, and writing. This commitment to Scripture expressed through a dynamic preaching and teaching style lies behind Moody's significance as one of the most outstanding Southern Baptist theologians. The capstone of his career was the publication in 1981 of his systematic theology, *The Word of Truth,* the first by a Southern Baptist seminary professor in over forty years.[3]

Biography

In many ways Dale Moody has remained a Texas preacher, filled with characteristic pietistic fervor, biblical fire, and dynamic personal presence. Born January 27, 1915, in Jones County, Texas, he was nurtured in a family with a rich Baptist heritage.[4] He grew up in Grapevine, Texas, present site of the Dallas-Fort Worth International Airport.[5] It was a pastoral ranch setting when as a twelve-year old he was riding his horse through the woods, stopped at a grove of trees, and committed his life to Jesus Christ.[6] Like many Baptists, this was a vivid experience for him, which he often recounts and revisits. At the end of that summer of 1927 he was baptized in the Grapevine Baptist Church. Moody's family then moved their membership to the nearby Coppell Baptist Church. By the time he was a senior in high school, he was called to preach and was called as pastor of that church.[7]

Subsequently, Moody followed a winding path until he found his theological home at The Southern Baptist Theological Seminary. He was attracted to Dallas Theological Seminary for a year because of a lifelong interest in premillennial views, but subsequently found it too confining.[8] Wherever he was, he distinguished himself academically, displaying even at Baylor University twin interests in science and the Bible.[9]

Moody inaugurated a relationship with Southern Seminary in 1937 that continues to this day as Emeritus Professor of Christian Theology, though not without plenty of *Sturm und Drang.* Moody received his Th.M. degree in 1941, which involved going back to complete his degree at Baylor. He began

539

work on his doctorate at Southern Seminary with the main mentor in his life, W. O. Carver. Carver represented for Moody the model of a person deeply committed to faith and to the Bible but who combined these with a remarkable breadth of knowledge and openness to the modern world. Carver as much as anyone accounts for the uniqueness of Moody as one who often appears to be simply a biblical literalist, yet who is remarkably open to modern critical methods, science, and philosophy.[10]

Study leaves in subsequent years with such notables as Paul Tillich (whom he served as fellow), Emil Brunner (on whom he wrote his dissertation), Karl Barth, Oscar Cullmann, and Walther Eichrodt[11] led to memorable expansions of his horizons. Two years at Oxford University and a book on baptism led to a second doctorate and wider ecumenical contacts.[12] Moody was a member of the World Council of Churches' Faith and Order Commission for two four-year terms in the sixties.[13] In 1969-70 he became only the second Protestant and the first Baptist to teach at the Gregorian University in Rome. He was invited to teach at The Ecumenical Institute for Advanced Theological Research (Tantur) in Jerusalem in 1973 and 1976. While being a quite conservative Baptist on many points, Moody possessed a liberal spirit second to none when it came to openness to other groups.[14]

Moody's influence lay not only in his writing and in his ecumenical contacts. In relation to Southern Baptists, one cannot underestimate the influence of a charismatic teacher whose classroom career spanned almost forty years. In talking with many people about Moody, one is ineluctably driven to the conclusion that he was an extraordinary teacher. My own estimation is that his greatest strength was as a teacher rather than as a writer. Several reviewers of *The Word of Truth* have commented on the way it draws on classroom experience.[15] He was consistently stimulating and provocative in the classroom. His style was not that of an objective and dispassionate expositor of various views. He would present the range of views on a subject but always in lively dialogical fashion, enlivened with a talent for illustration. He was intensely "interested" in the views he presented, and would energetically affirm or reject positions, always encouraging the students to take a position, too. When venturesome students would rise publicly to the challenge, Moody would often engage them just as if they were colleagues. Such a practice led to lively classes that were stimulating to some and understandably intimidating to others.

Always the reference point was Scripture. Baptist students who were accustomed to the Scripture as their final authority found Moody to be a person who started where they were but who led them into new paths. Debriefing after a controversial class session often went something like this: "I can't agree with him, but he sure does back it up with the Bible!"

Such an approach did not endear Moody to everyone, but it nonetheless resulted in an enormous influence in Baptist life—among students and also among the churches. Moody was a prolific guest preacher throughout his career. Beginning around 1970, each year he led from twenty to forty Bible studies on a single book and led two Holy Land trips, practices, he observes,

Dale Moody (1915-   )

Photo courtesy of The Southern Baptist Theological Seminary

that spurred on his biblical emphasis over the last decade of his teaching career more than anything else.[16] In addition to these he led conferences in the churches on theological topics and was a frequent speaker at student and other retreats. What is also significant about this immersion among local churches is that Moody did not hold back from challenging laypersons any more than he did the students. As he was accustomed to say, "The only difference between the classroom and the pulpit is that I get an hour in the classroom."[17]

As is evident, Moody has been a controversialist. His provocative style and his determination to judge tradition by Scripture led him into many a fray and finally to a bitter ending to a distinguished teaching career. Even as a student pastor in Texas in 1941 he initiated a conflict that would dog his steps thereafter by preaching that the New Testament teaches the possibility of apostasy.[18] After several interim clashes, conflict arose again in Arkansas in 1981 after the publication of *The Word of Truth*. Unfortunately, this was a fire that would not be doused. The controversy grew, resulting in Moody not being allowed to teach during the final year of his contract. Consequently, his last year of teaching at Southern Seminary was the 1982-83 academic year, although this did not prevent him from being named Emeritus Professor of Christian Theology in 1988.[19] In Moody's eyes the issue was whether or not he would place Scripture above tradition, purely and simply. It is to that single-minded passion that we now turn.

Exposition

The Biblical Theologian

Moody began his academic career in the heyday of the American biblical theology movement.[20] He had immersed himself in the thought of the continental scholars who most influenced that movement: Emil Brunner, Walther Eichrodt, and Oscar Cullmann.[21] While that movement lost its impetus in the sixties, Moody can best be understood as one who continued to embody its spirit. The first part of this section will consequently show Moody's affinity for that movement. Since a major dimension of the biblical theology movement was obviously its focus on the Bible itself, Moody's view of revelation and Scripture will be considered, followed by treatment of the way he moves from biblical theology to systematic theology.

Relationship to biblical theology.—Brevard S. Childs's classic study of the American biblical theology movement identifies several dominant characteristics, all of which are descriptive of Moody. First, Moody fully shared in the new emphasis on the theological dimension of critical study of the Bible, so much so that he is criticized for deriving his systematic theology from exegesis in much too direct and facile a way.[22] On the other hand, a general feature of the movement, which also characterized Moody's thought, was the direct relevance of biblical theology for the present.[23] If one could recover the biblical meaning, it was assumed that it would speak with fresh power today. The renewed focus on theology meant no repudiation of the historical-critical methodology per se, although it often meant less skeptical results for faith. Moody, too, has been adamant about not regressing to a precritical stage; rather, he is concerned to demonstrate the fruitfulness of historical study for understanding the Bible and for reforming theology.[24]

A second emphasis was the unity of the Bible, particularly the unity of the two Testaments, which was a unity in diversity that nevertheless attempts to do justice to the various theological perspectives in Scripture.[25] Moody was very likely one of the few scholars in the fifties who was able to do what many thought desirable, namely, to teach both Old Testament and New Testament theology.[26] As we shall see, Moody's theologizing constantly drew upon the dynamic unity that he perceived in the Bible.

A third area of commonality was an emphasis on revelation in history or *Heilsgeschichte* (salvation history).[27] This approach stressed the priority of revelation as God's personal self-disclosure as an event in the history of Israel over against revelation as the communication of information or timeless truths.[28] Usually a distinction was made between the event of revelation proper and the witness or record of revelation in Scripture. On the latter point, scholars differed as to whether the record, secondary as it is, has an infallible nature. Moody enthusiastically follows such an approach to revelation, while strongly asserting the infallibility of Scripture.

A fourth emphasis was on the priority of the conceptual and linguistic world of the Bible.[29] Biblical terms and categories were preferred. Theology was often based on word studies of key terms. A related point was the distinctiveness of the Hebrew mentality in contrast to its wider environment.[30] "The transition from the Biblical approach to the modern age required that modern man return to the Bible's way of thinking and acting."[31] This spirit is evident in Moody's preference for word studies, in using biblical terms whenever possible, and in his penchant for contrasting the biblical meaning, for example, of immortality, with meanings imposed by tradition.

On the other hand, two of Child's complaints about the movement are that it bore little fruit in systematic theology and in "sheer joy or spontaneous adoration for Scripture."[32] Moody perhaps escapes the indictment on both counts; he certainly cannot be faulted for trying. Moody's systematic theology is a unique genre because of the way he embeds it in biblical theology, and in the process of his teaching and writing ministry, he exhibited a contagious enthusiasm for the Bible. Out of this milieu of the early American biblical theology movement, Moody emerged as one who strikingly epitomizes its spirit and, rather than losing the initial vision in the disarray of the sixties, became if anything more determined to theologize on the basis of these tenets of biblical theology.

The "source" of Scripture.—Moody's greatest strength is that he is as much a biblical scholar as he is a systematic theologian, camping on what he calls at the outset of his systematic the "source" of Christian theology.[33] It is difficult to identify any modern systematic theologian who is more at home in biblical exegesis. Moody is as comfortable doing textual criticism or writing commentaries as doing systematic theology. One can perhaps find Moody at his best following an in-depth study of a text in his Romans commentary.[34] Indeed, most of his books are either explicit commentaries or *de facto* commentaries. *The Spirit of the Living God*[35] and *The Hope of Glory*[36] are perhaps more exegetical works on the pertinent biblical texts than they are reflective theology.

Ironically for one so committed to Scripture, Moody has written little on inspiration and his hermeneutics. Despite the context of intense interest in issues of inspiration during Moody's career, Dwight Moody points out, for instance, that "nowhere in Moody's published work is there a consideration of inerrancy and infallibility."[37] Moody has apparently been more comfortable doing exegesis than discussing it. In many ways, this is consistent with his oft-repeated complaint that people are too prone to talk *about* the Bible as opposed to simply "talking Bible."[38] Consequently, especially in the area of hermeneutics, one must judge as much by his practice as by his theory.

The order of priority for Moody is first revelation, then authority, and only then inspiration.[39] Likewise, interpretation comes before inspiration.[40] The importance of this order is that the fact of special revelation, the acceptance of biblical authority, and the actual practice of interpretation are much more important than being precisely correct on the nature of inspiration. This is why Moody has not been preoccupied with the nature of inspiration as have many twentieth-century evangelicals.[41]

Moody shows his affinity with biblical theology by stressing the historical nature of special revelation.[42] Moody states:

> Special revelation is historical revelation, because in the Bible revelation comes in historical events. It is not just ideas dropped down from heaven as a Moslem would describe the revelation of the Koran, but certain historical events take place in which God discloses Himself.[43]

For Moody, such revelation involves a scandal of particularity: a particular place, a particular nation, and a particular book.[44] He places the emphasis on God's activity but also stresses that special revelation is a dialogue. "Neither God nor man speaks to himself in historical revelation."[45] Thus, in order to understand the meaning of special revelation, one must perceive it with the eye of faith. It is *Heilsgeschichte,* which cannot be approached simply in terms of neutral historiography *(Historie).*[46]

As is apparent, when discussing revelation Moody customarily accents the neoorthodox categories of self-disclosure and personal relationship. Early in his career, under the influence of Brunner, he especially expressed himself in classical neoorthodox language.[47] Revelation is not a subject-object but a subject-subject relation. Like Brunner, he believes that the name of God stands for God's personal reality, not for propositional truth.[48] Moody consistently criticizes propositional approaches, which he tends to identify with a dictation theory of inspiration.[49] Even in *The Word of Truth* Moody describes Scripture as a "record" and "witness" of historical revelation.[50] These positions lead in neoorthodox thought to an emphasis on God's self-disclosure to which the Scripture fallibly points rather than to infallible propositions in Scripture.[51] The Bible is the supreme source for revelation but is not a revelation of doctrine.[52]

Such a sharp distinction between personalism over against a propositional approach to Scripture, however, is not reflected in Moody's practice. Moody consistently stresses the priority of relationship to God, but he does so on the basis of the biblical teaching. In his practice, there is no conflict between revelation as primarily existential and between the binding nature of the propositional content of Scripture. When the Bible is properly interpreted, Moody understands its teaching to be infallibly correct. The wedge between revelation and the Bible as fallible record or witness in much neoorthodox theology simply does not occur in Moody's use of Scripture.

Comments in a later unpublished interview help account for his greater emphasis on the propositional content of Scripture. In response to a question concerning the Bible as a record of revelation, Moody responds:

> It [the Bible] would be primarily a record of revelation. Although I would consider the Scriptures *as such* part of the revelation. I would not put the Scriptures outside the revelation. The writings and the canonization of the Scriptures would be part of the historical event. You wouldn't just have a historical event isolated, and then this is recorded without the help of the Holy Spirit. The stream of historical revelation would include the recording, not just the event itself, but the recording of the event and the initial interpretation of the event. So we get all of it; [sic] the event, the record, the inspiration and even the canonization of the documents that record the events.[53]

These comments indicate that the gap that can arise between revelation and the record or witness of revelation is mitigated due to the fact that Scripture itself is part of the historical event of revelation. In inveighing against propositional approaches to Scripture, Moody stresses that Scripture concerns an I-thou encounter, but in practice he regards the propositional content as authoritative, whether or not it concerns existential encounter.[54]

One can relate the two emphases in Moody's thought and practice by understanding the content of Scripture as *primarily* concerning historical encounters with God and personal encounter in the present. Scripture is at bottom confession, not doctrine, and it certainly is not a system. This fact, however, does not lessen the infallibility of the doctrinal content of Scripture. The relationship between revelation as historical event and as sacred Scripture is mediated by Moody's understanding of the *purpose* of Scripture. Like E. Y. Mullins before him, Moody regards the purpose of Scripture as salvific and not scientific.[55] Thus, he is not bothered by apparent errors in scientific or historical detail because providing such detail is not the purpose of Scripture. It is true, according to Moody, in what it "intends to teach."[56] In this light, Moody has been willing in some letters to refer to the Scriptures as inerrant and to subscribe to the Chicago Statement on Inerrancy.[57] However, Moody prefers to use the terms in this way:

> "Inspiration" refers to "the production of Scripture," "infallible" with the doctrine that the Scripture intends to teach, and "inerrancy" with "scientific matters, and historical matters, which don't really touch the heart of biblical revelation."[58]

Despite this definition of inerrancy, Moody takes the historicity of Scripture more seriously than much neoorthodox theology. He delights in harmonizing problematic passages and tends to accept factual historicity whenever it is at all possible in light of a conservative use of historical-critical methodology.[59] He is willing to use any critical methodology to interpret a text, but his results are decidedly conservative.[60]

Moody's approach to the interpretation of Scripture is thus clearly inductive.[61] One comes to the Bible without a priori commitments about what it "must" be but seeks to learn from Scripture what it is. As is already evident, a prime ingredient is serious study of the Bible as a historical document in its original language, utilizing all the tools available.[62] Nevertheless, study is not enough. The Holy Spirit must also illumine the understanding.[63] To illustrate the importance of both elements, Moody was fond of referring to the Southern Seminary seal, which depicts a dove hovering over an open Bible.[64]

Moody's approach to the nature of inspiration, though brief, is significant. As noted, he subordinates inspiration to revelation and authority, and he subordinates the inspiration involved in the canon to the prior inspiration of holy people. He describes the process of inspiration in a novel way as diverse. Moody first refers to A. H. Strong's description of four theories of inspiration:

> (1) the intuition theory that is but the higher development of natural insight into truth, (2) the illumination theory that aids the belief in the inspiration of the writer but not of the writing, (3) the dictation theory that regards the writers as passive, and (4) the dynamic theory that holds to both a human and a divine element in inspiration.[65]

Moody then proposes an eclectic view which subscribes to the truth of each approach. He bases this approach on an inductive analysis of Scripture in which he believes evidence exists for each type, even the dictation theory. He concludes, "A biblical view of inspiration must be broad enough to include the truth in all the historical theories. . . ."[66] "What really makes the difference," he adds, "is the fidelity with which the authority of Scripture is elevated above ecclesiastical traditions."[67] Again, authority and interpretation are placed above the vagaries of theories of inspiration.

Biblical theology and systematic theology.—One of the crucial issues for understanding Moody is to perceive how he relates his fundamentally biblical theology approach to systematic theology. Moody attempted the transition, producing a theology that is biblically shaped in a manner more marked than any previous Southern Baptist theology. Moody hammered home more rigorously than any of these predecessors the biblical foundation of theology and more radically attempted to allow Scripture to call into question his tradition. This does not necessarily mean that he was more successful or more correct in doctrine or that his is a better systematic theology. It does point to a distinctive approach not only to other Southern Baptists but also to the wider church community.

Moody's systematic theology can best be described as a biblical theology on the way to a systematic theology. Whereas most systematic theologians err on the side of dogmatics, if anything Moody errs on the side of biblical theology. This section will consequently scrutinize the way Moody integrates the two.

As early as 1949, in his inaugural address at Southern Seminary, Moody appealed to the historical study of Scripture as the norm for systematic theology.[68] On that basis, the three commentaries and two book-length biblical studies of the Holy Spirit and eschatology, respectively, in the seven-year period from 1963-70 paved the way for his own systematic theology. The opening lines of the preface to *The Word of Truth* reiterate that concern: "The publication of *The Word of Truth* is meant to issue a clarion call to the reformation and revival of theology on the basis of the historical exegesis which is so prominent a feature of recent biblical scholarship."[69] Moody's goal, therefore, is not only to root theology in historical exegesis of Scripture but to reevaluate tradition on the basis of Scripture. Moody has carried out this Protestant principle with unmatched fervor. In many ways, it is the passion of his life, leading him to significant revision in virtually every major area of systematic theology and also, predictably, to repeated controversy.

The typical way in which Moody develops any doctrine is to unfold its progressive development through the major sections of Scripture, usually in the form of word studies, keeping as much as possible to a chronological development. In the New Testament, where applicable, he usually begins with the Pauline literature, then Mark and Matthew, Luke-Acts, the Johannine literature, and the Catholic epistles.[70]

On such a biblical foundation, Moody desires to integrate Scripture with historical theology, modern science, and philosophy. Also in the preface to *The Word of Truth*, Moody states:

> This book thus represents a conscious effort to bring together the insights of several disciplines in a constructive harmony which is both biblical and systematic. Biblical theology, modern science, various types of biblical criticism, . . . historical theology, and the history of doctrine—all these have a significant part to play in the development of a systematic theology. . . .
>
> My use of the resources of these disciplines and my high degree of appreciation for the insights of the non-Christian religions of the world as well as the ideas set forth by philosophers of religion are all in the context of a higher view of the inspiration and authority of Scripture. Those who fear that using the findings of modern science and critical-historical method of Bible study is inevitably uncongenial to a strong view of biblical authority will, I hope, find the explorations of this book a pleasant surprise.[71]

As indicated in the biography, early in his college days Moody was confronted with the claims of science and the Bible. Since then he has been concerned to show the compatibility of the two.[72] This is most manifest in the striking section of his theology where he relates the creation stories to modern anthropology in terms of theistic evolution, a section that is likely unparalleled in any other theology, particularly an evangelical theology.[73]

Critics have accused him of a facile sell out to modern science in his theology, but this represents a serious misreading.[74] He critically appropriates modern science and its methodologies, often decisively rejecting skeptical results of biblical criticism or science that undermine the biblical witness.[75] When he is convinced that a clash exists, then he is eager to harmonize the results. The weight, however, is always on the primacy of Scripture in a stance that Moody designates as "critical conservatism."[76]

The comprehensiveness in the way Moody relates biblical theology to other disciplines struck many reviewers as especially impressive. For this reason, Clark Pinnock rated Moody's theology as the best of the recent theologies by several evangelicals. He remarks, "Even Bloesch, whose work comes a close second, does not appreciate the positive side of modernity as Moody does, nor does he integrate it into the theological vision."[77] In comparison with earlier Southern Baptist theologies and many other modern theologies, his theology includes both more Bible and more science. Nevertheless, the heart of his systematic theology lies in the starting point of a biblical theology.

The effect of his careful development of each doctrine on the basis of a historical study of the Bible, especially in light of his often independent analysis and when integrated with historical, philosophical, and scientific material, is often that of a tour de force. He is frequently able to uncover the biblical foundation of a doctrine at new and creative depths. Undoubtedly, this is the characteristic that appeals especially to evangelicals. Even when they disagree, they often praise him for his fidelity to Scripture.[78]

On the other hand, Moody is often criticized for failing to move beyond biblical theology to systematic. In the words of Alan Gragg, "He [Moody] seems to feel that his work as systematic theologian is done whenever he has uncovered the thought of one or more biblical writers."[79] Moody characteristically employs other disciplines to elucidate the biblical meaning, not to go beyond it. As noted previously, this hermeneutical confidence in the relevance of the biblical meaning was typical of the early biblical theology movement in general.

A related characteristic is the harmony of the various voices in Scripture. He affirms diversity in Scripture but not discordance, raising the specter of overharmonization. Again, the unity in diversity of Scripture was a shoal on which the biblical theology movement in general foundered. To some extent, also, this overharmonization is inherent in the task of systematic theology itself. The blessing and the bane of the systematic theologian is that the synthetic process may be a brilliant discernment of a hidden pattern that really exists or the forcing of recalcitrant materials into a Procrustean bed. In the tension between unity and diversity, Moody is at neither extreme but inclines towards unity.

Another contributing factor to Moody's biblicism is his conviction, shared with the Reformation and with the early Baptist movement, that Scripture has a plain meaning accessible to the ordinary believer. The principle of the priesthood of the believer and the Baptist emphasis on soul competency assumes a basic perspicuity in the meaning of the text.[80] Moody is fully persuaded of this belief. In connection with the apostasy and evolution controversies, Moody says:

> Really, I have very high confidence in the ability of the average person to interpret the Scripture when they come as Christians with the help of the Spirit and with a desire to know what it means. I get a great joy out of watching people discover what the text page says. . . . If people understand the historical meaning of the text, you don't have to spoon feed them as to what it means; they will immediately translate it over into their beliefs and behavior.[81]

In this sense, Moody has always been a populist; he has been comfortable taking his case "to the people." This conviction is consistent with the way he developed his theology and is basic, at least in some qualified sense, to the Baptist ethos. Moody was convinced that the gap between what the Scripture meant and what it means is not large. For him, explicating the biblical meaning was largely sufficient to convey its meaning *pro me* (for me). Thus, criticisms that Moody's theology is *merely* a biblical theology do not do justice to Moody's conviction about the transparency of the biblical meaning for the present (nor to the careful theological arrangement and dialogue with historical theology and the modern world). To discern what the Bible intends to teach in its own time is virtually what it teaches us in our time. Undoubtedly, this is the point at which Moody is most in tension with his contemporaries.[82]

Moody calls his theology a "real systematic *biblical* theology."[83] His approach is not reflective of an attempt to bypass the systematic task nor of a lack of understanding of it but is representative of a conviction about its nature. Carrying out this conviction lies at the heart of his entire career.

The Systematic Theologian

If for no other reason, Moody's systematic theology is historically significant because it is the first produced by a Southern Baptist seminary professor in nearly half a century. In addition to this fact, however, his theology is what one might hope for after all those years, a fresh and daring attempt to speak to a new situation while maintaining solid continuity with traditional Baptist emphases on biblical authority and piety. For good or ill, his systematic will be the legacy that most people will come to know.

General characteristics.—Based on his desire to reform theology on the principle of biblical exegesis, Moody is innovative in nearly every major doctrine. His views on theistic evolution and on apostasy have already been indicated. In addition, he argues on biblical grounds for the salvific potential of general revelation.[84] He also argues forcefully for Patripassionism or Theopaschitism, the view that God experiences and suffers with His creatures. In a later essay, Moody confesses, "To believe that God experiences all that happens in his universe, be it joy or pain, is one of the most personal and most important beliefs I have today."[85] Moody significantly establishes this dynamic view of God on the Old Testament, although he relates it to the emphases of process theology.[86] In anthropology he emphasizes the holistic or Hebraic unity of the self characteristic of biblical theology but couples it with the survivability of the spirit in an intermediate state.[87] In Christology he advocates a "skenotic" view, versus gnostic and kenotic approaches, based on the moral union of the Logos "tabernacling" or indwelling the human person Jesus.[88] Another notable characteristic is the broad ecumenical dialogue, particularly with Eastern Orthodox theology.

In terms of style, Moody's theology is designed for students. The general structure is clear, and he has a Hegelian gift for triads (which usually alliterate—often in Greek). In light of above criticisms that he frequently lingers too long in biblical theology, it should be said that Moody indeed has the systematician's skill in arranging diverse material in general categories. Fisher Humphreys, fellow Southern Baptist theologian, says that in comparison to earlier Baptist theologians, Moody's is "more organic, more a living body, where theirs were more like the scholastic *loci,* a series of topics dealt with sequentially like pearls on a string."[89] Some of this unity lies in basic themes and purposes that hold the various sections together. Some lies in the way Moody allows doctrine to flow out of the historical interpretation of Scripture. In many ways, the unity of his theology is the unity that he discerns in Scripture itself. In addition, some of Moody's innovation lies in arrangement of material, for example, placing the consummation of creation before the beginning of creation and placing Christology after soteriology.[90]

Despite the unity, what is sometimes lacking in comparison with earlier Baptist theologians is careful logical and conceptual development of ideas; in other words, the cement between the specifics of biblical exegesis and larger systematic theology is not as firm as some desire. Part of this is due to the strain of producing a one-volume systematic that tries to emphasize biblical theology more than other scholars and at the same time to dialogue with historical theology, modern science, and philosophy.[91] Moody acknowledges that most of the material he cut from an original of approximately one thousand pages was discussions in historical theology, although he still complains that he had to omit too much discussion of Scripture![92] The pruning of historical material is unfortunate because one of his strengths is the ability to set thought within its context. At other times, the sketchiness is partly due to the conversational and quasi-autobiographical nature of the work.

This personal nature of the book, however, perhaps accounts for one of its most commendable features: its vitality. Pinnock states, "Turning to Moody, I experience great pleasure. Here is a (Southern Baptist) evangelical who believes and loves his Bible. He writes with evident enthusiasm and joy."[93]

Moody indicates that throughout his career he has been concerned to debate three particular issues: Calvinism, Landmarkism, and dispensational premillennialism. Moody says, "In print, private correspondence and conversation, I have challenged the advocates of five-point Calvinism, five-point Landmarkism and three-point Dispensationalism on issues where they contradict Scripture."[94] His barbs against them in *The Word of Truth* account for most of the complaints of reviewers that the book is at times overly polemical and unobjective. Moody's opposition to these adversaries will guide a focused examination of three sections of his systematic: soteriology, ecclesiology, and eschatology.

Soteriology.—Moody disagrees with all the five points of Calvinism, but his energy was focused on refuting the last point, perseverence, popularly interpreted by Southern Baptists as "eternal security." Moody wrestled with the tension resulting from Baptists' dropping the previous four points, for example, unconditional election and irresistible grace, and yet retaining the fifth, which is logically based on them.[95] He was especially concerned that eternal security had come to mean that a person could be saved and then "live like the Devil."[96] His understanding of Scripture led him to oppose vigorously such a "transactional, punctiliar" view of salvation and to affirm apostasy with no possibility of restoration.

Moody's views on apostasy cannot properly be understood apart from his larger views on salvation. He follows the New Testament indications of salvation as a process with a past, present, and future tense, as opposed to a singular emphasis on a punctiliar event in the past.[97] Salvation also has two sides—grace and faith.[98] He especially argues against the Calvinist notions of an irresistible call and regeneration that precedes repentance and faith.[99] Rather, he appeals to the reciprocity—and vulnerability—inherent in personal relations as a model for the God-human relationship.[100] Sanctification is also a progressive idea, avoiding both perfectionism in Wesleyanism and false security among Calvinists.[101] Election or predestination Moody understands first of all as the predestination of Christ, which does not rule out human freedom.[102] Moody's soteriology is of a piece with his personalist approach to the doctrine of God and to the doctrine of persons. With this in mind, he interprets the New Testament passages as implying single predestination, the predestination of those who are being saved because they are "in Christ."[103] As he says, "God indeed has a program, but it is not programmed without a place for human freedom either before faith or after faith."[104]

And this brings us to his section on apostasy, one of the longest sections in the entire book (eighteen pages). As the biography indicated, the issue of apostasy has been central for Moody—and personally harmful. He observes that he has had major controversies over apostasy every twenty years, 1941, 1961, and 1981.[105] Especially in his later years of teaching, apostasy was a constant theme no matter what class he was teaching. Why was it so important? With the groundwork already laid, the answer may be evident. For one thing, it was at the heart of his most central conviction, the primacy of Scripture. He was convinced that apostasy was taught in virtually every book in the New Testament. To deny it for the sake of tradition, a confession of faith, job security, or popularity would be to violate everything to which he had given his life. For another, one can see how it was integral to his view of human beings as free, being in the image of the free God. It violated his understanding of salvation as consisting not in a legal transaction or a sovereign intrusion, but a free, loving relationship. The very structure of his entire theology would fall apart if one tore out this particular doctrine.

Another, more practical, reason may be mentioned. For many people, warnings of apostasy unsettle already uneasy consciences, robbing sincere Christians of needed assurance. On the other hand, Moody has often had just the opposite experience.[106] Preaching and teaching on apostasy consistently led to revival and spiritual awakening. Moody seemed to have a knack for running into people who rested on the laurels of "once saved, always saved." These were people who *needed* to be awakened and warned about presuming on the grace of God. Moody certainly affirms assurance and the primacy of God's grace. He is largely Arminian, but he is far from Pelagian or works-salvation. Given his emphasis on apostasy, however, some miss these counterweights. The conclusion that one may draw is that Moody's ardent espousal of this un-Baptistic doctrine was very much a part of his Baptist heritage in the sense of placing Scripture above any other authority and in the sense of promoting revival. Moody was often placed in the position of somehow being "for" apostasy, which is like a noninerrantist being in the position of being "for" errancy. This was far from the truth. His passion was to *prevent* apostasy, or to put it more positively still, to promote the full and abundant Christian life. Only when seen in that light, coupled with its interlocking into his whole theology, can one understand the fervor with which he would "preach" apostasy.

Ecclesiology.—Moody's treatment of Christology after soteriology is only in part due to the desire to elevate the work of Christ over the person of Christ. It is also in order to more closely relate Christology to ecclesiology (and to eschatology, centering around Christ's Parousia). Moody's dominant image for the church is the body of Christ. He significantly entitled his first book, a commentary on Ephesians, *Christ and the Church*.[107] Moody found in teaching that it made sense to group anthropology, sin, and salvation together and then relate Christology, the church, and the return of Christ in eschatology.[108] The church therefore represents the outworking of the new life in Christ.

In a related way, Moody's Baptist quarrel with Landmarkism centered on Landmarkism not doing justice to the one body of Christ, the universal church. Moody's ecumenicity is also involved here. As in the biblical theology movement generally, Moody hoped for unity among the churches centering around the historical study of the Bible. Secondly, as his colleague Wayne Ward points out, Moody discovered unity in spiritual relationship with other Christians.[109] One of the most ecumenical Southern Baptists, Moody sincerely attempted to champion truth wherever he found it, leading him to give critical support to the charismatic movement, Campbellism, and various positions historically deemed as heresies such as theopaschitism and Nestorianism.[110] Even in the case of disagreement, however, he was open to fellowship. Notable is his 1967 work on baptism, which allows for believer's baptism *and* pedobaptism as interim measures for the sake of the unity of the church. In contrast to Landmark views, therefore, Moody advocated the universal church, open communion, alien immersion, and ecumenical relations.

Concerning other issues in ecclesiology, Moody has, surprisingly for a Baptist, found a biblical basis for bishops, and, not surprisingly, for ordination in general and for the ordination of women.[111] The latter case and the case for bishops are interesting in that they reveal changes in his own earlier views and a progressive hermeneutic whereby the New Testament contains a trajectory towards an official ministry and for the ordination of women. Women's ordination, he agrees, is not found in the New Testament but is permissible because of the general openness to women's ministries in the early church in the New Testament.[112] Nevertheless, Moody insists on the difference in roles between men and women, upholding the Pauline teaching in Ephesians 5.[113] Although Moody is open to various practices for the sake of the unity of the church, he reveals a Baptist tendency towards restorationism, that is, toward a more New Testament form of worship, of communion, and of baptism.[114]

Eschatology.—Moody has had a lifelong affair with millennialism, accounting for the extensive work he has done on the subject of eschatology. E. Frank Tupper points out that Moody's book on eschatology, *The Hope of Glory*, was published in the same year as the books by Pannenberg and Moltmann that placed eschatology at the forefront of theology.[115] Moody rejected the dispensational premillennialism at Dallas Theological Seminary for being unbiblical but was not satisfied with the amillennialism dominant at Southern Seminary or the postmillennialism that was at one time dominant at Southwestern Seminary in his native Texas. Consequently, Moody developed a view that he terms historical premillennialism, due to the fact that he finds a similar view in an earlier theologian such as Irenaeus before it was swamped by the amillennialism of Augustine.[116] Moody accuses amillennial approaches of bordering on the allegorical method. Amillennialism, he asserts, "is really hard pressed when confronted with biblical literalism."[117] On another front, he states, "Many others, including myself, have found that Historical Premillennialism is far more literal on Revelation 20 than is Dispensationalism. It offers the best realistic response to atheistic Marxism."[118]

Accordingly, Moody enthusiastically endorses a Christian Zionism of a thousand year reign of Christ on earth at Jerusalem, which will be a fulfillment of God's promises to Israel and of Paul's tortuous reflections in Romans 9—11. These views represent his affirmation of historical eschatology as the hope of history, consisting first in the idea of the kingdom of God, which is immediate and imminent as it impinges on the present and is a future inheritance.[119] Second it includes the final *pleroma* (fullness) in the sense of the fulfillment of God's promises to Israel, mentioned above, and to the Gentiles.[120] Third, it includes the future *Parousia* or coming of Christ, which entails the previous coming of the Antichrist. Moody unabashedly states at this point:

> Belief in the literal fulfillment of 2 Thessalonians 2:1-12 in the future has led to a Christian Zionism that teaches (1) that Israel will return to the land promised to Abraham, (2) that the Temple destroyed in A.D. 70 will be rebuilt, and (3) that Jesus as the Messiah will return to destroy the Antichrist who will demand that he be worshipped as God.[121]

The millennial reign of Christ then begins Moody's treatment of cosmic eschatology, the hope of creation beyond this life. As he looks beyond the millennium, he suggests that because God is Creator and because miracle is possible in an open universe,[122] "Beyond cataclysm there is consummation, beyond woe there is weal in the wonders in the Holy City of God."[123] In contrast to his interest in the realistic fulfillment of history in the discussion of the millennium, he is interested here in the concordance between scientific views of the inevitable futility of the universe with the hope of re-creation in the Christian faith.[124] Moody's final poetic vision concludes with the new Jerusalem that fulfills the past earthly Jerusalem and the present heavenly Jerusalem.[125] In contrast to earlier strong words on biblical literalism, he concludes the mystery of eschatology with alternating biblical symbols and philosophical personalism.[126]

Moody has most often been engaged in dialogue on the above issues, but he actually begins the discussion of eschatology with individual eschatology.[127] His view of anthropology militates against the natural immortality of the soul and leads to a dependence on God for life. Human beings will perish without God's sustaining Being, but God does grant an intermediate state for good spirits in Paradise and wicked spirits in Hades. At the Parousia, the redeemed are clothed with spiritual bodies in the resurrection to life,[128] and the wicked are raised to face the second resurrection of judgment, which is the second death.[129] Moody advances then the idea of conditional immortality, which is received as a gift from God to those who choose to be in the presence of God. Conditional immortality means the unredeemed will simply perish as opposed to an immortal existence in Hell.[130]

Evaluation

Much evaluation has occurred in the process of exposition, but a general assessment is also in order. Despite the difficulty of estimating an influence so fresh, one can venture some probable judgments. Moody's impact will be significantly affected by both his thought and his personal influence.

Moody's Thought

The fact that Moody's theology has no real competition among Southern Baptists on the current scene guarantees it a significant hearing. For that reason it is considered by both Southern Baptists and those interested in Southern Baptist theology. Additionally, because it is judged to be a fresh and bold voice among evangelical theologies, with Pinnock rating it the best, it should continue to gain a hearing beyond Southern Baptist life. What are the qualities of his thought that will be of significance, and what are some of the questions that arise?

At this point, it should be clear that Moody's major issue has been methodological, that is, the reform of theology on the basis of Scripture combined with impressive openness. This concern is certainly not new for Protestants, not even for Catholics, but Moody has insisted on it to an extent that will remain challenging. Even if people disagree as to the content of his theology, the summons to the Protestant principle remains.

The genre of a biblical systematic theology is more controversial. Moody's appeal for unity in the church around the interpretation of Scripture and his dialogue around such interpretation has been and continues to be promising. This dream of the biblical theology movement, though it has foundered amidst other concerns, persists as a rallying point for the church. What Moody has done that is unusual is to follow through on this call in terms of a systematic theology, along with a willingness to revise any view on the basis of Scripture. For that he is to be commended. He is also to be commended for the courageous way in which he has reformed tradition on this basis of biblical interpretation, often at great personal cost. His systematic theology is biblical, but like Barth's theology, it is for the church, that is, the universal church. His concern is for the church to do its thinking and living correctly. In the words of the first article of the Abstract of Principles, an article with which he never had problems, *"The Scriptures . . . are the only sufficient, certain and authoritative rule of all saving knowledge, faith and obedience.* "[131] Moody meant it when he signed that document. He means for others to have the same commitment. And his life's work contributes to it.

Whether or not his method or hermeneutic will carry the day remains to be seen. As seen above, some are concerned that he is too open to modern science, while appreciating his biblicism; others believe he is overly biblical, never getting around to systematic theology proper; and others do not think he is biblical enough—in the sense that he does not understand the Bible. The latter position can be in terms of a specific such as not doing justice to assurance passages in John or of a general complaint that he overharmonizes the Scripture.[132] Moody would enjoy dialogue with the first and third groups, but not the second. The first and third groups can be dealt with on biblical grounds; the second group disagrees at a deeper level. Moody is convinced that by explaining what Scripture meant, it is a short step to what it means. Those who are more troubled by the hermeneutical gap will not be comfortable with Moody. Brevard Childs and James Smart both score the early biblical theology movement for its, in their view, minimization of the hermeneutical problem.[133] People of like mind would have similar problems with Moody. Those who find discordance in Scripture in terms of what it intends to teach will also not find Moody compelling. The fact of the matter is that there are large numbers who will find Moody's approach compelling and equally large numbers who will not, although both may subscribe to the final authority of Scripture. It is telling that no contemporary has done systematic theology quite like Moody, even among the conservatives.

In terms of specific issues, Moody is destined to have significant influence among Southern Baptists. He represents a trajectory from Boyce to Mullins to Conner on openness to historical-critical methodology, openness to modern science, and engagement with pluralism. Moody has carried out the movement of Southern Baptists towards a relational view of God and persons to its logical conclusions in several areas: a suffering God, conditional salvation and apostasy, and conditional immortality. Whether or not these conclusions will prevail or whether reassessment of the theological foundations in another direction will occur is impossible to say. What is possible to say is that debate on these issues will not be the same because Moody's voice will have to be considered.

Likewise, on numerous specific issues, Moody's voice will be considered. These are issues such as his redating of the New Testament in a way similar to John A. T. Robertson, his provocative views on authorship and amanuenses, millennial readings of New Testament passages, his harmonization of the resurrection appearances, and his emphasis on the Book of Hebrews. On all of these matters and many others, Moody has made a contribution.

Moody's Personal Influence

The pervasiveness in Southern Baptist life of Moody's charismatic personal influence has been emphasized already. This influence is more difficult to gauge but will perhaps be more weighty. Through this personal influence, many of the distinctives of his thought have had an impact. Additionally, due to his ecumenical interests, Moody has made a significant impression beyond Southern Baptist life. Hinson, an ecumenical Baptist himself, claims, "No other faculty member at Southern Seminary has been as open to or received as wide ecumenical notice as Dale Moody."[134]

In reality, it is too soon adequately to assess the thought and life of Dale Moody. History will determine whether he had the impact for which he dearly hoped, fought, and suffered, especially on Southern Baptist life.

Bibliography

˙Works by Moody
Books

Baptism: Foundation for Christian Unity. Philadelphia: Westminster Press, 1967.

Christ and the Church: An Exposition of Ephesians with Special Application to Some Present Issues. Grand Rapids, Mich.: Eerdmans, 1963.

The Hope of Glory. Grand Rapids, Mich.: Eerdmans, 1964.

"The Inspiration of Holy Scripture," ed. Dwight A. Moody. Unpublished manuscript, Boyce Centennial Library, The Southern Baptist Theological Seminary, 1981.

The Letters of John. Waco, Tx: 1970.

Scripture, Baptism, and the Ecumenical Movement: Two Lectures. Aurora, Ill.: European Evangelistic Society, 1970.

Spirit of the Living God: The Biblical Concepts Interpreted in Context. Philadelphia: Westminster Press, 1968. Revised edition: *Spirit of the Living God: What the Bible Says About the Spirit*. Nashville: Broadman Press, 1976.

The Word of Truth: A Summary of Christian Doctrine Based on Biblical Revelation.
Grand Rapids, Mich.: Eerdmans, 1981.

Contributions to Other Books

"Authority and the Holy Spirit." In *Commission on Baptist Doctrine of the Baptist World Alliance*. Washington, D.C.: Baptist World Alliance.

"The Authority for Faith." In *The Proceedings of Catholics and Baptists in Ecumenical Dialogue*, edited by J. William Angell. Winston-Salem, NC: Wake Forest University, 1973.

"The Bible and Homosexuality." In *Homosexuality*, Critical Issues. Nashville: Christian Life Commission of the Southern Baptist Convention, 1978.

"Christ and Freedom." In *Study Papers on the Meaning of the Free Exercise of Religion*. Washington, D.C.: Baptist Joint Committee on Public Affairs, 1964.

"The Church in Theology." In *The Theology of Emil Brunner*, edited by Charles W. Kegley. The Library of Living Theology, vol. 3. New York: Macmillan, 1962.

"The Fourth Exhortation (Hebrews 10:19-39)." In *The Way of Faith*, edited by James M. Pitts. Wake Forest, NC: Chanticleer Publishing Company, 1985.

"God Is Really Among You." In *Professor and the Pulpit*, edited by W. Morgan Patterson and Raymond Bryan Brown. Nashville: Broadman Press, 1963.

"Holding Fast that Which Is Good." In *God's Glory in Missions: In Appreciation of William Owen Carver*, edited by John N. Jonsson. Private publication, 1985.

"The Meaning of Salvation." In *Renewal in the Church*, edited by Findley B. Edge. Louisville: The Southern Baptist Theological Seminary.

"The Nature of the Church." In *What Is the Church?*, edited by Duke K. McCall.

"The New Testament Significance of the Lord's Supper." In *What Is the Church?*, edited by Duke K. McCall. Nashville: Broadman Press, 1958.

"The Origin of Infant Baptism." In *The Teacher's Yoke*, edited by E. Jerry Vardaman and James Leo Garrett, Jr. Waco: Baylor University Press, 1964.

"Pentecost." In *Upper Room Disciplines*, edited by Sulon G. Ferree. Nashville: Upper Room, 1969.

"A People Under the Word: Contemporary Relevance." In *The Concept of the Believers' Church*, edited by James Leo Garrett, Jr. Scottdale, Pa.: Herald Press, 1969.

"The Priestly Authority of Paul." In *The Pastor as Priest*, edited by Earl E. Shelp and Ronald H. Sunderland. New York: Pilgrim Press, 1987.

"Romans." In *The Broadman Bible Commentary*, edited by Clifton J. Allen. Nashville: Broadman Press, 1970.

Periodical Articles

"Baptism in Recent Research." *Review and Expositor* 65 (1968): 13-22.

"Charismatic and Official Ministries: A Study of the New Testament Concept." *Interpretation* 19 (1965): 168-81.

"The Crux of Christian Theology." *Review and Expositor* 46 (1949): 164-80.

"The Double Face of Death." *Review and Expositor* 58 (1961): 348-66.

"The Eschatology of Hal Lindsey." *Review and Expositor* 72 (1975): 271-78.

"The First Epistle of Paul to the Corinthians (A.D. 55)." *Review and Expositor* 57 (1960): 540-53.

"God Is Love." *Review and Expositor* 47 (1950): 427-33.

"God's Only Son: The Translation of John 3:16 in the Revised Standard Version." *Journal of Biblical Literature* 72 (1953): 213-19.

"The Good News Bible." *Review and Expositor* 76 (1979): 409-16.

"The Holy Spirit and Missions: Vision and Dynamic." *Review and Expositor* 62 (1965): 75-81.

"An Introduction to Emil Brunner." *Review and Expositor* 44 (1947): 312-30.

"Isaiah 7:14 in the Revised Standard Version." *Review and Expositor* 50 (1953): 61-68.

"The Man of God." *Review and Expositor* 56 (1959): 411-16.

"The Ministry of the New Testament." *Review and Expositor* 56 (1959): 31-42.

"The Miraculous Conception (Part I: The Old Testament)." *Review and Expositor* 51 (154): 495-507.

"The Miraculous Conception (Part II: The New Testament)." *Review and Expositor* 52 (1955): 44-54.

"The Miraculous Conception (Part III: The Church Fathers)." *Review and Expositor* 52 (1955): 310-24.

"The Nature of the Church." *Review and Expositor* 51 (1954): 204-16.

"A New Chronology for the Life and Letters of Paul." *Perspectives in Religious Studies* 3 (1976): 248-71.

"A New Chronology for the New Testament." *Review and Expositor* 78 (1981): 211-31.

"Perspectives on Scripture and Tradition: A Response by Dale Moody." *Perspectives in Religious Studies* 15 (Spring, 1988): 5-16.

"Present Theological Trends: A Review Article." *Review and Expositor* 47 (1950): 3-20.

"The Shaping of Southern Baptist Polity." *Baptist History and Heritage* 14 (July 1979): 2-11.

"Tabletalk on Theology Tomorrow." *Review and Expositor* 64 (1967): 341-56.

"A Texas Tumbleweed." (Written in collaboration with Clifton D. Harrison) *Elm Fork Echoes* 9 (April 1981): 10-15.

"The Theology of the Johannine Letters." *Southwestern Journal of Theology* 13 (1970): 7-22.

"On the Virgin Birth of Jesus Christ." *Review and Expositor* 50 (1953): 543-62.

Works about Moody

Debusman, Paul M., compiler. *Bibliography of Materials by Dale Moody*. Unpublished document, Boyce Centennial Library, The Southern Baptist Theological Seminary, 1986.

Gragg, Alan. "Dale Moody's *The Word of Truth," Perspectives in Religious Studies* 10 (Fall 1983): 269-78.

Hinson, E. Glenn. "Dale Moody: Bible Teacher Extraordinaire." *Perspectives in Religious Studies* 14 (Winter 1987): 3-17.

Marshall, I. Howard. "The Problem of Apostasy in New Testament Theology." *Review and Expositor* 4 (Winter 1987): 65-80.

Moody, Dwight A. "Doctrines of Inspiration in the Southern Baptist Theological Tradition." Ph.D. diss., The Southern Baptist Theological Seminary, 1982.

Simmons, Paul M. "The Ethics of Dale Moody." *Review and Expositor* 4 (Winter 1987): 125-38.

Ward, Wayne. "Dale Moody's Ecclesiology." *Perspectives in Religious Studies* 14 (Winter 1987): 81-97.

Youngblood, Clark Richard. "The Question of Apostasy in Southern Baptist Thought since 1900: A Critical Evaluation." Ph.D. diss., The Southern Baptist Theological Seminary, 1978.

Notes

1. One cannot remain long at The Southern Baptist Theological Seminary and not engage in conversation about Dale Moody. This is particularly true if one has been a student of his, as is true of the writer. I am indebted for background to this article to innumerable conversations. Particularly I would like to acknowledge the help of Karen Smith, Charles Scalise, and E. Frank Tupper in reading first drafts. Conversations with the aforementioned, Richard B. Cunningham, Marvin E. Tate, and Wayne Ward were also very helpful. I am especially appreciative of Dale Moody himself who provided the basic material as my doctoral supervisor and who graciously consented to a two-hour taped interview on December 12, 1988. This will be referred to as "Personal Interview." In addition, I gleaned information from Moody in phone conversations on December 30, 1988, and January 9, 1989, of which I have personal notes. Reference to these notes is designated by "Telephone Conversation." Additionally, Moody read this manuscript and checked it for factual correctness. The responsibility for accuracy and for the judgments expressed, of course, remains the writer's.

2. Tape of chapel address, The Southern Baptist Theological Seminary, October 30, 1979. The words that followed are also revealing, "He [Luther] could read the Hebrew. He could read the Greek. He translated both. And if we want to rejuvenate the church, and rejuvenate this seminary, and rejuvenate our own lives today, let us become captives to the Holy Scriptures and stop shouting shibboleths. Let's teach what the Bible *does* say. Let's preach what's on the page before us. And I am persuaded that the seal of this seminary [a dove hovering over an open Bible] will be meaningful. I don't need somebody's creed. I don't need somebody's confession. I don't need somebody's abstract. I need only the Holy Scriptures and the Holy Spirit, and I believe that when I stick with both, let the Spirit who inspired the Scriptures lead me, and follow what I see written there on the page, I believe that God will bless us."

3. Dale Moody, *The Word of Truth: A Summary of Christian Doctrine Based on Biblical Revelation* (Grand Rapids, Mich.: William B. Eerdmans, 1981). The previous theology was by W. T. Conner, *Christian Doctrine* (Nashville: Broadman Press, 1937). A larger, two-volume work was published in two parts, in 1936 and 1945, respectively. Frank Tupper alerted me to systematic theologies written by two other Southern Baptists in the sixties: Dallas M. Roark, *The Christian Faith* (Nashville: Broadman Press, 1969), and W. W. Stevens, *Doctrines of the Christian Religion* (Clinton, Miss.: n.p., 1965).

4. I am indebted in this section especially to two main sources. One is a brief autobiographical writing by Moody and Clifton D. Harrison, "A Texas Tumbleweed," *Elm Fork Echoes* 9 (April 1981): 10-15. The other is E. Glenn Hinson's lively, and fuller, biographical account, "Dale Moody: Bible Teacher Extraordinaire," *Perspectives in Religious Studies* 14 (Winter 1987): 3-17. Also helpful were two dissertations, which gave major sections to Moody's thought: Clark Richard Youngblood, "The Question of Apostasy in Southern Baptist Thought since 1900: A Critical Evaluation" (Ph.D. diss., The Southern Baptist Theological Seminary, 1978), and Dwight A. Moody, "Doctrines of Inspiration in the Southern Baptist Theological Tradition" (Ph.D. diss., The Southern Baptist Theological Seminary, 1982). Lack of space prevents a fuller account of Moody's life in this chapter. For more information, see Moody's and Hinson's articles.

5. Hinson, "Moody," 6.

6. Moody and Harrison, "Tumbleweed," 11.

7. Ibid.

8. Ibid., 10.

9. Hinson, "Moody," 7-9; and Moody and Harrison, "Tumbleweed," 11-12.

10. In a notable memorial tribute to Carver, Moody states that he was the last graduate student to major under Carver and that Carver's course on Christianity and Current Thought was "perhaps the most crucial course I ever had." Dale Moody, "Holding Fast that Which Is Good," in *God's Glory in Missions: In Appreciation of William Owen Carver,* ed. John N. Jonsson (Private publication, 1985), 85. The three foes of Carver that Moody identifies continued as major adversaries of Moody: "Landmarkism in ecclesiology, Dispensationalism in eschatology, and Fundamentalism in Christology" (ibid.).

11. Hinson, "Moody," 9-11.

12. Dale Moody, *Baptism: Foundation for Christian Unity* (Philadelphia: Westminster Press, 1967).

13. Telephone Conversation.

14. Hinson, "Moody," 11-12.

15. See especially Geoffrey W. Bromiley, rev. of Moody, "The Word of Truth," *Theology Today* 38 (July 1981). Cf. Bruce Demarest, rev. of Moody, "The Word of Truth, Themelios, *New Series* 8 (September 1982): 34; and David S. Dockery, rev. of Moody, "The Word of Truth," *Journal of the Evangelical Theological Society* 26 (December 1983): 459.

16. Telephone Conversation. Moody commented that he had done forty-three Bible studies on the Book of Philippians in the time span of approximately one year.

17. Hinson, "Moody," 3.

18. See especially Youngblood, "Apostasy," 150-55, for an account that was verified by Moody.

19. Hinson, "Moody," 14-17.

20. I am chiefly indebted on the description of the American biblical theology movement to the insightful work of Brevard S. Childs, *Biblical Theology in Crisis* (Philadelphia: Westminster Press, 1970). James D. Smart, *The Past, Present, and Future of Biblical Theology* (Philadelphia: Westminster Press, 1979), believes that Childs overplays the crisis and demise of biblical theology as well as the specifically American character of it. Despite other criticisms, Smart does not differ significantly on major characteristics, other than to caution concerning the diversity of people involved. Smart, however, does not do justice to the way Childs distinguishes between the early movement influenced by Walther Eichrodt and Oscar Cullmann as opposed to the very different influences of Gerhard von Rad and Rudolf Bultmann.

21. Childs, *Crisis,* 17, 62. See the remarkable tribute by Brunner concerning Moody in 1962, "I think I would not be in error if I call him the theologian best informed on my theological works." Emil Brunner, "Reply to Interpretation and Criticism," in *The Theology of Emil Brunner,* ed. Charles W. Kegley, The Library of Living Theology, vol. 3 (New York: Macmillan, 1962), 346.

22. Childs, *Crisis,* 33-6. See on Moody, Alan Gragg, "Dale Moody's *The Word of Truth,*" *Perspectives in Religious Studies* 10 (Fall 1983): 276-77.

23. Childs, *Crisis,* 34.

24. Moody, *The Word of Truth,* xi, 2; Childs, *Crisis,* 14-17, 28-29, 32-36.

25. Childs, *Crisis,* 36-9.

26. Moody, "Inspiration," 58.

27. Childs, *Crisis,* 39-44.

28. This point was best made in John Baillie's classic study primarily of neoorthodox thought, *The Idea of Revelation in Recent Thought* (New York: Columbia University Press, 1956), 83-125.

29. Childs, *Crisis,* 44-47.

30. Ibid., 47-50.

31. Ibid., 71.

32. Ibid., 53. The fuller quotation is as follows: "In all the writings of the biblical theologians one seldom heard expressions of sheer joy or spontaneous adoration for Scripture which abounded in the pages of Calvin, Luther, Bunyan, Wesley, and others. Somehow this side of Biblical interpretation had become identified with pietism and rejected," (53-54).

33. Moody, *The Word of Truth,* 2-6.

34. Moody, "Romans," in *The Broadman Bible Commentary,* ed. Clifton J. Allen (Nashville: Broadman Press, 1970), 153-286.

35. Moody, *Spirit of the Living God: What the Bible Says about the Spirit,* rev. ed. (Nashville: Broadman Press, 1976). Originally published in 1968.

36. Moody, *The Hope of Glory* (Grand Rapids, Mich.: Eerdmans, 1964).

37. Dwight A. Moody, "Doctrines," 190. Dwight Moody's chapter on Dale Moody in this work is a helpful guide, along with a collection of unpublished documents and an interview that he edited. Dale Moody, "The Inspiration of Holy Scripture," ed. Dwight Moody (Unpublished manuscript, Boyce Centennial Library, The Southern Baptist Theological Seminary). In a review of Moody's systematic, Fisher Humphreys notes the puzzling fact that "this most biblical of theologies has no discussion of inerrancy." Rev. of *The Word of Truth,* by Dale Moody, *The Theological Educator* 12 (Spring 1982): 110.

38. See Moody, "Inspiration," 43 (in a letter to Dr. W. A. Criswell, August 17, 1979).

39. Dwight Moody, "Doctrines," 194-95.

40. Ibid. See also Moody, "Inspiration," 65.

41. Cf. for example the long sections on inspiration and inerrancy in Millard Erickson, *Christian Theology* (Grand Rapids, Mich.: Baker Book House, 1986), 199-240.

42. Although general revelation is clearly subordinate to special revelation and to a high Christology in Moody's thought, he attempts to work out on a biblical basis the salvific possibility of general revelation. Moody, *The Word of Truth*, 57-67. As early as 1967, Moody was favoring Brunner over Barth on this point, and John Baillie, with his openness to salvific potential, over both of them. Dale Moody, "Tabletalk on Theology Tomorrow," *Review and Expositor* 64 (1967): 341-42.

43. Moody, "Inspiration," 58-59.

44. Moody, *Word of Truth*, 38-40.

45. Ibid., 40.

46. Moody, "Inspiration," 14 (from early lecture notes ca. 1950).

47. See Dwight Moody, "Doctrines," 183.

48. Moody, *The Word of Truth*, 61.

49. Moody, "Inspiration," 14, 59, 65; Moody, *The Word of Truth*, 38-47.

50. Ibid., 40.

51. For example, see the confrontation of E. J. Carnell with Karl Barth as documented in George M. Marsden, *Reforming Fundamentalism: Fuller Seminary and the New Evangelicalism* (Grand Rapids, Mich.: William B. Eerdmans, 1987), 194-95. Note that Baillie's classic exposition of the neoorthodox viewpoint of revelation and inspiration is adamant about the fallibility of the scriptural witness. Baillie, *Idea*, 83-125.

52. Ibid.

53. Moody, "Inspiration," 59. Moody later adds the redaction process, for example, in the synoptics, 61-2. Cf. Moody, *The Word of Truth*, 57.

54. Moody is extremely sensitive to the various genres in the Bible. For example, he points out the presence of hymns everywhere. One of the major items he desired in the indexes was the hymns he *quoted* in *The Word of Truth*, not just those to which he referred, a list that includes seventy-five in the New Testament alone! The hymnic quality, however, does not preclude him from deriving propositional content. For instance, he collates the hymns in 1 Timothy 3:16 and 1 Peter 3:18,22; 4:6 that celebrate Christ's death, descent into hell, and resurrection into a historical chronology of the events surrounding Christ's death and resurrection. Moody, *The Word of Truth*, 388.

55. E. Y. Mullins, *The Christian Religion in Its Doctrinal Expression* (Valley Forge, Pa.: Judson Press, 1917), 145, 150. Moody, "Inspiration," 64.

56. Moody, "Inspiration," 64.

57. For the letters, see ibid., 42, 45, 49. The qualified affirmation of the Chicago Statement is in ibid., 28-29. See also Dwight Moody, "Doctrines," 192-3. Moody would be closest to what Erickson, *Theology,* calls "limited inerrancy," 222.

58. Dwight Moody, "Doctrines," 68.

59. Ibid., 70-71.

60. Cf. his interest in an early dating of the entire New Testament, placing all of the Gospels before A.D. 70. Moody, "A New Chronology for the New Testament," *Review and Expositor* 78 (1981): 211-31.

61. Moody, "Inspiration," 65.

62. Ibid., 24, 65.

63. Ibid.

64. Ibid., 19. Cf. note 2, above. Note also the consistent openness and outright admiration that Moody evinces for those who emphasize the dynamic role that the Holy Spirit plays in the Christian life. Criticisms that Moody neglects the Holy Spirit in *The Word of Truth* can hardly be maintained, especially considering his book-length treatment of the Holy Spirit. See *The Word of Truth*, 36, 115-26, 393, 447-48, 474-80, 506-7, 558, 568, 575. See the criticism by Humphreys, rev., 110, and Henry W. Holloman, *Journal of Psychology and Theology* 10 (Spring 1982): 81.

65. Moody, *Word of Truth*, 46.

66. Ibid., 47.

67. Ibid.

68. Dale Moody, "The Crux of Christian Theology," *Review and Expositor* 46 (1949): 167.

69. Moody, *The Word of Truth*, xi.

70. A sterling example is Moody, *Spirit*.

71. Moody, *The Word of Truth*, xi.

72. Cf. Moody, "Inspiration," 71.

73. Moody, *The Word of Truth*, 198-212. See also 73-77.

74. See especially Carl F. H. Henry, rev. of Moody, *The Word of Truth, Eternity* 32 (October 1981): 43.

75. For example, see the sections on prayer, miracles, and angels. Moody, *The Word of Truth*, 158-69. Cf. also the discussion of the virgin birth and Christ's descent into hell, 417-8, 388.

76. Moody, *The Word of Truth*, 3, 23.

77. Clark Pinnock, rev. of Moody, *The Word of Truth, Christian Scholar's Review* 11 (1982): 159-60. The reference to Bloesch is to Donald Bloesch, *Essentials of Evangelical Theology*, 2 vols. (San Francisco: Harper & Row, 1979).

78. See, for example, the praise of Hinson and that of Criswell, who is cited by Hinson, "Moody," 17. Criswell "called Moody's *The Word of Truth* 'one of the finest volumes in present theological literature' and complimented Moody himself as 'truly and verily a learned man of God, . . . as learned as Karl Barth.' Moody has obviously not written as voluminously as Barth, but the remark rings true. Dale Moody represents the very best piety that persistent, painstaking, prayerful, and probing attention to the Bible can produce. If Southern Baptists have had a world-class Bible teacher and preacher, it has been Moody."

79. Gragg, "Dale," 276-77.

80. On the Reformation, see Robert M. Grant, *A Short History of the Interpretation of the Bible*, rev. ed.; (New York: Macmillan, 1963), 128-33. See also George M. Marsden, *Fundamentalism and American Culture: The Shaping of Twentieth-Century Evangelicalism: 1870-1925* (Oxford: Oxford University Press, 1980), 16, 110-11; and George, *Theology*, concerning Luther (79-82, 95-8), Zwingli (128), and Calvin (197). Cf. 315. George's work indicates that the Reformers did not apply the perspicuity of Scripture to the plain believer as did the later Reformed tradition. On Baptist tradition, see H. Leon McBeth, *The Baptist Heritage: Four Centuries of Baptist Witness* (Nashville: Broadman Press, 1987), 30-48, 63, 70-3, 105, and Herschel H. Hobbs and E. Y. Mullins, *The Axioms of Religion* (Nashville: Broadman Press, 1978), 75-90. Cf. George, *John Robinson and the English Separatist Tradi-*

tion, NABPR Dissertation Series, no. 1 (Macon, Ga.: Mercer University Press, 1982), 115-25.

81. Moody, "Inspiration," 67-68.

82. Similarly, Gragg also points out that in comparison to Moody's predecessors such as Strong, Mullins, and Boyce, Moody is less explicit concerning his own methodology. Gragg, "Dale," 276.

83. Moody, "Inspiration," 58. Moody makes this statement in the context of beginning his teaching career as a professor of both Old Testament and New Testament theology.

84. See note 41, above.

85. Moody, "Perspectives on Scripture and Tradition," *Perspectives in Religious Studies* 15 (Spring 1988): 9.

86. Ibid. Cf. Moody, *The Word of Truth*, 71, 80-81, 108.

87. Ibid., 170-74.

88. Moody, *The Word of Truth*, 421-26. Moody's appeal is to John 1:14. Here again Moody develops his view on a firmly biblical base but also appeals to process philosophy, for example, to explicate how "the concept of two static natures is replaced by a disclosure of the divine in the act of the human," 71. See also 425-26.

89. Humphreys, rev., 109

90. Moody's eschatological interest akin to Moltmann and Pannenberg shows up also where he places the postexistence of Jesus before the preexistence of Christ and the existence of Jesus Christ, *The Word of Truth*, 386-408. (Note also the intentional significance of the names in each case). However, he begins Christology from below by considering Jesus as the Messiah of Israel, 366-85.

91. Bromiley especially commends someone for "attempting a one-volume dogmatics in this day of theological specialization." Rev., 277.

92. Telephone Conversation. Moody's best historical theology work was *Baptism*. Moody was at home in historical theology as much as in biblical theology and systematic theology. His colleague Wayne Ward points out that scholars of other traditions with whom Moody has had contact "are often surprised to find him a walking encyclopedia, not only of biblical and Baptist theology, but also of their traditions." Wayne Ward, "Dale Moody's Ecclesiology," *Perspectives in Religious Studies* 14 (Winter 1987): 96.

93. Pinnock, rev., 160.

94. Moody, "Inspiration," 30.

95. Moody, *The Word of Truth*, 365-69. Clark Youngblood contends that Moody saw the biblical problem as did Robertson, and his systematic mind could not live with the tension between individual predestination and dropping the other four points of Calvinism, as could Robertson, Mullins, and Conner. "Apostasy," 149, 150-91, 295-99.

96. Personal Interview. Moody often referred to an opponent in Arkansas who responded to Moody's views on apostasy by saying, "Well, it may be Bible, but it's not Baptist." Such attitudes served to stoke the fires already burning in Moody's opposition to eternal security.

97. Moody, *The Word of Truth*, 311.

98. Ibid., 309-10.

99. Ibid., 314, 322.

100. An example is the concept of synergism in Romans 8:28, perhaps better understood as cooperation. Ibid., 314.

101. Ibid., 224-25.

102. Ibid., 340-41.

103. Ibid., 341.

104. Ibid., 344.

105. Personal Interview.

106. Personal Interview.

107. Frank Tupper's insights into the significance of ecclesiology in Moody's thought provided the foundation for these remarks.

108. Telephone Conversation.

109. Ward, "Ecclesiology," 83, 85.

110. See Moody, "Perspectives," 6-7, for remarkable, though qualified, affirmation of the Campbellite movement.

111. On bishops, see Moody, *The Word of Truth,* 457. See Moody, "Perspectives," 6-7, and Personal Interview for much stronger statements. The view on women's ordination comes from Personal Interview.

112. Moody, *The Word of Truth,* 458-59.

113. Ibid., 216-17.

114. For example, he says the elevation of area ministers to bishops "would be a complete return to the structure of the New Testament." Moody, "Perspectives," 6-7. Cf. Moody, *The Word of Truth,* 478, where Moody advocates the seven elements of New Testament worship for the present.

115. E. Frank Tupper, "Theology Christology, and Eschatology," *Perspectives in Religious Studies* 14 (Winter 1987): 99. Because of this eschatological dimension than runs through all their works, Moody states that he is closer to Moltmann and Pannenberg, especially Moltmann, more than any other contemporary theologians. Moody, "Perspectives," 14. Likewise, I think Moody is closer to them than to his earlier mentors Brunner and Barth because of their desire to dialogue with modern science. Moody indicated to me that his original manuscript for *Hope* was about one thousand pages, which he cut to three hundred for publication.

116. Moody, *The Word of Truth,* 549-50. Cf. Moody, *Hope.*

117. Ibid., 552.

118. Ibid., 553.

119. Ibid., 516.

120. Ibid., 530.

121. Ibid., 542.

122. Ibid., 567.

123. Ibid., 573.

124. Ibid., 557-58, 573.

125. Ibid., 576-94.

126. Gragg's complaint about Moody's failure to dialogue with science and philosophy in these sections is obviously not entirely on the mark. See Gragg, "Dale," 275. Nevertheless, one is left wishing for the kind of elaboration at this point that Moody provides in the doctrines of creation and of anthropology.

127. Moody, *The Word of Truth,* 487-515.

128. Ibid., 503.

129. Ibid., 512-14.

130. Ibid., 514. Note Moody's exception for the notoriously wicked, including the devil and his angels, who will be tormented forever and ever, based on some passages in Revelation. Ibid., 514-15. Moody has said recently that he is even more convinced of conditional immortality than when he published *The Word of Truth.* Personal Conversation.

131. The citation is from a commentary on the Abstract by Moody, which he underlined for the sake of emphasis, in Moody, "Inspiration," 33.

132. Concerning assurance, see Humphreys, rev., 110-11; Dockery, rev., 460; Demarest, rev., 34; and Gragg, rev., 277-78.

133. Childs, *Crisis,* 57-58, 70-72; and Smart, *Past,* 85-106.

134. Hinson, "Moody," 11-2.

$\boxed{29}$

George R. Beasley-Murray
R. Alan Culpepper

Biography

George Beasley-Murray's life has been a pilgrimage he could not have foreseen or shaped. His parents, who came from Irish Roman Catholic homes in London, eloped during World War I and married in the Anglican Church. George was born October 10, 1916. His father was killed during the war, when George was an infant. His father's name was George Alfred Beasley, and his step-father was George Murray; so he took the name Beasley-Murray.

George was baptized by a Roman Catholic priest—an event which he remembers—at the age of four, following the birth of his sister. Eighteen months later the family left London and moved to Leicester, where the Catholic Church was a long distance from his home. Since his step-father had no religious affiliation, George was out of touch with church life until he was fifteen. Then a providential event occurred. His parents gave hospitality to a stranger looking for a house in Leicester. The visitor, who's son was George's age, discovered a Free Church. In order for the boy to play football he had to go to the Bible class, and he prevailed on George to go with him. Two weeks later the man and his son moved away, and George has not seen them since.

George found a different kind of man in the Bible class and began going to preaching services. Shortly thereafter a revival was held by two students from Spurgeon's College. George was invited to a prayer meeting for the revival. A woman with a broad country accent poured out her heart in prayer to God, talking to Him as a friend. George went to prayer meetings the rest of the week and then to the revival meetings, which made very clear that Jesus' death was for him. It changed the direction of his life, and he came to the Lord that night.

As a boy he was fascinated with music. When he became a Christian he continued to put all his spare hours into playing the piano—playing four hours a day:

> At the romantic age of 16 the appeal of music was at its highest and I spent so many hours on the piano my mind was never free from music in any waking moment. I walked, cycled, worked, ate, and drank to its accompaniment (often in time to it!) and it invaded my sleep.[1]

Even after his conversion, he had a distinct feeling that he was being called to do something with his life for God.

At eighteen he concluded that he had to respond to the call to Christian ministry. He interpreted the call as a mandate to give up music, and for six months he did not play the piano at all. He began to preach and taught himself Greek using a classical Greek grammar for two years, preaching every Sunday. At the age of twenty George entered Spurgeon's College. When he entered Spurgeon's Beasley-Murray wanted to become an evangelist who could teach the Bible. He spent more time in the Old Testament than in the New during his first theological course. Later, in his teaching, he sought to enthuse students with the richness of the Bible.

Two years after he entered Spurgeon's World War II broke out. The final year of his four-year course of study coincided with the bombing of London. He felt he had to enter pastoral work immediately:

> . . . We remained in London throughout the war. When the bombing began and we on our high point in South London at night watched bombs exploding and houses disintegrating, it was not easy to perceive the relevance of some of the controversies of early Church history and the like which we were studying. Yet we realized that what was taking place before our eyes was precisely the result of the denial of the Faith for which we stood, and its replacement by godless philosophies and creeds, whose effect was destruction and misery. When I was asked by an acquaintance in those days, "how do you feel now about the ministry and Christianity?" I replied that I had never been so convinced of the need of the Christian faith and of ministers to proclaim it to the world. The passing of the years has deepened that conviction.[2]

A church in Ilford, Essex, the Ashurst Drive Baptist Church, called Beasley-Murray. Having completed a London University B.D. in 1941, he began his ministry in that church (1941-48). The church gave him his morning for study—not an uncommon pattern in England.

In 1942 he married Ruth Weston, and in time they had three sons and a daughter. The young pastor continued his studies, taking a Th.M. in New Testament (1945) with R. V. G. Tasker, a classicist at King's College, University of London, who drilled his students in reading the Greek New Testament and writing in Greek. As a young pastor he had started writing for Christian papers. Out of those writings he produced his first book—on resurrection—*Christ Is Alive* (1947). He also preached it.

Beasley-Murray's first scholarly article was on the two messiahs in the Testaments of the Twelve Patriarchs, which was published in the *Journal for Theological Studies* (1947). In 1948 Beasley-Murray went to Cambridge, and C. H. Dodd agreed to supervise a thesis on the eschatology of the Bible. A new regulation prevented Beasley-Murray from doing the Ph.D. while pastoring a church. He had accepted a call to pastor Zion Baptist Church in Cambridge (1948-50) and did not feel he could leave this responsibility. He therefore did general studies in New Testament criticism leading to a B.A. (1950) and an M.A. (1954). He attended meetings of the New Testament seminar chaired by his professor, C. H. Dodd. His immediate supervisor

George R. Beasley-Murray (1916-   )

Photo courtesy of E. C. Dargan Research Library
Sunday School Board of the Southern Baptist Convention

was P. Gardner-Smith, who made him work through a major commentary on each book of the New Testament. He also had courses from Dodd on John and on the Christology of the New Testament.

At this time Beasley-Murray's interest in Mark 13 was born. He had a Baptist Union scholarship, which was awarded on a competitive basis, to help with his fees. Beasley-Murray was then invited to go to Spurgeon's as a lecturer in New Testament (1950-56). It was a hard decision. After two and a half years at Cambridge he went to Spurgeon's and began a Ph.D. under Tasker, working on the "little apocalypse" theory of Mark 13. He completed the degree in 1952.

In 1956 he was invited to go to Rüschlikon. A week or two later Duke K. McCall wrote him a letter inviting him to come to The Southern Baptist Theological Seminary in Louisville, Kentucky. Beasley-Murray had met McCall at the Baptist World Alliance Executive Council. He also had conversations about becoming assistant secretary of the BWA with responsibility for Europe especially. Providentially, he had not received McCall's letter when he accepted the invitation to go to Rüschlikon. The experience at Rüschlikon (1956-58) gave him exposure to the Continent and brought him into the Southern Baptist fellowship.

When Beasley-Murray went to Rüschlikon in 1956 he expected to be there indefinitely. Spurgeon's lost its principal, however, and called Beasley-Murray back to lead the school (1958-73). He felt duty bound to return and rebuild Spurgeon's. Twelve months after returning to Spurgeon's he was invited to interview with a select committee for the Ryland's chair at Manchester. T. W. Manson had died. Beasley-Murray decided not to go to see them: "I felt that my whole life had been directed toward the service of the churches, and the theological seminary is an extension of the church."

The Resurrection of Jesus (1964) came out of BBC talks on the subject. Beasley-Murray then produced a lengthy response for the Baptist Union on Baptist and ecumenical relations (1965). The report contended that Baptists needed the insights of others, who needed the witness of Baptists. During this period he also served as president of the Baptist Union of Great Britain and Ireland (1968-69) and chairman of its first permanent council (1969). It was a period of great stress. Beasley-Murray gave himself to the demands of administrative duties and denominational service but all the while felt the need to give time to writing.

While he was teaching a one-month term at Southern Seminary, the seminary extended a second invitation for him to move to Southern. The time was right for him to lay aside administrative responsibilities and devote himself more fully to teaching and research.

In 1973 McMaster University awarded Beasley-Murray an honorary D.D. That January he was in the classroom. For the first time he felt that there was a contribution he could make among Southern Baptists. Previously he had thought there was such a wealth of ability among Southern Baptists there was no need for one to come from England. Now, the opportunity would allow him to make a contribution to Southern Baptist life and give more time to writing.

In 1977 Beasley-Murray was named the James Buchanan Harrison Professor of New Testament Interpretation at Southern Seminary, a chair which he held until his retirement and return to England in 1980. At that time he was named Elrod Senior Professor at Southern Seminary.

Influences

What books and teachers were the major influences on Beasley-Murray, and what did they contribute to the shaping of his mind?

(1) C. H. Dodd's influence on Beasley-Murray focused both the subjects to which he devoted his attention and the perspective and method with which he approached the New Testament. Beasley-Murray appreciated especially Dodd's work on the nature of the gospel and its relation to history, his teaching on the kingdom of God as the present power of God, his Christology, and his work on John. Dodd struggled with the text, writing on the text itself, not quoting other's opinions.

(2) B. F. Westcott, *The Gospel of the Risen Lord,* which related the resurrection of Jesus to the life of man in the cosmos; and his two commentaries on John.

(3) E. C. Hoskyns, *The Riddle of the New Testament,* which is an example of how the tools of criticism can be used in the service of New Testament theology. His *Commentary on John* showed how a commentary should be theological as well as philological.

(4) Adolf Schlatter, whose influence is evident in the introduction to Beasley-Murray's commentary on John. Schlatter opened his eyes to the importance of the theological implications of the New Testament and the Jewishness of Jesus.

(5) Strack-Billerbeck. Awakening to the Jewishness of Jesus led Beasley-Murray to the use of Strack-Billerbeck, *Kommentar zum Neuen Testament aus Talmud und Midrasch.*

(6) R. Newton Flew influenced Beasley-Murray while Beasley-Murray was at Cambridge. *Jesus and His Church* shows the importance of the church to Jesus. Flew asked him to represent Baptists at a Faith and Order conference. Beasley-Murray declined, however, because he did not think he knew Baptists well enough at that point. Flew, a Methodist, gave George an overview of the Baptist heritage. Von Hügel had taught Flew that one had to know a person of a given religious tradition in order to understand that person's tradition. Beasley-Murray began to read the giants of the Christian faith in other traditions. It shattered his stereotypes about others and his provincial exclusiveness toward other confessions.

Exposition

Jesus and the Future

Beasley-Murray's dissertation on Mark 13 was published as *Jesus and the Future*. In this volume he reviews every significant treatment of Mark 13 since 1864, the year in which Timothy Colani put forward the "little apocalypse theory." Mark 13:5-31, Colani argued, presents the eschatology of Jewish Christians, composed in the sixties. The crux of the issue is Colani's contention that the eschatology of the Jewish Christians differed sharply from the eschatology of Jesus. For 170 pages Beasley-Murray meticulously traces the development of this thesis and variations of it and the debate that it precipitated.

Chapter 5 constitutes Beasley-Murray's response, a tour de force demonstrating "that the teaching of the eschatological discourse approximates so closely to the otherwise attested teaching of our Lord as to preclude the necessity for postulating an extraneous origin for it."[3] One of the chief objections to the authenticity of the eschatological discourse has been the inconsistency of the suddenness of the end and the description of signs that will precede it. After analyzing the function of both of these elements in Jesus' teaching, Beasley-Murray explains the apparent inconsistency by appealing to "the pastoral care of the Chief Shepherd for his own":

> the end will come with unexpected suddenness, it will take the ungodly unawares, for they do not know the issue of their distresses; the believer also does not know when the end will come, but *the understanding of the nature of the times will encourage him to endure steadfastly and not lose his crown.*[4]

Beasley-Murray's response to the charge that Jesus was wrong in His prophecies of an imminent end, and that He is therefore discredited, reflects the author's personal struggle, his concern for the impact of his scholarship on the church's witness, and an admirable candor.

> Christian believers shrink from admitting that their Lord was mistaken in a major item of his preaching and not unnaturally cast about to see if there is any other explanation of the Gospel material. It will have become clear to the reader that the present writer inclines to conservative views; he freely admits that on this matter he hesitated long before capitulating before the facts. Yet facts they appear to be and the Christian must come to terms with them; to resist what appears to be truth is to deny the Lord in whose interests it is done.[5]

Since that time Beasley-Murray has modified his belief that Jesus expected His Parousia to occur before the end of the contemporary generation. Mark 13:30 reads, "This generation shall not pass away until all these things happen." Beasley-Murray draws attention to the close parallel in Matthew 23:36 and Luke 11:51, "Amen I tell you, all these things shall come upon this generation." That refers to the judgment of God upon the recalcitrant people of Israel. Beasley-Murray suggests that the Markan saying represents the form that the Q saying took when it was repeated apart from its context, and in its fresh (Markan) setting refers primarily to the coming of the "Day of the Lord" upon Jerusalem, its Temple, city, and people. While acknowledging that Jesus maintained a near expectation, Beasley-Murray now believes that Mark 13:32 indicates the real view of Jesus as to the time of the advent and consummation of the kingdom of God: "Of that day and hour no man knows . . . not even the Son."

Beasley-Murray's conclusion on this sensitive point is consistent with his resolution of the tension between the suddenness and signs of the end: His concern for His followers and His unique consciousness of the coming fulfillment of the kingdom: Jesus' *"conviction of the nearness of the victory was due to the clarity of that vision in his soul."*[6] Our author then quotes Bengel, the German pietist and expositor, with approval: "The summits of certain mountains are seen only at rare moments when, their cloud cap rolled away, they stand out stark and clear."[7] At one memorable meeting of the New Testament Colloquium at The Southern Baptist Theological Seminary, nearly a quarter of a century after he had completed *Jesus and the Future,* Beasley-Murray adapted and extended Bengel's metaphor by pointing out that from a high point one can see the ridges of mountain ranges in the distance. The ridges can be clearly seen, but one cannot tell how many miles separate them. Similarly, Jesus saw the coming fulfillment but did not know how many years lay between the resurrection, the destruction of Jerusalem, and the Parousia. Although Jesus may have given an eschatological discourse on the Mount of Olives, the text of Mark 13 is a compilation of fragments of Jesus' eschatological teachings.

Beasley-Murray returned to this issue in a paper presented to the Society for New Testament Studies in 1982 in which he affirms the composite nature of Mark 13. While continuing to reject the "little apocalypse" theory, he suggests that the Evangelist drew its elements from the early Christian catechesis wherein the teaching of Jesus was preserved: "It is reasonable to assume that Mark's prime function in the composition of the eschatological discourse, as in chapter 4 and 8:27—9:1, was to bring together the varied elements available to him in his tradition and to fashion them into a unitary whole in the light of the contemporary situation and needs of his church."[8]

Preaching the Gospel from the Gospels (1956) was an assigned topic for a conference of ministers. W. G. Kümmel and G. D. Kilpatrick challenged him to show how his view of Mark 13 works out in exegesis. In response, Beasley-Murray wrote *A Commentary on Mark Thirteen* (1957).

Beasley-Murray viewed Mark 13 and parallels as the most difficult section of the New Testament on eschatology. He saw this work as the first step toward a broader work on the eschatology of the New Testament, which he had begun in the mid-1950s, when the Baptist Union called on him to write a book on baptism.

Following Barth's lecture on baptism, other churches (Lutheran, Reformed, Anglican, Church of Scotland) began to examine their doctrines of baptism. Karl Barth had sought to demonstrate that the theology of baptism presumes the faith of the recipients. He called infant baptism a wound in the body of Christ, and called for the church to cease to baptize children. Joachim Jeremias, Oscar Cullmann, and the Church of Scotland maintained, in response to Barth, that in the New Testament, baptism was for families of believers. Barth concluded that apostolic baptism was for those who had responded to the gospel. Paradoxically, Baptists had not emphasized the doctrine of baptism in the New Testament so strongly. In response to these events, Beasley-Murray left eschatology and turned to baptism. While at

Rüschlikon, he was asked to represent Baptists in a commission of the World Council of Churches on Faith and Order which was charged with producing a statement on Baptism. These two invitations led him to write the book on baptism while in discussion with leading scholars representing other denominations.

Baptism in the New Testament

Beasley-Murray's interest in baptism can be traced back to his first article, "The Sacraments," published in *The Fraternal*, 70 (1948): 3-7, in which Beasley-Murray responded to an earlier essay which described baptism as an *ordinance* that expresses the Christian's dedication to God. Beasley-Murray maintained that baptism should be understood instead primarily as a *sacrament* which marks the bestowing of grace from God. In this regard, Beasley-Murray was building on the work of British Baptist scholars H. Wheeler Robinson (1872-1945) and H. H. Rowley (1890-1969), who laid the foundations for "evangelical sacramentalism" or "dynamic sacramentalism." Robinson had contended: "But if we do not make more of baptism than we are doing, I fear that we shall as a denomination, make still less, and that open membership may become a line of drift into Congregationalism, which I should personally deplore."[9]

A preliminary version of the chapter on "Baptism in the Pauline Literature" was published in a collection of essays entitled *Christian Baptism,* written by ten British Baptists.[10] Beasley-Murray's work on baptism was further developed in the Norton Lectures delivered at The Southern Baptist Theological Seminary, Louisville, Kentucky, March 17-20, 1959; lectures at Southeastern Baptist Theological Seminary, New Orleans Baptist Theological Seminary, and Southwestern Baptist Theological Seminary; and the Dr. W. T. Whitley Lectureship, for which Beasley-Murray delivered lectures at Regent's Park College, Oxford, in November 1959, and at the Bangor Baptist College at the University of Bangor, North Wales, in February 1960. The Adolph Olson Memorial Lectures delivered in 1965 at Bethel Theological Seminary, St. Paul, Minnesota, gave Beasley-Murray the opportunity to prepare a popular introduction to the baptismal controversy which was published under the title, *Baptism Today and Tomorrow* (London: Macmillan, 1966).

Baptism in the New Testament organizes Beasley-Murray's painstaking exegesis of all the New Testament references to baptism and his interactions with the relevant secondary literature (some 234 books and articles) into six chapters. The first four chapters provide historical survey of (1) the Antecedents (Old Testament, Qumran, Jewish proselyte baptism, and John the Baptist), (2) the Foundation (the baptism of Jesus), (3) the Emergence (baptism in the earliest church according to the Acts of the Apostles), and (4) the Development of Christian Baptism (in the Pauline literature, the Johannine literature, and in Hebrews and 1 Peter). The fifth chapter gathers up the theological themes related to the doctrine of Christian baptism in the New Testament: baptism and grace, faith, the Spirit, the church, ethics, hope, and the necessity of baptism. Chapter 6 constitutes an extended excursus dealing with the rise and significance of infant baptism, which, for Beasley-Murray, would not be, strictly speaking, an integral aspect of "Baptism *in the New Testament*."

The perspective on baptism which emerges from this careful exegetical study has been called Beasley-Murray's "bombshell in the baptistry."[11] While affirming that confession is essential for Christian baptism as it was practiced in the primitive church, Beasley-Murray maintains that baptism was "both an occasion of confession and itself a confession."[12] The one being baptized was baptized "in the name" of Jesus; baptism was a confession that "Jesus is Lord."[13] In response, "this desire of the baptized to number himself with the people who invoke the Name of Jesus is answered by his graciously being incorporated in baptism into the community of those who inherit the Kingdom."[14] Because of the unity of word and act, Beasley-Murray insists that baptism is an integral part of the conversion experience: "In baptism the Gospel proclamation and the hearing of faith become united in one indissoluble act, at one and the same time an act of grace and faith, an act of God and man."[15] "Baptism and conversion are thus inseparables; the one demands the other, for neither is complete without the other."[16] In Chapter 5 every aspect of conversion is related to baptism. Consequently, it follows that the New Testament attributes "the fullness of saving grace to the performance of . . . baptism."[17] Neither does Beasley-Murray separate baptism from either one's incorporation into Christ or into the church: "baptism to Christ is baptism to the Church"[18]; "the really important fact . . . is the indivisibility of the two aspects of baptism: it is baptism to Christ and into the Body. It is at once intensely personal and completely corporate, involving the believer in relationship simultaneously with the Head and with all the members of the Body."[19]

Beasley-Murray rejects the alternative that baptism is either symbolic *or* sacramental, for him it is *both:* "The idea that baptism is a purely symbolic rite must be pronounced not alone unsatisfactory but out of harmony with the New Testament itself. Admittedly, such a judgment runs counter to the popular tradition of the Denomination to which the writer belongs . . . ."[20] Both perspectives require careful qualification, however. Baptism is not "merely symbolic"; the apostolic writers show that baptism is "a symbol with power, that is, a sacrament."[21] On the other hand, Beasley-Murray rejects the logic of the argument that because "sacramentalism *can* be magical, therefore it is to be presumed that the sacramentalism of the primitive Church *was* magical."[22] Indeed, he points out clear warnings against a magical-sacramental view of baptism (1 Cor. 10:1ff.; 1 Pet. 3:21). As William E. Hull concludes in his summary of Beasley-Murray's view of baptism, whenever the normative New Testament doctrine is recovered,

> There, baptism is understood as a sacrament, or "symbol with power," because the grace offered in the event "is no impersonal influence, injected through material substances, but *the gracious action of God himself*" (p. 265). With this theocentric emphasis we reach the deepest level of Beasley-Murray's concern in his study of baptism.[23]

Perhaps one may add that this interpretation is claimed to be strictly exegetical, that is, an endeavor to set forth the *New Testament* teaching on baptism, not that of any denomination. Beasley-Murray believes that throughout the New Testament baptism remains what John the Baptist proclaimed it to be: "repentance-baptism" (i.e., conversion-baptism). This is why the theology of baptism and the theology of conversion in the New Testament are one. As soon as baptism is divorced from conversion it is misunderstood, and "sacramentarianism" arises through applying what is essentially the theology of conversion to a rite. Ernest A. Payne, secretary of the British Baptist Union, stated that Beasley-Murray had written an exposition of "ideal Baptism." Beasley-Murray approved that interpretation, but expressed the hope that Baptists would strive to approximate their practice to that New Testament ideal.

Beasley-Murray's exegesis of the biblical references to baptism will stand as the definitive work on the subject for years to come. Where issue is taken with the work it is usually not in response to its handling of exegetical matters but in its larger methodological, hermeneutical, and theological perspectives. Has Beasley-Murray exaggerated the significance of baptism in the New Testament and in the life of the early church in the course of such a monumental study of the subject? With the exception of ambiguous references in John 3:22; 4:2 there is no record that Jesus baptized others, nor was baptism a significant element of His teachings. Does Beasley-Murray adequately recognize the diversity of theological perspectives in the New Testament or the divergences between Jesus and the early church, Acts and the Pauline letters, John and the Synoptics, or Paul and John? Further work may show more clearly how the meaning of baptism changed and developed in the evolution of the church from Palestinian to Gentile soil, and from one trajectory of early Christian tradition to another. But such work will stand on the shoulders of the sturdy volume Beasley-Murray has provided as a guide for the church and its theologians.

For his book on baptism, the University of London awarded Beasley-Murray the D.D. (1963), which is viewed as a particularly valuable degree in England.

In 1965 the BWA world congress was held in Miami. Beasley-Murray presented a paper on "Baptism among Baptists." The meetings were open to all the delegates. Beasley-Murray affirmed the validity of Baptism in the name of the Father, Son, and Holy Spirit *for believers,* however it is administered. It is the intent, the gospel, and confession that make baptism valid—not immersion. The *Didache*, an early collection of directions for the church, shows that this was the belief of the church from a very early time. It specified that baptism should be administered in living water (running water), otherwise in a pool of cold water. The one being baptized was to be dipped three times. If there was not enough water, then water was to be poured over the candidate three times.

The Book of Revelation

Bringing solid scholarship to a much abused book, Beasley-Murray locates Revelation squarely in the tradition of Jewish and Christian apocalyptic literature, biblical prophecy, and the eschatological teachings of Jesus and the early church. In form, Beasley-Murray claims, it combines the genres of epistle, apocalypse, and prophecy: "John's adoption of the style of an apocalyptist in no way hinders him from thinking as a prophet."[24] Nevertheless, "he who seeks to compile from it a history-in-advance will be either disappointed or deceived, for it is not there to be written."[25] Indeed, as prophetic commentary on contemporary events and guidance for the church in difficult times, the imagery employed in Revelation has its closest modern parallel in the political cartoon, which employs symbols and human or animal representative figures whose meaning is readily understood.

Unlike other apocalyptists, John writes in his own name, not under a pseudonym. Taking Dionysius, the third-century bishop of Alexandria as his guide, Beasley-Murray rehearses the reasons why it is improbable that the same author wrote both Revelation and the Gospel of John: (1) John, the Seer, never claims to be an apostle or the Beloved Disciple; (2) there are distinct differences in content, though here Beasley-Murray demurs from Dionysius' sharp assessment that Revelation "scarcely, so to speak, has a syllable in common with them [the Gospel and Epistles of John]"; and (3) differences of style and language. The authors of these documents may have been disciples of the Beloved Disciple, but then John the Seer seems to have such authority that no further identification is necessary. Beasley-Murray therefore quotes with approval the judgment that "we know nothing more about the author of the Apocalypse than that he was a Jewish-Christian prophet by the name of John."[26] Following the early testimony of Irenaeus, Beasley-Murray endorses the view that Revelation was written ca. A.D. 95, near the end of the reign of Domitian.

In theme and emphasis, "the fulcrum of this book is not the parousia and the descent of the city of God, described in its closing visions, but the vision of God and the Lamb in chapters 4—5."[27] "the turn of the ages, therefore, lies in the past."[28] Whereas the commentary is replete with references to relevant parallels found in the Old Testament and in Jewish apocalyptic literature, Beasley-Murray states pointedly: "There is no analogy to the eschatological doctrine of Revelation chapter 5 in all Jewish apocalyptic, and that for a simple reason: it is an exposition of the gospel of the crucified and risen Christ, such as only a Christian prophet can give."[29]

The horrifying judgments on the world that follow after this chapter evoke the typology of the second exodus, and again "the crucial event is not the 'plagues' but the redemption which leads to the new world."[30] Chapters 6—19, moreover, are not to be read as a continuous narration of events leading to the Parousia; the three series of messianic judgments (the seals, trumpets, and cups of wrath) are parallel descriptions of a single short period in history, the time which precedes the coming of Christ's kingdom.[31] The episode of the seventh seal underscores the importance of the prayers of God's people. Chapters 12—14 set the conflict between church and state against the background of the age-long conflict between God and the powers of evil. The antichristian empire falls prey to its own forces of destruction (chs. 17—18), and then at last the revelation of Christ is portrayed (chs. 19—22).

The strength of Beasley-Murray's treatment of Revelation is that it places the book squarely in the context of the gospel and the great theological themes of the New Testament. Readers who are interested in learning or refuting dispensational theories of the rapture and the time of the millennium will be mystified or disappointed. Others may again respond that Beasley-Murray has exaggerated the continuity between Revelation and the other writings of the New Testament. To such objections Beasley-Murray responds:

> The Revelation calls on Christian people to take seriously the teaching delivered to the Church on the kingdom of God in history. For John that means the witness borne by Jesus to the kingdom of God as handed down by apostolic teachers and interpreted through the Holy Spirit and the Church.
>
> Is it possible to trace a connection between the teaching of Jesus and that of the Revelation? If we keep to the fundamental elements of eschatology, yes.[32]

The message of Revelation, therefore, is rooted in Jesus' proclamation of the kingdom and the imminent expectation of the end and the role of the Antichrist and the church as it is interpreted by Paul and the other apostolic writers.

Jesus and the Kingdom of God

At Southern, William E. Hull asked Beasley-Murray to take over the course on the kingdom of God in the teachings of Jesus. This request led to his doing what he had intended to do years before, a book on the eschatology of Jesus. He had to limit it to the Synoptic Gospels because of size, and saw it as a contribution to Christology. Books on Christology do not consider Jesus' views of His relation to the kingdom. The classical presentations of the doctrine of atonement neglect this area also. They are usually too heavily based on Paul. Similarly, theologians have generally done the same as Bultmann in neglecting Jesus when formulating Christology. The manuscript was completed in 1980, long before it was finally published in 1986.

For Beasley-Murray, the topic of this volume offers one the opportunity to understand the theme that dominated Jesus' life, and hence to see more clearly who Jesus was. The context and development of the theme of the kingdom of God in the Old Testament and contemporary Jewish literature is established first. Regarding the issue of the messianic interpretation of Daniel 7, Beasley-Murray contends that "the messianic interpretation of the one like a man is not demonstrable, but it is plausible and even probable."[33] Moreover, Beasley-Murray's review of the kingdom of God in apocalyptic literature leads to the observation that "the juxtaposition of present and future notions of the eschatological kingdom is not so foreign to Jewish eschatology as was once thought." Especially significant is his conclusion that the Similitudes of Enoch, which depict the Son of man as a messianic representative, were composed during or within a generation of the ministry of Jesus. In Jesus' teachings and the Similitudes, therefore, we have "two parallel movements of thought leading back to one source—namely, the vision of Daniel."[34]

Two major chapters survey the sayings and parables on the coming of the kingdom of God in the present. No single formula does justice to the relation of Jesus to the kingdom. Jesus is the Champion or Contender (Mark 3:27), the Initiator (Matt. 11:12), the Instrument (Matt. 12:28), the Representative (Luke 17:20-21), the Mediator (Mark 2:18-19), the Bearer (Matt. 11:5), and the Revealer of the kingdom (Matt. 13:16-17). Moreover, while Jesus does not claim the title *Messiah* in any of these passages,

> do not those sayings and functions indicate that he *assumed* for himself the function of Messiah? This is a point of no small controversy. The voice of critical scholarship either trails off into silence or becomes strident over it. In the end, however, we are compelled to say Yes for the simplest of reasons. . . . the function that Jesus assigns to himself in relation to the kingdom goes well beyond anything said of the Messiah in the Old Testament or in the apocalyptic and rabbinic teaching of his day. . . . It might be argued that the term is insufficient to convey *all* that he is in relation to the kingdom of God, but if that is so, then certainly nothing *less* than that will do to describe him.[35]

Responding to those who wish to dismiss "the Son of man" from the vocabulary of Jesus, Beasley-Murray demonstrates the appropriateness of this term as "a perfect vehicle for Jesus' proclamation of the message of the kingdom of God; it is a humble term with associations of divine glory."[36] It can be used in a generic sense ("man"), as a circumlocution for oneself, or to denote the representative and mediator of the kingdom. Jesus could therefore use the term in the context of references to His own death and vindication in the passion predictions:

> To look at the passion predictions in the light of this evidence is to view them in a fresh way. It does not prove that any single expression of an anticipated resurrection in the sayings is authentic, but it does show that in them we may see expressions of an assurance on the part of Jesus that after suffering he would be raised by God for further service and glory.[37]

The use of the Son of man in the Last Supper narratives shows further that "Jesus viewed his death as part and parcel of the process whereby the kingdom comes." Finally, while they do not allow us to describe it, the Parousia sayings point ahead to "an act of God in Christ for the salvation of the world and its judgment."[38]

Jesus and the Kingdom of God offers readers a painstaking analysis of the kingdom sayings, the Son of man sayings, and the Parousia sayings in the Synoptic Gospels. While some New Testament scholars will take issue with Beasley-Murray's insistence on the general reliability of the Gospel sayings for grasping the mind of Jesus, he has offered conservatives and evangelicals a majestic, scholarly reaffirmation of the view that Jesus was self-consciously the agent of the kingdom of God, the one in whose words and actions the kingdom of God was made present, the one by whose death the redemptive work of the kingdom was completed, and the one in whose future coming the kingly rule of God will be extended over all the earth.

When he completed this volume, Beasley-Murray began to bring his work on Mark 13 up to date. There had been only one work on Mark 13 before his (F. Busch in the 1930s). Subsequently, a half a dozen books had followed, as did the development of redaction criticism. The invitation to do a commentary on John for the Word Biblical Commentary, however, caused him to lay aside this project once more.

John

The Word Biblical Commentary has emerged as the leading edge of progressive evangelical scholarship. Beasley-Murray's commentary on John fits comfortably in this context and adds luster to the commentary series, which is designed to be both critical and theological in emphasis. For each unit of the text the author provides a carefully chosen bibliography of the most important treatments of that passage in English, German, and French; an original translation of the text; textual and lexical notes; detailed comment on the key verses; and then an explanation of the thematic developments and theological significance of the unit.

Beasley-Murray is skeptical of the identification of literary sources behind the Gospel of John, preferring to speak of its literary traditions. He rejects, for example, proposals that a signs source lies behind the Gospel[39] opting instead for the thesis that "the organizing of the traditions to form the Gospel took place through preaching, especially the preaching of the Evangelist."[40]

> The thought came to me when, as a student, I listened to Dodd expound his understanding of the structure of John's "Book of Signs" (chaps. 2—12). He believed that each episode of this part of the Gospel consisted of sign(s) plus discourse and that *each presents the Gospel in its wholeness,* namely, Christ manifested, crucified, risen, exalted, and communicating life (see Dodd, *Interpretation,* 383-86). To me this was as scales falling from the eyes, for this arrangement of the evangelic material was in all probability due to the Evangelist's use in his preaching, as he presented the episodes of the ministry in the light of their end in the redemptive death and resurrection of the Lord.[41]

The present order of the text, moreover, is intelligible, and the Gospel is "a remarkably unified and well integrated document."[42]

The roots of the Johannine tradition undoubtedly lie in Judea—and in this regard Beasley-Murray claims there is much to be said for Cullmann's view of the nature of the Jewish heritage that lay behind the Gospel. Indeed, one of the commentary's distinctive contributions is its extensive use of rabbinic materials to illuminate the text of John.[43] Throughout the exposition, Beasley-Murray is sensitive to the conflict between church and synagogue—

a view of the life setting of the Gospel whose most ardent advocate is J. Louis Martyn—and the relevance of the Gospel material to the setting in which it was written: "The Evangelist sets the historical ministry of Jesus in Palestine in indissoluble relation to the ministry of the risen Lord in the world."[44] Beasley-Murray therefore holds in tension and balance both the historical and the theological character of the Fourth Gospel:

> Our real concern, however, is to stress that the fundamental issue that determined the form of the Fourth Gospel is the theological one, namely, the unity of Christ's action in the flesh and in the Spirit. It calls for recognition of *both* components of the Lord's work and their mutual relations. In John's thought and writing their unity and distinctiveness are held in balance.[45]

In places Beasley-Murray acknowledges this blending of perspective means that we can no longer distinguish the words of Jesus from those of the Evangelist.

Beasley-Murray's discussion of the authorship of the Gospel reveals further development in his thought since the writing of his commentary on Revelation over a decade earlier. In the commentary on John, Beasley-Murray confidently adopts the view that the authors of these two writings were "fellow members of a Johannine 'school.'"[46] The Beloved Disciple, who was undoubtedly a real historical figure, was probably not one of the twelve, and hence not the apostle John. Neither was he the author of the Gospel. Rather, as an eyewitness, "the authority figure to which the Johannine communities looked, the Beloved Disciple appears to have had a group of teachers about him," among whom were the writers of the Gospel, the Epistles, and Revelation.[47] The identity of both the Evangelist and the Beloved Disciple remain unknown, but we may view "the Evangelist as a master interpreter of the school of the Beloved Disciple."[48] As to the provenance of the Gospel, Beasley-Murray arrives at a position very close to that of T. W. Manson, who suggested that

> The Fourth Gospel originated in a tradition which had its home in Jerusalem, and was taken to Antioch; there it influenced literature connected with that city, the liturgical usage of the Syrian church, the teaching of missionaries who went out from it (e.g., Paul) and its later leaders (e.g., Ignatius); from Antioch it was taken to Ephesus, where "the final literary formulation was achieved in the Gospel and Epistles attributed to John."[49]

Redressing recent emphases on the polemical features of the Gospel, Beasley-Murray maintains that the Fourth Gospel was written "with both evangelistic and didactic aims in view." He minimizes, therefore, the importance of the polemic against the movement of disciples of John the Baptist.[50]

One of the most rewarding aspects of the commentary is its nuanced handling of Johannine theology. Major theological themes and their distinctive Johannine development and expression receive balanced and illuminating treatment. For example, the importance of the "lifting up" sayings in 3:14; 8:28; and 12:32 is highlighted at relevant points in the exposition.[51] Similarly, Beasley-Murray gives due emphasis to the distinctive claim of the Gospel that believers already experience resurrection and eternal life through believing in Jesus, while not failing to recognize that John continues to hold forth a steadfast hope for the fulfillment of God's redemptive work in the future through the Parousia and a judgment in the last day. Even if such emphases come from the redactor, "they are in harmony with the fundamental theology of the Evangelists."[52] "Christ as the Resurrection gives hope for the future life, and the reality of that life in the present."[53]

Evaluation

In review, the scope and magnitude of George Beasley-Murray's contributions to the thought and life of the church place him among the most influential Baptist theologians in any generation. His experience as pastor, principal, and professor has kept him close to the pulse of the church. The impact of his work, moreover, has been heightened by the fact that Beasley-Murray has regularly chosen to deal with subjects that are of crucial significance not only for New Testament scholarship but also for the life of the church: Jesus and the future, baptism, and the kingdom of God. On each of these subjects he has provided the definitive monograph for this generation. Beasley-Murray has unerringly moved toward those parts of the New Testament that are the crux of the issues which have concerned him: Mark 13, Revelation, and John. Behind all of his work, however, one sees the enduring conviction that the New Testament puts us in contact with the teaching, the revelation, and the person of Jesus. Beasley-Murray's greatest, and one hopes most enduring achievement, therefore, is that he has helped the church (and four decades of ministerial students) to gain a clear and engaging understanding of the solid substance of the teachings of Jesus, and thereby a greater appreciation for both the Bible and the Lord whose revelation it contains.

Recognitions of Beasley-Murray's distinguished career and his contributions to New Testament scholarship and the church continue to come to him. In 1989 a Festschrift entitled *Eschatology and the New Testament: Essays in Honor of George R. Beasley-Murray* and edited by Hulitt Gloer was published (Peabody, Mass.: Hendrickson, 1988). Spurgeon's College has requested that the Council of National Academic Awards confer on Beasley-Murray an honorary D.Lit., and Cambridge University conferred on him the D.D. (1989) for his writings on the New Testament, especially his books on the kingdom of God and the Gospel of John.

Beasley-Murray has not laid down his pen, however. Having completed the commentary on John, he has recently produced a short book on the themes of the Gospel of John, and is currently working on a further volume on Mark 13 and another on the theology of John.

Bibliography

Books (chronological order)

1947   *Christ Is Alive*. Lutterworth Press.

1953   *Ezekiel*, in *The New Bible Commentary*, ed. F. Davidson. Tyndale Press.
Revelation, in *The New Bible Commentary*.
Jesus and the Future, An Examination of the Criticism of the Eschatological Discourse, Mark 13 with Special Reference to the Little Apocalypse Theory. New York, Macmillan.

1956   *Preaching the Gospel from the Gospels*. Lutterworth.

1957   *A Commentary on Mark Thirteen*. New York, Macmillan.

1962   "Philippians," in *Peake's Commentary on the Bible*, 2d edition. Nashville, Nelson.
Baptism in the New Testament. New York, Macmillan.

1964   *The Resurrection of Jesus Christ*. Oliphants.

1965   *The General Epistles*, in *Bible Guides*, ed. W. Barclay and F. F. Bruce. Lutterworth.

1966   *Baptism Today and Tomorrow*. New York, Macmillan.

1971   "2 Corinthians," in *The Broadman Bible Commentary*. Nashville, Broadman Press.

1972   *Highlights in the Book of Revelation*. Nashville, Broadman.

1974   *The Book of Revelation*, New Century Bible. Grand Rapids, Mich.: Oliphants/Eerdmans.

1977   *Revelation: Three Viewpoints*, with H. Hobbs and R. F. Robbins. Nashville, Broadman.

1983   *The Coming of God*. Exter: Paternoster Press.

1984   *Matthew*, in *Bible Study Commentary*. Scripture Union/Christian Literature Crusade.

1986   *Jesus and the Kingdom of God*. Grand Rapids, Mich.: Eerdmans/Paternoster Press.

1987   *John*, Word Biblical Commentary, 36. Waco, Word Books.

1989   *Word Biblical Themes: John*. Waco, Word Books.

Contributions to Books (chronological order)

1953   "The Apocryphal and Apocalyptic Literature," in *The New Bible Commentary*.

1959   "Baptism in the Letters of Paul," in *Christian Baptism*, ed. A. Gilmore. Lutterworth.

1963   "The Apostolic Writing," in *The Roads Converge*, ed. P. Gardner-Smith. E. Arnold.
"Introduction to the New Testament," in *A Companion to the Bible*, ed. H. H. Rowley. T. & T. Clark.

1964 "Die Taufe der Glaubigen," in *Die Baptisten*, ed. J. D. Hughey. Stuttgart: Evangelisches Verlagswerk.

1965 "The Diaconate in Baptist Churches," in *The Ministry of Deacons*, World Council Studies no. 2. Geneva: World Council of Churches.

1968 "My Call to the Ministry," in *My Call to the Ministry*, ed. C. A. Joyce. London: Marshall Morgan & Scott.
"The Holy Spirit and the Church," in *Sermons for Today*, ed. A. H. Chapple. London: Marshall, Morgan & Scott.

1970 "Jesus and the Spirit," in *Melanges Bibliques, Festschrift R. P. Beda Rigaux*. Gembloux: Duculot.
"The Child and the Church," in *Children and Conversion*, ed. Clifford Ingle. Nashville: Broadman Press.

1971 Articles on *Blut* (Greek *rhantizo*) and *Taufe* (Greek *baptizo, louo*), in *Theologisches Begriffslexikon zum Neuen Testament*. Wuppertal.

1974 "How Christian Is the Book of Revelation?" in *Reconciliation and Hope*, Festschrift for Leon Morris. Grand Rapids, Mich.: Eerdmans.

1975 "The Clue to the Meaning of Life" in *What Faith Has Meant to Me*, ed. Claude Frazier. Philadelphia: Westminster.

1979 "Faith and the Parousia," in *Science, Faith and Revelation: An Approach to a Christian Philosophy*, Festschrift for Eric Rust. Nashville: Broadman Press.

1980 "Jesus and Apocalyptic: with special Reference to Mark 14:62," in *L'Apocalypse johannique et l'apocalyptique dans le nouveau testament*, ed. J. Lambrecht, Bibliotheca/Ephemeridum Theologicarum Lovaniensum LIII. Duculot, Gembloux, Leuven University Press. Pp. 415-429.

1986 "John 12:31-34, The Eschatological Significance of the Lifting up of the Son of Man," in *Studien zum Text und zur Ethik des Neuen Testaments*, Festschrift H. Greeven, ed. W. Schrage and W. de Gruyter, Berlin and New York. Pp. 90-101.

1989 "Eschatology and Ethics in the Teaching of Jesus, with Special Reference to Matthew 6:33," in *Festschrift for Rudolf Schnackenburg*.

Articles in Journals (chronological order)

1943 "The Church and the Child." *The Fraternal*, Organ of the Baptist Minister's Fellowship, New Series, no. 50.

1946 "The Eschatology of the Fourth Gospel." *Evangelical Quarterly*, 18, 2 (April 1946).
"The Second Coming of Christ." *The Fraternal*, 61 (July 1946).
"The Relation of the Fourth Gospel to the Apocalypse." *Evangelical Quarterly*, 18, 3 (July 1946).

1947 "The Two Messiahs in the Testaments of the Twelve Patriarchs." *Journal of Theological Studies*, 48 (Jan.-Apr. 1947), 189-190.
"Doctrinal Developments in the Apocrypha and Pseudepigrapha." *Evangelical Quarterly*, 19, 3 (July 1947).
"Immortality." *Journal of the Transactions of the Victoria Institute*, 79 (1947).

1948 "A Conservative Thinks Again About Daniel." *Baptist Quarterly*, 12, Nos. 9 and 10-11 (1948).
"Biblical Eschatology, I, The Interpretation of Prophecy." *Evangelical Quarterly*, 20, 3 (July 1948).

"The Sacraments." *The Fraternal*, 70 (1948),
"Biblical Eschatology, II, Apocalyptic Literature and the Book of Revelation." *Evangelical Quarterly*, 20, 4 (October 1948).

1951 "The Second Coming in the Book of Revelation." *Evangelical Quarterly*, 23, 1 (January 1951).

1953 "A Century of Eschatological Discussion." *Expository Times*, 64, 10 (July 1953).
"The Rise and Fall of the Little Apocalypse Theory." *Expository Times*, 64, 11 (August 1953).

1954 "The Minister and His Bible." *The Fraternal*, 92 (1954).

1955 "Important and Influential Foreign Books: Gloege's Reich Gottes und Kirche." *Expository Times*, 66, 5 (February 1955).

1956 "The Church of Scotland and Baptism." *The Fraternal*, 99 (1956).

1957 "Demythologized Eschatology." *Theology Today*, 14, 1 (April 1957).
"The Significance of the Second Coming of Christ." *The Fraternal*, 103 (1957).

1958 "Das Reich Gottes und die sittliche Forderung Jesu." *Wort und Tat*, 12, 1 (Jan-Feb 1958).
"Gesetz und Geist in die christlichen Lebensführung (Die Ethik des Apostles Paulus.)" *Wort und Tat*, 12, 2 (March-April 1958).

1960 "Baptism in the New Testament." *Foundations*, 3 (1960).
"The Eschatological Discourse of Jesus." *Review and Expositor*, 57 (1960).
"Nya Testamentets Dopteologi." *Tro och Liv*, No. 6 (1960).

1961 "Interpretation av Rom. 6. 1-11." *Tro och Liv*, No. 1 (1961).

1963 "Ecumenical Encounter in Russia." *The Fraternal*, No. 127 (1963).

1965 "A Baptist Interpretation of the Place of the Child in the Church." *Foundations*, 8, 2 (1965).

1966 "The Holy Spirit, Baptism and the Body of Christ." *Review and Expositor*, 63 (1966).

1967 "Das Christusbild des Neuen Testaments und unsere Verkündigung." *Wort und Tat*, 21 (September 1967).
"I Still Find Infant Baptism Difficult." *Baptist Quarterly*, 22 (October 1967).

1973 "The Second Chapter of Colossians." *Review and Expositor*, 70, 4 (1973).

1974 "The Contribution of the Book of Revelation to the Christian Belief in Immortality, Drew Lecture on Immortality, 1972." *Scottish Journal of Theology*, (1974).

1975 "New Testament Apocalyptic—A Christological Eschatology." *Review and Expositor*, 72, 3 (1975).

1976 "The Preparation of the Gospel." *Review and Expositor*, 73, 2 (1976).

"The Righteousness of God in the History of Israel and the Nations: Romans 9-11." *Review and Expositor,* 73, 4 (1976).

1978 "Eschatology in the Gospel of Mark." *Southwestern Journal of Theology,* 28 (1978).

"The Parousia in Mark." *Review and Expositor,* 75 (1978).

1980 "The Authority and Justification of Believer's Baptism." *Review and Expositor,* 77 (1980).

1982 "Faith in the New Testament: A Baptist Perspective." *American Baptist Quarterly,* 1, (1982), 137-143.

"The Theology of the Child." *American Baptist Quarterly,* 1, (1982), 197-202.

1983 "The Interpretation of Daniel 7." *Catholic Biblical Quarterly,* 45, (1983), 44-58.

"Second Thoughts on the Composition of Mark 13." *New Testament Studies,* 29, (1983), 414-420.

1986 "John 3:3,5, Baptism, Spirit and Kingdom." *Expository Times,* 97, (1986), 167-170.

1988 "The Community of the New Life: John 13-17." *Review and Expositor,* 85 (1988).

Notes

1. George R. Beasley-Murray, "My Call to the Ministry," in C. A. Joyce, ed., *My Call to the Ministry* (London: Marshall, Morgan and Scott, 1968), 37-38.

2. Ibid., 39.

3. George R. Beasley-Murray, *Jesus and the Future, An Examination of the Criticisms of the Eschatological Discourse, Mark 13 with Special Reference to the Little Apocalypse Theory* (New York: Macmillan, 1953), 172.

4. Ibid., 180.

5. Ibid., 183.

6. Ibid., 190.

7. Ibid.

8. George R. Beasley-Murray, "Second Thoughts on the Composition of Mark 13," *New Testament Studies* 29 (1983): 418.

9. *The Baptist Quarterly* 1 (1922): 217.

10. George R. Beasley-Murray, "Baptism in the Epistles of Paul," in A. Gilmore, ed., *Christian Baptism* (Philadelphia: Judson, 1959), 128-49.

11. William E. Hull, "Baptism in the New Testament," an unpublished paper, 6. This paper has served as a valuable guide to Beasley-Murray's thought at a number of points.

12. George R. Beasley-Murray, *Baptism in the New Testament* (New York: Macmillan, 1962), 101; cf. Rom. 10:9-10.

13. Ibid., 100-12.

14. Ibid., 103.

15. Ibid., 272.

16. Ibid., 394.

17. Ibid., 264.

18. Ibid., 279.

19. Ibid., 202.

20. Ibid., 263.

21. Ibid.

22. Ibid., 264-65.

23. Hull, 19.

24. George R. Beasley-Murray, *The Book of Revelation,* New Century Bible (Grand Rapids, Mich.: Oliphants/Eerdmans, 1974), 22.

25. Ibid., 23.

26. Ibid., 37.

27. Ibid., 25.

28. Ibid.

29. Ibid., 26.

30. Ibid., 27.

31. Ibid., 30-31.

32. Ibid., 38-39.

33. George R. Beasley-Murray, *Jesus and the Kingdom of God* (Grand Rapids, Mich./Exter: Eerdmans/Paternoster Press, 1986), 35.

34. Ibid., 68.

35. Ibid., 146.

36. Ibid., 229.

37. Ibid., 247.

38. Ibid., 341.

39. George R. Beasley-Murray, *John,* in *Word Biblical Commentary* (Waco: Word Books, 1987), 152, 186.

40. Ibid., xli-xlii.

41. Ibid., xlii.

42. Ibid., xliii.

43. For example, ibid., 109, 120.

44. Ibid., xlvii.

45. Ibid., xlix.

46. Ibid., xliv.

47. Ibid., lxxiv.

48. Ibid., lxxv.

49. Ibid., lxxxi, citing Manson, "The Fourth Gospel," *Bulletin of the John Rylands Library* 30 (1946-47): 320.

50. Ibid., 23.

51. For example, ibid., 131.

52. Ibid., lxxvi.

53. Ibid., lxxvii.

Biographical

Bernard Lawrence Ramm was born in Butte, Montana, in 1916. As a young boy, one of his playmates was the son of a Russian engineer who had fled to this country during the Russian revolution. Ramm spent many hours in their home and sat in on numerous sessions in which his friend's father discussed Einstein and relativity theory, atomic theory, and chemistry. These discussions whetted Ramm's appetite for knowledge, and he purposed to spend his life in science. Accordingly, he took as much math and science as he could in high school and the university.

In the summer between high school and the university, however, Ramm experienced the transforming grace of Jesus Christ, and that "made a radical difference in every dimension of my life."[1] Ramm's brother, John, was the human instrument of his conversion. In a rare autobiographical statement, Ramm supported his view of Christian evidences with a reference to his own conversion:

> The writer himself experienced this power of the gospel to change life. He was a typical high school graduate with a mind stocked with what practically all high school graduates have when they leave high school—a profound respect for the sciences, a hope for a newer and better civilization, a toleration and mild respect for religion, a delight in sports and entertainment, and a desire "to make good" in the world. Then the gospel came to him. In one three-minute period his entire life perspective and basic personality were changed. He experienced the inflowing grace and transforming power of the grace of God. In a few moments he received a new philosophy, a new theology, a new heart, and a new life.[2]

Ramm continued with plans to study at the University of Washington, but he changed his emphases to philosophy and speech. After graduation, he attended Eastern Baptist Theological Seminary, and he also took graduate courses in philosophy at the University of Pennsylvania. From 1945-50 Ramm studied philosophy at the University of Southern California and was awarded the M.A. and Ph.D. degrees. His early interest in science, as well as philosophy, was evidenced by his M.A. thesis ("The Idealism of Jeans and Eddington in Modern Physical Theory," 1947) and his doctoral dissertation ("An Investigation of Some Recent Efforts to Justify Metaphysical Statements from Science with Special Reference to Physics," 1950). It is little

Bernard Ramm (1916-   )

wonder then, that one of Ramm's first books, and one of his most important, would be entitled *The Christian View of Science and Scripture*.

Ramm's work as a theologian and scholar has been balanced by his concern and love for the local church and practical Christian ministry. He pastored churches in New York, Washington, and California; and beginning in 1955 he taught summer courses at the Young Life Institute in Fountain Valley, California.

But Ramm will be best remembered as an author and teacher. He has authored twenty-one published books, several unpublished works, and dozens of articles for periodicals, such as *Christianity Today, Eternity,* and the *Journal of the American Scientific Affiliation*. (He also served as consulting editor of these publications.) Ramm has held professorships at Los Angeles Baptist Theological Seminary; the Bible Institute of Los Angeles; Bethel College and Seminary, St. Paul, Minnesota; Baylor University; California Baptist Theological Seminary, Covina, California (now the American Baptist Seminary of the West in Berkeley, California); Eastern Baptist Theological Seminary, Philadelphia, Pennsylvania, and the American Baptist Seminary of the West. Ramm taught at Haigazian Evangelical College in Beirut, Lebanon, from 1966-67; and he taught classes at Mennonite Biblical Seminary, Fresno, California; Simpson College in Modesto, California, and extension courses for Fuller Theological Seminary.[3]

At the present time Ramm lives with his wife, Alta, in their home in Irvine, California.

Exposition

Major Influences

Of the many influences upon Ramm's theology and career, the first and most important was his conversion. Second to that was Ramm's early love for science and philosophy. Ramm's scientifically trained mind has enabled him to view science and scientists without the naive suspicion characteristic of some of his contemporaries. He has continually warned evangelicals to beware of an obscurantism which would preclude their following truth, scientific or otherwise, wherever it led. Consequently, Ramm never approached the Scripture with a handful of a priori's concerning its nature (such as inerrancy); rather, he studied the Word itself to determine two things. First, Ramm wanted to know what the Bible says about itself. Second, Ramm wanted to understand the "phenomena" of Scripture as it stands. Thus, any theory of inspiration of Scripture, he believes, must be true to Scripture as it stands written, and not necessarily to some abstract and philosophical theory based upon certain a priori assumptions.

This openness to truth, rooted in his confidence that science and the Bible will ultimately tell the same story,[4] has driven Ramm to investigate the major theological and philosophical systems, ancient and modern, in order to learn from them and to critically evaluate his own thinking. He has a keen sense of the dynamics of history that have shaped evangelical thought, and he faults fundamentalists in general and Baptists in particular for their lack of historical awareness.[5] He has been willing to learn from anyone. Rather than writing off the "devil's hacks," such as Sartre, Nietzsche, Freud, Camus, Heidegger, Hume, and others, Ramm has consistently sought to "give the devil his due" (Ramm's term) by studying them, critically and dialectically engaging them, and learning from them.[6]

Theologically, Ramm is of the Reformed persuasion. The influence of Calvin and Dutch Reformed theologian Abraham Kuyper[7] is apparent upon nearly every page of his writings. His doctrines of the knowledge of God, the witness of the Spirit, religious authority, and the nature of Scripture, are consistently Calvinistic. Ramm writes boldly, "The truest expression of the Christian religion is the Reformed faith which seeks to preserve the best of Christian theology from the end of the Apostolic Age to the Reformation, and which cast the faith of the Reformation in its most biblical form."[8]

Another very important influence upon Ramm has been Karl Barth. In 1957-58 Ramm studied under Barth in Basel. Later Ramm was to read through Barth's *Church Dogmatics* "systematically every day according to a set schedule."[9] He was able, in so doing, to get beyond the caricatures, generalizations, and summaries of Barth with which so many evangelicals had politely dismissed Barth from their study. Interestingly enough, it was about this same time that Ramm began to study Abraham Kuyper and P. T. Forsyth, and he discovered many parallels in their theology, especially between Barth and Kuyper.

Barth's great impact upon Ramm was subtle at first. In his contribution to the book, *How Karl Barth Changed My Mind,* Ramm speaks of three "material changes" in the way he thought about theology. The first was that Barth helped Ramm to be fearless in his pursuit of truth. The Fundamentalist-Modernist controversy in America had tended to make many evangelicals defensive and suspicious. Ramm himself suffered from this anxiety over where science or biblical criticism may lead the theologian. Barth showed Ramm "the futility and intellectual bankruptcy" of his former approach and demonstrated that Ramm "could be just as free a person in theology as I would be if I were an experimental scientist."[10]

Barth's second material impact upon Ramm came from Barth's great respect for historical theology. Barth's knowledge and quotations of the Latin and Greek fathers were prodigious. Barth did not believe in "the tyranny of time"; and he "understood ecumenicity as a dialogue not only with one's contemporaries but with the theologians who have gone before."[11] Ramm's entire theological methodology was shaped by Barth's historical emphasis. One only has to read any of Ramm's works to learn that he never discusses any doctrine without first tracing its historical dimensions.

The third way that Barth changed Ramm's theological methodology was "the manner in which he correlated the critical study of Scripture with the inspiration and authority of Scripture."[12] Barth himself had struggled with the human and divine characteristics of Scripture and had early developed a bias against critical studies that stayed with him through his career. Yet he found a method of correlating the human and divine in Scripture that helped

Ramm at two points. First, Barth showed Ramm "that there is not a one-to-one correlation between the Word of God as it originates in the mind of God and the expression of that Word in the Old and New Testaments."[13] There is a *diastasis* or interval between the mind of God and the Word of God due to the accommodation of the Word to the specifics of the languages and cultures in which it was given. Second, Barth emphasized that "the way a portion of Holy Scripture came to be written or composed does not invalidate it as the Word of God."[14]

The full extent of Barth's influence upon Ramm did not become clear until the publication of *After Fundamentalism* in 1983. In this book, Ramm sought for a model or paradigm in theological methodology. Ramm says that the Enlightenment raised questions and created problems for conservative Christianity and that "fundamentalists" have not adequately responded to these issues. Many evangelicals act as if the Enlightenment never happened, as if biblical criticism did not exist, and as if they could dismiss the impact of modern science upon biblical studies without any serious intellectual engagement with the issues. Ramm found that *"Barth's theology is a restatement of Reformed theology written in the aftermath of the Enlightenment but not capitulating to it."*[15]

In successive chapters, Ramm illustrates how Barth handled various theological issues, such as preaching, apologetics, the human and divine in Scripture, and the doctrine of man; and he holds Barth's approach up as a model of theologizing. He does attempt to be dialectical and is critical of Barth at points; but his major reservations concerning Barth's method and theology are given only in a brief appendix. Ramm gives the shape of a Reformed theology patterned after Barth in his two 1985 publications, *An Evangelical Christology* and *Offense to Reason*.

The Nature, Task, and Method of Theology

Ramm has committed his entire adult life to the theological task. He believes that theology is a "science" in the sense that it deals with real knowledge.[16] Ramm answered the question as to whether revelation is personal or propositional by saying that it is both. By propositional revelation Ramm means that "there is a valid conceptual side to revelation."[17] Without this conceptual element there could be no theology.[18] Ramm feels that neither Barth nor Brunner made it clear how a nonconceptual revelation could be the basis for Christian theology.[19]

Ramm's view of the relationship of theology to philosophy is that of Augustine, Luther, and Calvin, in which philosophy is the "handmaiden" of theology and is ancillary to theology. Philosophy is useful, even indispensable, in theology, since the rules of discourse, the canons of logic, and the methodology of testing truth claims are philosophical in nature. But philosophy never dictates the substance of theology. Nor should theology be tied too closely to any particular system of philosophy (as Tillich and others have done). With characteristic insight Ramm warns: "If a theologian rests the case for Christianity completely on some philosophy, and that philosophy be discredited, then the whole case for Christianity is undermined."[20]

The theologian, Ramm believes, must be a Christian who "himself has participated in redemption through Christ and in revelation through the inner witness of the Holy Spirit."[21] The evangelical theologian must show that his "most fundamental motivation is passion for truth, no matter the cost, and not the prejudiced defense of an 'official' Evangelical position."[22] Ramm's commitment to "truth at any cost" is a leading idea in his theological methodology.

The theologian must use the tools and methods of scholarship developed during the Enlightenment, Ramm believes; textual criticism, literary criticism, and historical criticism all have their places in the task of theology. Ramm acknowledges the place of higher criticism as long as it is "reverent biblical criticism" (i.e., a criticism that respects the Bible as an inspired document).[23] Thus there is a limit to criticism, since criticism which destroys the notions of inspiration or authority has gone too far.[24] Yet criticism is both a possibility and a necessity since the Scripture has a dual authorship, human and divine.[25]

In his commentary on the Book of Exodus, in which Ramm demonstrated the practical application of his hermeneutical method, he acknowledged the legitimacy of source criticism and a reserved and cautious redaction criticism. He also found that "the sources J, E and P are not pure speculation but speak to phenomena in the text."[26]

However, Ramm cannot agree with the assumption that "faith elaborates" and that there are recorded deeds and sayings of Jesus which have no historical basis. There is indeed "church material," such as, possibly, the Trinitarian formula in Matthew 28:19-20. Yet the New Testament is not "interlarded" with church material, else the New Testament could not be an unimpeachable source of theology.[27] What is there is so for clarification, not distortion.

Ramm wrote that the "most acute theological problem today is to assess to what extent or degree culture determines the character of scripture, binding scripture to its own particular historical period."[28] The real problem is determining what in Scripture is trans-historical and trans-cultural. Ramm believes that the cultural aspect of revelation is its literary form or its language. Revelation is "anthropic" or "cosmic-mediated"[29] (i.e., it takes the form of human language and uses human analogies, metaphors, and anthropomorphisms). The language of the Bible which deals with scientific, psychological, and medical terms or with mathematical and measuring systems is purely cultural.[30] Thus the Bible does not *teach* a particular cosmology but merely expresses divine truth through the prevailing language of the day.[31] Ramm also believes that *theology* is culturally conditioned. He wrote that theologians must "be alerted by the Enlightenment to see what possible cultural elements have entered their theology and distorted it from its original biblical base."[32] It is the theologian's task to restate theology so it can be understood for each generation. "To be modern and yet biblical; to be biblical and yet contemporary; that's the rub."[33]

Apologetics

Early, Ramm disagreed with Barth that apologetics is a form of "unfaith" since it assumes that sinful man has the ability to test the revelation of God. Ramm feels that Barth does have an apologetic in his doctrines of revelation, the work of the Spirit, the signs of revelation, and the reality of God.[34]

Ramm presented his own view of the relationship between faith and reason in his first book, *Problems in Christian Apologetics*. He called his position "autonomous Christianity."[35] He believes that revelation is "self-established," yet reason may show that revelation is not inconsistent or illogical. Ramm agrees with Calvin that no human testimony or rational argument for the truth of the gospel is any benefit until first one grasps the gospel by faith. Certitude comes not by reason but by the persuasion of the Holy Spirit. Christian evidences or arguments for the existence of God are useful only to one who has faith.[36] Ramm discusses the traditional proofs for the existence of God, but he does not believe they "prove" anything. "When the biblical idea of faith in the living God . . . is contrasted with belief in God's existence by virtue of the theistic proofs, such belief appears pale and spiritless."[37] This statement is reminiscent of John Baillie's well-known statement: "The knowledge of God of which the New Testament speaks is a knowledge for which the best argument was but a sorry substitute and to which it were but a superfluous addition."[38]

Although the substance of Ramm's apologetic remained basically unchanged through the years, his later emphasis is more upon experience (the witness of the Spirit), God's acts in history, and "synoptic vision" (elements he calls "three concentric circles" of verification), which do not prove Christianity to be true but do make it probable.[39] His latest writings on apologetics show him agreeing with Barth that "if something external to the Word of God is necessary to establish the Word of God as true, then it is greater than the Word of God."[40]

Revelation

All theologians must address the issue of the nature of God's revelation of Himself to man, but few have majored on the doctrine to the extent that Bernard Ramm has. Nearly all of his books and many of his articles deal directly with some aspect of the doctrine. His most important venture into the subject is his book, *Special Revelation and the Word of God*, which Richard J. Coleman called "the best general book available which tackles the most important subjects" related to revelation.[41]

Ramm agrees with Calvin that there is a twofold knowledge of God—the knowledge of Him as Creator and the knowledge of Him as Redeemer. Today it is customary to speak of these two sources of knowledge as *general* revelation and *special* revelation. Ramm defines general revelation as "God's witness to himself for all men."[42] It includes the revelation of God in nature and in man. Traditional Roman Catholic theology holds to a belief in natural theology, a valid knowledge of God arising from nature and human reason. With Calvin, Ramm believes that there is a valid general revelation, but he argues that man does not profit from it as he should as a result of the noetic effects of sin. Thus there is no natural theology. In his sinfulness man suppresses and distorts the general revelation of God, even though the revelation is objective and real.

Special revelation, which is "God's word in concrete form to a specific person or group,"[43] is necessary for three reasons. First, the noetic effects of sin, or the "invasion of sin into reason,"[44] makes special revelation necessary. Second, the transcendence and incomprehensibility of God require special revelation. Ramm believes that the concepts of the "Unknown," "Wholly Other," *Deus Absconditus,* and the "Hidden God," which have come through Kierkegaard into neoorthodoxy, were needed correctives to the liberal views of divine immanence.[45] Third, the concept of God as personal requires a personal or special revelation. Persons can be known only as they choose to be known. God is never discovered; he discloses himself.

Ramm discusses special revelation under two major divisions—the modalities of special revelation and the products of special revelation. These forms or modalities are the methods by which God has mediated His revelation of Himself. The first modality is the "divine condescension" (i.e., the accommodation of revelation to man).[46] Revelation is not man rising; it is God stooping. As accommodated, revelation has human characteristics throughout, such as language, anthropomorphism, analogy. This "anthropic" nature of revelation assures that it will be understandable to man. Ramm disagrees with Bultmann that the principle of accommodation implies the loss of truth.[47]

The second modality or form is the "divine speaking," or revelation as the Word of God.[48] In some mysterious way, the Old Testament prophet received and delivered the oratorical word of the Lord. This is the first and most basic meaning of the word of God. Then the Word takes a written as well as oral form. Special revelation as written must assume some literary form, and Ramm believes that any genre of literature (including myth, saga, or legend) or any historical form (chronicling, geography, autobiography, etc.) are acceptable. In order to understand the Word of God, the literary vehicle must not be confused with the load of revelation it is bearing.

The third modality is "historical event."[49] Because sin is historical, revelation must be historical. Revelation is a reporting and reflecting upon the redemptive acts of God in history. Thus redemption is prior to revelation.

The fourth modality of revelation is the incarnation. Ramm believes in a real incarnation as stated in the historic creeds. Jesus is the God-man whose primary mission was to die on the cross as an atonement for sin. In the incarnation God has "come down" to man; He has stooped to put revelation on man's level. In His words, His character, and His deeds, Christ revealed the Father, and *"the Scriptures of the New Testament are the perpetuation within the Church of the apostolic experience of the incarnation."*[50]

Ramm believes that this cosmic-mediated revelation that finds its zenith in Christ has left "deposits" or "products," which he discusses as speech, the knowledge of God, Scripture, and translation. Speaking and writing are the attempts of the Christian community to preserve and communicate revelation. The knowledge of God which comes via revelation is both personal and conceptual, and involves truths which can be repeated through preaching, teaching, and writing.

Revelation also generated the Scriptures, which Ramm sees as an extension of the modality of the divine speaking.[51] The oral form of the word of God, or tradition, finds its summary and heart in the New Testament. Oral tradition alone could never have been self-sustaining and had to be written.[52]

What shall the theologian say about Scripture? There have been two approaches to determine the character of Scripture. One is the a priori method, in which one investigates biblical texts referring to the Scriptures and from these develops a theology of Scripture. The other method is the "phenomenological" method, by which one attempts "to first grasp the character of Scripture as it stands before us."[53] The former method assumes that if the Scripture is inspired it must have certain attributes; the latter method investigates the Scripture itself in all its "phenomena," human and divine, and comes to conclusions about its theological attributes. Ramm's method is the latter. Thus, he never reasoned from inspiration to some formal concept of inerrancy.

The phenomenological approach does not fear the humanness of Scripture. It allows for any genre of literature to be the bearer of divine revelation, including myth and saga. It encourages biblical criticism, and, as noted above, allows for "reverent" redaction criticism. It does not expect the Bible to be inerrant on matters of science, history, or geography. Ramm believes that evangelicals who have made inerrancy a watershed doctrine are wrong. He does not believe that one's view of Scripture is the most important part of one's theology.[54] Revelation is prior to and more important than inspiration; and one's *use* of Scripture is more important than his *view* of Scripture. A cultist may be an inerrantist, for instance.

Ramm does not minimize inspiration, however, but wants to understand it functionally. The function of inspiration is to preserve or "secure revelation in an authentic form."[55] No one knows how the Holy Spirit did this; therefore, there can be no a priori notions about scripture as it stands.

In his earlier writings Ramm does use the term "inerrancy" to describe Scripture, but he qualifies the concept considerably and limits it to matters of faith and morals.[56] In his later writings Ramm takes issue with Carl Henry's view of revelation. In a discussion of Henry's writings, Ramm asks, "What is the first thing one says about the Bible once he is convinced that it is the word of God?" Ramm answers, "Henry says that it is innerrant. In my research and thinking I do not think this is what should be said. What should be said is something about the message of Scripture."[57] In his most definitive treatment of revelation and Scripture, *Special Revelation and the Word of*

God, Ramm does not once mention the term "inerrant." He prefers the term "infallible," which means that the Scripture will not mislead, deceive, or disappoint. The power of the Scripture comes not from some characteristic such as inerrancy but from its authentic witness to Jesus Christ. It is an instrument of the Holy Spirit in revealing God to man. Ramm's mature view of inerrancy is presented in his book on Christology. The Christological content of Scripture, not inerrancy, is the "first line of defense" of God's authoritative Word. Ramm acknowledges his debt to Barth for this idea.[58]

Authority

Unlike many evangelicals, Ramm refused to locate authority in the Bible alone. To do so would mean there was no authority before Scripture. Also, in the New Testament witness Christ himself is the living authority of the church. Finally, this view would neglect the important role of the witness of the Spirit.[59] Instead of a "monistic principle" of authority, Ramm opts for a "pattern" or "mosaic" of authority, which includes the revelation of God in history, the incarnation, Scripture and the witness of the Spirit. "Thus the objective Word of the Father, and the subjective ministry of the Spirit intersect in the heart of the believer to create a true knowledge of God and to call into being the Christian principle of authority.[60] Ramm believes this approach is true to Reformed theology, and, in particular, to Calvin.

Scripture and Science

Ramm observed that the fundamentalist response to the Enlightenment and to modern science pitted Christianity in a battle with science which Christianity could not win. Throughout his career Ramm has sought a reasoned response to science which was not obscurantist on the one hand nor overly concessive on the other. While Ramm did seek to harmonize science and Scripture where he could, he did not seek to save Scripture from its culturally conditioned quality. The language of the Bible is popular, phenomenal, nontechnical. The Holy Spirit did not teach the writers of the Bible final science, although He did restrain them from serious errors which would have skewed revelation. Ramm argued that a partial flood, a figurative "long day of Joshua," and an ancient earth harmonized with the biblical record. A Christian, Ramm believes, can be a theistic evolutionist, and he himself holds to a view of "progressive creation."[61]

In one of his later books, Ramm wrestles with the results of the evolutionary theory of man and the biblical data concerning Adam and the fall of the human race. He suggests that Genesis 2—3 is narrative theology, and he follows Barth in seeing the Adam story as saga, which he defines as "an imaginative literary effort to recover the beginnings of a people."[62] Ramm sees Adam as "generic man," while at the same time he views him as the real person who is the head of the human race and the Jewish people. In this book Ramm's dependence on Barth has become even more obvious, in particular his Christological view of Scripture.

Christology

In Ramm's two latest books, *An Evangelical Christology* and *Offense to Reason,* he finally moved beyond questions of theological methodology to doing substantive theology. In these two works we see the breath of his reading, the depth of his scholarship, and the full impact of Barth upon his theology. *After Fundamentalism* (1983) was in a sense a prophecy that Ramm would be doing substantive theology from a Barthian perspective.

Ramm's Christology is that of the ancient creeds, although he knows that they did not solve all the problems in Christology.[63] Ramm affirms the deity and preexistence of Christ, the reality of the incarnation, the virgin birth, the real humanity and sinlessness of Christ (Christ did not assume sinful flesh and did not have a "sin nature"), the death and resurrection of Christ "according to scripture," and His second coming. Ramm strongly defends the biblical portrait of Christ against the radical critics; but he seriously engages their arguments. The passion of his life has been to make evangelicalism respectable, and his *An Evangelical Christology* is his attempt to show how this is done.

Ramm's other 1985 publication, *Offense to Reason,* likewise displays his theological erudition and his debt to Barth. Ramm shows that the Christian doctrine of sin makes sense of human life and history. The problem of sin is not just a Christian problem, since philosophers, psychologists, playwrights, secular authors, and the world's great religions have faced it in some fashion or other. He follows Barth in seeing Genesis 2—3 as saga and Adam as generic man. He goes beyond Barth in seeing Adam as a historic person and in holding that humanity was created in a state of righteousness from which it fell in a datable event in history.[64] Ramm never makes clear how, in his own thinking, Adam is both a generic name and also the name of a real individual in human history.

Ramm believes that the only basis for the salvation of any person is Jesus Christ. He also argues against Barth's universalism and maintains "an absolute distinction between saved and lost."[65] However, Ramm would not "slam the door" on all of those who had never heard the gospel, leaving open the possibility that the Spirit of God could apply the saving work of Christ to those who have not heard the name of Jesus.

Evaluation

Evangelicalism has undergone many challenges and changes within the last century. The effects of the Enlightenment and the rise of modern science have been two of the major forces that have shaped the debates. Ramm's mission has been to keep evangelicalism intellectually respectable and to rescue it from charges of obscurantism, while preserving the core of evangelical doctrine. To the extent that Ramm seriously faced the issues, read deeply and widely in the literature of philosophy, science, history, and theology, documented his study with a vast writing ministry, and engaged in honest dialogue with the proponents and opponents of Christianity, he has succeeded in his mission. Whether or not his conclusions are acceptable, in part or *in toto,* is not the point for Ramm. He admitted very early that there could be no final statements in theology and no "theology of glory."

The difficulty in Ramm's mission is that he attempted to steer a middle course between fundamentalism and liberalism. He has, consequently, been criticized by both sides: the fundamentalists accusing him of making too many concessions and the more liberal-minded saying he did not follow his ideas to their logical conclusions. Ramm, though sensitive to criticism, believes in following truth wherever it leads.

Ramm is a Baptist who has worked within the American Baptist Convention, more pluralistic than its Southern Baptist counterpart. Ramm saw no contradiction in being evangelical theologically as well as being a Baptist. But E. Glenn Hinson, a Southern Baptist, has argued that Ramm cannot be both.[66] Hinson listed four major differences between evangelicals and Baptists: Baptists disdain creeds, evangelicals use them; Baptists emphasize experience in response to the Word, evangelicals stress the objectivity of the Word; Baptists have acknowledged the positive influence of the Enlightenment, evangelicals have considered it an enemy; and Baptists place "priority on voluntary and uncoerced faith or response to the Word and Acts of God over any supposed objective Word and Act of God," while evangelicals have made the Bible into a paper pope.

To the first charge, Ramm would say that a study of Baptist history clearly shows that Baptists have used written confessions of faith from their earliest days. Ramm urged restraint and balance in their use, and noted that the confessions generally have a Reformed theological emphasis.[67] To the second charge, Ramm would plead guilty and would contend that it was Hinson who was out of step with solid Baptist theology. Ramm was suspicious of any attempt to make experience alone the authority in religion or the leading principle in a theological system.[68] Hinson's third point is clearly false, as is evidenced by Ramm's continual warnings against obscurantism[69] and his book, *After Fundamentalism,* in which Ramm calls for a positive response to the Enlightenment. The fourth charge against Ramm (viz., that he has erected a "paper pope"), is likewise a caricature of his opinion. One of Ramm's major contributions to theology, and in particular to the contemporary debates concerning the nature of Scripture and the structure of authority in religion, is his emphasis on a mosaic or pattern of authority as opposed to any "monistic" view.[70] Furthermore, Ramm's refreshing reemphasis of the internal witness of the Holy Spirit as the source of the believer's certitude in divine things has guarded him from an absolute objectification of the Word, which is done in much fundamentalist theology.[71]

Ramm's appreciation for Barth grew until he finally declared that the Swiss theologian should be the model for doing theology. One senses that his respect for Barth grew to near reverence. Perhaps it was Barth's influence that led Ramm to soften his claims for reason in establishing Christian truth. Perhaps, too, it was Barth's "christo-monism" that influenced Ramm to totter on the brink of universalism (without going over) and to open the door of salvation to many who have never heard the gospel.

Ramm's "open door" to the heathen came more, it may be suspected, from the slow progress of world evangelization and the relatively small number of Christians than from a serious engagement with the text of the New Testament. His exegesis of Romans 2 is suspect.[72] More importantly, Ramm seems not to take into account the total witness of the New Testament to the uniqueness of Jesus Christ and the importance of the *kerygma,* the gospel message, for faith and salvation. It is the gospel that is God's power unto salvation, Paul declares (Rom. 1:16); and it is through receiving the apostolic witness to the death, burial, and resurrection of Christ (the gospel) that one gives evidence of one's election by God (1 Thess. 1:4-5). Ramm himself argued repeatedly for the conceptual aspect of revelation. Faith is more than subjectivity.

To hedge on the importance of the preaching of the gospel for the salvation of the lost is a serious concession that, if pursued logically, could be the death knell for worldwide Christian missions. Furthermore, it seems but a short step from this view to that of Barth and universalism; and that doctrine would have serious negative consequences for evangelicalism. If the influence of Barth is to diminish the need or concern for world missions, then he is not the model that most Baptists will want to follow. Of course, Ramm was not thinking of just one particular doctrine when he held Barth up as a paradigm for theologians. But the tree is known by its fruit; and the bitter fruit of universalism, however pleasant to the eye, is poor fare for Baptist appetites.

Ramm has not been an original theologian. His legacy will not be that of the founder of a new system. He has influenced the thinking of a number of younger theologians,[73] but there appear to be no "Rammites" on the horizon. Perhaps J. I. Packer said it best when he remarked that Ramm will be remembered as "a pioneer in enriched synthesis,"[74] referring to Ramm's broad reading and his eclectic approach. Ramm has been a trailblazer whose passion for truth led him to break out of traditional molds.

There is much in Ramm to stimulate one's thinking, for he tries never to gloss an issue. Ramm should be read as he himself read others—dialectically and critically—accepting this and rejecting that. One does not have to agree with his approach to harmonizing science and Scripture or with his rejection of the concept of inerrancy in order to profit from Ramm. Perhaps this is his greatest contribution: he has modeled a love for truth, respect for the opinions of others, and fearlessness before the facts (as he sees them). It is too early to fully judge his life's work, and this writer for one hopes that there is more to come.

Bibliography

Books

After Fundamentalism: The Future of Evangelical Theology. San Francisco: Harper and Row, 1983.

A Christian Appeal to Reason. Waco: Word Books. Paperback, 1977. Originally published in hardback under the title *The God Who Makes a Difference: A Christian Appeal to Reason* by the same publisher, 1972.

The Christian College in the Twentieth Century. Grand Rapids, Mich.: Wm. B. Eerdmans, 1963.

The Christian View of Science and Scripture. Grand Rapids, Mich.: Wm. B. Eerdmans, 1954.

The Devil, Seven Wormwoods, and God. Waco: Word Books, 1977.

An Evangelical Christology: Ecumenic and Historic. Nashville: Thomas Nelson, 1985.

The Evangelical Heritage. Waco: Word Books, 1973.

A Handbook of Contemporary Theology. Grand Rapids, Mich.: Wm. B. Eerdmans, 1966.

His Way Out. Glendale, Calif.: G/L Regal Books, 1974.

Offense to Reason: A Theology of Sin. San Francisco: Harper and Row, 1985.

The Pattern of Authority. Grand Rapids, Mich.: Wm. B. Eerdmans, 1957. Paperback edition under the title *The Pattern of Religious Authority* by the same publisher, 1968.

Problems in Christian Apologetics. Portland: Western Baptist Theological Seminary, 1949.

Protestant Biblical Interpretation: A Textbook of Hermeneutics for Conservative Protestants. Boston: W. A. Wilde Co., 1950. Revised and enlarged by the same publisher, 1956. Revised edition under the title *Protestant Biblical Interpretation: A Textbook of Hermeneutics.* Grand Rapids, Mich.: Baker Book House, 1970.

Protestant Christian Evidences: A Textbook of the Evidences of the Truthfulness of the Christian Faith for Conservative Protestants. Chicago: Moody Press, 1953. Paperback edition by the same publisher, 1978.

Rapping About the Spirit. Waco: Word Books, 1974.

The Right, the Good and the Happy. Waco: Word Books, 1971.

Special Revelation and the Word of God. Grand Rapids: Wm. B. Eerdmans, 1961.

Them He Glorified: A Systematic Study of the Doctrine of Glorification. Grand Rapids, Mich.: Wm. B. Eerdmans, 1963.

Varieties of Christian Apologetics. Grand Rapids, Mich.: Baker Book House, 1962. Originally published under the title *Types of Apologetic Systems: An Introductory Study to the Christian Philosophy of Religion.* Wheaton, Ill.: Van Kampen Press, 1953.

The Witness of the Spirit: An Essay on the Contemporary Relevance of the Internal Witness of the Holy Spirit. Grand Rapids, Mich.: Wm. B. Eerdmans, 1959.

Contributions to Other Books

"Biblical Interpretations." In *Baker's Dictionary of Practical Theology,* edited by Ralph G. Turnbull. Grand Rapids, Mich.: Baker Book House, 1967.

"Biblical Interpretation." In *Hermeneutics,* edited by Ralph G. Turnbull. Grand Rapids, Mich.: Baker Book House, n.d.

"The Common Call for Human Dignity." In *Modifying Man: Implications and Ethics,* edited by Craig W. Ellison. Washington, D.C.: University Press of America, 1977.

"Ethics in the Theologies of Hope." In *Toward a Theology for the Future*, edited by David F. Wells and Clark H. Pinnock. Carol Stream, Ill.: Creation House, 1971.

"The Evidence of Prophecy and Miracle." In *Revelation and the Bible: Contemporary Evangelical Thought*, edited by Carl F. H. Henry. Grand Rapids, Mich.: Baker Book House, 1958.

"Fortunes of Theology from Schleiermacher to Barth and Bultmann." In *Tensions in Contemporary Theology*, edited by Stanley Gundry and Alan Johnson. Foreword by Roger Nicole. Chicago: Moody Press, 1976.

"The Glorification of the Soul." In *The New Life*, edited by Millard J. Erickson. Grand Rapids, Mich.: Baker Book House, 1979.

"Helps from Karl Barth." In *How Karl Barth Changed My Mind*, edited by Donald K. McKim. Grand Rapids, Mich.: Wm. B. Eerdmans, 1986.

"Is 'Scripture Alone' the Essence of Christianity?" In *Biblical Authority*, edited by Jack Rogers. Waco: Word Books, 1977.

"John Henry Newman." In *A History of Religious Educators*, edited by Elmer L. Towns. Grand Rapids, Mich.: Baker Book House, 1975.

"The New Hermeneutic." In *Baker's Dictionary of Practical Theology*, edited by Ralph G. Turnbull. Grand Rapids, Mich.: Baker Book House, 1967.

"The New Hermeneutic." In *Hermeneutics*, edited by Ralph G. Turnbull. Grand Rapids, Mich.: Baker Book House, n.d.

"The Principle and Pattern of Authority in Christianity." In *The Living God*, edited by Millard J. Erickson. Grand Rapids, Mich.: Baker Book House, 1973.

"Shifting University Education and the Evangelical College." In *About Schools*, edited by Mark Tuttle. New York: Houghton College Press, 1972.

"Special Revelation and the Word of God." In *The Living God*, edited by Millard J. Erickson. Grand Rapids, Mich.: Baker Book House, 1973.

Periodical Articles

"An Appraisal of Karl Barth." *Eternity* 20 (Feb. 1969): 36-38.

"Are We Obscurantists?" *Christianity Today* 1 (Feb. 18, 1957): 14-15.

"Baptist Theology." *Watchman-Examiner* 43 (Nov. 24, 1955): 1070-73.

"Baptists and Historical Theology." *Foundations* 2 (July 1959): 258-63.

"Baptists and Sources of Authority." *Foundations* 1 (July 1958): 6-15.

"Bernard Ramm's Confession of Christ." *Eternity* 31 (April 1980): 29.

"Biblical Faith and History." *Christianity Today* 7 (Mar. 1, 1963): 5-8.

"A Definition of Death." *Journal of the American Scientific Affiliation* 25 (June 1973): 56-60.

"Europe, God and Karl Barth." *Eternity* 10 (April 1959): 10.

"An Evaluation of Karl Barth." *Southern Presbyterian Journal* 7 (May 4, 1959): 8-11.

"Have You Discovered Thielicke?" *Eternity* 18 (May 1967): 19.

"Human Philosophy vs. Jesus Christ." *Eternity* 15 (Mar. 1964): 25-26.

"The Inscrutable Dr. Tillich." *Eternity* 14 (Nov. 1963): 28.

"Jesus Christ: Hallmark of Orthodoxy." *Christianity Today* 3 (Aug. 3, 1959): 9-11.

"Karl Barth and Analytic Philosophy." *Christian Century* 79 (April 11, 1962): 453-55.

"Karl Barth: The Theological Avalanche." *Eternity* 8 (July 1957): 4.

"Kierkegaard: Danish Timebomb." *Eternity* 9 (July 1958): 5-7.

"The Labyrinth of Contemporary Theology." *Christianity Today* 9 (July 16, 1965): 6-9.

"The Major Theses of Neo-orthodoxy." *Eternity* 8 (June 1957): 18.

"Moltmann and the Theology of Hope." *Eternity* 19 (Sept. 1968): 32-33.

"New Light on How God Speaks?" *Eternity* 25 (Oct. 1974): 79-80.

"The Relationship of Science, Factual Statements and the Doctrine of Biblical Inerrancy." *Journal of the American Scientific Affiliation* 21 (Dec. 1969): 48-124.

"Scripture as a Theological Concept." *Review and Expositor* 71 (Spring 1974): 149-61.

"Theological Reactions to the Theory of Evolution." *Journal of the American Scientific Affiliation* 13 (Sept. 1963): 71-77.

"Welcome 'Green-Grass' Evangelicals." *Eternity* 25 (Mar. 1974): 13.

"Will All Men Be Finally Saved?" *Eternity* 15 (Aug. 1964): 22.

Notes

1. Bernard Ramm, *The Christian View of Science and Scripture* (Grand Rapids, Mich.: Wm. B. Eerdmans Publishing Co., 1954), 7.

2. Bernard Ramm, *Protestant Christian Evidences: A Textbook of the Evidences of the Truthfulness of the Christian Faith for Conservative Protestants* (Chicago: Moody Press, 1953), 220-21.

3. The writer took this summary of Ramm's professional career from Ramm's *Vitae*, written by Ramm and sent to the writer in 1988.

4. Bernard Ramm, *Problems in Christian Apologetics: The Mid-year Lectures of 1948 of Western Baptist Theological Seminary* (Portland, Ore.: Western Baptist Theological Seminary, 1949), 92.

5. Bernard Ramm, "Baptists and Historical Theology," *Foundations* 2 (July 1959): 258-63.

6. Bernard Ramm, *The Devil, Seven Wormwoods, and God* (Waco: Word Books, 1977), 16.

7. See Bernard Ramm, *Special Revelation and the Word of God* (Grand Rapids, Mich.: Wm. B. Eerdmans Publishing Co., 1961), 7, for his tribute to Kuyper.

8. Bernard Ramm, *A Christian Appeal to Reason* (Waco: Word Books, 1972), 33.

9. Bernard Ramm, *After Fundamentalism: The Future of Evangelical Theology* (San Francisco: Harper & Row, Publishers, 1983), 11.

10. Bernard Ramm, "Helps from Karl Barth," in *How Karl Barth Changed My Mind,* ed. Donald K. McKim (Grand Rapids, Mich.: Wm. B. Eerdmans Publishing Co., 1986), 121.

11. Ibid., 122-23.

12. Ibid., 123.

13. Ibid., 124.

14. Ibid., 125.

15. Ramm, *After Fundamentalism*, 14. Emphasis is Ramm's.

16. Ramm, *The Christian View of Science and Scripture*, 46.

17. Ramm, *Special Revelation and the Word of God*, 154.

18. Bernard Ramm, *The Evangelical Heritage* (Waco: Word Books, 1973), 130.

19. Bernard Ramm, *A Handbook of Contemporary Theology* (Grand Rapids, Mich.: Wm. B. Eerdmans Publishing Co., 1966), s.v. "Revelation, Propositional."

20. Bernard Ramm, *The Devil, Seven Wormwoods, and God*, 142. See also *Types of Apologetic Systems*, 95; *Protestant Christian Evidences*, 33; *Protestant Biblical Interpretation*, 169.

21. Ramm, *Special Revelation and the Word of God*, 141.

22. Ramm, *The Devil, Seven Wormwoods, and God*, 60.

23. Ramm, *Special Revelation and the Word of God*, 191-92.

24. Ramm, *A Christian Appeal to Reason*, 66.

25. Bernard Ramm, *Special Revelation and the Word of God*, 179, and "Is Scripture Alone the Essence of Christianity?" in *Biblical Authority*, ed. Jack Rogers (Waco, Texas: Word Books, 1977), 117.

26. Bernard Ramm, *His Way Out* (Glendale, Calif.: Regal Books, 1974), 208.

27. Bernard Ramm, "Contemporary Theology and Church Material," *Christianity Today* 16 (August 11, 1972): 11-12.

28. Ramm, *Protestant Biblical Interpretation*, 157.

29. Ramm, *Special Revelation and the Word of God*, 36, 65-66.

30. Ramm, *The Christian View of Science and Scripture*, 65-76.

31. Ibid., 97 *ff.*

32. Ramm, *The Evangelical Heritage*, 72.

33. Ibid., 170.

34. Ramm, *A Christian Appeal to Reason*, 22.

35. Ramm, *Problems in Christian Apologetics*, 11.

36. Ibid., 25-30.

37. Ramm, *A Christian Appeal to Reason*, 108-9.

38. John Baillie, *Our Knowledge of God* (New York: Charles Scribner's Sons, 1939), 126.

39. Ramm, *A Christian Appeal to Reason*, 38 *ff.*

40. Ramm, *After Fundamentalism*, 61.

41. Richard J. Coleman, *Issues of Theological Warfare: Evangelicals and Liberals* (Grand Rapids, Mich.: Wm. B. Eerdmans Publishing Co., 1972), 105.

42. Ramm, *Special Revelation and the Word of God*, 17.

43. Ibid., 17.

44. Bernard Ramm, "The Labyrinth of Contemporary Theology," *Christianity Today* 9 (July 16, 1965): 8.

45. See Ramm, *A Handbook of Contemporary Theology*, s.v. "Other, Wholly," and *"Deus Absconditus."* See also *Special Revelation and the Word of God*, 24.

46. Ramm, *Special Revelation and the Word of God*, 31-52.

47. Ramm, *Protestant Biblical Interpretation*, 101.

48. Ramm, *Special Revelation and the Word of God*, 53-69.

49. Ibid., 70-105.

50. Ibid., 115. Emphasis is Ramm's.

51. Ibid., 161.

52. Ibid., 173-75.

53. Bernard Ramm, "Scripture As a Theological Concept," *Review and Expositor* 71 (Spring 1974): 150.

54. Bernard Ramm, "Is Scripture Alone the Essence of Christianity?" in *Biblical Authority,* ed. Jack Rogers (Waco: Word Books, 1977), 113.

55. Ramm, "Scripture As a Theological Concept," 158.

56. Ramm, *Protestant Biblical Interpretation, 202 ff.*

57. Bernard Ramm, "Carl Henry's Magnus Opus," *Eternity* 28 (March 1977): 62.

58. Ramm, *An Evangelical Christology,* 202.

59. Ramm, "Baptists and Sources of Authority," *Foundations* 1 (July 1958): 13-4.

60. Bernard Ramm, *The Pattern of Religious Authority* (Grand Rapids, Mich.: Wm. B. Eerdmans), 92.

61. See Ramm, *The Christian View of Science and Scripture.* See also *Offense to Reason: A Theology of Sin* (San Francisco: Harper & Row, Publishers, 1985), 74-75.

62. Bernard Ramm, *Offense to Reason,* 70.

63. Ramm, *An Evangelical Christology,* 16.

64. Ramm, *Offense to Reason,* 139-40.

65. Bernard Ramm, "Will All Men Be Finally Saved?" *Eternity* 15 (August 1964): 22-25, 33. See also *After Fundamentalism,* 165 *ff.,* 201.

66. E. Glenn Hinson, "Baptists and Evangelicals: What Is the Difference?" paper presented at the South Carolina Baptist Historical Society, Columbia, S.C., November 10, 1980.

67. Bernard Ramm, "Baptist Theology," *Watchman-Examiner,* November 24, 1955, 1070.

68. See Ramm, "Baptists and Sources of Authority," 6-15.

69. Bernard Ramm, "Are We Obscurantists?" *Christianity Today,* February 18, 1957, 14-5. See also *The Evangelical Heritage,* 70, for "an evangelical assessment of the Enlightenment."

70. See Ramm, "Baptists and Sources of Authority," 6-15, and also *The Pattern of Religious Authority* (Grand Rapids, Mich.: Wm. B. Eerdmans Publishing Co., 1957).

71. See Bernard Ramm, *The Witness of the Spirit: An Essay on the Contemporary Relevance of the Internal Witness of the Holy Spirit* (Grand Rapids, Mich.: Wm. B. Eerdmans Publishing Co., 1959).

72. Ramm, "Will All Men Be Finally Saved?" 25.

73. See Clark H. Pinnock, "Bernard Ramm: Postfundamentalist Coming to Terms with Modernity," *Perspectives in Religious Studies, (Festschrift* issue) (1990).

74. Packer made this statement during a conversation with the writer in November 1988.

Edward John Carnell

L. Joseph Rosas III

Biography

Edward John Carnell died in 1967 leaving a legacy of eight books, mostly on apologetics, numerous articles and book reviews, and a seminary he had helped shape during its formative years. Carnell was one of the preeminent evangelical leaders of his day. However, he also personified the tensions that would emerge in this new movement that sought to distinguish itself from sectarian fundamentalism on the right and liberal and neoorthodox theology on the left. This chapter examines Carnell's philosophical and theological perspective in that context. His emotional and psychological difficulties culminating with his untimely death are aspects of the darker side of his own reaction to that struggle.[1]

Fundamentalism Versus Evangelicalism: Carnell in Context

The nineteenth century saw a great ferment in both philosophy and science that would have a tremendous impact on theology. The epistemological divide in the philosophy of Immanuel Kant and G. W. F. Hegel's speculative and dialectical solution introduced a postcritical era in thought that changed forever the conceptual framework in which theology would seek to accomplish its task. The rise of rationalistic higher-critical studies of the Bible resulted in a radical reorientation of attitudes toward the divine origin and inspiration of the Scriptures with major implications for biblical hermeneutics as well. The widespread acceptance and popular dissemination of evolutionary theory also contributed to a growing polarization between conservative theology and science. The Princeton theology of B. B. Warfield and the Hodges was, in part, a reaction to these trends.[2]

Revivalism and dispensational millennial expectations abounded during this time, also occasioning conflict in the religious community. As conservative theological positions came under increasing attack, an informal alliance between the proponents of the old Princeton theology, revivalism, and dispensationalism was formed with the authority of the Scripture as their primary concern.[3] The differences between (and even within) these diverse groups was great. However, these differences were superficially submerged in the name of a literalistic hermeneutic dependent upon a completely reliable Bible.

The high-water mark of this loose federation was a series of articles published in 1911 under the heading of *The Fundamentals*. The concern was for

Edward John Carnell (1919-67)

Photo courtesy of Fuller Theological Seminary

orthodox theology on numerous points—the central issue being the authority of Scripture.[4] Gradually, the battle lines shifted and the fundamentalists themselves become the focus of attack within several mainline denominations. The "Modernist-Fundamentalist" controversies in the first quarter of the twentieth century saw the eviction or voluntary departure of the most vocal conservatives from their respective ecclesiastical fellowships.

Fundamentalism, as a movement, is difficult to define. There was no one standard confession ever universally adopted by this diverse group. As has been indicated, theologically it represented the wedding of the elaborate arguments of the old Princeton theology to the more simplistic biblicism of revivalism and dispensational theology. Thus, the movement is characterized by an insistence upon the inerrancy of the Bible in particular and "orthodox" theology in general. As many conservatives moved out of the mainline denominations, fundamentalism also became associated with a separatist ecclesiology.

The emergence of Bible colleges, independent mission boards, and various conservative parachurch organizations guaranteed the continued existence of a fundamentalist subculture. However, its sectarian mentality and numerous internal struggles for control of the movement contributed to the pejorative tone in which the term "fundamentalism" is often used.[5] This also seemed to ensure that the fundamentalist movement would never return to the ecclesiastical mainstream again.

Following World War II a new group of conservative leaders began to emerge. These "evangelicals," as they came to be called, were also committed to biblical authority (generally conceptualized as "inerrancy of the Scripture") and orthodox theology but displayed a desire to reclaim the mainstream of American Christianity. Their educational credentials, temperament, and scholarly output did much to commend their positions to the religious establishment.[6] Also, many evangelicals moved away from the dispensationalism, exclusivity, and divisiveness of their fundamentalist forerunners. Ambiguities on these and other issues made tension within the evangelical movement inevitable.

Carnell: The Man and His Influence

Edward John Carnell's life and work can best be understood against the backdrop of the emergence of evangelicalism out of the shadows of fundamentalism.[7] He personified many of the tensions which would characterize this new evangelical movement.

Carnell was born in Antigo, Wisconsin, June 28, 1919. He was raised in a conservative Baptist home; his father was a minister. Carnell would later complain about the cultic mentality of fundamentalism as "rigid, intolerant, and doctrinaire . . . ." yet there seems to be little evidence that this is a reaction to anything in particular in his childhood.[8] Indeed, there is little indication of any particularly intense religious sentiments or academic ability in young Carnell. However, his brooding, emotional moodiness, a tendency that would characterize his mature years, was in evidence.

Carnell received his undergraduate training at Wheaton College where he was influenced by Gordon H. Clark, a rigorous Christian rationalist and professor of philosophy who influenced an entire generation of Wheaton students.[9] During his days at Wheaton, Carnell devoted himself to a ministerial calling. He had a reputation as a serious and hardworking student who had some difficulty in social relationships. Carnell's basic seminary training (B.D. and Th.M.) was completed at Westminster Theological Seminary. At Westminster he came under the influence of Cornelius Van Til, who further stimulated Carnell's interest in apologetics and Calvinistic theology. He earned the Th.D. from Harvard Divinity School in 1948, writing his dissertation on "The Concept of Dialectic in the Theology of Reinhold Niebuhr."[10] A year later Carnell completed his Ph.D. dissertation on "The Problem of Verification in Søren Kierkegaard" at Boston University.[11] Here he came under the influence of Edgar Sheffield Brightman who served as another formative influence in Carnell's philosophical maturation.[12]

Carnell was ordained to the Baptist ministry in 1944. He served as pastor of the Baptist church of Marblehead, Massachusetts, as he completed graduate work and during which time he also taught at Gordon College and Divinity School. In 1948 he joined the faculty of the newly formed Fuller Theological Seminary in Pasadena, California. He remained a Baptist but attended the Lake Avenue Congregational Church, an early supporter of the seminary. Carnell spent the remaining nineteen years of his life at Fuller. He served as the first president in residence from 1954-59. On April 25, 1967, on the eve of a speaking engagement at an ecumenical gathering, Edward John Carnell died, apparently of a barbiturate overdose.

Exposition

While he was still a graduate student, Carnell's first book, *An Introduction to Christian Apologetics,* was published in 1948.[13] This award-winning book established his reputation as a rising star of the new evangelicalism. He also produced three other specifically apologetic works: *A Philosophy of the Christian Religion, Christian Commitment,* and *The Kingdom of Love and the Pride of Life. The Case for Orthodox Theology* was a summary and clearer elucidation of emphases in his earlier works. He also wrote *Television: Servant or Master?* and numerous articles and reviews, contributing regularly to *The Christian Century* and *Christianity Today.* Several articles and papers appeared in a posthumously published volume, *The Case for Biblical Christianity,* edited by a former student, Ronald H. Nash.

The focus of our study now shifts to a survey of Carnell's theological and philosophical insights gleaned from a survey of his major works. The chapter concludes with an evaluation of Carnell's significance as a Christian thinker, educator, and churchman.

It is difficult to classify Carnell's apologetic method. Although he considered himself a "Christian rationalist," several lines of argument are evident in his works.[14] Norman Geisler used the curious label "combinationalist" to describe Carnell's apologetic method while Ronald Nash called his approach "presuppositionalism."[15]

In his last apologetic work, Carnell noted the multiple lines of approach in his own works. He stated:

> In my own books on apologetics I have consistently tried to build on some useful point of contact between the gospel and culture. In *An Introduction to Christian Apologetics* the appeal was to the law of contradiction; in *A Philosophy of the Christian Religion* it was to values; and in *Christian Commitment* it was to the judicial sentiment. In this book I am appealing to the law of love.[16]

Kenneth Harper has suggested, in a useful distinction, that Carnell's apologetic may be seen as comprising a two-pronged approach: the early works embodying a Christianity for the "tough-minded" and the latter works a "tender-minded" approach.[17]

Apologetics for the Tough-Minded

The epistemological foundation for Carnell's thought is spelled out in *An Introduction to Christian Apologetics* subtitled *A Philosophic Defense of the Trinitarian-Theistic Faith*. This foundation is built upon in *A Philosophy of the Christian Religion*. *The Case for Orthodox Theology,* while accenting many of the same emphases of these early works, is also something of a bridge to Carnell's later "tender-minded" apologetic.

Carnell devoted the first of three sections of this work to the human predicament. Carnell saw his brand of Christian rationalism as a middle option between the extremes of rationalism and empiricism. He warned that if one "surrenders the *rationes aeternae* (the norms by which we judge), he ends up in skepticism; if he withdraws from a respect for the data of sense perception, he ends up with a high and dry philosophy."[18]

The "human predicament" is the existential precondition for appreciating the Christian world view.[19] The duality of human nature as both body and soul gives rise to the practical dilemma. The body, though fearfully and wonderfully made, is the source of sorrow. Physical ailments, deformities, and associated difficulties abound. Death appears to be the ultimate victor. It is the universal reality and fear of death that is the source of the greatest human anguish.[20] Temporality and transcendence comprise a person's "double environment," and according to Carnell, this is a "basic cause of soulsorrow."[21]

Just as the body, the environment of the soul, occasions anxiety, so the universe, which is the environment of the body, gives rise to anxiety. Carnell observed that Galileo had shown the infinite nature of the universe, Descartes its mechanical nature, Darwin its ateleological nature, and the second law of thermodynamics its ultimate destruction.[22] "In short," concluded Carnell, "modern man appears to be but a grown-up germ, sitting on a gear of a vast cosmic machine which is some day destined to cease functioning because of lack of power."[23] This soul sorrow is underscored by the conflict between the real and the ideal. The individual has four alternatives: (1) commit suicide, (2) live as if life had meaning without any rational evidence to support such a view, (3) make the best of a bad situation, or (4) opt for the "Christian-hypothesis"—presented at this point without any attempt at justification.[24]

Carnell argued that any cure for soul sorrow must restore one's faith in things and must include: (1) Hope—for personal immortality, (2) a logically intelligible view of the universe, and (3) a knowledge of what truth is.[25]

Human finitude is the practical problem of soul sorrow. The theoretical problem of the human predicament centers in the attempt to find a rational connection between the ideal and empirical worlds. It is the problem of the "one" and the "many" or of meaning and particulars and is illustrated by the problem of significant speech and action.[26] Refusing to concede an ultimate dichotomy between logic and experience, Carnell said that "Christ is the principle of the one and the author of the many. . . ."[27] Again, Carnell presented the Christian hypothesis without justifying it.

Having stated both the problem and a provisional solution, the second part of *Introduction* is an attempt to justify the Christian answer and way of knowing. Carnell rejected any definition of faith that separated it from truth. He stated: "Surely, if faith is not related to knowledge and truth, it is meaningless. It is more ouija-board than science. The Christian religion is indeed based upon the act of faith, but faith that is not grounded in knowledge is but respectable superstition."[28] Carnell saw faith as "whole-soul trust in God's word as true" and argued that the Holy Spirit is the power enabling one to see the Word as true.[29] Thus, the assurance of faith precedes the test for faith.

Testing is important for faith because of the possibility of error—which is also the problem for truth. Several traditional tests for truth are weighed and found wanting before Carnell introduced his principle of verification: "systematic consistence."[30] "Consistency" refers to "obedience to the law of contradiction" and is primarily a negative proof.[31] A hypothesis is tested in "systematic" fashion by measuring it against the facts of the real world.[32] Taken together, systematic consistence allows one to determine that a judgment corresponds to the mind of God and thus is true.[33] With this principle, Carnell treated both the problem of starting point and common ground.

Carnell argued that one's starting point controlled both one's method and conclusion in any philosophical system. According to Carnell, "Broadly speaking, *experience* is the only possible starting point for any philosophy."[34] Carnell distinguished between the logical, the synoptic, and the temporal starting point—the latter being one's predisposition and of relative unimportance. The logical starting point is, according to Carnell, "the coordinating ultimate which gives being and meaning to the many of the time-space universe."[35] The synoptic starting point provides the means for testing the logical starting point.[36] Both are presuppositions—the former being dictated by the system and thus ultimate, the latter determined solely by the criteria of verification for a given system.

Thus, Carnell sought to bridge the gap between rationalism and empiricism by accepting a dual criteria for testing truth. However, he does not suggest an adjudicating principle by which one could decide between two apparent contradictions. Rather, he was a priori committed to denying the substantial existence of such difficulties.

Carnell broadly defined general revelation, calling it, "every possible source that man has for knowing, save that of reading the Scripture."[37] Carnell saw general revelation as the common ground or point of contact between God and persons, however only special revelation—the Bible—could communicate salvation.[38]

Carnell flatly rejected the "Christian empiricism" of Saint Thomas. He argued that "effable external experience" is unable to provide immutable truth.[39] The Thomistic "proofs of God" relegate too much power of perception to the sin-stained intellect of the unbeliever. Carnell was sympathetic to the traditional critiques of the various arguments for the existence of God. Ultimately, Christian empiricism fails because it is grounded in nature and can never rise to the universal—it can rise no higher than its source.[40]

Carnell saw an analysis of the self as a more fruitful inquiry for general revelation. Following Augustine and Descartes, Carnell turned to mind's awareness of mind. He observed:

> The *cogito* establishes four things. First, it succeeds in drawing out attention from sensationalism to the mind, the source of knowledge to which rationalists appeal. . . . Secondly, it is a rebuttal to all who say that there is nothing in the intellect which was not previously in the senses . . . thirdly, the *cogito* provides us with a knowledge of God. Knowing what truth is, we know what God is, *for God is truth*. God is perfect consistency . . . . Fourthly, the *cogito* allows us to make univocal predications about God, for we are not limited in our *rationes* to those which can be abstracted from sensation. In properly knowing ourselves, we know truth; and God is truth.[41]

Carnell, citing Calvin's argument from the *sensus divinitatis,* argued that in knowing its own finitude and dependence the self also knows ". . . that Being over against whom we are perpetually set, upon whom we completely depend, and to whom we are finally responsible. All of this we know from a knowledge of our own finite, sinful, infelicitous condition."[42]

Carnell also cited Augustine's *rationes aeternae* or eternal concepts as the a priori frame of reference for categories such as the true, the good, and the beautiful. He said, "Without a knowledge a priori of the *rationes,* sense perceptions cannot report to us anything meaningful."[43] Finally, pointing to Paul's teaching that all know the Deity of God through nature, Carnell stated, "If man did not know what to look for when he observed nature, it would be pointless for Paul to look upon nature as a means to bring all men under condemnation."[44] However, the evidences from nature are not formal demonstrations of God's existence, rather they provide further proof by coherence. Carnell concluded, "The existence of God is the self-consistent hypothesis that the mind must entertain when it views all of the evidence which experience provides."[45]

However, according to Carnell, human reason is not only corrupted by sin, but it also lacks the ability and sufficient data to work out a complete view of God apart from special revelation.[46] This is not a transition from reason to faith, "for faith is the resting of the heart in the worthiness of the evidence."[47] Carnell claimed that, "Truth is systematically construed meaning, and if the Bible fulfills this standard, it is just as true as Lambert's law of transmission. Any hypothesis is verified when it smoothly interprets life."[48]

Carnell observed that, "the Christian operates under one major premise—the existence of the God who has revealed Himself in Scripture."[49] This premise is really a double hypothesis. Carnell said that "God is the *ratio essendi* (the ground for Scripture) while the Scriptures are the *ratio cognoscendi* (that through which God is apprehended)."[50]

Although Carnell developed his view of the Scripture somewhat in the final third of this volume as he dealt with various difficulties associated with the Christian world view; issues related to inspiration, authority, and hermeneutics are treated more systematically and theologically in *The Case for Orthodox Theology* which is examined later.[51] However, Carnell saw an authoritative and infallible Scripture as the only sufficient and reliable candidate for the status of special revelation. Carnell concluded *An Introduction to Christian Apologetics* with a Pascalian wager, for reason can only bring one to the threshold of decision, urging the uncommitted to opt for the gospel.

Carnell's *An Introduction to Christian Apologetics* was an evangelical attempt to deal with epistemology. Its companion volume, *A Philosophy of the Christian Religion,* was an attempt to deal with axiology or the problem of value systems. Carnell said, "Foolishness is to axiology as inconsistency is to logic."[52] Any value system must be examined as a whole before an intelligent commitment can be made. Carnell said, "Knowledge describes and orders the alternatives, separating the worthy from the unworthy . . . so that the heart may have an unambiguous place to rest."[53]

In this work Carnell surveyed a wide variety of philosophical systems that claim to deal with human need. Carnell began with the "lower immediacies" of physical pleasures and wants as supplied by hedonism and Marxism. Human transcendence denies contentment to anyone who lives simply for pleasure. The result of such an attempt is boredom which Carnell described as "that weariness of spirit which results when freedom is repetitiously related to an immediacy."[54] Frustration and guilt over the absence of any enduring purpose culminate in exhaustion when all hope for purposeful fulfillment is lost.[55] Carnell's discussion of materialism and Marxism is dated and reflects the cold-war mentality of the era in which it was written.[56]

Turning to the "higher immediacies" of intellectual satisfaction offered by rationalism and positivism, Carnell conceded that the astounding success of scientific technology, based upon a posteriori empiricism, has relegated a priori rationalism to a less than honorable status.[57] According to Carnell, scientific empiricism or logical positivism is the most consistent a posteriori philosophy and it is the logical conclusion of Kantian epistemology.[58]

The implications of positivism for metaphysics is devastating. Carnell noted that:

Because science cannot pass from the descriptive to the normative, one cannot formulate informational propositions about either ethics or metaphysics. There is no scientific operation which follows from either an ethical or a metaphysical assertion. Hence, neither has *cognitive* significance. Ethical sentences may be studied along with wishes or exclamations, but they cannot claim factual truth.[59]

However, he argued that an individual should bracket the positivist's criteria for meaningful speech and examine the system as a whole before becoming a convert.

Indeed, the positivist is faced with a dilemma. Either the positivist assumptions regarding "cognitive" language are based upon observation, which cannot be a universalized and thus cannot be applied with certainty, or they have the status of a belief, a metaphysical assertion, and thus do not conform to their own criteria for cognitivity.[60] Most of the early pioneers of science were, according to Carnell, "God-fearing" and "firmly persuaded that the true, good and beautiful were time- and space-transcending values. The scientific ideal is *judged* by these criteria; it does not presume to find them."[61]

Carnell also analyzed "threshold options"—humanism, deism, pantheism, and finite-theism—which stand at the border of Christian theism. Humanism shifts the focus from abstract principles to a devotion to humanity. Like Christianity, it defends values that terminate in persons, but the humanist refuses to go beyond the second table of the Ten Commandments.[62] The humanist also faces a fundamental difficulty. Committed to a scientific world view, the humanist denies any ultimate absolute (God, final authority, or absolute moral code) as binding. Yet as a philosopher, the humanist advances certain a priori ideals (such as love, justice, honesty, etc.) which, Carnell argued, entail at least the possibility of the existence of God.[63] Further, the collision between the individual ego and the collective good indicates the need for an ultimate point of reference if humanistic ideals are to have meaning.

Indeed, Carnell saw "God" as the ultimate point of reference for any fully satisfying value-system. However he would accept nothing less than the theistic Triune God revealed in Scripture.[64] In rejecting both deism and pantheism as proper views of God, he saw a need to restore the immanence-transcendence balance of the biblical view. Carnell observed:

One may not personally care to accept the Christian view of God and man, but at least he cannot deny the axiological advantage of a theology which, in addition to understanding God as Father, establishes both his immanence and his transcendence . . . . Transcendence insures the heart that God is far enough away from the world to save significance for history, while immanence assures it that he is near enough to hear prayer and receive worship.[65]

Carnell pointed to "kingdom clarifications," dealing with the subbiblical position of universalism and the Christian options of Roman Catholicism and Kierkegaardian existentialism before considering a fully biblical Christianity (i.e., Carnell's conservative evangelical reformation perspective). Carnell was convinced that the claims of Christianity were ignored mostly out of prejudice. He said:

> While each must judge the matter for himself, it is the conviction of the Christian philosopher that men turn from Biblical Christianity more by the leading of prejudgment than by the light gained from critical hypotheses. It is easy to misunderstand the simple system of Biblical truth by confusing it with a dissatisfying denominational or institutional system which pretends to come in its name. Consequently, men comb the world for data with which to deliver them from the uncertainties of the present hour, while by-passing a copy of the Scriptures which may be purchased for a few cents in a variety store.[66]

Carnell was also convinced that many reject the gospel because of an unfounded "fear that Christianity is an authoritative system of dogma" which somehow limits human freedom.[67]

Carnell's positive interaction with the Christian existentialism of Kierkegaard is of particular interest at this point because of the increased emphasis on inwardness in Carnell's later works. Although sympathetic to Kierkegaard's insistence on a concerned, inward response to God, Carnell thought that the Danish philosopher had gone too far in divorcing faith from reason. Carnell argued, "Unless faith is supported by a genuine authority, it will soften into an ephemeral expression of inwardness."[68] Further, he argued that "generic" faith (i.e., belief) "is the resting of the mind in the sufficiency of the evidences. Saving faith may go beyond this general expression, but it does not exclude it."[69] Arguing for a "healthy inwardness" Carnell concluded: "Truth as inwardness may be more important for fellowship than truth as a rational system, but apart from the guidance which inwardness receives from such a system it is a rudderless ship on a shoreless sea."[70]

Carnell concluded *A Philosophy of the Christian Religion* with the invitation, "taste and see that Jehovah is good."[71] Although he never repudiated the content or approach of these early apologetic efforts, Carnell's later works are more subjective in appeal and personal in tone.

Carnell's *The Case for Orthodox Theology,* although published after *Christian Commitment,* is a transitional apologetic work. Part of a trilogy published by Westminster in 1959, it displays a tempered rationalism.[72] This work is significant both because of what it says and what it doesn't say about Carnell's view of orthodoxy. It is an appeal both for tolerance toward and within the evangelical community.

Carnell defined "orthodoxy" as "that branch of Christendom which limits the grounds of religious authority to the Bible."[73] He argued that the twin elements of personal encounter and propositional revelation could not be separated. Carnell noted that "Orthodoxy has always insisted that the written Word does not commend itself unless the heart is confronted by the living Word."[74]

Carnell repeated the standard lines of evangelical thought with regard to the authority of the Bible. The Christian accepts the Old Testament on the authority of Jesus Christ.[75] The New Testament is substantiated by apostolic validation.[76] What is most significant about his discussion of biblical authority is that inerrancy is not discussed in any detail in this context. Carnell reserved a more extended discussion of inerrancy for a later chapter on "difficulties" for orthodoxy. Carnell remained committed to the Princeton theology view of inerrancy, however, he commented with considerable favor on the view of James Orr. Orr, in contrast to Warfield's emphasis on propositional truth, stressed that the communication of life, not knowledge, is the goal of the Bible.[77] Carnell saw the data of Scripture as giving rise to both positions and concluded that the dialogue between Orr and Princeton theology was never "successfully terminated."[78]

Carnell also advanced a fairly typical evangelical hermeneutic. He argued that while the whole of Scripture is plenarily inspired, the Bible is a "progressive revelation."[79] He condemned "cultic thinking" (i.e., fundamentalism) for imposing a uniformity on Scripture that the Bible does not justify.[80] He elaborated on five rules that govern biblical hermeneutics. These are:

> first, the New Testament interprets the Old Testament; secondly, the Epistles interpret the Gospels; thirdly, systematic passages interpret the incidental; fourthly, universal passages interpret the local; fifthly, didactic passages interpret the symbolic. If any rule is neglected, the harmony of Scripture is disrupted.[81]

Thus while Carnell insisted upon biblical authority he appeared to bracket the inerrancy question. This, combined with his rationalistic hermeneutic, left several areas of unresolved tensions. He cautiously applauded the insights of nondestructive higher criticism. Also, he acknowledged that evolution is a fact that is "here to stay."[82] Carnell was severely criticized for both granting concessions to "liberal theology" and his condemnation of the cultic and separatist mentality of fundamentalism.[83]

Carnell's identity as a Baptist was surprisingly insignificant in the expression of his evangelical identity. While at Fuller Seminary Carnell studiously avoided identification with any denominational expression of Christianity. In *The Case for Orthodox Theology* he cited various denominations' peculiarities as divisive. Further, as an example of "cultic mentality" he mentioned the fact that "Baptists often limit fellowship to those who have been immersed" and concluded, "This is unfortunate."[84] With regard to church government he said, "The apostles did not legislate a specific polity on the church."[85] This view would, no doubt, offend many Baptists. No major Baptists sources are cited in the suggested reading material at the end of each chapter in *The Case for Orthodox Theology*. Also, no Baptist sources are cited in his concluding "Bibliography of General Theological Sources."[86]

Apologetics for the Tender-Minded

Briefly, our attention turns to Carnell's later apologetic works. These were written during Carnell's tumultuous career as president at Fuller. Neither received a wide acceptance in the evangelical community. Carnell was particularly disappointed that *Christian Commitment,* his personal favorite, was a failure.[87]

Christian Commitment builds an apologetic case upon what Carnell referred to as the "third way of knowing"—the judicial sentiment or human moral perception.[88] It is an extended discussion of a modified "moral argument." Appropriating an autobiographical format as Carnell traced this third way of knowing through his own experience. Carnell's basic claim is that one demonstrates commitment to the truth of an ethical system by acting.

Carnell turned to Kierkegaard and observed, "no previous thinker has more energetically tried to interpret reality from the perspective of the free, ethical individual."[89] According to Carnell, Kierkegaard rightly pointed out that, "*Thinking* about duty is not the same as *doing* one's duty. Thought must yield to action."[90] Further, according to Carnell, "The only way to recognize duty is by morally submitting to the duties that already hold us."[91]

An individual's sense of right and wrong bears witness to a universal moral environment. When an individual's moral environment is violated by another, the offended judges the violator guilty. To act unfairly or to fail to act in response to an acknowledged need is universally unacceptable.

Carnell also saw the offended human conscience as an indication that the Divine judicial sentiment has been violated. He argued that ". . . the moral and spiritual environment on the finite level is precisely of the same stuff as the moral and spiritual environment on the divine level; and that it is also proper to say that God is perfectly held by standards that hold an upright man imperfectly."[92]

The essence of the imperative of this environment is love. God is good by nature whereas individuals are good insofar as they conform to the moral and spiritual environment share with God.

Indignation for wrong action and the moral predicament in deciding to act in the first place occasions the basic question:

> But how are systems verified? How can one decide whether one system is better than another? Here is the answer, and the answer once again applies to both theology and philosophy. Systems are verified by the degree to which their major elements are consistent with one another and with the broad facts of history and nature. In short, a consistent system is a true system. Were a person to demand a higher or a more perfect test than this, he would only show his want of education. This is about all that can be said. Christianity is true because its major elements are consistent with one another and with the broad facts of history and nature. The third method of knowing has shown that the human race is held in a moral predicament; and only Christianity can resolve this predicament without offending the larger features in man's fourfold environment—physical, rational, aesthetic, and moral and spiritual. Existence itself raises a question to which the righteousness of Christ is the only critically acceptable answer. Hence Christianity is true.[93]

The final third of *Christian Commitment* is devoted to a theological exposition of repentance based upon the judicial sentiment and an appeal to the finality of Jesus Christ.

In his last work, *The Kingdom of Love and the Pride of Life,* Carnell attempted to link the insights of Freudian thought with the gospel. The central theme of the book is that the fullest expression of one's personhood can be found by following Christ. A portion of the account of Lazarus's resurrection is treated at the outset of each chapter.[94]

The happy child is the systematic center of the work. The book's apologetic appeal is based upon the universal need for love and acceptance.[95] In the kingdom of love Carnell saw a "release from anxiety, fear, and the dread of not counting."[96] Throughout the book he traced the implications of childlike trust and faith. The Freudian psychoanalytical attempt to probe the childhood sources of neuroses is contrasted with Jesus' own admonition, "Unless ye become as little children. . . ."[97] The happy child is symbolic of the reasons of the heart, reasons of which the mind may be unaware. Carnell observed: "intellectual awakening has perils, for the mind can play tricks on us—and just when we think it is most dependable. It promises to lead us closer to reality, while all the while it takes us further away."[98] Carnell was more open to knowledge by intuition at this point. However, he continued to defend the trustworthiness of human reason and again stated his often repeated view that faith is "at least a resting of the mind in the sufficiency of the evidence."[99]

Carnell saw in Freudian psychoanalysis a proof that love is "the law of life."[100] He criticized Freud because he "could not articulate a philosophy of hope because he could not break from scientific detachment."[101] Carnell concluded that only Christianity offered a depth of love and hope that met the human need uncovered by psychotherapy. One hears Carnell's own personal need for hope in his final words:

> We were alone when we entered the world, but when we leave it we shall feel the abiding presence of the Lord. As death draws near and we dread the dark journey ahead, the Lord will assure us that our lives are precious in the sight of God. He will gently say, "Child, come home." Jesus has given his word that he will never leave us nor forsake us, and his word is as firm as his character.[102]

Kingdom of Love is also significant because it gives some clues to the direction of his thought at this time in his life. He chided conservative Christianity for being "so anxious to defend the Lord's divinity that it has slighted the Lord's humanity."[103] He expressed cautious favor of form criticism.[104] He admitted to a depth of human experience beyond the veil of human understanding.[105] And he chided orthodox rigidity claiming, "Competence in theology is never cited as a requisite for salvation."[106]

Evaluation

Carnell influenced the evangelical community in at least three ways. The roles of educator, scholar, and churchman all marked his ministry. His direction of Fuller Seminary during its formative years helped shape that institution in a moderate-evangelical mold. David A. Hubbard, current Fuller president, said of Carnell:

> During his years as president, Fuller Seminary made such remarkable advances in curriculum, faculty appointments, library holdings and financial stability that full accreditation was achieved. As much as any man he shaped the seminary's character.[107]

Indeed, at the time of Carnell's death, Aubrey B. Haines observed that Fuller would easily prove to be his greatest accomplishment.[108] Also, it is significant that Carnell was considered the most influential professor on campus throughout most of his tenure.[109] Ironically, it was the administrative burdens of the presidency at Fuller that contributed to Carnell's nervous breakdown, from which he never fully recovered.[110]

Second, Carnell also influenced the evangelical community at the scholarly level. His rationalistic orientation was fairly typical of a particular style of conservative apologetics.[111] However, Carnell was among the first evangelical scholars to positively interact with the work of Søren Kierkegaard and indicate some openness to insights of Christian existentialism.[112] Although he remained committed to the Princeton formulation of the inerrancy of the Scriptures, Carnell was at least appreciatively aware of the broader evangelical tradition on the issue.[113] Finally, Carnell attempted to engage difficulties and acknowledge uncertainties that conservative scholars frequently ignored. Thus, at the scholarly level, Carnell serves as a possible paradigm for understanding tensions in evangelical theology today.

He never achieved the popular status of many contemporaries in the evangelical community. He lacked the lucid and appealing writing style of C. S. Lewis. Although Carnell's works avoid the simplistic approach of some conservative apologists, as characterized by Francis Schaeffer, he failed to achieve the scholarly status of a conservative spokesperson like Carl F. H. Henry. Yet Carnell's work was substantial enough that many nonevangelicals saw in him an opportunity for dialogue between, as William Hordern expressed it, "fundamentalist and non-fundamentalist Christians" noting that, "The non-fundamentalist world cannot justify itself in ignoring a man of his stature."[114]

Carnell's basic philosophical weakness was his epistemology. The test of "systematic consistency" was in reality a dual criteria for truth. With both empiricism and deductive logic elevated to equal rank there is no provision made for their potential contradiction. At a theological level Carnell never distinguished Christian faith from other forms of belief. Carnell was attempting to demonstrate that the believer has adequate epistemic grounds for holding the Christian world view. In fact, the Christian is convicted by more than mere rational argumentation. Carnell was overly fearful of the existential and nonobjective aspects of faith.

In seeking to demonstrate the emptiness of non-Christian world views Carnell frequently attacked opponents of straw. He also underestimated the difficulties of the evangelical Christian world view. However, Carnell was surely correct in pointing out that the nonbeliever does not have to be persuaded of all the tenets of orthodoxy in order to hear and believe the gospel.

The third area of Carnell's influence was his churchmanship. Carnell warned of the "curious blend of classic and cultic elements" in contemporary orthodoxy.[115] He deplored the separatist view of the church and observed, "A spirit of divisiveness is not prompted by the Holy Spirit, for love is the law of life, and love remains unsatisfied until *all* who form the body of Christ are united in one sacred fellowship."[116] Carnell was irenic in temperament and was willing to dialogue with the larger theological and ecclesiastical community. He was the "conservative" representative on the board of questioners who queried Karl Barth at the University of Chicago in 1962. Carnell was also one of the few evangelicals to write regularly for the more liberal *The Christian Century,* which observed that it had in Carnell "a two-way bridge between itself [the editorial board] and one of the more conservative wings of evangelical Christianity."[117]

The tensions in Carnell's personal life and his theological thought are personifications of a generation of evangelicalism search for its identity. The lack of a significant relationship between Carnell's Baptist identity and his mature evangelicalism raises the question of the viability of the "evangelical" label in a denominational context.[118] Ronald Nash has offered a fitting epitaph for the life and work of Edward John Carnell. He said:

> The issue, it seems to me, is not whether Edward John Carnell was always biblically consistent in his teaching. Each of us unconsciously cultivates some heresy or other. The issue is whether Edward John Carnell was morally uneasy about his inability to be biblically consistent. As long as he was willing to know the right and be transformed by it, [we] can ask nothing more, for nothing more can be asked of [us].[119]

Bibliography

Works by Carnell
Books

The Burden of Søren Kierkegaard. Grand Rapids, Mich.: Eerdmans, 1965.

The Case for Orthodox Theology. Philadelphia: Westminster Press, 1959.

Christian Commitment: An Apologetic. New York: Macmillan, 1957.

An Introduction to Christian Apologetics. Grand Rapids, Mich.: Eerdmans, 1948.

The Kingdom of Love and the Pride of Life. Grand Rapids, Mich.: Eerdmans, 1960.

A Philosophy of the Christian Religion. Grand Rapids, Mich.: Eerdmans, 1952.

Television: Servant or Master? Grand Rapids, Mich.: Eerdmans, 1950.

The Theology of Reinhold Niebuhr. Grand Rapids, Mich.: Eerdmans, 1951.

Contributions in Other Books

How My Mind Has Changed, edited by Harold E. Fey. New York: Meridian, 1960.

"Fundamentalism." In *Handbook of Christian Theology*, edited by Marvin Halverson and Arthur A. Cohen. New York: Meridian, 1958.

"The Government of the Church." In *Basic Christian Doctrines*, edited by Carl F. H. Henry, Grand Rapids, Mich.: Baker, 1962.

"Niebuhr's Criteria of Verification." In *Reinhold Niebuhr: His Religious, Social, and Political Thought*, edited by Charles W. Kegley and Robert W. Bretall. New York: Macmillan, 1956.

"Reinhold Niebuhr's View of Scripture." In *Inspiration and Interpretation*, edited by John F. Walvoord. Grand Rapids, Mich.: Eerdmans, 1957.

"The Son of God." In *The Empirical Theology of Henry Nelson Wieman*, edited by Robert W. Bretall. New York: Macmillan, 1963.

Articles

"Barth as Inconsistent Evangelical." *The Christian Century*, June 6, 1962, 713-14.

"Beware of the New Deism." *HIS* (Dec. 1951): 14-6, 35-6.

"A Christian Social Ethic." *The Christian Century*, Aug. 7, 1963, 979-80.

"Conservatives and Liberals Do Not Need Each Other." *Christianity Today*, May 21, 1965, 6-8.

"Criterion of Love." Rev. of Nels F. S. Ferre's *Know Your Faith* (Harper). *Christianity Today*, Aug. 29, 1960, 42-43.

"The Government of the Church." *Christianity Today*, June 22, 1962, 18-19.

"The Grave Peril of Provincilizing Jesus." *The Pulpit* (May 1951): 2-4.

"How Every Christian Can Defend His Faith." *Moody Monthly*, Jan. 1950, 312-13; 343; Feb. 1950, 384-85, 429-31; Mar. 1950, 460-61, 506-7.

"Jesus Christ and Man's Condition." *Encounter* 21 (Winter 1960): 52-8.

"The Nature of the Unity We Seek: An Orthodox Protestant View." *Religion in Life*, 26 (Spring 1957): 191-9.

"Orthodoxy: Cultic vs. Classical." *The Christian Century*, Mar. 30, 1960: 377-79.

"Post-Fundamentalist Faith." *The Christian Century*, Aug. 26, 1959: 971.

"The Problem of Religious Authority." *HIS* (Feb. 1950): 6-9, 11, 12.

"The Secret of Loving Your Neighbor." *Eternity*, July 1961, 15-16.

"Should a Christian Go to War?" *HIS* (April 1951): 4-8, 10.

"The Virgin Birth of Christ." *Christianity Today*, Dec. 7, 1959, 9-10.

"Why Neo-Orthodoxy?" *The Watchman-Examiner*, Feb. 19, 1948, 180-81.

Other Works

"The Concept of Dialectic in the Theology of Reinhold Niebuhr." Th.D. diss., Harvard Divinity School, 1948.

"The Glory of a Theological Seminary." Inaugural Address of Edward John Carnell, president of Fuller Theological Seminary 1954-1959, delivered May 17, 1955.

"The Problem of Verification in Søren Kierkegaard." Ph.D. diss., Boston University, 1949.

Works Related to Carnell

Barnhart, Joe E. "The Religious Epistemology and Theodicy of Edward John Carnell and Edgar Sheffield Brightman." Ph.D. diss., Boston University, 1964.

Haines, Aubrey B. "Edward John Carnell: An Evaluation." *The Christian Century,* June 7, 1967, 751.

Harper, Kenneth C. "Edward John Carnell: An Evaluation of His Apologetic." *Journal of The Evangelical Theological Society* 20 (June 1977): 133-45.

Rosas III, Louis Joseph, "An Analysis of the Apologetic Method of Edward John Carnell," Th.M. Thesis, The Southern Baptist Theological Seminary, 1980.

Sailer, William S. "The Role of Reason in the Theologies of Nels Ferre and Edward John Carnell." S.T.D. diss., Temple University, 1964.

Sims, John A. "The Apologetical Odyssey of Edward John Carnell." M.A. thesis, Florida State University, 1971.

Sims, John A. *Edward John Carnell: Defender of the Faith*. Washington, D.C.: University Press of America, 1979.

_____. "The Problem of Knowledge in the Apologetic Concerns of Edwin Lewis and Edward John Carnell." Ph.D. diss., Florida State University, 1975.

Notes

1. Rudolph L. Nelson, *The Making and Unmaking of an Evangelical Mind: The Case of Edward Carnell* (New York: Cambridge, 1987) deals with the psychohistory of Carnell's life.

2. Ernest R. Sandeen, *The Roots of Fundamentalism* (Chicago: University of Chicago Press, 1970), 103-31. See B. B. Warefield, *The Inspiration and the Authority of the Bible* (Philadelphia: Presbyterian and Reformed, 1970). This is the classic statement of the old Princeton theology on biblical authority.

3. Sandeen, 162 *f.* Cf. George Marsden, "From Fundamentalism to Evangelicalism: A Historical Analysis," *The Evangelicals,* eds. D. F. Wells and J. B. Woodbridge (Nashville: Abingdon, 1975), 140, n. 8.

4. For a summary of these articles, see Sandeen, 203-6.

5. See Sandeen, 253 *f.* for a discussion of J. G. Machen's split with Princeton and the later split between his followers and Carl McIntire. Indeed, as Marsden has noted, "separatism" vs. inclusivism became a major dividing point between old style fundamentalists and the new evangelicalism of some at Fuller Seminary. See George Marsden, *Reforming Fundamentalism: Fuller Seminary and the New Evangelicalism* (Grand Rapids, Mich.: Eerdmans, 1987), 36-38.

6. William Hordern, *New Directions in Theology: vol. 1,* (Philadelphia: Westminster Press, 1966) chapter 4, "The New Face of Conservativism," 74-95.

7. Harold Ockenga apparently first coined the term "evangelical" as applied

in this context. George Marsden, *Reforming Fundamentalism,* 53 *f.* However, the distinction between "evangelicalism" and "fundamentalism" is not universally acknowledged. See James Barr, *Fundamentalism* (London: SCM Press, 1977).

8. Edward John Carnell, *The Case for Orthodox Theology* (Philadelphia: Westminster Press, 1959), 113. In fact he dedicated this book to his parents.

9. See chapter on Carl F. H. Henry, this volume.

10. Later published as *The Theology of Reinhold Niebuhr.*

11. Later published as *The Burden of Soren Kierkegaard.*

12. Cf. Joe E. Barnhart, "The Religious Epistemology and Theodicy of Edward John Carnell and Edgar Sheffield Brightman" (Ph.D. diss., Boston University, 1964) which develops the relationship between Carnell's and Brightman's thought.

13. See bibliography for a listing of Carnell's works with full bibliographic data.

14. Edward John Carnell, *An Introduction to Christian Apologetics* (Grand Rapids, Mich.: Eerdmans, 1948), 151.

15. Norman Geisler, *Christian Apologetics* (Grand Rapids: Baker Book House, 1976), 121. Ronald Nash, *The New Evangelicalism* (Grand Rapids, Mich.: Zondervan, 1963), 114.

16. Edward John Carnell, *Kingdom of Love and the Pride of Life* (Grand Rapids, Mich.: Eerdmans, 1960), 6.

17. Kenneth C. Harper, "Edward John Carnell: An Evaluation of His Apologetics," *Journal of the Evangelical Theological Society* 20 (1977): 137 *f.*

18. Carnell, *Christian Apologetics,* 7.

19. Ibid., 19, 29.

20. Ibid., 20.

21. Ibid.

22. Ibid., 21-22.

23. Ibid., 22.

24. Ibid., 24-55. Carnell's willingness to posit theoretically the Christian world view as a value to be tested by other criteria was strenuously opposed by Van Til. Carnell contended that Van Til failed to appreciate that Christianity can be better "with [the difference in value] absolute." Edward John Carnell, "Perfect Assurance," rev. of Van Til's *The Defense of the Faith* (Presbyterian and Reformed), *Christianity Today,* January 4, 1956, 15.

25. Ibid., 25-7.

26. Ibid., 30-31.

27. Ibid., 41.

28. Ibid., 65.

29. Ibid.

30. Criteria rejected include: instinct, custom, tradition, common consent, feeling, sense perception, intuition, correspondence, and pragmatism. Ibid., 48-56 *f.*

31. Ibid., 56.

32. Ibid., 59.

33. Ibid., 56.

34. Ibid., 123.

35. Ibid., 124.

36. Ibid.

37. Ibid., 157.

38. Ibid.

39. Ibid., 126 *f.* Carnell specifically repudiated Thomism and would no doubt

challenge John Newport's placing of him in that tradition. Cf. Newport, "Representative Contemporary Approaches to the Use of Philosophy in Christian Thought," *Review and Expositor* 82 (1985): 508, 518.

40. Ibid., 139.
41. Ibid., 158-59.
42. Ibid., 160.
43. Ibid., 169.
44. Ibid.
45. Ibid., 172.
46. Ibid., 157.
47. Ibid., 175.
48. Ibid., 173.
49. Ibid.
50. Ibid., 100.
51. Carnell dealt with issues such as biblical criticism, miracles and natural law, and the problem of evil. These continue to be intelligent evangelical responses to some traditional problems.
52. Edward John Carnell, *A Philosophy of the Christian Religion* (Grand Rapids, Mich.: Eerdmans, 1952), 21.
53. Ibid., 29.
54. Ibid., 58.
55. Ibid., 77.
56. Ibid., 83-128. Carnell was dependent upon secondary sources. He focused on the power-hungry leaders of the Soviet Union and viewed communism as static and monolithic. Further, Carnell displayed no knowledge of the early writings of Marx and little understanding of Marx's concept of alienation.
57. Ibid., 132. This would seem to be a dubious conclusion based upon an argument of straw that is a much easier target.
58. Ibid., 138.
59. Ibid., 140.
60. Ibid., 149.
61. Ibid., 163.
62. Ibid., 229.
63. Ibid., 243.
64. Ibid., 272.
65. Ibid., 293-94.
66. Ibid., 511.
67. Ibid., 512.
68. Ibid.
69. Ibid., 450.
70. Ibid., 453. Kierkegaard scholar Robert L. Perkins has correctly contended that Carnell did not really understand Kierkegaard's doctrine of subjectivity. Cf. Perkins, "Review of Carnell's *The Burden of Soren Kierkegaard*," *Scandinavian Studies,* 38 (May 1966): 160-61.
71. Carnell, *A Philosophy of the Christian Religion,* 516.
72. Also included were: William Hordern, *The Case for a New Reformation Theology,* and L. Harold DeWolf, *The Case for Theology in a Liberal Perspective* (Philadelphia: Westminster Press, 1959).
73. Carnell, *The Case for Orthodox Theology,* 13.

74. Ibid., 33.

75. Ibid., 35.

76. Ibid., 47.

77. Ibid., 100.

78. Ibid., 109. The tension in Carnell's thought on the issue of inerrancy is further illustrated by the fact that he is cited, with approval, by both sides in the ongoing evangelical debate. He is cited as supporting the mediating position of Jack Rogers and Donald McKim, *The Authority and Interpretation of the Bible* (New York: Harper and Row, 1979), 375, 401, 402. Also, Harold Lindsell, a strict inerrantist dedicated *The Battle for the Bible* to Carnell (among others) and cites him with approval. Lindsell, *The Battle for the Bible* (Grand Rapids, Mich.: Zondervan, 1976), 32, 70, 109, 112.

79. Ibid., 52.

80. Ibid., 53.

81. Ibid.

82. Ibid., 95.

83. Ibid., 113 *f.* Cf. John R. Rice, "Fuller Seminary's Carnell Sneers at Fundamentalism," *The Sword of the Lord,* October 30, 1959, 1, 7, 11.

84. Carnell, *The Case for Orthodox Theology,* 59.

85. Ibid., 22.

86. Ibid., 148. He listed the following headings with references under each: (1) the ecumenical creeds, (2) the standards of Greek and Eastern Orthodoxy, (3) the standards of Roman Catholicism, (4) the standards of Lutheranism, (5) the standards of the Reformed tradition, (6) the standards of Anglicanism, and (7) the standards of Arminianism.

87. Nelson, *The Making and Unmaking of An Evangelical Mind,* 103.

88. Edward John Carnell, *Christian Commitment: An Apologetic* (New York: Macmillan, 1957), x.

89. Ibid., 73.

90. Ibid., 74.

91. Ibid., 85.

92. Ibid., 138.

93. Ibid., 286.

94. Carnell, *Kingdom of Love,* 24, 36, 51, 65, 78, 94, 106, 122, 138.

95. Ibid., 10.

96. Ibid., 7.

97. Ibid.

98. Ibid., 17.

99. Ibid., 104.

100. Ibid., 59. Carnell had undergone extensive psychotherapy and electroshock treatment by this time in his life.

101. Ibid., 62.

102. Ibid., 160.

103. Ibid., 107.

104. Ibid., 107-8.

105. Ibid., 109.

106. Ibid.

107. David Hubbard, "Preface," to "The Glory of a Theological Seminary," the Inaugural Address of Edward John Carnell, President of Fuller Theological Semi-

nary 1954-1959, delivered May 17, 1955 (published as a portion of the Carnell Memorial established in 1969-70 by the Fuller Theological Seminary Alumni Association) 3.

108. Aubrey B. Haines, "Edward John Carnell: An Evaluation," *The Christian Century,* June 7, 1967, 751.

109. Marsden, *Reforming Fundamentalism,* Appendix.

110. Carl F. H. Henry, "The Loss of Two Great Leaders," *Christianity Today,* May 12, 1967, 30.

111. Similar approaches are associated with J. O. Buswell, Gordon Clark, Bernard Ramm, and Carl F. H. Henry, to name a few.

112. Carnell, *Commitment,* 73. Vernon Grounds also belongs in this category. Cf. Grounds, "Take Another Look at S. K.," *Christianity Today,* February 18, 1966, 33.

113. Carnell, *The Case for Orthodox Theology,* 99 *f.* The fact that Carnell continued to consider himself an inerrantist in the Princeton mold is confirmed by a letter to the editor published less than a year before his death. Carnell said, "I wholeheartedly agree . . ." with a recently published defense of biblical inerrancy, noting "the defense is actually a reconstruction of the procedure set down by . . . Warfield," which, concluded Carnell, "[is] the Bible's view of itself." (*Christianity Today,* October 14, 1966, 23.) Whether or not Carnell was a "consistent" inerrantist or would pass muster today is another question.

114. William Hordern, *A Layman's Guide to Protestant Theology* (New York: Macmillan, 1955), 75.

115. Ibid., 132.

116. Ibid., 137.

117. "Edward John Carnell Dies in California," *The Christian Century,* May 10, 1967, 612.

118. Cf. James Leo Garrett, E. Glenn Hinson, James Tull, *Are Southern Baptists "Evangelicals"?* (Macon, Ga.: Mercer University Press, 1983).

119. Nash, "Introduction," to *The Case for Biblical Christianity,* 9.

James Deotis Roberts

Gerald Thomas

Biography

James Deotis Roberts was born in Spindale, North Carolina, the son of a carpenter. His extensive education was obtained at Johnson C. Smith University located in Charlotte, North Carolina, from which he graduated with an A.B., magna cum laude, in religious education and English. He received a Bachelor of Divinity degree in 1950 from Shaw University in Raleigh, North Carolina. Roberts went to the Hartford Seminary Foundation in Hartford, Connecticut, where he earned another B.D. in 1951, and a Master's in Sacred Theology in 1952. His thesis topic was "The Problem of Faith and Reason in the Pascal, Bergson, and James."

This distinguished theologian studied abroad at the University of Edinburgh, which granted him the Doctor of Philosophy degree in philosophical theology in 1957. His dissertation topic was "The Rational Theology of Benjamin Whichcote: Father of the Cambridge Platonists." Roberts studied theology at Cambridge University as part of his university studies in 1956.

Roberts has developed one of the most extensive backgrounds and reputations of any contemporary black scholar. An ordained Baptist minister, Dr. Roberts has pastored churches in North Carolina and Connecticut and served as pastor-ad-interim of the Radnor Park Congregational Church in Scotland while working on his doctorate.

He was dean of Religion at Georgia Baptist College, Macon, 1952-53, the assistant professor of Philosophy and Religion and director of Religious Life and Activities at Shaw University from 1953-55, and an associate professor of Philosophy and Religion and College Minister, Shaw University, 1957-58.

In 1958 Mordecai Johnson, president of Howard University located in Washington, D.C., solicited the scholarship of this aspiring theologian in the history and philosophy of religion department at the "mecca" of black higher education. For fifteen years Roberts made his presence known in the academic arenas of theological development and religious education, both as an instructor and professor.

Following visiting professorships of religion during this time at The Catholic University of America, School of Sacred Theology (1968-69), Swarthmore College (1969-70), and George Mason College (University of Virginia, 1971-73), Roberts was elected dean of the School of Theology of Virginia Union University in 1973, one of the oldest black theological institutions in America.

After a one-year stint he returned to Howard University School of Religion and became professor of Theology and editor of *The Journal of Religious Thought* until 1980. During the summer of 1976 Roberts taught at The Southern Baptist Theological Seminary in the area of Black Theology: Liberation and Reconciliation. In the spring of 1978, he substituted for Professor John B. Cobb, Jr., as Visiting Professor of Theology at the School of Theology, Claremont, California.

The climax of his career came in 1980 when J. Deotis Roberts was elected president and Distinguished Professor of Philosophical Theology at The Interdenominational Theological Center, Atlanta, Georgia. He also has served as Visiting Professor at the Institute of Pastoral Ministry and Religious Education, Boston College, (1980), American Baptist Seminary of the West, Berkeley, California (1981), Candler School of Theology, Emory University, Atlanta (1983), and Columbia Seminary, Atlanta (1984).

Currently, Roberts is on the faculty at The Eastern Baptist Theological Seminary in Philadelphia as Distinguished Professor of Philosophical Theology. Roberts is married to the former Elizabeth Caldwell and they are parents of three daughters: Edin Charmaine, Carlita Rose, and Kristina LaFerne.

Exposition

Philosophical Theology

A modern penchant for the Christian interpretation between God as Redeemer and a people of faith inspired Roberts to propose credibility to the black experience as it encounters the realities of human suffering and racism. Although his initial publication, *Faith and Reason in Pascal, Bergson and James* emphasized a yearning for classical philosophy, he pursued the theological presuppositions of Pascal's life as they related to rationalistic and metaphysical approaches to physical science. But it was the "second conversion" of Pascal that proposed "the relationship of man to God is the basis of genuine knowledge" which appealed to Roberts.[1] He writes:

> Through this religious experience, Pascal realizes the futility of mere intellectual proofs for the existence of God. He speaks of knowing that God exists by the feelings of the heart. For this purpose, he urges men to search their hearts and observe the truth of what God speaks.[2]

The beginning of a heartfelt experience prompted the energetic scholar to pursue America's need for a cogent understanding of those who inhabited the "dark places" of her growing cities. The blatant racism within the "American way of life" met the prophetic voice of a young Reverend Martin Luther King, Jr., in the 1950s, as he mobilized Negro people to demonstrate against the injustices of inequality and segregation. Thus, a new theological frontier was about to be discovered for the depressed, despondent, and disenfranchised.

In 1968, during the zenith of outrage and rioting, Roberts made a major statement in Christian theology when his book *From Puritanism to Plato-*

James Deotis Roberts (1927-   )

nism in Seventeenth-Century England was published. Here was a major effort by a black theologian upon the intellectuals of Western culture. Being the first to write a dissertation on the life and thought of the founder of humanism, Benjamin Whichcote, the father of the Cambridge Platonists, brought Roberts notoriety as a bona fide theologian. From this effort, Roberts gained the respect of theologians both in Europe and America as one capable of presenting historical religious reflections through sound theological research.

Black Theology

In the discipline of black theology, J. Deotis Roberts stands as one of the premier contemporary theologians to develop systematically the religious experience of black people as equals. The reputation of Roberts reached new dimensions when he coedited a *Quest for a Black Theology* with Father James J. Gardiner. This effort was a collaboration of five black Ph.D's and the Reverend Albert B. Cleage, Jr., who all spoke directly to the issues of "black power" and its effect upon the black church.

Roberts wrote a chapter entitled "Black Consciousness in Theological Perspective as a Position Statement on Black Theology."[3] He states:

> This essay was for me "a maiden voyage in an uncharted ocean," but it is a "beginning" without which no further voyage would have been possible. The reader will discover many of the right questions and few of the right answers. If it provokes constructive criticism, it will have served a worthy purpose. Its "end" is a beginning.[4]

The essence of black theology was being defined by the likes of James Cone, Joseph R. Washington, Vincent Harding, Walter Yates, and others. They had focused on the necessity of understanding God and Scripture from the black perspective. The Commission on Theology of the National Committee of Black Churchmen issued a statement on black theology. In this document black theology is defined:

> For us, Black Theology is the theology of black liberation. It seeks to plumb the black condition in the light of God's revelation in Jesus Christ, so that the black community can see the gospel is commensurate with the achievement of black humanity. Black Theology is a theology of "blackness." It is the affirmation of black humanity that emancipates black people from white racism thus providing authentic freedom for both white and black people. It affirms the humanity of white people in that it says "No" to the encroachment of white oppression.[5]

Roberts posited a need for a black theology because "the black man in the United States has undergone a certain kind of treatment which produced a unique type of spiritual experience both personal and collective—an experience which deserves theological analysis and interpretation."[6]

Through a need for enlightenment and encouragement, Roberts has been a leading proponent of raising the spiritual consciousness of black people. He believes that "the theological task is to determine what it means to be at once black and Christian in the United States."[7] Since prejudice is a prejudgment at sight, observes Roberts, then the black man is highly visible.[8] The refusal to accept black people unconditionally is an apparent sin in the eyes of the examiner. Blackness is a matter of fact, a truth of life, a given that cannot be ignored, escaped, or overcome. Therefore, in order to avoid "faddishness," according to the writer, "black theology must have deep roots in Christian history and biblical faith."[9]

The document maintained that "there have been no breakthroughs by black scholars in theology. We have not produced no [*sic*] Barths, Tillichs, or Bultmanns, nor have we any creeds of our own."[10] This issue became a growing concerning for most black scholars during this era who had not "moved out" beyond the traditional European concepts of Christian theology. Joseph R. Johnson adds:

> We knew our Barth, Brunner, Niebuhr, Bonhoeffer and Tillich, but we discovered that these white theologians had described the substance and had elucidated a contemporary faith for the white man. These white scholars knew nothing about the black experience, and to many of them this black experience was illegitimate and unauthentic.[11]

Roberts and others sought to discover "an affirmation of faith that reflects their peculiar experience in American life."[12] The urgency of the hour seemed to fall upon the need for a "unity in blackness." He captured the true need of black people when he said:

> Our "getting together" as black Christians is to discover who we are. When we know our identity, have gained our self-respect, and are fully confident as a people, we will be in a position to be reconciled to others as equals and not as subordinates.[13]

From this belief of reconciliation J. Deotis Roberts launched his acclaimed book, *Liberation and Reconciliation: A Black Theology.* His position is one of responsibility upon whites as well as blacks to overcome the barriers of racism. He writes:

> Reconciliation, between blacks and whites, is a two-way street. It depends as much upon what whites will do to makes conditions in race relations better as it does upon what blacks will not do. Reconciliation must be based upon a oneness in nature and grace between all people upon the principle of equity. Equality belongs to the time of integration.[14]

The black theologian has the ethical task of pointing to the true demands of the Christian faith. One has the freedom to decide how the black experience will be "understood in view of black consciousness, black pride, black self-determination—in a word, Black Power."[15] This is the dividing line for Roberts between the radical extremes of "black power religion" and the Christian mandates apparent in black theology. He concludes:

> Many blacks who are not Christians are associated with "the religion of Black Power." A Christian theologian is not an interpreter of the religion of Black Power. He, as a black theologian, may be the interpreter of Afro-American

Christianity. He may be in tune with the meaning of Black Power. But he is attempting to understand the Christian faith in the light of his people's experience. The present writer takes his stand within the Christian theological circle.[16]

Here one finds Roberts's parameters for engaging in the process of doing black theology.

A black theology that takes reconciliation seriously needs strong intercommunication between blacks and whites. "Black and white Christians have been living an inauthentic life in this country in the area of race"[17] declares Roberts. The authentic concept for blacks is a movement through the dynamics of liberation to those of reconciliation. Authentic life for whites is a persistent engagement through humaneness to reconciliation.

Without hesitation, Roberts postulates that "liberation and reconciliation are the two main poles of Black Theology."[18] Since many view liberation as a revolutionary concept, Roberts strongly dismisses the idea of violence and bloodshed. He feels that there can be a revolution in race relations with reconciliation, but this goal must be sought through a joint effort by black and white Christians. Roberts offers the following as a method of overcoming the tensions:

> What needs to be changed is not merely individual relationships; the entire social pattern of racism must be changed. It must be attacked on the individual and social fronts at the same time. It should not be necessary for a black man to be a superperson to be accepted as a person.[19]

The task of the black church and black theology is the reexamining and rethinking issues upon black religion as it relates to freedom. The critical factors involved in determining a "biblical viewpoint" for equality and freedom is a major concern for every black theologian. Therefore, "it is the task of Black Theology to attempt a constructive statement of what it really means to be a peculiar people, an elect nation—the chosen of God."[20]

Indeed, the black experience of suffering is related to the biblical message of redemptive suffering as seen in the life of Moses and the people of Israel. But Roberts is not content with leaving the liberation themes in the Old Testament. "Black Theology must, I believe, move beyond this to a more comprehensive understanding of suffering in Jewish History down to the present."[21] The black theologian must be faithful to the biblical revelation while at the same time reinterpreting the needs of the black experience.

Understanding the needs within the framework of black theology, Roberts wrote *A Black Political Theology* in 1974 which continued to espouse his "holistic" themes concerning the redemption of black people. He believed that "black theology must not be a simple reaction to white oppression, but a constructive 'reconception' of the Christian faith."[22]

Black theology is existential, but it also bears the stripes of political ramifications. It is a theology of survival, of meaning, of protest against injustice.[23] The mission of black theology is plain; according to Roberts, "it is the alternative to a mass exodus of blacks from the Christian faith in this time of black consciousness, power, and liberation."[24] A black political theology must seek a positive balance between the quest for meaning and protest against racism and injustice.

The relationship of human pain to an omnipotent God is expressed by Roberts as "a symbol through which man is united to God."[25] He further suggests: "The suffering of God for and with man, the unity of love and wrath in God, and the manner in which love overcomes wrath and conquers pain are highly suggestive for reflection in black theology."[26]

God is a God of power, and God as power is a necessary and crucial concept for a black political theology. A powerless people being crushed by the ruthless abuse of power in a racist society needs a Christian understanding of God as power.[27] It is Roberts's belief that "this God of power is a God who delivers the oppressed from all forms of human bondage."[28] Racism is not a natural evil, but a moral evil that threatens one's relationship with God and all humanity. Therefore, it is necessary for a black political theology to attack and deal with power structures within an immoral society.

The late Howard Thurman makes a vital theological point as it relates to the black experience in his book, *Jesus and the Disinherited,* when he states "that an oppressed people can behold the human face of God only through the Jesus who as a man lived the very life of God."[29] The quest for a black political theology, observes Roberts:

> . . . is not to be discovered in a gentle, meek Jesus, but a Christ above culture who is at the same time at work in culture and history for redemptive ends— setting free the whole person, mind, soul, and body. Jesus speaks to the need of blacks to be whole persons in a society in which they are "mere faces in the crowd."[30]

The Jesus of the disinherited liberates humanity. He brings a message of conversion from the God who creates, redeems, and judges all. The Christian experience must resonate with the Jesus of the oppressed who enters into the true realities of life for the sake of humanity.

The schism between the black tradition and its people during the late 1970s led Roberts to explicate the needs and values of the black family in relation to the black church in *The Roots of a Black Future.* Roberts states that "while the main purpose of the treatise is to open up important ecclesiological considerations for black theology, it will share the writer's growing vision since *A Black Political Theology.*"[31]

Through this effort Roberts makes a break from the frustrations of the 1970s and outlines an appropriate theology for the black church in its contemporary setting. From the African background traditions through slavery, emancipation, and reconstruction Roberts offers a historical overview of the black church and its development. He brings an ongoing appreciation upon the struggles and victories achieved by black people as "the family and people of God." Hence, Roberts affirms the essence of black life when he writes:

> Throughout the African/Afro-American tradition the family system has been central to understanding the church—its purpose and mission. At the same time religion has been the core of fulfilled family life.[32]

Roberts points to the need of the black church being able to provide a holistic ministry to black families as his central motif. He reaches towards the most common and natural sector of the black experience in order to relate social concerns and their limitations on personal freedom. "When churches are involved in social transformation, states Roberts, we must be concerned with an adequate theology for praxis."[33] His overall agenda provides a healthy perspective for the priestly and prophetic ministry of the black church tradition.

In 1980 Roberts penned *A Theological Commentary on the Sullivan Principles,* which offered a means of leading American companies against apartheid in South Africa. Reverend Leon Sullivan, pastor of the Zion Baptist Church in Philadelphia, is founder of Opportunities Industrialization Center or OIC.

The book *Christian Beliefs,* written in 1981, provided laypersons, students, and busy pastors a means of gaining insights into the basic tenets of the Christian faith concerning God, Jesus, and the Holy Spirit.

The most exhaustive and comprehensive work completed by Roberts to date is volume 12 of the Toronto Studies in Theology for the National Council for the Church and Social Action entitled *Black Theology Today: Liberation and Contextualization.* One could easily substantiate the anthology as "Robert's Rules of Black Theology."

It is here Roberts demonstrates the superiority of his many years of scholarly research and writing. From the opening part on hermeneutics and method to his conclusion on black ministry, he splendidly projects the issues of the black tradition with a spirit of theological genius. He also observes:

> A theologian, as theologian, must work with the conviction, I believe, out of a belief-system. Faith should have first place, therefore, but there should also be a quest for understanding concerning what one believes. This means that theological assertions should be carefully and critically examined by means of all our logical and critical powers.[34]

This collection of Roberts's theology offers any serious scholar opportunity to digest the essence of black theology from its roots to fulfillment in the life and breath of its readers.

Robert's latest work, *Black Theology in Dialogue,* constructs the bridge for other cultures and liberation theologies to embrace the significance of black theology. Several chapters originated from lectures presented both at home and abroad which reflects the author's ongoing commitment to the discipline. Although he makes the observation that "black theology has come of age and is a dialogue partner with theological developments worldwide,"[35] it is still moving through a period of transition.

One immediately discovers an emphasis reconstructed upon new perspectives for doing theology. He writes:

> The new situation for theology is iconoclastic—it is not continuous. The climate is post-Barthian, cross-cultural, and interdisciplinary. Now enter theologies, including feminine, black and Hispanic programs. No longer is theology

accepted as prepared and prepackaged and shipped by theologians of the North Atlantic community. The market for Western theology is diminishing as Third World theologians develop their own programs.[36]

This breath of fresh air has moved Roberts into an era of appreciation of the past along with an anticipation for the future. Black theology still identifies with its African roots and Afro-American traditions and will remain "contexualized in the life of a community with all of its social, economic, political, and cultural aspects."[37] But an unfinished agenda still remains. Roberts goes on to say:

> We need an interpretation of the faith that treats holistically this critical theme (structural evil) of all theology. Adequate attention has not yet been given to how collective evils increase the personal suffering of the victims of oppression and how faith in God enables these people to find meaning at a survival level.[38]

The solution is adequately stated when the author affirms that "whatever we are able to do to turn this situation around in a constructive direction will depend upon black people themselves and especially black churches."[39] The clarion call to reevaluate the present conditions in order to reeducate the masses depends upon teamwork, mutual encouragement, and support.

Thus, regarding Roberts and black theology, the time has arrived to appreciate their contributions to all humanity. "Once black theology reaches an in-depth self-understanding, it does contribute significantly to cross-cultural theological understanding."[40] Such an endeavor is within the focus of all who believe.

Evaluation

J. Deotis Roberts has pioneered new territories for the black experience and its cultural traditions in theological education. Being on the cutting edge of black theology has enabled him to maintain a relationship for over twenty years with the most thought-provoking views on Christianity since the Renaissance.

Roberts exemplifies the conviction that racism is sinful not just because it prohibits equality, but because it thwarts the Christian concept of the "Imago Dei." However, he moves beyond the revolutionary mentalities of James Cone, Albert Cleage, Joseph Washington, Vincent Harding, and others. The earnestness of Roberts is vividly expressed in that while others confess an indifference toward whites, "he cares."

Even though he refuses to side with the zealots of black theology, Roberts uncompromisingly deals with the issues of oppression and injustice. Roberts has made a profound and universal impact upon the hearts of people via his liberation motif for black theology. He sees the contexualization for liberation within the framework of reconciliation. For him, it is a both/and, not an either/or. His reconciliation motif is the key component for all Christians to unify and eliminate mistreatment upon the powerless of our society. The Bible explicitly admonishes the "new creation" to concern themselves with the ministry of reconciliation.

Bibliography

Books

A Black Political Theology. Philadelphia: Westminster Press, 1974.

Black Theology in Dialogue. Philadelphia: Westminster Press, 1987.

Black Theology Today. Lewiston: Edwin Mellen Press, 1983.

Christian Beliefs. Atlanta: John Colton and Associates, 1981.

Faith and Reason in Pascal, Bergson and James. Boston: Christopher Publishing House, 1962.

From Puritanism to Platonism in Seventeenth-Century England. The Hague: Martinus Nijhoff, 1968.

Liberation and Reconciliation: A Black Theology. Philadelphia: Pilgrim Press, 1971.

Quest for a Black Theology. With Fr. James Gardiner. Philadelphia: Pilgrim Press, 1971.

The Roots of a Black Future. Philadelphia: Westminster Press, 1980.

A Theological Commentary on the Sullivan Principles. Philadelphia: International Council on Equality of Opportunity, 1980.

Contributions to Other Books

"The American Negro's Contribution to Religious Thought." In *The Negro's Impact on Western Civilization*, edited by J. S. Roucek and T. Kierman. New York: Philosophical Library, 1970.

"The Forgiveness of Sins." In *Christian Theology: A Case Study Approach*, edited by Evans and Parker. New York: Harper, 1976.

"Hermeneutics: History and Providence." In *Hermeneutics and Horizons: The Shape of the Future*, edited by Frank Flinn. New York: Rose of Sharon Press, 1982.

"Liberation Theism." In *Black Theology II*, edited by C. E. Bruce and W. R. Jones. New York: Bucknell Press, 1978.

"The Mind of Howard Thurman." In *God and Human Freedom*. San Francisco: Friends Press, 1983.

"Models of Christian Discipleship: An African/Afro-American Perspective." In *Christ's Lordship and Religious Pluralism*, edited by G. H. Anderson and T. F. Strausky. Maryknoll: Orbis, 1981.

Articles

"Afro-Arab Islam and the Black Revolution." *The Journal of Religious Thought* 28:2 (1972).

"Black Theologians' Conference." *Liberation and Unity*, a Lenten Booklet (1979): 5-7.

"Bergson as a Metaphysical, Epistemological and Religious Thinker." *The Journal of Religious Thought* 20:2 (1963): 105-14.

"A Black Ecclessiology of Involvement." *The Journal of Religious Thought* 32:2 (1975): 36-46.

"Black Perspectives on Theological Education and Global Solidarity." US/Canadian Consultation on Global Solidarity in Theological Education. Geneva's Programme on Theological Education, WCC, 1981.

"Black Theological Education: Programming for Liberation." *The Christian Century,* Feb. 6, 1974, 117-18.

"Black Theologies and African Theologies." *Insight: A Journal of World Religions* 3:1; 3:3 (1978-9): 14-27.

"Black Theology and the Theological Revolution." *The Journal of Religious Thought.*

"Black Theology in the Making." *Review and Expositor* 70:3 (Summer 1973).

"Christian Liberation Ethics: The Black Experience." *Religion in Life* 48:2 (Summer 1979): 227-35.

"Contextual Theology." *The Christian Century,* Jan. 28, 1976, 64-68.

"Ecumenical Concerns Among National Baptists." In *Journal of Ecumenical Studies,* edited by W. J. Boney and G. A. Iglheart. 17:2 (Spring 1980): 38-48.

"Folklore and Religion: The Black Experience." *The Journal of Religious Thought* 27:2 (1970).

"Gospel Particularity and Global Solidarity." *Grapevine* New York: JSAC, 1982.

"The Impact of the Black Church: Sole Surviving Black Institution." *The Interdenominational Theological Journal* 6:2 (Spring 1979): 138-47.

"The Implications of Black Theology for Campus Ministry." *Toward Wholeness* 1:1 (Summer 1972).

"Kierkegaard on Truth and Subjectivity." *The Journal of Religious Thought* 18:1 (1961): 41-56.

"Meditations on Reconciliation." *The Upper Room Disciplines* (Oct. 1972).

"Moral Suasion as Nonviolent Direct Action: The Legacy of William Stuart Nelson." *The Journal of Religious Thought* 35:2 (Fall-Winter 1978-9): 29-43.

"New Power for the Black Church." *Journal of the Society for Commons Insights* 2:2 (Nov. 17, 1978): 63-77.

"The Priestly and Prophetic Aspects of Black Theology." *Journal of the Society for Common Insights* 1:2 (Nov. 10, 1977).

"Religio-Ethical Reflections Upon the Experiential Components of a Philosophy of Black Liberation." *The Journal of the Interdenominational Theological Center* 1:1 (Fall 1973): 80-94.

"Traditional African Religion and Christian Theology." *Studia Africana* 1:3 (Fall 1979): 206-18.

Notes

1. J. Deotis Roberts, *Faith and Reason in Pascal, Bergson and James* (Boston: Christopher Publishing, 1962), 20.

2. Ibid., 21. Also see, Blaise Pascal, *Pascal's Pensees,* trans. H. F. Stewart (New York: Pantheon Books, Inc., 1950).

3. James J. Gardiner and J. Deotis Roberts, *Quest for a Black Theology* (Philadelphia: Pilgrim Press, 1971), xi.

4. Ibid.

5. "Black Theology: A Statement of the National Committee of Black Churchmen," June 13, 1969.

6. Ibid., 62.

7. Ibid., 63.

8. Ibid., 64.

9. Ibid., 65.

10. Ibid., 66.

11. Ibid., 100.

12. Ibid., 66.

13. Ibid., 79.

14. J. Deotis Roberts, *Liberation and Reconciliation: A Black Theology* (Philadelphia: Westminster Press, 1971), 10.

15. Ibid., 14.

16. Ibid., 21.

17. Ibid., 24.

18. Ibid., 26. Also see Alvin Pitcher, "White Racism and Black Development," *Religious Education* (March-April 1970): 84; and Joseph R. Washington, Jr. *Black and White Power Subreption* (City Beacon Press, Inc., 1969), 116-68.

19. Roberts, *Liberation and Reconciliation,* 33.

20. Ibid., 50.

21. Ibid., 55.

22. J. Deotis Roberts, *A Black Political Theology* (Philadelphia: Westminster Press, 1974), 40.

23. Ibid., 41.

24. Ibid.

25. Ibid., 102.

26. Ibid., 103.

27. Ibid., 111.

28. Ibid.

29. Howard Thurman, *Jesus and the Disinherited* (Nashville: Abingdon-Cokesbury Press, 1949), 22.

30. Ibid., 119.

31. J. Deotis Roberts, *The Roots of a Black Future* (Philadelphia: Westminster Press, 1980), 8.

32. Ibid., 86.

33. Ibid., 114.

34. J. Deotis Roberts, *Black Theology Today: Liberation and Contextualization,* vol. 12 (New York: The Edwin Mellen Press, 1983), 42.

35. J. Deotis Roberts, *Black Theology in Dialogue* (Philadelphia: Westminster Press, 1987), 7.

36. Ibid., 12.
37. Ibid., 47.
38. Ibid., 115.
39. Ibid., 116.
40. Ibid., 120.

Millard J. Erickson

David S. Dockery

Biography

The evangelical movement in America during the past four decades has basically been a trans-denominational movement. For example, Billy Graham and Carl Henry are more quickly perceived as evangelicals than Baptists. The same can be said for many others, including some theologians treated in this volume, especially E. J. Carnell. Likewise, James Dobson is more of an evangelical than a Nazarene, Mark Noll more of an evangelical than a Presbyterian, and Ron Sider more of an evangelical than a Brethren. Some have even questioned if one can be both an evangelical and a loyal denominationalist. Millard Erickson, by contrast, has not only become the most outstanding writing theologian in the evangelical world, but he has remained a loyal Baptist. Erickson's heritage is firmly rooted in Baptist life. This heritage, inherited from his Swedish grandparents, combined with his early attraction to "new evangelical" theologians like Bernard Ramm, Carl F. H. Henry, and particularly E. J. Carnell, has resulted in a new model for Baptist and evangelical theologians.

Millard J. Erickson was born on June 24, 1932, the youngest of four children in Stanchfield, Minnesota, near Minneapolis.[1] His father had come to the United States with many relatives, including his grandparents, when he was only six months old. His mother was born in this country only months after her parents arrived from Sweden.

Erickson was raised on the family farm that produced just enough food to feed the family of six, but not much more. A windmill provided running water, but the family had to heat water on the kitchen stove for their weekly baths. Erickson studied by the light of a kerosene lamp until he was in high school, because not until then did the farm have electricity.

Erickson, a well-rounded person who also participated in football, basketball, baseball, and music programs, demonstrated superior academic abilities throughout his life. Beginning his education in a one-room school a mile-and-a-half walk away, the bright, young Erickson was double promoted in the second grade. He graduated valedictorian from Braham High School in 1949.

His family heritage is firmly rooted in the Baptist tradition. His grandfather and grandmother became active in a Baptist church quickly after settling in Minnesota. Later his grandfather served for five years as lay pastor of a Baptist church they organized in their house. In this church, as a young boy,

Millard J. Erickson (1932-   )

Photo courtesy of Bethel Theological Seminary

in an unemotional experience, Erickson responded to the gospel message and was converted.

Following high school, Erickson enrolled at Bethel College. He originally planned to attend the University of Minnesota, but through providential circumstances and his pastor's encouragement, he decided to attend a Christian college. That summer his pastor received a concussion while participating in a church softball game. Because of the pastor's inability to preach, Millard filled the pulpit on a Wednesday evening. The pastor was so impressed that he encouraged Erickson to consider a commitment to full-time vocational Christian service. "I wondered at the time," Erickson relates, "if he had recovered from the blow on his head. But God planted the idea in my mind, and I could not ignore it."[2] During his initial year at Bethel College, following an important chapel message, Erickson knew God was calling him to preach. Though he was shy and afraid to speak in public, Erickson privately responded later that weekend. That Saturday he told the Lord that he would serve Him as a minister, but that God would have to supply what was lacking.

Following his sophomore year at Bethel, he transferred to the University of Minnesota in order to gain a wider exposure to secular thought. At Minnesota, he majored in philosophy and minored in psychology and sociology. Erickson graduated Phi Beta Kappa in 1953. He then returned to the Bethel campus where he enrolled in Bethel Seminary before transferring to Northern Baptist Theological Seminary in Chicago. While at Bethel Seminary, he met Virginia Nepstad, who was then a student at Bethel College. They were married on August 20, 1955. The Ericksons have been blessed with three daughters: Kathryn Sue, born February 23, 1959; Sandra Lynne, born May 1, 1962; and Sharon Ruth, born September 20, 1964.

Having encountered Bernard Ramm at Bethel Seminary, Erickson became attracted to the works of the new evangelical theologians, Carl Henry, E. J. Carnell, and others during this time. Erickson credits Carnell's works for shaping his theology and approach to Christian apologetics during this significant formative period in his life. His interest in these new evangelical theologians would continue to develop so as eventually to become the subject of his Ph.D. dissertation, as well as his first major publication.

Following graduation from Northern, Erickson was invited to become pastor of the Fairfield Avenue Baptist Church, a multiracial congregation in Chicago. On March 21, 1957, he was ordained to the ministry by this church. Erickson's lifelong desire to make theology both biblical and relevant to contemporary forms of thinking and life experience grew out of this important pastoral experience. Here he was challenged to relate the Christian message both to the urban intellectual and the blue collar worker. Erickson learned much from the correlation methodology of Paul Tillich while seeking to develop his own understanding of the theological task.

On completing his studies at Northern in 1956, he enrolled in a master's degree program in philosophy at the University of Chicago, graduating in 1958. Determining that he was more interested in theology than philosophy,

Erickson decided not to pursue doctoral studies at the University of Chicago. Instead, he enrolled in a joint Ph.D. program offered by Garrett Theological Seminary and Northwestern University under the supervision of William Hordern.

After completing his course work at Northwestern, Millard and Virginia, with their first child Kathryn, returned to Minneapolis where he accepted the pastorate of the Olivet Baptist Church. There he completed examinations for the Ph.D. and in 1963 finished writing his dissertation on the theology of Henry, Ramm, and Carnell. Though not without a genuine struggle and some misgivings about leaving the pastorate and a church he loved, Erickson, in 1964, accepted a position at Wheaton College as Assistant Professor of Bible and Apologetics. He was elected to the Department Chair in 1967.

Erickson revised his dissertation and published it under the title, *The New Evangelical Theology* (Westwood, NJ: Fleming H. Revell, 1968). In 1969 he accepted a position teaching theology at Bethel Seminary where he continues to serve as Executive Vice-President and Dean, as well as Professor of Theology. In addition to numerous articles, book chapters, and reviews, Erickson has authored or edited ten books including the impressive three volume *Christian Theology* (Grand Rapids: Baker, 1983-1985), which has become the standard systematic theology text in many Baptist and Evangelical seminaries.

Erickson also edited a trilogy of *Readings in Christian Theology* (Grand Rapids: Baker, 1973-1979) which serve as parallel readings in a host of theology classes. In 1974 he published *Relativism in Contemporary Christian Ethics* (Grand Rapids: Baker). This was followed by *Contemporary Options in Eschatology: A Study of the Millennium* (Grand Rapids: Baker, 1977). In addition to his *Concise Dictionary of Christian Theology* (Grand Rapids: Baker, 1986), he has written two popular works on soteriology: *Salvation: God's Amazing Plan* (Wheaton: Victor, 1978) and *Responsive Faith* (Arlington Heights, IL: Harvest, 1987). It is, however, his three volume theology that has placed him among the leading theologians of the day.

Volume one is dedicated to his first theology teacher, Bernard Ramm. The second volume is dedicated to his doctoral supervisor, William Hordern. Volume three is dedicated to his post-doctoral mentor, the eminent German theologian, Wolfhart Pannenberg of the University of Munich, with whom Erickson spent a sabbatical year in 1976. The *Christian Theology* volumes developed out of what Erickson perceived to be an intense need for an up-to-date textbook in systematic theology. The project began June 1, 1982, when he started writing a chapter per week. Volume one was completed by the end of November. The rough draft of volume two was completed over the next ten weeks while teaching the subject matter during the winter quarter. Volume three was soon begun and brought to completion during his sabbatical that year. The following year was used to revise volumes two and three. Erickson estimates that in addition to his 18 years of teaching, he invested over 4,000 hours in what his family calls "the book."

Erickson's theological interests are many, as evidenced not only by his previous work, but by his current projects focusing on third-world theology, process theology, black theology, and contemporary linguistic analysis. Yet, beyond this, he is primarily a churchman. He continues to serve interim pastorates, having served forty churches in the past twenty-five years. He is in demand as a speaker, and serves on important denominational committees and boards. For almost two decades, Erickson has been active in Baptist work outside of his own denomination, serving on positions with the Baptist World Alliance and lecturing at various Baptist seminaries.

This kind of commitment has made Millard Erickson one of the most respected Baptist and evangelical theologians of our time. His theological works will no doubt be used to shape the thought and life of the next generation of Baptist and evangelical church leaders.

Exposition

Shapers of Erickson's Theology

As indicated in the previous section, Erickson's theological thought and method has been shaped by his Baptist beliefs and practice. Beyond that, he has been influenced by commitment to the church, his apologetic orientation adopted from Ramm and Carnell, and his desire to relate theology to contemporary forms of thinking, so as to be both biblical and relevant. Erickson, however, is not a disciple, in the technical sense, of any particular theologian or theological school. His two years as a student at the University of Minnesota forced him to interact with contemporary philosophical currents. By his own admission, it was the writings of E. J. Carnell, particularly *An Introduction to Christian Apologetics* (Grand Rapids: Eerdmans, 1948) that shaped the apologetic orientation of his theology.[3] It is important to note that Carnell, Ramm, and Henry, the formative thinkers of the new evangelical theology, were all Baptists, who were, however, evangelicals first and Baptists second. Erickson's Baptist heritage and commitments have both directly and indirectly taken a higher priority in his life and in shaping his theology.[4]

Yet, while acknowledging his debt to Baptist theologians like John Gill, E. Y. Mullins, and particularly A. H. Strong, it cannot be said that Erickson's theology is necessarily consciously and distinctively Baptist. Erickson claims that his theology is intended to be broad in hopes of influencing an audience beyond the world of Baptists. His work is Baptist in its shape in the sense that it grows out of his church experience and commitments.[5] In this, he is not unlike theological giants Karl Barth and Paul Tillich, who were not Baptists, but their understanding of the theological task was largely influenced by their pastoral arenas. Erickson claims that Baptists, unlike Lutherans, who have Martin Luther; Presbyterians, who have John Calvin; and Methodists, who have John Wesley, have "no one shining light" and in some sense do theology from "an ideological ghetto."[6] Erickson believes that a theology emphasizing biblical themes with a corresponding commitment to the church will produce a theology emphasizing Baptist themes.[7]

Erickson's theology has also been shaped by his mentors. From Hordern, he received a concern for clarity of thought, as well as a writing style worthy of emulation. From Pannenberg, he learned to grapple fairly with differing positions. Erickson has only the highest praise for his teachers and claims that it is a demanding exercise to interact with Pannenberg, who "is in a league by himself."[8] But from the beginning, his work has been largely shaped by the influences of the new evangelicals.

In our exposition we shall note the context out of which Erickson's theology has developed. We shall focus on Erickson's major contributions to Baptist and evangelical theology which are his concern for theological method and his articulation of the doctrine of scripture. Other important matters will be surveyed followed by a brief analysis and evaluation.

Erickson's Context

Out of the bitter Fundamentalist-Modernist controversy of the twentieth century emerged a theological movement known as the new evangelicalism.[9] With roots in the Reformation, evangelicalism reached its zenith in the nineteenth century. In the early-twentieth century, however, evangelicalism went into a temporary eclipse. The success of the previous century resulted in a material prosperity, a loyalty to the nation that was confused with Christian commitment, and an over-emphasis on individualism that hampered the advancement of evangelicalism. The flood of new ideas such as Darwinian evolution, German higher criticism, Freudian psychology, Marxist socialism, and an overarching naturalism, undermined confidence in the truthfulness of the Bible and the reality of the supernatural. These ideological changes, resulting in the Modernist-Fundamentalist controversies, coupled with the blood baths of two World Wars, brought new challenges as well as new opportunities. Out of this void developed the new evangelicism, a term coined by Carl Henry and popularized by Harold J. Ockenga in 1947.[10]

In his expert analysis, Erickson observed that the new evangelical theology movement took issue with the older fundamentalism.[11] The new evangelicalism created a third stream in American Protestantism, running midway between the simplistic fundamentalism and the sophisticated faith espoused by the majority of the nation's best known theologians and denominational leaders. The new evangelical theologians argued that fundamentalism was wrong-headed in its suspicion of all who did not articulate every thought or practice Christianity exactly as the fundamentalists did. Also, it had an invalid strategy that promoted a strict separatism seeking to produce a totally pure church, both locally and denominationally. Lastly, fundamentalism had produced empty results since it had not turned back the tide of liberalism, had not impacted the thought worlds of the day, and had not dealt with the social problems of its time.[12] E. J. Carnell insisted that fundamentalism was orthodoxy gone cultic because its convictions were not linked with the historic creeds of the church, being more of a mentality than a movement.[13] Carl Henry contended that fundamentalists did not present Christianity as an overarching world view but concentrated instead on only part of the message. The fundamentalists were too other worldly, anti-intellectual and unwilling to bring their faith to bear upon culture and social life.[14]

The new movement emphasized several important themes such as social ethics, apologetical theology, evangelism, education, and Christian unity. Erickson noted that the movement sought unity on the basis of biblical doctrine. One of the goals of the movement was to restate the faith in a way which would command intellectual respect and heal the schism between the theological right and the left, at least to point to where meaningful theologue dialogue could be pursued.[15] These themes and emphases have characterized Erickson's own theological pilgrimage as evidenced in *Christian Theology*. These evangelical themes and emphases can be summarized as:

> A set of concerns and attitudes related to the needs of the present day, in continuity with vital orthodoxy of the past, and generally distinguishable from later fundamentalism, coupled with an orthodox Christology and an orthodox view of the scriptures.[16]

The Definition and Method of Theology

Erickson suggests that the study or science of God is a good preliminary or basic definition of theology.[17] But beyond that, it can be said that theology is "that discipline which strives to give a coherent statement of the doctrines of the Christian faith, based primarily upon the Scriptures, placed in the context of culture in general, worded in a contemporary idiom, and related to issues of life."[18] Theology then is biblical, systematic, related to the issues of general culture and learning, contemporary, and practical.

One of Erickson's outstanding contributions to the evangelical and Baptist worlds is his development of theological method. His process of doing theology is thoroughly grounded in Scripture, but it moves far beyond a simple "proof-texting" approach to theology. Also, while being thoroughly biblical, his theology is contextually relevant. His methodology attempts to bridge the gap between the then and now, a concern that developed in his pastoral days in Chicago.

Erickson acknowledges that there is a sense in which theology is an art as well as a science so that it cannot follow a rigid structure. Yet procedures can be suggested. For Erickson, biblical theology is developed before systematic theology, so that the sequence is exegesis—biblical theology—systematic theology[19] Erickson outlines nine steps in the process of doing theology.

1. *Collection of Biblical Materials*. This initial step involves not only the gathering of all the relevant biblical passages on the doctrine being investigated, but also an awareness of one's own presuppositions in interpreting these materials. Beyond this, Erickson notes the importance of knowing the presuppositions of the writers of reference books that might be used. Likewise, narrative texts as well as the didactic passages of scripture should be used.

2. *Unification of the Biblical Materials*. This means taking into account the whole of scripture when trying to find a common theme. Forced harmonizations should be avoided.

3. *Analysis of the Meaning of Biblical Teachings*. After attempting to find

the common teaching on a subject, these texts must be analyzed by asking, "What is really meant by this?" The theologian must seek to put the meaning of the Bible into clear and understandable language.

4. *Examination of Historical Treatments.* A recognition that we are not the first generation to examine a particular teaching will provide insight beyond our own viewpoint. It reminds us that we stand on the shoulders of those who have gone before us and helps us to ask the right questions of the text. Perhaps as helpful as anything, this step, suggests Erickson, calls for a measure of humility in presenting our conclusions.

5. *Identification of the Essence of the Doctrine.* Many biblical truths are bound up within the culture and context in which they are communicated. This does not mean dismissing the "cultural baggage." It does mean, for example, separating what Paul said to the Philippians as first-century Christians living in Philippi from what he said to them as Christians. Similarly, the sacrificial system in Leviticus is not the essence of the doctrine of the atonement. What is the essence is the concept that there must be vicarious sacrifice for the sins of humankind.

6. *Illumination from Sources Beyond the Bible.* The point of this step is the recognition that God has revealed Himself through general revelation as well as through special revelation. The Bible is the primary source for Christian theology, but it is not the only source. Erickson, consistent with his new evangelical heritage, suggests that experience and the sciences may add clarity where the Bible sheds little or no light. It is important to recognize that general (universal) revelation and special (particular) revelation are ultimately in harmony when both are properly interpreted.

7. *Contemporary Expression of the Doctrine.* The theologian must be mindful not only of the biblical message but also the contemporary context or situation in which the doctrine is being communicated. Both horizons must be observed. Yet, any theology which is designed only to meet the moods or issues of a particular time will quickly find itself outdated. Truths that can remain faithful to the biblical message and can communicate across different contexts, cultures, or traditions will be enduring.

8. *Development of a Central Interpretive Motif.* Like all coherent theologians, Erickson maintains that a particular theme or perspective should be formulated so that the various doctrines can be seen in relationship with one another. Yet, he warns that a central motif should never be used where it is not relevant, nor should eisegesis be used to make biblical teaching fit a particular system.

9. *Stratification of the Topics.* The final step in Erickson's method is an attempt to determine what issues are major topics and what issues are subtopics. The doctrine of the second coming is a major topic, while the question of the timing of the rapture is less important and certainly less emphasized in Scripture. An outline should then be made to help see the relationship of the importance of one teaching to another and to arrange the topics on the basis of their relative importance.[20]

Erickson develops his theology around the central motiff of the "magnificence of God."[21] This motif provides a sense of coherence to his system. Magnificence is understood as encompassing what has traditionally been associated with the expression "the glory of God," but without the connotation of self centeredness sometimes carried by that expression.

Erickson is not unaware of the problems involved in contextualizing the theological message, in developing a central motif, or communicating these matters through religious language. While wrestling with these matters, he opts for restating the classical themes of systematic theology without becoming overly creative so as not to overstep biblical revelation. He understands the difference between doctrine and theology and recognizes the need of permanence. His method lends healthy balance to his systematic approach.

Revelation

Consistent with his new evangelical heritage, Erickson presents God's universal and particular revelation in complete harmony with one another. Consequently, there can never be any conflict between the Bible, properly interpreted, and natural knowledge, correctly construed. If all the data were available, Erickson maintains a perfect harmony would emerge. This implies that it is possible to exhibit the truthfulness of the biblical view by appealing to evidence drawn from the created space-time universe.[22]

This conception of revelation also produces a positive attitude toward culture, thus his theology is culture-affirming rather than culture-rejecting. There is therefore a possibility of some knowledge of divine truth outside of special revelation. Erickson contends that God's universal or general revelation should be considered a supplement to, not a substitute for, special revelation.[23]

Because of God's universal revelation, Erickson believes God is just in condemning those who have never heard the gospel in the full and formal sense. He amplifies:

> No one is completely without opportunity. All have known God; if they have not effectually perceived him, it is because they have suppressed the truth. Thus all are responsible. This increases the motivation of missionary endeavor, for no one is innocent. All need to believe in God's offer of grace, and the message needs to be taken to them.[24]

Erickson distinguishes between God's universal and particular revelation. On the one hand, universal revelation "is God's communication of himself to all persons at all times and in all places.[25] On the other hand, God's particular revelation involves "God's manifestation of himself to particular persons at definite times and places, enabling those persons to enter into a redemptive relationship with him."[26] Particular revelation is available now only by consultation of sacred scripture. Universal revelation is inferior to special revelation, both in the clarity of the treatment and the range of subjects considered. The insufficiency of the universal revelation requires special revelation. Yet, because special revelation builds upon the universal, special revelation requires universal revelation as well.[27] Not only does Erickson propose the complementary nature of special and general revelation, but he also opts for a "both/and" answer to the question of personal or propositional revelation.[28]

Scripture

Since revelation includes propositional truths, then it is of such a nature that it can be preserved, written down, or inscripturated. Revelation is God's communication to humankind of the truth that they need to know in order to relate properly to God. Since God does not repeat His revelation for each person, there has to be some way to preserve it. Erickson differentiates between revelation and inspiration noting that revelation is the communication of divine truth from God to humanity, inspiration relates more to the relaying of that truth from the first recipients of it to other persons, whether then or later. "Thus, revelation might be thought of as a vertical action, and inspiration as a horizontal matter."[29]

Erickson wrestles with the issues involved in formulating a theory of inspiration, even raising the question of the legitimacy of doing so. He interacts with various theories and methods of formulating a theory of inspiration and concludes that it is possible to formulate a model of inspiration. To do so, he suggests that the church should construct its view of the inspiration of the Bible by emphasizing the teachings of the Bible regarding its own inspiration, while giving an important but secondary place to the phenomena of Scripture.[30]

Erickson maintains that inspiration involved God's directing the thoughts of the writers, so that they were precisely the thoughts that He wished expressed. At times these thoughts were quite specific; while at other times they were more general. When they were more general, God wanted that particular degree of specificity recorded, and no more. He contends that this specificity can extend to the choice of words, but does not necessarily become dictation.[31]

Erickson concludes God's Word is inspired, thus preserving God's special revelation. Inspiration is God's way of assuring that His Word will not be lost, but rather will be conveyed to His people in all ages. The result of inspiration assures God's people that the Bible is truthful, trustworthy, and reliable.[32] Likewise, the Bible has the right to command belief or action, but this should not be equated with a forced compliance. The Bible is authoritative because it is the dependable Word of God.[33]

The dependability of God's Word assures that the Bible is fully truthful in all its teaching. The theological term for this is inerrancy. Erickson defines inerrancy as follows: "The Bible, when correctly interpreted in light of the level to which culture and the means of communication had developed at the time it was written, and in view of the purposes for which it was given, is fully truthful in all that it affirms."[34] Erickson contends that inerrancy, while not directly taught in scripture, is the proper implication of the Bible's own teaching about itself. He claims that while inerrancy can be misunderstood, it must be maintained and argues for its importance theologically, historically, and epistemologically.[35]

Carefully, he avoids building his case on the "domino theory." Thus, he does not argue that one error would invalidate all other biblical teachings. Yet, he points out that if there are errors in Scripture, it would surely make it more difficult to show why we should believe those things taught therein. His view seeks to include and account for the pheonomenological language of scripture. Erickson suggests that the Christian would be unwise to give up the affirmation: "Whatever the Bible teaches is true."

God, Creation, and Providence

Erickson approaches the doctrine of God from the perspectives of "what God is like"[36] and "what God does."[37] These discussions are investigated from an orthodox Trinitarian perspective. He chooses God's majesty as the central focus when dealing with the attributes of God. He suggests that this, rather than glory, is a more appropriate way of describing God's greatness. After skillfully evaluating the various ways of dealing with God's attributes, he opts for the categories of greatness and goodness."[38] His conclusions on these matters are in line with classical formulations, though they are nuanced to account for the biblical data and the challenges of process theology.[39]

Erickson deals with "God's Plan" (traditionally defined as decrees) from a moderately Calvinistic model. He valiantly seeks to correlate human freedom and sovereignty.[40] This balance and consistency is generally reflected in his doctrine of salvation as well.

In line with Ramm and Carnell, *Christian Theology,* in volumes one and two, adopts a progressive creationist position.[41] Erickson believes that the Hebrew word for "day" (yōm) can mean a long period of time. Rejecting the "flood theory" on the one hand and "macro evolutionism" on the other, Erickson still strongly defends the historicity of the biblical Adam and Eve.[42]

Humanity and Sin

Similar to both Luther and Calvin, Erickson primarily opts for a structural and substantive understanding of the image of God, including relational and functional aspects,[43] while tentatively suggesting a "conditional unity" as the best way to describe the constitutional nature of humankind.[44]

In some of his most creative work, he devotes a chapter to the universality of humanity, extending to all races, both sexes, all economic classes, all ages, as well as to the unborn and unmarried.[45] Additionally, he fully treats the social dimensions of sin.[46]

Erickson defines sin as "any lack of conformity, active or passive to the moral law."[47] Sin is seen in terms of its negative effects on the sinner and the sinner's relation to others, in addition to the separation of one's relationship with God. The essence of sin is a failure to let God be God.[48] Regarding the transmission of sin, he opts for a conditional imputation calibrated according to the level of responsibility and maturity in one's life. He says that "human beings, while inheriting both a corrupted nature and guilt, first become guilty when they accept or approve of their corrupted nature."[49]

Perhaps motivated by his Baptist and pietistic concerns, he maintains that salvation requires a conscious and voluntary decision on our part. While suggesting that infants and children begin life with the corrupted nature and guilt that are the consequences of sin, he, nevertheless, says that our Lord does not regard children as basically sinful and guilty. Thus the act that ends childish innocence is every bit as voluntary as the act of accepting the offer of salvation at the age of moral responsibility.[50]

Christ, the Spirit, and Salvation

His Christology reflects a thorough-going commitment to Chalcedon with attempts to translate the meaning of Chalcedon for contemporary hearers.[51] Erickson, while obviously aware of issues surrounding the contemporary and critical discussion, depends on the treatment of Jesus' self consciousness in John's gospel for developing his Christology.[52] The Christological titles are thoughtfully treated, but their significance is not fully developed.

The work of Christ is treated around the themes of "revealer," "reconciler," and "ruler."[53] The various models of the atonement receive comprehensive attention, but primacy is given to the penal substitution model. Following his moderate Calvinism, he rejects particular redemption in favor of a universal atonement with limited efficacy. The decision accounts for a larger segment of the biblical witness with less distortion than does the theory of particular redemption.[54] Among the most impressive of the biblical statements, for Erickson, in this regard is 1 Timothy 4:10, which affirms that the living God "is the Savior of all people, especially of those who believe."[55] Apparently the Savior has done something for all persons, though it is less in degree than what He has done for those who believe.[56]

In one of his more controversial conclusions, Erickson suggests that Jesus' resurrected body did not undergo complete transformation until the ascension.[57] The point of this statement is not to detract from the resurrection, but somehow to give significance to the ascension. In a cautious and hypothetical manner, Erickson attempts to deal with the biblical teaching (Luke 24; John 20; 1 Corinthians 15) in a way so that the initial resurrection is somehow distinct from the glorified body of the ascended and exalted Lord.[58] This results in considering the forty days as a time similar to a resuscitation, like that of Lazarus. The eating with the disciples may have been out of a need to eat rather than a concession while with them. It must be remembered that Erickson suggests this only as a hypothesis and he cautiously concludes:

> But just as the virgin birth should not be thought of as essentially a biological matter, neither should the resurrection be conceived of as primarily a physical fact. It was the triumph of Jesus over sin and death and all of the attendant ramifications. It was the fundamental step in his exaltation—he was freed from the curse brought on him by his voluntary bearing of the sin of the entire human race.[59]

The work of Christ applied by the Spirit to the believer ultimately brings about the restoration of a proper relationship with God. For Erickson, the Spirit of God initiates the Christian life through regeneration and conversion and continues with empowering, illuminating, teaching, sanctifying, and the granting of spiritual gifts.[60] His conception of salvation follows a moderate Calvinistic *ordo salutis*. Yet, he goes against his usual Calvinistic tendencies opting for the temporal priority of conversion to regeneration.[61]

Church and Eschatology

Concerning the organization of the church, Erickson clearly favors congregational polity but with care "since the evidence from the New Testament is inconclusive."[62]

His baptistic commitments are quite obvious in his discussion of the church. He sees baptism as a token, an outward testimony or symbol of the inward change which has been effected in the believer.[63] Regarding the mode of baptism, immersion is affirmed, though without dogmatism, since he demonstrates openness to other modes.[64] The Lord's Supper is a time of relationship and communion with Christ. In the celebration, the Christian community comes with confidence to meet the risen Christ, for Christ has promised to meet with His people. The sacrament should be thought of as "not so much in terms of Christ's presence as in terms of his promise and the potential for a closer relationship with him."[65]

While emphasizing the local church, Erickson strongly affirms the universal church of God. Beyond this, he recognizes the church as only one manifestation of the Kingdom. He argues passionately for the unity of the church and rejects fundamentalists' emphasis regarding separation that tends to lead to division.[66]

Erickson's eschatology follows the line of a classical historic premillennialism.[67] An awareness of the apocalyptic elements in the biblical teaching concerning heaven and hell, and other areas of eschatology, including the messianic banquet of Revelation 19, is demonstrated. Yet, in no way does he hint at any form of universalism.[68]

Evaluation

Strengths

Millard Erickson's contribution to the theological enterprise is a significant milestone in Baptist and Evangelical thought. His careful work evidences diligent research, critical argumentation and a spiritually sensitive understanding of the biblical materials. His theology is of immense importance and his coherent and centralizing motif pervades the entire work.[69]

Erickson's theology is faithful to his Baptist and evangelical heritage. It is both orthodox and contemporary, yet it is neither faddist nor overly innovative. Generally, at every major issue, Erickson's theological construction can be considered biblical and classical.[70] The true strength of his work is the overall concern for the church and his doxological tone.[71]

His most noticeable strengths are his balanced theological method, his carefully nuanced view of Scripture, and his concern to relate orthodoxy to the contemporary issues of life. Also, he demonstrates the importance of coherence in systematic theology, the virtue of theological humility, and the tension between the timeless and time bound bibilical themes.[72]

He continually reflects an openness to various options and evidences a broad understanding of issues in contemporary theology.[73] While his theology is obviously born in a teaching context, it characteristically is irenic, fresh, and pastoral.[74]

Weaknesses

Yet, while there is so much to admire in Erickson's work, there are weaknesses that should be noted. For example, his doctrine of Scripture is a model for evangelicals and Baptists,[75] but there is no discussion of canonicity nor the relationship of canon to inspiration, authority, or hermeneutics.

His doctrine of God, which follows the line of Henry, Ramm, and Carnell, tends to be rationalistic, though not without clarification. He seems to reject paradox in theological thinking and discounts anthropomorphisms in constructing a doctrine of God. His moderate Calvinism, which influences his doctrine of God, has nevertheless been unsatisfying to those with more Arminian tendencies,[76] as well as more strict Calvinists.[77]

Erickson's classical Christology probably will not be satisfying to critical scholars because of its overdependence on a traditional reading of John's Gospel. His hypothesis concerning the resurrection and ascension is shaky at best and has not found a welcomed response among evangelical or critical scholars.

His Baptist concerns are evident at many places, including his doctrine of salvation and his emphasis on the church. Yet his openness regarding the mode of baptism might seem inconsistent to some Baptists, though the issue is being intensely debated in Baptist World Alliance circles. Similarly, to be faithful to his approach to salvation, it would be better not to construct a rigid sequence of events in the development of his *ordo salutis.*[78]

His emphasis on the doctrine of the church is not, however, well related to his eschatology, thus creating a lack of a theology of history. His view of the church seems to be emphasized to the exclusion of the kingdom of God.[79] There is a need to develop the theme of the kingdom of God and the consummation of God's work in history in the new heavens and new earth.[80]

Erickson's major contributions as we have noted are the creative construction of his theological methodology and his doctrine of revelation.[81] Overall, his theology is biblical, relevant, and practical. He demonstrates an openness to contemporary trends while being fully aware of the centuries of theologizing in the Christian church. He has managed to interact meaningfully with modern theological developments, while remaining faithful to his Baptist and evangelical heritage. The strengths of his work are many and the weaknesses are few. There is room for improvement in Erickson's theology, but to this date there is no finer evangelical theological work available. His work is more encompassing than Donald Bloesch and less intimidating than

Carl Henry, less daring than Hendrikus Berkhof and much less defensive than traditional evangelical theologies such as Louis Berkhof, J. Oliver Buswell, L. S. Chafer, and Charles Hodge. His theology is far more readable than A. H. Strong or Helmut Thielicke, and more engaging than Bruce Demarest and Gordon Lewis. The work is certainly faithful to Baptist emphasis in theology; yet it demonstrates a greater comprehensiveness than W. T. Conner, E. Y. Mullins, Dale Moody, or Morris Ashcraft. His work is a first rate achievement. While a Baptist and evangelical theology can probably be done better than Erickson has done it, it must be said that to-date, no one has done so.

Bibliography

Works by Erickson
Books
Christian Theology, three volumes (Grand Rapids: Baker Book House, 1983, 1984, 1985). One volume edition, 1986.

Concise Dictionary of Christian Theology (Grand Rapids: Baker Book House, 1986).

Contemporary Options in Eschatology—A Study of the Millennium (Grand Rapids: Baker Book House, 1977).

Ed. *The Living God, Readings in Christian Theology* (Grand Rapids: Baker Book House, 1973).

Ed. *Man's Need and God's Gift, Readings in Christian Theology* (Grand Rapids: Baker Book House, 1976).

The New Evangelical Theology (Westwood, N.J.: Fleming H. Revell Co., 1968 and London: Marshall, Morgan and Scott, 1969).

Ed. *The New Life, Readings in Christian Theology* (Grand Rapids: Baker Book House, 1979).

Relativism in Contemporary Christian Ethics (Grand Rapids: Baker Book House, 1974).

Responsive Faith (Arlington Heights, IL: Harvest Publications, 1987).

Salvation: God's Amazing Plan (Wheaton, IL: Victor Books, 1978).

Journal and Periodical Articles and Book Chapters
"Apologetics Today: Its Task and Shape," *Bethel Seminary Journal* 18 (Autumn 1969): 1-13.

"Authority of the Bible—Historical Basis," *Old Drums to March By* (St. Paul, MN: Bethel College and Seminary, 1971), 6-14.

"The Bible, Science and Creation—How to Interpret the Evidence," *The Standard,* July 15, 1968, 23-24.

"Biblical Inerrancy: The Last Twenty-Five Years," *Journal of the Evangelical Theological Society* 25 (December, 1982): 387-94.

"Christology from Above and Christology from Below: A Study in Contrasting Methodologies," *Perspectives on Evangelical Theology,* ed. Kenneth S. Kantzer and Stanley N. Gundry (Grand Rapids: Baker Book House, 1979), 43-55.

"The Church and Stable Motion," *Bethel Seminary Journal* 20 (Spring 1972): 9-17.

"Doctrine, Preaching, and the Preacher," *Proclaim the Good News: Essays in Honor of Gordon G. Johnson,* ed. Norris Magnuson (Arlington Heights, IL: Harvest Press, 1986), 43-57.

With Ines E. Bowers. Euthanasia and Christian Ethics," *Journal of the Evangelical Theological Society* 19 (Winter 1976): 15-24.

"The Holy Spirit and the Church Today," *The Standard,* May 1, 1975, 14-15.

"Hope for Those Who Haven't Heard? Yes, but . . . ," *Evangelical Missions Quarterly* 11 (April 1975): 122-26.

"How Do You Deal With Doubt?" *The Standard,* 77 July 1987, 21-23.

"Human Engineering and Christian Ethical Values," *Journal of the American Scientific Affiliation* 30 (March 1978).

"Immanence, Transcendence, and the Doctrine of Scripture," *The Living and Active Word of God,* ed. Morris Inch and Ronald Youngblood (Winona Lake, IN: Eisenbrauns, 1983), 193-205.

"Implications of Biblical Inerrancy for the Christian Mission," *The Proceedings of the Conference on Biblical Inerrancy 1987* (Nashville: Broadman Press, 1987), 223-36.

"Is Tongues-Speaking for Today?" *The Standard,* October 15, 1973, 18-19; November 1, 1973, 20-21.

"Narrative Theology: Translation or Transformation?" *Festscrift: A Tribute to William Hordern,* ed. Walter Freitag (Saskatoon: University of Saskatchewan Press, 1985), 29-39.

"The New Birth Today," *Christianity Today,* August 16, 1974, 8-10.

"A New Look at Various Aspects of Inspiration," *Bethel Seminary Journal* 15 (Autumn 1966): 16-26.

"Pannenberg's Use of History as a Solution to the Religious Language Problem," *Journal of the Evangelical Theological Society* 17 (Spring 1974): 99-105.

"The Potential of Apologetics" (two parts), *Christianity Today,* July 17, 1970, 6-8; July 31, 1970, 13-15.

"Presuppositions of Non-Evangelical Hermeneutics," *Hermeneutics, Inerrancy, and the Bible,* ed. Earl Radmacher and Robert D. Preus (Grand Rapids: Zondervan, 1984), 591-612.

"Principles, Permanence, and Future Divine Judgment: A Case Study in Theological Method," *Journal of the Evangelical Theological Society* 28 (September 1985): 317-25.

"Problem Areas Related to Biblical Inerrancy," *The Proceedings of the Conference on Biblical Inerrancy 1987* (Nashville: Broadman Press, 1987), 175-89.

"The Sting Is Gone," *The Standard,* March 23, 1970, 4-5.

"This Talk About the Millennium and the Tribulation—What's It All About?" *The Standard,* September 1, 1974, 16-17.

"Why I Believe in Jesus Christ," *The Standard.*

Dictionary Articles

"Absolutes, Moral," "Act Ethics," "Joseph Fletcher," "Norms," "Principles," and "Rule Ethics," *Baker's Dictionary of Christian Ethics,* ed. Carl Henry (Grand Rapids: Baker Book House, 1973).

"Jealousy," and "Joy," *Zondervan's New Pictorial Bible Encyclopedia,* ed. Merrill C. Tenney (Grand Rapids: Zondervan Pub. Co., 1974).

"Baptism," "Image of God," "Man," *Nelson's Illustrated Bible Dictionary,* ed. Herbert Lockyer, Sr. (Nashville: Thomas Nelson, Inc., 1986).

"Euthanasia," "Millennial Views," "Separation," *Evangelical Dictionary of Theology,* ed. Walter A. Elwell (Grand Rapids: Baker Book House, 1984).

"Christology in America," "Theories of Atonement in America," *Dictionary of Christianity in America* (Downers Grove, IL: InterVarsity Press, 1990).

Notes

1. Most of the other material in this initial section is drawn from several telephone conversations in November 1988. Also see the helpful material in Leslie R. Keylock, "Evangelical Leaders You Should Know: Meet Millard J. Erickson," *Moody Monthly,* June 1987, 71-73.

2. Ibid.

3. Conversation, November 1988.

4. Ibid., Also see Warren C. Young's observation at this point in his "Review of *The New Evangelical Theology,*" *Foundations* 12 (January 1969): 95-96.

5. Ibid.

6. Ibid.

7. Ibid.

8. Ibid.

9. See Millard Erickson, *The New Evangelical Theology* (Westwood, N.J.: Revell, 1968).

10. Ibid., 13-3. The popular claim that Ockenga coined the term "new evangelicalism" is disputed by Henry. Henry wrote three articles related to the "new evangelicalism" published in *Christian Life and Times* in early 1948. See George Marsden, *After Fundamentalism* (Grand Rapids: Eerdmans, 1987) 3, 167.

11. Ibid., 31-45. In an interesting observation, R. Hammer remarks that the American evangelicalism could be identified with British fundamentalism, pointing out the distinctions between the American and British scenes. See Hammer, "Review of *The New Evangelical Theology,*" *Expository Times* 81 (January 1970): 109-10.

12. Erickson, *New Evangelical Theology,* 22-30.

13. See E. J. Carnell, *The Case for Orthodox Theology* (Philadelphia: Westminster, 1959).

14. See Carl F. H. Henry, *The Uneasy Conscience of Modern Fundamentalism* (Grand Rapids: Eerdmans, 1947).

15. See S. Heavenor, "Review of *The New Evangelical Theology,*" *Scottish Journal of Theology* 24 (August 1971): 355-57.

16. As summarized in a review of Erickson's work by Richard N. Longenecker, "A Review of *The New Evangelical Theology,*" *Christianity Today* 13:1 (October 11, 1968), 19-20. All reviews of Erickson's early work were quite positive. The issues that were raised tended to focus around the definition of "evangelicalism." In addition to Longenecker, see Charles C. Ryrie, "A Review of *The New Evangelical Theology,*" *Bibliotheca Sacra* 126 (January 1969): 81-82; and Ralph Martin, "A Review of *The New Evangelical Theology,*" *Evangelical Quarterly* 42 (January 1970): 57-58.

17. Millard J. Erickson, *Christian Theology,* 3 vols. (Grand Rapids: Baker Book House, 1983, 1984, 1985), 1:21

18. Ibid.

19. Ibid., 1:66.

20. Ibid., 1:66-79.

21. Ibid., 1:78.

22. Ibid., 1:175-81.

23. Ibid., 1:173.

24. Ibid., 1:174. Also see Millard J. Erickson, "Hope for Those Who Haven't Heard? Yes, but . . . ." *Evangelical Missions Quarterly* 2 (1915): 122-126.

25. Erickson, Christian Theology, 1:153.

26. Ibid., 1:153-54, 175.

27. Ibid., 1:176-77.

28. Ibid., 1:191-96.

29. Ibid., 1:200.

30. Ibid., 1:207-10. See Millard J. Erickson, "Implications of Biblical Inerrancy for the Christian Mission" *Proceedings of the Conference on Biblical Inerrancy,* (Nashville: Broadman Press, 1987), 223-36.

31. Erickson, *Christian Theology,* 1:217.

32. Ibid., 1:221-40.

33. Ibid., 1:242-44.

34. Ibid., 1:233-34.

35. Ibid., 1:225-29.

36. Ibid., 1:263.

37. Ibid., 1:345.

38. Ibid., 1:266-67.

39. Ibid., 1:267-300. E.g. "God and time" (274-75); "constancy" (278-81); "faithfulness" (291-92); "love" (292-94); "love and justice" (297-98).

40. Ibid., 1:345-63.

41. Ibid., 1:378-86.

42. Ibid., 2:473-93. In our phone conversation, November 1988, Erickson suggests that flood geologists try to defend what is not required by Scripture to defend, and this can thus be classified as an "overbelief" on their part.

43. Ibid., 2:512-14.

44. Ibid., 2:536-39.

45. Ibid., 2:541-59.

46. Ibid., 2:641-58.

47. Ibid., 2:578.

48. Ibid., 2:580.

49. Ibid., 2:639.

50. Ibid., 2:636-39.
51. Ibid., 2:734-38.
52. Millard J. Erickson, "Christology from Above and Christology from Below: A Study of Contrasting Methodologies." *Perspectives on Evangelical Theology,* ed. Kenneth S. Kantzer and Stanley N. Gundry (Grand Rapids: Bauer, 1979), 43-55.
53. Erickson, *Christian Theology,* 2:762-69.
54. Ibid., 2:811-23.
55. Ibid., 2:834-35.
56. Ibid.
57. Ibid., 2:777.
58. The point was stressed in our phone conversation, November 1988.
59. Erickson, *Christian Theology,* 2:777.
60. Ibid., 3:872-77. Erickson suggests that it is difficult to determine whether the contemporary phenomena are authentic. He decides that charismata are sovereignly given and are not to be sought.
61. Ibid., 3:932.
62. Ibid., 3:1084.
63. Ibid., 3:1096-97.
64. Ibid., 3:1104-5.
65. Ibid., 3:1123.
66. Ibid., 3:1130-47. Also see Millard J. Erickson, "Separation," *Evangelical Dictionary of Theology,* ed. W. A. Elwell (Grand Rapids: Baker, 1984), 1002-3.
67. Erickson, *Christian Theology,* 3:1206-24. Also see his extensive discussion of these matters in Millard J. Erickson, *Contemporary Options in Eschatalogy: A Study of the Millennium* (Grand Rapids: Baker, 1977). This book grew out of a request of the Bethel Seminary classes for a course that would examine thoroughly and objectively eschatological options for today's churches. For evaluations and disagreements with Erickson's conclusions, see reviews by: Anthony Hoekema, "A Review of *Contemporary Options,*" *Calvin Theological Journal* 13 (1978): 208-11; D. K. Erlandson, "A Review of *Contemporary Options,*" *Christian Scholars Review* 9 (1979): 186-87; R. A. Coughenour, "A Review of *Contemporary Options,*" *Reformed Review* 32 (1979): 181-82; John Walvoord, "A Review of *Contemporary Options,*" *Bibliotheca Sacra* 137 (1980): 83-85.
68. Erickson, *Christian Theology* 3:1226-41.
69. Stanley Grenz, "A Review of *Christian Theology.*1," *Christian Scholars Review* 16 (1986): 93, 96.
70. David S. Dockery, "A Review of *Christian Theology.*1," *Grace Theological Journal* 5 (1984): 302-3.
71. David S. Dockery, "A Review of *Christian Theology.*2," *Grace Theological Journal* 7 (1986): 140-42.
72. Ralph W. Vunderink, "A Review of *Christian Theology.*3," *Calvin Theological Journal* 22 (1987): 144.
73. L. R. Bush, "A Review of *Christian Theology.*3," *Southwestern Journal of Theology* 28 (1986): 52; Charles Chaney, "A Review of *Christian Theology.*2," *Review and Expositor* 83 (1986): 134-35; R. H. Culpepper, "A Review of *Christian Theology.*3," *Faith and Mission* 3 (1986): 91-92.
74. David Wells, "A Review of *Christian Theology*1,2,3," *Eternity* 38 (Feb. 1987): 41; David Landegent, "A Review of *Christian Theology.*1," *Reformed Review* 39 (1986): 121.
75. Yet, Frederick Howe, "A Review of *Christian Theology,*" *Bibliotheca Sacra*

143 (1986): 75-76, among other more conservative evangelicals, has questioned his nuanced understanding of inerrancy.

76. So Clark Pinnock, "A Review of *Christian Theology* 1,2,3," *TSF Bulletin* 9 (1986): 29-30.

77. So Dale Sanders, "A Review of *Christian Theology* 2," *Calvin Theological Journal* 21 (1986): 111-13.

78. A helpful warning in this regard can be found in G. C. Berkouwer, *Faith and Justification*, trans. L. B. Smedes (Grand Rapids: Eerdmans, 1954), 25-38.

79. This is evidenced by the fact that the subject of the "kingdom" is treated as a special problem under the heading of the church, devoting less than a page to it. See the developed critique in Ralph W. Vunderrink, "A Review of *Christian Theology*," *Calvin Theological Journal* 22 (1987): 139-44.

80. I have noted in another place that the themes developed in volume 3 seem to have been treated more hurriedly and less thoughtfully, at least in their relationship to each other, than the themes addressed in volumes 1 and 2. See David S. Dockery, "A Review of *Christian Theology*.3," *Grace Theological Journal* 8 (1987): 295-96.

81. Some have pointed out the inconsistencies in the application of his method. See Bruce Demarest, "A Review of *Christian Theology*," *Journal of the Evangelical Theological Society* 29 (1986): 236-37; and David Landegent, "A Review of *Christian Theology*.2," *Reformed Review* 40 (1986): 67-68.

34

Clark H. Pinnock

Robert V. Rakestraw

Biography

Clark Harold Pinnock was born February 3, 1937, in Toronto, Ontario, Canada, and was reared there in a middle-class home. He was brought up in a liberal Baptist church that had mostly forgotten both the truth and the reality of God. He did, however, have a Bible-believing grandmother and a like-minded Sunday School teacher who led him to know Christ. He received further help in his Christian growth from Youth for Christ in Toronto and from working one summer at the Canadian Keswick Bible Conference. He was thus introduced to God in the context of fundamentalism, and he continues to appreciate his fundamentalist past.[1]

From the beginning of his Christian experience he developed a keen sense of dissatisfaction with diluted forms of Christianity and a high regard for what was indispensable. In the 1950s he came increasingly under the influence of the kind of mainstream evangelical theology associated with the old Princeton Seminary. Most of the authors he was exposed to in his early days as theologically "sound" were staunchly Calvinistic: John Murray, D. Martyn Lloyd-Jones, Cornelius Val Til, Carl Henry, James Packer, and Paul Jewett. Theirs were the books sold in the InterVarsity bookroom he frequented, and theirs were the books he was told to read if he wanted to learn correct theology.[2]

He graduated from high school in 1956, and four years later completed his B.A. with honors in the Ancient Near East Studies program at the University of Toronto. For his work at Toronto he earned both a Woodrow Wilson Fellowship to Harvard and a British Commonwealth Scholarship to England. Accepting the latter, he pursued Ph.D. studies at Manchester University, studying New Testament under the esteemed biblical scholar and apologist F. F. Bruce. After completing his dissertation on Pauline pneumatology in 1963, Pinnock remained with Bruce for two more years as an assistant lecturer in New Testament Studies. During these years he corresponded closely with apologist Francis A. Schaeffer, and in the summers was a student and worker at Schaeffer's L'Abri Fellowship in Huemoz, Switzerland, a study center which attracted troubled and doubting intellectuals from numerous countries.[3] Schaeffer's thirst for pragmatic truth left a deep and lasting impact upon the young Pinnock, although he saw even then the rather serious weaknesses in Schaeffer's method and thought.[4]

In 1965 he began teaching New Testament at New Orleans Baptist Theo-

Clark H. Pinnock (1937-   )

Photo courtesy of McMaster Divinity College

logical Seminary in Louisiana. After two years he moved to teaching systematic theology because of a need in that department as well as a growing desire to work in theology. At New Orleans he began to be noticed as a serious analyst and potential shaper of modern theological thought, and in 1967 he published *A Defense of Biblical Infallibility,* his first major theological writing. *Set Forth Your Case* appeared the same year, a defense of the Christian faith in light of biblical revelation and modern culture, with considerable indebtedness to Francis Schaeffer. He admits to having been bitten with the bug of "preoccupation with apologetic certainty" during this period of his life.[5]

In *A New Reformation: A Challenge to Southern Baptists* (1968), he appealed to his denomination to return to complete confidence in the written Word of God and even to take decisive steps to purge Baptist higher education of those professors who had jettisoned the historic high view of Scripture.[6] He showed the inseparable connection between *Evangelism and Truth* in a 1969 booklet in which he also declared the absolute necessity of a Calvinistic foundation for biblical evangelism. Further, in the late 1960s he was converted from amillennialism to premillennialism through influences at Dallas Theological Seminary.[7]

While Pinnock was demonstrating more and more confidence in his theological bases, he was feeling a lack of reality and power in his personal life due to his lopsided concentration on the intellectual side of truth. In 1967 in New Orleans he received what he calls "the infilling of the Spirit" when he asked some friends to lay hands on him and pray for him to receive the Spirit in power. "Being a Christian became an exciting adventure instead of a drag."[8] For a Southern Baptist leader in the conservative South in the 1960s this was a remarkable occurrence, indicating in him a thirst for God and His truth wherever that may lead and regardless of whose theological system it may violate.

His growing reputation attracted the attention of the newly revived Trinity Evangelical Divinity School in Deerfield, Illinois, and he was invited to join the growing number of avant-garde young scholars at Trinity. Here he taught systematic theology from 1969 to 1974. Even as he did in New Orleans, he devoured the writings of current theologians, whether conservative, neoorthodox, or liberal. (He has always been a voluminous reader in a wide range of subjects, reading about four books each week.) In 1971 two more works were published. *Biblical Revelation: The Foundation of Christian Theology* was hailed as "the most vigorous scholarly statement of verbal, plenary inspiration since Warfield."[9] *Toward a Theology for the Future,* coedited with David F. Wells, was written to indicate where the decisive action is taking place in the various fields of theological study, and to move toward a constructive, evangelical proposal. In the early 1970s, with the British Theological Students Fellowship model in mind, he started a North American division of the TSF which operated as an arm of InterVarsity Christian Fellowship until its discontinuance by IVCF in 1987. He continued very actively as its secretary throughout these years.

Robert M. Price, in a perceptive essay on Pinnock's theological development (approved, for the most part, by Pinnock himself[10]) correctly sees a new period in Pinnock's career beginning around 1971. Price considers that the publication of Pinnock's "Prospects for Systematic Theology," his chapter in *Toward a Theology for the Future,* marks the beginning of this second phase.[11] Clearly about this time major changes were taking place. While Pinnock is always on the move theologically, there are recognizable dividing lines between his major periods. Beginning with the new decade he called for a "post-liberal" or "Classical Christian" theology, a fresh evangelical alternative distinctive for its having listened seriously to and interacted with its opponents.[12] Whatever the influences on Pinnock at this time, they did not dampen his zeal for Christian witness nor his concern for vibrant Christian living. His brief evangelistic booklet, *Live Now, Brother,* and his *Truth on Fire: The Message of Galatians* both appeared in 1972.

Two areas in which Pinnock made dramatic changes in the early 1970s are his soteriology and his political/social ideology. As noted above, he began his theological life as a Calvinist, and did not question this view for many years. But around 1970, through his studies in the Book of Hebrews as part of his teaching on the perseverance of the saints, and through I. Howard Marshall's sturdy examination of the security issue, *Kept by the Power of God* (1969),[13] he found the logic of Calvinism to be seriously flawed.[14] His edited work, *Grace Unlimited* (1975), reveals his turnabout from Calvinism to a Wesleyan-Arminian position.

With regard to social and political issues, Pinnock notes that his quest for truth led him through several phases. From 1953 to 1969 he was "in the mainstream" of political conservatism, whereas from 1970 to 1978 he was "out on the edges." During these latter years, through the influence of Trinity student Jim Wallis and others, he adopted almost blindly a radical and subversive view of politics and culture. Spurred by John H. Yoder's *The Original Revolution,* he adopted to a considerable extent the outlook and agenda of the new left, and after moving back to Canada he even voted for Communist candidates in the Vancouver civic elections. In this second period he served as a contributing editor for the evangelical-left magazine *Sojourners* (formerly *Post-American*), edited by Wallis. The third phase (1978-present) is his "return to the center," in which he embraces and champions the spirit of democratic capitalism.[15]

He returned to his native land in 1974 to teach for three years at Regent College in Vancouver. During this time, amid other pursuits, he continued to examine and revise his views on scriptural inerrancy.[16] His questioning of the traditional expression, defense, and use of the inerrancy doctrine among conservatives earned him a stern rebuke from Harold Lindsell, the crusading former editor of *Christianity Today* who in his 1976 bombshell, *The Battle for the Bible,* had counted Pinnock an ally.[17] Many other conservatives were equally disturbed.[18]

In 1977 he was appointed associate professor of Systematic Theology at McMaster Divinity College in Hamilton, Ontario, where he remains to the present, now as professor. His tenure at McMaster, as might be expected, has not been without controversy.[19] Having settled at the age of forty into this position in his home area, he has become an even more bold, more innovative, yet seemingly more spiritually sensitive theologian than at any time in his career. His church membership is at the Westmount Baptist Church of Hamilton, a mildly charismatic congregation of the Baptist Convention of Ontario and Quebec. He and his wife, Dorothy, have one child, Sarah Katherine, born in 1967. Clark Pinnock is a member of the Society of New Testament Studies, Tyndale Fellowship for Biblical Research, the Evangelical Theological Society, and the Karl Barth Society of North America. He serves, among other responsibilities, as a Resource Scholar for *Christianity Today*.[20]

He has written considerably while at McMaster. In addition to over fifty articles, over fifty book reviews (almost all in the now extinct *TSF Bulletin* or its predecessor, *TSF News and Reviews*), and a number of chapters in books edited by others, he has written four more books and edited another. *Reason Enough* appeared in 1980, followed by *The Scripture Principle* (1984), *Three Keys to Spiritual Renewal* (1985), and *Tracking the Maze* (1990). He has also edited *The Grace of God, the Will of Man: A Case for Arminianism* (1989).

Except perhaps for *Reason Enough*, an apologetic effort midway between the old Pinnock and the new, these last five volumes represent his mature thought (Price suggests 1980 as the approximate beginning of Pinnock's third major period).[21] We will therefore discuss them in the next section of the essay, an exposition largely of Pinnock's views in the 1980s, with emphasis upon those areas in which he has changed over the years, and/or for which he has become noted. The following survey will group Pinnock's thought in four categories: Scripture, salvation, theism, and renewal.

Exposition

The God Who Speaks and Illumines

Pinnock has become known more for his doctrine of Scripture than for any other area of theological thought. Throughout his career he has argued vigorously and brilliantly for a high view of Scripture as the inspired foundation for Christian theology. But his views, especially on the divine-human balance in the composition of Scripture, have changed significantly.

In *Biblical Revelation* he writes that "inerrancy is to be regarded as an essential concomitant of the doctrine of inspiration, a necessary inference drawn from the fact that Scripture is God's Word."[22] If the biblical writers erred in one particular, we have no assurance that they did not err in many more, even in theological matters. Yet even in these early years Pinnock never held to a view of absolute or unqualified inerrancy, even though Lindsell seems to equate their views at that time.[23] He has always argued for a nuanced definition of inerrancy that allows some give and take.[24]

In *The Scripture Principle* he issues a carefully wrought argument (the book is a completely rewritten version of a 1981 draft) for the maintaining of a holistic doctrine of Scripture that will include divine authorship and authority, human character and fraility, and the spiritual dynamic so necessary for proper understanding. The "Scripture principle" is that this divine-human locus of the Word of God is the informative and authoritative message of God for people today, speaking truth whether doctrinal, ethical, or spiritual.[25]

Even though he favors retaining the term inerrancy, he moves significantly away from his earlier understanding of the concept. For example, while the historical character of the Fall must be preserved (Rom. 5:12), the story of it in Genesis 2—3 is probably an etiological inference drawn from the human experience of guilt and salvation in history and presented in a saga-like narrative form.[26] He notes that "there are cases in which the possibility of legend seems quite real," such as the incident of the coin in the fish's mouth (Matt. 17:24-27), which "has the feel of a legendary feature." Similar to this is Paul's escape from poisoning in Malta (Acts 28:1-6). "It is entirely possible that God delivered Paul in precisely this manner, though one should perhaps not count on it. But it is also possible that it forms part of a hero-narrative and is not an expression of fact."[27]

In *Tracking the Maze* he states that "there are things in the Bible that are history-like but not likely to be historical." We should not consider the historical value of the Sampson or Elisha stories, for example, on the same level as the accounts of the Exodus and the resurrection of Jesus. "We are not bound to deny the Bible the possibility of playful legend just because the central claim is historical." The resurrection had to happen for the gospel story to be true, but the same does not hold true for Elisha's axhead or the fate of Lot's wife. "I think we have exaggerated the supernaturalness of inspiration."[28] In the categories of inerrancy views formulated by Millard Erickson, Pinnock places himself today in that of "inerrancy of purpose," which understands the Bible to be inerrant only in that it accomplishes the purpose for which it was written.[29]

What might be considered by some as equally surprising is his growing understanding of "Scripture as sacrament." In the area of interpretation, Pinnock wants to hold to a middle way between the objective meaning of the text in the light of the author's original intention and the reader's subjective apprehension of that meaning as well as other meanings that may lie below the surface. He is not at all happy with the way conservatives in recent decades have omitted the illuminating work of the Spirit in interpretation just as surely as the liberals have.[30]

The God Who Seeks and Saves

While Pinnock has not yet published a monograph in soteriology, he has edited two very important volumes and written other items of significance on the topic (such as chapter 3 of *Tracking the Maze*). *Grace Unlimited*, with chapters by Vernon Grounds, Jack Cottrell, I. Howard Marshall, Grant Osborne, and others, calls for a new understanding of God's offer of salvation. In his introduction and his chapter on "Responsible Freedom and the Flow of Biblical History" (in which he acknowledges a great indebtedness to contemporary theologian Gordon Kaufman), Pinnock boldly asserts God's genuine desire to save all people. "We reject all forms of theology which deny this truth and posit some secret abyss in God's mind where he is not gracious."[31] This recognition underlies all of Pinnock's soteriology and emerges more recently in *Tracking the Maze* as the core truth of the gospel story from Genesis to Revelation. A related foundation stone concerns human freedom to accept or reject God's offer of salvation. "Universal man almost without exception talks and feels as if he were free. . . . This fundamental self-perception is, I believe, an important clue as to the nature of reality."[32]

His most recent work in this area is *The Grace of God, the Will of Man: A Case for Arminianism,* a collection of essays by an impressive team of evangelical scholars from many traditions. Here we find William Abraham, William Cra y, Bruce Reichenbach, and others, as well as some from his *Grace Unlimited* volume (Cottrell, Marshall, Osborne). These essays present and defend the proposition that God is a dynamic personal agent who respects the freedom he, by his sovereign choice, gives to his human creatures. In addition to his introduction, Pinnock contributes "From Augustine to Arminius: A Pilgrimage in Theology," in which he relates the changes in his view of redemptive truth.

Pinnock is excited about the current theological shift among evangelicals and other Christians away from determinism in the doctrine of salvation and toward a genuine human freedom. The Bible is more and more being read in a fresh manner, he believes, in dialogue with modern culture, with the emphasis being placed on autonomy, temporarility, and historical change. Pinnock discovered that there is no "horrible decree" (Calvin's term for predestination) after all. He acknowledges his indebtedness to Robert Shank in leading him to see election as a corporate matter rather than as the choice of individuals for salvation.[33] Predestination is to be understood as God's setting goals for people, not forcing them into predetermined patterns. He admits to a "paradigm shift" in his biblical hermeneutics as he views the Bible more and more from the vantage point of God's universal salvific will and significant human freedom.[34]

He also began to question the doctrine of total depravity. Because the Scripture appeals to people as those who are able and responsible to answer to God, he reasoned that it does so "because that is what they are."[35] Jesus died for the sins of all people. Yet Pinnock views the atonement more as Anselm and Grotius understood it, as an act of judicial demonstration rather than a strict or quantitative substitution as such. He does not want to abandon substitution, but seems unsure of how to retain the doctrine while holding to human autonomy.[36]

Pinnock's view of God's universal salvific will quite naturally affects his understanding of the precise nature of the individual sinner's response and destiny. In 1976 he wrote a controversial article entitled "Why Is Jesus the Only Way?" While strongly affirming the finality of Jesus Christ as the only Savior, he suggests that, for the multitudes who have lived and died without any knowledge of Christ, there may be occasion just after death to hear and believe the gospel. Drawing attention to 1 Peter 3:19 and 4:6, and noting that such reputable interpreters as Cranfield and Pannenberg present such a view, he contends that this is not a "second chance" theory, but involves a first chance at death.[37] Over a decade later he develops this view further, calling his proposal "a piece of disputed theology" on which he is not rigid, although he believes it to be sound and true.[38] As for those who do hear the gospel, either before or after death, but reject it, he argues for annihilationism. Opposing "the moral horror and exegetical flimsiness of the traditional view of hell," he sees the "extinction of the whole human person" as the meaning of "everlasting punishment" in Matthew 25:46.[39]

The God Who Lives and Responds

Pinnock's new understanding of the goodness of God in seeking and saving the lost led him to explore further the being and attributes of God. While he began to investigate these matters somewhat in the 1970s,[40] it was not until the 1980s that he developed his thoughts more fully.[41] While admitting that he agrees with much of the process *critique* of traditional theism, and in that sense expresses admiration for it,[42] he (as late as 1987) firmly rejects process theism.[43] He has, however, been influenced significantly not only by the process critique but also by the process construct.

On the traditional doctrine of the impassibility of God, he agrees with H. P. Owen that this is the most questionable aspect of classical theism.[44] To teach that God is incapable of being affected by anything outside Himself, and is unmoved by our sufferings and joys, is a serious distortion and denial of biblical truth. The Bible in general and the crucifixion in particular make it clear that God can experience sadness, pain, and love.[45] Concerning immutability, God "genuinely interacts with the world, responds passionately to what happens in it, and even changes his own plans to fit changing historical circumstances."[46] He is unchangeable in essence and character, yet changeable in His knowledge and actions.[47] Furthermore, God is not timeless. The Scriptures present God as exactly the opposite, as operating from within time and history. If God were not within time, "he would not be able to be with us on our journey, or freely relate to what goes on or make plans and carry them out or experience the joy of victory or the anquish of defeat, as Scripture says God does."[48]

What does Pinnock say, then, about divine omniscience? He has become increasingly uncomfortable with the view, held even by most Arminians like himself, that God has an exhaustive foreknowledge of everything that will ever happen. He found that he "could not shake off the intuition that such a total omniscience would necessarily mean that everything we will ever choose in the future will have been already spelled out in the divine knowledge register," thereby nullifying the belief that we make truly free, significant choices. He now contends that God knows everything that *can* be known, but free choices are not able to be known even by God because they are not yet settled in reality. "Decisions not yet made do not exist anywhere to be known even by God."[49] God can "surmise" what you will do next

Friday, but He cannot know it for certain. God is "dependent on the world for his information about the world."[50] But, does not predictive prophecy prove that God knows the future exhaustively? Pinnock says no, because a very high percentage of prophecy can be accounted for by one of three factors: "the announcement ahead of time of what God intends to do, conditional prophecies which leave the outcome open, and predictions based on God's exhaustive knowledge of the past and the present."[51]

The omnipotence and sovereignity of God must also be redefined. Omnipotence means that God can do what He chooses to do and what is logically possible to do. If He chooses to create a world of free beings instead of a race of automatons, this magnifies rather than denies His power. But once He has freely chosen such a world He is limited by the laws of that world. "His sovereignty is not the all-determining kind, but an omnipotent kind. God is certainly able to deal with any circumstances which might arise, and nothing can possibly defeat or destroy God. But he does not control everything that occurs." As to how God can bring His will to pass in a world where finite beings are free to resist Him, He can do it "because of his ability to anticipate the obstructions the creatures can throw in his way and respond to each new challenge in an effective manner." Somehow God works with and around the challenges to His kingdom rule. He is an "expert" who "sees a great deal more of what is going on than we can as finite creatures."[52] In addition, God calls us into partnership with Himself in running the universe. His plan is open, and prayer really can change the future. "If you believe that prayer changes things, my whole position is established. If you do not believe it does, you are far from biblical religion."[53]

On the Triune nature of God, he opposes the modalistic tendency of Western theology following Augustine, even in Rahner and Barth, and favors a social doctrine of the Trinity. Far from being irrational, such a view is actually very coherent and convincing, and makes good practical sense as well.[54]

The God Who Renews and Advances

While the previous three categories are in roughly chronological order of their emergence in Pinnock's thought and writing, the topics of renewal among God's people and the advancement of the kingdom on earth have occupied his attention throughout his scholarly career. This includes his concern for a clearer understanding of the nature, method, and content of theology. Our thoughts here will be grouped according to the categories in *Three Keys to Spiritual Renewal,* a small book (modest in size but not in importance) focusing upon the recovery and development of essential biblical theology, the return of Spirit-filled living, and the mobilization of God's people for the advancement of His kingdom. While we will look mostly at the first of these, the latter two emphases must be recognized as equally important to Clark Pinnock.

In his writings on the task and content of theology there is a notable evangelistic and pastoral tone. He sees theology as ministry. When asked "What is your chief concern in ministry?" he replied, "to blend my writing, speaking, teaching, witnessing, relating into one effective and relevant witness to Jesus Christ. To respond to those points where the witness is under a threat, and to give some helpful direction beyond current impasses."[55]

Pinnock's long-standing interest in apologetics demonstrates this concern for witness. He sees apologetics as a kind of preevangelism, and even as necessary for the survival of the church. In *Set Forth Your Case,* leaning heavily upon rational proof and verification, he sought to ground the Christian faith solidly in revelation as history, with the reliability of the New Testament documents in general and the resurrection of Christ in particular being the foundational evidences for the truth of Christianity.[56] In *Reason Enough,* he broadens his base of evidence from the more limited historical data to offer five circles of credibility: pragmatism, experience, natural theology, history, and community.[57] More recently he has become even less dependent upon rationalistic arguments. While over the years he has strongly objected to the presuppositional apologetics of Cornelius Van Til and his followers, he admitted in 1979 "Now I'm halfway between where I used to be and the Reformed fideists."[58]

The church's apologetic mission can only flounder, however, without a strong adherence to the essentials of our faith. Pinnock calls for new confessions of faith that present the essentials of Christianity as taught in Scripture. He thus wrote "A New Baptist Confession," composed in the context of the Baptist Renewal Fellowship of Canada. Here he presents the essentials in five categories: God has spoken; He is the living God; He is Creator, Sustainer, and Perfecter; God is our Savior and Redeemer; and, God is calling a new community. In this confession we find a clear but broadly worded affirmation of historic Christian truth.[59]

Tracking the Maze is Pinnock's most ambitious attempt to articulate his own theology systematically, with the hope of overcoming the liberal-conservative polarity of the past by moving toward a common center. He writes it, as he says, with fire in his bones, as one disturbed and perplexed by the accommodation to modernity evident in today's church. After a stimulating survey and analysis of the present pattern in Christian theology, and a masterful exploration of the historical roots for this pattern, he seeks in the final third of the book to ascertain what the essence of Christianity is.

In seeking to find the balance between fidelity to revelation and creativity in the modern context, he presents the general contours of a proposal that sees that Christian message as story. "In my judgment the central message of Christianity, and therefore its essence, is the epic story of redemption, enshrined in its sacred texts and liturgies, that announces the salvation and God's liberation of the human race." The narrative proclaims (as Tolkien called it) the great "eucatastrophe," the myth made fact, the intervention of God in history for the salvation of humanity which is at once historical and mythical. The gospel is both factual, with solid historical credentials, as well as alive with existential promise and symbolic wealth.[60] As for the sources or vehicles by which the story takes shape and is handed down over the centuries, Pinnock views the Wesleyan quadrilateral of Scripture, tradition, experience, and reason as most instructive, with revelation being the precondition of them all, and with each held in creative tension with the others.[61]

When asked "What is theology?" Pinnock stresses the secondary character of theological formulations. "Truth and meaning for Christianity lie with the narrative before it is expressed in the doctrinal form. Theology exists to serve the story and not the other way around." Christian theology, then, should not be primarily rational-propositional in form. Furthermore, "we should redefine heresy as something which ruins the story and orthodoxy as theology which keeps the story alive and devises new ways of telling it."[62] Such an approach to theology represents another paradigm shift for Pinnock, for he is expressing dissatisfaction with his earlier rationalistic self as much as with anyone.

From the beginning of his ministry Pinnock has been concerned for spiritual renewal. Changed by his experience of "infilling" in 1967, he began to call for a more favorable attitude on the part of noncharismatics toward Pentecostal teachings and practices.[63] His second key to reformation and renewal, following the rediscovery of essential biblical truth, is the opening of our lives and churches to the experiential renewing and empowering ministry of the Spirit. He laments that most Protestant churches today, including Baptist churches, are more at home in the Catholic liturgical stream where the order of service is written down and predictable than in the New Testament pattern where the freedom of the Spirit was unleashed, sometimes unpredictably, in the exercise of a wide range of spiritual gifts.[64]

The third key to a vital Christianity is obedience to all of God's commandments through lives of radical discipleship. Because he sees the first and most basic ethical imperative to be the command of Genesis 1 to exercise dominion over the earth, he is more and more growing away from premillennialism and favoring the old Puritan postmillennial eschatology and vision. Having moved from his earlier Anabaptist reading of the Bible to a Reformed hermeneutic with respect to the Old and New Testaments, he now emphasizes the need for the Mosaic law in society today and the value of the postmillennial view "as a practical policy to guide Christian action and morale."[65] He is excited about the resurgence of this theonomy teaching in the later writings of Francis Schaeffer, in the efforts of the New Right, and in the Chalcedon movement for Christian reconstruction, and he even urges Christians in his land to work hard to move the country "in the direction of a Christian commonwealth." He calls for Christians to take a bold stand for restitution instead of prisons, for the immediate restoration of the death penalty, and to work against such social evils as the breakup of the family, abortion, homosexuality, and radical feminism.[66] (As for those who espouse a biblical form of feminism, he is doubtful that a case can be made for such a position.[67]) In his fascination with reconstructionism, however, he is not uncritical of the West, nor does he claim that the Bible teaches capitalist economics *per se*.[68]

Evaluation

Theological Method

While only recently has Pinnock written of the quadrilateral of Scripture, tradition, reason, and experience as the fourfold source of theological truth, he has always operated within something like this framework. Of these, Scripture is the only infallible criterion of divine revelation for communicating the story of redemption. While his modified view of the phenomena of Scripture may cause some to question his faithfulness to Scripture as the supreme and absolutely authoritative source of theology, a wide reading of the new Pinnock finds him still every bit as stubborn on this point as in the 1960s.[69] Tradition guides Pinnock in his choice of confessional substance, but also in the overall development of his thought. While it might appear to be just the opposite at times, Pinnock always theologizes in light of historic Christianity. It is precisely because he is so aware of the tradition that he feels compelled either to defend it or modify it. When he departs from it it is not without considerable thought, although for him tradition is obviously no sacred cow. What does not accord with Scripture, reason, and experience must be rejected or reworked. Although he greatly respects and values tradition, it appears that for him it is the least binding of the four sources of Christian truth.[70]

If we ask whether reason or experience is the more important source of Pinnock's theology after Scripture, we would, for his earlier years, affirm reason. But as we follow his career we see the increasing importance and present ascendancy of experience (and with it personal desire and intuition) over reason and logic. On predestination, for example, he argues from the fact that "universal man talks and feels as if he were free."[71] He speaks of a postmortem opportunity for the unevangelized to hear the gospel as "a broad hint from the Lord that he will do what our hearts long for him to do."[72] Examples such as these (and there are many others) reveal that his heart often leads his head, both regarding his personal longing for a certain matter to be true, but also with regard to his desire to make the gospel appealing to outsiders or to Christians who are considering defection. Such motivation is not deleterious, but commendable, if experience is subjected to the unambiguous teachings of Scripture. Experience, intuition, and desire provide valuable empirical data that must not be discounted.

As for reason and logic, Pinnock has always relied upon these in building and defending his theology, but he now claims considerably less certainty for his views than in the past. He wisely admits that reason does not operate independently of history and culture, but is always embedded in it. Reason for him is not an autonomous, omnicompetent, or final judge of truth. While faith seeks to understand its rational expression, it also respects mystery and is aware of its limited ability to understand divine truth.[73]

The influences upon Pinnock are many and varied. Francis Schaeffer affected him greatly as an apologist, as a lover of truth, and as a model of Christian living. Donald Bloesch, Gabriel Fackre, and Millard Erickson, the three theologians to whom *The Scripture Principle* is dedicated, are, for him, examples of evangelical scholars who are both "valiant for truth and creative in expression."[74] Fackre's emphasis on narrative theology has particularly impressed Pinnock. I. Howard Marshall has been another significant influence, especially in moving Pinnock toward an Arminian interpretation of Scripture. He is enthusiastic about the work of Karl Barth and Wolfhart Pannenberg, seeing them as essentially orthodox, although not without their weaknesses.[75] And Dale Moody, through his book *The Word of Truth,* has become in Pinnock's view "something of an ideal evangelical theologian who combines critical thinking with conservative convictions."[76] Nonevangelical scholars such as Gordon Kaufman, Hans Küng, Schubert Ogden, and Langdon Gilkey have also affected Pinnock, as seen from the many allusions to them in his writings. He studies them not only to see what the "other side" is saying, but to learn from them. In 1982 he wrote, "Gilkey is still my favorite religious liberal whose work is always excellent and instructive."[77]

Theological Categories

On Scripture, Pinnock is to be applauded for his insistence in calling attention to the human face of the Bible. While liberals have, of course, overdone it here, conservatives have downplayed this truth and have thereby hindered accurate interpretation at times. His understanding of Scripture as sacrament is also a needed corrective to the tendency within evangelical scholarship to view exegetical precision as all-sufficient for doctrine and life.

He has gone too far, however, in his allowance for historical untruth in Scripture. His failure to give any solid basis or criteria for determining "playful legend" or scribal blunder is a considerable weakness. If the accounts of the coin in the fish's mouth, Paul's escape from poisoning in Malta, or Elisha's axhead are "not likely to be historical," how can we know this? It is not enough to say that they have "the feel" of legend. What constitutes this "feel"? Pinnock would most likely reply that the essentiality of the biblical passage in question to the overall gospel story, as well as the data within the account itself (or in comparison with parallel accounts) will reveal whether or not the likelihood of historical accuracy is high. If such criteria are to be used, however, how can they be developed and applied so as to avoid giving the impression that the controlling factor in such matters is really a desire to accommodate to modernity?[78]

On the doctrines of salvation, his move from Calvinism to an Arminian position on election, predestination, and human sinfulness is well within the range of evangelical thought. However, as in the case of Dale Moody at The Southern Baptist Theological Seminary,[79] Pinnock's abandonment of the eternal security doctrine will cause many to question his Baptist credentials. His new stress upon the gospel viewed primarily as story is a refreshing emphasis in the midst of an evangelical milieu often overly preoccupied with propositional truth. While his broadening view of Christ's atonement is welcome, he needs to clarify the sense in which he still sees it as substitutionary. Of major concern for traditional evangelicals is his espousal of a "second chance" for the unevangelized to respond to the gospel after death. He needs to work more thoroughly in developing this position. On this, as on annihilationism, his views go solidly against the mainstream of evangelical belief, Baptist or otherwise.[80]

It is in his semiprocess theism that Pinnock has departed most drastically from historic Christianity. While his embracing of a social trinity and his rejection of the philosophical doctrines of divine impassibility and timelessness can be construed as consistent with Scripture as a whole, his teaching of an immutable-mutable God needs further clarification and development. This last point is inseparable from his views of omniscience and omnipotence. Here, as Richard Muller has noted, Pinnock "leaves orthodoxy and traditional theism far behind."[81] If God does not know for certain what will happen tomorrow, and unexpected events arise that He did not foresee, how does this accord with such Scriptures as Deuteronomy 31:14-29; Psalm 139:4; Isaiah 40—48 (see, e.g. 46:10-11; 48:3-15); 2 Thessalonians 2; and the Olivet Discourse? Surely the language of Scriptures such as these is intended to convey a certain knowledge of the future on God's part, not a highly probable knowledge. The viability of alternative positions should be considered more fully.[82]

The themes of renewal and the advancement of God's kingdom on earth are a highlight, perhaps *the* highlight, of Pinnock's entire theology. It is like finding a gushing spring in the desert when we encounter a brilliant mind who is not afraid to be emphatic and even emotional, repeatedly, with regard to such matters as theological and ethical liberalism in the churches, the infilling and gifting ministries of the Holy Spirit, the dullness of "worship" services and church meetings, and radical obedience to all of God's commandments. His *Tracking the Maze* is an outstanding survey of the pattern of Christian theological thought, both as it exists today and how it came to be. In his own proposal, however, he seems at times to be setting doctrine and narrative almost in opposition to each other, rather than emphasizing their complementarity. He also may be overly optimistic in seeing significant moves toward reapproachment between liberals and conservatives.

Deficiencies and Merits

With Clark Pinnock, as with any major theologian, there are both strengths and weaknesses in his overall theological effort. Several inadequacies can be noted. His tendency to move so passionately in one direction may cause those who would otherwise follow his thinking to be somewhat skeptical, seeing that he has frequently reversed or drastically altered his position in the past.[83] For example, students of theology and ethics who are looking for guidance in developing their doctrine of salvation or their political/economic ethics may hesitate to study Pinnock as they should. To be fair, he has in recent years expressed himself with less certainty on many debatable issues, but his past will follow him for years to come. Closely related is his tendency to publish too quickly a debatable viewpoint without developing a fully adequate basis for that position. His allowance for historical errors in

Scripture without a method for ascertaining such errors, and his abandoning of divine foreknowledge without a satisfactory explanation for predictive prophecy are cases in point. It is not that he moves to such positions impulsively, with little thought. A study of his writings, particularly his book reviews, over the years will often reveal significant hints that such moves are being considered. But to go into print with a new position, especially a controversial one, when some key difficulties are not yet resolved, does not seem to be helpful.

Other weaknesses relate to the intensely pragmatic nature of his thought. He seems unable to allow much of a sense of mystery in conservative theological conclusions if such positions are not apologetically palatable. His rejection of divine omniscience because it seemingly destroys genuine freedom is an example. To be sure, conservatives have far too often resorted to "mystery" to escape from dilemmas, but Pinnock has perhaps gone too far the other way. Then too, the perceived practical value of a doctrine being considered by him sometimes seems to gain dominance over (or at least influences strongly) a thorough study of that doctrine in Scripture. In his move toward postmillennialism, for example, he gives the distinct impression that he has adopted the position as a working hypothesis, even though he is still searching Scripture for confirmation of the view. This is not entirely bad, and is the way many theologians develop their views, but before going into print it is best to have one's foundations more settled.

There are numerous strengths to Pinnock's theology. His desire to be biblical in doctrine and in life is evident throughout his writings. His emphasizing the human face of the Bible, while insisting stubbornly on divine inspiration and authority, is laudable. His approaching the Scriptures (most of the time) as they naturally unfold to the reader, rather than as theologians often predetermine them, is most helpful. His remarkable honesty and humility regarding his state of knowledge are refreshing, and do not appear to be self-serving.[84] Especially commendable is his willingness to change his position after reconsidering the evidence. In addition, he deserves highest praise for his passion for truth, wherever the "truth" (as he sees it) leads and regardless of whomever it disturbs. In this regard, his forward-looking attitude and riskiness is unusual, especially among evangelicals. In his own words, he "thirsts" for others to go out on a limb and indicate not only where we now stand in theology and where trends are likely to proceed, but also where we ought to be heading, and what we should be saying and doing.[85] Because so few conservatives attempt such risk taking, he feels compelled to do so.[86] This, too, is commendable. Another strength, perhaps the most important of all, is his concern for practical truth—truth that works in the everyday business of life with real people in a real world. He is no ivory-tower theologian.

Impact and Significance

How do we determine Clark Pinnock's impact upon Christianity in general and Baptist thought and life in particular? While his significance is not as easy to assess as those who are either deceased or retired, we can say without hesitation that his work has had and will continue to have considerable influence. His greatest impact has been, in all probability, upon the world of theological students, particularly those in his classes and in non-evangelical seminaries where his writings and ministry have become known. During the 1970s and most of the 1980s his chief influence among students was through TSF publications and conferences. Not only students, but many theologians and pastors had their horizons broadened and minds challenged significantly by the *TSF Bulletin* and the *TSF News and Reviews*. His books, of course, have been the chief means by which his views have spread to the Christian world at large. Unfortunately, in many conservative colleges and seminaries (Baptist and otherwise), he is now studied or referred to mostly negatively as one who has departed significantly from evangelical orthodoxy.

Wherever he has lived he has always held Baptist church membership, whether among the Southern Baptists, the Baptist General Conference, his present denomination, or some other group. His influence among Baptists will continue to follow the lines of the conservative-moderate debate of recent years among Southern Baptists. Conservatives will increasingly shun him for the reasons indicated in this chapter, while moderates will hail him even more as a model of creativity and relevance within the orthodox mainstream.[87] Surely he displays the considerable diversity to be found in North American Baptist circles.

As a creative theologian and risk taker, his influence on the content of evangelical theology at the end of the twentieth century will be more in forging new patterns of thought than in honing or defending established evangelical doctrines. He raises the questions that conservatives are often afraid even to ask, and he offers solutions that to him at the time seem most satisfactory. Although no one can predict Pinnock's future, we can almost certainly expect more surprises, both in his returning to greater orthodoxy in matters where he has moved too far from the center of biblical faith, and in his further questioning of cherished conservative beliefs that may not be grounded solidly in the quadrilateral of theological authority.

In spite of considerable weaknesses in his theology, Clark Pinnock is a major evangelical theologian in the latter third of the twentieth century. He is not likely to become Carl Henry's successor in North America as evangelicalism's chief theologian without significantly modifying his views on Scripture and theism, nor will he be embraced by the liberal camp as one of them. But he will continue to provoke and challenge all who study his work. And he will greatly reward those who can see beyond the inadequacies of his theology to the passion for living truth that is his gift to the people of God.

Bibliography

Works by Pinnock
Monographs and Edited Works
A Defense of Biblical Infallibility. Philadelphia: Presbyterian and Reformed, 1967.

Set Forth Your Case. Nutley: Craig, 1967; reprint, Chicago: Moody, 1971.

A New Reformation: A Challenge to Southern Baptists. Tigerville, SC: Jewel, 1968.

Evangelism and Truth. Tigerville, SC: Jewel, 1969.

Biblical Revelation: The Foundation of Christian Theology. Chicago: Moody, 1971.

Toward a Theology of the Future (edited with David F. Wells). Carol Stream, IL: Creation House, 1971.

Live Now, Brother. Chicago: Moody, 1972; reprint, *Are There Any Answers?* Minneapolis: Bethany, 1976.

Truth on Fire: The Message of Galatians. Grand Rapids: Baker, 1972.

Grace Unlimited (edited). Minneapolis: Bethany, 1975.

Reason Enough: A Case for the Christian Faith. Downers Grove: InterVarsity, 1980; reprint, *A Case for Faith*, Minneapolis: Bethany.

The Scripture Principle. San Francisco: Harper & Row, 1984.

Three Keys to Spiritual Renewal. Minneapolis: Bethany, 1985. (In Canada: *The Untapped Power of Sheer Christianity.* Burlington, ON: Welch, 1985.)

The Grace of God, The Will of Man: A Case for Arminianism (edited). Grand Rapids: Zondervan, 1989.

Tracking the Maze: An Evangelical Perspective on Modern Theology. San Francisco: Harper & Row, 1990.

Articles, Reviews and Contributions to Books (in chronological order)
"The Structure of Pauline Eschatology," *The Evangelical Quarterly* 37 (January-March 1965): 9-20.

"On the Third Day." In *Jesus of Nazareth: Savior and Lord,* ed. Carl F. H. Henry, 145-55. Grand Rapids: Eerdmans, 1966.

"The Inspiration of the New Testament." In *The Bible: The Living Word of Revelation,* ed. Merrill C. Tenney, 143-64. Grand Rapids: Zondervan, 1968.

"Cultural Apologetics: An Evangelical Standpoint," *Bibliotheca Sacra* 127 (January-March 1970): 58-59.

"The Harrowing of Heaven," *Christianity Today,* June 19, 1970, 7-8.

"Theology and Myth," *Bibliotheca Sacra* 128 (July-September 1971): 215-26.

"Truce Proposal for the Tongues Controversy," *Christianity Today,* October 8, 1971, 6-9.

"Prospects for Systematic Theology," In *Toward a Theology of the Future,* ed. David Wells and Clark Pinnock, 93-124. Carol Stream, IL: Creation House, 1971.

"The Living God and Secular Experience," *Bibliotheca Sacra* 129 (October-December 1972): 316-20.

"The New Pentecostalism: Reflections by a Well-Wisher," *Christianity Today,* September 14, 1973, 6-10.

"The Problem of God," *Journal of the Evangelical Theological Society* 16 (Winter 1973): 11-16.

"The Moral Argument for Christian Theism," *Bibliotheca Sacra* 131 (April-June 1974): 114-19.

"Baptists and Biblical Authority," *JETS* 17 (Fall 1974): 193-205.

"Faith and Reason," *Bibliotheca Sacra* 131 (October-December 1974): 303-10.

"Limited Inerrancy: A Critical Appraisal and Constructive Alternative." In *God's Inerrant Word,* ed. John Warwick Montgomery, 143-58. Minneapolis: Bethany, 1974.

"The Inspiration of Scripture and the Authority of Jesus Christ." In *God's Inerrant Word,* ed. John Warwick Montgomery, 201-18. Minneapolis: Bethany, 1974.

"Charismatic Renewal for the Radical Church," *Post American* (February 1975): 16-21.

"Responsible Freedom and the Flow of Biblical History." In *Grace Unlimited,* ed. Clark H. Pinnock, 95-109. Minneapolis: Bethany, 1975.

"Liberation Theology: The Gains, The Gaps," *Christianity Today,* January 16, 1976, 13-15.

"Inspiration and Authority: A Truce Proposal," *The Other Side* (May-June 1976): 61-65.

"Pannenberg's Theology: Reasonable Happenings in History," *Christianity Today,* (November 5, 1976): 19-22.

"No-Nonsense Theology: Pinnock Reviews Pannenberg" (second of two parts). *Christianity Today,* (November 19, 1976): 14-16.

"Why Is Jesus the Only Way?" *Eternity* (December 1976): 13-15, 32, 34.

"The Inerrancy Debate among the Evangelicals," *Canadian Baptist* (June 1977): 4-5, 11.

"Schaefferism as a World View," *Sojourners* (July 1977); 32-35.

"Three Views of the Bible in Contemporary Theology," In *Biblical Authority,* ed. Jack Rogers, 45-73. Waco: Word, 1977.

"Evangelicals and Inerrancy: The Current Debate," *Theology Today* 35 (April 1978): 65-69.

"Joyful Partisan of the Kingdom," *Sojourners* (December 1978): 26.

"A Call for Triangular Christianity." Address given at the annual Pastor's Conference of the Baptist Convention of Ontario and Quebec, 1979.

"An Evangelical Theology: Conservative and Contemporary," *Christianity Today,* January 5, 1979, 23-29.

"The Need for a Scriptural, and Therefore a Neo-Classical Theism." In *Perspectives on Evangelical Theology,* ed. Kenneth S. Kantzer and Stanley Gundry, 37-42. Grand Rapids: Baker, 1979.

"A Call for the Liberation of North American Christians." In *Evangelicals and Liberation,* ed. Carl E. Armerding. Phillipsburg: Presbyterian and Reformed, 1979.

"The Study of Theology: A Guide for Evangelicals," *TSF News and Reviews* (March 1980): 1-4.

"The Inspiration and Interpretation of the Bible," *TSF Bulletin* (October 1980): 4-6.

"A Pilgrimage in Political Theology: A Personal Witness." In *Liberation Theology,* ed. Ronald Nash, 103-20. Milford, MI: Mott Media, 1984. Reprinted in *Is Capitalism Christian?,* ed. Franky Schaeffer, 311-25. Westchester, IL: Crossway, 1984.

"A Response to Rex Koivisto," *Journal of the Evangelical Theological Society* 24 (June 1981): 153-55.

Review of *The Necessity of Systematic Theology,* by John Jefferson Davis. *TSFB* (September-October 1981): 22.

Review of *Message and Existence: An Introduction to Christian Theology,* by Langdon Gilkey. *TSFB* (January-February 1982): 20-21.

"Liberals Knock the Center Out of Theological Education," *Christianity Today,* February 5, 1982 32-33.

Review of *A Century of Protestant Theology,* by Alasdair I. C. Heron. *TSFB* (May-June 1982): 19-20.

"How I Use Tradition in Doing Theology," *TSF Bulletin* (September-October 1982): 2-5.

"Building the Bridge From Academic Theology to Christian Mission," *Themelios* (April 1984): 3-6.

"A Political Pilgrimage." *Eternity* (October 1984): 26-29.

"How I Use the Bible in Doing Theology." In *The Use of the Bible in Theology: Evangelical Options,* ed. Robert K. Johnston, 18-34. Atlanta: John Knox, 1985.

"Erickson's Three-Volume Magnum Opus." Review of *Christian Theology,* 3 vols., by Millard J. Erickson. *TSFB* (January-February 1986): 29-30.

"Catholic, Protestant, and Anabaptist: Principles of Biblical Interpretation in Selected Communities." *Brethren in Christ* (December 1986): 264-75.

"Assessing Barth for Apologetics." In *How Karl Barth Changed My Mind,* ed. Donald K. McKim, 162-65. Grand Rapids: Eerdmans, 1986.

"Biblical Authority and the Issues in Question." In *Women, Authority, and The Bible,* ed. Alvera Mickelsen, 51-58. Downers Grove: InterVarsity, 1986.

"God Limits His Knowledge." In *Predestination and Free Will,* ed. David Basinger and Randall Basinger, 141-62. Downers Grove: InterVarsity, 1986. Pinnock's responses to the other contributors are on pp. 57-60, 95-98, 137-40.

"Schaeffer on Modern Theology." In *Reflections on Francis Schaeffer,* ed. Ronald W. Ruegsegger, 173-93. Grand Rapids: Zondervan, 1986.

"Who Are the Evangelicals in Canada?" *Ecumenism* (March 1987): 4-5.

"Fire, Then Nothing." *CT* (March 20, 1987): 40-41.

Review of *Clark Speaks from the Grave,* by Gordon H. Clark. *TSFB* (May-June 1987): 37, 40.

"Parameters of Biblical Inerrancy." In *The Proceedings of the Conference on Biblical Inerrancy,* 95-100. Nashville: Broadman, 1987.

"What Is Biblical Inerrancy?" In *The Proceedings of The Conference on Biblical Inerrancy*, 73-80. Nashville: Broadman, 1987.

Response to James H. Olthuis in *A Hermeneutics of Ultimacy: Peril or Promise*, ed. Olthuis, et al. Lanham, MD: University Press of America, 1987.

"Between Classical and Process Theism." In *Process Theology*, ed. Ronald Nash, 309-27. Grand Rapids: Baker, 1987.

"Baptists and the Latter Rain: A Contemporary Challenge." In *Costly Vision: The Baptist Pilgrimage in Canada*, ed. Jarold K. Zeman, 255-72. Burlington, ON: Welch, 1988.

"The Finality of Jesus Christ in a World of Religions." In *Christian Faith and Practice in the Modern World*, ed. Mark A. Noll and David F. Wells, 152-68. Grand Rapids: Eerdmans, 1988.

"The Pursuit of Utopia." In *Freedom, Justice, and Hope: Toward a Strategy for the Poor and the Oppressed*, ed. Marvin Olasky, 65-83. Westchester, IL: Crossway, 1988.

"Climbing Out of a Swamp: The Evangelical Struggle to Understand the Creation Texts." *Interpretation* 43 (April 1989): 143-55.

"From Augustine to Arminius: A Pilgrimage in Theology." In *The Grace of God, the Will of Man: A Case for Arminianism*, ed. Clark H. Pinnock, 15-30. Grand Rapids: Zondervan, 1989.

Works about Pinnock

DeSmidt, Diane. "Clark Pinnock on Inerrancy: The Evolution of a Doctrine." Bethel Theological Seminary, Fall, 1988 (unpublished paper for Systematic Theology course).

Fuller, Daniel. "Daniel Fuller and Clark Pinnock: On Revelation and Biblical Authority." In *Christian Scholars Review* 2 (1973): 330-35. Reprinted in *JETS* (Spring 1973): 67-72.

Gilkey, Langdon. Response to "Langdon Gilkey: A Guide to His Theology." In *TSFNR* (April 1978): 7-8.

Gundry, Stanley N. "Response to Pinnock, Nicole and Johnston." In *Women, Authority and The Bible*, ed. Alvera Mickelsen, 59-64. Downers Grove: InterVarsity, 1986).

Koivisto, Rex A. "Clark Pinnock and Inerrancy: A Change in Truth Theory?" *JETS* 24 (June 1981): 138-51.

Lindsell, Harold. *The Bible in the Balance*. Grand Rapids:: Zondervan, 1979.

Muller, Richard. Review of *Predestination and Free Will: Four Views of Divine Sovereignty and Human Freedom*, ed. David Basinger and Randall Basinger. *The Reformed Journal* (May 1987): 31-34.

Nielsen, Glenn. "Clark Pinnock." The Southern Baptist Theological Seminary, Winter, 1982 (unpublished research paper for Trends in Modern Theology: Historical Criticism course).

Orser, Alan S. "An Interpretation of Dr. Clark H. Pinnock and His Contribution to the Baptist Convention of Ontario and Quebec, 1977-1985." Acadia Divinity College, November 12, 1985 (unpublished paper for Professor J. K. Zeman).

Price, Robert M. "Clark H. Pinnock: Conservative and Contemporary." In *The Evangelical Quarterly* 60 (April 1988): 157-83.

Reichenbach, Bruce. Response to "God Limits His Knowledge." In *Predestination and Free Will,* ed. David Basinger and Randall Basinger, 175-77. Downers Grove: InterVarsity, 1986.

Steen, Peter J. Review of *Set Forth Your Case.* In *WTJ* 31 (November 1968-May 1969): 101-9.

Taplin, Darcy. "Clark H. Pinnock: Growing Out of the Weaknesses of a Fundamentalist Past." The Southern Baptist Theological Seminary, December 3, 1980 (unpublished paper for Baptist Theologians in Historical Perspective course).

Wells, David F. "The Role of Tradition for Pinnock and Dulles: A Response." *TSFB* (May-June 1983): 5-6.

Wolterstorff, Nicholas. "Is Reason Enough? A Review Essay [of *Reason Enough*]." In *The Reformed Journal* (April 1981): 20-24.

Notes

1. Pinnock's testimony, in "I Was a Teenage Fundamentalist," *The Wittenburg Door,* December 1982-January 1983, 18. See also Clark H. Pinnock, *Three Keys to Spiritual Renewal* (1985), 18. Undocumented factual information in this chapter is from a phone conversation with Pinnock, January 1989.

2. "Pilgrimage in Political Theology" (1984), 107; Clark H. Pinnock, "From Augustine to Arminius" (1989), 17.

3. R. Price, "Clark H. Pinnock: Conservative and Contemporary," 158.

4. Schaeffer on Modern Theology" (1986), 173-93; *Three Keys to Spiritual Renewal,* 101, n. 3.

5. "A Response to Rex Koivisto" (1981), 154.

6. Harold Lindsell notes that in *A New Reformation* "Pinnock appeared like a tiger stalking his prey," who called for even more extreme steps than Lindsell himself! (Lindsell, *The Bible in the Balance,* 36, 38-39.)

7. "A Pilgrimage in Political Theology," 106, 108.

8. *Three Keys to Spiritual Renewal,* 50-51, 54.

9. Gordon R. Lewis, review of *Biblical Revelation* in *Eternity* (January 1972): 50.

10. Pinnock knows Price well and was on his Ph.D. dissertation committee for Drew University. He does not, however, agree with Price's comparison of him with Schleiermacher. "Just because a person sees more importance in experience than he used to, does not make him/her a liberal!" (Letter to Diane DeSmidt, Bethel Theological Seminary, November 11, 1988.)

11. Price, "Clark H. Pinnock," 173.

12. "Prospects for Systematic Theology," 96.

13. I. Howard Marshall, *Kept by the Power of God* (London: Epworth, 1969; now published by Bethany Fellowship, Minneapolis).

14. "From Augustine to Arminius," 17.

15. "A Pilgrimage in Political Theology," 103-20.

16. See, e.g., "Three Views of the Bible in Contemporary Theology" (1977), 45-73; and "Evangelicals and Inerrancy: The Current Debate" (1978), 65-69.

17. Lindsell, *The Bible in the Balance,* 36-43; Lindsell, *The Battle for the Bible* (Grand Rapids: Zondervan, 1976): 173-74, 201.

18. See, e.g., Rex A. Koivisto, "Clark Pinnock and Inerrancy: A Change in Truth Theory?"

19. Alan S. Orser, "An Interpretation of Dr. Clark H. Pinnock and His Contribution to the Baptist Convention of Ontario and Quebec, 1977-1985."

20. Some insights into Pinnock's theological development are given by Darcy Taplin in "Clark H. Pinnock: Growing Out of the Weaknesses of a Fundamentalist Past."

21. Price, "Clark H. Pinnock," 175.

22. *Biblical Revelation* (1971), 73-74. Pinnock now admits, "The deep reason I defended the strict view of inerrancy in my earlier years was because I desperately wanted it to be true." ("Parameters of Biblical Inerrancy" [1987], 96.)

23. Lindsell, *The Bible in the Balance,* 38.

24. "A Response to Rex Koivisto," 154.

25. *The Scripture Principle* (1984), xiii, 62.

26. Ibid., 67. See also "Climbing Out of a Swamp; The Evangelical Struggle to Understand the Creation Texts" (1989).

27. *The Scripture Principle,* 125.

28. *Tracking the Maze* (1990), 161, 175. Pinnock favors the Lausanne formula, which states that the Bible is "inerrant in all it affirms," and Article XIII of the Chicago Statement on Biblical Inerrancy, which reads (in part): "We deny that it is proper to evaluate Scripture according to standards of truth and error that are alien to its usage or purpose." ("What Is Biblical Inerrancy [1987], 74; "Parameters of Biblical Inerrancy" [1987], 97. The Chicago Statement is in *Inerrancy,* ed. Norman L. Geisler [Grand Rapids: Zondervan, 1980], 493-97.)

29. Phone conversation between Pinnock and Diane DeSmidt, as recorded in "Clark Pinnock on Inerrancy: The Evolution of a Doctrine," 12. See Millard J. Erickson, *Christian Theology* (Grand Rapids: Baker, 1983), 223. It is obviously with this nuanced definition of inerrancy that Pinnock continues to sign the yearly renewal statement for the Evangelical Theological Society, which requires members to affirm that "the Bible alone, and the Bible in its entirety, is the Word of God written, and is therefore inerrant in the autographs."

30. *The Scripture Principle,* 156, 192. Also "Reflections on *The Scripture Principle*" (1980), 10. Pinnock is not, however, favorable toward contemporary hermeneutical theories of interpretation as dialogical encounter between text and reader. See his negative critique of James H. Olthuis in Olthius et al., *A Hermeneutics of Ultimacy: Peril or Promise?* Lanham, MD: University Press of America, 1987.

31. "Introduction," in *Grace Unlimited* (1975), 11.

32. "Responsible Freedom and the Flow of Biblical History" (1975), 95.

33. Robert Shank, *Elect in the Son* (Springfield, Mo.: Westcott, 1970).

34. "From Augustine to Arminius," 20-21.

35. Ibid., 15.

36. Ibid., 17.

37. Why Is Jesus the Only Way?" (1976), 13-15, 32-33.

38. "The Finality of Jesus Christ in a World of Religions" (1988), 154. Pinnock adds that God "always sees to it that those responding to the light they have encounter Jesus Christ, whether before or after death (p. 163). Also see "Revelation" in *New Dictionary of Theology* (1988), 586.

39. "Fire, Then Nothing" (1987), 40-41. David F. Wells' rebuttal of Pinnock is on pp. 41-42.

40. *Grace Unlimited;* "The Need for a Scriptural, and Therefore a Neo-Classical Theism" (1979), 37-42.

41. "God Limits His Knowledge" (1986), 143-62; "Between Classical and Process Theism" (1987), 311-27; "From Augustine to Arminius" (1989).

42. "The Need for a Scriptural, and Therefore a Neo-Classical Theism," 37.

43. "Between Classical and Process Theism," 317-20.

44. Ibid., 323.

45. "God Limits His Knowledge," 155.

46. "From Augustine to Arminius," 24.

47. "God Limits His Knowledge," 155; "Between Classical and Process Theism," 323.

48. "From Augustine to Arminius," 25.

49. Ibid., 25.

50. "God Limits His Knowledge," 146, 157.

51. Ibid., 158.

52. Ibid., 146, 162.

53. Ibid., 152.

54. *Tracking the Maze,* 208-10.

55. Personal correspondence from Pinnock to Darcy Taplin, November 11, 1980, as recorded in Taplin, "Clark H. Pinnock: Growing Out of the Weaknesses of a Fundamentalist Past," 17.

56. A major negative review of *Set Forth Your Case* is by Peter J. Steen.

57. An appreciative but unfavorable review of *Reason Enough* is by Nicholas Wolterstorff. Pinnock replies in "Response by Clark Pinnock" (1981).

58. Lecture at New College, Berkeley, July 23, 1979. See Price, "Clark H. Pinnock," 181.

59. *Three Keys to Spiritual Renewal,* 30-33.

60. *Tracking the Maze,* 153-54.

61. Ibid., 170-71.

62. Ibid., 182-83.

63. "Truce Proposal for the Tongues Controversy" (1971); "The New Pentecostalism: Reflections by a Well-Wisher" (1973); "Charismatic Renewal for the Radical Church" (1975).

64. *Three Keys to Spiritual Renewal,* 42-44. In this volume Pinnock actually gives a "word of prophecy" (p. 56). See also his trenchant observations in "Baptists and the Latter Rain: A Contemporary Challenge" (1988), 255-72.

65. *Three Keys to Spiritual Renewal,* 104, n. 2; also "Baptists and the Latter Rain," n. 5. In 1983 he wrote, "I am not objecting to the premillennial expectation as such but only to the folly of placing a date on this hope" ("Having Ascension Eyes" [1983], 16).

66. "A Pilgrimage in Political Theology," 113; *Three Keys to Spiritual Renewal,* 77-78.

67. "Biblical Authority and the Issues in Question" (1986), 58. Stanley N. Gundry's response is on pp. 59-63.

68. *Three Keys to Spiritual Renewal,* 76. In fact, Pinnock is now on the editorial board of *Transformation,* a centrist journal of evangelical social ethics edited by Ronald Sider and others. He signed (as would be expected) the "Villars Statement on Relief and Development," a distinctly antisocialist document. See the statement in

Freedom, Justice, and Hope, ed. Marvin Olasky (1988), 141-48; and Pinnock's chapter in this book, "The Pursuit of Utopia," 65-83.

69. See, e.g., "How I Use the Bible in Doing Theology" (1985), 18-34. This is an excellent introduction to Pinnock's method of Scripture study.

70. "How I Use Tradition in Doing Theology" (1982), 2-5.

71. "Responsible Freedom and the Flow of Biblical History," 95.

72. "The Finality of Jesus Christ in a World of Religions," 166.

73. *Tracking the Maze,* 178-79.

74. *The Scripture Principle,* iv.

75. Price, "Clark H. Pinnock," 172. See Pinnock, "Assessing Barth for Apologetics"(1986), 162-65; "Pannenberg's Theology: Reasonable Happenings in History" (1976); "No Nonsense Theology: Pinnock Reviews Pannenberg" (1976).

76. Review of *Message and Existence: An Introduction to Christian Theology* by Langdon Gilkey (1982), 21. Dale Moody's book *The Word of Truth* (Grand Rapids: Eerdmans, 1981) is reviewed by Pinnock in *TSFB* (September-October 1981): 22.

77. Review of Gilkey, *Message and Existence* (1982), 21.

78. A major review of *The Scripture Principle* is by Kevin Vanhoozer. A helpful paper on Pinnock's use of historical criticism for understanding Scripture is by Lutheran Glenn Nielsen.

79. See the chapter on Dale Moody in this volume.

80. However, now that highly regarded John Stott has admitted to and defended annihilationism, many evangelicals will be taking a second look at this doctrine. See David L. Edwards with John Stott, *Evangelical Essentials* (Downers Grove: InterVarsity, 1988), 312-20.

81. R. Muller, "God Only Wise," 32. Pinnock acknowledges that among mainstream evangelicals he stands alone in his views of omniscience. A Seventh-Day Adventist, Richard Rice, presents the same view in *God's Foreknowledge and Man's Free Will* (Minneapolis: Bethany, 1985).

82. The following have argued recently that divine foreknowledge does not entail necessity or violate human freedom: Stephen T. Davis, *Logic and the Nature of God* (Grand Rapids: Eerdmans, 1983); Jonathan L. Kvanvig, *The Possibility of an All-Knowing God* (New York: St. Martin's, 1986); Bruce Reichenbach, "God Limits His Power," in *Predestination and Free Will,* eds. D. Basinger and R. Basinger (Downers Grove: InterVarsity, 1986); Alvin Plantinga, "On Ockham's Way Out," in *The Concept of God,* ed. Thomas V. Morris (Oxford University Press, 1987); William Lane Craig, *The Only Wise God: The Compatibility of Divine Foreknowledge and Human Freedom* (Grand Rapids: Baker, 1987). Pinnock is aware of the arguments presented in these works, and is considering them with an open mind.

83. On this point Pinnock writes, "It [Price's article] certainly showed up my propensity to change my mind. Although this is part of life which is dynamic, I do worry that I am too vascillating. I do not always like myself when I think how many changes I have had to make and am still making. I wish I was more stable. Part of that may be the fact that a postfundamentalist like me really has no set tradition and has to find or create one. How nice to be a comfortable Calvinist or Wesleyan or whatever. On the whole, though, as I think about the changes, in the areas of the Spirit, of determinism, of biblical inspiration, of political theology—I feel pretty good about the process. I have learned a lot and some people even say I have helped them." (Letter to Diane DeSmidt, Bethel Theological Seminary, November 11, 1988.)

84. (See, e.g., "A Response to Rex Koivisto," 153; and "A Pilgrimage in Political Theology," 118-19.) Pinnock can, however, be blunt concerning the work and

motives (as he sees them) of others. See his reviews of John Jefferson Davis, *The Necessity of Systematic Theology* in *TSFB* (September-October 1981), 22; Millard J. Erickson, *Christian Theology* in *TSFB* (January-February 1986), 29-30; and Gordon H. Clark, *Clark Speaks from the Grave* in *TSFB* (May-June 1987), 37, 40.

85. Review of *A Century of Protestant Theology* by A. Heron (1982), 20.

86. No doubt such risk taking is rare because, as Richard Mouw observes, "the evangelical community has tended to treat its theologians very badly. Theological scholars are watched more carefully than their colleagues in other disciplines." ("The Call to Holy Worldliness, *Reformed Journal* [January 1989], 8.)

87. Typical Southern Baptist examples of the two positions are seen in *The Proceedings of the Conference on Biblical Inerrancy, 1987*. For these see replies to Pinnock by W. Hull, J. Lewis, P. Patterson, and A. Rogers.

35

Baptist Theology and Theologians
David S. Dockery

From the beginning Baptists have been a varied group with a complex history and no single theological tradition. In this volume we have attempted to provide representatives from a variety of spheres of Baptist life, as well as theologians who practiced their art from different perspectives. Yet, many influential thinkers have not been included in the preceding chapters. The purpose of this final chapter is, in brief overview fashion, to survey numerous other significant voices in the history of Baptist theology. Certainly, some of the subjects in *Baptist Theologians* are very obvious choices. On the other hand, there have been and are other worthy theologians and shapers of Baptist life, including some of the contributors to this book, that deserve attention. From a historical perspective, we shall examine these important shapers of Baptist life and thought.

The Beginnings of Baptist Theology

Baptist theology, in common with Baptist churches, can be traced to two common English sources. From English Separatism arose General Baptists who sought asylum in the Netherlands around 1608-1609. One portion of this group, led by John Robinson (1572-1625), became famous as the "Pilgrim Church" that migrated to Plymouth Massachusetts in 1620. The other contingent, under the direction of John Smyth (d.1612), were exiled in Amsterdam. They rejected infant baptism and began *de novo* believer's baptism by affusion. Smyth continued to study the scriptures and offered new positions on church government and worship, in addition to baptism. These matters were outlined in his major works: *Principles and Inferences Concerning the Visible Church* (1607) and *The Character of the Beast* (1609).[1] The General Baptist theology was essentially Arminian in soteriological matters, stressing a universal or general atonement, thus the name General Baptists. Smyth's congregation included an independent thinker named Thomas Helwys (1570-1615), who was baptized by Smyth. Smyth attempted to unite the small band of followers with a Mennonite community, but Helwys and other leaders disagreed. Helwys, together with a small contingent, shortly returned to England and organized the first Baptist congregation on English soil at Spitalfields near London in 1612. He eloquently defended the case for religious liberty in his work, *The Mystery of Iniquity* (1612).[2]

In addition to General Baptists, there were also Particular Baptists, influenced by streams of Calvinism. Particular Baptists adhered to a particular understanding of the atonement and originated in Henry Jacob's Independent church. In 1638, several members from the congregation following the leadership of John Spilsbury formed the first Particular Baptist church. Over the next few decades this group grew rapidly.[3] They carefully articulated a Calvinistic confession of faith in the First London Confession (1644). A distinctive feature of the Confession called for baptism by single immersion. Soon General Baptists also adopted immersion.[4]

Similar paths were chartered in America, where in 1639, a year after Spilsbury formed the church in London, a Baptist congregation was started at Providence, Rhode Island by Roger Williams (1603-84). Actually, Williams was only a Baptist for a short time. Yet, due to the assessment of Williams in Isaac Backus' early history of Baptists, Williams' influence as a Baptist and pioneer in the arena of religious liberty looms large. Williams affirmed Baptist positions on scripture and baptism, at least for a short period, and blazed the trail for the Baptist position on religious liberty with his masterful work, *The Bloody Tenet of Persecution* (1644).[5] Between 1641 and 1646, a more stable Baptist community was established at Newport, Rhode Island by John Clarke (1609-76). His work, *Ill Newes from New England* (1652) secured the representation of Baptist views in the Charter of Rhode Island (1663), which paved the way for similar expositions in the following century for the colonies.

Back in England, following the Cromwell regime, new confessions of faith were adopted. The Second London Confession (1677), an altered form of the Westminster Confession of Faith, put forth a consistent Calvinistic position, with Baptist views of the Lord's Supper, baptism, and church polity. This statement has served as one of the most influential shaping documents for Baptist theology. The impact of this statement on the Philadelphia and Charleston associations indicates the significance of the confession. In other Baptist circles, the Orthodox Creed (1678) mediated Arminian and Calvinistic positions among General Baptists.[6]

Eighteenth-Century Baptist Theology

The next century saw two negative developments. General Baptists suffered from a deadening Socianianism, and Particular Baptists tended toward a rationalistic hyper-Calvinism.[7] The instrumental leader in the renewal of English General Baptist theology was Dan Taylor (1738-1816) of Yorkshire. In the days of his youth, Taylor was involved in the Wesleyan movement. Later he rejected Wesley's system of discipline and discovered a home among the General Baptists of Halifax. In 1770, Taylor called a special meeting of sympathetic General Baptists from the Midlands and laid the foundation for the New Connection of General Baptists. Central to Taylor's theology was a high Christology, believer's baptism, Arminian soteriology, coupled with evangelistic zeal. He wrote more than forty books or tracts in his development of these themes. Among the most important of his writings were *Fundamentals of Religion in Faith and Practice* (1775) and *The Truth and Inspiration of the Scriptures* (1790). At a time in Baptist history when both General and Particular Baptists faced spiritual and theological decline, Taylor's leadership brought renewal and paved the way for the establishment of the Baptist Union in 1813.[8]

In America great growth took place during the years surrounding the American Revolution. Much of the growth was a byproduct of the Great Awakening. The earliest system of Baptist theology in this country was primarily Calvinistic as evidenced in the Philadelphia Confession (1742). Moderating influences developed by the turn of the century, as can be observed in the New Hampshire Confession (1833).

Important contributions arose from a variety of sectors of Baptist life during the period at the end of the 18th and the beginning of the 19th centuries. Numbered among these were George Leile (ca. 1750-1800), Thomas Baldwin (1753-1825), and William Carey (1761-1834). Leile, the son of Virginia slaves, was baptized in 1773 and was given his freedom by his master in order to employ his several talents and spiritual gifts. He gathered together a group of believers near the Savannah River to begin the first Black Baptist church in America. He became the first Baptist missionary, serving in Jamaica, where he predated William Carey by a decade. He reportedly baptized over 500 converts in 1791. His ministry significantly advanced the case for the abolition of slavery.[9]

Thomas Baldwin, one of the leading lights among New England Baptists during this time, served as a pastor in Boston and as editor of the *Massachusetts Baptist Missionary Magazine* (1803-24). His theologizing and apologetic work greatly advanced Baptist causes. Among his most important works were: *Open Communion Examined* (1789), *Christian Baptism, as Delivered to the Churches* (1812), and *Catechism or Compendium of Christian Doctrine and Practice* (1816).[10]

William Carey led the development of the missionary movement at this time. Built on the theology of Andrew Fuller, this movement maintained a Calvinistic view of theology, including a particular view of the atonement, which was combined with a universal invitation to respond to the gospel message. This combination resulted in a new Baptist missionary theology and the advancement of the world missionary movement. The missionary movement continued through the efforts of Luther Rice (1783-1836) and Adoniram Judson (1788-1850). Rice, a great visionary and administrator, served in India with Judson, and later became a great Baptist statesman.[11] As Baptists moved into the nineteenth century significant gains were made in the renewal and shape of Baptist theology.

Nineteenth-Century Baptist Theology

Numerous important works were penned during the nineteenth century as Baptist theology matured and developed. John Leland (1754-1841) adeptly defended baptism by immersion, both historically and biblically. He regularly concluded preaching services with an invitation to be baptized. But it was religious liberty that dominated Leland's concerns and contributions.[12] These voluminous writings can be found in *The Writings of John Leland,* edited by L. F. Greene (1845).

Two shining stars during the first half of the nineteenth century were Jesse Mercer (1769-1841) and W. B. Johnson (1782-1862). Mercer, who achieved as pastor, educator, and administrator, was driven by the twofold desire to establish Baptist educational institutions and his prayer for God-sent revival. His major writing contribution, however, was his *History of the Georgia Baptist Association* (1838). Johnson, a Calvinist like Mercer, advanced numerous Baptist causes in the South. His lasting legacy can be found in his formative work on ecclesiology, *A Church of Christ with Her Officers, Laws, Duties, and Form of Government* (1844).

Francis Wayland (1796-1865) ranked as the premier intellect of his day. A pastor in Boston and Providence, he also taught theology at Andover Seminary, Union College, and Brown University. Like Johnson, his major contributions were in the area of ecclesiology, primarily his defense of autonomous congregations in *Notes on the Principles and Practices of Baptist Churches* (1856).

In the middle of the nineteenth century, Landmark theology sprang forth in the south through the controversial James Robinson Graves (1820-93). As editor of *The Tennessee Baptist* for over forty years, he strategically used the power of the press to advance his unique theological positions. Much of his work was strongly opposed by R. B. C. Howell (1801-68), who had preceded him as editor of the paper.[13] Graves defended the autonomy of the local church and the purity of the church based on an unbroken succession of believer's baptism. He articulated his theology in *Old Landmarkism: What Is It?* (1880). Graves also introduced dispensational theology into Baptist life in his *The Work of Christ in the Covenant of Redemption: Developed in Seven Dispensations* (1883). Graves's ongoing impact on Baptist theology has far surpassed his influence during his life.

Other theologians and shapers of Baptist life who helped form Baptist thought in the nineteenth century are numerous. John Newton Brown (1803-1868) contributed a major work on the church titled *The Baptist Church Manual* (1853), which included what has become a standard church covenant for scores of churches. Richard Fuller (1804-76), who was trained as a a lawyer, provided Baptists with a powerful theology of the cross called *The Power of the Cross* (1851). Though a popular preacher to the slave community, he nevertheless has been remembered for his defense of slavery. These wrong-headed views can be found in *Domestic Slavery Considered as a Scriptural Institution* (1845).

The foremost theologian of the day was Alvah Hovey (1820-1903), who served as professor and president of Newton Theological Institute. Strongly influenced by 19th century evangelicalism, he set forth a high view of biblical inspiration. His Christology was grounded in the norms established by the early church creeds. He provided his generation with a *Manual of Sys-*

tematic Theology and Christian Ethics (1877). Also, he served as editor of the *American Commentary* series. Another Baptist leader who was both influenced by, as well as a part of, the broad evangelicalism of this time was Adoniram Judson Gordon (1836-95). Primarily he served as a pastor, but also as president of the Boston Missionary Training School (later renamed Gordon College). His theological contributions came from his studies and teachings in pneumatology, exemplified in *The Holy Spirit in Missions* (1893).

Two Southern Baptist giants at the close of the nineteenth century, who significantly impacted Baptist thought were John A. Broadus (1827-95) and Basil Manly, Jr. (1825-92). Both were founding faculty members at The Southern Baptist Theological Seminary. The combination of their names has been joined together to provide the name for the book publishing arm of the Baptist Sunday School Board: Broad(us)Man(ly) Press. Broadus was a brilliant linguist, but he made his greatest contribution in the area of pastoral theology. His volume, *A Treatise on the Preparation and Delivery of Sermons* (1870) is still considered by many as a classic in the field. Manly's primary contributions included his influential work on biblical authority, *The Bible Doctrine of Inspiration* (1888), and his articulation of the Abstract of Principles (1859). This important statement served as the founding confession of faith for Southern Baptist Seminary.[14]

As the century drew to a close, British Baptists found themselves in the midst of a widespread controversy known as the Downgrade Controversy. The struggle involved two leading figures, John Clifford and C. H. Spurgeon. Clifford (1836-1923) advocated forms of biblical criticism and a theological-scientific synergism that was visciously rejected by Spurgeon's supernaturalism. Spurgeon withdrew from the Baptist Union in 1887 and Clifford continued as England's foremost statesman. Not only in the Baptist Union did Clifford exert strategic leadership, but also in the Baptist World Alliance at the turn of the century. The issues debated during the Downgrade Controversy set the agenda for ongoing controversies on both sides of the Atlantic in the twentieth century.

Twentieth-Century Baptist Theology

During the nineteenth century, the consistent Calvinism of the Philadelphia Confession was modified by the growing influence of the more lenient Calvinism of the New Hampshire Confession (1833). In turn, the New Hampshire statement became foundational for the 1925 and 1963 Baptist Faith and Message statements. Such modifications, resulting reactions, and continued diversity have characterized Baptist theology in the twentieth century.

Baptists were not exempt from the inroads of liberalism, as previously indicated and foreshadowed by the Downgrade controversy. Leading exponents of the liberal trends included: William Newton Clarke (1841-1911), Shailer Mathews (1836-1941), and Harry Emerson Fosdick (1878-1969). A social gospel theology was explicated by Walter Rauschenbusch and a mediating theology, influenced by personal idealism, was brilliantly expounded by A. H. Strong.

Clarke, for almost three decades, taught New Testament and Theology at Toronto Baptist Seminary and Colgate Theological Seminary. His many impressive works include: *The Use of the Scriptures in Theology* (1905), *Sixty Years with the Bible* (1909), and his classic contribution, *An Outline of Christian Theology* (1909). Clarke developed a semi-existential methodology that centered on Jesus' life and teachings as the revelation of God and the interpreter of human experiences.

Like Clarke, Shailer Mathews inherited a most impressive Baptist heritage. After studying at Newton Theological Institute, Mathews taught briefly at Colby College before a distinguished career at the University of Chicago Divinity School. More than any other twentieth-century Baptist, Mathews embodied liberal ideology. Shaped by German critical approaches to biblical and theological studies, by evolutionary understandings of religious history, and by a basic commitment to a social gospel, Mathews boldly defended modernism. His works on *The Social Teaching of Jesus* (1897) and *The Faith of a Modernist* (1924) expressed Christianity primarily in terms of human need and human freedom. His salient insights challenged traditional theological constructions and established the theological agenda for Baptists in the early years of the twentieth century.

The popular preacher who brought the thought of Clarke and Mathews to a wider audience was the pulpit giant, Harry Emerson Fosdick. Fosdick was a scholar who, at various intervals, taught at Union Theological Seminary for four decades while pastoring three churches in the New York city area. The peak of his popularity came while he served as the eloquent pastor of the Park Avenue Baptist Church (renamed Riverside Church). His challenge to traditional Christianity came in a 1922 sermon, "Shall the Fundamentalists Win?" He popularized liberal Baptist theology in his considerable writings. His thought can be observed in his two most famous works, *Christianity and Progress* (1922) and *the Modern Use of the Bible* (1924).[15]

Reaction to modernist thought came from Baptist fundamentalists especially William Bell Riley (1861-1947), John Franklyn Norris (1877-1952), T. T. Shields (1873-1955), and John R. Rice (1895-1980). By 1926 those who were militant for the fundamentals had failed to expel the modernists from Baptist conventions. They had, for the most part, lost the battles against evolution and historical criticism. The northern fundamentalists created new denominations in order to seek purity apart from the larger bodies they deemed apostate. They formed the General Association of Regular Baptist Churches, The Conservative Baptist Association of America, and The Baptist Bible Fellowship International.[16]

J. Frank Norris carried the banner as the most controversial and sensational of the fundamentalist leaders. Norris studied with B. H. Carroll at Baylor University and then ambitiously set out to preach regularly at the greatest pulpit in the world. Simultaneously he pastored churches in Fort

Worth, Texas, and Detroit, Michigan (1935-52). His primary vehicle of influence and the voice for his fundamentalist theology came through the editorship of *The Fundamentalist* (1909-52). He loathed evolutionary thought and the social gospel. Norris also raised premillennialism to the level of an essential theological belief. He maintained that theology, in all aspects, must be constructed from a literal hermeneutic. His work, *The Gospel of Dynamite* (1933), stressed a theological literalism that included a literal Christ, a literal salvation, a literal hell, and a literal heaven.[17]

T. T. Shields, editor of *The Gospel Witness* (1922-55) and president of Toronto Baptist Seminary (1927-55), joined with Riley and Norris to form the Baptist Bible Union of North America in 1923, and served as the first president of the BBU. A fourth major figure, John R. Rice, helped form the Southwide Baptist Fellowship. Raised a Southern Baptist, a close colleague with J. Frank Norris, Rice founded the *Sword of the Lord* in 1934. This publication became the most widely circulated and most important fundamentalist periodical in America. Through the *Sword of the Lord,* Rice exerted incredible influence which has been demonstrated through the expanding fundamentalist phenomenon, as well as the conservative resurgence that has taken place in the Southern Baptist Convention since 1979.[18]

Two extremely important women who pioneered women's causes and shaped Baptist life and thought were Susan E. C. Griffin (1851-1926) and Helen Barrett Montgomery (1861-1934). Susan Griffin was the first woman to receive ordination among American Baptists (1893) when she and her husband were called as pastors of the Elmira Heights Baptist Church in Elmira Heights, New York. For a decade prior to this call, the couple had served as missionaries in India. A gifted linguist, speaker, and administrator, she effected the union of the women's societies of the Free Baptist General Conference and the Northern Baptist Convention. Montgomery was another key figure in the developing role of women in Baptist life. She prepared numerous Bible study aids, but her most esteemed accomplishment was her *Centenary Translation of the New Testament* (1924). She organized the initial World Day of Prayer. In 1920, in the midst of the Modernist-Fundamentalist controversy, she presided over the national meeting of the Northern Baptist Convention.

Two prominent Baptists who served in the middle of the twentieth century and achieved status in different academic fields were Harold Henry Rowley (1890-1969) and Kenneth Scott Latourette (1894-1968). Rowley, an Old Testament scholar, treated the theological significance of the Old Testament from several perspectives including redemption, election, and worship. He contended that the Bible, the word of God, was both divine and human and yielded only to the ultimate authority of Jesus Christ, the living word of God. These views were adequately articulated in *The Relevance of the Bible* (1942), *The Authority of the Bible* (1949), and *The Unity of the Bible* (1953). Rowley, along with H. Wheeler Robinson, advanced the discipline of Old Testament theology among Baptists. Primarily he accomplished this with *The Faith of Israel* (1956) and *The Biblical Doctrine of Election* (1950). He argued persuasively that the Old Testament should be rediscovered and communicated in terms of its abiding significance for the church and Christian theology.

Latourette, a first-class church historian, especially in the area of the history of missions, served as professor of missions at Yale University (1921-53). His most famous work, a seven-volume study of *The History of the Expansion of Christianity* (1937-45), is still a classic, setting high standards for forthcoming Baptist historians. Latourette was a member of the American Baptist Foreign Mission Society for two decades, president of the American Baptist Convention for one term, and an ordained Baptist minister.

Two prophetic preachers whose pulpit theology challenged a generation of Baptist people were Carlyle Marney (1916-78) and Martin Luther King, Jr., (1929-68). Marney, born in Harriman, Tennessee was a prominent Baptist pastor and theologian. He pastored churches in Paducah, Kentucky; Austin, Texas; and Charlotte, North Carolina. The last decade of his ministry shifted Marney's focus to broader ecumenical interests while he served as Director of the Interpreter's House, a retreat center for ministers, at Lake Junaluska, North Carolina. His theology and ministry focused on ethical and social concerns. These themes are addressed in *The Structures of Prejudice* (1961); *The Recovery of the Person* (1963); *The Coming Faith* (1970); and *Priests to Each Other* (1974).[19]

Martin Luther King, Jr., son of the patriarchal Baptist minister Martin Luther ("Daddy") King, Sr., was the leading voice in the civil rights crusade of the 1960s and the foremost advocate of non-violent strategies for addressing social problems. He pastored churches in Montgomery, Alabama, and Atlanta, Georgia, before being assassinated in Memphis, Tennessee, in 1968. His theology was informed by the writings of Mahatma Gandhi and Walter Rauschenbusch. His Ph.D. dissertation focused on the theology of Paul Tillich. King founded the Southern Christian Leadership Conference in 1957, becoming the embodiment of its ideals. He worked with Gardner C. Taylor, a leading black pastor from Brooklyn, New York, to form the Progressive National Baptist Convention in 1961. In 1963 King was named the *Time* magazine Man of the Year. He received the Nobel Peace Prize in 1964, as well as over 300 other prestigious awards. The pastor was also a prolific writer. He wrote numerous articles and seven books. Among these, *Stride Toward Freedom* (1958) received the Ainsfield-Wolf Award. No single Baptist leader has done more to advance economic justice and racial reconciliation.[20]

Conclusion

Even with the addition of three dozen other voices that have influenced and shaped Baptist life, there are still many others worthy of notation. These include: William Whitsitt, J. B. Tidwell, William Rainey Harper, Robert Thomas Ketchum, Edwin McNeill Poteat, Jr., R. G. Lee, A. T. Robertson, John Brine, Alexander Maclaren, W. W. Stevens, John F. Carter, H. W.

Tribble, W. R. White, Louie D. Newton, Abraham Booth, George Truett, Ebenezer Dodge, Shubal Stearns, G. D. B. Pepper, Ezekiel Robinson, Nathan R. Wood, Jesse Louis Jackson, and Billy Graham.

Among contemporary Baptist theologians, several are writing or have written noteworthy volumes. Pride of place among these must go to James Leo Garrett, Jr. Garrett has taught at Southwestern Seminary, Southern Seminary, and Baylor University. He is well-known for his work on W. T. Conner, ecclesiology, evangelicalism, and the Believers' Church movement. An accomplished historian and theologian, Garrett's two volume systematic theology will surely be a standard for years to come. James McClendon has written the first volume of a multi-volume narrative theology from a baptistic perspective. Other multi-volume sets presently in progress include works by Bruce Demarest and Gordon Lewis, *Integrative Theology;* Thomas Finger, *Christian Theology;* and an ambitious project that is forthcoming by Gabriel Fackre.

Philosophical theology has been greatly enhanced by the prolific production of John Newport, longtime professor of theology and philosophy at Southwestern Seminary. Among dozens of books, his crowning achievement is *Life's Ultimate Questions* (1989). Aesthetic theology, a developing field of theology within Baptist circles, has been pioneered by William Hendricks. Hendricks, a brilliant and creative mind who has taught at Golden Gate Seminary, Southwestern Seminary, and Southern Baptist Seminary, is breaking new ground in the field of theology and the arts. Hendricks creativity has been demonstrated in his *A Theology for Children* and *A Theology for Aging*. Two biblical theologians, Wayne E. Ward and E. Earle Ellis, have attained international acclaim for their work in New Testament theology. Ward, an eclectic thinker, has popularized biblical theology with his dynamic pulpit presence. Ellis, a front-rank evangelical scholar, has authored numerous articles and commentaries, in addition to his recent outstanding volume on Pauline theology.

The major theologians treated in the chapters of the book, as well as those surveyed in this concluding chapter, are primarily North American and British Baptists. New insights, groundbreaking works, and the art and practice of contextualizing theology are taking place in Africa, Asia, parts of Europe, and the third-world. The development of these important contributions plus the fuller treatment due many in this final section must, however, be reserved for a future volume. Hopefully, this volume will help us all to realize the multi-faceted nature of Baptist theology and will enable us to recover the past history of Baptist theologians. Building on this foundation we can work to unlock the potential for creative and edifying theological work among Baptists in years ahead.

Notes

1. H. Leon McBeth, *The Baptist Heritage* (Nashville: Broadman, 1987), 30; cf. Timothy George, *John Robinson and the English Separatist Tradition* (Macon, Ga.: Mercer, 1982).

2. Ibid., 32-39.

3. Ibid., 39-44.

4. Ibid., 44-48.

5. Cf. Edmund S. Morgan, *Roger Williams: The Church and State* (New York: Harcourt, Brace and World, 1967).

6. Cf. William L. Lumpkin, *Baptist Confessions of Faith* (Valley Forge, Pa: Judson, 1959).

7. Cf. James Leo Garrett, Jr., "History of Baptist Theology," *Encyclopedia of Southern Baptists* (4 vols., Nashville: Broadman, 1958-1982), 2:1412-13. On the point of "hyper-Calvinism" see the discussion in Thomas J. Nettles, *By His Grace and For His Glory* (Grand Rapids: Baker, 1986) and Curt Daniel, "Hyper-Calvinism and John Gill," Ph.D. diss., University of Edinburgh, 1983.

8. McBeth, *The Baptist Heritage,* 154; also cf. William H. Brackney, "Dan Taylor," *The Baptists* (New York: Greenwood, 1988), 271-72.

9. Cf. E. A. Holmes, "George Leile: Negro Slavery's Prophet of Deliverance, *Foundations* 9 (1966), 333-45.

10. Cf. N. A. Baxter, "Thomas Baldwin: Boston Baptist Preacher," *The Chronicle* 19 (1956): 28-35.

11. Cf. H. W. Thompson, *Luther Rice: Believer in Tomorrow* (Nashville: Broadman, 1983).

12. Edwin S. Gaustad, "The Backus-Leland Tradition," *Foundations* 2 (1959), 131-52; also cf. Brad Creed, "John Leland: American Prophet of Religious Individualism," Ph.D. diss., Southwestern Baptist Theological Seminary, 1986.

13. Cf. Homer L. Grice and R. Paul Caudill, "Graves-Howell Controversy," *Encyclopedia of Southern Baptists,* 1:580-585; also see James E. Tull, *Shapers of Baptist Thought* (Valley Forge, Pa.: Judson, 1972), 129-51.

14. William A. Mueller, *A History of Southern Baptist Theological Seminary* (Nashville: Broadman, 1959), 61-100.

15. McBeth, *The Baptist Heritage,* 596-600; cf. R. V. Pierard, "Theological Liberalism," *Evangelical Dictionary of Theology* (Grand Rapids: Baker, 1984), 633-35.

16. Cf. George W. Dollar, *A History of Fundamentalism in America* (Greenville, SC: Bob Jones University Press, 1973); George M. Marsden, *Fundamentalism and American Culture* (New York: Oxford, 1980); and C. Allyn Russell, *Voices of Fundamentalism* (Philadelphia: Westminster, 1976).

17. Bobby D. Compton, "J. Frank Norris and Southern Baptists," *Review and Expositor* 79 (1982): 63-84.

18. Cf. Jerry Falwell, Ed Dobson, and Ed Hindson, eds., *The Fundamentalist Phenomenon* (Garden City: Doubleday, 1981); also see Bill Leonard, *God's Last and Only Hope* (Grand Rapids: Eerdmans, 1990).

19. Cf. John J. Carey, *Carlyle Marney: A Pilgrim's Progress* (Macon, Ga.: Mercer University Press, 1985).

20. Cf. Tull, *Shapers of Baptist Thought,* 209-35; also James M. Washington, ed., *A Testament of Hope: The Essential Writings of Martin Luther King, Jr.* (San Francisco: Harper & Row, 1986).

Index